Victor Emanuel, Cavour, and the Risorgimento

Victor Emanuel, Cavour, and the Risorgimento

DENIS MACK SMITH

LONDON
OXFORD UNIVERSITY PRESS
NEW YORK   TORONTO
1971

Oxford University Press, Ely House, London W.1

GLASGOW NEW YORK TORONTO MELBOURNE WELLINGTON
CAPE TOWN IBADAN NAIROBI DAR ES SALAAM LUSAKA ADDIS ABABA
DELHI BOMBAY CALCUTTA MADRAS KARACHI LAHORE DACCA
KUALA LUMPUR SINGAPORE HONG KONG TOKYO

ISBN 0 19 212550 8

Printed in Great Britain by
Hazell Watson & Viney Ltd, Aylesbury, Bucks

Contents

ILLUSTRATIONS

MAPS

Preface

VICTOR EMANUEL II began his political life in 1849 when his father unexpectedly abdicated and he was crowned 'King of Sardinia, Cyprus, and Jerusalem'. In 1861 he became King of Italy, and died in 1878. During these twenty-nine years, Italy not only was made into a united nation, but its parliamentary traditions were formed, the country's strength was tested in five wars, and the main guiding lines were set for Italian domestic and foreign policy. Yet no critical study has yet been written of the monarch under whose rule this new nation was born and took shape. Instead his character has been concealed behind a smoke-screen of boring and gossipy panegyric. A dozen short biographies have been published since 1878, though more as acts of praise and piety than serious history, and the more excessive of his biographers reach the point of claiming for him an improbable place among the great rulers of all time.

At first such adulation was a deliberate act of policy, for it was designed to overcome the challenge of republicanism and to help Victor Emanuel to over-shadow Garibaldi and Pope Pius IX in popular estimation. Partly it was a straightforward product of the flattery which no crowned head can ever escape. In particular it is to be explained by the fact that historians and archivists in Italy's strongly centralized educational system were obliged to recognize in the monarchy one of their most important founts of patronage and preferment. The result has been that, despite universal acceptance as the *padre della patria* and the *re galantuomo*, Victor Emanuel is entirely unknown to most Italians today except as a subject of anecdote and legend. His political significance has therefore been easy to ignore.

Count Cavour has been more fortunate, partly because the actions and thoughts of a minister are more in the public eye than those of a king, and also because he was a very attractive character who engaged the attention of a number of exceptional historians from Treitschke and Thayer to Omodeo and Romeo. Camille de Cavour was prime minister for only eight years. During this short period he proved himself to be one of the cleverer and more resourceful statesmen of the century, and one of the most successful, a man who for political skill and courage had few equals. By the time of his premature death in 1861, his good sense, pugnacity, and perseverance had become the admiration of all liberal Europe.

Nevertheless Cavour, too, has been preserved in part as a figure of legend, as someone who has had to be protected from the untempered winds of post-humous criticism. His papers were forcibly appropriated from his heir by the Italian government in 1876, and thereafter were seen by few. Some of them are said to have been transferred in 1878 to the royal archives and were seen by no one at all. When Senator Luigi Chiala's invaluable six-volume edition of Cavour's correspondence appeared in 1884–7, there were omissions and alterations in perhaps a third of the letters which he included. This censorship was forced on Chiala, whether willingly or not, and was designed to place Cavour and the king in a favourable light. In 1913 a special commission was appointed by Victor Emanuel's grandson to produce what was promised to be a definitive edition of Cavour's correspondence, but the immediate result was to make the original letters more inaccessible than ever. Alessandro Luzio, the moving spirit on the commission, who as head of the Turin archives did a great deal in other respects for historical scholarship in Italy, would not permit the Archivio Cavour to be seen, even by Adolfo Omodeo, the leading Cavourian scholar of his time.

The first volume of Luzio's new edition appeared only in 1926, and the slow pace of publication subsequently led some historians to protest that the commission was more interested in concealing than revealing the real Cavour. To an inquiry from myself after the Second World War, the answer came that some of the documents were 'too delicate' for publication or consultation. Apart from this slowness and secrecy, another criticism of the commission was that their principles of selection and presentation were fundamentally unsound, and that by refusing to accept a chronological sequence of letters they were considering rather their own convenience than that of their readers. Only after Luzio's death in 1946 was a new editorial commission appointed which introduced a more liberal policy. By 1960 the original scheme had been abandoned. Publication is now beginning all over again on a different and chronological plan, and by 1971 two volumes have so far appeared covering Cavour's early years before he entered politics. Probably this edition, which is mainly in the capable hands of Carlo Pischedda and Narciso Nada, will take another thirty years to complete, but the former principles of secrecy have at long last been modified, and it will now be possible for the most considerable personage in modern Italian history to be studied without concealment or reticence.

The archives of the royal house, on the other hand, are still protected by the heirs of Victor Emanuel, and this restriction is made the more onerous by a tradition that his letters to other people were, out of regard for the king, often destroyed or else returned to his possession on the death of their recipients. It can therefore be assumed that the key to a number of yet unsolved historical riddles lies buried at Cascais in Portugal where the royal archives were taken in somewhat mysterious circumstances after Italy became a republic in 1946. From a catalogue indiscreetly published fifty years ago by Luigi Cesare Bollea, a Piedmontese schoolmaster, we know something of Victor Emanuel's private papers. Bollea never succeeded in seeing the originals.

His request for less secrecy about them was refused, and so was that of another monarchist historian, Adolfo Colombo. Bollea had to face years of trouble with the police and the courts before he was allowed to produce his own edition of risorgimento documents, and when eventually his text appeared it had been severely censored and mutilated. Chiala, too, had planned an edition of the king's letters, but at his death in 1904 it was still unpublished and nothing more was heard of it. According to William Roscoe Thayer, Chiala used to tell in private of having once suffered imprisonment for revealing a letter written by Victor Emanuel. But this never became known outside a narrow circle.

On several occasions I have sought permission to consult the royal archives, without success. Copies of some 500 of Victor Emanuel's letters were eventually given by ex-King Umberto to Professor Cognasso and published in 1963, but this collection, though very useful, contains many obvious gaps which suggest that the motive for publication was as much political as historical. Other letters were secured by Ruggero Moscati for the *Documenti Diplomatici Italiani*, though the preface to the second volume of this monumental publication implies that the editors may possibly not have been permitted to see and use quite as much as they had hoped. Antonio Monti was allowed to work in the royal archives for the period before 1849, and his tendentious eulogy of the young Victor Emanuel is thus the most authentic work on the subject that we possess. Luzio had earlier seen a selection of documents covering the king's involvement in the events of 1862 and 1867. But a comparison of Cognasso's *Le Lettere di Vittorio Emanuele II* with these other publications and Bollea's catalogue suggests that there are many mysteries still to be cleared up.

Whatever the motives behind this sequestering of documents, that the truth has not been allowed to speak for itself is important, if only in explaining why sufficient detailed research has not yet been done on some of the central problems of Italian national history. Victor Emanuel and Cavour provide merely the most prominent instances of a much more widespread reluctance to probe into sensitive areas of the past. The *Documenti Diplomatici Italiani* for the years after 1861 are at last being published, but very slowly, and long after comparable series have appeared in other countries. Until the First World War, those who wanted to consult the main governmental archives of Italy were limited by law to the period before 1815, and some subjects even before that date were still kept secret. Giovanni Giolitti, speaking as prime minister in June 1912, at the time when Bollea was seeking permission to publish some of the documents in the Turin archives for the years after 1815, explained his government's view that the risorgimento was too recent to be freely studied; revelations might be inconvenient, and 'it would not be right to have beautiful legends discredited by historical criticism'. When the period of open access was at last extended, this was only as far as 1847; in other words it stopped short at a point before the patriotic movement had reached its critical phase.

Mussolini was more ready than his liberal predecessors to open the archives of the nineteenth century, but his law of December 1939, though it allowed publication of documents up to 1870, nevertheless provided ample safeguards wherever it might be thought that the national interest demanded concealment of certain varieties of source material, and he specifically exempted from public scrutiny the papers of Cavour and the king. The importance which Mussolini attributed to patriotic history and national mythmaking is shown by his creation of an official Directorate of Historical Research, as whose head he appointed no less a figure than Count De Vecchi di Val Cismon, one of the notorious quadrumvirate who had commanded the fascist 'march on Rome' in 1922. De Vecchi used his position to lecture the professors of risorgimento history on their duty to demonstrate that Victor Emanuel played a 'decisive' and beneficial part 'at every stage of the national movement'. As he stated it, the official fascist view was that Cavour was no true liberal, that Victor Emanuel was an ideological forerunner of Mussolini, and that their Kingdom of Piedmont-Sardinia had to be extolled as 'the most authoritarian, the most *reactionary*, the most military and indeed the most *militaristic* state in the Italian peninsula'.

De Vecchi could get away with this because Mussolini continued the practice of earlier liberal governments in inhibiting certain kinds of research and encouraging the advancement of 'safe' scholars in the academic hierarchy. Fascist historians nevertheless, though they took De Vecchi's directives with quite preposterous solemnity, did not go as far as their predecessors in the outright falsification of documents for political purposes. Of books published before 1900 which are still fundamental sources for risorgimento history, a great number are known to be unreliable in that their texts have been deliberately manipulated to endorse a particular interpretation of events. Chiala and Bollea were not alone in having to submit to this practice. Cavour's appointment of Michelangelo Castelli as head of the Turin archives had been an essentially political choice. So was the appointment of Castelli's successor, Nicomede Bianchi, whose eight volumes of documents on European diplomacy have still after a hundred years not been superseded. Bianchi's documents abound in errors and mistranslations, in altered names, in actual interpolations, in dates changed so as to justify the cause of Piedmont and that of the monarchy. Bianchi agreed with Cavour that Mazzini was as much an enemy as were the Austrians, and he did not scruple to twist historical truth if it would help the cause. When in 1856 the archives had first been opened to him by Cavour, this was so that he should write a political tract, and for many years he used his privileged position as the senior archivist in Italy to denigrate his enemies and justify his friends.

It is easy to accept the necessity for wartime propaganda, and such this was. But it would be equally easy to demonstrate the potential danger of per-petuating beautiful legends long after their main purpose has been served. Matching one political argument with another, I might suggest that the defeat of the liberals by Mussolini's fascism is not unconnected with historical self-delusions about the kind of nation and the kind of political system that was produced by the risorgimento. Politics aside, however, the more immediately relevant fact can surely be admitted that any reasons for continued secrecy ought no longer to apply after the lapse of a hundred years.

These few paragraphs of introduction may help to indicate some of the prob-lems facing an investigator in this field. They will explain some of the limitations of the book which follows. They may also explain some of the reasons for writing this particular book and for the form in which it has been cast.

The intention has been to choose a number of controversial episodes and problems which seem crucial to any general interpretation of the risorgimento, and then to see how they look in the light of the documentation which is now available. Some general conclusions are set out in Chapter 1, which differs from the rest of the book in being an introduction or outline history of the whole period. Each of the following fourteen chapters takes a single aspect or segment of this general outline and looks at it in detail. Some chapters deal with constitutional history, others with diplomacy, others with economic and social questions, two with military history, and one with the problems of administration and local government. Occasionally they overlap, as the same episode is seen in various contexts. The underlying theme is the personal contribution which two very different individuals—the two most politically powerful men of the risorgimento—made to the way that Italy became a nation.

D. MACK SMITH

All Souls College
Oxford
March 1971

Acknowledgements

FOR use of manuscript material I make grateful acknowledgement to Lord Clarendon whose family papers are in the Bodleian Library, Oxford; to the Trustees of the Broadlands Archives for the Palmerston papers; to Her Majesty the Queen for gracious permission to quote from the Royal Archives at Windsor; to the Controller of H.M. Stationery Office for documents in Crown Copyright from the Public Record Office; also to the archives of the Ministère des Affaires Étrangères at Paris, the Haus-, Hof- und Staatsarchiv at Vienna, the Deutsches Zentralarchiv at Merseburg, the Archivio Cavour at Santena, the Archivio Lamarmora at Biella, the Archivio Mordini at Barga, to the Biblioteca Classense at Ravenna for the Carte Farini, to the Biblioteca dell'Archiginnasio at Bologna for the Carte Minghetti, to the Senate library and that of the Ministero degli Affari Esteri at Rome, the Biblioteca Fardelliana at Trapani, the Biblioteca Nazionale at Florence for the Fondo Peruzzi, the Biblioteca Riccardiana at Florence for the Carte Galeotti, and the Archivi di Stato at Turin, Florence, Rome, Naples, and Palermo; also to the risorgimento institutes at Rome, Milan, and Florence; finally to the Duke of Norfolk for his family papers at Arundel, to the British Museum for the Gladstone papers, to Christ Church College, Oxford, for the Salisbury papers, and the Bodleian Library for the Villari papers deposited by Lady Berwick.

The number of libraries which I have used, and of scholars and archivists whose help I have exploited, is too large to list or even to remember. Among libraries, the British Museum, the Widener at Harvard, and the Bodleian are very rich for this field. To them, as well as to the curators and owners of the collections listed above, I give my particular thanks, and more individually to Noel Blakiston of the Public Record Office and Catharine Carver of the Oxford University Press.

Some of the material included has already been published elsewhere in casual articles. The first chapter of the book is for the most part translated from *Il Culmine della Potenza Europea* (Garzanti, Milan, 1970), and is a much altered and expanded version of an essay written for the Cambridge Modern History. Chapters 3 and 9 are based on articles which originally appeared in the *Cambridge Historical Journal*; part of Chapter 6 was included in *Inghilterra e Toscana nell'Ottocento* (La Nuova Italia, Florence, 1968); Chapter 7 is based on a contribution to *The Diversity of History: Essays in Honour of Sir Herbert Butterfield* (ed. J. Elliot and H. Koenigsberger, Routledge, London, 1970); an earlier version of Chapter 8 is in the *Atti del XXXIX Congresso di Storia del*

Risorgimento; and Chapter 10 is translated from *Studi in Onore di Gino Luzzatto* (Giuffrè, Milan, 1950). I am glad to make acknowledgement to the Cambridge University Press and to Messrs. Routledge, Garzanti, Giuffrè, and La Nuova Italia.

D.M.S.

BIBLIOGRAPHICAL ABBREVIATIONS

Azeglio-Galeotti	*Carteggio Politico tra Massimo d'Azeglio e Leopoldo Galeotti dal 1849 al 1860,* ed. Marcus de Rubris (Turin, 1929)
Azeglio, Rendu	*L'Italie de 1847 à 1865: Correspondance Politique de Massimo d'Azeglio,* ed. Eugène Rendu (Paris, 1867)
Azeglio-Torelli	*Lettere di Massimo d'Azeglio a Giuseppe Torelli con Frammenti di Questo in Continuazione dei 'Miei Ricordi',* ed. Di Cesare Paoli (Milan, 1870)
Bersezio, *Il Regno*	Vittorio Bersezio, *Il Regno di Vittorio Emanuele II: Trent'Anni di Vita Italiana,* 8 vols. (Turin, 1889–93)
Bianchi, *Storia Documentata*	Nicomede Bianchi, *Storia Documentata della Diplomazia Europea in Italia dall'Anno 1814 all'Anno 1861,* 8 vols. (Turin, 1865–72)
Bollea, *Una Silloge*	*Una Silloge di Lettere del Risorgimento,* ed. L. C. Bollea (Turin, 1919)
Carte di Lanza	*Le Carte di Giovanni Lanza,* ed. C. De Vecchi di Val Cismon, 8 vols. (Turin, 1935–41)
Carteggi E. d'Azeglio	*Carteggi e Documenti Diplomatici Inediti di Emanuele d'Azeglio,* ed. A. Colombo, 2 vols. (Turin, 1920)
Carteggio Castelli	*Carteggio Politico di Michelangelo Castelli,* ed. Luigi Chiala, 2 vols. (Turin, 1890–1)
Carteggi Ricasoli	*Carteggi di Bettino Ricasoli,* ed. Mario Nobili, Sergio Camerani, Gaetano Arfè (1939–70). In course of publication.
Cavour: Discorsi	*C. Benso di Cavour: Discorsi Parlamentari,* ed. Adolfo Omodeo, Luigi Russo, Armando Saitta (1932–69). In course of publication.

Cavour e l'Inghilterra	*Cavour e l'Inghilterra: Carteggio con V. E. d'Azeglio, a cura della Commissione Reale Editrice*, 2 vols. (Bologna, 1933)
Cavour-Nigra	*Il Carteggio Cavour-Nigra dal 1858 al 1861 a cura della R. Commissione Editrice*, 4 vols. (Bologna, 1926–9)
Cavour: Questione Romana	*La Questione Romana negli Anni 1860–1861: Carteggio di Cavour*, 2 vols. (Bologna, 1929)
Cavour-Salmour	*Carteggio Cavour-Salmour, a cura della R. Commissione Editrice* (Bologna, 1936)
De la Rive, *Cavour*	W. De la Rive, *Le Comte de Cavour: Récits et Souvenirs* (Paris, 1862)
Diario di Collegno	*Diario Politico di Margherita Provana di Collegno (1852–56)*, ed. A. Malvezzi (Milan, 1926)
Epistolario La Farina	*Epistolario di Giuseppe La Farina*, ed. A. Franchi, 2 vols. (Milan, 1869)
Giacomo Dina	*Giacomo Dina e l'Opera sua nelle Vicende del Risorgimento Italiano*, ed. Luigi Chiala, 3 vols. (Turin, 1896–1903)
Gran Bretagna e Sardegna	*Le Relazioni Diplomatiche fra la Gran Bretagna e il Regno di Sardegna*, ed. Federico Curato and Giuseppe Giarrizzo (Rome, 1961–71). In course of publication.
Lettere di Cavour	*Lettere Edite ed Inedite di Camillo Cavour*, ed. Luigi Chiala, 6 vols. (Turin, 1884–7)
Lettere di V. Emanuele	*Le Lettere di Vittorio Emanuele II*, ed. F. Cognasso, 2 vols. (*Biblioteca Storica Italiana, Nuova Serie*, vols. VIII and IX) (Turin, 1966)
Lettere Ricasoli	*Lettere e Documenti del Barone Bettino Ricasoli*, ed. Marco Tabarrini and Aurelio Gotti, 10 vols. (Florence, 1887–95)
Liberazione del Mezzogiorno	*La Liberazione del Mezzogiorno e la Formazione del Regno d'Italia: Carteggi di Camillo Cavour*, 5 vols. (Bologna, 1949–54)
Massari, *Diario*	Giuseppe Massari, *Diario dalle Cento Voci 1858–1860*, ed. Emilia Morelli (Bologna, 1959)
Matter, *Cavour*	Paul Matter, *Cavour et l'Unité Italienne, 1856–61*, 3 vols. (Paris, 1922–7)
Nouvelles Lettres	C. *Cavour: Nouvelles Lettres Inédites*, ed. Amédée Bert (Turin, 1889)
Nuove Lettere	*Nuove Lettere Inedite del Conte di Cavour*, ed. E. Mayor (Turin, 1895)

Omodeo, *Cavour*	Adolfo Omodeo, *L'Opera Politica del Conte di Cavour*, 2 vols. (Florence, 1940)
Pio e V. Emanuele	*Pio IX e Vittorio Emanuele II dal loro Carteggio Privato*, ed. P. Pietro Pirri, 5 vols. (*Miscellanea Historiae Pontificiae*, vols. VIII, XVI, XVII, XXIV, XXV) (Rome, 1944–61)
Rassegna	*Rassegna Storica del Risorgimento* (Città di Castello, Aquila, Rome), 1914–71
Ricordi di Castelli	*Ricordi di Michelangelo Castelli (1847–1875)*, ed. L. Chiala (Turin, 1888)
Sclopis: Diario	*Federigo Sclopis di Salerano: Diario Segreto (1859–1878)*, P. Pietro Pirri (Turin, 1959)
Scritti d'Azeglio	*Massimo d'Azeglio: Scritti e Discorsi Politici*, ed. Marcus de Rubris, 3 vols. (Florence, 1931–8)
Scritti di Garibaldi	*Edizione Nazionale degli Scritti di Giuseppe Garibaldi, a cura della Reale Commissione*, 6 vols. (Bologna, 1932–7)
Scritti di Mazzini	*Scritti Editi ed Inediti di Giuseppe Mazzini*, 100 vols. (Imola, 1906–61)
F.O.	Foreign Office (Public Record Office, London)
M. Aff. Étrangères	Ministère des Affaires Étrangères (Paris), Correspondance Politique, Sardaigne ('Italie' from 1861 onwards)
P.R.O.	Public Record Office (London)

ITALY
IN THE
RISORGIMENTO

THE REGIONS

N

FRANCE

SWITZERLAND

AUSTRIAN EMPIRE

TYROL

Savoy

LOMBARDY

VENETIA

PIEDMONT

PARMA

Istria

Liguria

MODENA

Nice

LUCCA

ROMAGNA

San Marino

Monaco

TUSCANY

MARCHES

UMBRIA

Abruzzi

CORSICA

SARDINIA

NAPLES

Apulia

Calabria

SICILY

PAPAL STATES

KINGDOM OF THE
TWO SICILIES

PIEDMONT-SARDINIA
(with Savoy and Nice)

LOMBARDO-VENETIA
(Austrian)

0   50   100 miles
0   80   161 km

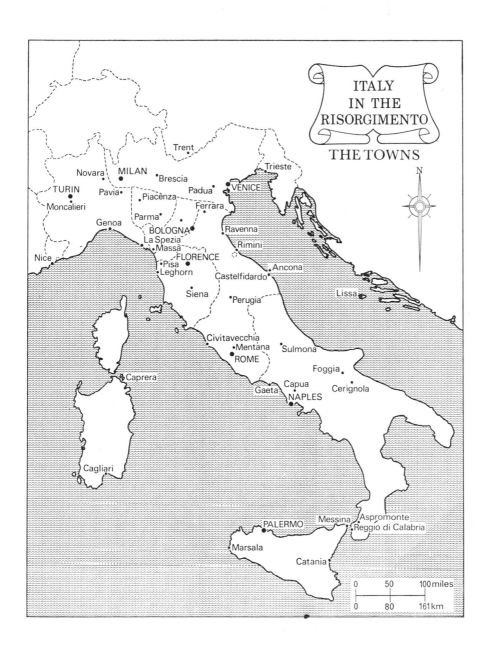

ITALY
IN THE
RISORGIMENTO

THE TOWNS

N

Trent

Trieste

Novara • MILAN • Brescia
TURIN • Padua • VENICE
Pavia • Piacènza
Moncalieri
Parma • Ferrara
Genoa
BOLOGNA • Ravenna
La Spezia • Massa • Rimini
Nice • Pisa • FLORENCE
Leghorn • Ancona
Castelfidardo
Siena
• Perugia • Lissa

Civitavecchia
• Mentana • Sulmona
ROME
Foggia
Caprera
Capua • Cerignola
Gaeta • NAPLES

Cagliari

Messina • Aspromonte
PALERMO • Reggio di Calabria
Marsala
Catania

0   50   100 miles
0   80   161 km

V.E.C—2

PRIME MINISTERS UNDER VICTOR EMANUEL

De Launay	27 March 1849	–	7 May 1849
Azeglio	7 May 1849	–	4 November 1852
Cavour	4 November 1852	–	19 July 1859
Lamarmora	19 July 1859	–	21 January 1860
Cavour	21 January 1860	–	6 June 1861
Ricasoli	12 June 1861	–	3 March 1862
Rattazzi	3 March 1862	–	8 December 1862
Farini	8 December 1862	–	24 March 1863
Minghetti	24 March 1863	–	28 September 1864
Lamarmora	28 September 1864	–	20 June 1866
Ricasoli	20 June 1866	–	10 April 1867
Rattazzi	10 April 1867	–	27 October 1867
Menabrea	27 October 1867	–	14 December 1869
Lanza	14 December 1869	–	10 July 1873
Minghetti	10 July 1873	–	18 March 1876
Depretis	25 March 1876	–	24 March 1878

I

An Outline of Risorgimento
History, 1840–1870

UNTIL after 1840 there were few people who believed that an Italian nation existed or should exist. Even inside Italy, all but a tiny handful of the population would have regarded the idea as not worthy of discussion. Ten distinct Italian states claimed to have an independent existence, and not one of them possessed a government with the resources or even the desire to revive Napoleon's partial experiment in national unity.

The political settlement of 1814–15 left regional divisions as strong as they had been before Napoleon's invasion. Austrian domination of the peninsula after 1815 did not have the effect of unifying popular sentiment but just made it difficult for Italians to play off their former oppressors against each other. The Habsburgs of Austria owned not only Lombardy but also Venice, and they controlled the central duchies of Tuscany, Parma, and Modena through a network of family relationships, while Austrian forces were also ready to quell any insurrections in the nominally independent kingdoms of Naples and Piedmont. Naples and Sicily under a Bourbon king formed a large single state, the kingdom of the Two Sicilies, but there was as little feeling of community between Sicily and Naples as between the south of Italy and the north. Naples and Palermo, the two largest Italian towns, seemed infinitely remote to anyone in Milan or Turin.[1] All these various regions, north and south, were further divided internally by mutually unintelligible dialects, so that people who lived fifty miles away from each other might be quite unable to communicate, and neighbouring villages might well have incompatible systems of measurements. The overwhelming majority of the common people indicated on many occasions that they desired good government rather than self-government, let alone national unification, and during the fifty years after the French occupation in 1796 they showed few patriotic preconceptions in response to successive invasions by Napoleon and Metternich.

---

[1] Letters were received in Milan much more quickly from New York or India than from Naples, wrote Giuseppe Sacchi in 1845; 'we have, as usual, to read the German newspapers or the *Allgemeine Zeitung* if we want to know what our so-called brothers are doing in Naples. They are as remote from us as China is' (*Annali Universali di Statistica* (Milan), 2nd ser. VI (1845), 118).

Between 1840 and 1870 Italy was to be politically unified. Yet the course of this risorgimento followed no preconceived plan; on the contrary it was a much more empirical and haphazard affair than later generations were to imagine. Many various and even contradictory forces aided it directly or indirectly. Much stronger than feelings of patriotism were individual motives of protest, against taxes and conscription, against clerical and aristocratic privilege, or the protest of class against class, region against region, country-side against town. Apart from these, a desire for political change was some-times consciously formulated, especially among the small class of military and civilian officials who, under the various Napoleonic regimes in Italy, had been encouraged to stand up against aristocracy and unenlightenment, but their voice was only one among many; or, rather, they spoke with many voices. Secret societies had grown up in the years after 1815, whose type was the *carboneria* with its vague and multi-faceted aspirations for liberation; such societies might well have some political motivation, but they could be politically in conflict with each other.

Social and economic protest often formed the most powerful of all incen-tives towards change. In almost all the major towns there were urban riots which helped to trigger off outbreaks of political revolution. Everywhere the peasants were ready to seize any opportunity to rise and better their lot, or at least to take revenge on landlords and city-dwellers for real and imagined grievances. Some far-sighted merchants wanted a wider national market and the removal of internal trade barriers: for example, there existed seven customs posts along the 120 miles between Bologna and Lucca, and each one of these could delay merchandise for several hours.[1] Anyone involved in commerce could see that the new railway age was going to need interlocking communica-tions and standardization of measures and currencies. More important still was that landowners, who were much more numerous than tradesmen and manufacturers, could recognize the advantages of creating a common metric system and an Italian customs union along the lines of the German Zollverein. Possibly the developing steamship routes from Bombay to Suez and Europe could be used to restore Italy to a privileged position on the main highway of world trade, provided only that Italians were sufficiently united and strong to press their claims.

At a different level altogether a cultural movement took its share in the general upheaval which accompanied the making of Italy. Gradually there was diffused through the different states a common literary language as defined by Alessandro Manzoni on the basis of the spoken vernacular of Tuscany. At last by 1830 there was in existence a real, though small, reading public. Books and magazines promoted a habit of retrospection and a cult of folk-memories held in common about the past greatness of Italy, about the

[1] Ibid. 1st ser. LXXVIII (1843), 198; LXII (1839), 103; goods could take over seven weeks to go the 200 miles from Florence to Milan, or longer in the winter.

Sicilian Vespers, the Lombard League, and the medieval guelphs who once fought against German invaders. Pamphlets were written about current affairs, legally or illegally. An educated minority was thus at hand to formulate present grievances in the struggle for individual freedoms, and also as a weapon to secure independence of the foreigner. Only after these two aims had been secured would there be much point in speculating about political unity. But already in 1839 the first 'Italian' scientific congress met at Pisa, and there was another each year until 1847, all testifying to the growth of a new cultural unity in Italy and to the economic and intellectual interdependence of its several states.[1]

The external context of this struggle for national self-identification was Franco-Austrian rivalry, and each Italian state tended to side with either France or Austria as part of the effort to stay alive and win power. Tangled diplomatic situations in Europe called for forceful statesmanship inside Italy and also needed effective support from other countries. The risorgimento would also require one Italian state prepared to develop a sense of aggression in order to annex its neighbours and aggregate a greater Italian kingdom.

Such a nucleus was eventually to be found in the kingdom of Piedmont-Sardinia, a country largely French by language and culture, yet which had been permeated less thoroughly than other parts of Italy by the liberalizing influences of the French Revolution, and which in the process of centuries had developed an effective military tradition. Until 1840 the royal house of Savoy which governed Piedmont showed little enthusiasm for either liberalism or Italian patriotism. Charles Albert, who was king from 1831 to 1849, agreed with his ministers that their small subalpine state was a nation of its own. They looked with some distrust on any idea of a merger with other states of northern Italy until it became quite clear that such a merger would be an absorption of other states into their own. They had been fortunate enough in the settlement of 1815 to be awarded Genoa and the Ligurian coast, and this made Charles Albert's kingdom much less French and more obviously Italian than it had been before. Though the republican aristocrats and merchants of Genoa had protested in 1815 against subjection to Turin, ultimately they helped to bring not only a more Italian consciousness but also a more liberal and commercial tone to the narrow court aristocracy of the capital.

Elsewhere in Italy there was no obvious competitor to Charles Albert. Duke Francis of Modena and Pope Gregory XVI in the Papal States ruled until 1846, Marie Louise of Parma and Charles Ludovic of Lucca until 1847, Leopold II of Tuscany and Ferdinand II of Naples until 1859; not one of these rose above mediocrity. The greatest competition to Piedmont was to be

---

[1] No Italian periodical gave nearly as much coverage to the Pisa meeting as did the German *Isis* (Leipzig), 1841, pp. 481–2. Four hundred scientists turned up on that occasion, mostly Tuscans; in 1841, at Florence, there were more than twice as many, of whom 97 came from Lombardo-Venetia, 93 from Piedmont, and 11 from the Two Sicilies; at Naples in 1845 there were over 1,700 inscribed members.

found in Lombardy and Venice which were governed by a succession of Austrian viceroys who were usually among the more efficient and enlightened rulers of the peninsula. Prince Metternich, the chief minister of Austria, was of course opposed to Italian patriotism because it would pose a direct threat to Austrian influence in Italy, but he had wanted to grant some autonomy to Lombardo-Venetia, and, though the Austrian emperor prevented this, a great number of Italians continued to serve the Austrian administration with loyalty and even enthusiasm.

Leopold of Tuscany was a relatively enlightened ruler whose absolutist ideas were modified by a well-meaning inefficiency. Though the influence of Austria was apparent in intellectual life and politics, Florence possessed a small English community and provided a home for many exiles from other Italian states. Interesting developments were to be found there in popular education and in the use of new agricultural techniques. The Tuscan legal system was in some respects more progressive than the Code Napoléon itself; and, largely owing to the naturalized Swiss, Vieusseux, Florence was for a time able to challenge Milan's claims to be the cultural centre of Italy. Tuscany was for these reasons, and because its language was the lingua franca of Italy, a preferred meeting ground for the all-Italian scientific congresses in and after 1839.

At Rome, on the other hand, cultural life was discouraged. There were few scientists in the Papal States, and Pope Gregory forbade his subjects to attend these scientific congresses. At Rome, if government was not consistently intolerant, at least it was arbitrary, sometimes corrupt, and always infinitely slow. There were no published accounts of government expenditure, and dissentient opinions had little chance of getting past the ecclesiastical censorship and the Holy Office. In the Roman countryside a counter-revolutionary and terroristic force of irregulars, the *centurioni*, had been given almost unlimited powers to suppress any sign of liberalism. The cardinal legates who governed the various regions gained materially from political abuses, and this was an additional reason why they should have had little inclination towards reform, while Pope Gregory's fear of losing the temporal power pushed the papacy into an especially anti-liberal policy. So long as he could count on Austrian troops, Gregory had nothing to lose by intransigence. This was the strength of his position, but it was an essential weakness of Metternich's political system, since papal misgovernment eventually forced the 'Italian question' upon other governments in Europe and gave them an excuse to intervene against Austrian predominance. French troops came to Ancona in 1832 in order to offset the presence of the Austrians in Bologna, and this was an important moment in recreating that balance of forces which was to prove so fruitful for the development of a nationalist movement in Italy. By this time there were also some British statesmen who realized that the Austrian domination of Italy might be a danger to European peace.

The one Italian who by the early 1830s had formulated a comprehensive doctrine of nationalism was Giuseppe Mazzini, a Genoese citizen far removed from the world of courts and governments. Mazzini had an uncompromising conviction that both French and Austrian influence must be removed from the Italian peninsula. All subsequent leaders in the risorgimento, however much they later differed with him and tried to deny his influence, learnt at the feet of this one man. The ultimate goal, in his opinion, was national unity no less, but his preaching of this theme to the pope and the king of Piedmont fell on deaf ears, because it was thought to be seditious and absurd. Imprisoned and exiled by the Piedmontese, Mazzini became a full-time revolutionary in London, from which place he tried to direct the Italian nationalist movement. Almost all his attempts at insurrection were to fail, but as an educative force the importance of his work of propaganda cannot be overestimated, and in practical politics he was often able to terrify his opponents and force them into taking the very steps he was prevented from taking himself. Mazzini's treatise on guerrilla warfare may not have been very important in itself, but it shows that he anticipated Garibaldi in recognizing a revolutionary tactic which was admirably suited to Italy, and Metternich promptly sent for a copy to study.[1]

If Mazzini was the leader of revolutionary Italy, Charles Albert aspired to be the leader of the conservative establishment. His conservatism was especially pronounced during the first two-thirds of his reign. He was not opposed to employing Austrian troops to stop revolution in Italy, and once told Metternich that his happiest hour would be when he could serve alongside Austrian soldiers against the liberal France of Louis-Philippe. Charles Albert's wife was an Austrian Habsburg. Far from looking southwards with a view to unifying Italy, he still had territorial claims beyond the Alps in France,[2] and he refused when the king of Naples suggested the formation of a league of Italian states. No wonder that high officials at Vienna continued to speak of Piedmont as virtually an outlying province of Austria and referred to its army as the advance guard of the imperial forces.[3]

Eventually Charles Albert was to change sides as fate and ambition pushed him in a different direction. He failed to gain territory from France, and hopes of annexing part of Switzerland were to collapse with the defeat of the seven Catholic cantons which formed the separatist Sonderbund. Instead he turned to Lombardy, long-time an object of ambition for the house of Savoy. Once he could be sure he would not need Metternich's help against liberals at home, he could see Austria as his rival, even a dangerous rival, especially when

[1] *Scritti di Mazzini*, III. 231–41; F. A. Gualterio, *Gli Ultimi Rivolgimenti Italiani: Memorie Storiche*, vol. I, pt. iv (Documenti) (Florence, 1851), p. 395.

[2] P. Silva, *Figure e Momenti di Storia Italiana* (Milan, 1939), p. 148.

[3] R. Romeo, *Dal Piemonte Sabaudo all'Italia Liberale* (Turin, 1964), pp. 42–4; Charles Albert's treaty with Austria was later transposed by court propagandists to the reign of his predecessor (see Gualterio, *Gli Ultimi Rivolgimenti*, vol. I, pt. i (1850), p. 606, and Bianchi, *Storia Documentata*, IV. 44–5); *Memorie R. Accademia delle Scienze* (Turin), LXVI (1923), no. 3, p. 1.

Austrian efficiency threatened the import trade of Genoa by building up the rival city of Trieste. By 1840, even his pro-Austrian foreign minister, Solaro della Margarita, was wondering whether revolutions might not one day break up the Austrian empire and leave Piedmont a free hand in Lombardy. Only the king's own character made him hesitate in hastening this consummation. As the French ambassador wrote, many people at Turin well knew that he 'will listen with pleasure to dreams about the future of Italy which promise him a great role in history. But at the moment of action it will all fade away.'[1]

Charles Albert possessed an almost mystical attachment to absolutism, but he genuinely favoured paternalistic reform to repair some of the deficiencies which made his one of the more backward states of Europe. Several different currencies still circulated in the component provinces of his realm, and internal trade barriers hindered commerce. Customs duties had multiplied by four times between 1815 and 1830, and hence Genoese trade had seriously fallen as a result of being annexed by Piedmont. Many Ligurians were emigrating to America because of economic hardship, while Genoa was being outstripped by Leghorn because of the more liberal economic policies adopted by Tuscany. Internal civic jealousies were such that some of the citizens of Turin deluded themselves that their own prosperity depended on lessening that of the Ligurian coast. Charles Albert was not among those who thought like this, and some restrictive tariffs were lifted after 1835. A number of advantageous commercial treaties were signed, one of which with the United States aimed to capture some of the transit trade in tobacco from America to Milan and Switzerland. A slight impetus was also given to constructing irrigation canals and port installations.

The cumulative effect of Charles Albert's reforms may not have been very considerable, but they mark an altogether new turn in the history of Piedmont-Sardinia. Among them was a not entirely successful attempt to break the shackles of feudalism in the island of Sardinia where private baronial courts and personal servitude were still in existence. A reform of the legal codes brought about a partial return to the Napoleonic system which Charles Albert's predecessors had inconsiderately abandoned after 1814. Then in 1842 permission was given for the creation of an Agricultural Society, which had a widely liberalizing influence through its two thousand members. Like earlier such bodies in Lombardy and Tuscany, this Agricultural Society helped to change the pattern of agriculture by experimenting with new breeds of farm animal, attacking plant diseases, reclaiming land, and improving the quality of wine. Piedmont was still an agricultural country, and its basic exports were silk, wine, rice, and oil; towards the end of Charles Albert's reign, however, banks were founded at Genoa and Turin, and a belated start was made with railway construction.

This reforming spirit was not peculiar to Piedmont. It was Naples and not

[1] *Rassegna*, XI (1924), 633–4.

northern Italy that produced the first Italian steamboat (1818) and the first railway (1839), while Naples was one of the first towns to adopt street lighting by gas. It was also Ferdinand II, the Bourbon king of the Two Sicilies, who talked of making a customs union among Italian states. A greater political tolerance was to be found in Parma than in Turin, and there were more liberal tariffs and laws in Tuscany, while Lombardy had a far more efficient system of administration. Only in Tuscany could non-Catholics easily attend university; only in Parma could Jews hold jobs in the public administration, whereas in Piedmont, as in the Papal States, they had to live in ghettos and could not own land.

Of all Italian states, Austrian Lombardy showed the greatest prosperity and the greatest advance in industrialization,[1] as it also boasted the finest system of irrigation and communications in continental Europe. Despite the usual allegations, it was not Austrian obscurantism so much as lack of capitalist enterprise and the municipal jealousies of Bergamo and Treviglio that held up the Milan-Venice railroad. Metternich was not hostile to this railway, though he would have liked it to be free of government control and finance, and he had hoped that local entrepreneurs would have shown more interest. Subsequently the Austrians were blamed for hindering its construction, but some Lombards praised the Austrian emperor for the speed with which the railway question was being tackled. Italian economists, by comparison, had a by no means universal enthusiasm for railways. A committee to consider railway building was appointed by a congress of Italian scientists, but apparently never took the trouble to meet.

Over other matters, too, Austrian Lombardy led the way. Elementary education was free and compulsory, and technical schools were far ahead of anywhere else in Italy. In 1830 Lombardy claimed 1 child in school out of every 13, as against 1 to every 16 in England and Scotland, and 1 to over 100 in the city of Naples.[2] The Austrian taxes were lower than those of their predecessors or successors in Lombardy, and the press laws allowed the existence of twice as many newspapers as in Piedmont or Tuscany. Carlo Cattaneo's *Politecnico* freely advocated revolutionary liberal reforms, and the *Annali di Statistica* possessed distinguished correspondents all over Italy who

[1] In 1830 a comparative table of figures gave:

	Population	National income in millions of francs
Austrian Italy	4,930,000	122
Kingdom of the Two Sicilies	7,420,000	84
Piedmont-Sardinia	3,800,000	60
Papal States	2,590,000	30
Tuscany	1,275,000	17
Parma	440,000	4·6
Modena	379,000	4

(*Annali Universali di Statistica*, XXXI (1832), 313.)

[2] Richard Hyse, 'Statistics in an Autocracy', *Il Risorgimento* (Milan), XVIII (Feb. 1966), 49.

could not publish in their home states. In 1842 a Piedmontese minister visited Lombardo-Venetia and was struck by its wealth: admittedly there was political discontent, and he reported that junior administrative officials were often unsympathetic; nor did he approve of the way that the Austrians were trying to educate the lower classes above their station; nevertheless he greatly admired their success in promoting prosperity.[1]

Metternich had lately been planning a close economic union of Austria with northern Italy as part of his drive against Mazzinian doctrines of Italian nationalism. Nor was such an idea entirely utopian, for feelings of Italian nationality did not stop the Milan Chamber of Commerce advocating entry into the German Zollverein as a means to greater prosperity, and even among the radicals there were some, for example Cattaneo, who thought that Austria might possibly be a more progressive and less overbearing ally than Piedmont. Metternich correctly identified these provincial jealousies as a dominant aspect of the Italian scene. Where the Austrian rulers failed was in preventing individual grievances from gradually developing into a larger desire for whole-sale renovation: and when the movement for reforms reached a certain point it inevitably became political, so playing into the hands of the patriots and the sects.

This imminent political revolution frightened Charles Albert as much as it frightened Metternich, and with reason, for the Albertine reforms were not so advanced that he ceased to be a main target of the radical Left, nor were they particularly effective in practice. The Jesuits remained more strongly entrenched at Turin than almost anywhere; the new codes of law did not abolish the separate ecclesiastical courts and still permitted rights of criminal asylum in churches. There continued to be serious discrimination against Waldensian Protestants and Jews; and fanatical orthodoxy was such that, when Paganini the famous violin-player died, even though visited on his death-bed by a priest, the body lay five years before being allowed burial. Solaro della Margarita even persuaded Gregory XVI in 1841 to restore ecclesiastical privileges in Piedmont which in Austria and Tuscany had been abolished fifty years earlier. The censorship at Turin insisted that the word 'country' had to be employed instead of such dangerous terms as 'nation' or 'Italy'; the words 'liberal' and 'constitution' were impermissible, and 'revolution' had to be replaced by 'anarchy'.[2] As late as 1845 it was forbidden for anyone to write about railways even in purely technical journals; and when Cavour published at Paris a famous article on the subject, Charles Albert told him to leave the country.[3] To a travelled man such as Camille de Cavour, to return from London to Turin was like entering 'une espèce d'enfer intellec-

---

[1] *La Politica Estera del Piemonte sotto Carlo Alberto secondo il Carteggio del Conte di Sambuy*, ed. M. degli Alberti (Turin, 1919), pp. 78–82.

[2] F. Predari, *I Primi Vagiti della Libertà Italiana in Piemonte* (Milan, 1861), p. 94.

[3] A. Manno, *Aneddoti Documentati sulla Censura in Piemonte dalla Restaurazione alla Costituzione* (Turin, 1907), pp. 46–7.

tu●●[1] and another distinguished Piedmontese, Massimo d'Azeglio, preferred
to live and write his novels in the much freer atmosphere of Milan.

Charles Albert himself was by temperament shifty, given to concealment,
even deliberately misleading his friends. His diary shows him distrusting
everyone and liking to play off one minister against another. Foreign ambassadors remarked on his love of mystification and his changefulness of view.
Metternich by 1848 regarded him as 'ambitious as well as vacillating: he
inclines towards despotism, and ridicules the liberals, requiring from them
only the incense which the literati burn to him; he detests not only France,
but also Austria which bars him from moving towards the throne of Italy'.[2]
Charles Albert had at first regarded ideas of national independence as merely
a disguise for hostility to throne and altar: to him they spelt Mazzini, in other
words republicanism and social revolution. Certainly he was irked by Austrian
intrusions into Italy, though as late as July 1844 his ministers had been discussing with the Austrian commander Marshal Radetzky the possibility of
forming a joint Austro-Piedmontese army under Charles Albert's command to
crush the forces of revolution. But by this time the king was also considering
the possibility of a very different kind of war. Anxious as he was to outdo
other Italian sovereigns and increase his own power in relation to theirs, he
eventually managed to find conservative and Catholic reasons for exploiting
Italian patriotism in a dynastic war against Austria.

The necessary intellectual stimulus for this change came from the 'neo-
guelph' writers who in the early 1840s made their kind of moderate and
Catholic liberalism almost obligatory for men of culture. Even though they
formed no organized party, the neo-guelphs collectively provided a respectable
alternative to Mazzini's patriotism, and gave themselves a firm intellectual
basis by linking up more effectively than he ever managed to do with previous
cultural traditions in Italy. Manzoni, Rosmini, and Tommaseo helped to
associate patriotism with liberal Catholicism. Others tried to involve the pope
by showing how the medieval papacy in an earlier age had fought for Italian
independence against the foreigner. In 1848 these Catholic writers and their
liberal friends were to enter practical politics: Farini and Minghetti became
ministers of Pope Pius IX, Gino Capponi became prime minister of Tuscany,
while Balbo, Gioberti, and Azeglio were each in 1848–9 to become prime
minister of Piedmont. Already before 1847, even when their books were not
allowed publication by the various Italian censorships, these moderates had
acquired a profound influence throughout Italy. They were individually
reluctant to defy the authority of existing states, but the *ancien régime* was
not so efficient that it could prevent the widespread circulation of these new
ideas.

[1] *Lettere di Cavour*, I. 328; *Camillo Cavour: Epistolario*, vol. I (1815–1840) (Bologna, 1962), p. 142.
[2] *Aus Metternich's Nachgelassenen Papieren*, ed. R. Metternich-Winneburg (Vienna, 1883), VII. 555–6;
Revue Historique (Paris), CLXIII (1930), 110.

Silvio Pellico's *Le Mie Prigioni* had appeared as early as 1832, describing ten tortured years in Austrian prisons. Although written in a spirit of religious resignation rather than of patriotic indignation, its great success labelled Austria as the major oppressor of the peninsula, to the surprise and embarrassment of its author. At Brussels in 1843 the Abbé Gioberti produced his *Del Primato Morale e Civile degli Italiani* and dedicated it to Pellico. He argued that there existed an Italian race united in blood, religion, and language, even if Mazzini's idea of political unity was unattainable; and in Gioberti's view the leader of this Italian community must be the pope. Although he had no great faith in papal politics, he hid his deeper thoughts because he was aiming at an audience which included conservative politicians and priests. He thus obtained permission to sell in Italy a book which reconciled religion and country; patriotism suddenly became orthodox and a matter for public discussion instead of for hole-and-corner conspiracy. Later Gioberti openly attacked the Jesuits and the narrow Catholicism of the *Curia*, but it was his earlier appeal to papal leadership which was remembered, and his theme of Italian 'primacy' helped to provide the necessary self-confidence for political revolution. The real trouble, according to him, was that Italians, despite their potential capacity to lead Europe, were in practice inert and unwarlike; they were too anxious to blame foreign governments for their plight, just as an excuse to avoid having to blame themselves, and to escape the inconvenience of having to take action. In stressing self-help and self-confidence, Gioberti was working parallel with Mazzini to carry out a fundamental act of national education.

Another educational writer was Cesare Balbo, especially in his historical writings which gave people a sense of continuity with the past and made them proud of the italianateness which they had in common. Balbo agreed with Gioberti, to whom he dedicated *Delle Speranze d'Italia*, that a loose federal state was the most they were likely to achieve, since the various peoples of Italy were so distinct that they were bound to need different forms of government. His own concern was less with general principles than practical possibilities, and he hoped that at some point Austria would expand eastward into the Balkans and leave Italy more free to arrange her own affairs. Italians were thereby encouraged to postpone self-determination and wait upon international events outside their control; and certainly Balbo was anxious to deter them from the dangerous alternative of national insurrection, since he could see no tyranny in Italy so great that it could warrant a general rising. Nor was he absolutely opposed to the Austrians: on the contrary, if Metternich would only accept an Italy free from foreign dominance, he thought that Italians would then help Austria to dominate other submerged nationalities. But independence must first be won, if necessary by war. 'We have reached such a point of decadence that our only hope is to fight a war, even a war in which we have no practical interest'; and every good Italian, added Balbo, would gladly sacrifice Dante, Michelangelo, and Raphael in return for a leader who could lead them to military victory.[1] As a loyal Piedmontese aristocrat, Balbo envisaged not the pope but Charles Albert as head of an Italian confederation. Giacomo Durando went still further by suggesting confiscation of most of the pope's temporal possessions, after which Italy might be redivided into three monarchies federated together.[2] It is noteworthy that, of these three Piedmontese authors, Gioberti published his volume in Belgium, while Balbo and Durando had to publish theirs in France and Switzerland.

Meanwhile, almost every year, in defiance of these startling but still essentially moderate counsels, minor insurrections were started by a quite different group of people who desired something more revolutionary. Their inspiration, though not always their direction, came from Mazzini, who made it an article of faith to want not a federation of monarchies but a single republic, not something imposed from above but autonomous self-determination from below. To Gioberti's and Balbo's objections that uncoordinated local insurrections would be wasteful and disheartening, Mazzini replied that only thus could you rouse ordinary people, and without popular involvement a revolution would fail and deserve to fail. The landing in Calabria by Attilio and Emilio Bandiera in 1844 might seem futile, but in fact their execution by King Ferdinand of Naples was another powerful act of patriotic education; and Mazzini argued that, until some Italians were prepared to die for their patriotic faith, patriotism would not be taken seriously. This exile in distant London, often with little encouragement inside Italy itself, continued to bend his whole energies to the generation of a powerful force against which (and subsequently for which) the liberal royalists were driven to compete.

Dramatic evidence of this competition came in 1845, when Charles Albert told Azeglio to hint to the subjects of the pope that, if only they would renounce republicanism and revolution, one day the Piedmontese army might fight for Italian liberation. In 1846, Azeglio's *Degli Ultimi Casi di Romagna* agreed with Balbo, to whom it was dedicated, that insurrection would be inexcusable. 'To call the present rulers of Italy tyrants would be a childish absurdity', wrote Azeglio.[3] Luckily, he thought, the poorer classes would not waste their time in petty risings, for such activity would only provoke another disastrous Austrian invasion. Guerrilla warfare, said Azeglio criticizing Mazzini, would be absurd in Italy for obvious geographic reasons; instead, the only hope was in Charles Albert and his regular army. In this very year, 1846, a commercial war broke out when the Austrians put a prohibitive duty on Piedmontese wines. Such a tax was serious for many Piedmontese agriculturists. Solaro continued in office until 1847, but before this date the hypothesis of a possible

---

[1] C. Balbo, *Lettere di Politica e Letteratura* (Turin, 1859), p. 445.

[2] G. Durando, *Della Nazionalità Italiana* (Lausanne, 1846), p. 97.

[3] *Scritti d'Azeglio*, I. 8; even this pamphlet could not be published in Piedmont, but came out in a clandestine edition at Florence and then in Corsica.

war one day against Austria was already being considered, even though no effective preparations were made for such a war. Piedmontese governments had for over a century kept at the back of their minds the idea that one day they might supplant Austria in Milan, and, now that moderates as well as Mazzinians were making public confession of national sentiment, this ambition was shortly to become one of the many explosive forces in Italy.

Just when the patriots were wanting action but uncertain what to do, a new pope was elected in June 1846. This proved to be the first major weakening in the power structure of the *ancien régime*, and Solaro later stated that without it Charles Albert would not have been emboldened to claim the national leadership.[1] Pius IX was not a political liberal, but he wanted to relax the tension which had grown up between the papal government and its subjects. His amnesty of some thousand prisoners and exiles, although only a customary act of clemency and fully approved by Metternich, was read as adhesion to the neo-guelph programme of liberty and independence. Wild scenes of enthusiasm greeted this amnesty, and Pius, no calculating politician but susceptible to applause, was thus encouraged to make other concessions. His statement in favour of railways and his decree announcing the grant of a *consulta di stato* were in response to popular demonstrations, and they were mistakenly interpreted as signifying his conversion to Gioberti's myth of a liberal and patriotic papacy. Concessions were made to local self-government, and a promising proposal was advanced for a customs union with other Italian states. The Jews were allowed outside the ghettos, and were no longer to be received during carnival with the formal kick which had symbolized their servile status—hitherto they had been forbidden by the Inquisition to spend a single night outside the ghetto and were even forbidden to maintain friendly contact with Christians.[2] Metternich became seriously alarmed, for the revolutionaries could now march under the unexceptionable slogan of 'viva Pio nono'; a guelph party was growing up again as in the Middle Ages, but this time with no ghibellines to contain it. Even the Sacred College of cardinals was upset by the pope's quite unexpected concessions to the laity, and among the conservatives at Rome there was wild talk of rebellion and possible schism.[3]

The year 1847 saw the sovereigns of Italy in general retreat, especially as the bad harvest of the previous summer brought food riots which built up pressure for economic reforms. This was one of those rare moments when ordinary people could feel politically powerful. Nevertheless opinion was of course far from clear or unanimous. Charles Albert's reluctance to make

[1] C. Solaro della Margarita, *Memorandum Storico Politico* (Turin, 1851), pp. 541–2.
[2] Decree of 1843, Achille Gennarelli, *Il Governo Pontificio e lo Stato Romano: Documenti* (Prato, 1860), I. 304–5.
[3] G. F.-H. and J. Berkeley, *Italy in the Making, June 1846 to 1 January 1848* (Cambridge, 1936), II. 75, 233.

concessions found support in the lack of enthusiasm for political reform among both peasants and nobility in Piedmont-Sardinia;[1] and he forbade his subjects to read the newly emancipated newspapers of Tuscany and Rome. But the king could not remain unmoved when, on the death of Duke Francis, Austrian troops entered Modena, nor when in July 1847 Radetzky (without waiting to consult Metternich) defied papal protests and for reasons of security occupied the garrison town of Ferrara. The Austrians had perhaps been relying on the undoubted fact that some Italians in papal Ferrara wanted annexation to Austria: but it was a bad miscalculation, for as well as provoking Piedmont, Austria lost her pretence to be the guardian of legitimacy and the settlement of 1815; it also impelled Pius further towards the liberals, and gave Turin the excuse for a war which could be justified as defensive and in aid of the Holy See.

By September the king was openly hinting at his desire for Italian independence of Austria, and in October, after hearing from Balbo that Leopold of Tuscany and Pius IX were both outbidding him for the moral leadership of Italy, he dismissed Solaro and introduced reforms in local government and a looser censorship. At the same time he reiterated his solemn promise to concede no more than this: Italian independence would be welcome, yet it would be quite incompatible with the grant of a constitution; in his view the achievement of independence would need soldiers not lawyers, it would need firm government rather than any experiment in popular representation. But these initial concessions proved, just as they had for the pope, to be a slippery slope. Balbo and Cavour began a new journal, *Il Risorgimento*, with a conservative point of view but advocating further political changes, and hinting that even the best laws were unworkable under absolutist government. When demonstrations took place at Genoa in December, the king at first thought they were an attempt to restore Genoese independence and ordered his troops to suppress them. Demonstrations were something unusual and unwelcome; they frightened him by raising visions of republicanism, especially when his soldiers fraternized with the demonstrators.

In southern Italy, if people had less idea of Italian patriotism than in the north, they were more revolutionary just because they were far poorer and had less to lose. King Ferdinand at Naples realized the need to meet this problem by providing cheaper food, but bureaucratic inefficiency held up action. His weakest point was Sicily, where the aristocracy resented his antifeudal legislation and where there was general dislike of his refusal to give Sicilians a monopoly of jobs in their own island. Moreover, although the moderates followed Azeglio's advice in looking askance on insurrection, the more radical elements in Sicily possessed no such scruples. All they needed

[1] M. Minghetti, *Miei Ricordi* (4th ed., Turin, 1889), I .307: G. Prato, *Fatti e Dottrine Economiche alla Vigilia del 1848* (Milan, 1921), pp. 369–70: 'In the villages the cry of "Long live Charles Albert and his reforms" was changed into "Long live Charles Albert and his uniforms".'

was for a rumour to circulate with the news that on 12 January 1848, under cover of celebrations for the king's birthday, there would be a demonstration at Palermo against the authorities: somewhat hesitantly, a few bold men then set an example; by degrees a demonstration grew into an insurrection; and finally, when after two days a revolution had taken firm hold, the well-to-do associated themselves with the movement in order to push the more democratic elements into accepting a constitution weighted in favour of the aristocracy. The price of success in this first great civic revolt of the risorgimento was a hundred dead. Unrest then spread infectiously through Sicily, even to Naples itself, until Ferdinand was forced in February to grant a constitution as 'spontaneous' and 'irrevocable' proof of his good intentions. This abject surrender testified to the surprising force of popular agitation, with the result that similar movements broke out elsewhere; and Leopold, Charles Albert, even Pius IX had to follow suit in March by conceding constitutions.

Until the last minute Charles Albert had insisted that such a concession would be impossible because of a promise on oath which he had once taken never to countenance constitutional government. He was furious with Ferdinand for granting a constitution, and at first spoke of using force to suppress any demand for one in Piedmont. But popular feeling ran so high that he finally sought episcopal permission to break his promise, and reluctantly a *statuto* was published.[1] All he could do to mitigate this retreat was to ensure that it would be as conservative a document as possible, reserving to himself foreign policy, the conduct of war, and a right of veto on legislation, as well as all executive power. He also retained exclusive rights of nomination to the senate, which he packed with *codini* (pigtails), as the more reactionary aristocrats were called. Since ministers remained answerable to him and not to parliament, he neither intended nor foresaw that parliamentary government might develop from this *statuto*. The details of the constitution had to be decided in a hurry without realizing what they would imply in practice; nor could it be appreciated that they contained latent contradictions which in later years would be used to whittle down the powers of the monarchy.

Another significant advance was the pope's repeated invitation to other Italian sovereigns to form a customs league together. It is perhaps strange that Piedmont had not yet anticipated that such a compact might be an excellent way to exclude Austria and win leadership in Italy. Tuscany and the Papal States arranged in 1847 to form an economic association, but Charles Albert had been reluctant to lower his tariffs to the Tuscan level; only several months later did he agree in principle, and without taking practical steps to implement the decision. Early in 1848 he made further difficulties about forming a defensive alliance among Italian states. Charles Albert would have liked to defeat Austria first, in the hope that he would then be in a position of

[1] D. Berti, *Scritti Varii* (Turin, 1892), II. 315; A. Colombo, *Dalle Riforme allo Statuto di Carlo Alberto* (Casale, 1924), p. 184: *Lo Statuto Albertino e la Sua Preparazione*, ed. G. Falco (Rome, 1945), p. 185.

strength where he could create and in effect dominate a federation. Hence the rest of Italy began to distrust what seemed his reluctance to co-operate. According to Luigi Carlo Farini, a liberal citizen of the Papal States, other Italian states were sometimes more afraid of him than of Metternich. Only when the Piedmontese realized the obvious point that they could not defeat Austria without help did Turin become more interested in an alliance.

Some liberals, Cattaneo for instance, and even Count Carlo Petitti, who was one of the most admired Piedmontese of his generation, still thought that complete independence from Austria might be unnecessary, or even undesirable since war carried the chance of destroying both liberty and prosperity. But a number of facts made a violent outcome seem likely: Sicily had not yet broken entirely free of Naples and its insular patriotism was very strong; Mazzini and his followers were quite unsatisfied by moderate reforms which left the main issue of nationalism unsettled; the Austrians were defying the pope's government by their continued occupation of Ferrara, and the Austrian embargo on Piedmontese wine was another crying grievance; food production in the various states, despite reduced taxation, had not been sufficiently increased; and there was still no constitution in Venice or Lombardy.

In the spring of 1848 a long-suppressed rebellion broke out in Lombardy, first among the peasants,[1] then in Milan itself. The Milanese patriots had learnt from the Boston tea-party that, since tobacco was a government monopoly, abstention from smoking might be a practically effective protest, and tension quickly mounted as people realized the strength of passive resistance and boycott. When petitions were submitted for more local autonomy, increasingly repressive measures were the response, because for Austria to yield in Italy might have detonated similar demands among the other subject peoples of her ramshackle empire. But then the Paris revolution of 25 February precipitated revolt in Vienna itself on 13 March. The news of this Viennese revolt reached Milan and Venice when both were surging with insubordination. Gabrio Casati, the mayor of Milan, tried to restrain people, and at first the radical Cattaneo was almost equally averse to using force; but a spontaneous movement resulted in hundreds of barricades blocking the streets, and Casati was obliged to head a provisional government in order to keep the revolt in bounds and give it some direction. During the heroic 'five days of Milan' the insurgents lost no more than 300 men, but they defeated a well-trained and well-armed force of 9,000–12,000 soldiers. Apparently it had not until now caused much concern in Vienna that a third of Marshal Radetzky's army in Lombardy was composed of Italians, and some of these deserted rather than fight. Faced with widespread and spontaneous street fighting, Radetzky could not easily supply all his troop units which were scattered throughout Milan. When the whole region broke out in rebellion he withdrew from Milan to the famous Quadrilateral of fortress-towns south of

[1] *Scritti Scelti di Cesare Correnti*, ed. T. Massarani (Rome, 1892), II. 6.

Lake Garda. Milan, like Sicily, had justified Mazzini's obstinate faith in popular initiative. 'Europe will take note of your courage', said Cattaneo to the citizens; 'the shame of thirty years has been wiped out. Long live Italy!'[1]

Subsequent legend notwithstanding, Charles Albert had made no serious preparations for the contingency of an offensive war against the Austrians. Often he had spoken in private of wanting to fight one day for Italian independence, but stronger still seemed to be his determination to fight against the revolution, and the 'five days of Milan' found his troops waiting not on the river Ticino to attack eastwards, but rather directed against the republican menace from France. Though he had lately sent arms to the anti-liberal forces in Switzerland, he could send none to Milan, and at first he even tried to halt volunteers who wanted to cross into Lombardy. At least he thought it would be prudent to wait and see if the popular rising at Milan was really strong enough to defeat the Austrians. But delay invited the charge of putting internal politics above national liberation, and Cavour had to warn him that, if he did not intervene now that the Austrians were being defeated, the dynasty might fall and Piedmont might have to forget for ever her hopes of acquiring Lombardy. Accordingly, but without enthusiasm, Charles Albert adopted the tricolour flag which was by this time accepted as the colours of Italy, and ordered his troops to cross the Ticino. Even now he was hesitant: his ambassador at Vienna was told to explain this step as designed to prevent the further spread of republicanism. Because of the slowness of the Piedmontese advance Radetzky was able to retreat through hostile country unhampered.

The untrained Milanese insurgents realized that they needed assistance from the Piedmontese army if they were to maintain their new independence, and the urgent need for disciplined troops persuaded even Mazzini to give grudging and temporary allegiance to the king. But Charles Albert was more alarmed than pleased at this unexpected support from the extreme Left. He also was horrified to find Daniele Manin at Venice reviving allegiance to the thousand-year-old Venetian republic which Napoleon had destroyed fifty years earlier. To the Piedmontese, republicanism represented as great a menace as did the Austrians. Worse still, the republicans were appealing for help from the new republican government in France. Other political disagreements arose between Charles Albert and the Tuscans, who were uneasy about his expansionist intentions and themselves wanted to annex Massa and Carrara on the Piedmontese frontier.

Equally serious, the initial enthusiasm in Lombardy began to wane. By no

---

[1] C. Cattaneo, *Le Cinque Giornate di Milano* (ed. Milan, 1931), p. 57. Of Radetzky's 62 infantry battalions, 24 were composed of Italians; the whole Austrian army in 1846 contained 52,700 Italians as well as 4,300 Friulani, compared with 128,200 Germans (*Handbuch der Statistik des Österreich-ischen Kaiserstaates,* ed. Joseph Hain (Vienna, 1852), I. 266); in the Austrian navy, most officers and almost all the ratings were Italian. Radetzky's dramatic account of his defeat is in *Archiv für Österreichische Geschichte* (Vienna), XCV (1906), 150–8.

means everyone was yet convinced that Austria was the national enemy. Some Milanese were suspicious of Piedmont, others were afraid of social convulsion resulting from the war. Cattaneo denounced Charles Albert as the man who had once before betrayed the cause of liberal patriotism in 1821, and who had tortured and executed other Piedmontese patriots in 1833. In the heat of the moment Cattaneo said he would prefer the Austrians to recapture Milan than see a renegade in command of Lombardy.[1] When the king insisted on a vote for immediate acceptance by Lombards of his rule, this caused a serious political division before the war had been won, and it also made other Italian sovereigns frightened at the prospect of Piedmontese aggrandizement. Charles Albert for his part was dismayed to encounter such suspicion. He could count on the support of Casati and the aristocratic party in Milan, with whose help a plebiscite was held which showed a decisive majority for fusion with Piedmont; but a proviso was inserted that unification be followed after the war by the summoning of a constituent assembly with powers to alter existing institutions, and this in turn infuriated the loyal monarchists of Turin. The plebiscite enabled Piedmont to join with Lombardy and Venice for a few days as a single state, but political and regional animosities had been exacerbated by controversy, and concentration on the war had been seriously weakened.

Meantime, as one of the radicals complained, while Charles Albert was collecting votes, Radetzky was collecting men. Leopold of Tuscany had declared for the Italian cause; so, somewhat reluctantly, had Ferdinand of Naples. But the Piedmontese refused an offer of collaboration from Giuseppe Garibaldi who had just returned with some of his Italian Legion from Montevideo to fight for national independence. Charles Albert showed no great eagerness to build up a potentially dangerous Lombard army; nor apparently did Casati and his friends disagree on this, for volunteers were thought likely to be politically unreliable, and the much-feared Mazzini had now arrived in Milan to be a potential focus for republican opposition. Charles Albert had an army of 60,000, but it now appeared that the commanding officers had no maps of Lombardy, and no serious study had been made of Austrian fortifications. Food, tents, and medical supplies were deficient; lack of horses hampered the artillery; troops had not been instructed in their firearms; while the officers, having mostly been appointed by family connection, did not know their job and sometimes not even the basic words of command. Charles Albert's personal courage was indubitable, and he insisted on directing operations at the front, but his chronic indecision and pre-Napoleonic ideas of generalship invited direct personal responsibility for the disasters that followed.

The initial slowness of advance, and the failure to watch the Alpine passes whence Radetzky obtained supplies, gave the Austrians a two months respite for consolidation and for a relief column to reach Verona. Until this moment

[1] Quoted in A. Monti, *Un Dramma fra gli Esuli* (Milan, 1921), p. 85.

their position in the Quadrilateral was fairly hazardous, and there had even been serious thoughts in Vienna over withdrawing altogether from Lombardo-Venetia. At one point Radetzky received orders to negotiate an armistice, but he disobeyed. In May he succeeded at Curtatone in checking the Tuscans and at Vicenza a contingent of soldiers from Rome. The Piedmontese reached the point of taking Peschiera, but in July they were soundly defeated at Custoza. This battle gave the Austrian empire a new lease of life, for it enabled them to reoccupy Lombardy and then to bring some of their troops back over the Alps where they were badly needed nearer home.[1]

Charles Albert still hoped for a miracle. In a fatalistic way he had been determined to win renown by a personal victory or else die in the attempt. A truce was offered to him which would still have left him Milan, but he refused. He also refused his generals' positive advice and fell back by way of Milan instead of through Piacenza. Once in Milan he promised the citizens to make a desperate stand, but in practice he abandoned the city at once, and in a way which gave the impression that his primary interest had been to prevent Milan saving herself again by inviting French help. His ministers advised him to appeal to France where Cavaignac was ready to provide 60,000 men, but he himself thought the French more dangerous than the Austrians. He therefore agreed to an armistice with Radetzky. In this armistice he promised to give no further assistance to the Venetians and Lombards whom a few days earlier he had accepted as citizens of his kingdom.

During 1848–9, in the first year of constitutional government at Turin, there were seven successive premiers, a fact which shows the difficulties of government with an untried constitution and parliamentary system. One particular difficulty was that Charles Albert's cabinet refused to ratify the 'unconstitutional' armistice which had been settled without any responsible minister being asked to countersign it. The radical majority at Turin wanted to resume hostilities; so did the king, too, want to retrieve his reputation by fighting, and even a conservative such as Cavour was eventually to accept that a resumption of the war would be a necessary means of re-establishing internal order.[2] It could be assumed that England and France would guarantee Piedmont against losing any territory even if she were once again defeated, for Europe positively needed this buffer state. Yet when war reopened in March 1849, the army was as unprepared as ever: the generals and the king himself had been so discredited that a Polish commander-in-chief was employed, but as a stranger he had an impossible task, and the ministers made it harder than ever by even failing to see that he knew in time of their declaration of war.[3]

---

[1] Cattaneo's strictures on Piedmontese policy and strategy have mostly been borne out by the documents, according to P. Pieri, *Studi sul Risorgimento in Lombardia*, ed. A. Monti (Modena, 1949), pp. 16–17; the defeatism at Vienna was described by Count Hartig, *Genesis der Revolution in Österreich im Jahre 1848* (Leipzig, 1850), p. 246.

[2] *Nouvelles Lettres*, p. 222.

[3] General Alfonso Lamarmora, *Un Episodio del Risorgimento Italiano* (Florence, 1874), p. 20.

Many officers fought indifferently because they were unenthusiastic or even opposed to the war,[1] and the other ranks followed their example. Radetzky won overwhelmingly at Novara, and the fact that the campaign lasted only three days is a measure of the quality of the army and of the politicians who had allowed war to be renewed. Meanwhile Brescia had broken into revolt in order to help the Piedmontese invade Lombardy, but suddenly found herself after Novara fighting a brave but hopeless battle on her own. Most of Lombardy remained passive.

The revolution in southern Italy had begun to collapse long before the end of 1848. Separation from Naples had been the only aim which most Sicilians possessed in common, whereas the Neapolitan liberals, however much they may have wanted liberty and constitutional government for themselves, were quite ready to use force to reimpose Bourbon dominion on the island. A separatist parliament met at Palermo, but most of the deputies turned out to have very different motives from those which had first inspired the citizens to man the barricades, and soon there were armed clashes between different elements of this Sicilian revolution. Likewise in Naples, though liberal intellectuals were partially satisfied by their acquisition of jobs and influence, the peasants were angry to find the landlords become stronger than ever a result of constitutional government, so that here too the main revolutionary forces were divided.[2] After May 1848, when riots occurred in Naples, Ferdinand altered the spirit of his 'irrevocable' constitution: he was criticized for bad faith, but equally it was the political immaturity and factiousness of the liberals which made the constitution patently unworkable.[3] Thereafter he withdrew his troops from Lombardy, for they were needed to suppress liberalism at home and to recapture the allegiance of Sicily.

A papal allocution on 29 April 1848 had also disowned any participation by the Papal States in the Austrian war, for Pius had been appalled to find himself pushed by his liberal ministers into fighting against a leading Catholic power. Azeglio had unwisely tried to force the pope's hand by announcing— and making it seem to come from Pius himself—that the soldiers of the Holy See were fighting a crusade against the evil forces of Austria; as a result of which Pius was compelled to withdraw. The pope had by now given clear evidence of his Italian sentiments. He had for instance shown far more enthusiasm than Charles Albert for an Italian league. But war could never form part of papal policy; nor could constitutionalism, if that meant that he would have to accept his ministers' advice and fight against Austria. At the

---

[1] A. Anzilotti, *Gioberti* (Florence, 1922), p. 232; A. Colombo, *Gli Albori del Regno di Vittorio Emanuele II, Secondo Nuovi Documenti* (Rome, 1937), p. 41.

[2] 'The poor began to ask, "If we have no work and are starving, what kind of liberty is that? Before the revolution broke out there was just one king with one man's salary, but now there are a thousand of them. It is high time for us poor people to think of our own interests" ' (L. Settembrini, *Ricordanze della mia Vita*, ed. E. Fabietti (Milan, 1941), p. 170).

[3] N. Nisco, *Ferdinando II ed il suo Regno* (2nd ed., Naples, 1888), pp. 195–6.

end of 1848 Pius fled to Gaeta after his minister, Pellegrino Rossi, had been assassinated. From now onwards he abjured all compromise with the liberals who had abused his good nature. Against the liberal Catholicism of Rosmini and Gioberti, the Jesuits were allowed to assert that liberalism derived from protestantism and was incompatible with true religion. Henceforward the risorgimento would be left to the anticlericals, with corresponding disadvantages for both church and state.

The pope's withdrawal enabled Mazzini to become ruler of a Roman republic for three months in 1849. This was Mazzini's greatest practical success, his one experience of actual government. He made some attempt to break up the large estates, to free trade, and to abolish serfdom, but he had little time to translate his doctrines of social reform into practice. Just as everywhere else, moreover, there was a stultifying cleavage in Rome between moderates and radicals, and undoubtedly his own policy made this worse. 'An abyss has now opened between the papacy and modern society', he proclaimed, 'and no human power can bridge it.'[1] But the papalists were far from acknowledging defeat, and the Catholic powers of Europe were summoned to restore Pius's temporal dominion by force.

When the Roman republic fell to the French in July 1849, lovers of law and order among the Roman citizenry gave General Oudinot a medal and a sword of honour to mark his victory. Nevertheless, from now onwards, papal administration would require despotic government and a foreign garrison to support its existence. In Florence the Tuscan moderates had already seized power from the radicals and invited the Grand Duke Leopold back into power. Sicily was overrun by King Ferdinand's Swiss mercenaries in May. In July, Garibaldi's gallant remnant of the defenders of Rome took refuge in San Marino. When Manin's Venetian republic collapsed in August after an admirable but desperate resistance, the Italian revolution of 1848–9 was over. The peninsula became occupied territory even more than before, for Austrian forces held Tuscany and Modena, and French soldiers remained in Rome as guardians of the papacy.

The great majority of Italians had placed local and partial aims of liberation before the more generalized ideal of patriotism. Neapolitan liberals had used force against the revolution in Sicily, as some Messinese had taken arms against the rival city of Palermo, and even some Palermitan liberals had thrown their support to Ferdinand when the revolution threatened personal property. Those who volunteered to fight against Austria had usually fought bravely, but volunteers had been few. Social and regional divisions had proved far stronger than any sense of national identity: thus the wealthier Tuscan liberals, Ricasoli, Capponi, Peruzzi, discovered that they were much closer to the grand duke than they were to Guerrazzi, Montanelli, and the 'socialist' Left who had formed the spearhead of the revolution; and when starving

[1] *Scritti di Mazzini*, XXXIX. 188.

Venice appealed desperately for aid, she received from the rest of Italy (said Tommaseo) but one day's supply. Without any doubt the revolution had occasionally helped to establish a common sense of *italianità*, but sometimes it had done almost the opposite. Azeglio, Balbo, and even Cavour spoke of the defenders of Rome in terms of jeering contempt. Nor did the Venetian republic give official recognition to their sister republic at Rome.

Disillusionment was inevitable. Charles Albert's policy of *Italia farà da se*, in other words the conviction that Italy could go it alone with her own unsupported forces, was clearly absurd, and evidently the making of Italy would have to wait upon the active interest of some other European state which could provide the resources and the determination which Italians lacked. As Bettino Ricasoli wrote, 'The national principle has vanished; Italy cannot possibly free herself without outside help'.[1] Azeglio, with exaggerated disillusionment, spoke of constitutional government as something 'for which Italians are not yet ready and which they will never properly understand'.[2] Gioberti henceforward, in his last three years of life, underplayed the myth of Italian primacy, and put his faith rather in republican France: the principal hope for the future, he thought, was for Piedmont to overcome its provincialism and make terms with democracy; the pope would also have to forfeit his temporal authority, for secular Italy could not permit the Papal States to keep the peninsula permanently divided into two.

After Novara, Charles Albert abdicated, and shortly afterwards died in Portugal. After so many years of combating liberalism, he had not been able in a moment to set aside his past. In spite of posthumous royalist mythology, he can be recognized as a weak character behind outward appearances, and his more amiable qualities were outweighed by indecisiveness and double-dealing. Perhaps Predari was right in saying that prolonged and cruel self-mortification had undermined his health to the point where he was deranged and hence incapable of ruling. Legends of the 'martyr of Oporto' were developed later, by the very people who had helped bring Piedmont to disaster.

Another political myth described how his successor, Victor Emanuel II, compelled an unwilling Radetzky to moderate his terms for an armistice, and how this young king resisted an Austrian attempt to circumscribe the *statuto*. Radetzky in fact did not wish to impose severe terms, especially as he wanted to bolster the new king against the Turin radicals. In return, Victor Emanuel secretly promised to override the radical majority in parliament. In defiance of that majority he appointed a conservative army general as premier, while another Piedmontese general bombarded radical Genoa into accepting the peace. He also ratified the treaty with Austria despite firm parliamentary opposition. By the 'proclamation of Moncalieri' in November, he personally

[1] 12 May 1849, *Carteggi Ricasoli*, III. 391.
[2] June 1849, cited by A. Filipuzzi, *La Pace di Milano (6 agosto 1849)* (Rome, 1955), p. 220.

commanded the electorate to return more amenable deputies, the implication being that, if the electors again returned a majority of the Left, he would revoke the constitution.

Victor Emanuel thus succeeded in re-establishing royal authority. If his remained more of a limited monarchy than other regimes in Italy, this was in large part because Custoza and Novara had damaged the prestige of the house of Savoy and shown the sheer inefficiency of absolutist government; though it was also due to Azeglio's wise moderation when he became chief minister. Even though taxes in Piedmont were sometimes still to be raised by royal decree, other Italian rulers behaved with far smaller concern for legal niceties. According to the French ambassador, most people in Piedmont did not greatly value their constitutional liberties;[1] yet the *statuto* was preserved intact and the tricolour flag remained as a pledge that Turin now intended to claim leadership in any future Italian revolution.

Once the generals had restored order, Azeglio became prime minister with a government of moderate conservatives, and in his administration during the years 1849–52 this man did as much as honesty and cautious good sense could do to restore confidence in the monarchy and recommence a policy of reform. Even though he began by defying the wishes of parliament and the electors, this was not of itself unconstitutional, and the deputies could not be allowed to prevent a realistic settlement with Austria. He also effected a noticeable reduction in the privileged position of the aristocracy at court and in the army. The development of parliament was meanwhile assisted by the gradual appearance of a small political class capable of taking an active share in government, and through the means of press and parliament a growing number of people thus received a training in public affairs. An important element in this class consisted of emigrants from other Italian states; for although Garibaldi, Mazzini, and others among the more dedicated patriots were not allowed to live in Piedmont, a cordial welcome was given to the more moderate of the refugees from Bourbon, Austrian, and papal Italy.

One of Azeglio's principal measures concerned the Piedmontese church, which after 1814 had been handsomely reimbursed for confiscations made during the French occupation, and whose vast wealth, as well as its system of separate courts and rights of sanctuary, gave it great power and were not easily compatible with that equality before the law decreed in the *statuto*. In 1850, therefore, the Siccardi laws abolished ecclesiastical jurisdiction. The number of holy days was reduced, and a limit was placed on ecclesiastical corporations acquiring land in mortmain. Archbishop Fransoni forbade his clergy to comply with these provisions, and tried to coerce the cabinet by withholding absolution and religious burial from those responsible. But since the church was now in full opposition to liberalism, there was little point in the laity offering a compromise, and the archbishop was imprisoned.

[1] Matter, *Cavour*, II. 134.

Azeglio was supported in this policy by Count Cavour, who, after losing his first parliamentary election, joined the ministry in 1850. Cavour was a rationalist in religion and a liberal-minded conservative in politics; he had been a journalist, and was a successful farmer as well as being involved in banking and railroad construction. He first debated whether to join the government or to overthrow it.[1] In 1850–1, he then successively held the departments of finance, naval affairs, agriculture, and industry, though even

Cavour in 1835, by his English friend William Brockedon, F.R.S.

after becoming a minister he continued to remain in touch with other politicians on both the Right and the Left until he could contrive to form a new parliamentary coalition of his own.

Cavour had to find the money to pay for the 1848–9 war and an indemnity to Austria; he had to pay for railways and for very necessary army reforms; he also revived an earlier scheme to build a naval base at La Spezia with the aim of making Piedmont inferior to no other Italian power at sea. Heavy increases in taxation over nine years eventually were to raise the annual revenue from 91 million to 164 million lire, but the public debt grew sixfold in the same period, most of this being managed by French banking houses. Cavour could never balance the budget, and indeed he lacked some of the

[1] *Cavour Agricoltore: Lettere inedite di Camillo Cavour a Giacinto Corio*, ed. E. Visconti (Florence, 1913), p. 282.

attributes of a truly successful financier;[1] but he did succeed in increasing the country's productive capacity. In this he had the support of a growing middle class whom he helped to educate in the principles of classical economy. This was a class which disliked existing economic restriction the more as they grew in wealth. Commercial treaties were therefore negotiated in 1850–1 with France, Austria, and England, and abolition of the duties on grain was a great victory for cheap food and for encouraging technical progress in agriculture.

Owing to Azeglio's debilitating war wound, Cavour became the most prominent member of the cabinet, and quickly set about undermining the position of his chief. Azeglio was not a man of finesse and tactics, nor was he a skilled parliamentarian. He was an amateur in politics, a painter and novelist by profession, and a statesman only by accident. Cavour was easily the more resourceful politician, and he could show ruthlessness and unscrupulousness if the situation ever called for it. Cavour first required a personal clientele in parliament. His general feelings would have led him to side with the aristocratic conservatives, but against such a union was his own religious latitudinarianism[2] quite apart from the loyalty of the conservatives to the existing premier. So early in 1852 he secretly made a private alliance or *connubio* with Urbano Rattazzi, the leading figure of what their common friend Michelangelo Castelli called the 'bourgeois party'. Then in a parliamentary speech Cavour suddenly committed the government to a breach with a section of the conservatives upon which Azeglio relied for support. He hoped that the prime minister would be obliged to accept this 'transformation' of the government majority and thereby acknowledge publicly that Cavour was chief minister in all but name.

The *connubio* set a durable tradition for Italian politics, which henceforth tended to see a succession of loose centre coalitions very similar to each other instead of an alternation between opposing parties. Cavour was acting in accordance with what he took to be English practice, for he greatly admired Sir Robert Peel and thought that Peel and Gladstone had been merging conservatives with whigs in order to carry out a reform policy; after close observation of the 1852 elections in England he also thought that Disraeli was possibly forming a *connubio* with Palmerston. Above all he was anxious to avoid the kind of parliament he had seen in Belgium where conservatives and progressives were organized in two strong parties which used to succeed each other in power. What he wanted was to exclude both the political extremes, so that he himself could remain in office with a permanently fluctuating political alliance that could be either conservative or progressive according to circumstances. Hence one of the English practices which he disliked was the voting procedure

---

[1] H. von Treitschke, *Cavour* (Leipzig, 1942), p. 207; F. Ruffini, *La Giovinezza di Cavour* (2nd ed., Turin, 1938), ii. 166–8, 174–9; R. Romeo, *Cavour e il suo Tempo (1810–1842)* (Bari, 1969), pp. 721–7.
[2] De la Rive, *Cavour*, pp. 302–3.

which aided the appearance of large clear-cut parties. Instead, in the electoral law which Cavour himself designed, the French system of *ballottage* allowed the small centre groups to assert themselves by combining on the second vote against the larger parties. This was the mechanism which helped to make possible his technique of coalition government. Of all his political actions, it was the *connubio* of which he was in later years most proud, and it did not fail to carry him into power. From 1852 onwards there was no parliamentary opposition worth the name; and the fact that the same system led later, under weaker direction, to a chronic instability of parliament was not something he could have been expected to prevent.

The issue on which Azeglio finally resigned was the king's refusal to approve a civil marriage bill which was supported by the chamber of deputies. Victor Emanuel mobilized support among his appointees in the senate to quash the bill, but then hit on the alternative of inviting Cavour to form a new administration on the understanding that it would not support Azeglio's opposition to this royal veto. Once firmly in power, Cavour was confident that he could restrict the use of the prerogative. When Cavour subsequently introduced further anticlerical legislation against the monasteries, Victor Emanuel again encouraged the senate to resist his prime minister; but this time the king found that, as a result of the *connubio*, there no longer existed any alternative party from which other political leaders could aspire to power.

Piedmontese laws continued in some respects to lag behind those of other Italian states, because Cavour's attention was taken up mainly with finance and with the long-term planning of war. He did not always have an easy time in his eight years as prime minister, and hence chose to limit his objectives. He had to meet personal opposition from the monarch; there was unpopularity arising out of his conservative past and his swingeing taxes; he had to fight aristocratic opposition in the senate, as well as some of the wealthiest and least enlightened prelates in Europe. The methods he used to overcome opposition were rigorous and occasionally novel. Sometimes he overrode his cabinet, and secret service funds were frequently employed to sway the press at home and abroad. Over some controversial measures he used to avoid asking parliament for money, but took action first and then sought retrospective consent. He developed the practice by which civil servants and local authorities were expected to use their influence to ensure that opposition candidates were not returned to parliament, and he recognized this as a necessary part of his system. Nor did he stop short of illegal measures when he wanted to suppress opposition newspapers.

And yet he was never tempted to abolish parliament, because parliament remained the most effective arena for defeating Mazzini and Garibaldi on the Left, as it also enabled him to withstand Victor Emanuel and the clerical extremists on the Right. Cavour was no tyrant. If sometimes he was accused of acting as a dictator, it was essentially a parliamentary and benevolent dictatorship. He preferred to disarm opposition wherever possible, presenting an issue frankly and accepting suggestions and amendments.

In foreign politics it was rather Mazzini who kept Italian discontent alive before Europe, yet Mazzini was immensely unpopular in Piedmont as the great enemy of religion, monarchy, and property. Cavour was so opposed to the radicals that he acted to forewarn Austria and other Italian states against Mazzinian activities. Although the radicals reacted by accusing Cavour of being *piemontesissimo*, and hence by implication un-Italian, he was only biding his time before he took over their more forceful policy, and meanwhile tried his hardest to discredit them so as to make his own alternative leadership the more palatable. The only solid advances, he used to say, were those which were slow and wisely ordered. He meant to isolate the Italian question from any chance association with democracy and social revolution, for only thus could he attract the support of the one class likely to solve it acceptably. This did not, however, prevent him from protesting with dignity when, in response to a Mazzinian rising in Milan, Austria in 1853 sequestrated the possessions of Lombards living in Piedmont.

On the other hand, his intervention in the Crimean War was not quite the brilliant *coup* of farsighted patriotism which subsequent generations thought it to be, but rather the indirect result of an attempt by the king to restore royal authority. Victor Emanuel looked forward to proving himself as a great military leader, and hostilities would permit him to cast off constitutional trammels. Cavour learnt by chance that the king was intending to dismiss his ministers and declare war on Russia, and was only just in time to forestall this by hurriedly announcing his own decision to fight. The cabinet was against such a decision, and so was public opinion, for war against Russia meant alignment with the national enemy Austria, and it meant spending scanty resources where no national interests were at stake. But Cavour's sudden announcement showed his courage, his gambling instinct, and his resourcefulness at making the best of a bad job.

The Crimean War ended before his small expeditionary force had fought more than one minor engagement in which a dozen soldiers were killed. Unwillingly Cavour then attended the peace conference in 1856, expecting he would be the scapegoat for a useless war, but half hoping to win one of the central duchies for his pains. All he obtained in the end was a short statement by the British representative that the present state of central and southern Italy was unsatisfactory. Cavour was disappointed, but it was useful to have this said formally by one of the Great Powers. Piedmontese prestige also gained from being the only Italian state represented at an international congress. One disastrous mistake Cavour made at Paris was to suggest secretly to Britain that she should join him in fighting Austria, and after this miscalculation he was never entirely trusted in London. But in compensation he established a close link with Napoleon III, and learnt the invaluable lesson that France might not be averse to such a war.

Another positive success was that Manin, who talked with him on three occasions in Paris, and who until a year previously had rather looked on the Piedmontese government as an ally of Austria,[1] took note that Cavour could speak as an Italian patriot and might possibly advance from merely seeking Piedmontese aggrandizement to the more revolutionary idea of wanting to create a new Italy. Cavour, in a private letter, sarcastically wrote of hearing Manin speak about 'Italian unity and other such nonsense',[2] but later he secretly offered encouragement to Manin's National Society on condition that they publicly abandoned republicanism and accepted the Savoy dynasty. Thus he sowed discord among his opponents and won a new source of strength, as yet without committing himself to anything. Italian unity was to him still an absurd notion, apart from being something which the French would never allow. He therefore had to accept, for instance, that if he wanted French help, Naples might have to become an apanage for one French prince and Tuscany for another. Only by degrees was public opinion in Piedmont being educated in *italianità*, and here an important role was played by the émigrés from other Italian regions. One estimate puts the number of these exiles as high as 100,000, but, even if there were only a quarter of this number, they still wielded a considerable influence in journalism, in the university, and in business circles. The National Society was led by three such exiles, the Venetian Manin, the Lombard Pallavicino, the Sicilian La Farina, and it soon exercised an important educative function not only in Piedmont but in central Italy and beyond.

It was a severe reverse when the 1857 elections doubled the clerical and right-wing representation in the Chamber of Deputies. Cavour admitted that in normal times this might have forced a change of government. But times were not normal, and he justifiably felt himself to be indispensable, so he discovered a somewhat arbitrary pretext to exclude some of the opposition deputies from parliament. Prompted by France, he also forced the resignation from the cabinet of Rattazzi. The government had lately been mysteriously in touch with Mazzini over a rising in the Lunigiana, and Cavour may have found it convenient to throw the blame on Rattazzi, as it was also useful to blame Rattazzi for a republican outbreak at Genoa in June 1857. The *connubio* thus ended in divorce as Cavour shifted the balance of his coalition towards the Right, for it was necessary to convince Napoleon that Piedmont would have no truck with revolution. Mazzini, who had already been condemned to death in 1833, was in his absence given the same sentence again. Cavour invited

[1] Nassau William Senior, *Conversations with M. Thiers, M. Guizot and other Distinguished Persons during the Second Empire*, ed. M. C. M. Simpson (London, 1878), II. 3.

[2] *Garibaldi, Vittorio Emanuele, Cavour: Documenti Inediti*, ed. G. E. Curàtulo (Bologna, 1911), p. 127; this phrase was thought too unflattering to Cavour, and so was excised by Chiala (*Lettere di Cavour*, II. 372), and by Bianchi (*Storia Documentata*, VII. 627).

French policemen into Piedmont to help catch this arch-conspirator, while Carlo Pisacane's fatal expedition to stir up revolution in Naples was discountenanced as an inexcusable embarrassment. Republican opposition to what opponents called Cavour's Prussian-style policy was failing, as repeated insurrections foundered on popular apathy and the disapproval of moderate liberals. Mazzini again offered to collaborate in the making of the nation, but Cavour's idea of a nation was quite different, and the Piedmontese ministers still needed Mazzini in opposition so as to frighten the Right into aiding their own more orthodox brand of revolution. Cavour on one occasion ungenerously spoke of Mazzini as more an enemy of Italy than the Austrian emperor himself. A deep incompatibility existed between the visionary agitator and the sceptical politician. Both were necessary for the making of Italy, but it was Cavour who now called the tune.[1]

In January 1858, an Italian refugee in France, Felice Orsini, tried to assassinate Napoleon III. This momentarily threatened the French support which was now the basis of Cavour's policy, so he reacted by even fiercer prosecution of the revolutionaries, and, when juries proved recalcitrant, he further restricted the press and passed legislation to get easier convictions in the courts. Scores of suspected agitators were deported to America, and Mazzini's paper, *Italia del Popolo*, which had already lost at least 150 issues by confiscation, was altogether suppressed. Fortunately Napoleon still needed Piedmont for his projected war against Austria; he had if possible to stop Austrian influence spreading in Italy, as he also meant to reinforce his new dynasty by military conquests for the greater glory of France. In return for helping Piedmont to win Lombardy and Venice, he intended that Cavour should cede substantial territory to France. Cavour correctly gauged French policy and therefore embarked confidently on a diplomatic duel with the Austrian premier, Count Buol. The Austrian administration at Milan had lately been trying to woo the Lombards with a promise of more local autonomy, and a number of former exiles from Lombardy were even returning home. Cavour had to stop this at all costs, and he countered it by deliberately picking a quarrel, hoping that he could induce the Austrians to act aggressively as they tried to meet this challenge to their authority in Italy.

When Cavour was invited by Napoleon to spend a brief holiday in France in order to plan their war, he hurriedly left Turin without even informing his cabinet because the utmost secrecy was needed. At Plombières, in July 1858, these two men in complete privacy arranged that Cavour should be responsible for bringing about hostilities the following spring. Their initial plan was that some citizens of the duchy of Modena should appeal to Piedmont for deliverance; Victor Emanuel's provocative reply would then force the Austrians to support their ally the duke of Modena, which would give France an excuse to intervene on Piedmont's side. In this way it was hoped to conceal

[1] Omodeo, *Cavour*, II. 231-2.

that the war would be one of blatant aggression. One objective would be to expand Piedmont into a state stretching across the whole of northern Italy and consisting of some eleven million people. There was also to be a new and enlarged kingdom of central Italy based on Florence, perhaps under Napoleon's cousin. Southern Italy would remain to the Bourbons, and the Roman states to the pope. In January 1859 a secret treaty confirmed that France should take Nice and the whole of Savoy in compensation.

Cavour then applied himself with dedication to make Austria declare war. Lombard refugees were ostentatiously enlisted in his army in the hope that Buol would be forced to demand their extradition; and the king, on Napoleon's suggestion, challenged Austria by speaking publicly of the cries of grief which came to him from the downtrodden inhabitants of other Italian states. But Cavour realized that it was important to prevent popular movements in Modena or anywhere else; there must be no repetition of social revolutions like those which in 1848 had so alarmed the conservatives; not popular revolt but regular war was what was needed, and Cavour's imagination here ran riot. He thought of possibly involving even Russia and the United States in a universal holocaust. In his excitement he told several friends that he was ready to set fire to Europe and, if necessary, to 'bouleverser le monde': Italy, he once said, has conquered the world before now, and will one day do so again.[1] The British, on the other hand, were horrified that Cavour, 'unassailed by any foreign power, and with no point of honour at stake', should thus deliberately seek to detonate a major European war from which everyone else was likely to suffer, and they finally succeeded in frightening Napoleon in recognizing that his aggressive plans were now clear for all to see and he had better call them off.

Cavour, with the greatest reluctance, submitted to what he saw as the collapse of his life's work. But his patient work of provocation was dramatically rewarded when Austria, instead of being grateful for this fortunate respite, decided to make Lombardy a test for the viability of her multi-national empire. There was now no statesman at Vienna with the vision and the essential realism and moderation of Metternich. Buol inadvisedly seized on Napoleon's withdrawal as Austria's chance to crush an isolated Piedmont,[2] and his ultimatum to Cavour enabled Napoleon to come to the rescue with every appearance of acting on the defensive.

By another stroke of fortune, the Austrian general failed to seize his chance and for several weeks remained almost inactive a few hours' march from Turin, so allowing the French enough time to bring their troops into action.

---

[1] Brassier de St. Simon, *Die Auswärtige Politik Preussens 1858–71*, vol. I, ed. C. Friese (Oldenburg, 1933), pp. 158–9, 272; Massari, *Diario*, pp. 116, 140, 142, 147–8, 206; *Lettere di Cavour*, III. 11; ibid. VI. 307.

[2] Among other mistakes, Buol counted on Prussian support (Egon Corti, *Mensch und Herrscher: Wege und Schicksale Kaiser Franz Josephs* (Graz, 1952), p. 213); F. Engel von Janosi, *L'Ultimatum Austriaco del 1859* (Rome, 1938); F. Valsecchi, *Italia ed Europa nel 1859* (Florence, 1965).

Early in June the French won at Magenta and forced the Austrians out of Lombardy. Another allied victory followed at Solferino. But in July, just as Mazzini had foretold, Napoleon stopped the war, and agreed by the armistice of Villafranca to leave Venetia and even a part of Lombardy in Austrian possession. Cavour desperately urged Victor Emanuel that Piedmont should continue the war on her own. But the king sensibly rejected such unrealistic advice.

In deciding for peace, France had been afraid that Prussia might rally to the Austrian side; nor did Napoleon III want Piedmont too strong in the Italian federation which he meant to create. He had been irked to find that Cavour, in defiance of their agreement at Plombières, was surreptitiously preparing to annex the central duchies; even worse, the Piedmontese were creating trouble in papal Umbria and the Marches. Cavour had defaulted by providing many fewer troops than he had promised in the treaty, and this left the French General Staff in grave difficulties. The emperor therefore felt justified in making peace, and to sweeten the pill for the Piedmontese he dropped his claim to Savoy and Nice. Cavour, faced with the collapse of the French alliance on which he had built his policy, was forced to resign. He had already antagonized Victor Emanuel by a tactless intrusion into the king's private life, and now in another violent scene he called the monarch a traitor for not wanting to continue the war. The more courteous and courtly Rattazzi formed an interim ministry under General Lamarmora. Lombardy was annexed by Piedmont, though the terms agreed at Villafranca stipulated that Tuscany, Modena, and Venice should be kept by their former rulers.

The settlement was soon to be modified by a spontaneous revolution in central Italy, for Baron Ricasoli in Florence, and Farini in Modena and Bologna, headed provisional governments which demanded annexation by Piedmont. The British government helped in this next stage, having fewer reasons than France to fear a strong Italy; the British even felt that an enlarged Italy might possibly act as a check on imperial France. At the same time there was in Britain a widespread admiration for Garibaldi and for Mazzini's idea of uniting the whole peninsula. Early in 1860, France was persuaded under pressure to agree that the central duchies and the papal Romagna could determine their own future by a succession of popular plebiscites. Supported by the British government, Cavour was reappointed prime minister in January to carry out this programme. His plan was once again to offer Savoy and Nice to Napoleon as the price of French support. Almost before the Piedmontese parliament knew what was happening, French troops occupied these territories[1] to arrange plebiscites in ratification of the accomplished fact, and by a remarkable *tour de force* Cavour then convinced parliament that Nice

[1] See the detailed evidence of an eye-witness, L. Oliphant, *Universal Suffrage and Napoleon the Third* (Edinburgh, 1860), p. 41.

was really more French than Italian. In the same month the annexation of Tuscany and Emilia (Modena, Parma, and Bologna) was effected, and plebiscites were carefully organized which showed almost unanimity for joining Piedmont.

Cavour's annexation of Bologna brought excommunication on himself and the king, while his surrender of Savoy greatly annoyed Britain and Switzerland; these difficulties apart, however, his diplomacy had been brilliantly successful. His next hope was to win Bourbon Naples as an ally and partner. He had no expectation of unifying Italy, but hoped in a few years' time to promote another European war in order to get Venice. In his opinion, popular insurrections in what was unredeemed Italy had still to be discouraged, for only if he remained strictly moderate and conservative would France help him to win Venice or Rome. This was one of the penalties of the French alliance, for Napoleon III could not afford to allow an Italy that was too strong or too revolutionary.

Mazzini, on the contrary, continued to believe with religious earnestness that Italy must be unified, and by her own exertions not by the condescension of interested foreigners. He and the other radicals resented that, since Cavour obviously depended on imperial France, Piedmont possessed only a limited power of autonomous decision. They regretted that so few Italians had volunteered to fight in 1859, as they regretted that Piedmont on French instructions had been less than enthusiastic about popular participation. From their point of view, if Italy were to be united, and especially if she were to be more than a puppet of France, action would have to be taken independently of and even against Cavour. Mazzini had long considered that a revolutionary situation existed in the south which he might use to recapture the initiative, and it was Sicily once again, just as in 1848, which in 1860 acted as the ignition point for a decisive act of rebellion. Feelings of Italian patriotism were far weaker in Sicily than Mazzini imagined, but two explosive forces were enmity against Naples and a latent peasants' revolt. The revolutionaries managed to exploit both of these when they touched off a precarious insurrection in April 1860.

Garibaldi, moreover, though he had had his own strong disagreements with Mazzini, was so incensed by Cavour bartering away his home town of Nice that he, too, was in thoroughly rebellious mood. Garibaldi had been twice deported from Piedmont as an undesirable, and had spent twenty years of his life as an exile, mostly in South America. In Brazil and Uruguay he had learned a technique of guerrilla warfare with which European armies were untrained to contend. In 1848, and again in 1859, he had been given a poor share in the Lombard wars, since officers of the regular Piedmontese army regarded his irregular volunteers with a mixture of contempt, jealousy, and fear. In May 1860 he therefore decided to act on his own. While Cavour was still trying to persuade parliament to accept the cession of Nice, he took his chance and led a thousand followers to where a fitful insurrection spluttered in Sicily. Cavour did all he dared to stop the thousand sailing, but in the end procrastinated. The other ministers were prepared to use the Piedmontese navy against Garibaldi, but Cavour was in two minds, partly because parliamentary elections were being held and he feared to lose votes. At this very moment, moreover, his coalition was threatening to break over the question of Nice. He also knew that the king half sympathized with Garibaldi and was seeking an excuse to appoint a new premier. For these various reasons he preferred to let events take their course, hoping to be able to exploit them whether Garibaldi won or, as was much more likely, lost.

Before the Turin government could make up its mind, Garibaldi had done the impossible and captured Palermo. The conservatives had ridiculed the idea of guerrilla warfare in Italy, but they were wrong. Garibaldi with a sure instinct appealed directly to the Sicilian peasants, and a fearful *jacquerie* helped to terrify a large army and police force into submission. On receiving the news from Palermo, Cavour allowed reinforcements to be sent and tried to annex the island to Piedmont before Garibaldi could cause any more trouble. But the Garibaldians knew that Cavour would wish to halt the volunteers before they crossed to Naples, and they therefore refused to surrender the base which they would need for further operations on the mainland. This placed Cavour in difficulties, for he would have preferred to be defeated by Austria rather than let this popular leader unite Italy and offer its crown to the king.[1] Worse still, if the rebels continued to advance, they were likely to clash with the French garrison defending the pope in Rome. In July, therefore, further reinforcements were stopped from joining Garibaldi. Cavour was at this point engaged in negotiations for a treaty with the Bourbon government at Naples. It was no time for orthodox measures. Though he continued ostensibly with these negotiations, his ambassador in Naples simultaneously instigated a conspiracy aimed at overthrowing the Bourbons, because such a conspiracy would both displace a rival dynasty and also forestall Garibaldi's conquest of the south. Several of the more important generals and ministers of the Bourbon king were bribed into betraying the regime, but the conspiracy failed because Cavour's agents carried no conviction at all in their unaccustomed role of revolutionaries.

When Naples fell to Garibaldi in September, Cavour reacted with a far more imaginative project. Garibaldi's extraordinary success had so quickened enthusiasm for immediate Italian unification that Cavour himself was carried away by this one-time Mazzinian heresy; and it did not escape his notice that here was perhaps his only remaining chance to stop Garibaldi and regain the initiative. On the papal frontier, incidents were hurriedly manufactured which would give him a pretext to invade Umbria and the Marches on the pretence of saving the pope from a radical revolution. The incidents were a lamentable

[1] *Cavour-Nigra*, IV. 122–3.

failure, but the invasion was a success, and victory over a small papalist force at Castelfidardo was magnified in a brave attempt to snatch some of Garibaldi's prestige away from him. Having occupied the Papal States it was also possible to invade Naples, explaining to France that this and this alone would bring Garibaldi to heel. Faced with the prospect of civil war, Garibaldi submitted with a good grace, and the usual plebiscites then gave the inevitable massive majorities in favour of annexation by Victor Emanuel.

The word 'annexation' was used deliberately by Cavour, for there was to be no repetition of Charles Albert's injudicious acceptance of a constituent assembly in which Italians could debate their new form of government. He intended the new Italy to be as much as possible a projection of Piedmont. Far better to adopt laws which had already been tried and proved at Turin; and better still if this could be effected without wasting time in parliamentary discussion. The decision was taken to extend to southern Italy some quite fundamental legislation which had originally been imposed on Piedmont without parliamentary debate. There was some opposition when Cavour decided that the king's title should remain Victor Emanuel II instead of Victor Emanuel I, but not so much that he felt he should yield to criticism.

This gesture to themselves by the Piedmontese helped to sweeten for them the not always grateful task of organizing the rest of Italy. But the process of 'Piedmontization' was often irksome to other Italian regions which felt reduced to the status of being conquered and annexed. Some Sicilians had looked on association with Piedmont just as a means to winning autonomy from Naples and certainly without any wish to be annexed by another Italian state. Some Neapolitans had equally been given to understand that an affirmative vote in their plebiscite would still allow them to keep local autonomy; they were the more displeased when they had to accept the abolition of many venerable traditions and institutions, and a fairly rigid centralization based on Turin. Another kind of disillusionment affected those of the Garibaldians who had been fighting for more radical objectives, and Garibaldi himself was disgusted at the meanness shown to his volunteers who had won half Italy for Cavour. Niccolò Tommaseo, Giuseppe Ferrari, Carlo Cattaneo, and Giuseppe Montanelli were other distinguished Italians whose preference for an Italian federation now had to be disregarded in the interests of uniformity and a speedy return to ordered government.

A different kind of opposition came from social groups disturbed by the revolution. Not all the old aristocracies accepted with pleasure absorption into a new middle-class state. As for the peasants, who were the great majority of the population, few can have had much idea what the word *Italy* meant; in some places they had lent their powerful aid to the rebellion hoping to obtain land and economic security, but discovered too late that the *ancien régime* had been on their side against the lawyers and farm-owners whom they had now unwittingly helped into power. Many devout Catholics were also appalled that

Cavour and Victor Emanuel had defied excommunication to make war on the Holy See: not only was nearly all the pope's territory annexed by conquest, but on it were now to be imposed the anticlerical laws of Piedmont which must have been abhorrent to most of the population.

One further source of malaise was economic. Taxes had at once to be greatly increased, for there was still the war of 1859 to pay for; there was the debt which Cavour had incurred over ten years of unbalanced budgets in Piedmont, and the new Italy was thought to require a large increase in the number of troops and naval ships. There was also the fact that the extension of low tariffs from Piedmont to economically backward provinces—sometimes a sudden reduction by 80 per cent—could result in completely extinguishing local industries. The fusion of provinces which were at such different levels of development made it hard to avoid this kind of problem, especially as there was insufficient time to gather the information on which policy should ideally have been based; and inevitably it was the south, with its lack of markets and communications, with its comparative lack of industry, which suffered most. Northern industries, on the other hand, had already had time to adjust to free trade, so that tariff equalization was an unexpected bonus for them. On the other hand, many existing job-holders at Turin strongly resented the process of dilution by southerners who were used to more clientelistic and less efficient methods of public administration. Sometimes this mutual incomprehension was total. Azeglio even recommended that the south should again be separated off from Italy, because it was clear to him that the plebiscites had been a mere ruse which gave an entirely fraudulent idea of public enthusiasm for Italy. According to Cavour's representative in Naples, there were not a hundred believers in Italian unity out of seven million inhabitants.[1]

Although many people were to a greater or lesser extent unhappy about the outcome, the forging of national unity had been a great achievement. Despite the fact that probably a numerical majority of Italians had been more or less indifferent to the process at the time it was happening—despite, indeed, the fact that many had been against it, for the risorgimento had been a series of civil wars as much as of national wars against Austria—before long the result was to alter everyone's lives in a positive way. The skill and noble ambition of a few brave men, a fortuitous moment in European diplomacy, the obstinate convictions of a small but growing class of intellectuals, and a sudden wave of enthusiasm which equated unity with everything that was noble and profitable, all these in fortunate combination turned Mazzini's utopian dream into practical politics just when Mazzini himself was utterly disillusioned and forced out again into the bitterness of exile. 'This is only the ghost of Italy', wrote Mazzini just before he died,

[1] *Scritti d'Azeglio*, III. 399–400; *Liberazione del Mezzogiorno*, IV. 56.

it is an illusion, a lie. Our natural frontiers with France and Austria are in the hands of foreigners; and even if we ever reach the point of occupying Trent, Trieste, and Nice, it would still be only the material husk that would be ours, it would still be a corpse without a truly living soul inside it. Italy has been put together just like a mosaic, piece by piece, and the battles for this cause have been won on our behalf by foreigners who were fighting for their own reasons of dynastic egoism, foreigners whom we should properly regard as our enemies.[1]

Early in 1861 the existence of a Kingdom of Italy was formally proclaimed in a new parliament to which deputies from all over Italy had been elected. Unluckily the session was marred by an unseemly brawl between Garibaldi and Cavour over the decision taken by the army authorities to disband the volunteers. Few of the immediate and intricate problems of unification had been solved when, in June, Cavour was taken with a severe fever: the doctors bled him many times until his last resistance was sapped; Fra Giacomo charitably defied an ecclesiastical interdict and gave him the last rites of the Church. Cavour died still some months before his fifty-first birthday—the main architect of the Italian union, and the one man equipped to understand the baffling difficulties attending reconstruction.

Victor Emanuel had had three prime ministers in twelve years, but now he was to have one a year: Bettino Ricasoli in 1861, Rattazzi in 1862, Farini and then Marco Minghetti in 1863, Lamarmora in 1864, Ricasoli again in 1866, then Rattazzi, Menabrea, and Lanza. Without Cavour's strong hand, the system was evidently unstable. If political life lacked clarity and balance, that was partly because no adequate party organization existed which could focus differences of opinion: for Cavour had not been interested in parliamentary opposition, and when out of office had preferred to leave Turin so as to be able to resume power with fewer policy commitments in the next emergency. After his death it was evident that the many small personal groups in parliament had become used to an unhealthy dependence on a single man. Nor had he possessed the time to train any successors in his own highly personal techniques of government. Inevitably, moreover, the risorgimento had been a process which depended essentially on force, on wars and civil wars, in other words on methods that hampered the development of liberal institutions; the remarkable fact was not that these institutions were imperfect in Italy, but rather that Cavour left them as healthy as he did.

There was general agreement on what were the main political problems to be solved after 1861. To most good patriots the first requirement was to win Venice and Rome, and this meant heavy military expenditure. Impossible to reconcile with this was the parallel need for financial equilibrium. Official figures did not immediately reveal the extent of the deficit, but the annual budget almost at once seems to have doubled the sum total of the individual state budgets before 1860, and expenditure ran almost 50 per cent above

[1] *Scritti di Mazzini,* XCI. 162–4.

revenue. As a result the currency had to be devalued and ecclesiastical property nationalized and sold, while extra taxes raised food prices until there were starvation riots. One quite unexpected expense was that the army had to quell another frightening civil war which dragged out for years in the south as a protest against the defeat of Bourbon Naples. Bourbonists and papalists exploited the wish for local autonomy and the hatred of northern conscription and taxes, while economic discrimination by government and landlords kept the southern peasantry all too often a revolutionary force. Martial law had to be applied quite generally, and in some areas half the quota of military recruits disappeared into the hills to become a veritable army of outlaws. In 1866 an armed rebellion succeeded in capturing the town of Palermo and holding it for a week. The casualties in this cruel and wasting series of civil wars were probably to be as many as those lost in all the wars fought against Austria for national independence.[1]

The last chapter of this short history lacks the glamour of the previous decade.[2] Austria at one point prudently offered to cede Venice to Italy, but the offer was refused, because Lamarmora aimed also to win the Trentino and Trieste, and he incidentally thought that Italy needed the prestige of an armed victory. War against Austria broke out in 1866, but the king had kept military affairs away from public scrutiny, and the higher command was totally inadequate. Despite superior numbers, the army was completely outmanoeuvred at Custoza. Off the Adriatic island of Lissa, though first announced as an Italian victory, a larger and better equipped Italian navy was convincingly beaten by good leadership and disciplined competence. Nor was this gloomy picture relieved by any serious liberation movement breaking out in Venice against the Austrians. Ordinary citizens demonstrated what Garibaldi called a shameful apathy as they waited to see who would win.[3] But Italy's much smaller ally, Prussia, scored an overwhelming victory, as a result of which Austria ceded Venice to Napoleon III, who gave it to Victor Emanuel in time for another plebiscite to show that 99.99 per cent wanted annexation by Italy.

Rome was also to be, as it were, a present to Italy, in this case a present from Bismarck. The problem here was more difficult than with Venice, for the pope was less amenable than the Austrian emperor, and with extremists on

---

[1] The total cost of national independence between 1846 and 1870 was worked out as 6,000 Italian dead and 20,000 wounded (Giustino Fortunato, *Il Mezzogiorno e lo Stato Italiano* (Florence, 1926), II. 470); C. Cantù, *Della Indipendenza Italiana: Cronistoria* (Turin, 1877), III. 685, gave the figure of 27,804 dead between 1848 and 1866; whichever figure is more correct, it can be compared with 20,000 French casualties in May and June of 1859 while fighting in Lombardy, of whom 7,668 were killed (*Mémoires du Maréchal Randon* (Paris, 1877), II. 15).

[2] As Ricasoli admitted in 1870, 'Once we proclaimed the existence of a new kingdom of Italy, our history after 1861 has not been particularly splendid, but Italians suddenly seemed to be a race of pigmies. . . . What, after all, has this kingdom achieved? Nothing historic, nothing that is wise or felicitous, nothing that can serve as an example for others' (*Lettere Ricasoli*, X. 131–2).

[3] *Scritti di Garibaldi*, V. 336. Later nationalists took a wry pride in the fact that the victorious Austrian fleet at Lissa was still composed of Italians, so that it was really an Italian victory (*Il Nazionalismo Italiano: Atti del Congresso di Firenze* (Florence, 1911), p. 134).

both sides there were no very obvious possibilities of compromise between clericals and anticlericals. Garibaldi tried again to march on Rome in 1862, having been encouraged by the prime minister to think that the government might stand aside. But exposure of this collusion forced the royal troops into action against the volunteers, and Garibaldi was gravely wounded by them at Aspromonte. Something very similar happened again in 1867, when the government secretly gave Garibaldi money and arms to stir up a revolt in Rome, but then had the humiliation of watching a French expeditionary force trounce Garibaldi's volunteers at Mentana.

Most parliamentarians—though Azeglio and a number of other leading liberal elder statesmen did not agree—had been taught by Mazzini and later by Cavour to feel that, without Rome, Italy would not be complete. Apart from sentimental considerations, possession of Rome would settle the contest for precedence between Turin and the other regional capitals. But any official Italian initiative to acquire Rome was barely conceivable so long as the city was protected by French troops, and indeed the king had to promise Napoleon that he would defend the pope against any attack. Nor did the inhabitants of Rome show any serious sign of wanting to rebel in favour of annexation to Italy. In 1870, however, an unexpected defeat of France by Prussia forced the French protecting garrison to withdraw, and, a few months after papal infallibility had been proclaimed a dogma, the Italian army marched into the Holy City. They encountered just token resistance, and some seventy people lost their lives in this culminating battle of political unification. It was not quite Mazzini's idea of national redemption by popular initiative; but what to Mazzini still seemed but the ghost or the corpse of Italy, to others appeared vital enough. What Metternich had disparagingly called a 'geographical expression'[1] had come to life. With the acquisition of Rome, the risorgimento seemed, for the time being, to be complete.

---

[1] Metternich said he coined this famous phrase when arguing with Lord Palmerston in the summer of 1847, and he added that the same term could also be used of Germany (*Aus dem Nachlasse des Grafen Prokesch-Osten: Briefwechsel mit Herrn von Gentz und Fürsten Metternich* (Vienna, 1881), II. 343).

2

The King and the
Constitution, 1849–1855

THE *re galantuomo* was moderately popular in his lifetime, especially in his native Piedmont. After his death he was going to be enshrined as the first hero of the risorgimento, and given a colossal monument which dominates the skyline of Rome, dwarfing all the other monuments to emperors, popes, and kings. He was to be called one of the great monarchs of history, a man whose successes were unequalled.[1]

Good qualities he certainly possessed. His affability and simplicity of behaviour attracted the loyalty of conservatives and revolutionaries alike, and this had great advantages for the country at a time when parliamentary government was taking shape. He was good-natured, and he also possessed common sense and even some capacity for political finesse. He showed physical courage in four wars. Compared with these qualities his laziness and coarseness of character were minor faults. No doubt he was always happiest in either the barracks, the stables, or the hunting field, but he also took the trouble to play a leading if not always obvious role in national politics. This role was not so noble or purposeful as a succession of official historians has led us to believe. Too often his inveterate boasting about his political and military prowess was taken at face value. On the other hand some people who knew him well, and especially foreigners beyond the reach of censorship, could call him a weak character, and in general a devious, untrustworthy, and mediocre man.[2] How far he deserved his popularity is, in other words, doubtful. What is less in doubt is his importance as a politician, for during his reign many of the enduring traditions of Italian political practice were established, and he was involved both negatively and positively in their establishment.

Until Victor Emanuel was twenty-eight years old, Piedmont-Sardinia was

---

[1] G. Ardau, *Vittorio Emanuele II e i Suoi Tempi* (Milan, 1939), I. 140; Bianchi, *Storia Documentata*, VIII. 10; A. Monti, *Figure e Caratteri del Risorgimento* (Turin, 1939), pp. 247, 249.

[2] G. A. H. de Reiset, *Torino 1848: Ricordi sul Risorgimento*, ed. R. Segàla (Milan, 1945), pp. 235–6, 287–91, where, among other stories, Victor Emanuel told de Reiset he had once killed someone over an affair with a woman; H. d'Ideville, *Journal d'un Diplomate en Italie: 1859–1862* (Paris, 1872), I. 53–8; Pompeo Provenzali, quoted by C. Pellegrini, *Nuova Antologia* (Rome), Sept. 1968, pp. 29–30.

under an absolutist form of government, and his own political education, such as it was, had therefore been aimed at producing a monarch to rule by divine right. His schooling had been minimal, and mainly military at that. Reports by his teachers contain such remarks as 'thoroughly bored and indolent', 'always asleep', 'an hour's lesson is not enough to get across to him the simplest point'.[1] His family was closely related to the other reigning houses of central and southern Italy which, in course of time, he was to dispossess. Another curious fact is that the man who was destined to be an enemy of Habsburg Austria had a mother and wife who were Habsburgs, and later he tried to marry his son to another. More significant for the future history of the house of Savoy may be that he, like his son Umberto after him, married a first cousin. Some psychological significance may also be read into the fact that he remained entirely subject to his father until he became king at the age of twenty-nine. Charles Albert treated him without much affection and showed a manifest preference for his younger brother.[2] Victor Emanuel was allowed no part at all in practical politics until the moment when, in March 1849, defeat in the three-days' war against Austria forced his father into abdication.

His first action as sovereign was to negotiate an armistice with Marshal Radetzky. This was to become the subject of the first serious historical criticism of his qualities as a politician, when the Austrian archives were quoted to show, in reports by Radetzky, Baron von Metzburg, and Baron d'Aspre, a very different picture from that painted in Italian historiography.[3] The accepted view was that the new king's firmness in the armistice talks at Vignale saved the Piedmontese constitution which Radetzky had hoped to make him renounce. But this story was a later fabrication, since the Austrians, who themselves had a constitutional government of their own, did not try to make Piedmont give up the *statuto*. If the country secured fairly easy terms of peace, that was due not to any courageous stand by the king so much as to Austria's need to be generous in order not to drive Victor Emanuel into the arms of France. Radetzky needed a friendly Piedmont in order to obtain a lasting peace in the Italian peninsula. He needed above all to restore confidence in the monarchy, which Charles Albert, by political concessions and military fecklessness, had done much to damage.

Far from defending the constitution, Victor Emanuel privately assured the Austrians that he was determined to crush the liberal tendency of the Turin parliament; he further explained that he had not been in favour of fighting against them, and indeed that he was determined to make a clean break with

[1] Ed. G. Oxilia, *Nuova Antologia*, Aug. 1907, pp. 376–7; O. Vimercati, *Carteggio Castelli*, I. 317.

[2] Azeglio was sure that the king had been a supposititious child (G. Barbèra, *Memorie di un Editore, 1818–80* (Florence, 1930), pp. 342–3).

[3] H. McGaw Smyth, 'The Armistice of Novara: a Legend of a Liberal King', *Journal of Modern History* (Chicago), 1935, pp. 141–74.

his father's domestic and foreign policy. If Radetzky would help him, he would restore some of the monarchical authority which Charles Albert had surrendered. The Austrians in reply made it clear that he could rely on their military support if he needed it. In other words, Victor Emanuel was not patriotically saving the constitution, but on the contrary undertaking to befriend the Austrians and restore a greater degree of royal power. But this conclusion was too much for dedicated monarchists and champions of the historical legend to accept. Of the two most reputable recent biographers of the king, Professor Cognasso asserted confidently that a man of Victor Emanuel's sincerity and openness could not conceivably have acted in such a way; Professor Monti agreed, and added that there could not even be any doubt about the matter; in their opinion this new view could not be correct for the reason that it would vitiate the patriotic and monarchic interpretation of the risorgimento which was at the heart of national self-consciousness.[1]

A much more plausible defence of the king would have been to stress the fact that he had to act hurriedly in a very difficult and totally unexpected situation. Brought up to believe in the virtues of monarchical absolutism, he inherited a constitution granted only a year earlier and which no one yet knew how to work. The military defeat of Novara was a national humiliation, and there were good reasons to seek scapegoats for something which seemed incredible. Victor Emanuel thus put the blame on his father and on parliament. The military establishment rather singled out General Ramorino, who was tried and publicly executed for disobedience in face of the enemy, and this execution helped to cover the fact that the new king himself was under some suspicion for misconduct as a soldier during the war. The conservative reactionaries, by blaming parliament for seeking war against Austria, were hoping to use the occasion to recover some of their former power and privileges, whereas the radicals, who preferred to blame the incompetence and defeatism of the army, began to talk of introducing universal suffrage and even of creating a republic.

In such a threatening situation the king's behaviour towards Radetzky at Vignale showed courage and realism when he acted on the assumption that peace must be made at almost any cost. Equally courageous and dignified was his conduct in facing the people of Turin on 27 March, when there were threatening scenes in Piazza Castello and a disipiriting absence of applause for their new sovereign. Genoa went further and broke into open rebellion at his refusal to continue the war, and armed force had to be used in the very first days of his reign to bombard this rebel town into submission. In fulfilment of his undertaking to Radetzky, he at once dismissed the 'democratic' adminis-

---

[1] F. Cognasso, 'Il Colloquio di Vignale', *Atti della Reale Accademia delle Scienze di Torino* (Turin), LXXVI (1941), pt. ii. 155; A. Monti, *La Giovinezza di Vittorio Emanuele II (1820–1849)* (Milan, 1939), pp. xxi, 246; *Il 1848 nella Storia Italiana*, ed. E. Rota (Milan, 1948), II. 986, where it is still maintained that Monti is beyond question correct; but, against these authors, a fundamental book is A. Filipuzzi, *La Pace di Milano (6 agosto 1849)* (Rome, 1955), pp. 14–16, 22, 44.

tration which had been appointed by Charles Albert. To replace them his choice as prime minister was General De Launay who had the reputation of being a reactionary and possibly even pro-Austrian.

Elsewhere in Italy, Victor Emanuel's brother sovereigns had to use forceful repression on a yet wider scale, and this fact in the end made his own action less objectionable. In Tuscany and Naples the Austrian victory prepared a return to a modified absolutism, with the suppression of parliament and of a free press. Victor Emanuel might have been tempted to follow suit, for even in Piedmont many thought that popular government must have come too soon and that Charles Albert's experiments in constitutionalism would have to be abolished.[1] But the new king, at least for the moment, lacked any firm basis for a re-establishment of personal power. The army had collapsed and some of its units had totally disintegrated; the primary seaport of his realm was in open rebellion; the finances of the country were in terrible disarray, and parliament was effectively dominated by an unrealistic and doctrinaire majority of the Left. In such a situation, even some of the leading conservatives, among them Count Balbo and Count Ottavio di Revel, having helped to devise the *statuto*, still believed that constitutional government offered the best hope for withstanding republicanism and social disorder.

For himself, the king was secretly hoping for a resumption of war soon; war, as he explained, was his true *métier*.[2] This meant that he would have to be careful not to antagonize public opinion nor to offend other constitutional states who might be prepared to support him. These were arguments for retaining the *statuto*. On the other hand he privately continued to reassure both French and Austrians that the real reason for rebuilding his army was that he needed a military regime in order to defeat the democrats.[3] In both these superficially contradictory views we can find something of the king's personality. Nor can he be criticized for wanting to keep on good relations with Austria until a satisfactory peace settlement was reached. Nor by any means could he yet be sure that he would not one day need Austrian military help against the revolutionaries. It is therefore not hard to explain why he asked to be allowed to fight alongside the Austrians and French in defeating Garibaldi at Rome and restoring Pius IX to his temporal throne.[4] He had to play for time, and he could not afford to offend anyone he thought he might sometime need as a friend. To the French ambassador he produced another *argumentum ad hominem*, putting the blame on his own father who 'trompait

[1] Gioberti, quoted by C. Gioda, 'Vincenzo Gioberti e Francesco Crispi', *Nuova Antologia*, May 1901, pp. 321–3; Massari and Collegno, quoted by Nassau William Senior, *Journals Kept in France and Italy from 1848 to 1852* (London, 1871), I. 301–2; Carlo Petitti, quoted by A. Codignola, *Dagli Albori della Libertà al Proclama di Moncalieri* (Turin, 1931), p. 660.
[2] De Reiset, *Torino 1848*, p. 286.
[3] Apponyi, in *Le Relazioni diplomatiche fra l'Austria e il Regno di Sardegna (1848–1860)*, ed. F. Valsecchi (Rome, 1963), III. 46–7; Murat, ed. C. Vidal, in *Rassegna*, XXXVII (1950), 530; *Sclopis: Diario*, p. 75.
[4] *Pio e V. Emanuele*, I, pt. i. 23–4.

tout le monde' with his 'régime déplorable', and he also blamed those Italians who pursued 'le fantôme, de l'indépendance italienne qui a perdu notre malheureux pays'.[1] In the eyes of Professor Monti, Victor Emanuel's dedication to the cause of Italian independence was a sacrosanct dogma, and yet in fact the king could speak in a very different sense on occasion. If indeed he thought national independence a tolerable goal, it was as an expedient to be used, with great caution, in order to destroy the supreme evil of liberalism which was leading the country to ruin.[2]

One consideration in his mind must have been that the monarchy, without needing to change the constitution, already possessed plenty of powers under the terms of the 1848 *statuto*. Not only was he commander-in-chief of the armed forces, but he had the sole right to declare war and make treaties; he alone nominated the members of the upper house of parliament; he alone chose and dismissed ministers, who were responsible to him rather than to the chamber of deputies; and he also had a fair latitude in using royal decrees, since the constitution stated, with perhaps studied vagueness, that while he shared the legislative power with parliament, 'the king alone has the executive power'.[3] From the very first, Victor Emanuel used to preside at cabinet meetings, or at least the newspapers were told to say he was presiding even if he might be away hunting; he did not mean to let the existence of a constitution make people think that he was content to act King Log.

Almost at once he realized that General De Launay had few of the qualities needed by a peacetime government, so after a month he dismissed this prime minister and instead appointed Massimo d'Azeglio. When the radical majority in parliament attacked his armistice as unconstitutional, he held elections in July, and intervened personally to ask the electors for a parliament which would allow a peace treaty to be signed. But another strong Leftist majority was returned, so he encouraged Azeglio simply to ignore parliament. The first necessity was to turn the armistice of Vignale into a longer-term peace settlement: it was with this in mind that he had told Radetzky of his willingness to use force against the democrats in parliament, and now the Austrians were again reassured by Azeglio that constitutional government had been a deplorable mistake, since Italians were not politically mature enough for it.[4] Disregarding the elected deputies, king and minister together proceeded to negotiate peace on their own responsibility. When attacked for acting illegally, they signed the treaty and again dissolved parliament.

Victor Emanuel did not abolish the constitution as other Italian sovereigns had done, but he allowed no constitutional scruples to stop him intervening

[1] Bois le Comte, 14 Apr. 1849, M.Aff. Étrangères.   [2] *Pio e V. Emanuele*, I, pt. ii. 4–5.
[3] Most of the *statuto* is translated in *The Making of Italy 1796–1870*, ed. D. Mack Smith (New York, 1968), pp. 136–9; taxation without parliamentary consent is discussed by M. Mancini and U. Galeotti, *Norme ed Usi del Parlamento Italiano* (Rome, 1887), pp. 425, 437–8.
[4] Filipuzzi, *La Pace di Milano*, p. 220.

personally in the elections. It seemed to him that parliament had been quite unreasonable in opposing his policy of making peace with Austria. At the same time as he continued to collect taxes without waiting for parliamentary consent, in November 1849 he issued another appeal to explain that it was his duty as monarch to 'save the nation from the tyranny of parties' and to ask the electorate to return a more conservative chamber.[1] Some people, including Cavour, even when they accepted it as necessary, regarded this second royal intrusion into party politics as a risky adventure, for, if the new election turned out badly, there would be no alternative except abdication or else to overturn the constitution.[2] But while this 'Proclamation of Moncalieri' might have looked odd at Westminster, it did not violate the letter of the Piedmontese *statuto*. On the contrary one could argue that the constitution was thereby saved from breakdown, and so a way was left open for the later development of 'constitutional' into 'parliamentary' government.

Azeglio was without doubt the man whose advice prevailed with the king on this delicate issue. In Azeglio's view at the time, Victor Emanuel was a man of courage whose main lack was experience and who was not a despot at heart; indeed it was to be assumed that the king would almost always end by taking good advice if it were backed by a judicious threat of resignation. Azeglio was one of those liberal conservatives who recognized the desirability of keeping and if necessary improving the parliamentary system. Under his guidance this particular crisis was resolved when, by the use of considerable and possibly questionable pressures, he succeeded in obtaining a conservative majority which gave the king what he wanted.[3]

In analysing Victor Emanuel's attitude it must be noted that his private remarks, as those at other times, can be interpreted in different ways. Possibly he was deceiving the constitutionalists into thinking that he had liberal instincts; or he was deceiving the Austrophiles and reactionaries into a contrary opinion; or he may have been deceiving both sides at once while ready himself to move in either direction as events should develop. The British minister was convinced that Victor Emanuel was 'sincere, frank and chivalrous', and had set his face firmly against a reactionary policy;[4] but this was a minority view in diplomatic circles. The French minister thought he was just biding his time until he could overturn the constitution, in other words that he was basically illiberal and accepted parliamentary government only as a temporary expedient.[5] The Prussian minister, too, was shown the autocratic

[1] The proclamation is translated in *The Making of Italy*, ed. Mack Smith, pp. 168–70.
[2] *Nouvelles Lettres*, p. 357.
[3] *Azeglio*, Rendu, p. 70; *Lettere di Massimo d'Azeglio a sua Moglie Luisa Blondel*, ed. G. Carcano (Milan, 1870), p. 417; *Azeglio-Galeotti*, p. 22; A. Brofferio, *Storia del Parlamento Subalpino* (Milan, 1867), III. 338–44; G. Sardo, *Storia del Parlamento Italiano* (Palermo, 1964), II. 305–6; A. M. Ghisalberti, *Massimo d'Azeglio: un Moderato Realizzatore* (Rome, 1953), pp. 174–82.
[4] *Gran Bretagna e Sardegna*, II. 300–6; ibid. III. 35.
[5] Dispatch translated in *The Making of Italy*, ed. Mack Smith, pp. 170–1.

side of his character.[1] To the papal nuncio, Victor Emanuel made it quite explicit that he disliked constitutional government and was quietly acting to abolish it, while Bishop Charvaz, the king's former tutor and friend of twenty years' standing, reported that, just in case the new elections proved a success for the Left, the king was ready with plans to suspend parliamentary government.[2]

Possibly this was the real truth, or possibly it was a blind, or possibly he genuinely did not know what to think and was waiting to see what chances presented themselves. The king's language to Apponyi, the Austrian minister, was very firm indeed, for he insisted that he was inexorably opposed to 'ces canailles de démocrates'—'on tombe sur cette canaille et on l'écrase, comme des mouches. . . . Je les ferai pendre tous.' Apponyi was convinced that the king not only disliked the Lombards and the *italianissimi*, but frankly resented his father's regrettable concessions to liberalism, and was determined that when war broke out again Piedmont would be fighting in alliance with Austria against the revolution.[3] On the other hand, to those of the *italianissimi* with whom he was acquainted he could talk as early as 1850 of fighting a '*guerra italiana*'; and the following year he let it be known that he liked the chapter on 'Piedmontese hegemony' in Gioberti's *Del Rinnovamento civile d'Italia*.[4]

There were some Piedmontese in aristocratic and clerical circles who were anxious to push the king in the direction of a *coup d'état* in order to restore the old regime,[5] and it is hard to think that his own instincts were firmly against a return to the more authoritarian past. His Habsburg wife and her circle at court had little direct political influence, but indirectly they must have been a focus of pro-Austrian and reactionary opinions. His private household at Moncalieri was essentially one of army officers, few of whom were noticeably enthusiastic about constitutional government. No single civilian minister during his reign was as close to him as these army officers of the *casa reale*, and many of them he was able to bring into the cabinet. At least five generals were invited to become prime minister during his reign, and he seems to have turned instinctively to the army in moments of great emergency. Some twenty-five generals and admirals, people who had sworn a very special obedience to himself, became cabinet ministers, and no administration was without one or more of them. In particular, ministers of war were almost always his personal choice; they were invariably generals, and all or almost

[1] Canitz, quoted by F. Valsecchi, *L'Alleanza di Crimea* (2nd ed., Florence, 1968), p. 406.

[2] *Pio e V. Emanuele*, I, pt. ii. 29–30, 48, 60; and see the interpretation by later fascist historians, C. M. de Vecchi di Val Cismon, *Bonifica Fascista della Cultura* (Milan, 1937), p. 68, and G. Volpe, *Momenti di Storia Italiana* (Florence, 1925), p. 296.

[3] *Relazioni fra Austria e Sardegna*, ed. Valsecchi, III. 46–7, 84–5, 130, 181.

[4] *Memorie di Giorgio Pallavicino* (Turin, 1886), II. 305–6, 444.

[5] Pralormo and Marshal de la Tour, quoted in Monti, *Giovinezza di V. Emanuele*, p. 508; M. Minghetti, *Miei Ricordi* (Turin, 1890), III. 14.

all had been among his private aides-de-camp. He was quite capable of appointing a minister of war by personal fiat and on the advice of his private military household, allowing the premier to learn of such an appointment through the newspapers.[1]

Not that there was anything strictly unconstitutional about this, but it does reflect on the kind of constitution Piedmont possessed and on the king's attitude to government. Some of his private threats against parliament were no doubt empty boasting and designed just for effect. While he was undeniably a great boaster, it seems in retrospect that he lacked the drive and imagination to go far in playing the tyrant. Though he sometimes fancied himself as a dictator, this was probably another day-dream, since he did not like taking decisions, and for the most part was only too pleased if a prime minister would spare him the duty of presiding at cabinet meetings; especially was this true once he learnt the convenience of thus being able to shift the blame to his ministers when plans went wrong. Private remarks to Apponyi and the nuncio are not by themselves convincing evidence to the contrary, as the fact that the king habitually said quite different things to different people was common knowledge among those who saw him often.

All his life long this remained a handicap under which he suffered, because, despite the carefully tended legend of frankness and trustworthiness, his more forceful statements were treated with doubt by the professional politicians. They knew that his heart was never really in politics and that he lacked any capacity for protracted seriousness. Observers thus used to report that his ministers had much greater influence on affairs than the king himself liked to think.[2] They knew also of his appetite for popularity; and this desire for popular acclaim is another of the reasons why, unlike other Italian rulers of the time, and despite his frequent impatience with parliamentary government, he in fact preserved representative institutions and gradually, unenthusiastically, allowed them to assert themselves in the constitution.

Far the most important reason for the ultimate triumph of parliamentarism was the influence of two remarkable chief ministers, Azeglio until 1852, then Cavour until 1861. Azeglio was liked only moderately by the king; Cavour was liked by him hardly at all; but both these Piedmontese aristocrats he treated on the whole with good sense and good humour, and usually he possessed enough political awareness to submit to their superior intelligence and character. Neither was in any sense a courtier;[3] both were men of strong views, and both realized that only a firm basis of parliamentary power would enable them to control the king's occasionally extravagant whims so that they could claim for Piedmont the moral leadership of Italy.

[1] Gen. E. Della Rocca, *Autobiografia di un Veterano* (Bologna, 1897), I. 313; *Lettere d'Azeglio a sua Moglie*, ed. Carcano, p. 417.

[2] *Relazioni fra Austria e Sardegna*, ed. Valsecchi, III. 84, 242; *Pio e V. Emanuele*, I, pt. ii. 65; Bayle St. John, *The Subalpine Kingdom* (London, 1856), II. 126; *Diario di Collegno*, p. 86.

[3] *Azeglio*, Rendu, p. 197; R. Romeo, *Cavour e il suo Tempo* (Bari, 1969), pp. 219-22.

The first of them was the man who invented the legend of the king as an honest man of integrity whose word could always be trusted. Azeglio was determined to save the middle way of the *statuto* from disruption by either the democrats or the reactionaries, and under his guidance Victor Emanuel gained invaluable experience of the sheer effectiveness of constitutional government. When the king was irritable he was frank enough to tell Azeglio that he did not very much like being advised, and that his idea of kingship left him responsible to no one;[1] but here, too, such a remark was possibly intended mainly to impress, to strike an attitude, and in practice he knew his own limitations too well to go against his ministers beyond a certain point. When he added that a prime minister was merely expected to play grand vizier to the royal tyrant, this was said in jest.

Azeglio's major success as premier was the Siccardi laws in 1850 which abolished the church courts and other surviving ecclesiastical privileges which looked inappropriate under a constitutional regime. The king's decision to accept these particular laws suggests that the religious question had a decisive effect on the development of parliamentary government, for this was one of the areas of public life in which he more or less shared the attitude of his ministers. He himself was a moderately good Catholic. He used to hear mass regularly, and by his own testimony he was strongly superstitious in his beliefs, but he was no *dévot*, and indeed his private life made it impossible for him to remain on completely good terms with the church. His quoted utterances contain little reference to religion or god, and he looked on the *partito pretino* with as much distaste as he did on the democrats.[2] The papacy was thus shocked to learn that this inexperienced king meant to use his powers to reform some of the scandals and deficiencies in the Piedmontese church,[3] and the Siccardi laws were the result.

Victor Emanuel listened respectfully to the pope, and managed to remain in not unfriendly correspondence with him despite repeated excommunication, but Azeglio in 1850 found a useful ally in the king when some of the clergy tried to separate the monarch from his ministers.[4] The queen and the queen mother, no doubt under clerical pressure, used the argument that the dead Charles Albert would suffer in purgatory if these anti-clerical laws were passed, and even that God might visit the royal children with sickness or death; but against these crude threats the king wrote to explain to Pius that, at any rate for the moment, he was bound by his oath to the *statuto*, and he boldly maintained not only that the pope might err, but that excommunication

[1] N. Vaccalluzzo, *Massimo d'Azeglio* (Rome, 1930), pp. 395–7.
[2] Bollea, *Una Silloge*, p. 36; U. A. Grimaldi, *Il Re 'buono': la Vita di Umberto I* (Milan, 1970), p. 103, where it is recorded that Victor Emanuel used to keep a walking stick with a note attached to say that he had once used it to thrash a priest.
[3] *Pio e V. Emanuele*, I, pt. i. 34; pt. ii. 30–4, 41.
[4] M. de Rubris, *Confidenze di Massimo d'Azeglio* (Milan, 1930), p. 63.

in temporal matters could be disregarded as invalid.[1] When in the space of a few weeks there occurred the deaths of his mother, his wife, his brother, and his youngest son, it was too much to hope that some of the clergy would not use this as evidence of divine vengeance, but he held firm, and the archbishop of Turin, who persisted in defying the new laws, was imprisoned. As the king said jokingly, the monarchy was covered in this instance by the signature of a responsible minister, so that it was Giuseppe Siccardi who would be sent to hell for any defiance of the Holy See.[2] This was the first occasion on which he found the constitution to be a useful 'alibi', and the lesson was not wasted. After these laws were passed he softened the blow by promising the pope that he would allow no further legislation against the church.

The year 1852 saw Cavour's somewhat unscrupulous displacement of Azeglio after making a personal alliance with deputies of the Left Centre. First, by a dexterous parliamentary move in May, this junior but influential minister managed to have Rattazzi elected speaker of the lower House, and though the king tried through his chief aide-de-camp, General Durando, to stop the election, he acted too late.[3] Cavour proceeded quickly and secretly in order to foil what he called the plotting of court circles, and correctly guessed that the king would not dare make an open protest once parliament was publicly committed by a vote. This episode was an early sign of how someone who had studied the working of parliament in France and Britain could outmanœuvre a king who was unfamiliar with the rules. It was also an indication to both Azeglio and the king that Cavour was a dangerously ambitious character who not only was somewhat unprincipled, but who would not be satisfied until he had taken their power for himself.[4]

This sign of independence in the lower House was perhaps responsible for the king's attempt in June to galvanize the senate into greater action. When he wrote asking the senators for more exertion, this was resented by many elderly gentlemen who valued their quiet life of dignified ease, and their resentment in turn led the king to threaten that, if they were not careful, he would nominate 60 middle-class citizens to the senate and so outnumber the existing aristocratic majority.[5] This not very well documented episode suggests that the king foresaw difficulties ahead with the *camera*, and was hoping to prepare a firmer basis of power in the nominated upper House; although in practice he lacked the staying power and the political tact to succeed.

Azeglio chose this moment to challenge Cavour's alliance with the anti-clerical Left. To outbid him he proposed to follow up the Siccardi laws with

---

[1] *Lettere di V. Emanuele*, I. 322–3, 393–4; *Pio e V. Emanuele*, I, pt. ii. 95.

[2] G. Massari, *La Vita ed il Regno di Vittorio Emanuele II di Savoia* (Milan, 1878), I. 161.

[3] *Il Conte di Cavour: Ricordi di Michelangelo Castelli*, ed. L. Chiala (Turin, 1886), pp. 44–5.

[4] *Diario di Collegno*, p. 447; Butenval, on 28 Oct. 1852, reported it as well known that Cavour was 'antipathique' to the king (M. Aff. Étrangères); Minghetti, *Miei Ricordi*, III. 55, remarked on Azeglio's poor opinion of Cavour.

[5] Bollea, *Una Silloge*, p. 458; *Lettere di V. Emanuele*, I. 392–3; *Diario di Collegno*, p. 451.

a bill introducing civil marriage. This measure obtained a decisive affirmative vote in the *camera*, but then came up against an outright refusal by the king to accept his ministers' advice if it meant violating his recent promise to the pope. Such a sacramental issue provided a good occasion to exercise the right of royal veto. Azeglio countered by resigning in order to confront the monarch with the full responsibility for his action. The latter then tried to form a cabinet with Balbo and di Revel of the Right. One difficulty here was that his agreement to the Siccardi laws had partially blocked his lines of communication with these conservative Catholics. The Right were also encumbered by the fact that they wanted economies in the armed forces, and some of them tended to look on Austria as an ally in preserving the old order. What was more, they had little support in parliament. Nevertheless the king had to admit that the best hope of exerting his own authority was to bring the conservatives into office, and hence he acted for a moment as though parliament were irrelevant.

Only when these men failed to form a government did he turn to Cavour, and it was fortunate for him that Cavour was ready to make some compromises in order to obtain power. One such compromise was to accept some of the king's friends as ministers. Another was his agreement not to press the civil marriage bill despite the fact that the *camera* had already approved it. Cavour continued to speak publicly in favour of marriage-law reform, but in private he encouraged the senate to vote against what was technically a government bill; so doing he earned the monarch's gratitude.

Once he had won office in this somewhat back-door manner, Cavour had less reason in future for such obsequiousness. Though he stopped short of treating the king with familiarity, his attitude was sometimes marked by impatience and even condescension. He might let Victor Emanuel have his way over parts of the wording of a document, or he would agree to find jobs for relatives of the king's mistresses, or send royal love letters through the diplomatic bag, but he tried hard to prevent the monarch altering the substance of policy. Occasionally the ministers badly needed the king's support, in particular when the 1857 elections had revealed the existence of a dangerous conservative revival, or again when Cavour needed to work without parliamentary consent on some delicate matter of finance or rearmament: on such occasions the minister was genuinely appreciative, and hence tried to avoid flouting the royal wishes too openly.

Cavour was too much of an intellectual and a civilian for the king, too little a flatterer or a courtier, and in general too clever and guileful. At the same time, though Victor Emanuel went on talking in private of how easy it would be to carry out a *coup d'état*, and of how the *statuto* had been 'une des sottises que nous avons faites',[1] he usually recognized that he needed the cleverness and resourcefulness of this powerful minister. While he tried to defend the

[1] *Relazioni fra Austria e Sardegna*, ed. Valsecchi, IV. 26; *Lettere di V. Emanuele*, I. 409–10; G. A. H. de Reiset, *Mes Souvenirs* (Paris, 1901–3), II. 300–1.

royal prerogatives when Cavour seemed to be whittling them away,[1] he no doubt realized that he lacked the talent and the industry to carry out all his threats. He continued to annoy Cavour by using his orderly officers to carry private messages to foreign courts, and so doing he sometimes made foreign policy unnecessarily difficult; but though he used to boast to his military entourage that, when he differed from his ministers, it was Cavour who surrendered, the generals had reason to know that the true balance of power was the other way round.[2]

One occasion on which these two men differed was in 1854 when the king made a bid to get rid of the masterful Cavour before the latter became too powerful. The issue was that of entry into the Crimean War.

Victor Emanuel always had a romantic idea of warfare, and his military entourage flattered him into thinking that he was a talented general. In wartime he knew he would recover an almost absolute power by virtue of his constitutional position as commander-in-chief. This was one reason why he wanted war, almost any war. Several times he darkly hinted that he was ready to touch off a major explosion in Europe and was looking forward enormously to the prospect.[3] He spoke to the Austrians of possibly fighting as their ally, just as he secretly told the French he was ready to join them in fighting against Austria; or else he was prepared to join both of them against Russia. A still further possibility was put to him by the Marquis Pallavicino, one of the radical patriots whom Cavour so despised, who suggested that many people in other parts of Italy would rally behind *casa Savoia* if only Piedmont would pugnaciously raise the flag of Italian nationalism.[4] It was this last possibility which in the end was to convince Victor Emanuel that the cause of Italian independence might not be so dangerous or so harmful to Piedmont as he had once imagined.

When the Crimean War broke out, another and more immediately practicable alternative presented itself, for the British were soon worried by their losses in Russia and anxious to find additional troops in Spain or Italy. The king was delighted with the idea. He even reached the point of offering, on certain conditions, to take personal command of both the French and British armies in the Crimea; when this particular offer was taken less seriously than he had hoped, he was extremely angry, and remarked that the British were jealous of him and feared a strong Italy that would mean their decline as a great power.[5] Another more serious problem was that Cavour found great difficulty

[1] Omodeo, *Cavour*, I. 200–2; A. Monti, *Vittorio Emanuele II (1820–1878)* (Milan, 1941), pp. 149–50.

[2] Della Rocca, *Autobiografia*, I. 377–8.

[3] *Lettere di V. Emanuele*, I. 409; *Il Piemonte nel 1850–51–52: Lettere di Vincenzo Gioberti a Giorgio Pallavicino*, ed. B. E. Maineri (Milan, 1875), p. 55; *Memorie di Pallavicino*, II. 362, 365.

[4] Ibid. II. 460–3; *Diario di Collegno*, pp. 89–90; *Daniele Manin e Giorgio Pallavicino: Epistolario politico (1855–1857)*, ed. B. E. Maineri (Milan, 1878), pp. xxxix, 328–9.

[5] L. Cipriani, *Avventure della mia Vita*, ed. L. Mordini (Bologna, 1934), II. 172; L. Chiala, *Ancora un po' più di Luce sugli Eventi politici e militari dell'Anno 1866* (Florence, 1902), p. 564; *Diario di Collegno*, p. 265.

in persuading his cabinet to undertake such a remote and obviously unprofit-
able war, so the king decided to seize his chance and replace Cavour by a more
conservative administration. This would kill two birds with the same stone.
When he privately told the French of his intention, the French minister communicated this startling news in confidence to a friend, who broke the confidence and informed Cavour; and the latter then brilliantly retrieved the
situation by disregarding his cabinet and suddenly deciding for war before the
king could put his alternative plan into effect.

Some people might have labelled this a constitutional impropriety on
Cavour's part, while others subsequently have preferred to think that he
thereby saved Piedmont from a monarchist coup. The king must have been
indulging in one of his self-adulatory day-dreams, because it is hardly conceivable that any other minister except Cavour, and especially not the conservatives, would have agreed to support him in entering this war on the
distinctly ungenerous terms which now had to be accepted. Some politicians
thought that the king should and could have negotiated much better terms, in
particular to obtain from Austria some concessions in Lombardo-Venetia
which would have been a diplomatic victory for Turin; and we now know that
the British were so anxious for Piedmontese help that they were ready to
bring pressure on Austria.[1] But the king, by his tactless remarks to the French,
had compromised the monarchy by committing himself to war, and hence
deprived his ministers of their main bargaining counter.[2] Intervention by the
court in politics was proving to have certain disadvantages.

Equally unfortunate was a second intervention by the court against Cavour,
this time over a law to dissolve the monasteries. Almost everybody agreed,
including some of the senior clergy and the king himself, that there were too
many monasteries in Piedmont, and that some of them were scandalous in
their laxity and uselessness. Cavour's proposal to dissolve just over half of
them was part of a compact with Rattazzi in return for the latter's reluctant
agreement to support Cavour's new policy of fighting in the Crimea. Victor
Emanuel did not at first disagree, but on second thoughts he saw it as another
chance to make his peace with Rome, to displace Cavour, and at the same time
to score a success for his personal diplomacy by forcing the pope to make
some concessions. Secretly, without telling his ministers, he sent some of the
bishops to discuss at Rome the possibility of a new concordat. He wrote personally to remind the pope that he, the king, had been the one who stopped
parliament passing the civil marriage bill, and adding that, if only the pope
would help by making some plausible concessions, Cavour could be dismissed
and replaced by a more obediently Catholic administration.[3] Just as the

---

[1] *Gran Bretagna e Sardegna*, IV. 360.
[2] P. Silva, *Figure e Momenti di Storia Italiana* (Milan, 1939), pp. 293–4; Valsecchi, *L'Alleanza di
   Crimea*, pp. 393, 430–1; *Memorie e Lettere di Carlo Promis* (Turin, 1877), p. 126; other documents
   translated in *The Making of Italy*, ed. Mack Smith, pp. 195–9.
[3] Ibid., pp. 185–7.

marriage law in 1852 had provided the occasion to get rid of Azeglio, so the monasteries bill in 1855 would do the same service in getting rid of the still more intrusive and ambitious Cavour. But the pope, to the king's disgust, refused to yield to this concealed threat and replied by the counter-threat of excommunication.

When the lower House of parliament passed Cavour's bill on the monasteries, the king ordered the president of the senate to ensure that it would be rejected in the upper House, and Bishop Calabiana was encouraged to propose its rejection. Cavour thereupon resigned, just as Azeglio had once done, in order to confront the monarch with the responsibility for such a dangerous and unparliamentary procedure. The ministers knew they were on difficult ground, for the bill was not particularly popular, but they were saved by the fact that Azeglio was not the man to take his revenge on Cavour by copying the manœuvre which Cavour had used against him in 1852. When the king invited General Durando to form a new cabinet, Azeglio strongly supported Cavour and asked for a private audience: the king realized the danger and refused to talk to him. Azeglio did not accept Cavour's request to join the cabinet, for he would not associate himself again with such an unscrupulous and untrustworthy man, but he did write to warn the king roundly against what he called a ruinous violation of the constitution. Victor Emanuel was told that he was losing his reputation in the country. Never again after this brave and frank letter was there a welcome at court for Azeglio, the conservative elder statesman who had been the king's chief political mentor and the creator of his reputation as the *re galantuomo*.[1]

General Durando's difficulty in forming a ministry was that he could not rely on the Right, because the conservatives were mostly against the idea of Piedmont joining the Crimean War, and that made them unacceptable at court.[2] Victor Emanuel had to admit that there was no other alternative available which would give him both his war and his concordat; and of the two, he preferred war. In particular he was worried when he witnessed a threatening demonstration outside the palace: as the mob gathered numbers, he spoke of using force against them, but his aides persuaded him that this would be dangerous, and he realistically gave up and recalled Cavour.[3] If he wanted his war, this was the only answer. Though the king still spoke bravely of perhaps having to close parliament, Cavour explicitly called in question the issue of royal intervention in politics, and even made an ominous speech recalling how Charles I had been deposed in England for resisting the trend of his times. The hint was taken; the senate was discreetly permitted to

[1] *Diario di Collegno*, pp. 224, 244, 253, 259–60; Ghisalberti, *Azeglio*, pp. 190–1; E. Borghese, 'La Crisi Calabiana', *Bollettino Storico Bibliografico Subalpino* (Turin), LV (1957), 458–80.
[2] De Reiset, *Mes Souvenirs*, II. 304.
[3] *Ricordi di Castelli*, pp. 84–5; E. di Nolfo, *Storia del Risorgimento e dell' Unità d'Italia* (Milan, 1965), VIII. 792–6; A. Brofferio, *Giacomo Durando* (Turin, 1862), pp. 85–6.

Above and on facing page:
Two sketches of Victor Emanuel made from life
by Queen Victoria in December 1855.

change its mind; and the dissolution bill received the royal assent, so bringing
the 'Calabiana episode' to an end. The king had deliberately tried to defy the
majority in parliament, and had suffered a resounding defeat.

Evidently Victor Emanuel lacked the conviction or the courage, or the
political weight, to push his defiance of parliamentary government too far, and
the result of these two half-hearted attempts to assert himself was rather to
to diminish monarchical authority in the practical working of the constitution.
On 27 July 1855 the pope issued his allocution *Cum Saepe* with a major excommunication against those who had either proposed this dissolution of the
monasteries, or who tried to enforce it. The king was angry with Cavour for
forcing him into such a situation, but far more angry with the clergy for their
disobedience and their interdict, and angry also with the aristocracy who
ought to 'se grouper autour de son roi au lieu de subir l'influence du clergé et
de l'Autriche'. Henceforward Cavour was able to exploit the fact that a probably

unbridgeable gulf divided the excommunicated sovereign from the conservatives and the *partito clericale*.[1]

Though the king disliked travel, at the end of 1855 he was persuaded to visit France and England to celebrate Piedmontese participation in the Crimean War. Cavour and Azeglio accompanied him, and their first diplomatic success was to persuade him to cut off ten centimetres of his ferocious-looking upturned handlebar moustache. Even so diminished, he struck Queen Victoria as a very strange sight: 'He is *ein ganz besondere, abenteuerliche Erscheinung*, startling in the extreme in appearance and manner'; yet he was an agreeable companion, brusque and shy in society, but 'straightforward, liberal and tolerant'.[2] The diarist Greville was not quite so charitable. Note was taken that some people thought the king intelligent, but he looked rather like 'a chief of the Heruli or Longo-bardi':

His Majesty appears to be frightful in person, but a great strong, burly, athletic man, brusque in his manners, unrefined in his conversation, very loose in his conduct, and very eccentric in his habits, ... the most debauched and dissolute fellow in the world.[3]

There had in fact been considerable apprehension in London that Victor Emanuel might frighten the queen by addressing her in the same barrack-room language that he had used at the Tuileries.[4] Cavour obviously warned him about this, and he behaved well on the whole. Prince Albert took him to see Woolwich arsenal. He worried the Catholics by receiving a deputation from the Y.M.C.A., though he retrieved the situation by making a quite impressive

[1] La Tour d'Auvergne, 1 Jan. 1858, M. Aff. Étrangères; *Conversations with Napoleon III*, ed. V. Wellesley and R. Sencourt (London, 1934), p. 99, where the king is quoted as saying, 'Tous les prêtres sont de la canaille! Si on avait suivi mon conseil je les aurai fait fusiller tous! Ils ne méritent pas autre chose.'

[2] *The Letters of Queen Victoria (1837–61)*, ed. A. C. Benson and Viscount Esher (London, 1907), III. 198.

[3] C. Greville, *A Journal of the Reign of Queen Victoria from 1852 to 1860* (London, 1887), I. 303.

[4] Cowley, 27 Nov. 1855, F.O. 519/217: 'He'll frighten the Queen out of her senses if he goes on so with her'; Clarendon, 3 Dec., F.O. 519/172; M. Paléologue, *Cavour* (Bologna, 1929), pp. 60–1.

speech at the Guildhall. He also worried his ministers by dropping a number of minor bricks which showed a considerable ignorance of affairs outside Piedmont, and at one point Cavour even threatened to leave him and go home.[1] Deliberately, or out of *gaucherie*, he tried to make trouble by mentioning to the British some of Napoleon's imprudent criticisms of them, and then in return telling an infuriated Napoleon of Palmerston's remark that the imperial court was run by a parcel of adventurers. In apologizing for this, Cavour made things even worse by explaining to the British foreign office that the king had been set against Palmerston by Queen Victoria herself.[2] According to the latter's diary, however, the true story was that Victor Emanuel had tried to set the queen against Palmerston. He had startled her by exclaiming that 'Austria would have to be exterminated'. He did not like being a king, he told her; fighting was the only thing he had learnt how to do. 'He said this in a tone of desperation and that singular strong voice, and with those rolling eyes. Poor man. I think he is unhappy and *much* to be pitied. He is more like a knight of the Middle Ages who lived by his sword, than a king in present days.' But the queen does not seem to have entirely believed him when he confided to her that the duties of a sovereign allowed him only two hours of sleep each night.[3]

Later in life Victor Emanuel used to amuse his courtiers by telling them that Queen Victoria's eldest daughter fell in love with him on this visit, and indeed wanted to marry him, but he had felt he would look too much of a fool with a wife who knew Greek and Latin.[4] This is a strange story, all the more so in that the fifteen-year-old Princess Victoria was by this time already engaged to the future emperor of Germany. The truth is that Victor Emanuel secretly sent a proposal of marriage to Princess Mary, younger sister of the Duke of Cambridge, who had recently turned down an offer from Prince Napoleon (the king's future son-in-law). The princess saw him four times, but eventually refused him, politely, but 'for some very excellent and weighty reasons'. She noted, what the queen had also perceived, that the king's abrupt and almost *farouche* behaviour concealed an innate shyness in society.[5] She was inclined

to make more allowances for his want of education than others I could name. . . . [But] from all one hears, my comfort and happiness as his wife would be very problematic. He has, I feel convinced, a good heart, but this does not make up for

---

[1] Massari, *Diario*, p. 413; A. Gallenga, *Italy Revisited* (London, 1876), I. 393; E. di Nolfo, *Europa e Italia nel 1855–1856* (Rome, 1967), p. 473; *Cavour e l'Inghilterra*, I. 141–6.

[2] Ibid. I. 150, where Napoleon is quoted as saying 'Le Roi de Sardaigne est un brave sous-officier, qui ne passera jamais officier'; Clarendon, 5 Dec. 1855, F.O. 519/217; Cowley, 10 Dec., F.O. 519/218; Cowley, 25 Jan. 1856, ibid., reported Napoleon's reaction to the king's words, and 'I never saw a man more chagrined'.

[3] Queen Victoria's Journal, 30 Nov., 1 and 3 Dec. 1855, Royal Archives (Windsor).

[4] G. Finali, *Memorie*, ed. G. Maioli (Faenza, 1955), pp. 354, 496.

[5] C. Kinloch Cooke, *A Memoir of H.R.H. Princess Mary Adelaide Duchess of Teck* (London, 1900), I. 228–9; *Cavour e l'Inghilterra*, I. 112; *The Letters of Queen Victoria*, III. 262.

want of principle and noble breeding, and how *could* I ever respect or esteem a thoroughly *coarse minded* man? one who has not even the polish and refinement of the gentleman to make up for his *faiblesses*.[1]

Being rebuffed, albeit with tact and delicacy, must have been damaging to his pride, and that may explain how the true facts were later concealed and improved in order to turn the story of his own advantage.

The main interest of this episode, apart from the casual light it may throw on the king's character, is that the incident was hidden at the time from the cabinet. This was not the last occasion on which he played at dynastic politics on his own. Subsequent decades were to show that in international affairs he enjoyed having a personal policy which was different from, or even contrary to, that of his ministers, and this fact was to create a very special constitutional problem for Cavour and his successors.

[1] Princess Mary to the Duke of Cambridge, 14 Sept. 1856, Royal Archives, C.27/54. J.12.

3
Cavour and Parliament

CONSTITUTIONAL history has not bulked large in risorgimento studies, because events of greater dramatic impact have been accorded precedence on this particular stage. The 1848 constitution of Piedmont was a haphazard document drawn up hurriedly by inexperienced lawyers, and the history of the next hundred years showed that it was open to either liberal or illiberal interpretation. A great deal was to depend on the formative period between 1848 and 1861, during which first Azeglio and then Cavour created traditions of parliamentary and cabinet rule. Cavour was the most successful and authoritative parliamentarian in the whole span of Italian history. On his development of the constitution, however, we possess little more than the provocative but fragmentary essays of Adolfo Omodeo, a lack which must be partly due to the fact that the Cavour archives have been kept secret. The modern Italian parliament grew out of Cavour's theory and practice, and what he understood by liberal government is therefore important.

Cavour was a gentleman farmer who, only in his late thirties, entered active politics. He stood for parliament in 1848, being rejected in four constituencies. Elected shortly afterwards, he took his seat on the Right. By late 1850 he was a minister, and by 1852 prime minister, a post he retained almost continuously until his death in 1861. This was a short but brilliant political career. At first he had assumed that political economy was an exact science like physics,[1] yet in time his practical bent turned him into a supple realist adaptable to any situation. He remained an indifferent administrator, and said he disliked diplomacy, but the management of parliament brought out his greatest gifts, and constitutional history is therefore a good field for observing his political technique.

The British minister at Turin called Cavour's 'the first true parliamentary government which Piedmont has seen'.[2] And Cavour himself once made a profession of faith as follows:

I believe that with a parliament one can do many things that would be impossible under a system of absolute power. . . . So long as you have no intention of being intimidated by the violence of parties, you have nothing to lose from parliamentary

[1] Early 1845, *Gli Scritti del Conte di Cavour*, ed. D. Zanichelli (Bologna, 1892), II. 355.
[2] Sir James Hudson to Lord Cowley, 6 Nov. 1852, F.O. 519/194.

strife. I never in fact feel weak except when parliament is in recess. . . . The Mazzinians, for instance, are less to be feared inside parliament than outside it . . . for the heavy atmosphere of Turin would always calm them down.[1]

This carries some conviction. Cavour, after an unpromising and unpopular start, truly came to represent the tiny ruling class of liberal-conservatives which a narrow tax qualification allowed to vote, or the 1 per cent of the population who in practice voted.[2] Parliament was therefore his preferred field of battle against those who represented other elements in the nation, Garibaldi and Mazzini for instance, or the pope. In parliament he could usually depend on a solid vote, and there he alone knew all the tricks of government.[3]

Cavour when he was a mature statesman was seldom doctrinaire, not even in his liberalism. Experience taught him that there were no absolute political maxims after all, and he came to be a utilitarian even in his attitude to parliament. He blamed his chief rival for 'exaggerating the parliamentary system',[4] and took pride in being 'less liberal than the Americans'.[5] He admired Pitt, Canning, and Peel, but also thought Cromwell a supreme political genius.[6] Cavour was an opportunist and pragmatist. His belief in representative institutions was not so simple and forthright as he liked people to think, and carping critics could call it just a means to his own kind of personal power.

Although Cavour said he felt strongest in parliament, in fact he kept sessions short. His greatest moments were elsewhere. Parliament was a useful rostrum for publicity, or for focusing and welding opinion, but it is hard to find a single occasion when parliamentary criticism made the prime minister alter his policy. When, for example, it was decided in 1855 to enter the Crimean War, this was without reference to parliament and directly against both a cabinet decision and public opinion.[7] Cavour refused to discuss with his ministers the policy to be followed at the Congress of Paris,[8] nor were they allowed to see the dispatches which told how the congress was going.[9] In 1858 the French alliance arranged at Plombières was not only quite extra-parliamentary, but Cavour consulted only one cabinet minister.[10] In January 1859 the dramatic provocation of Austria in the king's speech was by private suggestion of Napoleon III overriding a unanimous cabinet, and Cavour himself called this procedure 'passablement extraparlementaire'.[11] These actions were not strictly unconstitutional, but they can hardly have strengthened cabinet and parliamentary government. Cavour was thus less able to

[1] *Cavour e l'Inghilterra*, II, pt. ii. 284–5.

[2] *L'Opinione* (Turin), 18 Dec. 1857; fuller details in G. Sardo, *Storia del Parlamento Italiano* (Palermo, 1964), II. 165.

[3] 6 Apr. 1860, *Atti del Parlamento*, p. 47.   [4] *Lettere di Cavour*, VI. 184.

[5] *Cavour: Discorsi*, VIII. 203.   [6] De la Rive, *Cavour*, pp. 160–1.

[7] *Cavour-Salmour*, pp. 82–3; *Nuove lettere*, p. 591.

[8] Hudson to Cowley, 28 Jan. 1856, F.O. 519/194.

[9] *Lettere di Cavour*, II. 183.   [10] Matter, *Cavour*, III. 95.

[11] *Cavour-Nigra*, I. 289; Massari, *Diario*, pp. 105, 111.

protest when the settlement of Villafranca in July 1859 was negotiated without any reference to himself. This, too, was not unconstitutional.

In 1860, however, Cavour confessed to having committed 'un acte haute-ment inconstitutionnel' which invited impeachment.[1] This was the secret treaty signing away Nice and Savoy to France. A plebiscite was held later to justify this cession, carefully designed to take place when parliament was not sitting. Napoleon had insisted on taking Savoy in exchange for Cavour annexing Tuscany. If Cavour had been ready for a more loose federal organi-zation of Italy, he might well have been able to keep these two border provinces or at least one of them; but he wanted the outright annexation of Tuscany and so paid the extra price, while it was also essential not to let parliament see that there was any choice. He admitted that the accusation of impropriety could be levelled against this constitutional behaviour, more indeed than against the actual cession of national territory,[2] but he was confident that parliament would not denounce an accomplished fact. National emergency and parlia-mentary incompetence entitled him to act on his own.

The plea of national emergency could be raised in defence of many other decisions taken during this decade. When the fortification of Casale was begun in 1851, no prior approval was sought for the necessary expenditure, though parliament was then sitting. Cavour subsequently asked for indemnifica-tion, admitting that his action had not been strictly legal or constitutional,[3] and threatened resignation if any blame was imputed. This time he obtained only the narrowest majority. In 1856–7, when his parliamentary system was better rooted and an identical situation arose over fortifying Alessandria, Cavour again kept parliament in the dark,[4] for which he was later excused by 106 votes against 14. He had not wanted to risk submitting these military preparations to debate until they were well advanced. The minister of war apologized for such an unconstitutional action, but Cavour, to the general embarrassment, publicly disavowed this apology. Mamiani, a future colleague of Cavour's, then summoned the deputies to 'save the dignity of parliament' by renouncing discussion and rising to their feet to cheer the government's 'holy' action. Certain individual members, however, even while voting for Cavour, admon-ished him that parliament would atrophy if treated like a rubber stamp. People should not be taught that the constitution was a mere piece of paper, nor should ministers learn that automatic absolution would follow any governmental illegality.[5]

Cavour was evidently not a man to let constitutional niceties stand in his way. He welcomed discussion and criticism up to a certain point, but he was

---

[1] *Cavour-Nigra*, III. 167.
[2] Ibid. 258.
[3] *Cavour: Discorsi*, V. 359, 425.
[4] A. Lamarmora, *Agli Elettori del Collegio di Biella* (Turin, 1860), pp. 6–7.
[5] Ferrero-Ponziglione, Corsi, Brofferio, Mamiani, Lamarmora, and Cavour in parliament, 14 Mar. 1857.

equally fond of legislating by decree during parliamentary vacations.[1] An educational bill could drag out for weeks, but only two days were allowed for debating the treaty of Paris. In education, too, a distinguished political opponent, Carlo Cattaneo, had to find a job in Switzerland; and when the economist, Francesco Ferrara, criticized the government in his lectures, he was suspended from his university chair and had to seek a post in Tuscany. Cavour appreciated the free conflict of ideas, but liked to be able to alter the rules when pressed too hard. He avoided acts of force where he could, knowing that they often defeated their purpose, but did not scruple to use repressive measures when in real difficulties, and used to say that one should never be half-hearted about it.[2]

Theory and practice must clash sometimes with every politician. Against what he called an over-democratic government in 1849, Cavour's mind had even turned to instigating a military *coup*, and from this idea he had to be dissuaded by his friends.[3] When out of office he had advocated a free press, but twice later he introduced press laws which, though mild enough, were inroads upon liberties guaranteed by the constitution. He said, for the record, that he preferred to meet the Mazzinians openly, but in practice kept them outlawed; and when the courts repeatedly acquitted them, he persuaded parliament to alter the 'detestable' system of freely selected juries. Nor was this enough. Intendants were ordered to sequestrate the solitary Mazzinian newspaper, if necessary every day, without troubling too much about legality. Printers could be bribed or threatened, contributors expelled from the country, and trade unions bullied into submission. *Italia del Popolo* was thus harried out of existence. Cavour's chief press officer, Giuseppe Massari, could not understand why most newspapers at Turin criticized the government's conduct as undignified and illiberal.[4]

This extreme Left round Mazzini was never more than a lunatic fringe, but the extreme Right had firm bases of support in a Catholic population. Here the elections of November 1857 came as a sharp shock to the liberals. Cavour had taken little trouble. Few of the liberal-conservatives had been near their electors or had even issued any electoral statement.[5] As many as five different liberal candidates could be competing in one constituency, without electors being given any help by the government in choosing between them. In consequence nearly a third of the 204 deputies proved to be clericals of the Right.

Cavour had stated that if the elections were not 'entièrement ministérielles'

---

[1] Cavour in the senate, 26 May 1854; Nicolucci in the chamber, 4 Apr. 1861; Mazziotti in the chamber, 3 Apr. 1861.

[2] Cavour in parliament, 28 Nov. 1848.

[3] *Il Conte di Cavour: Ricordi di Michelangelo Castelli*, ed. L. Chiala (Turin, 1886), pp. 28–9.

[4] Massari, *Diario*, p. 22; *Lettere di Cavour*, VI. 63, 130, 135, 145, 240; *Rivista Storica Italiana* (Turin), XLVIII (1930), 16.

[5] *Il Piccolo Corriere d'Italia* (Turin), 22 Nov. 1857.

he would resign,[1] but he now interpreted this acknowledged 'solemn defeat' not as a personal failure but as another national emergency which forced him to increase his own power. He argued that the use of confessional and pulpit had been unfair and unconstitutional,[2] and some elections were accordingly annulled. Furthermore, as the constitution made ecclesiastics with cure of souls ineligible, it was proclaimed, against clerical authority and contrary to previous practice, that canons had such a cure and could not sit. This expulsion of opposition members seemed the more arbitrary in that the government admitted supporting the original candidature of at least one of these canons.[3] In earlier elections, moreover, episcopal intervention had even been encouraged, but that was only when the bishops backed the government. Many weeks of 1857–8, and over 500 pages of parliamentary proceedings, were now taken up with using these newly-coined constitutional dogmas in order to redress the balance of parties in parliament. Cavour refused to refer the matter to a judicial tribunal. The Piedmontese judges, he said unguardedly, were insufficiently impartial to see his point of view; moreover, they would consider only what was the law and not the political factors involved.[4]

The upshot was that 10 per cent of seats in the *camera* were declared vacant by means which even one of Cavour's cabinet colleagues called illegal,[5] and then filled with tame government supporters by the strong use of official influence. Cavour knew what he was about. He had decided on war, and this depended on convincing Napoleon III that Italians were overwhelmingly anti-Austrian, so a strong opposition was a luxury he could not afford. What patriotism gained, however, liberalism lost, and the political education of the electorate must have suffered. Henceforward a government of the Right could not be tolerated, for it would possess a precedent for retaliation which might destroy parliament. The lack of an organized conservative party in post-risorgimento Italy was not unconnected with these events, for the clericals were gradually being pushed into a position where they had more to gain than lose from boycotting parliamentary institutions.

Evidently Cavour's statements about welcoming opposition in parliament should not be taken too literally. He genuinely believed in representative institutions, or at all events he did so in so far as they bolstered his own position; and here he was copied later, as historians built up Cavour's to be the golden age of liberalism, in imitating which one could do no wrong. If he liked parliament, it was not to restrain the executive, nor to help formulate policy, but more to reinforce his own authority and perhaps also to enhance

---

[1] *Lettere di Cavour*, VI. 69 (a different date is given to the same letter in vol. II, p. 277); ibid. 87.
[2] Cavour in parliament, 30 Dec. 1857.
[3] Rattazzi and Costa di Beauregard in parliament, 13 Jan. 1858.
[4] Cavour in parliament, 19 Jan. 1858.
[5] Quoted in *La Vita e i Tempi di Giovanni Lanza: Memorie Ricavate da suoi Scritti*, ed. E. Tavallini (Turin, 1887), I. 179.

his reputation in parliamentary countries abroad.[1] Parliament could be used either to publicize his designs or to colour them for public consumption. Furthermore, it was his main weapon when he clashed with Victor Emanuel.

One of Cavour's finest constitutional achievements was to stand up against the king and habituate him to the practice of liberal government. Often he had to allow the sovereign an important or even a decisive voice in policy: for example, over the civil marriage bill, over the appointment of certain ministers, over entry into the Crimean War, over the armistice of Villafranca, over Garibaldi. But so long as the king was indulged into thinking that he possessed the reality of power, in practice he could be deceived into confusing reality with illusion. If Victor Emanuel was sometimes a beneficial restraint upon Cavour, so Cavour unobtrusively built up parliament as an even more beneficial counter-restraint upon the king.

Mme Rattazzi, who had been a mistress of the king and spoke with direct knowledge, commented in retrospect that he 'subissait la dictature morale de Cavour'; and the same word was used by others who accused Cavour of creating a 'parliamentary dictatorship'.[2] Liberal historians, for example Omodeo, have utterly rejected such an accusation, just as Cavour himself firmly disclaimed any liking for ministerial despotism. Yet others said that he possessed an excessive love of power and liked flatterers and nonentities in the cabinet as a means to greater personal dominion.[3] Perhaps these views may be reconciled in the paradox that the victory of constitutional Piedmont depended on the pseudo-dictatorship of someone who was a true liberal at heart. This brought with it a danger that the means might condition the end and liberal institutions might remain shallowly rooted. Even some of Cavour's friends recognized him as a necessary man who deliberately built up a system of personal rule and whose very irreplaceability made the government a practical dictatorship.[4] The French minister once wrote that

Le Président du Conseil, on ne peut le contester, domine la situation par sa haute popularité. La fiction que le Piémont décore du nom de gouvernement constitutionnel, repose en entier sur sa personne; il jouit en ce moment d'un pouvoir sans contrôle et d'autant plus absolu qu'une Chambre docile en accueille toute la responsabilité, comme le souverain en accepte aveuglément toutes les conséquences. Il y a loin de cette concentration de tous les pouvoirs à l'équilibre constitutionnel qui est censé faire la base des' institutions sardes, mais telle est la force des illusions agréables, que les hommes d'état du Piémont, et le Comte de Cavour le premier,

---

[1] *Cavour e l'Inghilterra*, II, pt. i. 12: 'cette discussion, faite pour rehausser notre réputation parlementaire'.

[2] Mme Rattazzi, *Rattazzi et son Temps: Documents Inédits* (Paris, 1881), I. 443; R. Bonghi, *Come Cadde la Destra*, ed. F. Piccolo (Milan, 1929), pp. 85–6.

[3] *Il Diritto* (Turin), 8 Dec. 1858, 22 Jan. 1860.

[4] *Cavour-Salmour*, pp. 93–4; Massari, *Diario*, p. 72; *L'Opinione*, 13 June 1861; Oldofredi, 13 July 1861, MSS. Archivio Lamarmora (Biella), XCVI. 154; *Azeglio-Torelli*, p. 130.

s'imaginent vraiment pratiquer le gouvernement constitutionnel dans toute sa
pureté et servir, avec l'Angleterre, d'exemple aux autres peuples du monde.[1]

Particularly useful was the trend of elections in showing Cavour whether he
needed to adjust his policy in order to prevent the growth of any rival party.
His idea of parliament was not to have a second party waiting with an alternative programme for the electors. Cavour preferred the broad government
majority, possessed of more than one alternative policy and prepared to alter its
programme rather than resign. In the 1880s, under the premiership of Agostino
Depretis, this type of government acquired the name of 'transformism'.
But transformism was only the rationalization of an already traditional
practice. The word 'party' had never quite lost the pejorative implication of 'faction'.[2] Cavour in 1849 welcomed the king's promise to save the
nation from the tyranny of parties. His own parliamentary following was less
a party than an amalgam of groups, conservative and radical, nationalist and
'campanilist'. It included centralizers and regionalists, Catholics and irreligious, as it also included various shades of opinion between free trader and
protectionist, '*giurisdizionalisti*' and '*liberisti*'; and the balance between these
different elements could be unobtrusively shifted if need be. His own favourite
phrase, the '*juste milieu*', reflects his urge to move towards any strong opposition and absorb its programme by a compromise. This emasculated his
opponents and kept himself at the head of a variously transforming majority.

Cavour's most instructive experiment in transformism was the *connubio*,
the marriage he made in 1852 between his own moderate conservatives and a
break-away group on the Left under Urbano Rattazzi. Cavour himself called
the *connubio* his political masterpiece.[3] The initiative for this alliance seems to
have come from the Left when in 1849 some people asked him to join an
alliance against the other conservatives.[4] Cavour debated whether to back the
prime minister, Azeglio, or overthrow him, and eventually chose to join the
conservative cabinet—sacrificing *amour propre* to patriotism, as he oddly put
it.[5] Subsequently he tried to make his new colleagues accept a more radical
programme in alliance with Rattazzi. They refused, and there followed a
petulant scene in which Cavour threw crockery about the room.[6] But instead
of resigning, he determined on a *coup*; for this junior minister was already the
driving force of the ministry and felt strong enough to dictate terms. He began

---

[1] Gramont to Walewski, 22 July 1857, M. Aff. Étrangères.
[2] Cavour in parliament, 9 July 1848. Depretis in parliament, 30 Nov. 1862, boasted that the independent Left had thought of itself not as an opposition but just as a stimulus to Cavour; another
speech by Depretis of 1 Dec. 1862 shows that the 'transformation' of parties had already become a
customary phrase (*Discorsi Parlamentari di Agostino Depretis*, ed. G. Zucconi and G. Fortunato
(Rome, 1891), IV. 235, 249).
[3] Cavour in parliament, 6 Feb. 1855.
[4] 24 Aug. 1849 (wrongly printed 1842), *Nouvelles Lettres*, p. 329.
[5] *Cavour Agricoltore*, ed. E. Visconti (Florence, 1913), pp. 282, 292.
[6] Matteo Ricci, *Azeglio e Cavour* (Florence, 1882), pp. 18–19.

to disregard cabinet decisions and discuss secret government business with the opposition.[1] He was quite ready to contradict his colleagues on the floor of parliament and irresponsibly assume pledges for the whole cabinet. Finally, without consulting even the prime minister, he publicly accepted on behalf of the government the support of the twenty-four deputies of the Left Centre; and followed this by opposing his colleagues in backing Rattazzi's election as speaker.[2]

Given its worst interpretation, this simply reflected Cavour's 'amour du pouvoir', as the French minister called it.[3] The Abbé Gioberti was possibly right to think that, in weakening Azeglio, the *connubio* risked allowing the anti-constitutional Right into power.[4] Certainly it showed a highly individual conception of cabinet government. Later generations might have recognized a typical *combinazione* aimed to win a new clientele of deputies personal to Cavour, a new centre-grouping of the professional and commercial classes who, in alliance with the liberal urban aristocracy, were to carry through the national revolution. Uniting the Centre, it isolated both the extremer radicals and the conservatives round Azeglio, and so diminished the danger from clericalism or revolution. It split Rattazzi away from his more extreme friends, Depretis and Valerio, making him just a fellow-traveller with Cavour. In the long run, by keeping the opposition divided at two remote extremes, this *connubio* provided maximum possibilities for parliamentary manœuvre; it allowed Cavour to veer towards the Right when he needed support for muzzling the press, and leftwards when public opinion became more nationalist or anticlerical. In the short run it secured him appointment as prime minister when he permitted a royal veto on Azeglio's civil marriage bill as the price of an invitation by the king to supplant his former leader. By another transformist gesture, Cavour retained most of Azeglio's ministers, since his new coalition had to include as much as possible of the old.

Cavour studied British politics closely and often quoted British examples and Erskine May to his own parliament in Turin.[5] But in the 1850s it was hard to understand party politics at Westminster,[6] and perhaps, when making the *connubio*, his superficial acquaintance with British precedents confused rather than instructed him. In France he had discerned a 'transformation' of parties which reinforced the centre against the extremes,[7] and the same trend was visible with the Peelites and anomalies such as Gladstone and

[1] Memoirs of Galvagno, *Lettere di Cavour*, I. 577–8.
[2] L. Chiala, *Une Page d'Histoire du Gouvernement Représentatif en Piémont* (Turin, 1858), pp. 4, 187.
[3] His de Butenval to Drouyn de Lhuys, 16 Nov. 1852, M. Aff. Étrangères.
[4] *Gioberti-Massari Carteggio (1838–52)*, ed. G. Balsamo-Crivelli (Turin, 1920), p. 539.
[5] Cavour in parliament, 14 Aug. 1849, 16 Oct. 1849, 26 Nov. 1850, 14 Apr. 1851, 28 Apr. 1851, 7 July 1851, 10 Mar. 1853, 26 May 1854, etc.
[6] *Cavour e l'Inghilterra*, II, pt. i. 19.
[7] *Lettere di Cavour*, I. 285–7; F. Ruffini, *La Giovinezza di Cavour* (2nd ed., Turin, 1937), I. 238–9.

Palmerston. Cavour reasoned that the future lay not with an alternation of parties but with a central liberal coalition. He further argued that Britain and France might be encouraged to underwrite his aggressive foreign policy if the only alternative to his centrum was an anarchic vacuum of power at the two extremes.[1] Wellington had compromised over Catholic emancipation, Grey over parliamentary reform, Peel over free trade, and had thus created a middle way which saved Britain from chartism or rightist authoritarianism. Cavour would do likewise. Peel should even have gone further and transformed his coalition by bringing in the whigs; he would then have remained in office and kept the governing classes united.[2] This was more or less how Cavour saw the *connubio*.

The marriage with Rattazzi was not, as is often thought, something final. The ideal of a *juste milieu* rather implied a continuous rhythmical oscillation of group alliances to stabilize each changing parliamentary situation.[3] Thus the heirs of Azeglio always hoped that Cavour would return to a slightly more conservative allegiance, and indeed such a new piece of parliamentary alchemy seemed within sight once the king was prised away from the clericals over the Calabiana controversy in 1855. As the danger of clerical reaction receded in 1856, so it seemed that Cavour might swing back to the Right.

Transformism worked more subtly than this however. Cavour later invented an explanation for his *connubio*, namely that the imperialist *coup d'état* in France in 1851 had made him join the Left Centre in order to counter-balance the growth of reaction.[4] One difficulty in this explanation is that for most of his political life he was a client of imperial France. Another difficulty is that, on Cavour's reasoning of balance and equilibrium, the clerical victories in the 1857 elections should then have pushed him back further towards the Left; instead of which he dissolved the *connubio* and moved rightwards to absorb this new opposition.[5] Instead of either resigning or accepting the new challenge in parliament, he disarmed his opponents by transforming his majority in their direction. The elections had shown him that the constitutional Left was weaker than at the time of Rattazzi's defection in 1852. As this parliamentary group was now worth little to his coalition, he divided them further by abandoning Rattazzi while retaining Giovanni Lanza,[6] and for a time it seems that the Left ceased meeting together to concert policy.[7] This dropping of Cavour's chief colleague was the price demanded by the moderate Right for their support. As the French minister now noted of Cavour: 'Il profite volontiers des occasions qui se présentent de rallier individuellement à

---

[1] Cavour in parliament, 7 Mar. 1850; *Cavour e l'Inghilterra*, I. 154–5.
[2] Cavour in parliament, 26 May 1857.
[3] Omodeo, *Cavour*, II. 126.
[4] Cavour in parliament, 6 Feb. 1855.   [5] *Lettere di Cavour*, VI. 101–2.
[6] La Tour d'Auvergne, 19 Nov. 1857, M. Aff. Étrangères; *Lettere di Cavour*, II. 285; ibid. III. 177; *Carte di Lanza*, II. 157.
[7] *Il Diritto*, 1 Jan. 1858.

lui les hommes qui passent pour appartenir à la fraction de la droite modérée'.[1]

This was not exactly a new marriage with the Right, although the possibility was much discussed in the press. It was rather a deliberate confusion of the parliamentary spectrum. The need for a French military alliance had forced Cavour to seek Napoleon's advice, and the advice had been that he should break with Rattazzi.[2] This breach with his chief lieutenant shocked some of Cavour's closest friends [3] who feared to disrupt the coalition and were upset by French interference. But Cavour manœuvred with skill. His system of fluid group alliances depended on minimizing political conflict, so he now promised to 'base himself on the whole of parliament without making distinction between parties'.[4] The moderate Right fell before this sweet reasonableness. Furthermore the king saw several leaders of the extreme Left, and won their qualified support by telling them confidentially of the plan to conspire for a war against Austria.[5]

These methods rendered the existing groups '*fractionnés*' and '*dissipées*'.[6] Cavour could assert that all parties had disappeared, and that Right and Left were each so divided that there was nothing more for him to fear.[7] He had never accepted the existence or the necessity of an equilibrium of powers in the constitution.[8] He boasted now that the breadth of his coalition took away all reasonable pretext for opposition to him. He was even proud that Piedmont had had no ministerial crisis for nine years while England had seen four.[9] Cavour's parliamentary majority had seemed perilous in 1857, but grew bigger and bigger through 1858 as he trimmed his sails to the prevailing wind. What opposition remained was soon as much regional as political. After the loss of the essentially conservative region of Savoy in 1860, the Right almost ceased to exist; this meant that Cavour no longer had any need to court the Left as an anti-conservative counterweight; it was noted that he even ceased listening to speeches by the opposition, since the disappearance of any parliamentary equilibrium had taken most of the point out of parliamentary discussion.[10]

Some of Cavour's statements reflect a theoretical predilection for a two-party system. He might say in public that he believed in a systematic opposition and parliamentary conflict;[11] he had subtle reasons for wanting a strong

[1] La Tour d'Auvergne, 6 Dec. 1857, M. Aff. Étrangères.
[2] Ibid., 11 and 17 Dec. 1857; *Cavour-Salmour*, p. 145; Massari, *Diario*, pp. 310–11.
[3] *Ricordi di Castelli*, pp. 50–1.
[4] La Tour d'Auvergne, 23 Apr. 1858, M. Aff. Étrangères.
[5] Ibid., 1 June 1858.
[6] *Lettere di Cavour*, VI. 204, 243.
[7] *Cavour e l'Inghilterra*, II, pt. ii. 245, 252.
[8] Cavour's article in *Il Risorgimento* (Turin), 27 May 1848, in *Camillo Cavour: Scritti politici*, ed. G. Gentile (Rome, 1930), pp. 202–3.
[9] *Nuove Lettere*, p. 591.
[10] P. Duprat, *Il Parlamento Italiano* (Turin, 1862), p. 43.
[11] Cavour in the *camera*, 21 Apr. 1858; *Cavour-Nigra*, III. 26; Cavour to the senate, 9 Apr. 1861.

opposition of Garibaldian deputies, and even a ministry of the Right might one day 'perhaps' be admissible.[1] This casual insertion of 'perhaps' is surely significant. For despite verbal statements of belief in opposition and parties, in fact Cavour tried hard to dissolve them and prevent a party system arising. He recognized that there was often good reason for using pacific tactics with opponents, as when in 1861 he allowed Rattazzi, then the leading opposition deputy, to become speaker of the lower house. Believing in the *via media*, and disdainful of opponents and colleagues, he cast himself as both sides of the dialectic at once.

This helps to explain the occasional ambiguity of Cavour's policy and the apparent deceitfulness of his methods. His confusion of parties was considered deliberate.[2] The Right saw it as his motive for the *connubio*, while the Left saw it as his motive for annulling the *connubio*. Luigi Menabrea of the Right, one of Cavour's successors as premier, publicly condemned his 'essentially eclectic policy . . . as he navigates now towards the Left and now to the Right'.[3] Giuseppe Saracco of the Left, another future prime minister, deprecated the 'game of political see-saw' which made Cavour so untrustworthy.[4] People as different as Garibaldi and Lord John Russell said that they never would take him at his word again, and Hudson thought that few in his own parliament really trusted him.[5] Massimo d'Azeglio reached the point of saying: 'Quant aux affirmations de Cavour, personne ne les prend au sérieux. Le cher homme en est arrivé à ce que, quand il parle, la seule chose qu'on croit impossible est précisément celle qu'il affirme.'[6]

A broad, mobile government majority had much to recommend it, especially in Cavour's skilful hands. It made for strong government, able to overcome faction and regionalism in order to plot long ahead for war. It gave Cavour a free hand to modernize Piedmont and make this Frenchified province more acceptable to other Italians. It let him crush all signs of social or political revolution. His mild parliamentary dictatorship was a barrier against any monarchic or Garibaldian dictatorship, and excluded any possibility of a radical Mazzinian republic, as it also ruled out the kind of federal Italy that would have appealed to Ferrari and Cattaneo. As a result the risorgimento was kept sufficiently conservative to win the allegiance of the socially dominant classes, and this made the national movement respectable.

But there were some incidental drawbacks. In one important respect, political education was retarded. History was also to show that parliamentary institutions languished under this treatment, for such a personal union of forces went to pieces when the master hand was gone. Omodeo praised a

[1] *Cavour: Questione Romana*, I. 243; *Lettere di Cavour*, II. 288.
[2] *L'Opinione*, 11 Feb. 1852; *La Gazzetta del Popolo* (Turin), 4 Dec. 1853.
[3] Menabrea in parliament, 5 Feb. 1852, 16 Apr. 1858.
[4] Saracco in parliament, 14 May 1858.
[5] Hudson to Russell, 12 Apr. 1861, P.R.O. 30/22/68.
[6] *Azeglio*, Rendu, pp. 189, 297.

system which went on producing single 'representative' figures such as Cavour, Depretis, and Giolitti;[1] but the same process also produced Crispi and Mussolini. These monolithic representative figures were necessary to make transformism work, yet checks and balances should therefore have been needed all the more, and Cavour was, understandably enough, not interested in checks upon himself. His system worked well enough in 1852–61, for he was a moderate man and a liberal who understood the intricate techniques required; but the years 1895–1900, 1914–15, and 1919–25 saw men in power who were less skilful and less well-intentioned. Cavour's views could be carried even by his own collaborators to the point of saying that only one party was needful in the state.[2] There was in fact almost no parliamentary restraint on his ministry, and independent liberals naturally recognized this as dangerous.[3] 'The Chambers', said Hudson, 'believe Cavour to be infallible.'[4] His enemies had been divided and conquered; and were either absorbed innocuously into his coalition, or else left isolated and sterile, vainly protesting that Cavour was turning Piedmontese politics into a concealed one-party despotism.

Another drawback was the difficulty of maintaining a coherent cabinet policy. Right and Left were mixed up in almost every future government, just because prime ministers found this the best way of achieving and staying in office. Such a coalition demanded that many important decisions be shelved because they might divide and destroy the government, or because any unambiguous statement on policy might hinder individual ministers in joining another subsequent coalition. For a similar reason, parliament sometimes had to be kept in the dark. Thus in April 1855, when Bishop Calabiana and the king acted to frustrate Cavour's project to dissolve the monasteries, Cavour resigned without waiting for a parliamentary vote, partly because a debate might have exposed the crown, but also because a vote might have gone against him and prejudiced his return to power. Again in July 1859 his resignation had no connection with any parliamentary vote; nor was his reappointment in January 1860 the result of any parliamentary decision. Furthermore, when out of office, whether in 1859 or 1852, Cavour neither co-operated actively with the government nor organized an opposition party, but kept himself

---

[1] Omodeo, *Cavour*, I. 144.

[2] *L'Opinione*, 18 June 1856; *Piccolo Corriere*, 10 June 1860.

[3] *L'Indipendente* (Turin), 5 Mar. 1858, 6 July 1858; C. Boncompagni, *L'Unità d'Italia e le Elezioni* (Turin, 1861), pp. 37–8; Duprat, *Parlamento Italiano*, p. 45; Bayle St. John, *The Subalpine Kingdom* (London, 1856), II. 57–8: 'The various ministries come and go according to palace arrangements or intrigues, and with scarcely any reference at all to what takes place in parliament. I believe that there has never been but one minister overthrown by a vote. On many other occasions, mutations have occurred for mysterious or personal reasons; but no explanation is offered to the chambers, and no change of policy is a necessary consequence. M. Cibrario succeeds to M. d'Azeglio, M. Rattazzi to someone else; it matters not. There is always a majority, generally the same majority, receiving its orders from anyone but its constituents.'

[4] Hudson to Russell, 11 Mar. 1861, P.R.O. 30/22/68.

remote, uncommitted, ready to reassume power when conditions were ripe; and in 1859–60 he returned to active politics only when Rattazzi struck at his electoral system by appointing administrative officials from the Left. According to Cavour's example, the duty of an opposition was less to oppose than to lie doggo. When Giolitti followed this example in the very different circumstances of 1914–15 and 1922–4, the result was disastrous for constitutional government.

Because Cavour had studied foreign parliamentary systems, he passed in Turin for an infallible constitutional expert. Inevitably, however, his knowledge was limited, and on his visit to London in 1856 he had to plead ignorance of the conventions when caught intriguing against Palmerston with the parliamentary opposition. In 1848 he had advised avoiding 'the slowness, the infinite formalities and rancid traditions' of the British parliament,[1] but later he held up British practice as an object-lesson for dispatch and the French for slowness.[2] The parliamentary standing orders at Turin, he stated, were about the worst anywhere: Cavour would have liked a 'radical reform', for these standing orders were an incentive to rhetoric and to the making of innumerable procedural points.[3] The legal quorum was so large that it demanded the presence of an absolute majority in either house, and this often meant that business could not proceed, though parliament met only in the afternoons and for half the year.

Cavour in office introduced no reform bill, and the old *octroyée* constitution was simply extended to the other Italian provinces as they were annexed, because the Piedmontese were proud of it and feared that an alternative might suit them less. Yet in miscellaneous statements we can piece together that Cavour would have liked an elective senate.[4] He thought he would prefer the British practice of expert committees and three readings to the Piedmontese practice of committees (*uffizi*) drawn by lot, but rejected the idea of a committee of the whole house.[5] He opposed the introduction of evening sessions.[6] He would have preferred a larger number of deputies in parliament, but a much smaller quorum than the regulation prescribed.[7] He decidedly favoured the British system of small constituencies against the French method of block-voting for large provincial lists, and would even have liked to exclude any deputy who obtained votes from less than 1 per cent of the population in his area.[8] He was against the payment of deputies.[9] He disliked the British electoral procedures, which aided the formation of large parties, and preferred the French system which made for a much more fluid parliament and less of

---

[1] *Cavour: Scritti politici*, p. 165.   [2] Cavour in parliament, 26 Nov. 1850, 4 May 1852.
[3] Ibid., 24 Jan. 1848, 29 Aug. 1849, 3 Oct. 1849.   [4] *Cavour: Scritti politici*, p. 205.
[5] Cavour in parliament, 17 Mar. 1857.   [6] Ibid., 14 May 1851.
[7] *Carteggio Castelli*, II. 577.   [8] Cavour in parliament, 4 and 9 July 1848.
[9] Ibid., 14 Jan. 1852.

a two-party structure.[1] Sometimes he favoured an open ballot,[2] sometimes a secret ballot;[3] for Cavour was always ready to change his mind. The same person who had opposed the 'dangerous sophism' of universal suffrage[4] was thus the man who eventually in 1860 unified Italy by mass plebiscites; and if there had to be a mass vote, he had learnt from Napoleon III that a public ballot could more easily be manipulated to give the required result. In the north, Cavour wanted the vote to be confined to those with the education and wealth to be politically middle-of-the-road and socially conservative;[5] but in the south, where the wealthy were reactionary and the intellectuals revolutionary, he might prefer the suffrage of the illiterate poor who disliked both these extremes.[6]

Cavour inherited a not particularly liberal constitution, but in the course of years he, second to no one except possibly Azeglio, made the elected chamber in practice the very centre of government. Most Italians, however, were still given little encouragement to believe in parliament. The restricted suffrage excluded nearly everyone from elections and was weighted to produce an anticlerical, bourgeois house. Hence the papalists, the Catholic peasantry, the Garibaldians, the intellectual federalists and Mazzinian revolutionaries, all these had cause to resent parliament as a disguised minority dictatorship. Even inside the exiguous *pays légal*, enthusiasm was weak. Surprisingly little can be found in memoirs and letters to show any widespread interest in parliamentary business, nor did people take pains to put their names on the voting register. Cavour mentioned that some deputies were being elected by only five or six voters apiece,[7] and once no one at all turned up at a polling booth.[8] Such facts reinforced the contention that 'le Piémont est indifférent au régime qui le gouverne, pourvu qu'il soit gouverné'.[9] Half the deputies might be new to parliament after each election, and the complications of parliamentary procedure baffled them. Cavour's benevolent instruction and masterful technique were therefore generally welcome, and in his absence the House (to his surprise and annoyance) was sometimes reluctant to proceed with business.[10]

Cavour did much to make parliament work, and much by precept and example to make debate orderly and reasoned. He was no orator himself. His speaking was usually slow and difficult,[11] his voice cold and metallic,[12] and his gallicisms and grammatical solecisms when speaking Italian were often painful

[1] G. Maranini, *Storia del Potere in Italia 1848–1967* (Florence, 1967), pp. 181–2.
[2] *Diario del Conte di Cavour*, ed. L. Salvatorelli (Milan, 1941), p. 198.
[3] *Cavour: Scritti politici*, p. 63.   [4] Ibid., pp. 71–2.
[5] Ibid.; *Lettere di Cavour*, III. 213.   [6] Ibid. IV. 238.
[7] Cavour in parliament, 9 Nov. 1849, 10 Jan. 1850.   [8] Ibid., 13 Aug. 1849.
[9] Lucien Murat, 21 Nov. 1849, quoted in Matter, *Cavour*, II. 134.
[10] *Cavour e l'Inghilterra*, I. 193.   [11] *Ricordi di Castelli*, p. 21.
[12] Petruccelli della Gattina, *I Moribondi del Palazzo Carignano* (Milan, 1862), p. 61; Duprat, *Il Parlamento Italiano*, p. 30.

to hear.[1] Nevertheless, partly perhaps because of his early mathematical training, his speeches were usually a model of logic and lucidity. Occasionally he resorted to rhetoric and made the galleries applaud,[2] but usually he was staid and unemotional. He spoke with few gestures and few notes, always preferring facts and figures to generalities. He tried hard to be friendly even with political opponents,[3] though he had a tendency to caustic sarcasm and occasional outbursts of temper and so did not always succeed. Hudson once remarked that, 'although Cavour is admired and feared and followed, he is not loved';[4] but his usual courtesy and good humour set an excellent example, and even critics recognized in him 'le terrible don de la familiarité'.[5] In the conduct of business the few vocal opposition deputies were incomparably less persuasive. Parliament to them was rather a platform for playing to the gallery. Even if in some respects more liberal than Cavour, they were almost invariably less balanced, and were certainly less experienced and effective as politicians.

The criticisms advanced by these opposition deputies are nevertheless interesting, for, though often extravagant, they show Cavour's work through other eyes than his own. Angelo Brofferio, for instance, the most vocal of all, accused him of not accepting private members' bills; monopolizing the right to initiate legislation, he upset the balance between executive and legislature. Brofferio gratuitously hinted that Cavour, in neglecting the chamber, might be deliberately discrediting the parliamentary system—the very same accusation which Cavour with even less reason levelled at Brofferio.[6] The prime minister was said to be a follower of the tyrannical Napoleon III, with liberty on his lips but not in his heart. The electoral system was geared in his favour, and unfair representation was accorded to small rural constituencies more accessible to 'influence'. As high a proportion as a third or more of the deputies were salaried employees of the establishment in their capacity as civil servants, army officers, magistrates, professors, or pensioners. Others aspired to such jobs and pensions and were thus on good behaviour. These placemen dominated the chamber, for they were hand-picked and organized for the purpose. Patronage, pensions, promotion, and decorations were at their service. All they had to do for their pains was 'to rise to their feet when the minister rises, to sit when he sits, to call "Bravo" when he speaks, and to chatter when anyone speaks against him . . . or to cry "Ai voti", "Alla questione", "Basta", "La chiusura", "Ah! ah!", "Oh! oh!"'[7]

[1] *Il Conte di Cavour in Parlamento: Discorsi*, ed. I. Artom e. A. Blanc (Florence, 1868), pp. xviii-xix; A. Brofferio, *Storia del Parlamento Subalpino* (Milan, 1866), I. 146-7; G. Massari, *Il Conte di Cavour* (ed. Turin, 1872), p. 221.

[2] *Lettere di Cavour*, II. ccliv.   [3] Ibid. VI. 127.

[4] Hudson to Russell, 12 Apr. 1861, P.R.O. 30/22/68.

[5] Mme Rattazzi, *Rattazzi et son Temps*, I. 580.

[6] Cavour in parliament, 3 Mar. 1854.

[7] A. Brofferio, *Fisionomie parlamentari* (Turin, 1853), pp. 16-19, 38; A. Brofferio, *Il Conte di Cavour* (Turin, 1861), pp. 33-9; G. Briano, *La Congiura di Genova* (Turin, 1857), p. 8; G. Briano, *Francia e Piemonte* (Turin, 1858), p. 11.

Another target of opposition deputies was governmental interference in elections, though it must be remembered that the critics were usually defeated candidates who had an axe to grind. There is no simple conclusion on this matter. Cavour created a special government department charged with seeing that officially sponsored deputies were returned.[1] At first, as an independent deputy, he had not been so keen on the use of official pressure,[2] but when he found the Left with a solid majority he changed his mind.[3] In 1849 he welcomed the proclamation of Moncalieri in which the king appealed personally to the electors to overthrow the existing parliamentary majority which 'unconstitutionally' had refused to vote as the king asked them.[4] Yet Cavour also spoke against using material favours and against the electoral corruption which he discerned in America and France.[5] Government employees, he said, ought to be permitted to vote how they liked, but if in opposition they must keep quiet about it.[6] In practice he used government officers as part-time party agents: alongside their impartial administrative functions they had to aid his candidates and run the local party organization. These officials could be dismissed if they differed from Cavour over politics. Here some people already foresaw another dangerous precedent.[7]

Cavour made himself minister of the interior in January 1858 expressly to organize the elections, and his first action was a stiff electoral circular to the provincial intendants.[8] When the next parliament was about to be summoned early in 1860, he took over the same ministry, again 'to direct the elections', but trying to make a show of impartiality.[9] In 1861, too, there were further complaints about the use of police by the minister at election time.[10] It became the usual practice that elections brought either promotion or removal for prefects, according to their diligence or negligence in backing the official nominees. Solaro della Margarita, Charles Albert's former prime minister, said that this electoral procedure made Cavour more absolute than the king had ever been. Solaro accused the liberals of altering electoral lists in their own favour, and of bribing the constituencies with the promise of schools, bridges, and railways if only a government candidate were returned.[11]

Another criticism was of Cavour's attitude to his ministers. Not only was the cabinet not consulted about some of his most important decisions, but his broad coalition sometimes made collective cabinet responsibility impossible.

---

[1] Correspondence of F. Guglianetti, MSS. Archivio di Stato (Turin), Gabinetto Ministero Interni 1848–60, cartella 40.
[2] Cavour in parliament, 9 July 1848.   [3] Ibid., 22 Dec. 1849.
[4] *Nouvelles Lettres*, pp. 357–65; Massari, *Cavour*, p. 50.
[5] Cavour in parliament, 14 Nov. 1855.   [6] Ibid., 4 Apr. 1854; *Lettere di Cavour*, VI. 105, 270.
[7] Ibid. 109, 118–19, 282–3; *Il Diritto*, 19 Jan. 1858.
[8] *Lettere di Cavour*, II. 423.
[9] *Liberazione del Mezzogiorno*, V. 450, 465.
[10] E. Artom, 'Il Conte di Cavour e la Questione Napoletana', *Nuova Antologia* (Rome), Nov. 1901, p. 151; Mellana in parliament, 5 Apr. 1861.
[11] C. Solaro della Margarita, *Discorso alla Nazione* (Turin, 1857), pp. 24–35.

Cavour could override a unanimous vote by his colleagues, and it is rare to find even one of them ever having an important say over policy. The composition of the cabinet was Cavour's responsibility, whatever the court might think. He might appoint ministers without waiting to see the results of an election,[1] and, in various *rimpasti*, ministers joined and resigned more because Napoleon insisted than because of parliamentary decisions.[2]

Much more important was the protest, made sometimes even by his colleagues, against Cavour's keeping too many portfolios himself.[3] Even those who approved of such pluralism agreed that it was too dangerous to be copied by others after his death.[4] Several times he was simultaneously foreign minister and minister of the interior, as well as prime minister, and he was always the chief cabinet authority on economic and financial matters. During several critical months of 1859 he was minister of war and of marine in addition to these other posts, so controlling most departments himself. Under his immediate successor, Bettino Ricasoli, there were nine ministers in the cabinet; Cavour had preferred seven ministries shared among only five ministers. His pluralism therefore made him all the stronger, and the check of personalities rubbing against each other inside the cabinet was lacking. No doubt this is partly explained by the fact that there were too few politicians of ministerial calibre, but it was also deliberate choice on his part, a preference for pliability and even mediocrity in subordinates and colleagues. Sometimes he took an extra portfolio himself just because to appoint another minister would imply a shift to Left or Right,[5] and that might have helped to recreate an opposition and a party system which would challenge his monopoly of power. Perhaps more fundamental was that he did not work well with other men of forceful character. All the leading contemporary parliamentarians were at one time his colleagues, but he broke with each in turn: Balbo, Azeglio, Rattazzi, Lamarmora, and Ricasoli, not to mention the king whom in the end he could hardly abide.

This is why Cavour, despite his success in personal relations, sometimes earned the reputation in politics of being a '*mauvais coucheur*',[6] of 'always wanting to be the boss, of exploiting his colleagues, and then throwing them away like a squeezed lemon, and so creating for himself a kind of solitary eminence . . . where people could live neither with him nor without him'.[7] One result was that, in the absence of strong colleagues, he came to be all the more dictatorial and uncompromising. A second result was that he worked

[1] *Lettere di Cavour*, IV. 153.   [2] Valerio in parliament, 23 Apr. 1858.
[3] Ibid., 27 Apr. 1858; Lamarmora, in *Lettere di Cavour*, III. 94.
[4] *L'Opinione*, 10 June 1861; *Piccolo Corriere*, 11 Nov. 1861.
[5] *Lettere di Cavour*, II. 292.
[6] Hudson, 9 Feb. 1856, Clarendon MSS. (Bodleian Library, Oxford), dep c 55.
[7] *Lettere di Cavour*, IV. 256–7; *Massimo d'Azeglio e Diomede Pantaleoni: Carteggio Inedito*, ed. G. Faldella (Turin, 1888), p. 338.

himself to death.[1] A third was that no one at all after his death possessed enough experience of affairs. As a friend said: 'His moral dictatorship . . . was a good thing in that it kept liberty within certain bounds; but it was a disaster in that all power was concentrated in himself, so that at his death we are now left in front of a gaping void.'[2] These were hardly conditions calculated to foster the growth of liberal parliamentary government.

A catch-phrase of Cavour was that nationalism in foreign policy implied liberalism at home.[3] In practice, however, nationalism came to take precedence over liberalism and even to thwart it, especially when he set himself to beat Naples in the race for national leadership.[4] The 'aggrandizement of Piedmont' was a phrase he began to use more frequently. A close relative, who was also one of his least partisan friends, thought that he changed quite radically after Rattazzi was turned out of the cabinet in 1858. Though Cavour remained liberal and 'constitutional', all the powers of the state became concentrated in himself. 'Policy . . . was more imperiously imposed upon parliament, who obeyed him as a master rather than followed him as a leader. . . . There was but one policy—I had almost said one religion—namely, the will of Cavour. . . . The constitution was reduced to a mere machine.'[5]

As foreign policy came to take precedence over internal policy, so parliamentary government came under strain, and the 'Italian question' made it ever more desirable to avoid gratuitous dissension at home. The amount of domestic legislation was soon noticeably reduced.[6] Cavour had decided privately on war, but both this decision and also the necessary expenditure on war preparations had to be kept away from close parliamentary scrutiny. As early as 1857 he declared that a national emergency forced him to ignore ordinary constitutional procedure.[7] Independent newspapers of the Centre suggested that he had abandoned his earlier reform programme and was on the road towards absolutism.[8] French pressure forced him to introduce cabinet changes and a partial censorship. Not that this was despite parliament, since no vote went against Cavour; only that parliamentary government suffered by the very fact that it should have been found necessary and done at all. The submissiveness of the deputies was ominous, and Cavour's continual assumption of their submissiveness equally so. They too wanted a nationalist foreign policy. They too wanted Piedmontese troops to remain in occupation of

---

[1] De la Rive, *Cavour*, pp. 323-7; *Carteggio Castelli*, I. 346.

[2] Oldofredi, 13 June 1861, MSS. Archivio Lamarmora, XCVI. 154.

[3] Cavour in parliament, 20 May 1858; *Cavour in Parlamento*, ed. Artom e Blanc, p. xxii.

[4] Massari, *Diario*, p. 47; *Nuove Lettere*, p. 372; *Lettere di Cavour*, III. 22; *Piccolo Corriere*, 18 Dec. 1859.

[5] De la Rive, *Cavour*, pp. 373-4. Omodeo notes this without comment (*Cavour*, II. 140).

[6] *L'Opinione*, 19 June 1856.

[7] *Lettere di Cavour*, VI. 87.

[8] *L'Indipendente*, 1 June 1858; *Gazzetta del Popolo*, 4 Dec. 1853.

Monaco,[1] although this was as unjustifiable as the Austrian occupation of Venice which they so claimed to resent. In the parliament of 1860 the National Society became an important influence, and this fact is one further index of an important change in temper. Cavour out of office had recognized the danger to liberalism in such a quasi-governmental revolutionary body, and had turned against this National Society.[2] But, once prime minister again, it was a different matter. Members of the National Society were soon organized as a block in the chamber and became a highly successful pressure group for returning their friends to parliament.[3]

This patriotic fervour reached its peak at the approach of war against Austria in 1859. For some months a dangerous frenzy had grown inside Cavour's following. Massari, one of his close friends, had even advocated war in order 'to raise the declining moral standards of Europe'.[4] Cavour talked of starting a world war against Britain and Austria in order to further the expansion of Piedmont.[5] The British, for their part, were worried that Cavour, through a policy of forceful aggrandizement, might create an Italy which was altogether too authoritarian.[6] Evidently internal freedom and reform mattered far less than national independence; the 'stato forte' was universally desired.[7] Cavour now decided that he would admit no discussion. He had determined to assume 'a kind of dictatorship', and he would stay in office despite any constitutional opposition.[8]

One must accept that Cavour came to think the unification of Italy more important or at least more urgent than fine shades of liberal sentiment. According to Cattaneo, Cavour's choice of war and strong government was bound to attenuate liberal feelings. Historians must not lightly suggest that Cavour should have acted otherwise—though the king, for one, thought that the same results might have been achieved with less risk 'and without alarming all Europe'.[9] But the procedure he chose carried certain disadvantages. The liberties of the subject could not flourish in a period of war fever: newspapers might have to be suppressed, deputies expelled from parliament, the jury system modified, people kept in prison without trial, and political opponents exiled to South America. Parliamentary government took shape in an emergency when overwhelming votes of confidence were thought to be imperative. Parliament was useful as a dramatic stage where, for instance, Cavour in one of his last great speeches could declare for the annexation of Rome and so again steal the programme of his enemies on the Left. But it was less welcome as a place for discussing social, religious, and other questions of internal politics. The important thing was to create a new nation, the rest could

---

[1] *Lettere di Cavour*, VI. 191.   [2] Ibid. III. 134.   [3] *Piccolo Corriere*, 1 Apr., 27 May 1860.
[4] Massari, *Diario*, p. 62.   [5] Ibid., pp. 140–2, 147, 206, 388.
[6] Hudson, quoted by Massari, ibid., p. 130; Russell to Corbett, 25 Aug. 1859, P.R.O. 30/22/109.
[7] Massari, *Diario*, p. 184.   [8] *Lettere di Cavour*, III. 45, 76, 92, 96.
[9] Hudson to Russell, 30 June 1861, P.R.O. 30/22/68.

follow afterwards; and any tensions incidentally built into society were unfortunate, but presumably inescapable.

Most present-day scholars tend to accept Cavour's own picture of himself as a simple, straightforward man, who was too impulsive to be a calculating Machiavellian. But those who disagree with this view will not accept uncritically his own statements about parliament. A good end, for him, justified the means. He excused Pitt's parliamentary corruption on the grounds that statesmen could do what for others would be immoral—and Pitt was one of his favourite exemplars. War, dictatorship, confiscation of private property, even a rule of terror, all would be proper if necessary to make Italy free and independent.[1] One deputy described Cavour as a cross between Peel and Machiavelli,[2] and no doubt all successful liberal statesmen have something of this mixture and must sometimes be unprincipled in their liberalism. Cavour had few if any immovable principles. The anti-revolutionary preached revolution in the Papal States. The admirer of British local government then modelled Italy on the French administrative system which he had once execrated. The champion of individual freedom became authoritarian in Naples. The man who demanded self-determination for Sicily would not allow a plebiscite in Monaco, but revived antiquated feudal rights there to justify what other people labelled as his tyrannical police rule.[3] He also supported dynastic projects in Greece and Bessarabia which would have made him righteously indignant had they come from Austria and been designed for Italy. Cavour called the British unprincipled for allying with illiberal Austria, at the same time as he eagerly cultivated the alliance of illiberal Russia; and he, of all people, castigated Austria for breaking treaties and plotting war.

Cavour's great success was to achieve a high common factor of liberalism and statesmanship. He tried to convince himself and others that Piedmont was the most progressive liberal state in Europe,[4] and his own liberal ends were kept surprisingly undefiled by the severity and deceit and warmongering which he was forced to practise. A narrowly representative parliament gave him an admirable footing against those like Garibaldi and Victor Emanuel who put their faith in other methods; hence Italy was united without altogether disregarding parliament, or in other words by a different method from that which Napoleon and others would have preferred.[5] The cost, however, was that Cavour left the country with governmental traditions formed in a period of crisis. He had trained no one who could work the system as he had done, and his successors sometimes took as a norm what for him may have been an exception.

Cavour had used a national emergency to curb the deputies and impose on them an artificial unity. There is not a great deal of point in speculating over

[1] *Cavour: Scritti politici*, p. 288.   [2] Della Gattina, *I Moribondi*, p. 58.
[3] Gramont, 17 Feb. 1857, M. Aff. Étrangères.   [4] Cavour in parliament, 13 Feb. 1851.
[5] *Carteggio Castelli*, I. 348.

what he would have done when domestic problems again became paramount. Possibly he would not have survived in office, and Hudson at least thought that parliament was turning against him.[1] A broad coalition would probably have cohered less easily once Italy was created and when every deputy could afford to hold his own views on administrative and financial matters. Time would show that there were certain disadvantages in a lack of party structure: for example there was the absence of disciplined debate and collective attitudes; fragmentary discussions and partial proposals thenceforward dragged out the business of the House; there was a lack of a strong and critical opposition, at the same time as numerous shifting groups made governments too powerless and too short-lived. Once Italy was unified there would be no easy escape from taking fundamental decisions on domestic policy, though each such decision threatened to weaken the existing coalition. When the country was launched subsequently into an armaments race and a scramble for national prestige and colonies, it sometimes seemed as though an artificially forceful foreign policy was the only way to unite people sufficiently to make this type of parliament work. In some ways Cavour had an easier time than his successors. The Italian parliamentary system had been forged by him almost as a weapon of war, and this fact can sometimes be seen as a burden on later generations.

[1] Hudson to Russell, 12 Apr., 24 May 1861, P.R.O. 30/22/68.

4

Cavour, Clarendon, and the Congress of Paris, 1856

THE Congress of Paris in 1856 marks an important stage in Cavour's foreign policy. It was the first time that he had appeared on the wider European stage, and he learnt there many lessons that he was later to turn to good use. It is interesting to speculate on what he acquired there of diplomatic technique. It is also interesting to see why he failed to reach at the conference the objectives he wanted.

Cavour's great personal likeability made him a popular but not an important person during the few weeks he spent at Paris. Italian affairs were only a small side-show in the work of the congress, and on other subjects he kept well in the background. One Italian journalist, Count Oldofredi, wrote home with a description of Cavour as 'the lion of the congress and most eminent delegate of them all',[1] but it can now be seen that he played an unobtrusive role. At the time, Cavour himself thought he had produced an 'electric effect' on Lord Clarendon, the British foreign minister who was then at Paris, and yet Clarendon's dispatches mention him hardly at all.[2] Count Buol and the Austrians were also liked by the British, much better liked at least than Cavour imagined.[3] The armistice had been a diplomatic victory for Austria, and the congress itself was as much a success for Buol as for Cavour.[4]

Before the delegates met in Paris, an interesting letter arrived in London from Sir James Hudson, the British representative in Turin, explaining to Lord Clarendon what sort of a man was Cavour.

Cavour is quick, suspicious, hot tempered, liable to 'coups de tête', but if cooled down by a few hours reflection very sagacious, bold and practical, with an intimate knowledge of the financial position of all the states of Western Europe. When he finds frankness and fair play he is frank and fair; otherwise he is close, cautious,

---

[1] *Diario di Collegno*, p. 478.
[2] Of the 32 letters dated March 1856 from Clarendon to Palmerston in the Palmerston archives at Broadlands, Cavour is mentioned four times, and only in connection with Italian affairs.
[3] Clarendon to Palmerston, 23 Mar. 1856, Broadlands.
[4] *Lettere di Cavour*, II. 175; *Cavour e l'Inghilterra*, I. 444; J. A. von Hübner, *Nove Anni di Ricordi* (Milan, 1944), p. 386.

suspicious, sarcastic, unsparing, a 'mauvais coucheur' and very difficult to 'corner' as the Yankees express it. He is a great whist player, a great eater, a great worker, and in ordinary life what we should call a very 'jolly fellow', delighting in farming and finance, and abominating diplomacy and everything connected with it, generally speaking.[1]

The British plenipotentiaries were strongly predisposed in Cavour's favour, and they took a leading share in getting him accepted by the congress on more or less equal terms. Piedmontese diplomacy began by underrating their sympathy. Cavour had concentrated on France instead of England to help secure his inclusion in the conference. He promised that he would always act 'as an auxiliary of France' if France would only sponsor his acceptance, and he particularly stressed the usefulness of a Piedmontese vote in supporting Napoleon against the British.[2] In practice, however, it turned out to be Clarendon who chiefly pushed Cavour's claims. Clarendon feared that the British might otherwise have to stand alone at Paris,[3] and hence, when the French talked of excluding Piedmont, he tried to insist on Cavour's admission 'on a footing of perfect equality'.[4] The British minister privately acknowledged that there was a debt of honour to be paid.

Sardinia should be upheld as much as possible in the general estimation of Europe, and . . . the greatest care should be taken to avoid wounding her susceptibilities by insisting too vigorously on the exact observance of the limitations assigned to the part she is to take in the negotiations for peace. . . . But the Western Powers have certainly reaped substantial advantages from their alliance with Sardinia. . . . Whenever the period, whether remote or near at hand, for an improvement in the social condition of the Italian peninsular [*sic*] shall arrive, it will be of the utmost importance that . . . Sardinia . . . should present an example to the other states of the peninsular of a well-ordered constitutional government.[5]

On the other hand, the French minister, Count Walewski, wanted Cavour to attend the conference only when Italian interests were under discussion. Under pressure he was ready to consider equality of status, but had made up his mind not to stand up for Piedmont against the determined opposition which he expected from Austria.[6] Cavour met this by playing off Britain against France. He hinted to Walewski that Britain was only pushing Sardinian claims 'in order to earn for herself an extra leverage and popularity, which could only be at French expense', and he promised the French not to turn up at meetings if the big powers ever wanted to discuss the more important

[1] To Clarendon, 9 Feb. 1856, Clarendon MSS. (Bodleian Library, Oxford), dep c 55.
[2] Gramont to Walewski, 2 Feb. 1856, M. Aff. Étrangères; *Cavour e l'Inghilterra*, I. 167.
[3] To Cowley, 30 Jan. 1856, F.O. 519/173.
[4] Palmerston to Clarendon, 3 Feb. 1856, Clarendon MSS., dep c 49; Clarendon to Cowley, 6 Feb. 1856, F.O. 519/173.
[5] To Cowley, 4 Feb. 1856, F.O. 167/87.
[6] Cowley to Clarendon, 7 Feb. 1856, F.O. 519/218.

issues on their own.[1] It was Clarendon who most strongly fought for Piedmontese rights.

I stood up for perfect equality. I said that Sardinia had behaved towards us with chivalrous boldness, and had launched into the war without enquiring about principles or caring for consequences, and that we English were not people to abandon our friend because we might not stand in want of him at the moment, or to permit any slight to be put upon him.[2]

I am not prepared to affirm that she is not as much interested as ourselves in the internal organisation of the [Danubian] Principalities. Her object in joining the alliance was to prevent the aggrandizement of Russia. . . . The opinions of such a man as Cavour would be valuable in the committee.[3]

If Cavour wanted territorial acquisitions from the congress, he did not have a strong case. The chief belligerents had agreed in advance on asking for no annexations, and to this agreement Cavour too had adhered, explaining that he wanted no territorial aggrandizement but just hoped that at the peace he 'would be entitled to some political consideration'.[4] The war had not been popular at Turin.[5] Piedmont had participated much less fully or successfully than Cavour had wanted; almost all her casualties in the Crimea had been from disease, and a bare thirty soldiers had been killed or died of wounds.[6] Nevertheless, despite his prior undertaking and his small part in the war, Cavour was hoping to annex territory in central Italy.[7]

The atmosphere of the congress brought out all his tremendous self-confidence, for it was a kind of situation he loved, in which charm and finesse were the really important requisite qualities, and these he had in abundance. He was soon playing off not only France against Britain but Walewski against Napoleon, and sending secret notes to the emperor behind the back of the French foreign minister. He also proceeded behind Clarendon's back to work on Palmerston, the British prime minister, and behind Palmerston to Lady Palmerston and Lord Shaftesbury. Sometimes his excess of subtlety and enthusiasm betrayed him. For example, he thought that, by supporting Russian claims in Bessarabia, he might shake the very existence of the liberal government in England, and so force Palmerston to seek popularity by giving Piedmont both Parma and Modena.[8] This was bad logic. Russia was the enemy against whom Cavour had lately declared war. It is true that he had never had any genuine quarrel with the Tsar; Russia had been his enemy only by the

---

[1] Gramont from Turin to Walewski, 10 Feb. 1856, M. Aff. Étrangères.
[2] To Palmerston, 21 Feb. 1856, Clarendon MSS., dep c 135; to Hudson, 23 Feb. 1856, F.O. 167/87.
[3] To Cowley, 24 Feb. 1856, F.O. 519/173.
[4] Hudson to Clarendon, 15 Dec. 1854, F.O. 67/201.   [5] *Nuove Lettere*, pp. 590–3.
[6] Lamarmora in parliament, 16 Mar. 1857; C. Rubiola, *L'Armata Sarda in Crimea (1855–56)* (Pisa, 1969), p. 53.
[7] *Cavour e l'Inghilterra*, I. 215–16.   [8] Ibid. 232.

accident that he needed a war, and he now saw his interest as making friends with the Russians at Paris if he could do so without attracting attention.[1] Nevertheless, far from making Clarendon more sympathetic, coquetting with Russia helped to antagonize Britain unprofitably.

This is to anticipate. In early March 1856, the British still trusted Cavour implicitly and sought Piedmont as a useful ally. Clarendon, after seeing Cavour, described him as 'one of the most moderate but at the same time most practical men I have ever had to do with'. He added, 'I should not mind taking the initiative in the conference about the state of Italy, which was a scandal to Europe and which a European congress ought to consider'; however, in his view little was likely to be gained for Italy, because Napoleon III was halting between two different opinions.[2] Palmerston was ready, in Cavour's favour, to forget that the belligerents had decided on no annexations, or at least was willing for Piedmont to be the sole exception and acquire Parma or even Lombardy.[3]

The stumbling-block in the way of what the Italians called '*piani ancien régime*' was Buol's firmness and Napoleon's indecision.[4] In a meeting on 19 March, Clarendon pushed the emperor as hard as he could to get something for Piedmont,[5] but without much result. Napoleon did not entirely exclude that Piedmont might get Parma, but 'Cavour was much dissatisfied with the Emperor's tone'.[6] Palmerston then sent formal instructions from the cabinet in London to insist that the congress must settle a date for evacuating Austrian troops from Italy. As late as 30 March, Palmerston thought it might be possible for the Piedmontese to buy out the Duchess of Parma, or possibly to push her on to the throne of Greece.[7] But Napoleon was not prepared to give public support to any such idea.

Cavour gradually became more desperate. Public opinion at Turin had been allowed and even encouraged to expect territorial gains, and he feared that his government might be defeated if he returned empty-handed. Victor Emanuel was also threatening to come incognito to Paris and teach his minister a lesson in diplomacy.[8] For a moment Cavour even meditated using the Anglo–Italian legion to capture Sicily.[9] This was an extraordinary project, and is another example of how his imagination now carried him away. But in calmer moments he knew that he must not antagonize France. By 3 April, Clarendon was ready to ask on behalf of Piedmont more than Cavour was ready to accept. As he informed Palmerston,

[1] Ibid. 240.   [2] To Palmerston, 13 Mar. 1856, Broadlands.
[3] 7 Mar. 1856, Clarendon MSS., dep c 49.
[4] Clarendon to Palmerston, 13 Mar. 1856, Broadlands; Matter, *Cavour*, II. 368.
[5] *Cavour e l'Inghilterra*, I. 347.
[6] Clarendon to Palmerston, 19 Mar. 1856, Broadlands; *Cavour e l'Inghilterra*, I. 372.
[7] 19 Mar. 1856, Clarendon MSS., dep c 49.
[8] *Carteggio Castelli*, I. 141; *Cavour e l'Inghilterra*, I. 374, 380, 424; *Cavour-Salmour*, p. 94.
[9] *Cavour e l'Inghilterra*, I. 355.

My note in answer to Cavour upon the Italian question was written in the terms of your despatch, but Cavour asked me to modify it, because, if it once became public, he should be reproached for having suggested much less than the English government thought right. He of course would have liked a great deal more, but he confined himself to what was practical and would not frighten the Emperor.[1]

Not until one week after peace had been signed was Italy mentioned officially at the conference. The signature of peace had put the plenipotentiaries in such a good humour that the Englishman decided to force the pace. Clarendon explained to Palmerston that the Piedmontese representatives were the only other liberal members of the conference.[2] The British delegates had in private made three further attempts to settle Italian affairs with Napoleon, for they realized that Italy would gain nothing unless France and Britain were acting in concert; but their approaches met vague and indeterminate replies. 'Poor Cavour is very low about it.' Napoleon was too embarrassed to ask Buol about evacuating foreign troops, for the highly delicate reason that there were French soldiers in Rome as well as Austrian soldiers in Lombardo-Venetia. Clarendon therefore chose to raise the matter himself. With regard to the Papal States, 'Buol admitted the evils of clerical government but declared that the laymen would do worse'. It looked as if the British would have to bring the Italian question forward 'singlehanded', and unfortunately that would do Italy no good.[3] Cavour 'is in low spirits' because Napoleon was going back on his promise. Cavour 'of course wants me to take the labouring oar in the matter,' wrote Clarendon. On 6 April at the Tuileries, 'I begged H.M. to instruct Walewski to take a firm tone about Italy'. He replied that he would try to fix a date for evacuating foreign troops, but Clarendon still doubted if the French would do anything positive.[4]

He was wrong, for Walewski was given instructions to raise the question in general terms on 8 April, and this gave Clarendon his chance to intervene, which he did by criticizing the pope, criticizing the Bourbons for misgoverning southern Italy, and by implication criticizing Austria too. This one speech was to be Italy's chief gain from the whole congress. Cavour was agreeably surprised to find Clarendon so energetically pro-Italian, yet was still greatly disappointed at receiving nothing more tangible. In parliament Cavour spoke some weeks later as though no one could ever have hoped for any territorial annexations,[5] but at the time he himself had certainly hoped for some. He failed to get them chiefly because France was in two minds, while the Russians, from whom he had hoped so much, sided with the Austrians in refusing to discuss the question of Italy.

---

[1] 3 Apr. 1856, Clarendon MSS., dep c 135.
[2] 6 Apr. 1856, ibid.   [3] Clarendon to Palmerston, 27 Mar. 1856, Broadlands.
[4] To Palmerston, 5 Apr., 7 Apr. 1856, Clarendon MSS., dep c 135.
[5] 6 May 1856, *Cavour: Discorsi*, III. 356–7; *Cavour e l'Inghilterra*, I. 444.

Clarendon alone shared Cavour's disappointment with the lack of any practical result. Clarendon's report on this occasion was that,

We have made bad work of it today with the Italian Question. Walewski made a long speech not in a very high tone, and though he declared that the Emperor wished the occupation of the papal dominions by foreign troops to cease as soon as might be, yet he did not specify any time nor indicate the measures which would render the withdrawal of the troops practicable and safe. I followed in rather stiffer terms, and whether my speech was good or bad it completely satisfied Cavour and made Buol angry. The latter declared that the Congress had no power to treat of such questions, and his language was intemperate and unsatisfactory, as might be expected from a man in a passion. Cavour said a few words correcting some of Buol's misstatements, and the observations of the other P.P.s were unimportant. I shall take care that a proper record of what passed is made in the protocol, and that will serve as a *point de départ* for future remonstrance, which is all we shall have done for Italy. It is a poor result, but Cavour thinks that the opinion of England will fructify.[1]

Palmerston echoed this grave disappointment and the failure to do anything material for Italy.[2] When the time came to draw up the written minutes of this meeting on 8 April, as Clarendon reported it, Buol asked to be allowed to leave out of the protocol

most of his very objectionable opinions. To please the Emperor I have left out a good deal of what I said about the Pope and clerical government, as well as some remarks on Bomba [King Ferdinand of the Two Sicilies]. I could not well do otherwise in a protocol that was to be signed by all, and if necessary I can always say the same things again *in another place*.[3]

Omodeo, the most reliable historian of Cavour, is unkind when he criticizes the British for not helping Piedmont more strongly against the Austrians. According to Omodeo, Cavour was trying to free England from her 'insular egoism and a somewhat over-crude utilitarianism'. Omodeo here forgets that Austria was England's ally; and he proceeds to the astonishing conclusion that England could and should have 'decided for war in the Adriatic, for the simple reason that she had nothing to lose there'. Such an aggressive policy (continues Omodeo) 'after eighty years seems to us better attuned to British interests and altogether much more shrewd than the purely empirical policy of Clarendon and Palmerston'.[4] This was a somewhat ungrateful attitude after Clarendon's efforts on 8 April; but, chiefly, such speculation is as diplomatically unrealistic as it is *antistorico* and beside the point. It would have been asking too much for England to launch a European war just to pull Cavour's chestnuts out of the fire, and what Cavour had in mind on 9 April was nothing less than *'une guerre générale'*. The only basis for Omodeo's view is the undoubted fact that Cavour somehow persuaded himself that England ought to

[1] To Palmerston, 8 Apr. 1856, Broadlands.
[2] 10 Apr. and 14 Apr. 1856, Clarendon MSS., dep c 49.
[3] 14 Apr. 1856, ibid., dep c 135.   [4] Omodeo, *Cavour*, II. 110–12, 122.

fight and was indeed ready to fight just such a war. Other historians will be more preoccupied with the problem of how the Piedmontese minister came to such a surprising conviction.

Cavour was undeniably thrown a little off balance at this moment, partly by his disappointment at not securing Parma, partly by the fear that returning empty-handed would weaken his parliamentary position at home, partly by his disappointment with Napoleon and Russia. In this mood he self-defensively took refuge in exaggerating the force of italophile public opinion in England; and likewise he read too much into the unexpected forcefulness of Clarendon's intervention in favour of Italy. As a result he miscalculated, and dreamt of burying his relative failure at Paris under a war against Austria. This miscalculation in turn did him a lot of harm.

Cavour was a brilliant opportunist in politics, but opportunism has its dangers, especially with someone who can take important decisions so lightly. There is little doubt, whatever some historians may say, that he did not even begin to understand the basic principles of British foreign policy at this time;[1] and his fantastic notion of using the Anglo-Italian legion to attack Sicily is all of a piece with his new idea of using the British for a war against Austria. Here he ignored the plain warnings from his ambassador at London that British statesmen would never commit themselves in advance, let alone to such a belligerent and revolutionary plot, and certainly not to war against an ally.[2] Early in April he reached the point of hoping that Britain, France, and Russia would all aid him in war against Austria.[3] 'Le canon seul peut nous tirer d'affaire.'[4] Such was his state of strain and excitement, that he wrote a provocative note with the deliberate intention of causing his foreign minister, Luigi Cibrario, to send an immediate resignation.[5]

What seems fairly clear is that, in a moment of great excitement, Cavour abandoned his customary calm and judgement. A close friend described how,

led into error by a variety of circumstances, by the tone of the English press, by the fact that the Whigs were in office, by his private conversations with the English he met, by his intimacy with the English minister at Turin, by his relations with Lord Clarendon, deceived also, it must be said, by his own optimism, which naturally gave a colour to the opinions expressed by others, dazzled by the prospect which suddenly opened before him, carried away by his own impulse, Cavour had fancied that, although separated from the English Cabinet, he was not the less certain of being supported by England in any enterprise which had for its object the independence of Italy.[6]

[1] *Cavour e l'Inghilterra*, I. 331; ibid. II, pt. i. 70, 125, 157; a failure of perception is indicated by the boasting about his own invariable *loyauté*, frankness, and liberalism, at the same time as he was stigmatizing foreign statesmen for their egoism, inequitability, and ungenerousness.
[2] Ibid. I. 357.
[3] Ibid. 406, 444, 461; *Diario di Collegno*, p. 487; Bianchi, *Storia Documentata*, VII. 622–3.
[4] *Cavour e l'Inghilterra*, I. 424.   [5] Ibid. 433.
[6] De la Rive, *Cavour*, pp. 361–2 (the translation is that by E. Romilly).

It was on 11 May that Cavour had a private talk with Clarendon about which there was to be much speculation. The Piedmontese statesman was quite positive that Clarendon on this occasion specifically promised to help him in an aggressive war against Austria; though, if Cavour really believed this, it is incredible that he did not consult Clarendon before going to England on 18 April to win support for his warlike plans in London, and Cavour's subsequent apology for not having so consulted him is significant.[1] There is not a word in Clarendon's contemporary dispatches which would confirm Cavour's interpretation of their talk. When Cavour's private letters were later published, Clarendon was forced in self-defence to comment on them, and he described their meeting quite differently. Though we would naturally believe what Cavour wrote at the time rather than what Clarendon said from memory six years later, Clarendon's remarks in the House of Lords carry some plausibility.

First, said Clarendon in 1862, Britain's firm policy had been to uphold the settlement of 1815, not to overthrow it by war against England's ally, Austria, and this was a fact which he had repeatedly impressed on Cavour. Secondly, it was unthinkable that Britain could have irresponsibly advised Piedmont to commit what seemed like national suicide in provoking Austria to war. Thirdly, he added, if he (Clarendon) had said anything about helping Piedmont, it could only have been in reference to a defensive war against Austrian aggression; whenever Cavour talked of the '*terza riscossa*', it had been mentioned as a purely defensive war. And, fourthly, it might be that Cavour had exaggerated Clarendon's remarks when writing to Turin, for he would have had an understandable desire to find some positive result with which to confront his king and parliament.

That, without the shadow of authority for doing so, I should have given any pledge for the support of England on such a policy as would have embroiled us with half Europe, is an absurdity so palpable that I hope your Lordships will think it carries with it its own refutation.[2]

This is a difficult controversy, and several different interpretations are possible. Omodeo concluded that 'Clarendon was bewitched' by Cavour into making indiscreet threats against Austria. Or it might even be the other way round, that Cavour was outwitted by Clarendon. Or it might have been that they were both speaking French and misunderstood each other. Perhaps Cavour was privately confident that he could manufacture an aggressive war which he could make to seem defensive. Certainly he based his expectations on an entirely mistaken view about British public opinion and must have relied excessively on his own ability to sweep Palmerston into war. He did not

---

[1] *Cavour e l'Inghilterra*, I. 452, 461; Hudson, 3 June 1856, Clarendon MSS., dep c 55.

[2] Clarendon's speech of 17 Feb. 1862 is reproduced in *The Making of Italy 1796–1870*, ed. D. Mack Smith (New York, 1968), pp. 206–8. Lord John Russell to Clarendon, 15 Feb. 1862, Clarendon MSS., dep c 104: 'You never could have said that we should support Sardinia in a war against Austria.'

question the stereotype assumption prevalent in Italy that anti-Catholicism in Britain would help him to annex the papal Romagna. Evidently he also thought he could plot with Clarendon in the same way as he was later going to plot with Napoleon, and in this belief he was wrong, as he was also wrong in his conception of British interests and British foreign policy.

Possibly this was another of those moments, as Hudson put it, when Cavour had 'a rush of blood to the head', moments attended by undoubtedly morbid symptoms and about which the king said that Cavour used to lose all recollection. Either by his own failure or Clarendon's, he undeniably began to hope that England would fight provided that Piedmont could provoke a war against Austria. Clarendon's letters show that he was aware of Cavour's new belligerent mood, but for some reason he chose to take it not too seriously.

Cavour is very indignant. He told me just now that 2 courses were open to him, either to resign and make way for men friendly to Austria and base to Rome, or to bide his time and to declare war against Austria on the first favourable opportunity and to proceed to the liberation of Italy. He seemed to have little doubt as to the latter course being the right one. This congress I can see won't separate without leaving behind it the seeds of some mighty pretty quarrels.[1]

Clarendon explained that Cavour was obsessed with how to justify himself in Turin. He 'thinks only of his Chambers but we must not forget ours. However he is an excellent fellow and the more I see of him the more I like him.' Cavour was drafting an angry 'philippic' to send to Britain and France, but Clarendon advised him to modify it, on the grounds that it would later 'make him rather ashamed'.[2]

One contributory feature in this misunderstanding was that Clarendon could not be completely frank with Cavour and must accordingly have been slightly embarrassed and inexplicit. The reason was that he was at this very moment arranging the secret treaty which was signed on 15 April between Austria, Britain, and France. Cavour had convinced himself that he could rely on the alliance of England and France against Austria, but in fact Austria had got in first.[3] The British documents suggest that Palmerston had been even more anxious than Austria or France for this tripartite agreement of 15 April, and it was not a last-minute improvisation but had been his object from the first.[4]

Before he knew about this treaty, Cavour on 18 April travelled to England and stayed there a week, a visit which he quickly regretted when he found that his confident assumptions about British opinion had been unjustified.[5]

[1] To Palmerston, 11 Apr. 1856, Broadlands; to Lord Panmure, 27 Mar. 1856, Clarendon MSS., dep c 135.
[2] To Palmerston, 15 Apr. 1856, Broadlands.
[3] Matter, *Cavour*, II. 390; Bianchi, *Storia Documentata*, VII. 282.
[4] Clarendon to Palmerston, 24 Mar., 31 Mar., 12 Apr. 1856, Broadlands.
[5] *Cavour e l'Inghilterra*, II, pt. i. 1.

Apparently he did not consult Clarendon first, and this fact may arouse some suspicion. He certainly intended to see Queen Victoria, and quite possibly he thought that he could play her off against her ministers in the same way as he was doing with Napoleon.[1] He dined with the queen on the 19th, but all she noted about the occasion in her diary was that 'Count Cavour was very agreeable, and very amusing about the conference'.[2] He saw Palmerston, who authorized him to assure Napoleon that Britain would probably take one and a half steps for every step France took in Italian affairs.[3]

Cavour also met the leaders of the tory opposition and privately encouraged them to raise a motion in parliament against Palmerston's government.[4] This tactless step was to do the Piedmontese grave damage in the eyes of Clarendon and the liberals. Cavour subsequently tried to explain that he had met the opposition leaders accidentally while dining with the queen; he added implausibly that he had given instructions that Palmerston should first be consulted about this proposal to criticize the government, but could not recall if his orders had been carried out.[5] Having expected great things from Disraeli, he was hurt to find the tories so strongly pro-Austrian, and they had simply been using him for party purposes.[6] Cavour's warlike talk in England thus did much more harm than good. The impression he had intended to convey was that, if moderate men like himself thought in terms of war against Austria, then Italy must really be oppressed. But instead he gave almost a contrary impression, namely that he, Cavour, was a dangerous man who must not be too far encouraged or trusted when he talked about oppression. His private talks with the opposition, despite what his friends and disciples used to say, did not show much familiarity with the British party system and conventions of constitutional government. They were bad manners and bad tactics, 'on principle thoroughly wrong', said Clarendon, and Cavour eventually realized this and sent a full apology.[7]

Talking to Massari in later years, Cavour recalled how in April 1856 he had based his policy on the assumption that the peace was so unpopular in Britain that Palmerston would be obliged to play the card of italophilia in order to keep in power.[8] This assumption had been quite incorrect. Britain was pro-Italian, but not to that extent. Furthermore, this misunderstanding made Cavour behave in such a way as lost him the enthusiastic support of those British politicians whom he had captivated by his moderation and friendliness during the congress. Another thing he told Massari was that the tripartite treaty of 15 April subsequently convinced him that Britain 'was changing

---

[1] Ibid. 1. 452; Hudson, 3 June 1856, Clarendon MSS., dep c 55.
[2] 19 Apr. 1856, Royal Archives (Windsor).
[3] Palmerston, 30 Apr. 1856, Clarendon MSS., dep c 49.
[4] Hudson to Clarendon, 3 June 1856, Clarendon MSS., dep c 55.
[5] Ibid.; *Cavour e l'Inghilterra*, II, pt. i. 5–8.   [6] Ibid. 43.
[7] Ibid. 19; Clarendon to Hudson, 28 May 1856, Clarendon MSS., dep c 136.
[8] Massari, *Diario*, pp. 46–7, 52.

sides', and hence that he had adjusted his policy accordingly. Here again he was incorrect, for Britain's association with Austria was not something new but was merely a development of her traditional policy; hitherto and henceforth Britain hoped to reconcile a strong Austria (as bulwark against Russia) with a liberal and independent Italy. Cavour failed to see that British favour towards Italy had little to do with Palmerston trying to win public opinion at home; it was a genuine sympathy combined with the desire to avoid revolution and European war.

Clarendon continued to bring pressure through the British ambassador in Vienna for improvements in Italy.

I hope that some of our ships on their way home [from the Crimea] will call to enquire after his [the King of Naples'] health, and whether Poerio and Co. are *at home* or still *lodging with* Bomba [in prison]. The Italian question is *palpitante* and will soon occupy a large share of public attention, European as well as English. Buol behaved very foolishly about it at Paris and took a tone which did him much harm. It was the only matter upon which he and I disagreed. With regard to all others we were the best of friends. . . . He really however ought to put us in a position to say to the numerous interpellators that Austria means to evacuate the papal territory as soon as she can. *Bologna 8 years in a state of siege* is an unendurable scandal![1]

Clarendon and Palmerston now began a serious diplomatic campaign to make the French and Austrian troops leave central and northern Italy.

The Italian question excites intense interest here, for everybody feels that, peace being now established, things should in different countries be placed as far as practicable in a position not to disturb the general tranquillity, and that the occupation by French and Austrian troops of a large portion of Italian territory is not in accordance with treaties, and that if it is to be considered an *état normal*, the equilibrium of Europe will be deranged and a revolutionary effervescence will be maintained. . . . It is difficult to talk to Buol on these matters because he disputes one's right to do so and straightway flies into a passion. The only conversation I had with him was upon a previous arrangement that he would not be angry, and then we got on famously. I wish you would try to find out what he meditated with respect to Italy, and whether Austria and France really will come to an understanding as to preparing the way for evacuation.[2]

Would it be possible to get the Emperor of the French to join with us in declaring that after a given day say six months hence all military occupation in Italy must cease, never under any circumstances to be renewed, and that in Tuscany, Parma, Modena, Rome and Naples, sovereigns and people must settle their differences as best they can without any interference from foreign powers, just as the French and English would do? If such a rule were laid down and enforced, the Italian question would at once be settled.[3]

---

[1] To Sir Hamilton Seymour, 22 Apr. 1856, Clarendon MSS., dep c 135.
[2] 29 Apr. 1856, ibid.   [3] Palmerston to Clarendon, 12 May 1856, ibid., dep c 49.

This policy of non-intervention would of course have led, as Palmerston realized, to Piedmontese domination of the peninsula. British policy in May 1856 had thus accepted the idea of a Piedmontized Italy almost more fully than Cavour did himself, and only quarrelled with the means which the more aggressive Italian patriots intended to use.

It was over this question of method that British and Piedmontese policy diverged. News of the secret treaty of 15 April came as an unexpected blow to Cavour. Until this moment he thought that he had conquered the heart of Clarendon by flattery. He thought of himself as the deceiver not as the deceived.[1] His strong speech to parliament of 6 May probably reflected his justifiable annoyance after discovering about the tripartite treaty, and Clarendon in his turn was antagonized by the sharp note of that speech.[2] Cavour had decided now that war alone could solve the Italian question, and by this decision he inevitably nullified any British attempts now or later to push Austria out of Italy by peaceful means.

Britain wanted peace more than she wanted a united Italy, and when Cavour threatened to fight, this forced Britain against her will to turn against him. She also feared Russia more than she liked Italy, and her system of alliances against Russia had to come first. Britain wanted to help Italy, said Clarendon, but not at the cost of quarrelling with Austria or France. Far from bearing Cavour any ill will, 'I have a real regard and friendship for him, but he must let us help him in our own way'.[3] Cavour, for his part, was right to put Sardinian interests first, but would have done better to study British interests less superficially before he tried to elicit British aid. As Massari once commented,

unfortunately we Italians are made in such a way that we believe the rest of Europe has nothing else to do except to think about us and to agree with our way of thinking; and hence we blacklist as rascals or worse any foreigners who fail to make Italy the *Standpunkt* of their policy.[4]

How, then, in conclusion, was British policy changed as a result of the Congress of Paris? First of all, British sympathy for Italy continued unabated. On 13 May, Clarendon brusquely wrote a note to his representative in Vienna to say that the Austrian occupation of Italy was both contrary to international law and also a provocation to revolution; and on both these counts he insisted that the British had a right to intervene and to demand that the Austrians should withdraw.

Count Buol was indisposed to discuss with me the questions connected with Italy, and he continues the same system with you. I am sorry because it prevents a good understanding between the 2 governments upon matters important to both. Public

---

[1] *Cavour e l'Inghilterra*, II, pt. i. 10–11.
[2] Hudson to Clarendon, 13 Mar. 1856, Clarendon MSS., dep c 55.
[3] To Hudson, 28 May 1856, Clarendon MSS., dep c 136; *Cavour e l'Inghilterra*, II, pt. I. 15, 31.
[4] Massari, *Diario*, p. 5.

opinion is so strong here about Italy that even if the government desired to blink it, it would be impossible; but we have no such desire, and when we see any portion of Europe occupied in a manner contrary to treaties, which are the international law of Europe, we have a right to ask for explanations, and when we see a state of things established which is likely to lead to revolution, against which *on principle* the English government is as firm as that of Austria, we are entitled to enquire whether in the common interest such a state of things cannot be put an end to. So that all attempt to exclude us from the consideration of Italian questions is unwise and short-sighted and is sure to fail. I told Buol that speaking to him as a friend, and looking at matters from his *point de vue*, I thought he had mismanaged the question of Italy at Paris. If he had not been so *boutonné* and so angry, but had displayed a little more frankness, all the sour feelings with Sardinia and all the diatribes of the press that we have been and shall be exposed to, might have been avoided, and Austria and France would have had much more leisure to set about things in their own way, and to prepare for a *safe* evacuation of the Papal dominions.

Clarendon hoped Buol would follow him in sending a strong note to Naples, and hoped the Austrians would provide a statement about troop evacuation in time for a parliamentary debate at Westminster on 27 May. On 20 May he wrote again to complain that Rome and Naples would evidently not take advice.

Sardinia, and small blame to her, will keep the flame alive, though I conscientiously believe without any wish for territorial aggrandisement, or anything else than a bona fide amelioration of Italy. England is determined that something should be done in the right direction. . . . But if they [the Austrians] will say that on this day six months one half of our troops shall withdraw and the remainder shall follow in 12 months, the thing would be done.[1]

Clarendon repeated much the same in a message to Cavour, saying that Austria and France, by keeping troops in Italy, were disturbing the European equilibrium, endangering peace, as well as promoting discontent and popular revolution.[2] Palmerston at the end of May was yet more threatening.

Buol like all Austrians is fond of *Bullying*, but he must be made to understand that in the next war between Austria and Sardinia, if it is brought about as it will be by the fault of Austria, Sardinia will not be left alone as she was last time.[3]

Palmerston would have liked to call a special conference in London to discuss the Italian question. He himself was quite ready to see the Romagna made into a republic, to see northern Italy united, and 'to see the pope reduced to the condition of the Greek patriarch of Constantinople'; but, at the very least, Austrian and French troops must leave Italy in the next six or twelve months, and both Naples and the Papal States must agree to some liberal reforms.[4]

Italians disagreed. Mazzini did not want reforms if they would lessen the

[1] To Seymour, 13 May, 20 May 1856, Clarendon MSS., dep c 136.
[2] To Hudson, 26 May 1856, F.O. 167/88.   [3] 27 May 1856, Clarendon MSS., dep c 49.
[4] 29 June 1856, ibid.

desire for unity. Cavour did not hope for the withdrawal of French troops, but on the contrary wanted even more of them to come and fight on the plains of Lombardy. Cavour did not even want Austrian troops to leave, for he needed them as a provocation for the *terza riscossa*. Palmerston's policy of peaceful reform and Cavour's of war were, therefore, mutually exclusive, and in June 1856 Clarendon had to confess that he saw no way to reconcile them. 'The Italian question is certainly a most embarrassing one and if we had carte blanche for cutting the Gordian knot we should hardly know how to set about it.' 'We keep running in a vicious circle upon these Italian questions. The sovereigns never will take the initiative in reforms. Why should they? . . . So if France and England can't or won't combine to force improvement, the only change to be looked for is that the present state of things will if possible become worse.'[1] Italy was going to be made not peaceably, but by war; not by evolution, but by revolution; not by non-intervention, but by French arms: and there is no point in speculating about other possibilities that did not in fact happen.

The consequences of the Paris congress were less disastrous than Cavour had at one point feared even if less advantageous than he had once expected. On the one hand British sympathy continued, and the British government was made even more conscious that there was an Italian problem that needed solving. On the other hand, Britain found herself pushed into opposition against the methods by which the risorgimento finally took place. Cavour's real success at Paris was not with Britain but with the Emperor Napoleon. If the British refused to 'tirer les marrons du feu', the French would do so at a price. It was at Paris that Cavour learnt *le vrai secret de l'Empereur* which he turned to such good account two years later.

With Britain, on the other hand, he reached an impasse. First of all his coquetting with Russia leaked out, and the British were bound to be put off when they discovered this underhand dealing with their great enemy.[2] Secondly, he failed to understand the British interest in the integrity of the Ottoman empire and of Austria as a joint bulwark against Russia. Thirdly, he made the political and psychological error of thinking that Britain would fight against Austria: so doing he gave the game away to Palmerston and forced the British more to the Austrian side than they wanted. Fourthly, Cavour earned a reputation for unreliability and mendaciousness. Though the congress had voted to keep its discussions secret, he deliberately broke this pact and secretly spread mischievous tales against Austria all over Europe.[3] Fifthly, he made the mistake of secretly intriguing with the parliamentary opposition

[1] To Cowley, 9 June, 25 June 1856, F.O. 519/173.
[2] *Cavour e l'Inghilterra*, I. 161; *Lettere di Cavour*, II. 396.
[3] *Cavour e l'Inghilterra*, I. 243, 344, 346–8.

in London, and so gratuitously annoyed Clarendon, without even impressing the opposition leaders.[1]

Having made these minor qualifications, one can return to the conclusion that the Congress of Paris marked a significant moment in Piedmontese and Italian history. Its real importance was not as a diplomatic triumph for Cavour, but as a unique experience in which he for the first time was able to feel the pulse of European politics. At Paris, Cavour learnt that British statesmen were too much aware of their own interests to pull his chestnuts out of the fire, and this was a useful lesson. He also learnt that Clarendon was as *rusé* a diplomat as he was himself. But Napoleon, on the other hand, might be manipulated; and it was at Paris that Cavour learnt how to do it. Before long he had adjusted his whole policy accordingly. He then saw himself fighting not alongside Britain but actually against her; and his fertile imagination was envisaging a Grand Alliance of France, Russia, even Switzerland as well, and possibly the United States of America, against Britain and Austria. While he was in that mood, he neither could hope for a British alliance, nor did he need it.

[1] Clarendon to Palmerston, 25 Oct. 1856, Broadlands: 'I had a long talk with Malmesbury yesterday who is just come from Turin. He says he is all for the Sardinians, but that he never saw people so cocky and puffed up or who more wanted to be taken down a peg. Cavour's nonsense about nationalities is incredible he says.'

5

Victor Emanuel
and the War of 1859

IN the three years before 1859, what chiefly bound Cavour and the king together, despite their personal differences, was the growing hope of being able to provoke a war against Austria. Their aim was to annex Lombardy, Venetia, and the duchies of Parma and Modena, thus creating a kingdom of northern Italy stretching from Savoy to the Adriatic. Obviously this would need massive foreign help. When the British in 1856 were scandalized at the suggestion of a joint war against the Austrians, the only alternative was to turn to France and pay Napoleon III whatever price he asked. This would inevitably include ceding to France the considerable stretch of territory which Piedmont still owned on the French side of the Alps. A minor but still necessary condition was that Victor Emanuel should give his daughter in marriage to the emperor's cousin, Prince Napoleon. The king was quite distraught at such an unwelcome demand, for Clotilde was only fifteen years old and deeply devout, while the prince was middle-aged, irreligious, and a notorious roué; but Cavour was inexorable, and reproved the king for his weakness when the prospective winnings were so considerable. As he complained to a friend, the king 'has an extraordinarily weak character'.[1]

Another way in which the king made things hard for Cavour was through an inability to refrain from dropping hints in public as he became increasingly excited at the prospect of war. Though he was able on occasion to lie brazenly and deny he had any even remote idea of fighting Austria, the secret of Piedmontese military preparations eventually leaked out by way of his military cronies, so that his denials were not taken seriously.[2] Moreover his lack of subtlety allowed foreign diplomats to compare his conversation with Cavour's and so see when they were being deceived.[3] Yet he made up for this by being able to attract a wider spectrum of support than Cavour could have done on his own: on the Left there were the various groups round Rattazzi, Garibaldi,

[1] *Cavour-Nigra*, I. 132–3, 146.
[2] Brassier de St. Simon commented on 'ses imprudences habituelles' (*Die Auswärtige Politik Preussens 1858–71*, vol. I, ed. C. Friese (Oldenburg, 1933), p. 82). On 12 March the king told Hudson, 'I have no intention of attacking Austria' (*Gran Bretagna e Sardegna*, VI. 390.)
[3] Massari, *Diario*, p. 155.

Brofferio, and Pallavicino, who trusted the monarch where they did not always trust Cavour; while to the conservatives the king was a guarantee that the war would be anti-revolutionary, monarchist, and would put Piedmontese considerations before Italian if there were a conflict of interest between the two. With great panache, Victor Emanuel on 10 January 1859 delivered to parliament the most famous speech of his life, containing a provocative reference to the 'cries of grief' which came to Piedmont from other parts of Italy. Nothing did more than this phrase to establish his reputation as a national leader: its authorship was ascribed in court circles to him personally, but in fact the words were suggested by Napoleon.[1]

In order to enlarge the alliance, Cavour further thought at one point of a marriage between the widowed Victor Emanuel and a Russian princess, Marie de Leuchtenberg. The monarch had other ideas. His private life was often to be a worry to his ministers, not least because it cost a great deal of money, much of which fell ultimately on the state budget. For the previous decade his chief mistress had been Rosina Vercellana, a lady who during the four years since his wife's death he considered virtually his wife; but he had had many other affairs, which caused scandalous jealousies between the ladies at court, and sometimes even more scandalous rumours of physical violence.[2] At the end of January 1859 the news leaked out that the king, perhaps to counter Cavour's plans for a dynastic alliance, was threatening to marry the drum-major's daughter, Rosina; and this shocked the *bien pensants* much more than his liaison had done previously.

To prevent it, Cavour, apparently against the wish of his colleagues, tactlessly used the argument to both Rosina and the king that the other was unfaithful and had secret lovers. But his diplomacy for once failed. An actress to whom he offered a large sum of money to support his story refused to do so; and Rosina easily won the day by flattery of Victor Emanuel, protesting that his embraces were so frequent and vigorous that she had no strength left for other men.[3] Neither of the two ever forgave Cavour for such a lapse in taste and finesse, nor did Cavour forgive Rattazzi to whom the king turned for advice

---

[1] L. C. Bollea, 'Il "grido di dolore" del 1859', *Bollettino Storico-Bibliografico Subalpino* (Turin), XVI (1911), 232; the opposite view is in Bianchi, *Storia Documentata*, VIII. 10–11.

[2] *Sclopis: Diario*, p. 59; U. A. Grimaldi, *Il Re 'Buono': La Vita di Umberto I* (Milan, 1970), p. 103. Hudson to Clarendon, 4 Jan. 1856, Clarendon MSS. (Bodleian Library, Oxford), dep c 79/332: 'We have had another batch of court scandal. The king amidst his innumerable amours is still constant to his Rosina, the daughter of an officer of low extraction, a great thumping woman talking broad Piedmontese, the most awful jargon in or out of Xtendom. The other rival is the Countess della Rocca, wife of the general of that name, the Chief of the King's État Major.' The two recently had come to blows when they accidentally met, and Rosina had been pronounced the victor.

[3] A. Luzio, *Aspromonte e Mentana: Documenti Inediti* (Florence, 1935), pp. 90, 101; a partial index to the Royal Archives lists a document headed 'biographical notes on Mme de Maintenon' (*Il Risorgimento Italiano: Rivista Storica* (Turin), X (1917), 481); Marie de Leuchtenberg thought Victor Emanuel a ridiculous figure (E. Corti, *The Downfall of Three Dynasties* (London, 1934), p. 103); Cavour's attempted bribery of Laura Bon is discussed by G. Piccini, *Memorie di una Prima Attrice* (Florence, 1909), p. 159; *Cavour-Salmour*, p. 118.

and support on this delicate issue. From now onwards Rattazzi became the political favourite at court, and, partly by means of Rosina herself, built up a potential challenge to the prime minister. This dangerous division between the two leading politicians in the country occurred at one of the most critical periods in Piedmontese history. Censorship of the official archives helped to bury the whole episode, and the story only emerged forty years later when D'Ideville published his memoirs in France.

War was to break out towards the end of April. In the last few hectic weeks Cavour's plans were almost foiled when pressure from London and finally also from Paris was brought to bear against his project of calculated aggression. It was the king rather than the minister who remained calm in these difficult days. When the former threatened to abdicate if war did not come, this was not intended seriously. Victor Emanuel recognized, correctly, that Piedmont might still win a good deal even without war, and hence was ready to accept the alternative of a European congress to discuss the troubled state of Italy. He criticized the prime minister for a failure of realism and optimism on this point. What happened behind the scenes during these weeks is known only in part, but the breach between the two was not healed in response to the state of national emergency. Cavour later said, justifiably or not, that if the king had had his way there would in the end have been no war. On the other hand the king wrote on 14 April to his son-in-law that people of sense were turning against Cavour because of his uncontrollable temper and inability to choose efficient subordinates: 'Azeglio is much more level-headed than Cavour, and his political judgement is always right.' Anyway, boasted the king, Cavour's failings no longer mattered all that much, since everyone now realized that the monarch had taken effective government into his own hands.[1]

Once war broke out this boast became almost true. Victor Emanuel as commander-in-chief felt himself a new man, powerful again, and free from interfering civilians. Parliament voted full powers to him personally, not to his government. He had had little practical training or experience as a serving officer,[2] but his military entourage lacked either the courage or the wish to remind him of this fact. Cavour, who had himself been a professional soldier for five years as a young man, dropped some hints that the king should retain only nominal command as his father had done in 1849, and he hoped that the generals would have full powers to act on their own. This was a quite vital point which no doubt should have been raised and settled earlier, especially as

---

[1] 'L'Italie Libérée (1857–1862): Lettres et Dépêches du Roi Victor Emmanuel II et du Comte de Cavour au Prince Napoléon', ed. F. Masson, *Revue des Deux Mondes* (Paris), Feb. 1923, pp. 558–9; Massari, *Diario*, p. 389; La Tour d'Auvergne, 10 Apr. 1859, M. Aff. Étrangères, reports the king's criticism of Cavour 'de se laisser aller trop facilement aux illusions et au découragement'.
[2] A. Gatti, *Uomini e Folle di Guerra* (Milan, 1929), pp. 35–43; F. Cognasso, *Vittorio Emanuele II* (Turin, 1942), p. 154; Matter, *Cavour*, II. 108; N. Rodolico, *Carlo Alberto negli anni 1843–1849* (Florence, 1943), p. 553.

serious problems were involved when a constitutional and politically 'irresponsible' sovereign assumed an active command for which he might eventually be called to book. But Victor Emanuel had no intention of yielding. In his opinion the essential fact about the war was that he would be leading his subjects to victory. The most he would permit, and with great reluctance, was that General Lamarmora could accompany him as a cabinet minister attached to army headquarters.

This concession, moreover, was not intended seriously. The king at once overrode Lamarmora on a major point and appointed as chief of staff Count Morozzo Della Rocca, who was essentially a 'court general' and had little enthusiasm for the niceties of constitutional government. Della Rocca was also a noted personal opponent of both Lamarmora and Cavour: he made a point of not speaking to Lamarmora during the campaign, and no doubt this was at the king's instance.[1] Lamarmora held the title of minister of war, and his absence from Turin was thus to place an intolerable burden on Cavour, who had managed to rid himself of the ministry of finance, but was still prime minister, foreign minister, and minister of the interior, and now had to cope suddenly with the huge additional task of running the navy and the war office. The fact that this was decided only at the outbreak of war made efficient administration almost impossible. Cavour performed wonders in providing supplies for the army, but inevitably some important matters connected with mobilization were forgotten in the general haste. He was also compelled to let some of the foreign office work go by default, and his lack of contact with foreign capitals was to have some unfortunate results as the war developed.[2]

Evidently the chief lesson of 1848–9, that careful preparations were necessary before provoking another war against Austria, had been forgotten. The authorities at Turin were relying on the French coming to their rescue and did not want to disrupt society by full-scale conscription. The regular Piedmontese officers, with the self-confidence of an élite, had opposed any idea of a large army, partly because of finance, partly because there was a real fear of training citizens to arms. Cavour had been advised in January to call up more men, but had refused on the specific grounds that he had to avoid the threat of popular agitation that had been present in 1848.[3] Immunity from military service was allowed to anyone rich enough to buy himself off, and some 15 per cent of Piedmontese citizens continued to take advantage of this even despite the conditions of emergency. Instead of the 150,000 troops which

---

[1] Gen. E. Della Rocca, *Autobiografia di un Veterano* (Bologna, 1897), I. 337, 414.
[2] Brassier de St. Simon to Schleinitz, 18 May, MSS. Geheimes Staats-Archiv, Auswärtige Angelegenheiten (Merseburg), 426/45, shows that the Prussian minister saw Cavour rarely; the Piedmontese representative in London regretted that Cavour had no time to write (*Carteggi E. d'Azeglio*, II. 195–6); *Il Diritto* (Turin) of 21 July complained that Cavour had taken most of the ministries under his personal hand to set up 'un governo personale'.
[3] Casaretto's report of 17 Jan. 1859, *La Guerra del 1859: Documenti*, ed. Ufficio Storico del Corpo di Stato Maggiore (Rome, 1910), I. 24–5; *Lettere di Cavour*, III. 80.

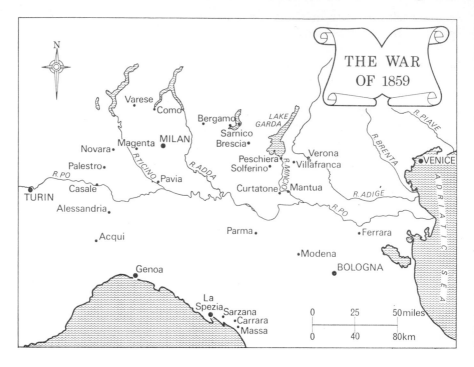

Cavour had been expecting, which would have produced the 100,000 front-
line soldiers that had been promised to the French, the numbers of front-line
Piedmontese troops thus reached only 60,000 at the height of the campaign.
Of the conscripts called to the colours in March, only half showed up, and
the call-up of a further draft in June had to be deferred because there were no
uniforms ready for them, while the 50,000 reservists of the age-group 25–30
were never called upon at any stage during the war.[1] As for the volunteers
from other regions of Italy, Victor Emanuel had boasted that 200,000
would at once rally to him,[2] whereas in fact he obtained barely a tenth of this
number.

   The same absence of preparation could also be found elsewhere. Cavour
had been minister of finance continuously between 1850 and 1858 except for
one gap of six months, and as such he had engaged in continuous battle to
keep the army estimates within bounds. The minister of war, Lamarmora,
had sometimes carried out military preparations on his own authority without
telling his colleagues.[3] But there were many deficiencies in supply. The lack

[1] C. Pischedda, *Problemi dell'Unificazione Italiana* (Modena, 1963), pp. 79, 91–7; P. Pieri, *Storia militare del Risorgimento* (Turin, 1962), pp. 745–6.
[2] Brassier, 23 Apr., MSS. Geheimes Staats-Archiv.
[3] A. Lamarmora, *Agli Elettori del Collegio di Biella* (Turin, 1860), pp. 14, 61.

of horses was to be serious in 1859, and in the end was to prevent any artillery attack being launched against the Austrian fortresses of the Quadrilateral.[1] Not nearly enough maps of Lombardy had been printed.[2] Neither Cavour nor Lamarmora, and certainly not the royal commander-in-chief, had any military plans ready except to wait for an Austrian attack or for the French to arrive and take over. The somewhat casual scale of preparations is shown by the fact that, until the very eve of hostilities, workers were crossing the frontier from the Piedmontese side to help the Austrians build the fortifications of Pavia, just because wages were higher there.[3]

Cavour had recently talked of fighting single-handed against Austria if necessary, but this was ridiculous braggadocio, and his lack of seriousness is indicated by his failure to make the general staff work out the implications of his policy in military terms. He himself did what he could to remedy the deficiencies once he had taken over as acting minister of war, but by then the fighting had begun and it was not so easy to impose any central direction. He suddenly realized that Turin looked almost indefensible, and General Cialdini pointed out that the Austrians would have a walk-over if they attacked during the two weeks before the French appeared. General Fanti disagreed, but more by faith than reason. A kind of panic seized the capital city, and Cavour sent urgent requests for the army to fall back and save Turin from a major disaster.[4]

The king had other ideas. From the moment of his taking up command of the army there had begun a dangerous divergence between ministers and generals, between Turin and headquarters, a divergence of view and of policy which was to last all through the war. When he heard that an improvised evacuation of Turin had commenced, he was so angry that Della Rocca had to tone down his language before dispatches could be sent. To the request that troops should defend the city, he contemptuously replied that army dispositions were his responsibility and would not be altered. Cavour began to fear that the king's lack of military sense was going to prove disastrous, and he tried all the more to assert his own equally amateurish strategic views in a peremptory and not altogether tactful manner. The king reacted very sharply indeed, and this led for one vital week to a complete severance of communication between prime minister and command headquarters.

---

[1] Ibid., p. 12.

[2] *La Guerra del 1859: Narrazione*, ed. Corpo Stato Maggiore (Rome, 1910), I. 129.

[3] *Il Diritto*, 17 Mar.; N. Tommaseo e G. Capponi: *Carteggio inedito dal 1833 al 1874*, ed. I. Del Lungo and P. Prunas (Bologna, 1923), IV, pt. i. 387–9; General Woinovich, quoted in *Alcuni Fatti del Risorgimento Italiano da Documenti Inediti*, ed. Corpo Stato Maggiore (Rome, 1911), p. 360; compare Napoleon's far more serious preparations, G. Bapst, *Le Maréchal Canrobert: Souvenirs d'un Siècle* (Paris, 1904), III. 199–203, 210, 213.

[4] G. Cecconi, *Torino è in pericolo: Storia di Diciotto Giorni* (Turin, 1882), p. 29; H. d'Ideville, *Victor Emanuel II: sa Vie, sa Mort, Souvenirs Personnels* (Paris, 1878), pp. 89–90; Massari, *Diario*, p. 210; Bapst, *Canrobert*, III. 244–8; Della Rocca, *Autobiografia*, I. 402, 412–13; *La Guerra del 1859: Documenti*, I. 437–8, 479, 481.

Victor Emanuel had here taken a calculated risk, emboldened by talks with the French Marshal Canrobert; and he was probably right not to fall back, while Cavour was probably wrong. Another strategic decision, to override Lamarmora's initial dispositions and retreat southwards to Acqui, was less sensible. The king's orders for a retreat were, by his explicit instructions, concealed from Lamarmora and Cialdini, for he was determined to prove his own generalship without interference. The movement was well under way when Lamarmora, perplexed by what was happening, rushed to headquarters to persuade the king that he was leaving the way wide open for an Austrian attack. The general was at first refused entry to the royal presence, but was brave enough to insist, and Victor Emanuel sensibly if reluctantly changed his mind when it was pointed out to him that his manœuvre would seem to others like retreat in face of the enemy.[1]

This proximity of Lamarmora, a more experienced soldier and one with cabinet rank, was irksome to the commander-in-chief, who now took full advantage of the fact that Lamarmora's powers had in the general rush been left undefined. Instead of showing gratitude for being saved from what he himself admitted to be a dangerous error, the king was soon angrily complaining that Lamarmora was interfering too much in strategy. The most senior of all the generals in the Piedmontese army was effectively kept in isolation, uninformed about what was going on, and powerless to intervene on any subsequent occasion throughout the whole campaign. The one effective restraint on the sovereign was that Napoleon III arrived on 12 May and took over supreme command of the allied armies. Again there were complaints from the king that his own strategic schemes were being ruined, and that Napoleon and Cavour were both amateurs by comparison.[2] Victor Emanuel was anxious to distinguish himself by some great victory, and restriction on his initiative seemed to him wrong; but in the end, having made his purely verbal protest, he prudently accepted as inevitable that Napoleon should be in charge.

The main strategy of the war was therefore devised at Marshal Vaillant's headquarters. There is no evidence that Victor Emanuel was allowed much say: he was left with occasional tactical decisions to make, never of any importance, so he had no real chance to show his mettle. Napoleon had said of him that he would make an admirable *sous-officier* but lacked the qualities of a commander, and he now found himself treated as such. On 22–23 May, Victor Emanuel visited the front and came under fire. He was most reluctant to leave this scene of battle, even when Della Rocca tried to insist that his rightful position was at a fixed headquarters where the French emperor could find him

---

[1] *Schiarimenti e Rettifiche del Generale Alfonso Lamarmora* (Florence, 1868), p. 15; Verax, *Alfonso Lamarmora: Commemorazione* (Florence, 1879), pp. 71–8, 171; *La Guerra del 1859: Narrazione*, I. 198–200.

[2] *Cavour-Nigra*, II. 186–7, 189, 195, 206.

with any urgent orders; his constant preoccupation was lest other people should think him afraid. Again at Palestro, on 31 May, he abandoned his staff in order to be near his troops, though he was careful to leave the conduct of this small engagement in the hands of Cialdini.

After crossing the Ticino, on 4 June at Magenta there came the first big victory of the campaign. Niccola Nisco, whose history of Italy was commissioned by the king, contrived to attribute the success of this day mainly to the Piedmontese, but in fact it was entirely a French victory and not a single Piedmontese soldier lost his life. The true facts were deliberately concealed from the Italian public. Complaints were made by the French that the bulk of Victor Emanuel's army had made no attempt to move towards the sound of gunfire which lasted all day. This may have shown lack of imagination and initiative on the king's part; it was not lack of courage. General Lebœuf heard the emperor rebuke him after the battle for disobeying orders.[1] An alternative story, from second-hand Piedmontese sources, described this incident as a rebuke for showing reckless bravery under fire.[2]

The result of Magenta was that the allies reached Milan on 8 June. In deference to the French, and perhaps somewhat abashed by the events of Magenta, Victor Emanuel let Napoleon have pride of place and take the salute as they entered the Lombard capital, while he himself stood back.[3] The acquisition of Milan was a great occasion for Cavour, but he was still only partially mollified over his treatment at the king's hands. He had complained that he was sent almost no news from the front, and in normal times he would have resigned rather than allow a prime minister to be so completely disregarded. The king for his part resented what he called Cavour's mismanagement of the political developments in central Italy and the appointment of lawyers rather than soldiers to administer the newly conquered areas of Lombardy. He especially disliked Cavour's gratuitous advice on military strategy with its ill-concealed implication that the king did not know his job. Cavour, when he realized this, was enough of a diplomatist to send congratulations to the king on his courage and military skill, and a touch of sarcasm was barely apparent.[4] He now came to Milan and was once again told not to interfere in military matters. It was put to him that he should give up the ministry of war and find someone else to run it: the efficient running of the war was suffering just because he himself had too many portfolios, and his tempera-

---

[1] É. Ollivier, 'Napoléon III, Général en Chef: Magenta et Solferino', *Revue des Deux Mondes*, May 1899, p. 335; N. Nisco, *Storia Civile del Regno d'Italia* (Naples, 1883), IV. 78–9; A. Guarnieri, *Otto Anni di Storia Militare in Italia (1859–1866)* (Florence, 1868), pp. 168–70; the fact that the only serious Italian forces at Magenta were on the Austrian side is never stated.

[2] *Azeglio*, Rendu, p. 104.

[3] G. di Revel, *Il 1859 e l'Italia Centrale: Miei Ricordi* (Milan, 1891), p. 69; Cols. Claremont and Cadogan both noticed that the cheering in Milan was more for Napoleon than for the king (*F.O. Confidential Print*, no. 802, pp. 2, 4).

[4] *Lettere di Cavour*, III. 90, 92; *Cavour-Nigra*, II. 207, 214.

mental *prepotenza* made it very hard for some of his colleagues to work with him.[1]

The prime minister did not yield on this point. He always found it hard to share power, and his opinion of other alternative ministers was low. One such possibility, Rattazzi, had in Cavour's opinion ruled himself out by his intriguing at court. It was the more annoying that Rattazzi was now summoned to the royal headquarters: observers noted that he arrived there at the same time as Cavour but separately, and that he remained behind after Cavour had returned to Turin.[2] This was highly provocative, and perhaps intended to be so. It was taken by the prime minister as one more sign that he could not trust the king.

Piedmontese war aims must surely have been discussed on this visit to Milan, but not enough for everyone to be clear about them. For some reason Cavour decided that it would be wise to be secretive about his own intentions. The future of central Italy was an immediate problem which required a political answer, since the battle of Magenta forced the duchess of Parma and the duke of Modena to abandon their states, at the same time as Austrian garrisons withdrew from the papal legations in the Romagna. Parma and Modena were easily occupied by the Piedmontese, but papal territory presented a much harder question, and it soon appeared that Cavour, having been told to keep out of military affairs, was playing politics on his own account without due reference to His Majesty or to France. He also evidently had ambitions on other territory across the Apennines which it could not be in Napoleon's interest to let him annex.

What he did was to let former members of La Farina's National Society use the withdrawal of the Austrian garrisons as a pretext for popular insurrections, his intention being to prove to the French that the patriotic urge of the Italian people was uncontrollable. This caused trouble: first, because papal diplomacy was able to protest that it reflected no patriotic urge but simply Piedmontese aggression; secondly, because the French were bound by an agreement to the pope; and thirdly, most important of all, because the insurrections turned out to be disappointingly feeble. Instead of proving the force of Italian patriotism, their failure proved rather its weakness, and they merely alerted Napoleon to the fact that the Turin government was pursuing secret aims of its own. The fact that these aims were prejudicial to French interests was soon made abundantly clear to Victor Emanuel, who remarked that his prime minister must be crazy to be playing about with revolution in the Papal States at a time when French assistance was so necessary.[3]

To Cavour's consternation, even when Austrian troops had retreated and

---

[1] Lamarmora to Dabormida, 10 June, MSS. Archivio Lamarmora (Biella), XCII/145; Dabormida to Lamarmora, 13 June, ibid. XCIV/150; *Carteggi E. d'Azeglio*, II. 195.
[2] *La Guerra del 1859: Documenti*, I. 1136; *Sclopis: Diario*, pp. 153–4.
[3] *Cavour–Nigra*, II. 222–3; *Lettere di V. Emanuele*, I. 540.

revolt would have been relatively easy, sometimes there was no popular rising at all. Most people outside the big cities, and again this surprised him, showed little interest in the national movement, or at all events preferred to remain as spectators and leave everything to be settled one way or the other by the French and Piedmontese forces.[1] There was not even much co-ordination between one town and the next, while often the revolutionaries showed that they were rather concerned just to replace the Austrian troops and keep order than to promote a real political uprising.[2] In some places the papal forces found it easy to restore their authority. On the other hand, in Bologna and other main towns, revolutionary committees boldly declared for Piedmont and sent deputations to invite the king to take over government; but someone must have omitted to tell them that such an offer would offend the French, and might be more embarrassment than help. It seems that there had been no pre-arranged policy on this vital point. To some extent Cavour was trying to force the pace on his own account; but to some extent, too, his dissolution of the National Society had left his own followers without advice or direction, so that the more revolutionary patriots were displacing the moderates with a policy which was aimed to force the pace more than he can have wished.

Partly the trouble was that there were several different policy-making centres which were not entirely open with each other, as Cavour was not entirely open with the king, nor Napoleon with his own ministers in Paris. The French foreign minister, despite his conviction that the Papal States had to be kept out of the war, soon began to fear that the emperor might have given some secret undertakings of a different sort. True enough, Napoleon had given some latitude to Cavour to encourage recruitment of volunteers in the northern provinces of the pope's dominions. Perhaps he still had an open mind on the possibility of Piedmontese occupation of this area as the Austrians withdrew. Whether or not this is true, he must have been hoping that what happened would happen quickly before he was personally compromised and before protests could arrive in Paris: any insurrection should preferably appear to be spontaneous and so not involve him in any direct responsibility; it should also be speedy and overwhelmingly successful. When direct Piedmontese instigation could be proved, and when there was no quick solution and no overwhelming success, he had reason to be annoyed, especially when very few volunteers were forthcoming and popular support was obviously half-hearted. He was further upset when Cavour's agents were found to be working in Perugia and in the Marches, for there could be no excuse that Piedmontese occupation so far south would assist military operations.

The king's attitude to the policy of insurrection was not without its ambiguities. He was glad to be able to blame Cavour for opposing French policy

[1] G. Finali, *Memorie*, ed. G. Maioli (Faenza, 1955), p. 120; G. Finali, 'Le Marche: Ricordanze', *Atti e Memorie della R. Deputazione di Storia Patria per le Marche* (Ancona, 1897), III. 15–18.
[2] R. Grew, *A Sterner Plan for Italian Unity* (Princeton, 1963), pp. 211, 215.

in central Italy, but it is clear that he had sanctioned at least some of Cavour's plans in advance, and likely that he had at least hinted at them to Napoleon.[1] Since the emperor preferred to have this kind of thing agreed only by word of mouth, or indeed left without any formal and compromising agreement, it is not easy to discover the whole truth. But French opinion became explicitly hostile as soon as it could be seen that Cavour was secretly trying to prevent any French preponderance in Italy. Napoleon also informed the king of his extreme embarrassment when the pope threatened to excommunicate them both for causing these political disturbances in papal territory.[2] When papalist troops recaptured Perugia, this was another unwelcome sign that the patriotic movement was insufficiently strong, as it was also an equally unwelcome indication to the local patriotic movement that the king could not or would not support the insurrections which people speaking in his name had been instigating. Papalist 'atrocities' in retaking Perugia were deplored in Turin: one Turin newspaper, on the other hand, excused them as no worse than Victor Emanuel's bombardment of Genoa in 1849, but the newspaper was suppressed and its editor sent to prison.

The victory of Magenta brought the allied forces almost to the river Mincio, and here they were at last confronted with the large fortified towns known as the Quadrilateral. The Piedmontese forces were allotted the task of assaulting Peschiera. For some reason, this need for complicated and slowing siege work came as a surprise and perhaps had been simply forgotten. Cavour blamed this on the king as commander-in-chief,[3] but he as acting minister of war was equally responsible. Possibly they both had once again been relying too much on French power to overrun these fortresses. The Austrians had by now blown up most of the railway bridges, and supply lines were already badly disorganized, as a result of which for some days the armies could not move forward at all. It was noted that both king and emperor looked seriously worried, and still on 22 June no siege artillery had left Turin.[4]

On 23 June the king met Napoleon near Lonato, just before what was to be the battle of Solferino, and heard that it was now likely that they would have to make peace on the Mincio and without further conquests in the Veneto.[5] Despite later denials, there can be little doubt of the broad lines of what was said on this occasion. The two motives evidently adduced by Napoleon were, first, that Germany might not stand by idly while Austria lost Venetia; second,

[1] *Il Principe Napoleone nel Risorgimento Italiano*, ed. A. Comandini (Milan, 1922), pp. 128–9.
[2] Brassier de St. Simon to the Prussian Regent, 17 July 1859, MSS. Geheimes Staats-Archiv, no. 72; *Lettere di Cavour*, VI. 414; *Cavour-Nigra*, II. 233.
[3] *Lettere di Cavour*, III. 103.
[4] *La Guerra del 1859: Narrazione*, II. 390–1; ibid. *Documenti*, II. 297; Correspondence relating to the Peace of Villafranca, July to August 1859, *F.O. Confidential Print*, no. 881/802/2, p. 12; ibid. 881/802/4, p. 3.
[5] *Sclopis: Diario*, p. 165; *La Guerra del 1859: Documenti*, II. 338; Della Rocca, *Autobiografia*, I. 458–62, 468; G. Massari, *Il Generale Alfonso Lamarmora: Ricordi biografici* (Florence, 1880), p. 236.

that insurrections inside the Papal States were upsetting the Catholics in France.[1] To neither of these arguments was the king in any position to demur.

June 24 was the date of Solferino. Strictly speaking this, like Magenta, was a French victory, while the Piedmontese won what was almost an ancillary engagement some miles away at San Martino. The events of this day have been claimed by Professor Monti as the chief proof of Victor Emanuel's military skill.[2]

Early on the 24th, the Piedmontese stumbled into a surprise engagement with insufficient strength and in two quite different places, after which a disorganized battle took place which lasted indecisively for ten hours or more and over a very wide front. There were very few signs of any central direction of any kind. Later paintings of the king with drawn sword leading his troops up the hill of San Martino are certainly without historical foundation,[3] for he seems to have been at Castel Venzago some miles away. General Solaroli, one of the king's aides, recounts in his 'diary'—written subsequently and not entirely trustworthy—that until fairly late in the day the king was in a state of some confusion, unable to decide how or where to concentrate his forces so as to bring the battle under control.[4] Only in the afternoon of this hard-fought day, after the French had won at Solferino and the Austrians had been ordered to retreat,[5] did Victor Emanuel realize how vital it was for the Piedmontese to have some share of the victory before the day was done; the emergency forced him to take his one important decision, something which he should almost certainly have done earlier, and that was to order Lamarmora to take over command of two divisions in another attack on San Martino.[6] Until now his jealousy of Lamarmora had resulted in this general being not used and not even asked for his advice.

Late in the evening, San Martino was captured, very creditably to the Pied-

[1] Bollea, *Una Silloge*, p. 168.

[2] A. Monti, *Vittorio Emanuele II (1820–1878)* (Milan, 1941), p. 237. M. Ciravegna accepts this, *Rassegna*, XXIX (Nov. 1942), p. 867.

[3] Capt. Carlo Rocca, 'Il Re Vittorio Emanuele alla Battaglia di San Martino', *Alcuni Fatti del Risorgimento Italiano*, pp. 67, 72–5; P. Pieri, 'I tre Enigmi della Guerra', *L'Osservatore Politico Letterario* (Milan), June 1959, p. 107. For a conventional view of the king's heroism, C. Bergamaschi, *La Guerra del 1859 in Italia* (Voghera, 1909), p. 131; O. Pio, *Vita Militare di Vittorio Emanuele II Re d'Italia* (Rome, 1879), pp. 127–8; P. C. Boggio, *Storia Politico-Militare della Guerra dell'Indipendenza Italiana (1859–1860)* (Turin, 1867), III, appendix p. 3; *Constance d'Azeglio: Souvenirs Historiques*, ed. E. d'Azeglio (Paris, 1886), p. 593.

[4] Solaroli's diary is in *Ricordi di Castelli*, p. 305; *La Guerra del 1859: Narrazione*, II. 171–2.

[5] Benedek had been ordered to fall back two hours before the Piedmontese attack (*Benedeks Nachgelassene Papiere*, ed. H. Friedjung (2nd ed., Leipzig, 1901), p. 242; *Der Krieg in Italien: Generalstabs-Bureau für Kriegsgeschichte* (Vienna, 1876), II, pt. ii. 346–7; W. Ramming, *Ein Beitrag zur Darstellung der Schlacht von Solferino* (Vienna, 1861), p. 129; W. Rüstow, *Der Italienische Krieg* (Zurich, 1859), p. 324. This is denied, on no evidence, by de Vecchi, 'La Battaglia di San Martino', *Rassegna*, 1934, p. 457.

[6] Reports on the engagement by Gen. Lamarmora, Capt. Driquet, and Capt. di Robilant, in *La Guerra nel 1859: Documenti*, II. 479, 507, 520; Verax, *Alfonso Lamarmora: Commemorazione*, p. 83; one anonymous author dared to say that the lateness of the king's order was the one really unfortunate mistake of the day (*La Guerra in Italia nel 1866: Studio militare* (Milan, 1867), p. 36).

montese forces, but only after Benedek had, as commanded, begun to withdraw many Austrian troops, and the French were left with serious doubts about the Italian army and its higher command under Victor Emanuel. Cavour concluded that the only hope of continuing the war was to persuade the king to give up his post as effective commander, but the prime minister's acid comments to Lamarmora were either altered or deleted from Chiala's edition of Cavour's letters.[1] The official volume of war history produced by the Prussian general staff went so far as to describe San Martino as a victory for the Austrians against superior Piedmontese forces.[2] Solaroli, himself a fervent monarchist, commented on the day that, if only Victor Emanuel possessed a fraction of the ability that he had courage, he would have made a splendid general; whereas the truth was that he had no memory, no eye for terrain and tactics, and just could not apply himself with sufficient concentration.[3] The official account of course had to tell a different story: Napoleon had been personally in command at Solferino, so Victor Emanuel had to be made into the victor of San Martino.

One cannot positively assert that doubts about Victor Emanuel's leadership were one of the factors which persuaded Napoleon on 6 July to make peace, but some people thought so.[4] The Italians were later to accuse Napoleon of treachery in concluding the armistice of Villafranca, and this fact makes it worth noting that a number of different reasons made his action logical and far from treacherous. He had by now discovered that Cavour's ambitions in the war went beyond what had been agreed between them, as they certainly went beyond what was in the interests of France. Possibly Napoleon might still have been content for Cavour to annex the Romagna provided that it could have been done quickly and without obvious signs of Piedmontese imposition; but these two conditions were evidently unrealistic. On 20 June the pope issued a bull of excommunication and thereby made Victor Emanuel an embarrassing ally. Almost as bad was what was happening in Tuscany. The French had insisted that the revolution 'should not cross over the Apennines',[5] and yet Cavour, it was now clear, had been working in secret for the annexation of

---

[1] *Lettere di Cavour*, III. cxcix, 103, 105; the original letters are in the Archivio Lamarmora; Marshal Randon, the French minister of war, called the battle a defeat for the Piedmontese, where 'they were ill disposed, ill commanded, and fought ill' (Nassau William Senior, *Conversations with Distinguished Persons during the Second Empire from 1860 to 1863*, ed. M. C. M. Simpson (London, 1880), I. 114); *Der Krieg im Jahre 1859 nach offiziellen Quellen* (Bamberg, 1894), p. 193; Guarnieri, *Otto Anni di Storia Militare*, pp. 204, 212.

[2] *La Campagne d'Italie en 1859, rédigée par la division historique de l'état-major de Prusse* (French transl., Paris, 1862), pp. 181–2; and of course the Austrians agreed, e.g. J. A. von Hübner, *La Monarchia Austriaca dopo Villafranca*, ed. Maria Cessi Drudi (Rome 1959), p. 45.

[3] *Ricordi di Castelli*, p. 309.

[4] *La Campagne d'Italie en 1859*, pp. 195–6; the author is indicated by its later publication as *Moltkes Militärische Werke: Der Italienische Feldzug des Jahres 1859* (Berlin, 1904), III. 274.

[5] Walewski, 2 July, M. Aff. Étrangères; E. Forcade, 'Chronique de la Quinzaine', *Revue des Deux Mondes*, July 1859, p. 503.

Tuscany. Nationalism was in this way being mixed up dangerously with revolutionary ambitions which could not be welcome to France.[1] Cavour had had so many administrative tasks that he had failed to keep sufficiently in mind what the real national interests of France were; hence he was caught unawares when the French backed down from the fight, and he had to find an explanation for Villafranca in terms of French treachery and deceit.

Another reason in Napoleon's mind may have been financial, since it had been stipulated by treaty that Piedmont would pay for France's expenses in the war, but France had already incurred 360 million francs of expenditure and her ally some 80 millions more, sums immensely beyond Piedmont's foreseeable taxable income. He had discovered, according to his cousin, that his generals were not good enough to achieve a full victory. There had also been the dreadful sight of the carnage at Solferino: when Victor Emanuel revisited San Martino the following day, he found some of the wounded still lying on the battlefield untended; the great heat must have caused appalling distress, and pillagers were already at work on the dead and wounded.[2] Soldiers were dying of sunstroke, and there was mention of typhus. Furthermore the French were bound to be preoccupied by the partial mobilization of the Prussian army. Possibly the Prussians would not have intervened to save Venice, but they were alarmed at the increase in French power; they were also worried by Garibaldi's troops nearing the Tyrolese frontier of the German Confederation and by Cavour's plans to provoke revolution north of the Alps.[3] Several communications from Russia were also received advising Napoleon to make peace.[4] Every European country with an interest in the balance of power had reason to fear a France which was too victorious or an Austrian empire threatened with destruction.

All these were factors in the decision which led to Villafranca, but purely military considerations would have been enough by themselves. The railways were jammed and in disrepair;[5] hence, after ten weeks of war, the Piedmontese had not been able to bring up the siege artillery which they now needed, and most of these guns were no nearer than Alessandria 150 miles to the rear.[6] Napoleon was particularly upset by this, and was dismayed when on 5 July

---

[1] Napoleon's proclamation in Luigi Zini, *Storia d'Italia dal 1850 al 1866: Documenti* (Milan, 1869), II, pt. ii. 282; Moltke, *Der Italienische Feldzug*, p. 274. Jules Richard, *Napoléon III en Italie* (Paris, 1859), pp. 169–70, said that Cavour was 'aveuglé par l'exclusivisme national', and had made the fatal error to 'confondre le principe des nationalités avec celui de la révolution'.

[2] J. Henry Dunant, *A Memory of Solferino* (London, 1947), pp. 23–4; *La Guerra del 1859: Documenti*, II. 878; Boggio, *Storia Politico-Militare*, III, appendix p. 7; *Revue Historique* (Paris), March 1904, p. 283.

[3] Schleinitz, *Auswärtige Politik Preussens*, I. 561, 686–8; Brassier, MSS. Geheimes Staats-Archiv, 426/45.

[4] Corti, *Downfall of Three Dynasties*, p. 114; Solaroli's diary, *Ricordi di Castelli*, pp. 314, 317; É. Ollivier, *L'Empire Liberal: Études, Récits, Souvenirs* (Paris, 1899), IV. 216.

[5] *Cavour-Nigra*, II. 213–14; Napoleon's note, 8 July, MSS. Ministero Interno, Archivio di Stato, Gabinetto, Versamento 1927 (Rome).

[6] *La Guerra del 1859: Narrazione*, II. 343, 390–1.

he learnt that lack of artillery would prevent his Piedmontese allies from attacking the first minor target assigned to them in the next stage of operations.[1] Until Mantua and Peschiera had fallen, there would be no chance of advancing beyond the Mincio. On 6 July Napoleon therefore agreed to an armistice.

Cavour claimed that he was shocked and surprised when the French gave up the fight, but his surprise must have been partly feigned, for he had already admitted that this might happen if he could not put more Italians than Frenchmen into the fight: in fact there were twice as many Frenchmen fighting as Italians, and the French had suffered twice as many casualties.[2] Napoleon was fully justified in complaining that he had found less support than Victor Emanuel had bound himself by treaty to provide. The French had to conclude that the Piedmontese army was just not good enough, and Italians were not ready to make the sacrifices required.[3] Two months after the liberation of Florence there was not a single unit of Tuscan troops at the front. To attack the Quadrilateral would need a new force double or treble the size of the existing Piedmontese army, and there was not the smallest sign that such a force was being collected.

Some people say that Cavour had counted on receiving more volunteers from the rest of Italy, but he had done little to encourage their recruitment, and Garibaldi was indignant at the way Cavour had prevented so many volunteers from fighting.[4] Possibly it had been hoped that the 50,000 Italians enrolled in the Austrian army would change sides: many of them did in fact desert, but many others had continued to fight fiercely against the Piedmontese; very few recruits had been picked up in Lombardy, and one British observer noted a 'total apathy' on the part of the local population.[5] Sometimes, furthermore, the Lombards had shown positive hostility to the French and Piedmontese.[6] Mazzini and Cattaneo compared the active enthusiasm shown

[1] *Campagne de l'Empereur Napoléon III en Italie*, ed. Général Blondel (Paris, 1862), p. 348; Bollea, *Una Silloge*, p. 169; *La Guerra del 1859: Documenti*, ii. 886; Nassau Senior, *Conversations with Distinguished Persons*, i. 69.

[2] *Mémoires du Maréchal Randon* (Paris, 1877), ii. 15; *Lettere di Cavour*, iii. 54.

[3] Massari, *Diario*, pp. 301, 316; *Cavour-Nigra*, ii. 239; *Il Risorgimento Italiano: Rivista storica*, iv (1911), p. 431; Napoleon's statement to Malmesbury, *Memoirs of an Ex-Minister* (London, 1885), p. 503; Gens. Fénelon and Trochu agreed that the Piedmontese army was no more than 'good third-rate' (Nassau Senior, *Conversations with Distinguished Persons*, i. 106–7, 288), while General Chrzanowski said that 'the officers are worth nothing. They are ignorant, conceited, undisciplined, and careless': and Chrzanowski thought that 50,000 Austrians would be able to beat three times as many Piedmontese (Nassau William Senior, *Conversations with M. Thiers, M. Guizot and other Distinguished Persons during the Second Empire*, ed. M. C. M. Simpson (London, 1878), pp. 300–1).

[4] *Memorie di Giorgio Pallavicino* (Turin, 1895), iii. 564.

[5] Claremont, 9 July, *F.O. Confidential Print*, no. 802/7, p. 2; Loftus, in *Parliamentary Papers* (London), xxxii (1859), 177; Massari, *Diario*, p. 262; *Carteggio Politico di L. G. De Cambray Digny, Aprile-Novembre 1859*, ed. G. Baccini (Milan, 1913), p. 53; Lamarmora, *Agli Elettori di Biella*, p. 24. É. Ollivier, *Revue des Deux Mondes*, June 1899, p. 550: 'L'apathie invincible des Italiens l'avait déçu; l'indiscipline du roi de Sardaigne l'avait contrarié; la facilité des Lombards à reprendre, sur l'apparence d'une défaite, les couleurs autrichiennes l'avait froissé.'

[6] *Lettere di V. Emanuele*, i. 545; *Cavour-Nigra*, ii. 219; Claremont, 8 June, *F.O. Confidential Print*, no. 802; *The Times* (London), 15 July; Richard, *Napoléon en Italie*, p. 173.

in the revolutionary wars of 1848 with the passive or mainly vocal support given to the monarchist war of 1859, and they blamed this on Cavour's deliberate policy of discouraging popular involvement. Milan in 1848 had risen against fearful odds, whereas in 1859 there was no rising in this city to support the allied advance.[1]

It has been customary to accept Cavour's version of these events and blame Napoleon for breaking his 'promise' to liberate the whole of northern Italy; whereas broken promises on the Italian side have gone unremembered. It has furthermore been customary to accept Victor Emanuel's version of how he strongly disapproved of Napoleon's desire for an armistice, because this story alone seemed to fit the legend of a liberal, patriotic king. Victor Emanuel also tried to convince people that he was not even consulted about the decision and knew nothing of it until called upon for his signature.[2] The truth is that he had been notified of the possibility almost three weeks earlier, and when on 6 July the emperor spelt out to him in more detail why the dangers of the situation made an armistice desirable, he evidently made no complaint. He was in fact present when General Fleury was ordered to take a letter to Austrian head-quarters, and the letter had first been read to him without any recorded protest. That evening king and emperor dined together: one may guess that they talked of little else, and afterwards the king let people think that he agreed an armistice was desirable.[3]

One advantage in a truce would be that it would give time to conceal the disastrous omission to bring up the Piedmontese siege artillery. The absence of these guns would in any case have meant a three weeks' wait.[4] The king felt very guilty on this point; only three days earlier had he discovered that the guns had been forgotten, and his first reaction had been horror of what Napoleon would say if he found out.[5] On the 7th, after hearing that the Austrians would accept the proposal for an armistice, Napoleon told the king as though this was something that the latter could be expected to welcome, and Victor Emanuel expressed himself in writing as pleased about it.[6] Colonel Claremont, who dined with them at Valeggio, noted that Napoleon was in

---

[1] *Scritti di Mazzini*, LXIII. 259–60; C. Cattaneo, *Il Politecnico: Repertorio mensile di Studi* (Milan), VIII (1860), 271.

[2] C. Belviglieri, *Storia d'Italia dal 1814 al 1866* (Milan, 1869), v. 163; C. de Mazade, *Le Comte de Cavour* (Paris, 1877), p. 265; Bersezio, *Il Regno*, VII. 252; Brassier de St. Simon, 17 July, MSS. Geheimes Staats-Archiv, LXXII, that the king told him 'ils ont fait la chose sans me consulter'.

[3] *La Guerra del 1859: Documenti*, II. 938, 984; Prince Napoleon, 'Les Préliminaires de la Paix (11 Juillet 1859): Journal de ma Mission à Vienne', *Revue des Deux Mondes*, Aug. 1909, p. 483; *Souvenirs de Général Cte Fleury* (Paris, 1898), II. 113; Cadogan, 14 July, P.R.O. 30/22/66. Walewski told Cowley (*F.O. Confidential Print*, no. 881/810, p. 10), that 'the King of Sardinia had been, if possible, more in favour of peace than the Emperor himself; that he had urged both the conclusion of the armistice and the signature of the preliminaries; and that he had expressed himself to be completely satisfied with the conditions obtained'; *Il Problema Veneto e l'Europa 1859–1866*, vol. II, ed. N. Blakiston (Venice, 1966), pp. 33, 38.

[4] *Lettere di V. Emanuele*, I. 557–8.   [5] *Lettere di Cavour*, III. 409.

[6] *La Guerra del 1859: Documenti*, II. 984; *Lettere di V. Emanuele*, I. 548.

'great spirits' that evening; Victor Emanuel was 'as peaceably inclined as anybody', and said he was ready to settle for no more than Lombardy.[1] On the 8th, which was the day the armistice was signed, Prince Napoleon was also said to be 'very much pleased at the prospect' of peace, and this has some importance in that Prince Napoleon himself said that he was less pleased than the king his father-in-law.[2] On the 9th, Victor Emanuel made another written statement that he would be content to accept Lombardy and make peace 'so as to save useless expense'.[3]

The king's attitude to constitutional government was such that, during these three days in which he encouraged the emperor to negotiate, he sent no communication to inform Cavour. He had been given full powers for the duration of the war, and he intended to keep his ministers in the dark. Perhaps he had heard by now that Cavour was wanting to deprive him of effective command of the army. Possibly he remembered the armistice of Vignale in 1849, since which date he had been flattered by his courtiers into thinking that he had saved the country by negotiating brilliantly in a private talk with Radetzky. The one cabinet minister present at the royal headquarters, Lamarmora, was equally and deliberately kept from knowing anything until the 8th. During these two days, whenever Lamarmora tried to see the king, he was fobbed off with excuses that the sovereign was resting or was away: even on the 8th when Lamarmora heard about the armistice, still the king would not say anything about the political terms which he hoped to obtain.[4] This refusal to consult or inform Lamarmora is all the more inexcusable in that Victor Emanuel told other people that he just could not understand what the French leaders were up to,[5] and hence he presumably must have needed all the advice he could get. When he later pretended that he had not been consulted by Napoleon, this no doubt was just a device to cover the fact that he himself had not consulted his own ministers but had allowed himself to be completely outmanœuvred by the French.

Cavour, whatever else he tried to make people think, had known for at least ten days that the French were thinking of making peace.[6] When he finally heard about the armistice through telegrams sent on 8 July by Prince Napoleon and Lamarmora, for some reason he still waited a day in Turin before taking action. He had been nettled, and justifiably, by the fact that the king had summoned Rattazzi and consulted with him, in other words with the opposition leader in parliament.[7] Perhaps this same fact made him the more

[1] Claremont, 7 July, *F.O. Confidential Print*, no. 802/7, p. 2; 10 July, ibid. 802/8, p. 2.
[2] Claremont, 9 July, ibid., p. 2; Prince Napoleon, *Revue des Deux Mondes*, Aug. 1909, p. 503.
[3] *Lettere di V. Emanuele*, I. 550.   [4] Bollea, *Una Silloge*, pp. 168-9.
[5] *Ricordi di Castelli*, p. 313; *Lettere di V. Emanuele*, I. 549.
[6] *Cavour-Nigra*, pp. 289-90; *Lettere di Cavour*, III. 105; A. J. Whyte, *The Political Life and Letters of Cavour* (London, 1930), p. 321, refused to believe this evidence because it did not accord with his opinion of Cavour's honesty and Napoleon's dishonesty.
[7] Massari, *Diario*, p. 413.

cautious before he showed his hand, and no doubt he also feared to confront Napoleon now that the latter knew of his own revolutionary activity in central Italy.

Cavour arrived at royal headquarters only in the early hours of the 10th. Once there, he first went to see Lamarmora, the minister *ad latus*, and found that this general had still been told very little of what was happening. When he met the king there was no dramatic confrontation, but he was content to wait until more details had been provided in a meeting with the emperor on the 11th. This was the meeting already arranged for settling the preliminaries of peace, and Cavour agreed that he should not accompany the king to it.[1] Almost certainly Victor Emanuel wanted the credit for completing the negotiations on his own: the emperor had no ministers present, so neither would he. Nevertheless it is unlikely that he could have persuaded Cavour to stay quietly behind unless he had convinced the minister that he was capable of getting the best possible terms. Probably Cavour must have assumed furthermore that a confrontation between himself and Napoleon would be unhelpful.

The day of 11 July began with a private meeting between Napoleon and Franz Joseph at Villafranca. Towards midday Napoleon spent more than two hours with Victor Emanuel at Valeggio, telling him the terms on which the Austrians were ready to settle; and the king was still said to be quite pleased with it all, even though he now knew that he would get no more than Lombardy and would have to accept the pope as honorary president of an Italian confederation. It was only at this point, when he knew the king's reaction, that Napoleon made up his mind definitely to make peace.[2] After lunch the emperor sent Prince Napoleon to see Franz Joseph again, in order to confirm and enlarge the details which in Victor Emanuel's presence he had already written down. That evening, Napoleon and Victor Emanuel met again for two hours to discuss and confirm the results of Prince Napoleon's mission. From this meeting, according to General Solaroli, the king emerged in considerable distress. 'We are ruined,' he said, 'our frontier is to be not the Adige but the Mincio, and without Mantua, Peschiera or Modena.' Suddenly he realized that Napoleon had made a fool of him. He had hoped to get the credit for a diplomatic success. Instead, since he had deliberately kept his ministers in ignorance, he had saddled himself with direct responsibility for a failure. His own statement on the matter tried to place himself in a better light by in-accurately stating that he had refused to agree to these terms for two more days.[3]

---

[1] *Cavour-Nigra*, II. 290.

[2] Prince Napoleon, *Revue des Deux Mondes*, Aug. 1909, pp. 483–4; F. Salata, 'Napoleone III e Francesco Giuseppe alla Pace di Villafranca: un carteggio inedito', *Nuova Antologia* (Rome), Dec. 1923, p. 292.

[3] *Ricordi di Castelli*, p. 317; 30 August, *Lettere di V. Emanuele*, I. 558; the king's interest in concealing some of the truth can be seen in *Cavour-Nigra*, III. 64.

At midnight, in a meeting at Monzambano, Cavour was informed of the result in a terrible interview witnessed only by Costantino Nigra, his protégé and favourite assistant, who never could bring himself to tell the full story. The heat was stifling; the king was in his shirt sleeves and greatly embarrassed as he communicated to Cavour the results of his private diplomacy.[1] Cavour was purple in the face with anger and gasping for breath. It must have been what Hudson called one of his usual attacks of blood to the head. Arrivabene of the *Daily News*, who was waiting for them outside, noted Cavour's apoplectic colour: the prime minister had completely lost all self-control and 'seemed almost to have lost his mind'.[2] This occasion must have been in the king's mind when he later spoke to Sir James Hudson about Cavour:

'In his passion (said H.M.) he has sometimes kicked over every chair in this room. He has called me "traitor", and worse, but I knew this was merely the effect of temper, and I used to sit quietly making my own notes of the particular matter which had driven him to this extremity of heat, and when he cooled I used to read them to him. After his bursts of temper he was cool and collected: I believe his reason forsook him in those moments, for he seemed to have no recollection of them: and hence I often doubted whether he were a safe guide, tho' I am the first to do justice to his immense courage and his great capacity for details of business. I am not at all sure (he continued) but what we might have attained the same end with less labour and without alarming all Europe: just as I propose to conclude in peace the union of Italy.'[3]

What Cavour had advised in this meeting was that the king should refuse peace on such terms, and that he should continue the war on his own, if necessary giving up Lombardy. This was a counsel of absolute despair, but Cavour was in no mood to be judicious and diplomatic. The king refused to accept such advice, and the minister thereupon resigned. Refusing to take a prime minister's advice was not unconstitutional, though it could be thought dangerous and 'unparliamentary', and it certainly involved the sovereign in a degree of personal political responsibility which might have been fatal to the constitution if events had gone badly. Yet the king was ready to take the risk. From his point of view one of the compensations for a not very satisfactory peace was that it got rid of this tiresome minister, and he told Napoleon that he would gladly pay a million francs to get Cavour to go off to America.[4] Cavour must have spoken his mind very fiercely. Among other things he accused the king of accepting these bad terms just as a means of getting Rat-

[1] D. Orsi, 'Il mistero dei "Ricordi diplomatici di Costantino Nigra",' *Nuova Antologia*, Nov. 1928, pp. 149–50; *Cavour-Nigra*, II. 291–2; there is some evidence that Cavour had threatened resignation earlier on the 11th (*La Guerra del 1859: Documenti*, II. 992, 994).
[2] C. Arrivabene, *Italy under Victor Emmanuel: A Personal Narrative* (London, 1862), I. 271; Hudson, 1 June 1861, P.R.O. 30/22/68.
[3] Hudson, 30 June 1861, P.R.O. 30/22/68; the king told Prince Napoleon that Cavour was a 'tyrant' and he had 'lost his head' (Ollivier, *Empire Libéral*, IV. 249).
[4] *Il Problema Veneto*, II. 33.

tazzi into office again, and he threw in some additional insults about the permanent dishonour which would now attach to the house of Savoy.[1]

One Englishman at the royal headquarters at Monzambano was Colonel Cadogan of the Guards, who was British military attaché to the Piedmontese forces. He had a long talk with the king a few hours after this dramatic encounter, and his evidence is thus about the most direct and immediate we possess. There was possibly less reason for the king to put on an act with a friendly and neutral foreigner than with the politicians and generals of his suite. Cadogan was told that the king had wanted an armistice in order to gain time and recruit more men: 'The advantage in an armistice therefore was all on our side but I objected to being the first to ask for such a thing.' What chiefly annoyed him was the refusal of the Austrians to negotiate directly with him, for this showed that they recognized the French but not the Piedmontese as victors; and he had naturally been upset when they surrendered Lombardy not to him but to Napoleon, and minus Peschiera and Mantua. Yet 'His Majesty seemed to me personally quite contented with what had been done'. At least Cavour had been pushed aside. As the monarch commented:

C'est un brouillon qui est toujours à me fourrer dans quelque guêpier; il est fou, je lui ai bien souvent dit qu'il était fou; il va tremper dans des bêtises comme celle de la Romagne et Dieu sait quoi. Son temps est fini: il a bien servi, mais il ne peut plus servir.[2]

When the king later spoke to Sir James Hudson about Cavour, he remarked that 'vanity and pride had turned his head'; the minister had imperilled the national cause by playing with revolution in central Italy, and had done so without any authority from his sovereign.

He [Victor Emanuel] said the Count had taken too much upon himself and had acted too independently of him in the question of the Romagna. He [the king] had desired to quiet Italy and not to raise it, to settle the question by a pitched fight and not by intrigue and revolution. But Cavour during 20 days had never communicated with him and had taken the bit between his teeth.[3]

These complaints may have been up to a point justified, but it is hard to avoid the suspicion that the king was trying to find excuses for the failure of his own negotiations. As Hudson reported it, 'This sovereign has been completely bamboozled by that sharp practitioner Louis Napoleon'. The king was now trying to persuade people 'that he had never been consulted or spoken to by the Emperor of the French on the subject until His Imperial Majesty

[1] Massari, *Diario*, p. 466; Cowley, 19 July, *F.O. Confidential Print*, no. 881/810, p. 10, reported Napoleon's story that Victor Emanuel had told him 'he would give a million out of his own pocket to induce him [Cavour] to go to the United States'; G. A. H. de Reiset, *Mes Souvenirs* (Paris, 1903), III. 11, quoted the king on 30 July saying that he was satisfied with the acquisition of Lombardy as it would give him 'une situation prépondérante dans la confédération italienne; il ne désirait pas avantage. Il paraissait plutôt soulagé qu'attristé par la retraite du Comte de Cavour.'
[2] Dispatch reproduced in *The Making of Italy 1796–1870*, ed. D. Mack Smith (New York 1968), pp. 288–91.
[3] *Gran Bretagna e Sardegna*, VII. 163, 220.

V.E.C.—9

informed him that he had settled the terms with the Emperor of Austria'. The king added that he had little idea 'how, when and where the treaty was made and by whom. . . . Nor was his consent asked upon any part of it until called upon to sign it.' When eventually he signed, it was 'against his convictions'. These few phrases show how the legend of Villafranca came to be created by Victor Emanuel. He had been treated, he said, 'comme un chien' by the emperor; 'but I am not, by nature, suspicious and the truth only flashed upon me when too late. I had no one to advise me and I am no politician.'[1] He claimed credit, however, for signing the preliminaries of peace with the qualifying phrase 'en tout ce qui me concerne', and he clearly stated that this had been done by him against Napoleon's strongly-expressed wishes.

The king's account of events was not entirely correct. The face-saving formula *en tout ce qui me concerne* was almost certainly suggested to him by Napoleon.[2] The emperor had consulted him on a number of occasions since 23 June when he had first broached the possibility of peace. Between 6 July, when it was decided to treat for an armistice, and 11 July when the terms were settled, the two men saw each other every day at least once. Nor was Victor Emanuel without advisers. The truth was that he had two ministers at hand but purposely kept them out of negotiations and paid little attention to their views. Since Napoleon did not need advice, Victor Emanuel would lose face if he asked for any himself. Kingly dignity demanded that he should sign before showing the armistice terms to Cavour.

Such was the strain of this exceedingly difficult moment that neither Cavour nor the king appeared at their best. At their meeting late on 11 July at Monzambano it was, however, the king whose judgement was the more cool and sensible. If the allied army of 250,000 men was bogged down in front of the Quadrilateral, it was inconceivable that 60,000 Piedmontese could have continued the war profitably on their own, and Cavour's suggestion of giving up Lombardy might have been disastrous for the cause of Italian patriotism. What constitutionalism lost at Villafranca, nationalism gained. A few months later Cavour frankly confessed that his resignation had been a mistake, since Villafranca was far from being the catastrophe which in a moment of hysterical aberration he had imagined it to be.[3]

[1] Ibid. 148–50, 161–2; it seems that the king was intercepting the dispatches from the British Legation, perhaps in order to see how these conversations with Hudson and Cadogan were reported ('L'Archivio Personale di Vittorio Emanuele II', ed. L. C. Bollea, *Il Risorgimento Italiano: Rivista Storica*, x (1917), 461).

[2] Bollea, *Una Silloge*, p. 170.

[3] La Tour d'Auvergne to Walewski, 29 Dec., M. Aff. Étrangères, that Cavour had said that 'si après la paix de Villafranca il eût un seul instant pensé que les choses dûssent aller comme elles ont été, il n'eût pas cru nécessaire de se retirer'; *Lettere di Cavour*, vi. 540.

6

Radicals and Moderates
in Florence, April 1859

THE morning of 27 April 1859 was a turning point in Tuscan history, for it was then that the *ancien régime* was overthrown. This was the day when the Italian patriots in Florence evicted the Grand Duke Leopold of Lorraine and opened the way towards joining a united Italian nation. The success of this revolution has been attributed to the work of two separate elements inside the patriotic movement, both of whom helped Cavour to achieve the success which he had planned. One of these was the National Society, now run by Giuseppe La Farina, which was the more forward and active of the two; the other was the circle known as the Biblioteca Civile, a more aristocratic and academic group which acknowledged the leadership of Bettino Ricasoli, Ubaldino Peruzzi, and Cosimo Ridolfi.

The moderates who belonged to the Biblioteca Civile included the best-known Tuscans of the day, people who were, by fairly general consent, the leading personalities of the duchy whether by reason of wealth, intelligence, or social position. Ricasoli himself, in May 1859, was going to establish an almost personal rule over Tuscany which endured for the following year, and in retrospect this makes him easily the most significant figure in the movement which annexed Tuscany to Piedmont. Yet the part Ricasoli played in the initial insurrection of 27 April was not so straightforward as it was made to look in retrospect. Later he used to speak of what happened that day as if there had been a universal movement in which all social classes had been united against a discredited dynasty,[1] but this was not entirely true, and until the 27th he and other members of the Biblioteca Civile did their best to preserve the grand duke and the independence of Tuscany.

The autocratic government of the old regime had been milder and more tolerable in Florence than almost anywhere else in Italy. The richer citizens and moderate liberals of Florence, appalled by the revolution of 1848, had been happy when the grand duke returned in 1849 and exiled Montanelli, Guerrazzi, and the radical firebrands of Leghorn. This restoration involved them in a six-year occupation of Tuscany by Austrian troops. Throughout the

[1] *Carteggi Ricasoli*, XII. 65.

1850s they continued to accept Leopold's autocracy out of fear that the extreme radicals and republicans might recover power. Among these moderate liberal-conservatives, Marquis Ridolfi admired Cavour and resented Tuscan subservience to Austria, but to him the real enemies were Guerrazzi, Mazzini, and the *italianissimi* rather than Leopold.[1] The blind Gino Capponi, one of the most generally respected elder statesmen in all Italy, showed his Italian patriotism by gladly contributing to the Piedmontese war loan, but still accepted Leopold's divine right to rule; so did the Marquis Corsini di Lajatico; all these men were anxious not to provoke further Austrian counter-measures against Tuscany, and hence feared to side unequivocally with Cavour. Nor were they entirely happy with the idea of Piedmontese hegemony, let alone the unthinkable idea of annexation by Piedmont. The other leading Tuscan moderates, for instance Peruzzi, Salvagnoli, Giorgini, Galeotti, and Cambray-Digny, all qualified their belief in Italy by a panic fear that the radicals might profit most from any revolution, or that Leghorn would rebel against the dominant position of Florence as had happened in the terrible days of 1848–9.

Baron Ricasoli, almost alone among the grandees who dominated Tuscan society, had long since possessed a clear vision of the peninsula being unified at some time in the future; but he too was chiefly preoccupied with the immediate need to avoid revolution, and hence was far from being opposed on principle to the reigning house of Lorraine.[2] Ricasoli, Ridolfi, and Peruzzi, together with a few politically more advanced non-aristocrats, had formed the 'Biblioteca Civile dell'Italiano', which was a group of savants who intended to publish a monthly volume to educate Tuscans in *italianità*; but they found less enthusiasm and a much more restricted audience than they had hoped, and in practice could produce only two books a year. Some of this group continued to be distantly in touch with Cavour,[3] but they often disagreed with him, and in general they assumed that, even if or when an Italian nation was formed, an autonomous Tuscany would continue to exist inside it.

When we look closely at the events which took place on the morning of 27 April in Florence, it is surprising to find that, out of all these moderates, only Ridolfi and Corsini took a prominent part or even showed much sign of life; and both these men were working hard not to evict Leopold but to keep him on his throne. Ricasoli had left the city during the night as soon as he saw signs of imminent revolution, and he refused the urgent request of his friends to return and give citizens some kind of lead in this emergency. He had also

[1] *Cosimo Ridolfi e gli Istituti del suo Tempo*, ed. L. Ridolfi (Florence, 1901), p. 373.
[2] *Atti della Reale Accademia delle Scienze di Torino* (Turin), Nov. 1929, pp. 25–6; *Le Assemblee del Risorgimento: Toscana* (Rome, 1911), III. 604–5; Ricasoli's unitarist faith is discussed by Carlo Pischedda, 'Appunti Ricasoliani', *Rivista Storica Italiana* (Naples), LXVIII (1956), 66–8.
[3] P. Cannarozzi does not make out any case at all when he describes their policy from 1857 to 1859 as inspired by Cavour (*La Rivoluzione Toscana e l'Azione del Comitato della Biblioteca Civile dell'Italiano* (Pistoia, 1936), p. xiii).

been away on his country estates during the ten days before 21 April when others had been discussing how far they could support Cavour.[1] He and his associates were chiefly worried by the fear of popular insurrection, as they also feared what might happen if the army should be disloyal to Leopold or if he were forced to abdicate. Their first priority was the preservation of order.[2] Good patriots as they were, the immediate unification of Italy was far from their minds, and in the final two days before the rising took place they became more ambiguous politically, less effective, and even more conservative and anti-revolutionary than ever.

The generally accepted explanations of what happened on 27 April do not dwell on this fact; they rather insist that Ricasoli and Peruzzi were the acknowledged leaders of the revolution, that La Farina and the National Society had been responsible for its preliminary organization, and that the general plan had been prepared by Cavour. The rising has indeed been called one of La Farina's greatest successes.[3] Raymond Grew, however, has recently demonstrated that the National Society worked fairly well as a force of propaganda, but not so well as an effective instrument of action, and at Cavour's behest it operated on this occasion rather to put off any insurrection and to quieten revolutionary zeal.[4] Instructions occasionally arrived in Tuscany from La Farina during April, but not often, and they sometimes could seem hesitant or even to contradict each other; what is more, when orders did arrive from him which were clear and urgent, they had no practical results at all.[5] Almost certainly the National Society was far less large and active than has been generally believed. The Tuscan police, which evidently knew a fair amount about the forces of subversion, hardly bothered about it. The National Society seems almost to have been paralysed by fear of a popular tumult just as the moderates were; and no wonder, for Cavour's orders to them were that at all costs a tumult must be avoided.[6] Only later did it become clear that popular agitation had been a prior requirement before Cavour's policy could

[1] *Carteggi Ricasoli*, VI. 267–71; ibid. VII. 344.

[2] Peruzzi, 'Cavour e Guerrazzi', ed. Luzio, *Atti della Reale Accademia*, LXV (1930), 48; *Cronaca degli Avvenimenti d'Italia nel 1859*, ed. A. Zobi (Florence, 1859), I. 149; sometimes war against Austria was feared just because it would mean disorder (*Le Relazioni Diplomatiche fra la Francia e il Granducato di Toscana*, ed. A. Saitta (Rome, 1959), III. 121).

[3] G. B. Giorgini, quoted in *Il Rivolgimento Toscano e l'Azione Popolare: Ricordi Familiari del Marchese Ferdinando Bartolommei*, ed. M. Gioli Bartolommei (Florence, 1905), p. 247; Cannarozzi, *La Rivoluzione Toscana*, p. 16; S. Camerani, 'La Toscana alla Vigilia della Rivoluzione', *Archivio Storico Italiano* (Florence), 1945–6, pp. 148, 155, where these events are discussed under a chapter-heading 'The Victory of the National Society'; *Il Movimento unitario nelle Regioni d'Italia* (Bari, 1963), pp. 24, 38–41; A. Salvestrini, *I Moderati Toscani e la Classe Dirigente Italiana (1859–1876)* (Florence, 1965), p. 2.

[4] R. Grew, 'La Società Nazionale in Toscana', *Rassegna Storica Toscana* (Florence), 1956, pp. 77–96; R. Grew, *A Sterner Plan for Italian Unity* (Princeton, 1963), pp. 96, 118, 170, 196–7.

[5] B. Manzone, 'Cavour e Boncompagni nella Rivoluzione Toscana del 1859', *Il Risorgimento Italiano: Rivista Storica* (Turin), 1909, p. 209; *Epistolario La Farina*, II. 128, 192–3, 248; Grew, *A Sterner Plan*, p. 170.

[6] *Epistolario La Farina*, II. 91, 151; Manzone, *Il Risorgimento Italiano*, 1909, p. 212.

succeed, and the National Society, like members of the Biblioteca Civile, was then able retrospectively to claim paternity for something which at the time they had both tried to avoid.

What happened on 27 April was precisely one of those mass popular demonstrations in the streets that Cavour had been afraid of and which were so reminiscent of the unfortunate days of 1848. The demonstration was accompanied by a fraternization between the populace and the grand-ducal soldiers, and it was this combination of citizens and soldiers which defeated the grand duke; but the prospect of such fraternization had greatly worried the moderates, for they had looked on Leopold's army as the chief safeguard of law and order. The crowds in the street on 27 April probably knew little or nothing about the National Society. The crowd leaders were the *capipopolo* who normally had a function in their various suburbs as popular spokesmen and unofficial trades-union leaders. On 10 April there had been a meeting of such popular leaders, probably in the Borgo San Lorenzo, when some kind of decision had been taken to co-ordinate popular action in the event of a rising.[1] Most prominent among them was the baker, Giuseppe Dolfi, a friend of Mazzini, a man who wielded considerable power among the poorer citizens of Florence and whom even Ricasoli treated with great respect. Dolfi is sometimes called a member of the National Society, but he himself wrote that he had never belonged to it.[2]

Associated with Dolfi were two other men of a different stamp, Ermolao Rubieri and Piero Cironi. Cironi was a republican, a dedicated disciple of Mazzini for whom the National Society was an obstacle not a help to the revolution.[3] Rubieri is usually considered to have been another of La Farina's followers, but his name does not figure among the 200 Tuscans whom Professor Grew has identified as certain members of the National Society. No doubt such an argument is inconclusive, but it is confirmed by the fact that Rubieri in parliament voted on the opposite side to members of the National Society on major issues of policy when La Farina organized his men in support of Cavour.[4] In Rubieri's memoirs, furthermore, the name of La Farina stands out by its absence. Rubieri was neither a Mazzinian nor a social revolutionary, but he used to describe his own associates as the '*partito di azione*' or the '*partito nazionale*', and these names have a certain significance, for La Farina

---

[1] Cironi's diary for 4 and 11 April, *Rassegna Storica Toscana*, 1959, pp. 253, 256.

[2] Jessie White Mario, *Agostino Bertani e i suoi tempi* (Florence, 1888), II. 138; C. Cecconi, *Il 27 Aprile: Narrazione* (Florence, 1892), p. 29; *Biografia di Giuseppe Dolfi* (Florence, 1869), p. 17; Grew, *A Sterner Plan*, p. 199. W. K. Hancock assumed that Dolfi belonged to the Society (*Ricasoli and the Risorgimento in Tuscany* (London, 1926), p. 185).

[3] G. Valeggia, *Giuseppe Dolfi e la Democrazia in Firenze negli Anni 1859 e 1860* (Florence, 1913), p. 115.

[4] 29 May 1860, *Atti del Parlamento* (1860), pp. 399–400, shows Rubieri voting against the solid National Society, including La Farina, Corsi, Malenchini, Cempini, Tanari, and Fenzi.

insisted on using the word '*società*' to make a differentiation from the '*partito nazionale*' which was a term employed by Mazzini.

Rubieri and Dolfi were the inspiration of the rising which took place on 27 April, for they had no scruples about planning an *émeute* in alliance with Cironi and the republicans; whereas the *lafariniani*, led in Tuscany by the Marquis Ferdinando Bartolommei, were much less prominent. Bartolommei was someone much respected on all sides, but his attitude in the previous few days is not completely clear. He had lately been strongly supporting the moderates, for instance in their attempt to collect money and signatures for a manifesto. He also took a prominent part in assembling volunteers and sending them to join Cavour's forces for the prospective war against Austria; this, too, he did in conjunction with the main body of liberal aristocrats,[1] and it is interesting that the grand-ducal government raised no serious opposition to recruitment. Rubieri and the radicals, on the contrary, disapproved of sending these volunteers to Piedmont, because they wanted them available in Florence for a revolution, and indeed they suspected that the moderates and the National Society were deliberately sending away the more active among Tuscan youth in order to weaken the unruly elements at home. Here was a fundamental difference of opinion. The moderates were absolutely against a revolution; so, up to a point, were members of the National Society, for they took their orders from Cavour, and Cavour feared what might result from a popular insurrection. The Piedmontese government was more concerned to persuade the grand duke into an alliance with Turin, whereas the radicals were determined to overthrow him. Rubieri therefore believed that Cavour's Piedmontese preconceptions and his undertakings to Napoleon III made him a less than wholly effective guide for the rest of the nation.

Bartolommei's position differed from that of both Ricasoli and Rubieri in various meetings among the various groups which took place secretly on and after 19 April. In these meetings, Rubieri's friends proposed to the others a compromise, namely that, provided all would agree to remove the grand duke, they themselves would accept Ricasoli and Ridolfi as leaders of a provisional government. The moderates replied to this that they would oppose any rising against the grand-ducal government. Bartolommei on this point stood between the moderates and the radicals, for he at least was determined to associate Tuscany with Piedmont in the war, yet he was under orders from Turin to avoid a popular revolution, and it still seemed probable that Leopold would accept Cavour's offer of an alliance. Bartolommei was thus in a situation where he could do nothing positive, and this may explain why not one of the

---

[1] Bartolommei, 24 Mar., MSS. Fondo Peruzzi, Biblioteca Nazionale (Florence), V/30/2; Bartolommei, 21 Apr., MSS. Carte Galeotti, Biblioteca Riccardiana (Florence), 2/72/3; *Rassegna*, 1936, p. 1088; *Carteggio del Conte Senatore L. G. de Cambray-Digny e della Contessa Virginia, dal 16 Maggio al 13 Luglio 1859*, ed. G. Baccini (Florence, 1910), pp. 110-11, 114-15, where it appears that Cambray-Digny and Galeotti, though in general opposed to the National Society, were friendly with Bartolommei.

reports of these meetings records that he ever opened his mouth. When those at the meetings who wanted action had to name one of their number as spokesman or representative, they chose Rubieri and not Bartolommei. The chief source quoted by those who assume the National Society to have been important at this moment is the book written by Bartolommei's daughter some forty years later. Other contemporary sources hardly regard him as the head of the Left, but thought of him as another aristocrat who was a welcome guest in Ricasoli's house. The part he took in these meetings convinced Cironi that he was in fact a member of the moderate Biblioteca Civile, and Rubieri regarded him as a waverer on whom they had better not count.[1]

The planning centre for the Florentine revolution was not in the Palazzo Bartolommei, but rather in the Trattoria La Fenice and in Dolfi's bakery. Bartolommei joined the revolution in the end, but between 19 and 27 April he and the National Society were not particularly prominent, and the probability is that they were waiting for orders from Turin which did not come until the last moment. La Farina remained in touch with them, but he was simultaneously in direct communication with Ridolfi and the moderates, and his orders were merely that Tuscany should be ready to take some action as soon as the war began.[2] La Farina had prepared no proper plan for an insurrection: he sent only general remarks about unspecified future action, and hence his practical effect was small until Malenchini arrived in Florence late on the 26th. Members of the National Society at Turin had many other things to bother about as the war came closer, and to organize a revolution at Florence would have seemed unimportant if not positively undesirable. A complete lack of central direction by La Farina can be inferred from the fact that the National Society at Leghorn, as also in other towns, was left to decide its own policy on sending volunteers and encouraging desertion among the grand duke's soldiers.[3]

The Biblioteca Civile had this in common with the National Society, that both feared social disorder and both were hoping that there would be no need to overturn the existing dynasty. Admittedly there was one big difference between them, that the former placed Tuscan autonomy at the head of its requirements for the future, while the latter was mainly concerned to obey whatever orders came from Cavour. Apart from this, the two groups were not so very far away from each other. No one noticed for instance that, of the six founder members of the Biblioteca Civile, two, Cempini and Corsi, were also

---

[1] *Rassegna Storica Toscana*, 1959, p. 259; *Lettere di Giuseppe Mazzini ad Andrea Giannelli*, ed. A. Giannelli (Prato, 1888), I. 97; E. Baldasseroni, 'Giovanni Baldasseroni, Uomo di Stato', *Bollettino Storico Livornese*, V (1941), 130; E. Rubieri, *Storia Intima della Toscana dal 1 Gennaio 1859 al 30 Aprile 1860* (Prato, 1861), p. 35.

[2] Camerani, *Archivio Storico Italiano*, 1945–6, p. 167.

[3] *Rassegna*, 1929, pp. 455–6, 458; *Il Rivolgimento Toscano*, ed. Gioli, p. 232; *Carteggio Castelli*, I. 188.

members of the National Society;[1] nor that the man who first conceived this same Biblioteca Civile, Carlo Fenzi, was another of the *lafariniani*; nor indeed that the moderates at one point chose Fenzi as their spokesman when the moment arrived for negotiations with Rubieri and the radicals.[2]

Probably neither of the two associations was as united or possessed such a coherent objective as might be thought. Ermolao Rubieri had a far more coherent and positive policy than either of them, and he criticized both for their inability to decide one way or the other at this urgent moment. He later described how, in the middle of April, he and everyone else looked upon the members of the Biblioteca Civile as leaders of liberal Tuscan society and were waiting for the decision which it seemed that only such men could make. As the days went by, with no decision taken, it became apparent that the imminence of revolution was paralysing the moderate liberals, who clearly thought that the grand duke's continued presence in Florence was their best hope of avoiding anarchy. This was why Rubieri, Dolfi, and Cironi, protesting against such timidity, finally met on their own to formulate a programme of action. Usually this meeting is described as a session of the National Society which was about to take the initiative away from the moderates, but Bartolommei does not seem to have been present, and we know at this moment that Cironi regarded Bartolommei and the National Society as working rather with the moderates to delay action.[3]

No doubt the Biblioteca Civile represented too many different opinions to be able to formulate any positive policy. Its members, according to Ricasoli's secretary, Marco Tabarrini, 'were weak people, men of words, not deeds, who will probably end up as before by giving way to the republicans'.[4] Since Ricasoli, their leading figure, was so much away from Florence, Peruzzi was the person who succeeded in convincing his colleagues that they would still be wise to temporize and avoid any programme of action.[5] Ricasoli himself, far from seeing any need to organize a revolt, was still mainly concerned to persuade the grand duke to change his attitude and join Piedmont: this, to Ricasoli, was vital before war broke out and brought with it the danger of another 1848-style revolution.[6] At one point the possibility was discussed between liberals and court officials that Leopold might revive the abolished Tuscan constitution, or at least that he might appoint a liberal administration under Corsini.[7] This fact was kept secret because it would have horrified Rubieri and the activists.

[1] Grew, *Rassegna Storica Toscana*, 1956, p. 86. One historian who realized that there were no hard and fast lines between them was Hancock (*Ricasoli*, p. 185).

[2] The fact that Fenzi first had the idea of forming the Biblioteca Civile is not mentioned in Cannarozzi's book on this institution, but is admitted by Ricasoli (*Carteggi Ricasoli*, VI. 57).

[3] *Rassegna Storica Toscana*, 1959, pp. 257–8; Rubieri, *Storia Intima*, pp. 26, 28, 42, 198.

[4] M. Tabarrini, *Diario 1859–1860*, ed. A. Panella (Florence, 1959), p. 9.

[5] *Carteggi Ricasoli*, VI. 262.   [6] Ibid. 266.

[7] Manzone, *Il Risorgimento Italiano*, 1909, p. 218; Salvagnoli, 24 April, MSS. Carte Galeotti; *Rassegna Storica Toscana*, 1960, p. 151; ibid., 1958, p. 43.

At the same time Peruzzi agreed to hold meetings with Rubieri and Cironi, for it was important to know the plans of the opposition and to hold them in check as long as possible. On 23 April, the leading radicals were invited to Ricasoli's house, but clearly with no intention that any compromise could be offered to such dangerous men. Rubieri at this meeting countered the moderates with a suggestion that a popular demonstration be organized in order to put pressure on the government, but the assembly broke up without ever taking this proposal into serious consideration. Instead, all that Ricasoli's friends could agree upon was to send a petition to the grand duke asking him to give up his alliance with Austria.

Such timidity convinced Rubieri that the radicals should now break formally from aristocratic leadership. His decision then showed Ricasoli that the feared moment of anarchy had arrived, and the result of this was that the Biblioteca Civile, far from taking the lead in any revolution, decided on 25 April to dissolve itself. The motive can hardly have been, as some say, to leave the way open for other more active patriots to act, because these others could and would have acted anyway. Rather it was that the more conservative of the group wanted to be free from those of their activist liberal colleagues who were beginning to accept that there was no alternative to revolution. Most of the moderates were reluctant to accept responsibility or agree about action, and they still had no reason to believe that France would give Cavour more than purely diplomatic help in any war. Hostilities might mean rioting and social disintegration; hence they looked on the independent initiative of Dolfi and Rubieri with disdain and horror.[1] War might even bring the unmitigated disaster of another Austrian invasion.

Ridolfi, Peruzzi, and Galeotti reacted to this new development by each individually getting in touch with the grand-ducal government to beg for a clear break with Austria as the one way to save the country and the dynasty.[2] This was obviously a concerted policy, for the same action was also taken between 24 and 27 April by Corsini, Matteucci, Capponi, Salvagnoli, and Cambray-Digny, and all of them, one can assume, must have been acting with the full approval of the Piedmontese minister, Carlo Boncompagni.[3] Ricasoli and Salvagnoli, the two closest to Cavour of the group, were so far away from Rubieri's policy that they were ready to accept merely a constitution, and were now willing not to press Leopold for an active alliance with Piedmont against

---

[1] *Carteggi Ricasoli*, VI. 265–6; *Relazioni fra Francia e Toscana*, ed. Saitta, III. 121; Rubieri, *Storia Intima*, pp. 50–1, 57–60.

[2] L. Galeotti, *L'Assemblea Toscana: Considerazioni* (Florence, 1859), pp. 90–4; *Cronaca degli Avvenimenti*, ed. Zobi, I. 109–17; A. Panella, 'Un po' più di Luce su una "Storia di Quattro Ore" ', *Miscellanea di Studi Storici: ad Alessandro Luzio* (Florence, 1933), II. 257–65; Anon. (Peruzzi), *La Toscane et ses Grands-Ducs Autrichiens* (Paris, 1859), pp. 112–3.

[3] Panella, *Miscellanea ad A. Luzio*, II. 265; *Rassegna*, 1929, pp. 466–8; *Rassegna Storica Toscana*, 1958, p. 44; M. Carletti, *Quattro Mesi di Storia Toscana, dal 27 Aprile al 27 Agosto 1859* (Florence, 1859), p. 22.

Austria.[1] The important thing was to avoid revolution. As Giorgini put it, the moderates feared that 'once let the people loose in the streets, and you will never get them back home again'.[2]

Ricasoli himself spoke privately to the government in the same sense as his other aristocratic companions, and as late as the evening of the 26th, at the very moment when in Dolfi's house the time-table of the revolution was being drawn up, Ricasoli paid a personal visit on Leopold's chief minister in order to see if they could not save the dynasty.[3] Meanwhile, in Dolfi's house, the radicals, in other words those whom the moderates liked to think of as 'dangerous reds', were deciding once more to ask Ricasoli himself if he would preside over their revolutionary junta. Ricasoli again refused the invitation, for he had no wish for revolution or to be associated with such men.[4] His meeting with Giovanni Baldasseroni, the minister, had at last convinced him that it might not in the end be possible to save the grand duke's government, and in that case he would go to Turin to ask for the assistance of troops from Piedmont; these troops he needed to control the very revolution that Rubieri was trying to organize. Ricasoli therefore left overnight for Turin, hurriedly abandoning the revolution to take its course.[5] In his absence, Ridolfi was so alarmed by the news of what was happening in Dolfi's house that he not only refused to join the insurrection, but went so far as to warn the grand duke of what was about to happen unless he took steps to prevent it.[6] Cipriani also went to warn the head of police, while Ferdinando Martini and others in the early hours of the 27th woke up Leopold's other ministers to put them on their guard.[7] Evidently the moderates had not yet given up the grand-ducalist cause as lost.

In the evening of the 26th, the radicals decided to go ahead with their revolution on the following day.[8] By this time the National Society had, like

[1] Salvestrini, *I Moderati Toscani*, p. 15; *Relazioni fra Francia e Toscana*, ed. Saitta, III. 121, 128.

[2] *Carteggi Ricasoli*, VI. 267–8, 270; Massari, *Diario*, p. 226; Tabarrini, *Diario*, p. 18.

[3] Cironi's diary, *Rassegna Storica Toscana*, 1959, p. 128.

[4] Rubieri, *Storia Intima*, pp. 74–5; the contrary view, that Ricasoli at once supported the revolutionaries, was accepted by Rodolfo della Torre, *La Evoluzione del Sentimento Nazionale in Toscana dal 27 Aprile 1859 al 15 Marzo 1860* (Milan, 1915), p. 37.

[5] Ricasoli's movements can now be followed in 'Un Carteggio Inedito di Bettino Ricasoli', ed. A. Sapori, *Rivista delle Biblioteche e degli Archivi* (Florence), XXXVI (1926), 4–6; *Carteggi Ricasoli*, VI. 267–71; ibid. VII. 344; and Panella shows that Ricasoli altered one of the relevant documents later to show himself in better light (*Miscellanea ad A. Luzio*, II. 262).

[6] C. Ridolfi, *Breve Nota a una Storia di Quattro Ore, Intorno ai Fatti del 27 Aprile 1859* (Florence, 1859), pp. 9–12.

[7] Cecconi, *Il 27 Aprile*, pp. 44–5; memoirs of Sardi, *Rassegna Storica Toscana*, 1960, pp. 158–9; Ferdinando Martini, *Confessioni e Ricordi: Firenze Granducale* (Florence, 1922), pp. 158–9.

[8] Camerani calls this 'the last meeting of the National Society' (*Archivio Storico Italiano*, 1945–6, pp. 181–3); but the choice of *casa* Dolfi instead of *casa* Bartolommei, taken in conjunction with the recollections of Cironi and Rubieri, and the absence from this meeting of Fenzi, Corsi, Cempini— all this speaks in a different sense; Bartolommei may have been present, but if he spoke no one records it, while the neutral Cecconi, who names the other participants, did not see him there (*Il 27 Aprile*, pp. 40–3).

the Biblioteca Civile, formally ceased to exist, and some of its former members decided to join Dolfi's insurrection. Their decision was almost certainly influenced by the arrival from Turin of Malenchini, who probably brought last-minute orders from Cavour to dissolve the Society and co-operate with the popular movement. Malenchini would have convinced some of the lukewarm that it was now too late to hold back,[1] and that they would have to take some practical part in the popular demonstration if they wished to have any say in a revolutionary government. Towards midnight there was busy activity. In particular, individual contacts were made with the more open-minded of the army officers to convince them that they should let the revolution take its course without offering resistance.

The army, and in particular Major Danzini who was commandant of the artillery, were to play an important part on the 27th. Some of the younger officers obviously had liberal and patriotic sentiments. Others must have feared for their jobs if they were caught on the losing side. The silence of the relevant documents suggests that Danzini was not among the known liberals and patriots. On the contrary, he was the favourite of the Austrian general, Ferrari da Grado, and he was close to the grand-ducal family through his friendship with the Archduke Charles; nevertheless he had also been in some kind of contact with Boncompagni and the Piedmontese.[2] Boncompagni had orders from Cavour to win friends among the grand duke's army officers, and the choice of Danzini on the 27th to be a member of the provisional government, as also his subsequently rapid promotion to the rank of general at the early age of thirty-six, suggests that he had already discussed with the Piedmontese the possibility of changing sides.

Far greater than that of the army, however, was the role of Dolfi and Rubieri, because without the enormous crowd in the Piazza Barbano there would have been no chance at all of a mutiny, nor would either Boncompagni or Danzini have had any opportunity to intervene. The whole of the city's inhabitants were in the streets early on the 27th. Lieutenant Cecconi later recalled how Dolfi was to be seen among them, 'surrounded by a group of bold and tough working-class men under the command of the master bricklayer, Morandi, who formed his bodyguard'.[3] The correspondent of the London *Times* was astonished by

the perfect command which the leaders of the people seemed to possess over each and all. They might be seen going from group to group recommending order and

---

[1] For the activity of Malenchini on the 26th, there is a tantalizing single sentence by Boncompagni (Manzone, *Il Risorgimento Italiano*, 1909, p. 222); another in Yorick, *Uomini e Fatti d'Italia* (Florence, 1921), p. 62; another in *Lettere di Mazzini a Giannelli*, I. 103; another in *Ricordi di Castelli*, p. 226. Cironi suggests that Malenchini's action was chiefly addressed to introducing Victor Emanuel's name into the revolutionary proclamation (Ludmilla Assing, *Vita di Piero Cironi* (Prato, 1865), p. 167); Rubieri mentions him only *en passant*, *Storia Intima*, pp. 66–9.

[2] E. Montazio, *L'Ultimo Granduca di Toscana* (Florence, 1870), p. 124; *I Casi della Toscana nel 1859 e 1860 Narrati al Popolo* (Florence, 1864), p. 37; *Rassegna Storica Toscana*, 1960, p. 152.

[3] Cecconi, *Il 27 Aprile*, p. 47; Rubieri, *Storia Intima*, pp. 81–2.

tranquillity. Throughout the entire day no single act of turbulence occurred as far as I have been able to discover.[1]

The tricolour flag was first hoisted in the Piazza Barbano. Then the grand duke, obviously very frightened, made the main concession sought by the moderates and agreed to accept a policy of war against Austria. Not even then, however, did the crowd go home, and it was the constancy and discipline among this huge mob of citizens which made possible further revolutionary demands and brought the dynasty down.

Towards midday on the 27th, Leopold agreed under pressure not only to accept the Italian cause but to appoint a liberal government. Rubieri was for refusing this concession, because he and the radicals wanted to proceed to the overthrow of the dynasty, but at this point Boncompagni intervened to speak for Cavour. First he asked the opinion of the army officers, because he did not want to go too far without assurance of their support; and when it was clear that even the more liberal-minded officers still supported Leopold, the Piedmontese minister encouraged Corsini and Ridolfi to accept the offer to replace Baldasseroni and form a government under the grand duke. The liberal-conservative aristocrats seem to have been fully behind this move, for it would have kept Leopold on the throne, and there was still no alternative to the grand duke as a defence against 'the reds'.[2] In Ricasoli's absence from Florence, Corsini therefore agreed to Leopold's request to form a ministry.

Rubieri and Malenchini both disliked this. They gave way reluctantly, and only when Ridolfi agreed to a compromise: this compromise was that Corsini should first make a condition before accepting Leopold's offer, namely that he abdicate in favour of his son Ferdinand. Corsini thought such a condition excessive, and agreed only when this seemed to be the one chance of saving the dynasty. What subsequently defeated this consensus and gave Rubieri and Dolfi their victory was the unexpected decision by Leopold to leave the country rather than accept abdication. Rubieri noted how, at Boncompagni's house, the moderates were at first stunned by the news and what they must have taken as the defeat of their policy.[3]

When Ridolfi later tried to recall the sequence of these events, he made no reference to the principal characters who made possible the triumph of the Italian cause. Nor, incidentally, did Ricasoli make any mention of the serious and concerted attempts by himself and his friends to keep the grand duke on his throne; on the contrary he went out of his way to conceal them. In this way the moderates fed the myth which developed about the revolution of

---

[1] *The Times*, 3 May; and see Adolphus Trollope, *Tuscany in 1849 and in 1859* (London, 1859), p. 283.

[2] 'Lettere di Neri Corsini a Leopoldo Galeotti', ed. B. Biagiarelli, *Rassegna Storica Toscana*, 1958, p. 43; Peruzzi, quoted in Salvestrini, *I Moderati Toscani*, p. 33; the uncertainty prevailing in Boncompagni's house was described in a letter to Cavour (Manzone, *Il Risorgimento Italiano*, 1909, pp. 222–3).

[3] *Storia Intima*, p. 92.

27 April. As they looked back, they could see it as in their own interest to exaggerate their motives of patriotism and to describe how they had led a united Tuscan people in rising to turn Leopold out and create a unified Italy. Only a few weeks later, Ricasoli's secretary was referring to the happenings on the 27th as a revolution organized by the aristocrats. What had occurred in the meantime to create such an illusion was that the aristocracy, as soon as they saw that revolution could no longer be avoided, changed their attitude so that the insurrection should not get out of hand. As Tabarrini put it,

when they saw that the patriotic cause was going to prevail, they changed sides, terrified of being condemned by the rest of the community. They would stoop to anything rather than expose themselves to the anger of the people. Cowardly as always, they deserted the grand duke who had humiliated them, and instead they espoused the cause of democracy.[1]

Ricasoli, the unchallenged hero of the next twelve months, changed more speedily than anyone. The Marquis Corsini, on the other hand, the moderate liberal who, far more than Ricasoli, had been at the centre of events on 27 April, looked at the happenings in the Piazza Barbano not with pleasure but with fright. As he wrote to his son at the time, 'One o'clock struck on the 27th, and all was over, after four hours in which everything could have been saved but everything was in fact lost.'[2] Ridolfi, too, spoke of Leopold's decision to abdicate as a 'grave misfortune' for the country.[3] Peruzzi privately agreed with the French minister at Florence that the events of the 27th, despite later myth, had been a victory for a dangerous group of democrats over the Biblioteca Civile.[4] Corsini and Peruzzi waited anxiously for Piedmontese military support, but not so much to help complete the revolution as to arrest it 'and stop the victory of the reds'. And, by the reds, they meant Dolfi and the *popolani*. All of them did their best in the meantime to enlist French and British help in preventing Cavour from using this occasion to destroy the autonomy of Tuscany.[5]

A few days later, Count Cambray-Digny and his wife wrote of wanting Piedmontese troops to put down the revolutionaries, and, with unconscious irony, justified their request by stating that they, the moderates, had been responsible for the revolution of 27 April, and hence Piedmont had a reciprocal 'obligation' to help them against Dolfi and 'the mob'. Had Cavour known it, the 'reds', the 'jacobins', the *parti demagogique*, these were the very people

---

[1] *Diario*, pp. 68, 76.

[2] Neri Corsini di Lajatico, *Storia di Quattro Ore, dalle 9 antimeridiane alle 1 pomeridiane del 27 Aprile* (Florence, 1859), p. 16.

[3] *Breve Nota a una Storia*, p. 14.

[4] Ferrière-le-Vayer, 30 April, 4 May, *Relazioni fra Francia e Toscana*, ed. Saitta, III.139, 142; Corsi, 8 May: 'Remember that it was the common people who carried out the revolution, while we just watched from the window' (*L'Unità d'Italia nel Pensiero e nell'Azione del Barone Bettino Ricasoli*, ed. M. Puccioni (Florence, 1932), p. 31).

[5] Ferrière, 10 May, *Relazioni fra Francia e Toscana*, III. 148; Scarlett to Malmesbury, 6, 11 May, F.O. 79/204.

who in fact had forced a reluctant aristocracy into accepting a revolution which the moderates had not wanted; these same democrats were now described by the moderates as a dangerous enemy, to crush whom Piedmontese troops ought to abandon the battlefields of Lombardy.[1] The fact that they were not in any sense 'reds' was beside the point. Only by giving them such a label could the moderates justify their own passiveness on 27 April and retain their position as acknowledged leaders of Tuscan society.

Usually in the risorgimento the moderates were able, justly, to take pride in their sense of realism and their ability to temper the idealism and the impetuousness of the radicals. Nevertheless it is possible to think that, in this case, the true realism, as also the true sense of moderation, was not on their side. The way in which Dolfi and Rubieri won, and then refused to cause division by pushing their victory any further, is remarkable. When Boncompagni later on the 27th formed a provisional government and wanted, for obvious reasons, to exclude the 'party of action', Rubieri agreed to stand down in the interests of patriotic union and went off to fight in Lombardy.[2] One contemporary commentator was therefore moved to look back on these few dramatic hours as *la journée des dupes*, since 'opponents of the dynasty, though they won the day, did not capture power, while the *dinastici* were soundly beaten and yet were able to take over government'.[3] The revolution of 27 April was in fact, despite what all the moderates feared, easy, calm, even conservative. The people came out into the streets, but without committing any excesses, and they cheerfully returned home when all was over. This much feared '*moto di piazza*' was one more proof of the good sense of the Florentine people.

[1] *Carteggio del Cambray-Digny e della Contessa Virginia*, pp. 69–71; L. Galeotti, *I Toscani del '59*, ed. R. Ciampini (Rome, 1959), p. 92; Lambruschini, *Carteggi Ricasoli*, VIII. 51; Salvagnoli's dislike of Dolfi, Rubieri, and Malenchini can be seen in *Il Risorgimento Italiano*, 1911, p. 428, and ibid., 1925, p. 658.
[2] *Storia Intima*, pp. 100–2.
[3] 'Opinioni e Problemi in Toscana nel 1859–60', ed. R. Carmignani, *Rassegna*, XLVI (1959), 398.

7

Cavour and the Tuscan
Revolution of 1859

THE peaceful revolution in Florence at the end of April 1859 had, as its long-term effect, the Piedmontese annexation of Tuscany and the displacement of Leopold by his nephew, Victor Emanuel. This was the more remarkable in that such a result had been opposed by France as well as Austria. It was possible for some to conclude that the events of 27 April effectively decided that Italy should become a unitary rather than a federal state.[1] Others were able to conclude further that, since Cavour was the ultimate gainer from the revolution, he must have planned and organized it.[2] But his attitude was not so simple. Further study of his policy during the months leading up to this moment can throw light on his political technique, as well as on the nature of his patriotic beliefs, and on his attitude towards the different political currents inside Italian patriotism.

Before 1859, Cavour's thoughts had not often travelled beyond the boundary of the Apennines. He had never been in central Italy. He had no intimate friend in Tuscany and possessed fewer contacts there than in most other Italian regions. His ideas about its future had been changeable, nor were they the result of any profound thought. When Palmerston once suggested enlarging the grand duke's domain, he had opposed the idea,[3] because he wanted Turin to be the only focus for Italian patriotism; yet when Napoleon III later repeated the suggestion, Cavour agreed that Tuscany could be allowed to annex Umbria and the Marches.[4] In negotiations with the emperor he bid to annex Venice, Modena, Parma, and the Romagna, but not for Tuscany. The continuance of Leopold's dynasty evidently met no rooted objection on his part, and he once seems to have considered a marriage alliance between the houses of Lorraine and Savoy.[5] He even showed solidarity with Leopold by

[1] L. Salvatorelli, *Spiriti e Figure del Risorgimento* (Florence, 1961), p. 318; G. Spadolini, *Firenze Capitale, con Documenti Inediti* (Florence, 1967), p. 344.
[2] R. della Torre, *La Evoluzione del Sentimento Nazionale in Toscana* (Milan, 1915), p. 23; S. Camerani, 'La Toscana alle Vigilia della Rivoluzione', *Archivio Storico Italiano* (Florence), 1945–6, pp. 159 181; E. Passerin d'Entrèves, *Il Piemonte l'Italia Centrale e la Questione Romana nel 1859–60* (Pisa, 1960), pp. 54–6, 59.
[3] 21 Jan. 1856, *Lettere di Cavour*, II. 176.   [4] 24 July 1858, *Cavour-Nigra*, I. 105.
[5] F. Martini, *Confessioni e Ricordi: Firenze Granducale* (Florence, 1922), p. 227.

helping him suppress Mazzini's nationalist agitation.[1] Yet on another occasion he could also consider giving Tuscany to the Bourbons of Parma so as to leave Parma available for that advancement of Piedmont which was his first political principle. As late as December 1858 he was not unfavourable to the strange notion of imposing a Hohenzollern prince on Tuscany, for it would please the Germans and bring into Italy what he oddly called 'une race qui a encore de la force et de la vigueur'.[2] All this shows a notable disinclination towards political dogmatism or doctrinaire Italian patriotism.

Cavour's instructions to his diplomatic representative in Tuscany, Count Boncompagni, were that Piedmont's principal aim there was to support political reform and detach the grand duke from his existing alliance with Austria.[3] Boncompagni also had orders to befriend the Tuscan liberals. In November 1858, Cavour was angry to find that these liberals were in independent touch with Napoleon and had the 'absurd' notion of enlarging Tuscany; for, although he himself had secretly agreed with the emperor to enlarge Tuscany, this was to be *his* decision, and any interference with his plans was unwelcome. His indignation was tempered only by his contemptuous belief that 'the Etruscan race' was too timid to rival Piedmont as the driving force in Italy. He privately notified Ricasoli that Piedmont was preparing war against Austria, but added that he did not want any revolution at Florence; and when it was suggested that an artificially contrived revolt in Tuscany might serve to spark off his war, Cavour disagreed, for, despite some of his biographers, it was alliance not enmity that he required from Leopold. Massa, Carrara, and the Romagna—in other words, Modenese and papal territory—were where he intended to 'detonate the explosion'; these areas, unlike Tuscany, were marked down for Piedmontese annexation.[4]

Ricasoli's circle, or the group known as the Biblioteca Civile, did not know Cavour's more secret thoughts. In January 1859, when rumours of war became common knowledge, they sent to ask him what they could do to help, and explained that lack of information and advice was embarrassing Piedmont's friends in central Italy.[5] Their request arrived at a time when Cavour was beginning to want something more positive, for he had undertaken to give the French a plausible pretext for hostilities by creating the illusion that it would be a spontaneous war of liberation, not something planned, nor a war of Piedmontese aggression. When he ordered one of his officials to sound out

[1] Gramont to Walewski, 26 Aug. 1856, M. Aff. Étrangères.   [2] *Cavour-Nigra*, I. 250.
[3] 13 Jan. 1857, Bianchi, *Storia Documentata*, VIII. 77–80; Carlo Boncompagni, *Considerazioni sull'-Italia Centrale* (Turin, 1859), pp. 36–8; *Cavour-Salmour*, p. 149.
[4] Massari, *Diario*, p. 71; 25 Nov. 1858, *Cavour-Nigra*, I. 213–14; Della Torre asserts that Cavour in October 1858 prepared a plan for a revolution in Tuscany (*Evoluzione del Sentimento Nazionale*, p. 23), and is supported in this view by W. K. Hancock (*Ricasoli and the Risorgimento in Tuscany* (London, 1926), p. 189), but in fact this plan, if indeed it was ever approved by Cavour, concerned not Tuscany, but Massa, Carrara, the Romagna, and the smaller central duchies (*Epistolario La Farina*, II. 83–5).
[5] Corsi, *Carteggio Castelli*, I. 179; *Carteggi Ricasoli*, VI. 211–12.

the grand duke's army to test its allegiance, this had to be concealed from the Florentine liberals who valued the army's loyalty. His reply to Ricasoli's friends was just that they should try to make Leopold grant a constitution, and Marquis Gualterio was sent to explain why.[1]

This advice was received with some disappointment. It suggested that Cavour meant to leave Tuscany out of his territorial realignment of Italy, or even that he favoured the Tuscan radicals—the same extremists who, in 1848–9, had won power through a constitution very similar to that which he was now trying to revive. Probably Cavour's advice arose in fact from no deeply laid plan. The abruptness of its presentation, however, did indicate that he put no great value on consulting Tuscan opinion; hence the suspicious reaction among Florentines was that they should do nothing until Piedmont committed herself publicly and irrevocably to war. Cavour was furious when they would not take his advice about a constitution. He was not even mollified when Vincenzo Salvagnoli sent him an advance copy of a pamphlet advocating an alliance with Piedmont against Austria. The diplomatic situation was already complicated enough without these self-important Tuscans refusing to do as he required.[2]

This minor contretemps exposed a potentially dangerous weakness in Cavour's lines of communication, for evidently his officials were out of touch with liberal opinion in Florence. Detached from Turin, the Tuscan moderates were developing ideas of their own which threatened to upset his schemes. Cavour therefore moved away from these moderates and turned in the direction of La Farina's National Society, whose members were pledged to support Piedmont and whom he knew to be a younger, more activist, more middle-class element. La Farina, who had already given Cavour to believe that his society had many disciplined supporters in Tuscany, now instructed his principal agent there, Marquis Ferdinando Bartolommei, to agitate with the aim of forcing Leopold into alliance with Piedmont. Cavour said that failure in this task would not matter provided agitation was obvious enough to convince Europe of widespread Italian backing for his war. Yet to those more extreme patriots who would have preferred to dethrone the dynasty, it was explained that revolution might be the aim elsewhere, but not in Tuscany; here a military alliance with Turin was preferable, for it would unite moderate and extreme patriots, together with those who wanted an independent Tuscany, and would even attract many supporters of the grand duke.[3] To La

---

[1] Massari, *Diario*, pp. 107, 120–1; Bollea, *Una Silloge*, p. 139; *Carteggi Ricasoli*, VII. 344.

[2] Salvagnoli, 11 Jan. 1859, *I Toscani del'59*, ed. R. Ciampini (Rome, 1959), p. 181; Massari, *Diario*, p. 133; *Lettere ad Antonio Panizzi di Uomini Illustri e di Amici Italiani*, ed. Luigi Fagan (Florence, 1880), p. 288.

[3] *Epistolario La Farina*, II. 127–8, 133; *Il Rivolgimento Toscano e l'Azione Popolare*, ed. M. Gioli Bartolommei (Florence, 1905), pp. 239–40; La Farina's secret orders of 4 March are, once again, said to have been directed at Tuscany, e.g. by P. Cannarozzi, *La Rivoluzione Toscana e l'Azione del Comitato della Biblioteca Civile dell'Italiano* (Pistoia, 1936), p. 273, when in fact they were sent to Sarzana for use in Massa and Carrara.

Farina's great chagrin, however, no demonstrations took place in response to his urgent plea.

Cavour knew that the Tuscan aristocrats feared he might be using other channels to promote a more revolutionary policy than he ever spoke of to them. There would have been outrage had they also known that he had no qualms about getting in touch even with Guerrazzi and Montanelli. This was Cavour's natural instinct, to play different policies independently of, or indeed against, each other. While Nigra was sent to Paris to ask how far Tuscan agitation could be allowed to go, Cavour kept up a more moderate and moderating correspondence with his ambassador, Boncompagni; he also maintained indirect contact with the Biblioteca Civile, though still trying to conceal from them the extent of his parallel relations with the National Society. Boncompagni sometimes found that other people than himself in Florence claimed to speak for the Turin government, which was not only undignified for him, but confusing for everyone else; and there was even a junior secretary in his own embassy who for a time, no doubt on orders from Turin, seems to have been secretly working at complete cross-purposes against Boncompagni's official policy. Cavour at one point tried to find a new ambassador who possessed a 'less scrupulous political conscience';[1] but he could think of no one suitable, and so Boncompagni was recalled to Turin at the end of February for talks. With him, at their own request, came Ridolfi and two others connected with the Biblioteca Civile.

Ridolfi, Carega, and Corsi had not met Cavour before; they now had three talks with him. Marquis Carega's account of their meetings, many years later, is not entirely trustworthy; but he thought he recalled Cavour's 'exact words', that Tuscans 'should do nothing except induce the dynasty to ally with Piedmont and grant a constitution', and on this point his testimony is confirmed by Ridolfi's later attempt to carry out this policy, as it is also supported by a contemporary account from Corsi.[2] Cavour strongly opposed what they told him of Ricasoli's wish to start a newspaper, strangely arguing that it would divide opinion and frustrate action. Perhaps this shows that Cavour had been nettled by Ricasoli's use of the very same argument against Turin's advocacy of a campaign for a Tuscan constitution. It also exemplified Cavour's scornful attitude to Tuscans and to their inability to act in concert. In the upshot the Tuscan delegation agreed to put out a booklet in favour of Tuscany allying with Piedmont, and Boncompagni also promised to be less timid

[1] Massari, *Diario* (28 Jan.), pp. 127–8; *Lettere di Cavour*, III. 23; Boncompagni's protest is in Bianchi, *Storia Documentata*, VIII. 81; for the confusion in embassy policy, cf. the police report of 15 March in *Rassegna*, 1929, p. 469; *Il '59 in Toscana*, ed. R. Ciampini (Florence, 1959), p. 51.

[2] F. Carega, 'Dal Conte di Cavour nel Febbraio 1859', *Fanfulla della Domenica* (Rome), 31 Jan. 1892; F. D. Guerrazzi, 'Diary', 2 May 1859, *Nuova Antologia* (Rome), June 1933, pp. 330–1; Camerani correctly shows (*Archivio Storico Italiano*, 1945–6, pp. 143–5) that both accounts must have been occasionally wrong over details where they disagree, but it would need further corroboration to conclude from this, as he does, that they must therefore both have been wrong on major points where their testimony concurs.

about the morals of using his diplomatic immunity as a cover for conspiracy.

Ricasoli was upset by Cavour's unwillingness to accept a newspaper: far from causing divisions, a newspaper in his view would be a rallying point for all who opposed Austria; on the contrary it was Cavour who was dividing liberals by imposing policy from a distance where local conditions were not understood. A newspaper would educate public opinion, at the same time as it would create a useful initiative for manufacturing a crisis at any desired moment. Ricasoli accepted Cavour's decision, but here he had new evidence of an unwillingness at Turin to be seriously interested in Tuscans. Cavour just wished them to agitate, which they did not like, so as to obtain a constitution, of which they were suspicious, and in association with unknown radical forces of whom they were deeply afraid. Cavour's mind was merely set on annexing Italy north of the Apennines, and he wanted Ricasoli to help him do this and no more. 'These Tuscans are unbearably doctrinaire', he said to Massari; if they continued with their foolish plan to start a newspaper he would wash his hands of them.[1]

By mid-March, however, Cavour needed Tuscan help more than he had anticipated, for in the papal Romagna La Farina's friends once again were failing to produce the required detonating mechanism. As it was imperative to show Napoleon and Europe that Italy was in a state of complete dissolution, the evidence for seething patriotic revolt might be more easily manufactured under the tolerant regime of the grand duke than under the eye of Austrian soldiers in Bologna. Moreover, Cavour suddenly saw a possible danger if England succeeded in persuading Leopold to give up his Austrian alliance: the Piedmontese had, on French advice, told England they wanted just this; but, now that the options were narrowing, a continuance of the Austro-Tuscan alliance might turn out to be the only available pretext for the war which he so badly needed. Once again, therefore, Gualterio mysteriously reappeared in Florence and the National Society was again ordered to produce some agitation, while the burgraves of the Biblioteca Civile were accused by Turin of cowardice and told to choose more active leaders than Ridolfi and Ricasoli. Cavour then tried hopefully to persuade Napoleon that Tuscany must be in a ferment of unrest,[2] but his case was unconvincing.

A more authentic success was that the Biblioteca Civile on 21 March published a much-applauded manifesto of liberal, pro-Piedmontese opinion. *Toscana e Austria* stated that Tuscany should accept Cavour's lead in excluding Austria from the peninsula. Ricasoli, Ridolfi, and Peruzzi put their names publicly on this pamphlet, but they made difficulties when Cavour asked further

[1] Massari, *Diario* (8 Mar.), p. 164.
[2] 13 Mar., B. Manzone, 'Cavour e Boncompagni nella Rivoluzione Toscana del 1859', *Il Risorgimento Italiano: Rivista Storica* (Turin), 1909, pp. 210–11; *Cavour-Nigra*, II. 78, 99, 117; *Il Risorgimento Italiano nell'Opera, negli Scritti, nella Corrispondenza di Piero Puccioni*, ed. M. Puccioni (Rome, 1932), p. 61.

for a collectively-signed letter which he could publish as proof that the best-known persons in Tuscany were behind him. They were reluctant to compromise themselves in such a way, partly because it might be read as political criticism of Leopold, but partly because Capponi, Corsini, and Galeotti feared that others among this loose group of moderates were going too far. This was a most unfortunate division. When time went by with nothing which Cavour could show to the emperor as evidence of agitation, and indeed almost no communication from Tuscany of any kind, he sharply accused the moderates of *lèse patrie*.[1]

Lack of communication went both ways. On Cavour's side it was understandable, for this was perhaps the most difficult month of his whole life; yet it had unfortunate results which suggested that his type of empirical statesmanship carried some inherent defects. Boncompagni on 18 March asked how he ought to act if Leopold fled from Florence or if popular insurrection broke out; but Cavour had no time to answer, and anyway counted on Leopold remaining as grand duke. The Turin government still had established no unified chain of command, and advice continued to reach Florence in various senses through various agencies: the regular Tuscan postal service had been bribed by the Piedmontese so that it would also deliver secret messages, which may explain why the Tuscan police could read Ricasoli's letters and even Boncompagni's dispatches.[2] A much more serious difficulty was that, though Cavour repeatedly demanded incessant 'agitation', he once again specifically barred any *émeute*. Legal petitions were needed, but never on any account *moti in piazza*; street demonstrations would not only revive fears of another 1848, but they could easily get out of control, and above all they would antagonize Napoleon who needed to feel that Cavour was fully in charge of what was a socially conservative movement. The advice against mob demonstrations was repeated often and firmly.[3] In effect, however, much as this advice delighted the Tuscan moderates, it disarmed the activists among Cavour's followers, at the same time as it strengthened those dangerous anti-French radicals who had no scruples about defying Cavour and taking revolution into the streets.

Uncertainty also existed over what attitude should be taken towards the volunteer soldiers who were leaving in small batches to join Garibaldi and the regular army in Piedmont. Capponi, Peruzzi, Bastogi, Ricasoli, and above all Bartolommei, subscribed to help these volunteers, but Cavour's attitude changed more than once. He needed volunteers, especially (so he said) from

---

[1] Manzone, *Il Risorgimento Italiano*, 1909, p. 213; Boncompagni's earlier reports are given in *Il '59 in Toscana*, ed. Ciampini, pp. 43–4, 49; *Epistolario di Luigi Carlo Farini*, ed. L. Rava (Bologna, 1935), IV. 246.

[2] Diary of Landucci, 'La Toscana alla Vigilia del 27 Aprile 1859', ed. G. Lumbroso, *Rassegna*, 1933, p. 96; report of police spy, Cannarozzi, *La Rivoluzione Toscana*, p. 203.

[3] *Cavour-Nigra*, II. 47, 122, 150; *Epistolario La Farina*, II. 91, 151; *Il '59 in Toscana*, ed. Ciampini, p. 45.

the upper classes; he knew his shortage of troops in Piedmont, and the arrival of central-Italian recruits would incidentally be a welcome demonstration of support for his cause. But sometimes his agents preferred to discourage enlistment, partly because there were counter-arguments for keeping the activists at home, but partly because the regular Piedmontese army was suspicious and jealous of any volunteer units.[1] Early in April, however, Cavour was again worrying that the volunteers from central Italy were too few to impress the French. Such vacillation helped to create uncertainty about what was required and so contributed to inhibit action.[2] It was this confusion over the volunteers and over the permitted limits of agitation which left the field open to the radical elements around Rubieri and Dolfi, for such people had fewer inhibitions than either Biblioteca Civile or National Society about disobeying orders from Turin.

Cavour was not intending to annex Tuscany; he still hoped for central Italy and possibly even Naples to ally with him against Austria. On 12 April he therefore decided to let Leopold into the biggest secret of all, and explained to him privately, perhaps injudiciously, that France had secretly promised to join Piedmont in a war to liberate Italy; also that moral support had been promised to this alliance by Russia, Prussia, and England; and hence Tuscany would be wise to join the big battalions. Leopold was unimpressed, having checked with the Russians that the story was untrue.[3] Apparently Boncompagni was not informed of this move by Cavour, but, after reminding Turin that he still had no orders what to do in an emergency, the Piedmontese ambassador at last received the positive instructions which he had requested a month earlier. He was now told that, when war began, he should formally ask Leopold for an alliance.[4] If repulsed, he should try to terrify the grand duke into leaving the country. Failing success in that, he should still not promote anything so dangerous as a revolution by the local Italian patriots, but as a last resort should incite the army to a pronunciamento, after which

[1] Provenzali's report from Turin to Lenzoni, 30 Mar., Archivio di Stato (Florence), Sardegna no. 60; but Boncompagni was already trying to discourage recruitment (*Pasqua di Liberazione, Raccolta di Documenti . . . sul 27 Aprile 1859*, ed. V. Soldani (Florence, 1909), p. 55).

[2] *Epistolario di Farini*, IV. 247; Bardesono (Cavour's secretary), edited by E. Masi in *Fra Libri e Ricordi di Storia della Rivoluzione Italiana* (Bologna, 1887), pp. 113–14; *Carteggio Castelli*, I. 188.

[3] Canofari's dispatch from Turin to Naples and Provenzali's to Florence were both published by Bianchi, 'Il Conte Camillo di Cavour: Documenti Editi e Inediti', *Rivista Contemporanea* (Turin), Apr. 1863, pp. 29–30; the denial by Russia is in Bianchi, *Storia Documentata*, VIII. 87.

[4] An alliance, of course, would have excluded any chance of Piedmont annexing Tuscany; Chiala, perhaps for this reason, is sure that Cavour had no wish for an alliance (*Lettere di Cavour*, III. clxvi). Camerani similarly thinks that Cavour felt safe in offering an alliance because he was quite certain that Leopold would never accept (*Archivio Storico Italiano*, 1945–6, pp. 155–9); but it is hard to explain, if so, what there was to gain in allowing Boncompagni to go on trying for an alliance until the last moment (Bianchi, *Storia Documentata*, VIII. 84, 90–1). Napoleon certainly would have liked Leopold to join the Franco-Piedmontese side, and to secure this was ready to guarantee the grand duke's throne (*Cavour-Nigra*, II. 172); Nerli from Paris, 26 Apr., *Rivista Contemporanea*, Apr. 1863, p. 29; an alliance would, equally, have been good politics for Cavour, quite apart from the fact that he was still allowing France to dictate policy.

he would intervene to proclaim the dictatorship of Victor Emanuel. Cavour now realized that it might prove wrong to have taken so many volunteers from Tuscany where they might have exerted a useful pressure at this critical stage.[1] Boncompagni, who had reported that efforts to win over the army were proving ineffective, was now instructed to be more deceitful and give the army officers a private reassurance that there was not the least intention of promoting a pronunciamento or undermining their loyalty to the grand-ducal throne.

Some historians still argue that, whatever may be true of the aristocratic liberals in Florence, Cavour had designed an insurrection against Leopold, even down to details, and indeed that a fortnight earlier he had ordered the National Society to put a long-prepared plan into action. But Cavour did not want a real insurrection in Tuscany; he would certainly have liked to avoid the dangerous *moto in piazza* of 27 April, and his note of a fortnight earlier made this quite clear. Not only had Napoleon insisted on Cavour keeping the Tuscan movement within legal and constitutional bounds, but the National Society had shown itself to be too disorganized, too small and unpractical to make a reliable instrument of revolt. If there did exist any plan, it was not carried out, and members of the society acted in ways which showed that there was still no effective central direction from Turin. Cavour was not sure until 21 April that the war would even start. Certainly he hoped that, if hostilities began, there would be sympathetic movements elsewhere in Italy; but any independent rising by the party of action was to be rigorously avoided, while his own preparations for a revolt were in practice confined to a modest operation in the Modenese districts of Massa and Carrara adjoining the Piedmontese frontier.

On 24 April, Boncompagni followed instructions and again asked Leopold for an alliance after giving his word that Piedmont had no intention of violating Tuscan sovereignty.[2] Meanwhile, at Turin, Mezzacapo was told to enlist volunteers from the Papal States, and Ulloa had to hold himself ready to reorganize the Tuscan army in the event of joint action. Cavour further informed Paris that he had sent agents to Tuscany to prepare a movement in support of the war,[3] but we know nothing that these anonymous people can have done, and probably his communication was merely a ruse to help frustrate any eleventh-hour attempt by the French to stop the fighting. From La Farina, who would surely have publicized any official call by Cavour to revolt, there came only the news that the National Society no longer existed.[4] Not until late on the 26th did Malenchini arrive with orders to support the radicals, and this must have been a last-minute change of plan by Cavour, for Malenchini had been unexpectedly diverted to Florence when on his way to join

---

[1] Manzone, *Il Risorgimento Italiano*, 1909, pp. 215–16; Camerani, *Archivio Storico Italiano*, 1945–6, p. 167; *Lettere di Cavour*, VI. 384.

[2] *Cronaca degli Avvenimenti d'Italia nel 1859*, ed. A. Zobi (Florence, 1859), I. 393, 395.

[3] *Il Principe Napoleone nel Risorgimento Italiano*, ed. A. Comandini (Milan, 1922), p. 118.

[4] Camerani, *Archivio Storico Italiano*, 1945–6, p. 177; Masi, *Fra Libri e Ricordi*, p. 118.

Garibaldi. Cavour probably took this decision when he heard from Crespi that the party of action had the upper hand in Florence and it was too late to resist it. Malenchini's orders were that Cavour urgently wanted the various parties to settle their differences and win over the army; but, as can be seen from Boncompagni's conduct the next day, Malenchini must also have brought confirmation of the belief that an alliance with the grand duke would still be welcome.

On the 27th there took place the huge popular demonstration which Rubieri and Dolfi had arranged and which the leading aristocrats still refused to countenance. Boncompagni's role that day was mainly to provide an extra-territorial residence where revolutionaries could meet with Ridolfi and Peruzzi to see if they could find a compromise policy.[1] At one point Boncompagni intervened decisively against Rubieri and Malenchini in an attempt to keep Leopold on his throne, and certainly must have felt that such was Cavour's wish.[2] Only Leopold's obstinacy permitted the revolution to run its full course.

The collapse of the dynasty was greeted with joy in the crowded streets, though, despite subsequent legend, it was far from welcome to Corsini, Ridolfi, Peruzzi, and those who now found themselves the leaders of free Tuscany. We may assume it was also not particularly welcome to Cavour, but he was seldom one to be caught entirely by surprise, and quickly adapted his plans to this new situation. General Ulloa was already waiting near Genoa to come to organize the Tuscan army, and was provided with funds from Cavour's secret service account. When news arrived of the grand duke's departure, the cabinet in Turin impetuously decided that Ulloa should proceed to Florence and if possible assume 'une espèce de dictature militaire'.[3] The French, when they heard of this, realized that it would be wrong to spoil the general appearance of spontaneity by thus imposing a dictator from outside, and an urgent telegram from Paris stopped Cavour's abrupt decision to confer full powers on such an entirely incompetent man.

Meanwhile, Boncompagni, improvising on his own initiative and despite his embarrassing position as ambassador to the grand-ducal court, assumed a

---

[1] Passerin d'Entrèves accepts that both Boncompagni and La Farina's National Society played a dominant role in the revolt as part of a master plan by Cavour to confront Napoleon with a convincing example of Italian patriotism (*Il Piemonte, l'Italia Centrale . . . nel 1859–60*, p. 55); but Cavour and La Farina had too many other things to think of, and were not closely enough in touch with events in Florence, while Boncompagni, perhaps wisely, merely tried to keep the options open until he could exert some influence as a mediator.

[2] Manzone, *Il Risorgimento Italiano*, 1909, p. 223; M. Carletti, *Quattro Mesi di Storia Toscana* (Florence, 1859), p. 22.

[3] Cabinet minute for 27 Apr., edited by Ernesto Artom in *L'Opera Politica del Senatore I. Artom nel Risorgimento Italiano* (Bologna, 1906), p. 246; 'L'Italie Libérée', ed. F. Masson, *Revue des Deux Mondes* (Paris), XCIII (1923), 570–1; Cavour's telegram to Boncompagni, and a note about funds for Ulloa, are in Archivio di Stato (Turin), Gabinetto Min. Interno 1848–60, cart. 29.

certain degree of power to make the change-over as easy as possible. It may even be that he prevented a last-minute change of mind by Leopold who tried to save the day for his son by abdicating at the last minute.[1] Boncompagni also helped to form a provisional government and threw his weight against the inclusion of Rubieri and the party of action. Peruzzi's election as head of government was decided inside the Piedmontese embassy. With a forbearance and good will that may have surprised the conservatives, Rubieri then secured pseudo-legitimacy for this election by obtaining public approval of such members of the Florentine municipal administration as could be induced to agree.[2]

Cavour soon knew that Ricasoli's friends, however fearful of absorption by Piedmont, were far more afraid of the radical Left,[3] and he learnt from Ricasoli that extra troops were badly needed to prevent further popular agitation.[4] On the 28th he agreed to send these soldiers on condition that Peruzzi formally asked for French and Piedmontese protection.[5] But Boncompagni, following previous instructions, had already persuaded Peruzzi to request that Victor Emanuel should act as dictator and not merely as protector of Tuscany: Peruzzi clearly explained to Turin that this dictatorship would be offered just for the duration of the war and on condition of preserving, or later restoring, local autonomy. Cavour in reply, changing his former policy in response to French wishes, would accept no more for the king than full powers over the Tuscan army; he further agreed to appoint Boncompagni as royal commissioner to exercise an undefined protectorship over Tuscany, allowing local self-government, and specifically stating that Tuscans would be left free to decide their own future when the war was over.

Cavour later admitted that it would have been better to accept the offer of dictatorial powers, and he blamed this mistake on Paris, as he later blamed Boncompagni for not disregarding the letter of his instructions and acting as a dictator.[6] If a mistake was made, part of the explanation is that Cavour was trying to run five ministries himself, so that he had little enough time for these unexpected developments so far away from Turin. His first principle had to be that he could not afford to antagonize Napoleon who wanted a conservative

---

[1] G. Cecconi, *Il 27 Aprile* (Florence, 1892), p. 54; Boncompagni says that, after securing the army's consent, he intervened to prevent a printer publishing Leopold's final protest (Manzone, *Il Risorgimento Italiano*, 1909, p. 224); a few hours earlier he was playing whist with the grand duke's family, according to Provenzali's diary, ed. C. Pellegrini, *Nuova Antologia*, Sept. 1968, p. 32.

[2] After some difficulty, Rubieri got the consent of one-third of the council members (*I Casi della Toscana nel 1859 e 1860* (Florence 1864), p. 84).

[3] Peruzzi, quoted in Lilla Lipparini, *Minghetti* (Bologna, 1942), I. 299.

[4] Ricasoli had warned Turin on 18 April that Piedmontese troops might be needed in an emergency (*Carteggi Ricasoli*, VI. 266); his notes of a meeting with Cavour on 28 April were published by Jarro (G. Piccini), *Vita di Ubaldino Peruzzi* (Florence, 1891), p. 108.

[5] Cabinet minute quoted in Artom, *Opera Politica del Artom*, p. 247.

[6] *Epistolario di Farini*, IV. 253; that it was a mistake was agreed by Pallavicino, *Memorie di Giorgio Pallavicino* (Turin, 1895), III. 520; by Cavour, *Cavour-Nigra*, II. 215; and by the king, *Le Relazione Diplomatiche fra la Francia e il Granducato di Toscana*, ed. A. Saitto (Rome, 1959), III. 186.

policy in Tuscany; nor would he wish to add to his other troubles a gratuitous fight with the Tuscan aristocrats who firmly believed in local autonomy. Peruzzi tried to persuade him that the revolution of 27 April had been the work not of the liberals but of dangerous radicals who were far from reconciled to Piedmontese policy; to defeat them he would need to back their strongest opponents—in other words, the autonomists who wanted Florence a capital city with its own separate court life. Cavour can at first have been in little doubt about this alliance, for he still had few ambitions on the Tuscan side of the Apennines; Modena, Bologna, and Ancona were rather the places which he was anxious to annex.[1] The usefulness to him of Tuscany was, first, for its moral support, secondly, for its army, which he badly needed in Lombardy, and, thirdly, as a base from which General Mezzacapo could prepare another 'spontaneous' movement in the papal Romagna.

It is almost certain that Cavour, had he planned to annex Tuscany instead of letting policy wait on events, would have chosen more decisive men than Ulloa and Boncompagni, and would have briefed them better about Piedmontese intentions; moreover, he would hardly have waited until war was beginning before he appointed Marco Minghetti, an outsider from central Italy, as chief secretary at the Turin foreign office; nor, if he could have foreseen these events, would he have left it till May to set up Luigi Carlo Farini in a new department dealing with 'annexed and protected' provinces. The likelihood is that the Florentine revolution was largely unexpected by him, and hence that the events of 27 April reinforced his natural liking for an empirical policy with few fixed points or precise expectations. This would help to explain why his emergency decision to assume dictatorial powers was subsequently changed, and later changed back again.

Early in May, Boncompagni did try to obey Cavour's changed orders and recover greater authority, but he could not find a single person in Florence who combined being acceptable to Piedmont with a willingness to co-operate in what must now have seemed to other Tuscans as a threat to self-government and local autonomy. Capponi, Matteucci, Galeotti, Corsini, and Peruzzi were all working actively to secure Tuscany's right to remain autonomous. Perhaps, if the National Society had been as important as is usually said, the royal commissioner might have found enough support from the *lafariniani*, but they had produced not a single leader of real stature, and in general were still treated by the aristocracy and by Boncompagni as of little account. As for the real radicals, those who it was now admitted had done most to bring about the revolution,[2] their brief grasp of power had at all costs to be loosened, especially since their talk of a much larger Italy resembled Mazzini's doctrine of national

---

[1] *Epistolario di Farini*, IV. 260–1.

[2] Ferrière reported that the *parti unitaire* was very weak in Florence, and that Cavour's best allies there should have been, paradoxically, the old republicans (*Relazioni fra Francia e Toscana*, ed. Saitta, III. 153–4).

unity. As Cavour reassured the French minister, 'la cause de l'indépendance de l'Italie ne pourrait qu'être compromise par le concours du parti dema-gogique'. 'Son langage, à cet égard', reported the minister, 'a été des plus explicites.'[1] Failing to obtain respectable local support for a non-political administration under his own control, Boncompagni on 11 May had to change direction and fall back on what Ricasoli termed 'the usual people', in other words, on an autonomous government led by Ricasoli, Ridolfi, and Salvagnoli.

Not a single one of the leading names in Tuscany yet subscribed to any policy of fusion with Piedmont. Nor, probably, did Cavour himself. He knew that he had, if possible, to avoid repeating the mistake of 1848, when so many Italian patriots had been alienated by the fear of Piedmontese ambition; nor should he antagonize too early those who wanted a federal solution for the Italian problem. The Tuscan autonomists were, as Cavour himself admitted, the most widely admired Italians in Europe. Also their roots were deep. 'Tuscany is small', wrote Galeotti, 'but it is all we have': the common cause of Italian patriotism would merely be undermined if Piedmont were to treat this province as annexed and subordinate territory.[2]

So Ricasoli's government now received Cavour's renewed promise that Tuscan autonomy would be respected. Moreover, two official representatives from Florence, Marquis Corsini and Count Cambray-Digny, were individually reassured on this head by Minghetti, Farini, and also by Napoleon III himself. The bait was even held out that an independent Tuscany, possibly under a relative of Victor Emanuel, might be expanded after the war to include Modena, Umbria, and the Marches.[3]

At first Cavour must have thought this a minor matter. From his point of view, an infinitely more serious problem was to hasten the arrival of Tuscan soldiers to help in the war. These soldiers were urgently needed, though the delay in sending them was more his own fault than he would acknowledge, for he had deliberately retained for himself and Victor Emanuel full powers over the Tuscan army: General Ulloa, the military commander, was Cavour's personal choice and had been imposed on the Tuscan army without consulta-tion; General Mezzacapo was also appointed by Turin to a separate military command in Florence, so incidentally causing much confusion, and another Piedmontese officer was sent to become military governor of the strategically

---

[1] La Tour d'Auvergne, 5 May, M. Aff. Étrangères.

[2] *Azeglio-Galeotti*, p. 136; *Cavour-Nigra*, II. 197; *Lettere di Gino Capponi e di Altri a Lui*, ed. A. Carraresi (Florence, 1899), III. 239. Poggi, a ministerial colleague of Ricasoli's, recalls a 'tacit agreement between the various parties that Tuscany would not be joined to Piedmont' (E. Poggi, *Memorie Storiche del Governo della Toscana nel 1859–60* (Pisa, 1867), I. 67).

[3] *Rassegna Storica Toscana* (Florence), 1958, p. 44; Poggi, *Memorie Storiche*, III. 14; *Carteggio politico di L.G. de Cambray-Digny (Aprile-Novembre 1859)*, ed. G. Baccini (Milan, 1913), p. 34. The idea of an enlarged Tuscany was quite widespread: Cavour had toyed with it favourably at Plombières; so had Salvagnoli (Bianchi, *Storia Documentata*, VIII. 15–16), Corsi (*Nuova Antologia*, June 1933, p. 330), and Guerrazzi (Agostino Savelli, *Leonardo Romanelli e la Toscana del suo Tempo* (Florence, 1941), p. 409); so at various times did Ridolfi and Peruzzi.

vital port town of Leghorn. Peruzzi and Ricasoli repeatedly and urgently begged Cavour to send yet another experienced Piedmontese soldier to act as minister of war in Florence, but there was a month's unaccountable delay before he arrived, and in the meantime no one in the Tuscan government understood enough about military matters to give orders which made much sense.

To this extent Piedmont was responsible for the disorganization in this vital field. It is equally true, however, that Ricasoli delayed the dispatch of troops by putting preservation of domestic order above fighting against Austria. He feared to introduce mass conscription or increase recruitment above the normal 2,000 a year out of a population of nearly 2 million, since army service was highly unpopular even for this war of national liberation, and there was a fear that the grand duke's supporters would stage a counter-revolution if the war went badly.[1] Ricasoli therefore thought it unwise to arm the peasants, and he had to recognize that middle- and upper-class citizens regarded it as their traditional right to buy themselves out of military service. Even a civic guard would be too dangerous to permit, because it would give too much power to ordinary townsmen. On the other hand, he not only insisted on appointing many more policemen than had been required by the former government of the authoritarian Leopold, but he thought it prudent in the interests of security to raise police pay above that of comparable rank in the army. It was also ordered that punishments for offences against property had to be especially severe and publicly administered.[2] All this showed a certain mistrust of the revolution and a less than single-minded enthusiasm for the war. Not until 25 May, four weeks after the revolution, did Ricasoli decide to declare war on Austria—the declaration contained an unfortunate reference to Cavour having 'initiated hostilities', which caused some embarrassment in Turin where the accepted story was one of Austrian aggressiveness against peace-loving Piedmont.

Ricasoli's unwillingness to recruit enough Tuscans was aggravated in Piedmontese eyes by his reiterated demand for 2,000 troops from Turin to help him keep order. Cavour, though at first he agreed to send this force, had to back down as soon as serious fighting began and he discovered what modern war meant in practice. But without troops, warned Galeotti and Lambruschini, the reds and blacks would create havoc in Tuscany. 'Cavour understands nothing of the situation', complained an indignant Ricasoli.[3]

It was also resented at Florence that the Piedmontese declined to receive an official Tuscan embassy. Cavour had not in fact fully appreciated that, by

---

[1] F. Martini, *Confessioni e Ricordi 1859–1892* (Milan, 1929), II. 6–8; Peruzzi in May, Lipparini, *Minghetti*, I. 299.

[2] *Atti e Documenti Editi e Inediti del Governo della Toscana dal 27 Aprile in poi* (Florence, 1860), I. 123, 129, 133; when a militia was finally set up, after the war was over, all those in receipt of daily wages were excluded as too dangerous (23 July, ibid. 361).

[3] *Carteggi Ricasoli*, VIII. 44, 85.

refusing Tuscany's offer of dictatorship, he had permitted or even encouraged the setting up of a largely independent administration with its own foreign office and diplomatic representatives. When told by Boncompagni that Salvagnoli was coming to Turin as an official representative, he refused in blunt terms to accept him as such.[1] So Salvagnoli decided to stop instead at Alessandria, an intermediate railway station on the way to Turin, the place where Victor Emanuel and Napoleon had their headquarters. This was an unexpected misfortune for Cavour, who had told the king almost nothing about the revolution in Florence; for Victor Emanuel, who did not know Cavour's policy, was ill-equipped to argue against Salvagnoli's suggestion that he send French soldiers to Tuscany if Piedmont had none available. Cavour had intended to subordinate Florence to Turin, but here was Turin having to follow Florence. Documents have recently been published which show that Salvagnoli, in requesting French soldiers, was speaking officially for Ricasoli, and almost certainly it was with Boncompagni's approval. Bringing French troops to Tuscany was no new idea, but had long since been suggested to Turin by Salvagnoli, and the possibility had been readily admitted by Cavour when Ricasoli saw him on 28 April. The Tuscans could not be expected to know that Cavour's views had changed in the interim; nor had they any reason to think that Piedmontese policy, which desperately required French troops in Lombardy, might object to them further south.[2]

On 17 May it was decided at Alessandria that Prince Napoleon would lead a French force to Tuscany, and this fact gave rise to the story that the emperor aimed to place his cousin on the Tuscan throne. In view of later events it is unlikely. Military considerations had already compelled the French to think of sending troops to create a diversion in Tuscany on the Austrian flank.[3] If Napoleon also had a political motive, more likely it was that he guessed—from the king's inability to tell him about Cavour's policy—that Piedmont might herself have secret ambitions in central Italy.[4] French interests were against making Piedmont too large, and Cavour knew it: to permit annexation of Tuscany by Cavour was no part of Napoleon's plan, and indeed it would have seemed a breach of the Plombières agreement; nor were the French eager to see revolution spreading through the Papal States. Prince Napoleon's force would be an insurance against this, at the same time as it would help to

---

[1] Massari, *Diario*, pp. 237, 240–1.

[2] Ricasoli's letter of 21 May to Salvagnoli (*Carteggi Ricasoli*, VIII. 85) shows that the latter's request must have been previously concerted in Florence; the contrary view was maintained by Aurelio Gotti, *Vita del Barone Bettino Ricasoli* (Florence, 1894), p. 280, by D. Guccerelli and E. Sestini, *Bettino Ricasoli, i suoi Tempi, la sua Opera* (Florence, 1950), pp. 84–5, and by Della Torre, *Evoluzione del Sentimento Nazionale*, p. 113.

[3] *Principe Napoleone*, ed. Comandini, p. 120; this was common knowledge at Florence (*I Toscani del '59*, ed. Ciampini, p. 90).

[4] Cavour's preparations to invade the Papal States are shown by several notes of 2 May to General Mezzacapo (Ugo Pesci, *Il Generale Carlo Mezzacapo e il suo Tempo* (Bologna, 1908), pp. 61–3).

organize military provision in Tuscany and stop the kind of socialist or Mazzinian movement which was the emperor's private nightmare.[1]

Military considerations are probably enough to explain why Napoleon, after
consulting the king and the prince, decided to send not 2,000 but 10,000
troops: to deceive the Austrians, he even called it a full army corps.[2] The fact
that he could decide this within a few hours of Salvagnoli's arrival suggests
that it was premeditated and that Ricasoli's request for help was merely a
pretext for what had already been decided. The emperor must have guessed
that Cavour would be annoyed, for Prince Napoleon received his orders
twenty-four hours before Turin was so much as informed. Cavour would not
want his French ally calling the political tune in central Italy, especially as
this was exactly what Mazzini had prophesied would follow from Piedmontese
subservience to the emperor. Quite likely Cavour had deliberately not co-
ordinated his Tuscan policy with the French, hoping that they would be too
preoccupied with the war to notice how he proceeded with his secret ambitions
in central Italy. More likely still, he had no time to devise any policy: at all
events, if a credible policy did exist he had concealed it not only from the
French, but from the king and Ricasoli. Whichever explanation is true, he had
allowed the initiative to be taken out of his hands.

Only late on 18 May did Salvagnoli reach Turin and inform Cavour about
Prince Napoleon's expedition. Presumably he also brought the information
that the emperor had spoken of a possible long-term solution which preserved
an independent and enlarged Tuscany under a new and probably non-French
dynasty.[3] Cavour's public anger over this news may well have been wholly or
partly feigned, for he quickly saw some possible advantage to be gained from
it.[4] The next day he hastened to Alessandria to discovered the emperor's views
at first hand. He told others he was hoping to stop the expedition, but more
likely he was merely determined not to let the political future of Tuscany go
by default. From Alessandria he travelled to Genoa to see Prince Napoleon,
who, friendly as ever to Piedmont, had already sent to advise Cavour to use

[1] *Principe Napoleone*, ed. Comandini, p. 126; the prince's subsequent report on his mission was
published in *La Nazione* (Florence), 19 July 1859, p. 1. Massari as early as 19 May thought that
Napoleon must have had antecedent plans to send troops to Tuscany, and noted the interesting
point that Salvagnoli was not expecting Cavour to be annoyed (*Diario*, p. 245).

[2] It is still quite generally assumed that an army corps was sent, though in fact the greater part of
the Fifth Corps remained in Lombardy; with equal implausibility it is also still asserted, in explanation of Cavour's anger, that Salvagnoli *persuaded* the French to send such a large force (Passerin
d'Entrèves, *Il Piemonte, l'Italia Centrale . . . nel 1859–60*, p. 59; S. Camerani, 'Il Principe
Napoleone e la Toscana', *Miscellanea in Onore di Roberto Cessi* (Rome, 1958), III. 336–8).

[3] *Il Risorgimento Italiano*, 1925, p. 658; the telegram quoted here is not included with Salvagnoli's
three letters of this week to Ricasoli in *Carteggi Ricasoli*, VIII. 69–70.

[4] Cavour's exchange of telegrams with Lamarmora on 18 May, indicating that there were no dis-
advantages and some positive advantages in this new development, is in *La Guerra del 1859:
Documenti*, ed. Corpo Stato Maggiore (Rome, 1910), II. 25; according to Massari's diary, this was
after Cavour had shown his displeasure to Salvagnoli. He had good reasons for wanting to bully
Salvagnoli, and certainly would not have wanted to tell him, as he told Lamarmora, that Prince
Napoleon's expedition could be welcomed as hastening plans for a revolution in the Romagna.

the emperor's change of plan as a pretext for demanding outright annexation of the grand duchy.[1] Returning to Alessandria, the prime minister was able to obtain an undertaking that France had no political ambitions in central Italy. It is always assumed that he also persuaded the emperor that only by allowing Piedmont to push her alternative claims would the rest of Europe be reconciled to the existence of French troops in Tuscany. Almost certainly, however, this clever suggestion by Prince Napoleon was accepted by the emperor merely as a ruse to deceive the diplomats, for there is no reliable indication that he entertained the possibility of actual Piedmontese annexation.[2] Cavour seized on the fact that French troops in Tuscany would mean strong British counter-support for Piedmont as an alternative claimant. So he now told Boncompagni to change direction and prepare the ground secretly for 'fusion', while not showing too much regard for anyone who might think this improper or unwise.[3] The French foreign office was privately reassured that, since there were not many 'fusionists' in Tuscany, no one could possibly assume that Piedmont meant to annex Tuscany; if facts ever appeared to suggest the contrary, they were to be considered merely a blind to allay any fears about French intentions.[4]

Nigra and Cipriani were at once sent to support Boncompagni in working for Piedmontese annexation, and this was certainly no blind but serious evidence of intent. The sudden vision of new possibilities was such that, in the excitement of the moment, Cavour sent secret and vastly over-optimistic orders for an uprising to begin all through Lombardy and in the Papal States.[5] Meanwhile, in Piedmont, he tried to convince Salvagnoli and Corsini that, if avoidance of anarchy and sedation of revolution was their wish, these would

[1] *Cavour-Nigra*, II. 200.

[2] *Principe Napoleone*, ed. Comandini, p. 131; 25 May, Ernest d'Hauterive, *Napoléon III et le Prince Napoléon* (Paris, 1925), pp. 171–2, a dispatch which was not printed by Comandini. The possibility that Cavour was in league with Prince Napoleon against the emperor would square with the fact that Cavour told Salmour not to discuss Piedmont's Italian policy with Napoleon, but to see the prince instead (*Cavour-Salmour*, pp. 188–9).

[3] *Cavour-Nigra*, II. 202–3.

[4] La Tour d'Auvergne, 20 May, M. Aff. Étrangères; Massari thought that he still did not intend seriously to annex Tuscany, but just to sacrifice it at a peace conference for something better (*Diario*, pp. 248–9). The French foreign office did not recognize the authority exercised by Sardinia in Tuscany, wrote Cowley from Paris to Malmesbury, quoting Walewski (Further Correspondence Respecting the Affairs of Italy, *Parliamentary Papers* (London), XXXII (no. 2527, p. 25). Camerani rather assumes that Cavour's campaign for annexation arose out of a mistaken but sincere fear of Prince Napoleon's ambition, and does not consider the possibility that Cavour had arranged with the prince to use the latter's suspected ambition as a pretext for annexation by Piedmont ('L'Annessione in Toscana', p. 21 of offprint from *Atti del Convegno Tosco-Romagnolo Tenuto a Forlì e Rocca San Casciano l'11–12 Giugno 1960*); Camerani's view that Prince Napoleon had no serious ambitions in Tuscany is now broadly accepted, though not entirely by Carlo Pischedda, 'Il '59 Toscano', *Rivista Storica Italiana* (Naples), LXXII (1960), 74.

[5] Pallavicino, *Memorie*, III. 520; Boncompagni, quoted in Lipparini, *Minghetti*, I. 149; Cipriani was hardly a good choice of agent, for on 29 July he was telling Walewski that he would do anything to help France if French interests demanded the return of Leopold to Tuscany (M. Aff. Étrangères).

best be gained by temporarily surrendering their now anachronistic Tuscan autonomy. Fear of the Left, the same fear which had made these moderates try to save the grand duke until 27 April, now pushed them closer to Piedmont; and, to gild the pill, they were allowed to go on thinking that, after the war, Tuscany might regain her independence under a prince of Savoy, even perhaps with more territory than before.[1]

At Florence, however, the moderates were quickly disillusioned when they found Nigra apparently plotting with the very 'reds' against whom they sought protection. When Nigra did not accept Ricasoli's invitation to come and explain his mysterious visit, it could only seem that this was on Cavour's orders—in other words, that the Piedmontese were using Nigra and Prince Napoleon to by-pass the burgraves and undermine Ricasoli's government. When the prince openly spoke at Leghorn in favour of Piedmontese annexation, Cavour's excuse about French ambitions could be seen as a mere cover, and suspicion of Piedmontese 'aggrandizement mania' was thereby increased, while Nigra's furtive activity antagonized 'toutes les notabilités aristocratiques, scientifiques, littéraires et politiques du pays et le sentiment général'.[2] Boncompagni quickly warned the king that Nigra's annexation propaganda was having this unfortunate effect; Victor Emanuel thereupon informed the emperor, who sharply told his cousin to obey orders and leave such political questions till the war was won. The king, too, evidently without consulting Cavour, informed Florence that the annexation campaign was mistaken and must cease. Nigra beat a hasty retreat.[3]

Cavour was evidently caught unawares by this reaction; he had quite underestimated the feelings of *toscanità* which lay behind Salvagnoli's mission and Nigra's fiasco. When he changed his policy and advocated 'fusion' and 'annexation', possibly this may have pleased his friends at Turin, but it was poor tactics with Tuscans who resented being bossed and who (said Ridolfi's secretary) 'by tradition and language think themselves more Italian than other Italians'. *The Times*'s correspondent noted irritation at the idea of ultra-civilized Tuscany being annexed to semi-barbarian Piedmont. One contributory mistake, said Galeotti, was that Cavour had too easily accepted La Farina's self-justificatory propaganda about the strength of the National Society in Tuscany and its campaign for Italian patriotism. Ridolfi rather believed that it was the same mistake as Piedmont made in 1848, namely, to

---

[1] Poggi, *Memorie Storiche*, III. 17, 19; *Carteggio Politico di Cambray-Digny*, pp. 45–6.

[2] Ferrière, 24 May, *Relazioni fra Francia e Toscana*, ed. Saitta, III. 158; 'aggrandizement mania' was Cambray-Digny's phrase, *Carteggio Politico*, p. 48.

[3] Minghetti's note after a foreign office meeting is in 'Un'Agenda di Marco Minghetti (26 Maggio–11 Giugno 1859)', ed. U. Marcelli, *Convivium* (Turin), July 1959, p. 460; *Carteggio del Conte Senatore L. G. de Cambray-Digny e della Contessa Virginia*, ed. G. Baccini (Florence, 1910), pp. 31–3; M. Tabarrini, *Diario 1859–1860*, ed. A. Panella (Florence, 1959), p. 42; Boncompagni tactfully tried to retrieve the situation by telling Tuscans that the idea of annexing Tuscany to Piedmont came not from Cavour, but from Prince Napoleon (dispatch to Cavour, *Cavour-Nigra* II. 211).

set up gratuitous antagonism by trying to swallow Tuscany as a snake swallows a frog. Corsi thought much the same. So did Peruzzi, who pointed out the damage done by Piedmont going back on her pledged word to allow Tuscany to decide her own future after the war. Others, so Prince Napoleon explained, were particularly alarmed to find that the main supporters of annexation were their *bêtes noires* on the Left, 'la canaille (c'est à dire les patriotes)'; and there was even a reaction towards considering surrender to France or Leopold as a possible refuge. The only convinced 'fusionists' in Tuscany, said another observer, were Ricasoli and Bartolommei, and even they were now wavering.[1]

Ricasoli's belief in *un'Italia forte* was known and appreciated in Turin; but unfortunately he was one of the people Cavour could not abide, and this mutual dislike must be the explanation of why these two men repeatedly seemed to be going out of their way to thwart each other. The 'iron baron' lacked finesse as much as he lacked subservience. He had strong views. He had presumed to disagree with Cavour over several issues in February and March. Now he condemned as a 'massive error' Cavour's devious decision to campaign through Nigra for annexation, as it merely weakened what had been a growing enthusiasm in Florence for the Italian cause. He concluded that Cavour would be wise to speak more of 'Italy' and less of 'Piedmont'; the demand for annexation had been 'a far worse example of municipalism than they can ever find to criticize in Tuscany', and it demonstrated Cavour's 'great lack of political sense'. Ricasoli probably intended that these wounding phrases should be seen by the king. On 27 May he put out a public statement that Tuscan policy still remained true to the original agreement with Piedmont, which postponed all political matters until the war was over.[2]

Cavour must have been annoyed to discover that the king had overruled him and taken Ricasoli's part, but, as always, at once accepted the inevitable. He confessed that the Tuscan question was unexpectedly proving the most intricate question raised by the war.[3] Worst of all was that the French had been alerted by Nigra's mission to Cavour's wish for more territorial acquisitions than had been stipulated either at Plombières or in the secret treaty of January 1859. Napoleon had promised the British that it would not be a revolutionary war, yet now he found the Piedmontese belying his words and encouraging revolution for purposes of aggrandizement. In central Italy they had incorporated Massa and Carrara and were trying to annex the Lunigiana. In the Garfagnana they were already refusing petitions for local autonomy. The annexation of Lombardy and Modena was just about to be proclaimed, and

[1] *Carteggio Politico di Cambray-Digny*, pp. 27–8, 36–7; Peruzzi, quoted in A. Salvestrini, *I Moderati Toscani e la Classe Dirigente Italiana* (Florence, 1965), pp. 39–43; Vieusseux, in Arturo Linaker, *La Vita e i Tempi di Enrico Mayer, con Documenti Inediti* (Florence, 1898), I. 270–1; Galeotti, in *I Toscani del '59*, ed. Ciampini, pp. 89–90; Prince Napoleon, in *Cavour-Nigra*, II. 210.
[2] Eugenio Albèri, *La Politica Napoleonica e Quella del Governo Toscano* (Paris, 1859), p. 8; *Carteggi Ricasoli*, VIII. 103–4, 137–8, 232.
[3] Manzone, *Il Risorgimento Italiano*, 1909, p. 226.

there was clearly some idea of taking part or most of the Papal States.[1] But Napoleon, on whom the main burden of the war had fallen, cannot have been pleased to find Cavour secretly playing at revolutionary politics instead of giving France anything like the help he had promised; certainly this fact was not unimportant in preparing the French decision to back out of the war and leave him isolated.[2]

The Piedmontese meanwhile had the sorrow of realizing that their brief annexation campaign had probably been unnecessary as well as inopportune, for Tuscany 'lacked the elements needed for a separate existence', and the pro-autonomy burgraves were obviously a small minority. Much more urgent than these untimely schemes of political union was how to obtain immediate Tuscan help against Austria; and such help was, for some incomprehensible reason, simply not forthcoming. Ulloa's volunteer division was looked upon suspiciously by some people in Tuscany as a potential political danger from the Left, and Ricasoli would not even recall reservists for fear of provoking opposition from public opinion: these were two reasons why the grand duke's army (which had been only about 13,000) could not now be substantially enlarged. Cavour asked for 15,000 effectives; Ulloa said he could possibly produce 12,000; and Boncompagni, supporting Ulloa, agreed that no more could be found without large-scale conscription, which would mean using force and so prejudicing the fortunes of the revolution. Prince Napoleon, who was the senior military commander in Florence, thought on the other hand that 35,000 men should and could have been quickly sent to the front: he told Cavour that Tuscany was making no serious preparations at all for the war, but was simply hoping that France and Piedmont would do all the fighting that was needed.[3]

Cavour reacted scathingly. If Tuscany could have sent even 15,000 men, the moral effect in Europe would have been so great that he was still ready to divert 3,000 Piedmontese troops to keep order at Florence. But if the Tuscans rejected annexation and sent no help, he would not provide a single policeman. Since they had preferred to invite French soldiers, let them ask France. He was sarcastic over their lack of military ardour. He spoke harshly of his own nominee, Ulloa, and not too well of his chief ally there, Prince Napoleon. Even more he blamed Boncompagni, who had first favoured annexation without guessing that this was against Cavour's wishes, then opposed it only to find that Cavour was now favourable, and was about to change his mind

[1] *Epistolario di Farini*, IV. 264; Walewski, 26 May, 4 and 8 June, M. Aff. Étrangères; Ferrière's reports from Florence, *Relazioni fra Francia e Toscana*, ed. Saitta, III. 163-4, 173; Minghetti's notes, *Convivium*, July 1959, pp. 461, 465, 467. Minghetti, secretary-general of the Turin foreign office, still insisted that Piedmont did not want to annex Tuscany, only the Romagna.

[2] *Lettere di Cavour*, III. ccxxxviii; in another version, Massari, *Diario*, p. 301.

[3] G. Ulloa, *Observations sur l'Ouvrage 'Campagne de l'Empereur Napoléon III en Italie'* (Paris, 1865), pp. 11–16; *Cavour-Nigra*, II. 209–10; *La Guerra del 1859: Documenti*, II. 43; General Niccolò Giorgetti, *Le Armi Toscane e le Occupazioni Straniere in Toscana (1537–1860)* (Città di Castello, 1916), III. 582–91.

once more just when Cavour was changing his back again. Cavour belatedly decided that Boncompagni ought to have disregarded formal orders and set up a *de facto* dictatorship. Cavour was an exacting taskmaster.

Ricasoli and his colleagues, unaware of these problems, were full of pride over their achievement. They were delighted when Cavour gave up his campaign for annexation, for this would attract Tuscans to a much more confident support of the Italian cause. They now realized, moreover, that active support for the war was needed for selfish reasons, because the French victory at Magenta on 4 June and the capture of Milan warned them that they might arrive too late to claim any credit for their help. The emperor's proclamation from Milan on 8 June was addressed to 'Italians' (whereas Victor Emanuel's on 9 June made the mistake of being just to 'Lombards'), and this was inaccurately interpreted to mean a significant change in French policy. As Austrian rule in central Italy crumbled, allowing Parma and Modena to be liberated, there was mounting patriotic enthusiasm at Florence; and enthusiasm apart, if any Italian nation was really going to be made, even if reaching no further south than Ancona, *Toscanina* would have to join it or else be left impotent against revolution or reaction.

Among those Tuscans who responded readily to this message were Dolfi and the democrats who had long since learnt from Mazzini to believe in a united Italy. After Peruzzi on 27 April had refused to share office with them, these radicals had remained politically in the background; now some people thought their mood more dangerous than in April as they reacted against this feeble behaviour by the moderates. The French minister in Florence described how Dolfi, 'le président de la société de secours mutuels des boulangers', was now the Ciceruacchio of Florence and in a position to terrify the moderates by threatening 'la vengeance des clubs';[1] and Ricasoli well knew the danger of letting these Jacobins keep a monopoly of the unitarist faith. As the French troops in Tuscany were now moving northwards into Lombardy, Florence was left unarmed; there was a sudden fear of social unrest, of patriotic demonstrations by the mob, a fear of the *rossi* who had already defeated the *onesti* on that memorable 27 April and might do so again.[2] The middle-aged men in power at Florence were afraid of being displaced by a younger, more radical generation of Italian patriots if they did not emerge from their lethargic irresolution and modify their autonomism to fit the quick march of events.[3]

---

[1] *Le Relazioni fra Francia e Toscana*, ed. Saitta, III. 178.

[2] Salvagnoli, 20 June, *Il Risorgimento Italiano*, 1925, p. 659; Corsini, 16 June, *Carteggio Politico di Cambray-Digny*, p. 76; Cambray-Digny, quoted by Massari, *Diario* (17 June), p. 273; Salvagnoli, 16 June, *L'Unità d'Italia nel Pensiero e nell'Azione del Barone Bettino Ricasoli*, ed. M. Puccioni (Florence, 1932), p. 71.

[3] This age-differential was raised by the *Times* correspondent on 30 May (issue of 6 June), when tilting against the 'arcadian doctrinaires of the Georgofili society' who monopolized government under Ricasoli.

Parallel to this was a fear that Leghorn, Siena, Lucca, and Pisa, by tradition impatient of Florentine hegemony, might get ahead of the regional capital in declaring for Italy, and indeed might see this as a way of depreciating Florence. The Leghorn municipality was in fact quick to pass a vote for Italy on 10 June by nine votes to six, whereas Florence could not be persuaded to follow suit until six weeks later.[1]

Ricasoli was a fervent unitarist after the battle of Magenta, seeing how Tuscany could help to pave the way to a new state of Italy and so avoid the indignity of Piedmontese annexation.[2] When he discovered that there was an address of loyalty in circulation which prophetically hailed Victor Emanuel as king of Italy, he and Salvagnoli boldly signed it, and on 8 June asked the other ministers in Florence to sign too. He must have known that this would meet opposition; Ridolfi and Enrico Poggi, the minister of justice, were in fact very hostile, and the French minister, by threatening to break off relations, forced the withdrawal of the address.[3] Four days later, however, Ricasoli persuaded the cabinet to approve a more noncommittal appeal to Italian patriotism after warning a reluctant Ridolfi that anything less might precipitate another *moto in piazza*.

Boncompagni informed Turin by telegram of this development. He himself signed the new appeal, though he felt guilty about acting in a hurry and without instructions. As he explained to Cavour, Tuscans must not be allowed to think Piedmont indifferent to the national idea; moreover, Ricasoli's proposal would be the one sure method of dishing the democrats who were now a real danger. Unfortunately, Cavour had just been seeing Napoleon in Milan and had been roundly told not to go on providing the rest of Europe with gratuitous evidence of Franco-Piedmontese intentions of aggrandizement. He therefore had to answer Boncompagni that he could not accept Ricasoli's patriotic proclamation of 12 June. Apart from French views against it, there was in any case a growing feeling in Turin that Tuscany, by virtue of Boncompagni's presence as royal commissioner, had a dependent status and must not take such autonomous initiatives on its own. There was resentment also at Ricasoli's back-door welcome for Mazzini's notion of a united Italy instead of 'fusion' with Piedmont; and it seemed particularly impertinent at a time when Ricasoli's government was still begging for Piedmontese money and soldiers.

It is ironic to find former autonomists furious with Cavour for this new veto on their appeal to Italian patriotism. Twice now he had refused what they had thought of as almost over-generous acts of self-sacrifice by Florence; and once he had shown his own preference for forcibly imposing annexation on

[1] *Archivio di Note Diplomatiche, Proclami, Manifesti, Circolari . . . Referibili all'Attuale Guerra contro l'Austria* (Milan, 1859), p. 232; Bartolommei's apology for not being able to persuade Florence to act earlier is in *La Nazione* of Florence, 20 July 1859.
[2] *Carteggi Ricasoli*, VIII. 186.
[3] Georges Bourgin, in *Bollettino Senese di Storia Patria* (Siena), LVIII (1953), 284–7; Poggi, *Memorie Storiche*, I. 81–99.

them by somewhat underhand means. They could resent all this, yet they had to admit that he now held most of the cards. A new kingdom of 12 million people was suddenly taking shape, and Tuscany, if she did not join, would be left behind as another insignificant Monaco. At last the burgraves of Florence were able to feel the true realities of the situation, to understand what was involved in the war, how it required from them, if they were not to be submerged, an active participation which would cost money, men, and the acceptance of discipline and sacrifice. Only the Piedmontese army could defend them against Austria in future; and they also feared that Tuscany might be financially unviable on her own.[1] Even Ridolfi and Capponi, who until lately had still envisaged the possibility of the war creating an enlarged grand duchy under Ferdinand of Lorraine, were changing their minds, and the presence of Ferdinand at Austrian headquarters now made his succession almost impossible.[2]

One motive for this change was a growing fear that the *parti avancé*, the *unitari rossi*, might use what Ricasoli contemptuously called the *popolaccio* to organize further *émeutes* and snatch power from the moderates. Aristocratic circles must have noted with alarm that Boncompagni was trying to get in touch with Dolfi. Owing to their fear of arming the citizenry in a civic militia, no force existed to control the mob once Prince Napoleon had departed. Piedmontese help was all the more necessary. Even Bartolommei and the relics of the National Society saw good reason to forestall Dolfi's patriotic demonstrations in order to avoid the appearance of yielding to popular coercion. As Tabarrini, Ricasoli's faithful follower, noted in his diary, the bulk of the non-political aristocracy at last began to fear what might happen if the Italian cause should win without their co-operation, and fear was a powerful incentive to action. Pazzi, Gherardesca, Ginori, Strozzi, Franceschi, old and famous names not much in evidence in April and May, now emerged to associate themselves with the benefits of a revolution which they had done more to hinder than promote.[3] The whole basis of the revolution had been rapidly changing since 27 April. There was already a move by interested parties to use this brief interregnum to reduce mortgage rates, taxes, and welfare pay-

[1] *Lettere Ricasoli*, III. 102–4; *Carteggi Ricasoli*, VIII. 202; *Rassegna Storica Toscana*, 1958, pp. 47–8; Poggi, *Memorie Storiche*, III. 23–4; *Carteggio Politico di Cambray-Digny*, pp. 110–12.

[2] *The Times* of 18 June (p. 12) printed Scarlett's dispatch from Florence of 2 June, which quoted Ridolfi's private communication about supporters of the old dynasty being in a majority at Florence; Ferrière later confirmed that Ridolfi had once spoken in the same sense to him, but that by 14 June he was changing (*Relazioni Diplomatiche fra Francia e Toscana*, ed. Saitta, III. 179, 197); Ridolfi, however, made a public disclaimer of Scarlett's statement (23 June, *Atti e Documenti . . . del Governo della Toscana*, I. 247); Scarlett on 26 June, in another private dispatch, confirmed the accuracy of his original report; but he too, in his dispatch of 16 June, noted that Ridolfi and Capponi were changing their views (F.O. 79/205).

[3] These names had been notably absent from the *Consulta* appointed on 11 May (*Atti e Documenti*, I. 88–9), but they were among the deputies chosen on 7 August (*Le Assemblee del Risorgimento: Toscana* (Rome, 1911), III. 657–8); Tabarrini, *Diario*, p. 76; L. Galeotti, *L'Assemblea Toscana: Considerazioni* (Florence, 1859), p. 46.

ments as well as to diminish the power of the clergy.[1] Now there was also a
rush by these noble families to become *italianissimi* before the main political
issue could be decided by popular vote of their tenants—and by 'i pizzicagnoli,
i medicuzzi, i dottoruzzi di legge' that they both despised and feared.[2]

The attitude towards Piedmont, too, was a mixture of admiration, gratitude,
but also real fear and resentment. Many were the complaints at Florence
against what was held to be Cavour's ill-defined, changeable, and indeed
dishonest and double-faced succession of policies.[3] Even now it was changing:
though on 13 June Cavour ordered that Ricasoli's appeal to Italian patriotism
must be suppressed, two days later he gave this order a quite different twist,
hinting that a 'spontaneous' manifestation by Tuscan citizens in favour of
fusion with Piedmont might still be acceptable, so long as it did not come from
Ricasoli and the government and so long as it could be privately brought to the
emperor's attention.[4] More interestingly still, Cavour on 14 June seems to
have tried to outbid Ricasoli in a confidential circular which spoke of his own
aim to make an Italian kingdom united by race, language, and geography.[5]
Ricasoli was quite unaware that he might have stimulated such a remarkable
development in Piedmontese policy, but refused to be deterred by Cavour's
veto on his own proclamation of *italianità*; on 17 June he declared publicly for
a strong, united Italy. In private he repeated his repudiation of such politically
insulting words as 'annexation' or 'fusion'. Despite Salvagnoli's objections,
he privately and bravely sought the help of Dolfi, whose influence in Florence
was enormous and who had strong views on this matter. Forcibly suppressing
alternative manifestations of opinion, Ricasoli spent a week obtaining from
individual municipal councils an impressive list of patriotic declarations to
support that already published by Leghorn.[6] Boncompagni protested, but
vainly. All he could do was to summon the 'principal agitators' and beg them
to cry for Victor Emanuel not as 'king of Italy' but as 'the Italian king'—this

---

[1] *Atti e Documenti*, I. 203–5, 282; Ginori to Ricasoli, *Carteggi Ricasoli*, VIII. 95–7.

[2] This phrase was in Corsini's letter to Capponi of 10 June, *Lettere Ricasoli*, III. 103; Massari, *Diario*,
pp. 271–3; *Carteggio del Conte Senatore L.G. di Cambray-Digny*, pp. 69, 78; *Carteggio Politico di
Cambray-Digny*, p. 120.

[3] Giorgini to Cambray-Digny, 21 June, ibid., pp. 113–14; Lambruschini to Cambray-Digny, 28
June, ibid., p. 138; Peruzzi to Cambray-Digny, quoted in Salvestrini, *I Moderati Toscani*, p. 50.

[4] Cavour to Boncompagni, 15 June, Bianchi, *Storia Documentata*, VIII. 507–8; Cavour's feelings about
Ricasoli are partly explained by the apparent paradox that Boncompagni could describe the strong
man of Tuscany as representing at once 'il concetto più toscano', and 'la parte più fervida nelle
idee Italiane'—which made him doubly suspect (Boncompagni to Cavour, 14 June, ibid. 506);
Boncompagni to Minghetti, 21 June, Salvestrini, *I Moderati Toscani*, p. 44.

[5] *Cronaca degli Avvenimenti*, ed. Zobi, I. 735–6.

[6] Ricasoli's declaration, 17 June, *Atti e Documenti*, I. 228–30, and his note to the prefects, 19 June,
ibid. 236–8; Rubieri referred to Ricasoli's meeting with Dolfi, *Storia Intima*, pp. 259–61; Corbett
accused the government of using 'unscrupulous' police measures to secure a favourable vote
(dispatch of 20 July, Correspondence relating to the Peace of Villafranca, July to August 1859,
F.O. Confidential Print, no. 881/810, p. 43); Tabarrini mentioned his secret refusal to obey Boncompagni, *Diario* (18 July), p. 53; Ricasoli's own attitude is forcibly expressed in letters, 20 June–
3 July, *Carteggi Ricasoli*, VIII. 221, 242–3, 256, 273, 280.

formula would perhaps placate Turin by its disassociation from Mazzinian notions of national unity.[1]

But by this time Cavour had been forced by the French to back down yet again and oppose even the spontaneous declarations for Piedmont which he had wanted a few days before. The emperor had been becoming increasingly reproachful of the Piedmontese leaders, especially for the poor military support which he was receiving and which was in flagrant breach of the Franco-Piedmontese treaty. Moreover, La Farina's adherents in occupied territory, interpreting Cavour's orders too strictly, were still in all appearance more anxious to stop *émeutes* than to encourage popular movements against Austria. Ulloa's Tuscan army was not ready for action; nor could rich Tuscany produce even enough money to buy munitions, because Ricasoli feared that higher taxes would lead to a counter-revolution. This was an awkward commentary on the patriotic movement. Far from contributing effectively to the common cause, the Tuscans were still asking for French soldiers to be left in Florence as preservers of law and order, which made nonsense of Cavour's promise to the French about eager popular support for a war of national liberation.

Not only was Napoleon bearing the brunt of hostilities, but the French foreign office was shocked to discover that Piedmont had been working against France for a policy of annexation in Tuscany and the Papal States. The Catholic world would be outraged as soon as this became widely known, and it was a personal blow to the emperor, for the pope had been given formal assurances that his sovereignty would be inviolable.[2] The French were also offended by Ricasoli's talk of Italian unity.[3] Moreover, Cavour's note of 14 June, as well as hinting at a stronger Italian kingdom than France wanted to admit, also declared that the great powers ought not to emerge from the war with enlarged frontiers, and this could be read as intending to deny France her stipulated pound of flesh in Savoy and Nice.[4] Cavour tried to parry some of the more obvious French criticisms by again putting the blame on Boncompagni and promising to dismiss him; in the meantime, urgent orders were sent to Florence that Ricasoli's campaign for Italian unity was intolerable and indeed that no further political decisions of any kind could be permitted.[5]

It was easy for him to blame subordinates, but what the French objected to was the policies of Turin, or rather the lack of consistent and effective policy.

---

[1] Boncompagni to Cavour, 16 June, *La Guerra del 1859: Documenti*, II. 114–16.

[2] Walewski, 18 June and 2 July, M. Aff. Étrangères.

[3] Tabarrini, *Diario* (22 June), pp. 55–6; 27 June, *Lettere di Cavour*, III. 97–8; Peruzzi, in Salvestrini, *I Moderati Toscani*, p. 52; Corsini from Milan, 17 July, *Lettere Politiche di Bettino Ricasoli, Ubaldino Peruzzi, Neri Corsini e Cosimo Ridolfi*, ed. A. Morpurgo and D. Zanichelli (Bologna, 1898), p. 120; *Ricordi di Castelli*, pp. 314, 318.

[4] Walewski's anger at this note, and his ominous reply that Cavour 'fait le compte sans l'hôte', was reported by Antonini to the Neapolitan government, 1 July (ed. Bianchi, *Rivista Contemporanea*, Apr. 1863, pp. 31–2).

[5] Corsini, 30 June, *Carteggi Ricasoli*, VIII. 267–8; Massari, *Diario* (6 July), p. 292.

In the Romagna, for instance, there were two unwelcome changes of policy when the active patriots, having first been told to expect Piedmontese support, were left in the lurch once they were brave enough to rebel. Turin continued to express disapproval of popular insurrection and of an indiscriminate increase in the volunteers, yet also was grieved at the implications of poor recruitment and humiliated when the Austrians were allowed to escape unharassed by local insurgents.[1] This seemed to show muddle on Cavour's part and an unwillingness to support France adequately. Nor, to the great astonishment of the French, were Ulloa and Mezzacapo able to bring the armies of central Italy into action even during the last stages of the war. Gualterio, Torelli, De Cavero, and Cipriani were all sent to Florence by Cavour to supervise these troops; but, whatever their instructions, they also brought with them an irremediable confusion, for there was both an absence of central planning and at the same time a distrust of local initiative. If the Tuscan army remained disorganized, this was largely due to Cavour's ill-considered demand that its whole structure and regulations had to be altered before it was sent to the front. Prince Napoleon, partly because of this fact, could make no impact on the incapable Ulloa, and eventually was also astonished to find that Mezzacapo had secret and quite inexplicable orders from Turin not to fit into the French plan of attack.

Mezzacapo's force had been left, perhaps on purpose, as an anomaly, with orders arriving sometimes from Boncompagni, sometimes from Prince Napoleon, La Farina, or Gualterio; and at the end of May another inexplicable command from Cavour suddenly overruled Boncompagni and ordered its transference to Piedmont.[2] This order was militarily questionable and administratively impossible to execute: worse still, its motivation must have been partly anti-French, for Prince Napoleon was kept completely in the dark and encouraged to go on thinking that Mezzacapo came under his immediate command. The prince had once been Cavour's most loyal supporter, but lack of support in Tuscany now turned him into an advocate of ending the war,[3] and no doubt his views on this subject had an important impact on the emperor in the days leading up to the latter's decision to make peace. When a disorganized revolt finally broke out in the Papal States, Mezzacapo's division,

---

[1] Cavour in conversation to Gaspare Finali, G. Finali, *Memorie* (Faenza, 1955), p. 120; Cavour to Farini, 3 July, *Liberazione del Mezziogiorno*, v. 435; for his dislike of volunteer units, *Lettere di Cavour*, III. 80.

[2] Telegrams of 26 and 29 May, *La Guerra del 1859: Documenti*, II. 96, 116–20; Minghetti's note of 30 May, *Convivium*, July 1959, p. 463; Boncompagni, 25 May, and Pepoli, 22 May, Lipparini, *Minghetti*, I. 159–60.

[3] Peruzzi, 16 June, *Carteggio Politico di Cambray-Digny*, p. 78; Massari, *Diario* (14 July), p. 300; É. Ollivier, *L'Empire Libérale* (Paris, 1889), IV. 232; *The Times* of 4 August mentioned the effect of Prince Napoleon's melancholy tale to the emperor about 'the want of any real sympathy on the part of the people of Central Italy in the cause for which they were alleged to be so enthusiastic'; Peruzzi reported from Paris on 26 July about the feeling there against Piedmontese 'egoism', 'ambition', and 'desire for aggrandizement' (*I Toscani del'59*, ed. Ciampini, p. 17).

whose original function had been to stand ready to help such a movement, had orders to do nothing and in fact stood idle while papal forces mounted their counter-revolution.[1]

Cavour evidently did not excel as an administrator. He was unwilling to go far enough in delegating minor executive responsibilities; yet, as his colleagues knew, he held too many portfolios in his own hand,[2] with inevitably adverse effects upon efficiency, and subordinates were sometimes left alone to improvise major points of policy independently of or even against each other.[3] He himself was able to keep an open mind on most issues and be ready for whatever changes events might suggest; but a procedure which worked excellently in peacetime, when the problem could be tackled on the single level of diplomacy, worked less well when the skills required were those of wartime administration. Lack of time to think and plan was one reason for his contrariness with Ricasoli and for Tuscan policy being sometimes allowed to go by default. So far as we know, his cabinet colleagues did not particularly want to bring Tuscany into the new kingdom of northern Italy,[4] and probably they were not even presented with the issue as one that required decision. As for Minghetti, the chief executive in the foreign office, he had to agree that Cavour's policy towards Tuscany was worse than just empirical: it was muddled and hence ineffective.[5]

What Minghetti had particularly in mind was the repeated changing of plans which resulted from an attempt to follow the whims of the French emperor. The tremendous burden of administration left Cavour's great talent for subtle diplomacy with little other field of action than that of Franco-Piedmontese relations. Nor could he resist the temptation to magnify complexities. The first problem was how to understand Napoleon, then how to defer to him without losing all political autonomy, and, thirdly, how to deceive him and still keep that deceit secret. Cavour's long-term policy in central Italy had to be kept concealed because it was far from being identical with that of France: hence, perhaps, the continuous anxiety to modify his public short-term policy to conform with Napoleon's wishes; and the results of this

[1] Cavour's attitude to Mezzacapo's division is discussed by Giulio del Bono, *Cavour e Napoleone III: le Annessioni dell'Italia Central al Regno di Sardegna (1859 60)* (Turin, 1941), pp. 87–101; and by Umberto Marcelli, *Cavour diplomatico, dal congresso di Parigi a Villafranca* (Bologna, 1961), pp. 352–61.

[2] Dabormida to Lamarmora, 10 June, *Lettere di Cavour*, III. 94; Minghetti to E. d'Azeglio (wrongly dated here, but perhaps c. 21 June), *Carteggi E. d'Azeglio*, II. 195.

[3] His ambassador in England, for example, was left largely on his own; one dispatch of 24 June, omitted for some reason from the official *Carteggio Cavouriano*, shows Azeglio suggesting to Palmerston that an independent state of central Italy might possibly be created to balance an enlarged Piedmont in the north (Bianchi, *Storia Documentata*, VIII. 515); Palmerston, on the contrary, was already way ahead of Azeglio and looking to the union of Tuscany and the papal Romagna with Piedmont (Azeglio to Cavour, 4 July, ibid. 526).

[4] General Fanti, 16 Oct. 1862, *Carteggio Castelli*, I. 452.

[5] Minghetti to Farini, 30 June, in Marcelli, *Cavour Diplomatico*, p. 372; *Carteggi E. d'Azeglio*, II. 196.

changeableness and duplicity were an indecisiveness of action and an absence of programme. This indecisiveness he imposed on successive Tuscan governments after the revolution of 27 April, a fact which not only caused frustration and misunderstanding among Tuscan liberals, but created a vacuum of power in which it was hard for him to control events or to recapture the initiative. A pragmatic strategy based on expediency and intuition, though hitherto he had shown that it could sometimes work admirably in the hands of a single master politician, could not possibly be so effective when events became too complex for one man's mind and energy.

Cavour had to resign in July when the French, on whom he had built his war policy, concluded the armistice of Villafranca and revived Leopold's claim to Tuscany. The news of this setback arrived in a Florence which was already angry, divided, and suspicious: the last two envoys sent to Tuscany by Cavour, Massimo d'Azeglio and La Farina, were received frostily, because there was by now a conviction that the interests of Tuscany were never much of a consideration at Turin.[1]

Ricasoli, too, had been meeting quite strong opposition from his colleagues. Peruzzi, Ridolfi, Poggi, Capponi, Giorgini, Lambruschini, Galeotti—all had doubts about what seemed his undue partiality towards Piedmont.[2] Many Tuscans, following Ricasoli's lead, would now have been ready to accept what they preferred to call 'union' with Turin, as distinct from 'fusion'; but, as Cavour's chances of forming a large Italian kingdom receded, there was a revival of all the old feelings against becoming just 'an appendix of Piedmont'. Better than union perhaps would be the old project of a prince of the house of Savoy ruling an autonomous Tuscany; failing that, the duke of Parma would do; and some of the moderates were even able once again to recognize Ferdinand of Lorraine as a possibility if this would win European sanction for an enlarged grand duchy incorporating the other central Italian states.[3]

Eight months later, Piedmontese annexation of Tuscany at last became a fact. It was then possible to see that, during the interim, Ricasoli's energy

---

[1] Salvagnoli to Ricasoli, 8 July, 'Carteggio Inedito Salvagnoli-Ricasoli', *Il Risorgimento Italiano*, 1925, p. 661; 26 July, *Epistolario La Farina*, II. 193.

[2] Tabarrini, *Diario* (26 June), pp. 57–8; Ferrière's reports of 22 June and 6 July, *Relazioni fra Francia e Toscana*, ed. Saitta, III. 186, 202; as Corbett wrote some months later, 'The Tuscans are proud of their history and of their civilization, which they consider superior to that of any other part of Italy, and are not, I believe, generally disposed to see their country absorbed by a kingdom which they have only lately become accustomed to look upon as Italian, and whose inhabitants they consider as their inferiors in intelligence and intellectual culture' (Jan. 1860, F.O. 79/213).

[3] Ridolfi, 31 July, *I Toscani del'59*, ed. Ciampini, p. 32; Jarro, *Vita di Ubaldino Peruzzi*, p. 79; Binda to Walewski, 5 Aug., ed. S. Mastellone, 'Gli Agenti Francesi in Italia e la Politica del Walewski dopo Villafranca', *Rivista Storica Italiana*, LXIII (1951), 390–2. The return of the old dynasty met a fair amount of support even at Turin (Massari, *Diario*, 24 July, p. 311, and 11 Aug., p. 334); indeed, Victor Emanuel tried to trade this as a concession in return for Austrian surrender of Venice to Piedmont (Hudson from Turin to Lord John Russell, 1 Oct. 1859, *Gran Bretagna e Sardegna*, VII. 219).

and obstinacy had kept a larger concept of Italy vigorously alive at Florence as a programme of practical politics; and Cavour himself, though his personal feelings towards Ricasoli became even more hostile, was deeply appreciative of this fact. The revolution of 27 April, the handiwork of the despised and hated radicals, could then be seen to have been a decisive event in the political education of the Tuscan aristocracy. Under Ricasoli's guidance they had been enabled to take and keep power as a result of Austria's defeat by France and Piedmont. Finally, in 1860, when the balance of power in Europe had changed again, and when Cavour took his next step towards merging Piedmont into a greater Italy, they overcame their former fears and accepted the political implications of a common nationality.

8

Palmerston and Cavour: British Policy in 1860

ALTHOUGH public opinion in Great Britain was in general well disposed towards the risorgimento, there were some who misunderstood or positively disapproved of it. Queen Victoria, for instance, looked at events in Italy from a German or even an Austrian point of view. Her attitude to Italians, wrote Palmerston, was 'what business had they to want to be free?'[1] Garibaldi was in her eyes a pirate, Cavour an unscrupulous adventurer. The tory party, like the queen, was deeply suspicious of revolution. Disraeli seems at one point to have been intriguing secretly with Napoleon III to undermine official British policy on Italy, and Lord Malmesbury, the tory expert on foreign affairs, was temperamentally pro-Austrian.

Drive Austria out of Italy and leave Italy to govern herself—Italy will become a second Mexico. . . . The prejudices and even dislike of the various provinces to one another is ingrained by centuries, and if a man could have been found fit to rule even a simple department of state, he would have appeared in 1848. The only decent one was Manin.[2]

Not only conservatives, not only Catholics of all political opinions, but also some of the liberals and whigs in office looked upon Cavour as a man moved not so much by the desire to liberate Italy as to enlarge his own region of Piedmont at the expense of other states in the peninsula. They judged from the paucity of volunteers that Piedmont was not widely supported by other Italians. The larger this one state grew, the less liberal she might become in her domestic policy; or, in other words, Italian national independence might be the enemy of true liberty for Italians.[3]

These views were those of a minority and were not of primary importance in the formation of British policy. In 1860 and 1861, the decisive years for Italian unification, Cavour found an unusually sympathetic group of politicians in power at London. Palmerston was prime minister, with Lord John

---

[1] Palmerston to Russell, 16 Aug. 1859, P.R.O. 30/22/20.
[2] Malmesbury to Cowley, 7 Dec. 1858, F.O. 519/196; G. B. Henderson, *Crimean War Diplomacy and Other Historical Essays* (Glasgow, 1947), pp. 280–2; 6 Oct. 1859, Aberdeen to Gladstone (British Museum, Add. MSS. 44088), called Victor Emanuel 'a profligate blackguard'.
[3] Cowley to Malmesbury, 28 Mar. 1859, F.O. 519/9; Russell to Corbett, 25 Aug. 1859, P.R.O. 30/22/109; Clarendon in the Lords, 18 Apr. 1859.

Russell his foreign minister, and Gladstone the most vocal other member of his cabinet; and these three were convinced italophiles who spoke Italian and kept up a friendship with many Italians. Lord Shaftesbury, the prominent Protestant leader, might be named as a fourth enthusiast for Italy who wielded considerable political influence. All four of them kept open house to the envoys of Cavour. Palmerston's wife used to pass on private information to Emanuele d'Azeglio, the Piedmontese ambassador, and may well have been having some kind of mild affair with him.

On a number of occasions it was important for Cavour to make split-second decisions, and for this the up-to-date information he received from his friends in London was invaluable. Lord Shaftesbury's son, who was the prime minister's private secretary, on at least one occasion stole secret papers from Palmerston's desk for Cavour to see.[1] Cavour himself seems to have intercepted confidential messages which were being sent back from Italy by British official representatives.[2] Sir James Hudson, despite his position as British diplomatic representative in Piedmont, used to show Cavour confidential official documents within minutes of receiving them. One can only conclude that Hudson on some occasions was deliberately sabotaging his government's policy where he thought it not sufficiently favourable to Italy. For instance in the spring of 1859, when Britain was trying to threaten Cavour into dropping his plans for war, Hudson betrayed confidential information to the Piedmontese which showed them that these threats were pure bluff, and Cavour was thus able to ignore Russell's warnings without risk. Cavour sometimes repaid Hudson's kindness somewhat churlishly and nearly ruined his career by telling tales against him to the foreign office,[3] but that is another story. The important fact is that some of the English italophiles took their enthusiasm for Italy very far indeed. The queen would have been shocked to know that Palmerston and his foreign minister used the secret service funds to help fit out one of Garibaldi's piratical ventures against Naples.[4]

Palmerston had formed his government in June 1859. Officially his policy towards Italy was one of 'non-intervention', but the word did not mean what it said. Lord John Russell was not hindered by it from giving some fairly threatening advice to Naples. He hinted at breaking off diplomatic relations if King Ferdinand held out against introducing reforms, and claimed that the restoration of the Bourbons in 1815 had been conditional on their maintaining parliamentary government in Sicily.[5] Britain had, on this view, a diplomatic right to intervene. At a court reception Palmerston shocked the Neapolitan

[1] *Cavour e l'Inghilterra*, II, pt. ii. 142.
[2] Copies of such dispatches are in the archives of Ricasoli at Florence and Minghetti at Bologna; Massari, *Diario*, p. 464; *Cavour e l'Inghilterra*, II, pt. i. 13.
[3] Massari, *Diario*, pp. 120–1; Cowley to Malmesbury, 28 Mar. 1859, F.O. 519/225.
[4] Henderson, *Crimean War Diplomacy*, pp. 238–41.
[5] Russell to Elliot, 11 Aug. 1859, P.R.O. 30/22/111; Correspondence Respecting the Affairs of Naples, June 1859–March 1860, *F.O. Confidential Print*, no. 881/862, pp. 16, 51.

minister by telling him publicly that the whole world would rejoice if his government fell.[1]

Where the new British prime minister placed his hopes for Italy was on Piedmont and the person who was shortly to become once again her chief minister, Count Cavour. Palmerston thought that 'on general principles the larger and stronger Piedmont could be made, the better it would be for the happiness of the people united to it, and for the peace of Europe depending on the tranquillity of Italy';[2] and Gladstone thought that, while the aggrandizement of Piedmont was not *per se* a good thing, it might avert more pressing evils.[3] The prime minister advocated that Austria should evacuate north Italy and leave the peninsula under the influence of Piedmont;[4] and when the French put forward a plan for an Italian confederation in which Austria should have a part, the British government was the decisive force in ensuring its repudiation so that Italy should be freed from Austrian influence.[5] In Palmerston's view, Britain had in 1856 at the Congress of Paris formally and publicly undertaken to better the position of Italy: therefore she had a right to intervene in 1859, and she also had an indisputable right to take steps to prevent war breaking out again in Europe.[6] Italy must be pacified and something done about removing the causes of unrest in the peninsula: by which he meant tackling both the misrule of the Bourbons of Naples in southern Italy, and the alien rule of Austrian Habsburgs in the north. Two subsidiary causes of discontent were recognized to be papal misgovernment and the continued presence of French troops in Rome.

Palmerston's government decided, accordingly, that Piedmont should ideally replace Austria in Lombardy and Venice. An independent kingdom of northern Italy, free of both Austria and France, was thought to be in British interests. As early as the autumn of 1859 the British were ahead of the Piedmontese government in thinking it was possible for Piedmont to annex Tuscany and the Romagna. Russell explained to the queen that

by the doctrines established in 1688 . . . the authority of the King of Sardinia over Tuscany and Romagna is supported and his troops are as well entitled to be at Bologna as those of the Emperor of Austria at Venice. . . . The right of deposing princes who violate their word and subvert the fundamental laws, and the right of each nation to regulate its own internal affairs, were . . . established by the revolution of 1688.[7]

Annexing the Romagna would mean an encroachment upon the temporal

---

[1] *Cavour e l'Inghilterra*, II, pt. ii. 60.
[2] Palmerston to Russell, 18 Aug. 1859, P.R.O. 30/22/20.
[3] 30 June 1859, Gladstone's cabinet memorandum, British Museum, Add. MSS. 44748; Gladstone to Russell, 22 Aug. 1859, P.R.O. 30/22/19.
[4] Lord Fitzmaurice, *The Life of the Second Earl Granville* (London, 1905), I. 325–6; Palmerston cabinet memorandum, 28 June 1859, Broadlands archives.
[5] *The Later Correspondence of Lord John Russell*, ed. G. P. Gooch (London, 1925), II. 244.
[6] Ibid. 238.   [7] Ibid. 241, 243, 254–5.

sovereignty of the pope. One of the reasons why so many people in England were enthusiastic supporters of either Cavour, Garibaldi, or Mazzini was that these three had in common a strong anticlericalism, and to this extent Italian nationalism coincided not only with British liberal sympathies, not only with British political interests against France, but also with Protestant anti-Catholicism. As Russell added, 'Italy has outgrown the Papacy. The Pope would be a saint at Madrid, Valencia or Majorca. In Italy he is only an anachronism.'[1]

On 3 January 1860, Palmerston and Russell made the remarkable suggestion to the cabinet that Britain ought to be ready to go to war against Austria in the interests of Italy, since only by excluding Austria from the peninsula would Europe be allowed rest from this Austro-Italian tension.[2] This readiness for a possible war, and war against an ally, Austria, throws interesting light on the so-called doctrine of non-intervention. Palmerston went on in more detail to consider the possibility that the British navy might move up the Adriatic to bombard the Austrian part of Venice. But the cabinet and the queen were on this occasion more cautious. The queen indeed was very annoyed with the revolutionary policy of her government towards Italy. Russell had to remind her more than once, and he did it with some effrontery, that she herself owed her throne to a revolution. The queen's objection, however, helped to restrain Palmerston from further thoughts of actually fighting for Italy. All that he gained for Cavour in January 1860, and it was by no means a negligible gain, was an undertaking from Austria to let Italian affairs take their course and not to use force to stop Piedmont annexing Tuscany.[3]

On 21 January 1860, Cavour returned to power in Piedmont, there to remain as prime minister until he died the following year. Cavour began this last phase of his life with a high reputation in England. Russell had gone to unusual lengths in pressing Victor Emanuel to bring Cavour back into affairs, but France advised differently and the king was at first adamant in stating that he would never be so foolish.[4] Then on 9 January, Hudson asked Russell to intervene positively in Piedmontese internal affairs so as to force the king to make up his quarrel with Cavour and dismiss the previous cabinet. Hudson did in fact proceed to take what could be deemed a highly improper share in the political crisis which finally brought Cavour back.[5] The opposition press at Turin criticized 'this intervention by a foreign ambassador which is offensive to the dignity and independence of our government and people', but Russell expressed himself highly satisfied with the results of Hudson's manœuvre. 'I am delighted', he said, 'to have Cavour's sense and ability to conduct

[1] Ibid. 240, 250; Russell to Cowley, 25 June 1859, F.O. 519/197.
[2] Evelyn Ashley, *The Life of Viscount Palmerston* (London, 1876), ii. 174–80; *Later Correspondence*, ed. Gooch, ii. 250.
[3] Ibid. 253, 257.
[4] *Rassegna*, 1934, p. 691; Walewski to La Tour d'Auvergne, 29 Nov. 1859, M. Aff. Étrangères.
[5] Hudson to Russell, 9 and 16 Jan. 1860, P.R.O. 30/22/66.

matters at Turin instead of the late incapables.'[1] Victor Emanuel a year later confessed to a friend that he had taken Cavour back in order to please the British.[2] Under these strange auspices began the final and most dramatic phase in the risorgimento.

Cavour's first task on his return to office was to secure the annexation by Piedmont of Tuscany and the central duchies. Here France was against him, still preferring the arrangement which she had made at Villafranca for the return of the old dukes and the grand duke; but Britain from the start hoped for Piedmontese annexation of central Italy. Even before Cavour's return, British pressure had gone some way towards making France yield ground on this issue. Cavour's predecessor as foreign minister, Giuseppe Dabormida, is never given much credit for the fact, but he had already helped to prepare the ground. By 12 January, indeed, Russell thought that the matter was virtually settled,[3] and on taking up office Cavour therefore found the annexation of central Italy a good deal easier than he later made out.

But on one important matter Britain disagreed with Cavour, being anxious that the annexation should not involve Piedmont in yielding Savoy and Nice to France as Napoleon wanted. Dabormida supported the British on this point; he agreed that Savoy should belong to France in strict logic, but only if France were prepared to extend the same nationalist principles to Venice, and he added that, if he were to surrender Nice as well as Savoy, he would be giving Piedmont an indefensible frontier against France.[4] Russell went further still and on 15 January suggested that the French should not only drop their claim to Nice and Savoy but should altogether withdraw their troops from Italy, leaving the Italians to work out their own salvation. (French troops had remained in Lombardy after the war of 1859.) France did not accept this proposal, and Napoleon made alternative suggestions designed if anything to increase French authority in Italy. Among other things he restated his wish that Tuscany should remain an independent state. Here he met firm opposition from Palmerston, for while it was French policy to keep Italy weak, the British were determined that the new kingdom should be strong enough not to depend on foreign support.

It was this stance taken by Palmerston which neutralized France and eventually allowed Cavour to carry out the annexation of central Italy.[5] Even when Napoleon gave way on the question of annexation, it remained French policy that Florence and Bologna should keep some local autonomy, and here too the

---

[1] *Il Diritto* (Turin), 21 Jan. 1860; *Gran Bretagna e Sardegna*, VII. 315; Spencer Walpole, *The Life of Lord John Russell* (London, 1889), II. 317.

[2] *Rassegna*, 1934, p. 1203; Hudson to Russell, 14 Mar. 1861, P.R.O. 30/22/68, refers to 'when by your orders I brought him [Cavour] from his retirement at Leri'.

[3] Desambrois to Dabormida, 6 Jan. 1860, and E. d'Azeglio to Dabormida, 12 Jan. MSS. Ministero degli Affari Esteri (Rome), Régistre des pièces chiffrées.

[4] Dabormida to Desambrois and De Launay, 13 Jan., ibid.

[5] *Cavour-Nigra*, III. 92; *Cavour e l'Inghilterra*, II, pt. ii. 54–5.

British helped to strengthen Cavour's hand. Palmerston was determined that all the provinces of the new Italy ought if possible to have a unified constitution and system of laws. This was the moment, rather than any other, when it was settled that Italy would be a unitary and not in any sense a federal kingdom, and British policy here had a distinct contribution to make.

Until this moment Palmerston had done a great deal for Cavour. But the whole situation was changed when Cavour decided in the spring of 1860 that it would be more prudent to cede Savoy and Nice to France. The surrender of these transalpine provinces was to be the cause of a serious breach between Britain and Piedmont. Until this moment, British politicians had not only helped to bring Cavour back to power, but had been preparing to help him annex Tuscany and Venice and even part of the Papal States. Palmerston had reached the point of advocating war against Austria as the only way of settling the future of Italy. But now this policy changed abruptly; and the reason was that to the British the sacrifice of Savoy and Nice seemed unnecessary, since Tuscany could have been annexed without it; they furthermore thought it positively dangerous, because it would both increase the power of France and also show that the alliance of France and Piedmont went much deeper than they had thought.

This was a decided diplomatic victory for Napoleon. When he had raised the question of Savoy and Nice in January, Dabormida had refused to give way, on the grounds that acceptance of Napoleon's demands would be both improper and unnecessary. Napoleon raised the same point privately with Cavour later in the month. Unfortunately the news received some unwelcome publicity in the French press, and the British at once protested, asking France to drop her request in the interests of European peace. Simultaneously Russell told Cavour that to surrender Savoy in this manner would disgrace him in the eyes of Europe. Shaftesbury warned Cavour that it 'would throw a stain on the whole effort for national independence and entirely alienate the affections of Englishmen'.[1] Cavour's first reaction was to feign ignorance, saying that he knew nothing about any suggestion for giving up Savoy. He even agreed, when talking to Hudson, that the cession of these ancient possessions of the house of Savoy would be a disgrace, and pronounced that 'the Sardinian government had not the slightest intention of either ceding, exchanging or selling Savoy'.[2] This was the statement which was to cause particular offence; for unfortunately Napoleon at the same time was telling Britain the true story and explaining that Cavour and he had secretly agreed on the matter several years back.

By the middle of February the British were seriously alarmed. They already suspected that Napoleon was trying to involve Cavour and Europe in another

---

[1] *Gran Bretagna e Sardegna*, VII. 334; *Cavour e l'Inghilterra*, II, pt. ii. 15.
[2] Hudson to Russell, 3 Feb. 1860, F.O. 67/255; *Gran Bretagna e Sardegna*, VII. 338; *Cavour e l'Inghilterra*, II, pt. ii. 46.

general war, and here was an additional cause of suspicion. According to Lord Cowley, the British ambassador in Paris,

It is difficult to reconcile the positive, unqualified denial made by Count Cavour to Sir James Hudson of there being any understanding between the French and Sardinian Governments on the subject of Savoy, with the Emperor's admission made to me through M. Thouvenel, that communications had passed between the French and Sardinian Governments before the war, in which there had been a question of the cession of Savoy to France under certain eventualities. . . . Count Cavour's solemn declaration sets this story at rest.[1]

Napoleon next gave three undertakings which were soon seen to be fraudulent. First, he promised that he would not annex Savoy without consulting the other great powers, but then showed that he meant to do just the reverse. Secondly, he tried to obtain British acquiescence in this annexation by promising that Chablais and Faucigny, two districts of Savoy which were under an international guarantee of permanent neutrality, would not be taken by France but would be united to Switzerland.[2] Thirdly, he tried to delude Cavour into thinking that, contrary to appearances, France and England were working in complete harmony over Savoy.[3] Cavour of course sent to London for confirmation of this, and the reply came that, on the contrary, French plans were altogether 'subversive of Italian independence' and must not be allowed to prevail.

Evidently Napoleon was so anxious to annex Nice and Savoy that he was ready to break with England. These annexations would be the only gain he could show to his country for all the cost and the casualties of Magenta and Solferino. He could not afford to pay any attention to diplomatic protests. He even announced in advance that the plebiscites which Cavour proposed to hold in both Nice and Savoy were pointless and would not count with him at all if they showed a hostile majority;[4] nor could he approve of the matter being discussed in the Turin parliament.

Cavour was in an embarrassing position. Now that the news had leaked out, he could not be quite so pleased with the French alliance which he had made and from which he had no hope of breaking free. Hitherto he had relied on trying to balance Britain against France, and hence had had something to bargain with, but henceforward such a policy would be more difficult. He was furious with the British and claimed that he could not understand their feelings about Savoy.[5] For a time he played with the idea of getting Palmerston

[1] *Il Problema Veneto e l'Europa 1859–1866*, vol. II, ed. N. Blakiston (Venice, 1966), p. 212.
[2] Correspondence respecting the Proposed Annexation of Savoy and Nice to France, July 1859 to February 1860, *F.O. Confidential Print*, no. 881/948, pp. 29, 40, 43; G. Pagés, 'The Annexation of Savoy', *Studies in Anglo-French History*, ed. A. Coville and H. Temperley (Cambridge 1935), pp. 96–7; E. Rossier, 'L'Affaire de Savoie en 1860', *Revue Historique* (Paris), xc (Jan. 1906), 25, 56–7; E. Bonjour, *Histoire de la Neutralité Suisse* (Neuchatel, 1946), p. 248.
[3] Thouvenel to Talleyrand, 27 Feb. 1860, M. Aff. Étrangères.
[4] 1 Mar., ibid.; Massari, *Diario*, p. 504.
[5] Ibid., pp. 507–9.

to help him retain Nice;[1] but Napoleon insisted on having both territories, and Cavour, who had realized since 1856 that the French alliance was the one indispensable basis of his foreign policy, decided to yield. In view of Dabormida's contrary conviction, it seems possible that Napoleon had privately specified these acquisitions as his price for allowing Cavour's return to power.

The emperor's tactics over Savoy and Nice led Palmerston to look with much greater distrust at both France and Piedmont. Only two months before, he had concluded a commercial treaty with France, but now the two countries fell out of step; the *entente cordiale* was at an end, and for the first occasion since 1815 France had openly defied England. Britain and France so far had both looked benevolently on the risorgimento, and a breach in the Anglo-French *entente* was therefore a most awkward factor for Cavour to reckon with, especially as it limited his freedom of action just at the moment when Garibaldi was planning an armed raid on Sicily.

Napoleon's desire to round off the natural frontiers of France carried a distinct menace to European peace, for an extension of French territory to the Rhine and the Alps posed a direct threat to Belgium, Luxemburg, Switzerland, Prussia, and other states of the German Confederation.[2] The emperor was in fact considering the possibility of a war from which France might gain the Rhineland and Piedmont win Venice. Both Palmerston and Cavour were aware of his ambitions to redraw the map of Europe, and this helps to explain British suspicions about Piedmontese policy. Palmerston and the pro-Italian party in London believed that the cession of Savoy and Nice by Cavour was being carried out against positive undertakings on Cavour's part: secondly, they knew that, once admit Napoleon's arguments about natural frontiers, and a major European war was round the corner. France was also known to look favourably on the collapse of the Turkish empire, though England was pledged to its maintenance in the interests of European stability. Palmerston was convinced that France, instead of wanting European stability, was determined to effect the collapse of both the Austrian and Turkish empires. Moreover, he had recently heard of French agents working in Belgium towards annexation of the Rhineland by France, as also of attempts to stir up anti-British sentiment in Ireland.[3] This explains why the cession of Savoy and Nice generated such a sudden sense of alarm, for it justified the queen's belief that Napoleon had a secret plan to restore as much as he could of his uncle's European empire.

---

[1] *Gran Bretagna e Sardegna*, VII. 340; Hudson to Russell, 9 Mar., P.R.O. 30/22/66; Massari, *Diario*, pp. 491, 506; P. Guichonnet, 'La Réunion de Nice à la France', *Revue d'Histoire Diplomatique* (Paris), LXXVI (1962), 45-6.
[2] *Cavour e l'Inghilterra*, II, pt. ii. 39, 58-9; Further Correspondence relating to the Peace of Villafranca, March 2 to April 23, 1860, *F.O. Confidential Print*, no. 881/895, p. 21.
[3] *Cavour-Nigra*, III. 61, 142, 227; ibid. IV. 76-7; *Cavour e l'Inghilterra*, II, pt. ii. 137-8.

This change in British policy also affected Italy, since Cavour had allowed himself to become identified with these French ambitions. The possibility existed that further secret arrangements had been made in which Piedmont might have agreed to join France in another war against Austria. Russell did his best to counter the queen's hostility and to explain that an independent Italy would be 'far more valuable than Savoy and Nice'. Palmerston continued to speak of Cavour as 'one of the most distinguished patriots who have adorned the history of any country. [Italy] will owe to him as great obligations as any nation ever owed to any of its members.'[1] But it is also clear that the British now considered Cavour deceitful and dangerous. At the very moment when Cavour (to use his own words) badly needed Britain to do for the south of Italy what France had already done for the north, Palmerston's suspicion had unfortunate results for the Italian cause.

Cavour's ambassador in London wrote on 14 April to explain this change. The British, he explained, still thought of Italy as 'une terre de prédilection' and would like nothing better than for Piedmont to annex the whole peninsula; but the cession of Savoy was something which looked to them as little better than the eighteenth-century partition of Poland; such a barter of national territory was disreputable, and also unnecessary, since Cavour backed by England could have annexed central Italy without it. Azeglio went on to explain that British politicians now regarded Cavour as someone who would use any means to reach his end, and who must henceforth be considered a puppet of Napoleon.[2]

From Turin, Hudson reported that 'Cavour, certainly, is much changed since the annexation of Tuscany and Emilia. The French seem to have got one rope round his neck and another round his legs, and he is alternatively choked and held back as suits them.'[3] Russell's acid comment was, 'I can only hope that the independence of Italy will not always consist in selling small provinces to get large ones—profitable as the traffic may be.'[4] As Russell saw the matter, Cavour had ceded Savoy and Nice in contravention of an international treaty, despite a formal obligation of Piedmont towards Switzerland, and furthermore despite a guarantee by Britain and others which dated back to 1815. Cavour had not seen fit to consult the other countries concerned; on the contrary he had violated an undertaking which Piedmont had recently made; and, since only a month earlier he had promised Hudson that he would not cede Savoy, at least it would be a counsel of prudence not to trust him in future.[5] Palmerston still thought that the expansion of Piedmont was desirable in theory, but, so long as the French regarded this north Italian state as 'forcément attachée à la France comme un satellite', it was safer to assume that any increase in the territory of this satellite might also imply the aggran-

---

[1] Palmerston in parliament, 13 Mar. 1860; Russell to the queen, 26 Mar., P.R.O. 30/22/14.
[2] *Cavour e l'Inghilterra*, II, pt. ii. 65–7.   [3] 6 Apr. 1860, P.R.O. 30/22/66.
[4] 19 Apr., to Marliani, P.R.O. 30/22/110.   [5] *Gran Bretagna e Sardegna*, VIII. 51, 66.

dizement of France and hence a major European war.[1] Russell wrote to Hudson
that

I quite agree with you as to Cavour's past services. But it appears to me that he has
cancelled them and placed his country in the hands of France by the Treaty of
Turin. The peace of Villafranca was ten times more honourable for Sardinia. . . .
Nor can Cavour with any face pretend that he cannot bear foreigners in Italy, when
he himself has given up Italian towns to French domination. . . . To submit to force
is one thing; to participate in a measure lowering and degrading one's country is
another.[2]

Palmerston voiced his suspicions to Russell:

Now we should perhaps have no strong objection to the union of all Italy and of the
island of Sicily into one monarchy. But to the cession of Genoa to France we should
have the strongest objection. . . . Cavour if he were asked about it would gravely
assure us that the King of Sardinia will never cede, sell or exchange Genoa, though
he Cavour may have in his drawer an engagement with France to do these things.[3]

Cavour soon knew that he had placed himself in a false position with regard
to Britain and that Russell was bound to be furious when he found out about
these deceptions.[4] But it was too late to draw back, and if British support for
him was henceforward going to be doubtful, his only recourse was to attach
himself yet more firmly to the fortunes of France. Plans therefore went ahead
for his next move in the expansion of Piedmont, and these included preparations for precipitating another European war alongside France. He and the
French were once again smuggling arms into eastern Europe.[5] He was quite
ready for France, as her share of the profits, to annex Belgium, Luxemburg,
and the Rhine frontier,[6] though he understandably went on trying to persuade
Russell into thinking the contrary. He reassured the British that he meant to
take no step towards annexing Venice, but in fact he was stirring up insurrection for this very purpose in Hungary, and on 8 April he stated in private that
he would seize Venetia as soon as there was any possibility of success. In these
weeks, while Garibaldi was working towards an invasion of Sicily, Cavour's
counter-plan was to precipitate another European war over the Eastern
Question and so to make his cession of Nice and Savoy less conspicuous.[7]

---

[1] *Cavour e l'Inghilterra*, II, pt. ii. 72, 83–4, 95, 103; Russell to Hudson, 16 Apr., P.R.O. 30/22/109;
Le Conferenze e la Pace di Zurigo nei Documenti Diplomatici Francesi, ed. A. Saitta (Rome, 1965),
p. 346.
[2] 29 Apr., P.R.O. 30/22/109.   [3] 17 May, P.R.O. 30/22/21.
[4] *Cavour-Nigra*, III. 146.
[5] Ibid. 148–9; report by Raffaele Benzi, Piedmontese consul in the Danubian principalities, 17 Oct.
1859, MSS. Ministero degli Affari Esteri, Affari Politici Vari 1815–61.
[6] *Cavour-Nigra*, IV. 57.
[7] *Cavour e l'Inghilterra*, II, pt. ii. 14; compare the statements by Cavour and Farini to Pulszky on
8 Apr., 19 Apr., and 25 Apr., *Politica Segreta di Napoleone III e di Cavour in Italia e in Ungheria,
1858–61*, ed. L. Chiala (Turin, 1895), pp. 93–7; Bollea, *Una Silloge*, p. 285.

Cavour's closest collaborator, Nigra, came to think that 'a prolonged war would be the best hope for Italy'.[1]

The British government knew about this only in part, though information later reached them that Cavour was actively fomenting revolution in Hungary.[2] In conjunction with what Palmerston knew about Napoleon's intentions, their suspicions were quite enough to cause a distinct change in the way the British government viewed the risorgimento. A few months earlier, Palmerston had been thinking of possible war against Austria in the interests of Italian liberation; but in May 1860, the British were talking of the possibility that, in the interests of European peace and British interests, they might rather be compelled to fight alongside Austria against Cavourian ambitions.[3] For a short time Russell was hoping that Cavour might fall from power, as 'he is too French and too tricky'.[4] Then, after Garibaldi upset the whole pattern of events by setting out with his Thousand, the British minister had to admit that 'Cavour is still the best minister for Italy, though he has sadly shaken my confidence in him.'[5]

I fear Cavour is little more than a Prefect of the Department of the Po. It is a great pity, as he is so able and has rendered such service to his country. The Emperor said at Baden that the cession of Savoy was a matter of prearrangement before the war began. Who can tell what prearrangement may now exist? Does it include Sardinia, Genoa, Malta, Gibraltar? If he would but run straight, all might be well.[6]

In Russell's view Cavour was not 'straight'; and this belief proved important for British foreign policy, because, whatever else could be said about Garibaldi, he was certainly 'straight', and that was one of the reasons why the British switched from backing Cavour to backing his professed enemy. May 1860 was the month in which Garibaldi, strongly against Cavour's wishes, set off on his Sicilian expedition. The sailing of the Thousand was deliberately intended as an 'Italian initiative'; its leaders were absolutely opposed to Cavour's policy of solving the Italian problem as part of another Napoleonic conquest of Europe. When England went wildly enthusiastic over such a revolutionary venture, this was partly because Garibaldi, who had shown himself consistently to be Napoleon's enemy, could not possibly be working secretly for the aggrandizement of France.

Unlike France and Russia, Britain did not protest to Turin against Garibaldi's expedition. *The Times* unambiguously called him a hero defending the cause of humanity against tyranny. Subscriptions poured in to help the Sicilian rebellion, from the rich, but also from Working Men's Committees.

---

[1] *Cavour-Nigra*, IV. 152.   [2] Russell to Hudson, 25 July, P.R.O. 30/22/109.
[3] Russell to Hudson, 22 May, P.R.O. 30/22/109.
[4] To Palmerston, 1 May, Broadlands.   [5] To Hudson, 14 May, P.R.O. 30/22/109.
[6] 25 June, ibid.

About £3,000 had been left over from British contributions to help the Sicilian revolution of 1848, and had been invested to wait for the next movement of liberation.[1] To increase this sum Charles Darwin sent £5, Florence Nightingale £10, the widow of Lord Byron £40, the Duke of Wellington £50. Lady Palmerston, Lady Shaftesbury, Mrs. Gladstone all helped. A sum of £300 was collected in one evening at the Athenaeum, and at Birmingham the mayor presided over a meeting to raise funds for Garibaldi.[2] One Italian living in London said that it felt like being at home in Italy.[3] There were no Englishmen in the original Thousand, but at a later stage several hundreds flocked illegally to join Garibaldi's troops in Sicily, including a son of one of Palmerston's cabinet colleagues. The British consuls at Genoa, Palermo, and Catania gave help to the revolutionaries without any permission from the government to do so. British naval officers also seem to have given help by covertly assisting the disembarkation at Marsala; this has been the subject of some controversy, but the failure of the Neapolitan navy to prevent the landing is otherwise inexplicable. Other British officers while on leave brought Garibaldi important information about the Bourbon defence positions in Palermo.

These were the actions of private individuals. The government was more cautious. Before Garibaldi set sail, Lord John Russell said he would use his influence 'to prevent any aggression on Naples and Sicily on the part of Victor Emanuel',[4] but at the same time he insisted with the queen that she had no right to interfere by force or cast any moral reprobation when Italians were fighting for their freedom.[5] Garibaldi's invasion was at least a guarantee that France would not be the gainer, and Palmerston thought that on this condition the British might be ready to accept a united Italy which included Sicily.[6] Russell disagreed with the prime minister on this particular point, and expressed the view that a union of north and south Italy in one state might corrupt and spoil the north. Russell rather hoped, at least to start with, that Garibaldi would preserve Sicilian autonomy inside a larger Italian federal union, but he welcomed Garibaldi's success and refused the request of Naples to help put down this pirate. As he said, 'the quarrel in Sicily is one between Italians, and until the balance of power is in question we cannot properly interfere'.[7] 'The falsehoods and treachery of the Neapolitan Government towards the Sicilians, much to our discredit, make me unwilling to stand sponsor for them now.'[8] Russell's view of the Neapolitan Bourbons was expressed to the queen in no unsure terms, since 'a government so false and corrupt does not exist anywhere'.[9] A strong protest was sent when the

[1] Letter from Michele Amari to Mordini, MSS. Archivio Mordini (Barga, Lucca), B. 30.
[2] L. Scalia to Fardella, 25 May, Biblioteca Fardelliana (Trapani); 22 June, F.O. 70/326.
[3] *Mattia Montecchi nel Risorgimento Italiano*, ed. E. Montecchi (Rome, 1932), p. 147.
[4] To the queen, 28 Apr., Royal Archives (Windsor), J.28, no. 55.   [5] 1 May, ibid.
[6] Elliot to Russell, 29 May, P.R.O. 30/22/85.
[7] To Hudson, 26 May, P.R.O. 30/22/109; to Elliot, 26 and 27 May, F.O. 70/312.
[8] To Elliot, 28 May, P.R.O. 30/22/111.   [9] 21 May, Royal Archives, J.28, no. 124.

Neapolitans bombarded the town of Palermo after Garibaldi had entered it; such an attack on civilians was 'an expedient opposed to the system of modern warfare amongst civilized nations, and which could in no way accomplish the result you are so desirous to attain'.[1]

Events in the south moved so fast that neither Cavour nor Palmerston found it easy to formulate a policy in the weeks which followed. On the whole, through June and July, Russell tended to believe that British interests would best be served if southern Italy were not united to Cavour's kingdom in the north, though this was a matter which Italians and not Englishmen should decide.

I think Naples and Sicily must be kept, if possible, from Sardinia. If the Neapolitans and Sicilians could agree on a prince worthy to wear the crown, we should be glad to recognize him. It is of no use for you or I to think of such a prince; he must be the choice of the Italians of the south themselves.[2]

If the Bourbon government could avert this by themselves granting reforms in time, so much the better.[3]

At Turin, however, Sir James Hudson had been converted by Garibaldi's capture of Palermo to a belief in the possibility of national unification at once. Not until this moment had national unity seemed feasible to Cavour's friends, but Garibaldi had now altered the whole pace and direction of the risorgimento. Hudson pointed out to Russell that henceforth the policy of non-intervention was likely to work in favour of national unity whether Britain liked it or not.[4] 'Either Italy must be Italian, or she will again be either Austrian or French.'[5] Hudson was now going to become an important personage in this drama, both through his support of Cavour at Turin, and even more by the advice he sent back to London. Cavour admitted that Hudson was the one foreign representative at Turin who was now backing the national movement. Yet once again Cavour had no scruples in letting Hudson down when it suited his policy, and he let it be generally known that the British minister was disobeying Russell's instructions.[6] Queen Victoria thought Hudson disloyal and dangerous and wanted him dismissed. But Russell, who knew quite well that Hudson was privately encouraging Cavour far beyond the limits of official policy, did not comply. He just told the minister to 'be very careful to keep the interests of Great Britain always in sight and not be led too far by your Italian sympathies. But *evviva l'Italia* nevertheless.'[7]

---

[1] Russell to Elliot, 21 June, F.O. 70/312; Adm. Mundy to Gen. Lanza, 25 June, F.O. 165/135.
[2] To Elliot, 25 June, P.R.O. 30/22/111.
[3] To Elliot, 27 June, F.O. 165/132; Russell in parliament, 12 July; *Cavour e l'Inghilterra*, II, pt. ii. 113–14.
[4] 31 July, P.R.O. 30/22/66.   [5] 28 June, ibid.
[6] Talleyrand to Thouvenel, 23 June, Matter, *Cavour*, III. 358; *Cavour e l'Inghilterra*, II, pt. ii. 102.
[7] Russell to Hudson, 25 July, P.R.O. 30/22/109; one element in the queen's opposition to Hudson may have been that he was privately believed to be an illegitimate son of King George IV.

Palmerston and Russell by no means had it always their own way in London. The queen had the absolute right to be consulted before her ministers could send important dispatches, and she could insist, if she disagreed with them, that these dispatches be first discussed by the whole cabinet. This gave her a power of delay; and since the rest of the cabinet were not nearly so pro-Italian as the prime minister and foreign minister, it also had an important effect in making British policy sometimes seem muddled and indecisive. The queen believed that Napoleon was a threat to European peace, and also believed, not without reason, that Cavour was another. She was not wholly illiberal in her views about Italy, and she agreed that Britain ought not to advise Sicily to submit to Naples,[1] but she disapproved of sending encouragement to the Piedmontese.

If *we* are a *little determined* with this *really bad* unscrupulous Sardinian government and show them that we will *not encourage* or countenance *further piratical* and filibustering proceedings, they will desist, the Queen doubts not.[2]

The Queen wishes that she could join with Lord Palmerston in rejoicing at the Unity of Italy.[3]

Palmerston and Russell threatened resignation over this difference in policy,[4] and for the most part they succeeded in winning their point, but there is no doubt that Queen Victoria acted as a brake on the strong Italian sympathies of British public opinion.

Both the queen and her government feared that at any moment the Italian revolution might start another European war in which Britain would be involved. In such an event Palmerston was worried that, though British sympathies would be on the side of Italy, British interests (if Cavour had his way) might conceivably force British intervention on the side of Austria or at least would demand a non-benevolent neutrality. His constant aim, therefore, was to avoid such a war. The so-called doctrine of non-intervention had been adopted just because it was in fact a concealed but powerful form of intervention, as the best means of stopping other nations interfering in Italy and precipitating war. The one essential was that Italians 'must work out their own salvation'.[5] Earlier in the year, despite the official talk about non-intervention, Palmerston had intervened to arrange the annexation of Tuscany to Piedmont; then again he had intervened to try to stop the annexation of Savoy and Nice to France; more recently he had intervened against both Austria and France in order to stop them supporting the Bourbons in Sicily and Naples. More than once in 1860 he considered the possibility of actually using force in order to counter either Austria or France. On these various occasions the

[1] To Russell, 14 July, P.R.O. 30/22/14.   [2] To Russell, 11 Dec., P.R.O. 30/22/14.
[3] To Palmerston, 3 Jan. 1861, Royal Archives, J.32, no. 25.
[4] Palmerston to Russell, 24 and 25 Aug. 1859, P.R.O. 30/22/20.
[5] *The Times* (London), 9 Apr.; *Cavour e l'Inghilterra*, II, pt. ii. 84.

distant but serious threat from London was without doubt a significant element in Italian affairs.

One important decision could not be postponed long after June, and this was whether British politicians should use their influence either to restrain Garibaldi or to encourage him. France early in June had proposed a joint intervention with England in order to stop Garibaldi before he could do too much harm; the proposal was refused.[1] More than this Palmerston would not do, for events in Sicily were moving too rapidly to let him make up his mind, and sources of information from there were limited. Napoleon, on the other hand, knew his own mind more clearly. French policy at this moment was more positive and consistent, and it was anything but favourable to Garibaldi.[2] Cavour was informed by the French ambassador that Napoleon had made Italy independent, and therefore Piedmont was showing ingratitude when she moved away from Napoleon's pleas for a divided or federal Italy.[3]

Russell and Palmerston were enthusiastic Garibaldians in general, yet they were anxious lest he should try his luck too far or provoke Europe to intervene and stop him. They would not help Cavour strongly, because they were afraid that he was planning a major war. At the same time they were certainly not prepared to oppose him if he was able without such a war to take over the south, and indeed they guessed that by now a further instalment of the unification of Italy was more than due.[4] They were inclined to believe that 'Italy would be stronger under two sovereigns, one in the north and the other in the south, than under one crown';[5] yet by 23 July it seemed likely that Piedmont might find it too hard at this late date to stand out against the movement to unite all Italy.[6] Russell for a time hoped that Garibaldi would stop at Messina and not invade Naples, but his main reason was the fear that an invasion of Naples might fail.

On 24 July, Napoleon made a second attempt to secure a joint Anglo-French policy. He officially proposed that the navies of Britain and France should intervene by force to stop Garibaldi crossing the Straits of Messina. Russell was again firm in his refusal. As he explained, if Italians were behind Garibaldi, then such intervention would be wrong, and might even help the Bourbons to stage a counter-revolution which would saddle Britain with responsibility for the triumph of reaction. If Italians were against Garibaldi, he would fail whatever action were taken. For a brief moment the French seem to have debated whether to intervene on their own against the spread of revolution, but decided that without British support it would be too risky.[7]

[1] Ibid. 79, 82.
[2] *Cavour-Nigra*, IV. 76–7, 90.   [3] Talleyrand to Thouvenel, 12 June, M. Aff. Étrangères.
[4] *Gran Bretegna e Sardegna*, VIII. 147, 152.   [5] Russell to Elliot, 23 July, F.O. 165/132.
[6] *Gran Bretegna e Sardegna*, VIII. 150–1.
[7] Further Correspondence relating to the Peace of Villafranca, July to October 1860, *F.O. Confidential Print*, no. 881/900, pp. 41, 46.

Russell had witnessed the disastrous results of French intervention in Rome during 1849, and did not wish to repeat the error; nor did Napoleon wish to chance his arm alone. This refusal by Russell to join France in policing the Straits of Messina was therefore an important fact, since only an Anglo-French intervention could now have stopped Garibaldi on his triumphant march.

Meanwhile British public opinion, becoming more and more favourable to Garibaldi, was gradually pushing the government away from its indecision and in favour of positively helping the revolution.[1] The court and the Catholics might disagree, but the public in general were reacting very favourably to the possibility of a unified Italian peninsula. The *Morning Post* advised Garibaldi to go on fearlessly and complete his revolution, and most of the other London papers agreed. By 6 August, if not earlier, Russell had been won round to the fact that the Bourbons would lose, and would deserve to lose, whereas Piedmont would probably annex southern Italy and make Italy almost a single state.[2] Later in August he reached the point of writing to tell Cavour to come out openly and declare war on Naples: though he added that this was a private view and might well not receive the full backing of the British government.[3]

Official policy in London was by now ahead of official policy in Turin in wanting Garibaldi to invade and conquer Naples. But the possibility that he might move on beyond Naples to Rome was a more difficult matter, for this would be an attack on the Catholic Church. The risorgimento had turned out to be essentially an anticlerical movement, and Piedmontese statesmen were involved in the penalties of a major excommunication against what Pius IX called Cavour's *abbominevoli disegni*. Cavour did not mind much about this anathema of the church, for he felt that ordinary Italian Catholics and even the lower priesthood would in the last resort side with him against the pope. To him it was a useful means of stirring up Protestant feeling against the papacy, and he tried to convince the British that Pius was training Irish soldiers for subsequent use in the cause of Irish independence.[4] *The Times* itself showed the temper of Protestant opinion when it published a leading article on 10 September about Garibaldi's arrival in Naples:

We hope [that Garibaldi] will possess himself of the mixture called the blood of St. Januarius, and cause it to be submitted to a searching chymical analysis, and make the results, whatever they may be, known to the civilized world. It is worthy of the

---

[1] *Cavour e l'Inghilterra*, II, pt. ii. 89, 115; *Mémoires du Duc de Persigny* (Paris, 1896), p. 274.

[2] Russell to Odo Russell, 6 Aug., P.R.O. 30/22/111; to Elliot, 6 Aug., ibid.: 'The Bourbons of Sicily seem determined to be faithless to the end. The trick about evacuating Sicily shall be the last that they shall play me. . . . Do not follow the King to Gaeta, or any other place where he may lay his false head on his uneasy pillow.'

[3] Russell to Hudson, August: 'It would be a manly course, likely to rouse all the sympathies of Italy' (P.R.O. 30/22/109).

[4] *Cavour e l'Inghilterra*, II, pt. ii. 75; Hudson to Russell, 2 Nov., P.R.O. 30/22/66.

hand which has just emancipated the people from the fetters of temporal oppression to expose one of the grossest and most impudent frauds which even the priesthood of the South of Italy ever practised on the credulity of a semi-barbarous population.

The many obvious defects in the pope's governmental system had often been the subject of gratuitous advice from both France and Britain, but, as the pope had always refused to change, Russell was able to explain that he could not support such a system against the powerful forces of liberalism and nationalism. He hoped that Napoleon would not support it either, except to preserve the city of Rome for the pope.[1] Russell said that he thought Florence preferable to either Rome or Turin as a capital city for the new Italy, especially as the centuries had made of Rome a clerical city which would hardly be a helpful environment for a lay and liberal state.[2] He specially criticized the presence of French troops in the Papal States.

Her Majesty's Government regret that the French occupation of Rome ever took place, and that none of the many opportunities which have occurred for putting an end to it have been taken advantage of . . . by reason of the deeply rooted discontent which the system of government carried on in his [the pope's] name has inspired. . . . While the practical administration of the pope is confessedly bad, the theory upon which the French occupation rests is obviously untenable.[3]

The question of Rome was less immediately important in British eyes than that of Venice. Venice was generally recognized in Britain to be Italian by rights, despite having been under Austrian sovereignty since the time of the first Napoleon. Yet disaster was feared if Italy and France should be tempted to fight a war against Austria for possession of Venice; such a war would be disastrous for Europe, since 'unless Venice remains with Austria, all Germany will stir'; possibly it would also be self-defeating for Italy, since the war might well not be won.[4] At the end of August Russell sent a note to Cavour hoping that Venice was not a proximate object of Piedmontese ambitions, for otherwise it might be another point where Piedmontese and British interests would clash. Russell warned Garibaldi that an attack on Venice might bring great calamities on his country.[5] It is clear that the British foreign minister was here speaking for himself alone, and Cavour published the note in order that Russell's censorious sermonizing should become generally known in London. British public opinion was ahead of their foreign minister on this point, and newspapers at London were beginning to say that Garibaldi should liberate the whole peninsula.[6] So Gladstone and Palmerston had considerable support

[1] *Il Problema Veneto*, II. 307.

[2] *Cavour e l'Inghilterra*, II, pt. ii. 125, 131; Russell to Hudson, 11 Oct., P.R.O. 33/22/109.

[3] 22 September, Further Correspondence relating to the Peace of Villafranca, July to October 1860, F.O. *Confidential Print*, no. 881/900, p. 152.

[4] *Cavour e l'Inghilterra*, II, pt. ii. 131, 136; Russell to Palmerston, 18 May, P.R.O. 30/22/30.

[5] Russell to Elliot, 6 Sept., F.O. 70/312; Elliot to Russell, 10 Sept., F.O. 165/133.

[6] *Morning Post*, 28 Aug.; *Daily News*, 24 Aug.; Miriam B. Urban, 'British Opinion and Policy on the Unification of Italy, 1856–1861' (Ph.D. diss., Scottdale, Pa., 1938), pp. 507–8.

behind them when they contradicted Russell and succeeded in over-ruling him in cabinet. Palmerston thought that Italy would soon win Venice from Austria with the support of Europe. 'Until Austria is out of Venice', wrote Gladstone, 'the Italian question remains unsolved, the danger to the peace of Europe continues, and Austria will never, I suppose, be able to square her accounts.'[1]

Cavour in fact, as we know now, was not thinking about Venice so much as about Umbria and the Marches in what was left of the Papal States, and here he was going to find even stronger support in London. Ever since May, the British government had assumed that these provinces of central Italy would not delay long after Bologna and Tuscany before they too wanted to break free from papal rule.[2] At last on 7 September, the day of Garibaldi's triumphant entry into Naples, Cavour explained privately to the British government that he was planning an invasion of the Papal States in the next few days. This plan had in fact been known in London eight days earlier, since Cavour, perhaps in order to prepare the Paris bourse, had told his Rothschild bankers in Turin, and they had at once leaked the information to the British government.[3]

The pretext which Cavour now gave was that otherwise Garibaldi would move quickly up the peninsula and so be able to threaten the Austrian frontier. This explanation was shrewdly aimed at winning over British opinion against Garibaldi and in favour of Cavour's invasion of papal territory.[4] British opinion was, in fact, once again most favourable to Cavour, and partly no doubt just because he was able to give this plausible if somewhat disingenuous pretext. Another reason was that the French ambassador had been withdrawn from Turin in protest at the violation of papal sovereignty, and this protest by France was welcomed in London as suggesting that Cavour was no longer involved in Napoleon's dreams of aggrandizement. Once again Britain therefore provided Cavour with his chief foreign support, and Cavour wrote that, at this difficult moment when European diplomacy was against him, British support clinched the success of his dramatic new step in the process of national unification.[5] As Russell saw it, the pope's government was tyrannical, corrupt, and demoralizing, and this was sufficient justification for Cavour's bringing the temporal sovereignty to an end.

Meanwhile Garibaldi was still the hero of the London press, Garibaldi far more than Cavour.[6] Cavour mistakenly imagined for a time that British opinion was deliberately setting up Garibaldi as a rival to him and a curb on

---

[1] Gladstone to Russell, 15 Sept., P.R.O. 30/22/19; Palmerston to Russell, 21 Sept., P.R.O. 30/22/21.
[2] Russell to Odo Russell in Rome, 14 May, P.R.O. 30/22/111.
[3] Hudson to Russell, 7 Sept., P.R.O. 30/22/66; Hammond to Palmerston, 31 Aug., Broadlands; Cowley in Paris told Russell on 1 September that Cavour was going to invade Naples against 'the Mazzinists' (F.O. 519/10).
[4] *Cavour e l'Inghilterra*, II, pt. ii. 123–5.   [5] Ibid. 126; *Cavour-Nigra*, IV. 215.
[6] John Walter (owner of *The Times*) to its editor Delane, 14 Sept.: 'I doubt whether, in all history, there has been such another instance of the right man in the right place' (*The History of The Times* (London, 1939), II. 230).

Turin. On the contrary, though the London press thought Garibaldi a hero, they were not sorry to see him checked by the Bourbon troops before Capua, for this check forced the revolutionary leader to modify his zeal and work more harmoniously with Cavour.[1] People in London saw more clearly than did many people in Turin the need for harmony between these two such different yet complementary characters. The British were anxious that Cavour, when his army encountered the Garibaldian forces in the south, should not show himself ungrateful to Garibaldi and should not perpetuate divisions between conservatives and radicals which could only weaken the new state.[2] Cavour disagreed. His view was that he could not drag the crown of Savoy in the gutter by treating with an adventurer. Cavour had decided that he must be ready to fight a civil war against Garibaldi if the latter would not surrender; if necessary the Piedmontese army would have to throw the Garibaldians into the sea. Cavour once described Garibaldi as 'the bitterest enemy I possess'.[3] Palmerston was genuinely sorry about this division, especially as Garibaldi had shown his good will by never wavering in his loyalty to the king and by gratuitously handing over the Neapolitan fleet to Cavour.

This was the stage when, on 27 October, Russell sent his famous note applauding both Garibaldi's revolution in southern Italy and Cavour's invasion of the Papal States. Cavour had begged for some sign of British support to counter the general disapproval of Europe and to deter the rulers of Russia, Austria, and Prussia who were now menacing him at their congress in Warsaw. It was a dangerous time for him, since not only did he think that Austria was on the verge of attacking, but his ally France was intervening actively against him by withdrawing her ambassador and by her naval blockade at Gaeta. He also learnt from Paris that French public opinion was becoming much more hostile to the risorgimento as it came closer to Rome.[4] So Russell's note was, as Cavour put it, an immense service to Italy. It certainly went far beyond what *The Times* thought proper. Russell was able to supplement it with a useful guarantee to Cavour that Austria would not attack in Italy;[5] and he went so far as to say that, if Austria was so foolish as to provoke a war, then England might well take action in defence of Italy.[6] This continued to be Russell's policy, and it is a reminder of a fundamental fact of the risorgimento: namely that Piedmont and then Italy were necessary to the working of the balance of power, and hence neither Britain nor France could let them suffer as a result of defeat in war. Cavour knew this, and it enabled him to be provocative and aggressive, in the knowledge that he had not very much to lose.

After their note of 27 October, Palmerston and Russell went yet further,

---

[1] *The Times*, 21 Sept.; *Cavour e l'Inghilterra*, II, pt. ii. 139.   [2] Ibid. 120, 129–33.
[3] Ibid. 133; *Cavour-Nigra*, IV. 221, 240.   [4] Ibid. 264; *Cavour e l'Inghilterra*, II, pt. ii. 146.
[5] Ibid. 145–6, 148–9.   [6] Ibid. 154–5.

and on 2 November prepared to send another strong dispatch saying that Venice and also Rome should shortly be annexed to Italy. They even threatened that Britain might intervene if any other power attempted to stop this happening. But once again a message arrived from the palace, this time to say that 'the Queen for one is not prepared to decide to go to war to ensure the success of the Italian Revolution'.[1] The dispatch was not sent, but as early as 13 November the British cabinet decided to approve the title of King of Italy if Victor Emanuel should ask for it.[2] A further protest was entered against French action in favour of the Bourbons at Gaeta, and Cavour acknowledged that it was British protests which finally made Napoleon give way on this point.[3] The French were told that their continued presence in Rome was 'to the great detriment and danger of the Italian people'; and the suggestion was made that perhaps the pope could go to Spain until his successor 'in a more accommodating spirit' could return home at a later date.[4] Russell went further still: on 8 December he proposed to the cabinet that Britain should intervene with Austria in order to secure the peaceful cession to Cavour of Venetia, his argument being that without this cession Italy would remain in a permanent and dangerous state of turbulence.[5] Palmerston's idea was that Austria should sell Venice to Italy.[6] Victor Emanuel himself some months earlier had secretly proposed to the British that he should buy Venice, and in December Russell began negotiations to obtain this end.[7]

Cavour, however, disagreed, and hence British and Piedmontese policy once again began to move in opposite directions. There was already a slight division between them over the subject of Garibaldi, for the British regretted that Cavour was not behaving with more generosity towards the radical leader; Cavour, on the other hand, had been trying to make Garibaldi look ridiculous in English eyes, though without much success.[8] A second point of disagreement, and much more dangerous, was that the two countries looked with very different eyes at the possibility of a general European war. Cavour told a friend at the end of November that he wanted to fight. Purchasing Venice would look too easy and would be in fact too expensive. This is a strange moment in Cavour's secret diplomacy. He needed a war, as he said, 'for reasons of internal policy' and in order to cement the new nation which

[1] *The Letters of Queen Victoria*, ed. A. C. Benson and Viscount Esher (London, 1907), III. 411.

[2] Russell to the queen, 13 Nov., P.R.O. 30/22/14: he chose not to ask.

[3] *Cavour e l'Inghilterra*, II, pt. ii. 173.

[4] Further Correspondence relating to the Affairs of Italy, December 1860 to June 1861, *F.O. Confidential Print*, no. 881/874, pp. 64–5, 251.

[5] Russell's draft memorandum to the cabinet, 8 Dec. 1860, P.R.O. 30/22/27; Clarendon to Russell, 26 Dec., P.R.O. 30/22/29.

[6] *Cavour e l'Inghilterra*, II, pt. ii. 142, 165; Palmerston to Russell, 6 Oct., P.R.O. 30/22/21, that for Austria to say that her honour forbids her to sell Venice 'is all *bosh*'.

[7] Massari, *Diario*, p. 366; Solaroli, *Rassegna*, 1934, pp. 1192–3; *Il Problema Veneto*, II. 411–12.

[8] *Cavour e l'Inghilterra*, II, pt. ii. 159, 167.

he was in the process of creating. Once again the Napoleonic ambitions for a greater France could be harnessed to the cause of making a greater Italy.[1]

Hudson desperately tried to convince Russell of the very opposite, and in particular insisted that Cavour was not trying to instigate a Hungarian rebellion; but London had other sources of information which indicated that Napoleon and Cavour were working in concert for an explosion in the Balkans.[2] Cavour had sent one of his trusted officials on a mission to eastern Europe, ostensibly to inspect the Piedmontese consulates, but Russell knew the man to be a professional revolutionary.[3] A consignment of guns which Cavour was smuggling into the Balkans was also captured early in December. Cavour denied on his word of honour that he was connected with these arms, and tried to blame their shipment on Garibaldi, but the British knew all about them,[4] and the crates bore the notice 'fatto nell'arsenale di Torino, "Al Comando Generale della R. Marina in Genova".'[5] Russell commented that Piedmont had now grown up and should act like a responsible government: 'the arms sent to the Danube, the tampering with Couza, Roumanians, Hungarians and Montenegrins make Sardinia very bad company for gentlemen.'[6] Russell's conclusion, that the Piedmontese were not to be trusted, was confirmed when the Austrians intercepted incendiary correspondence between Cavour and the Hungarian revolutionaries.[7]

After this exposure, Cavour changed back abruptly to more pacific councils. One reason for the change was that in the meantime he had learnt that the forces available to him in Italy were smaller than he had hoped and were insufficient to win Venice by war.[8] A few weeks earlier the British had been ready to help him obtain Venice, but by now they had been sufficiently antagonized to drop their former plan of trying to make Austria yield this region in peace. As a result it was impossible for Cavour to take the unification of Italy any further before his death.

Looking back over the year 1860 it is clear that the British government was more suspicious of Cavour at the end than it had been at the beginning. His policy over Savoy and Nice had been against British interests, and so was his belligerent policy over Venice. Also his attitude to Garibaldi was thought ungenerous. But though the British were often irritated by Cavour, on the other hand they were highly favourable towards the risorgimento. Palmerston and Russell had given perhaps too much unsolicited advice to Italy in this period,

---

[1] *Politica Segreta di Napoleone e Cavour*, pp. 155–8; *Cavour e l'Inghilterra*, II, pt. ii. 168–9; *Carteggio Ricasoli*, XIV. 27.

[2] *Cavour e l'Inghilterra*, II, pt. ii. 165–7, 170–1.

[3] Ibid. 175–6; *Cavour-Nigra*, IV. 158.   [4] *Rassegna*, 1934, p. 1201.

[5] Cerruti from Galatz to Cavour, 9 Dec., MSS. Ministero degli Affari Esteri, Affari Politici Vari 1815–61, no. 116.

[6] To Hudson, 24 Dec., P.R.O. 30/22/109.

[7] Further Correspondence relating to the Affairs of Italy, December 1860 to June 1861, *F.O. Confidential Print*, no. 881/874, p. 128.

[8] *Politica Segreta di Napoleone e Cavour*, pp. 163–4.

but their advice had never been insistent. As for British public opinion at large, possibly it was as enthusiastic over Italian unification as over any other issue of foreign politics in the whole century.[1] Lord Shaftesbury was able to write to Cavour that 'your revolution is the most wonderful, the most honourable, and the most unexpected manifestation of courage, virtue and self-control the world has ever seen'.[2] Few others would have gone as far as that, but the enthusiasm was both widespread and deep, and this made Cavour's task easier than it would otherwise have been.

[1] This is discussed fully in D. Beales, *England and Italy 1859–60* (London, 1961), especially pp. 20–34, 159–60.
[2] Shaftesbury to Cavour, 12 Sept., *Cavour e l'Inghilterra*, II, pt. ii. 123; *The Letters of John Stuart Mill*, ed. H. S. R. Elliot (London, 1910), I. 243.

9

Cavour and the Thousand, 1860

CAVOUR was one of the first great statesmen to live in the telegraph age when the minute-to-minute study of history becomes possible, yet there is still room for disagreement over what his policy was at any one moment. Whenever he had time to look back, he himself like the rest of us tended to rationalize his career, idealize his motives, and superimpose a pattern on the past. His biographers went even further in trying to convert a tangle of facts into a simple shape. But there is no necessary reason why truth should be beautiful or simple, and if we examine Cavour's attitude at the moment when Garibaldi set out with his piratical venture on 5–6 May 1860, his reactions can hardly be summarized in any formula or pattern that is consistent with all the facts. Cavour used to say that history is a great improviser. Part of his own personal success was due to his ability at improvisation, to a capacity to co-operate with events when he could not coerce them, to his instinctive desire to keep an open mind and freedom of action as long as possible. It was his habit to be not too rigid about formulating policy. He was always ready to change his opinion, and sometimes he could alter his attitude even on points of principle.

In so far as there may be said to be any general view of events in May 1860, it is that Cavour gave to Garibaldi every help consistent with diplomatic prudence. On this interpretation Cavour was by now convinced of the possibility of unifying Italy, and was already himself forming plans for invading the south. La Farina thus claimed that 'Cavour's friends helped the expedition with every possible means.'[1] When the evidence seems to show both persecution of, at the same time as assistance to, Garibaldi, this is generally explained as real but secret assistance which was merely disguised by pretended persecution. The most balanced supporters of this view, for instance G. M. Trevelyan, do add that it is still impossible to make all the facts fit such a pattern, and confess that they cannot fully fathom his motives—indeed, that Cavour probably changed his mind more than once.[2]

[1] G. La Farina, *Atti Parlamentari: Camera, Discussioni*, 18 June 1863; I. Nazari-Micheli, *Cavour e Garibaldi nel 1860* (Rome 1911), pp. 194–5; Matter, *Cavour*, III. 342–3; D. Zanichelli, *Cavour* (Florence 1905), pp. 376–7.
[2] G. M. Trevelyan, *Garibaldi and the Thousand* (London, 1909), pp. 196–8.

Alternatively, it might be held that on this matter Cavour scarcely had any mind to change, and that, possibly like most politicians for much of the time, he rather drifted before events. His motives on this view would seem a little more ascertainable, though still complicated enough; and it was partly because of their complexity that he was unable to confront the dramatic events of May 1860 with a policy that was entirely clear and consistent. One inherent weakness of the empirical statesmen who co-operate with rather than force events is that, when history moves too fast, they may not be ready to make up their minds in time to influence those events. Adolfo Omodeo was able to suggest that there was a hiatus in Cavour's policy,[1] and this hiatus came at one of the more critical moments in the whole risorgimento, when Italy was near to foreign invasion and civil war, and when Cavour's government, on his own confession, was tottering. It might further be argued, though Omodeo would not have agreed, that such influence as Cavour did have on events in these few days was used less to help than to deter and thwart Garibaldi.

This was a view once propounded by the radical politicians in opposition to Cavour, and it was subsequently discredited along with their politics for reasons which were political rather than historical. In post-risorgimento Italy, under the liberals and much more under the fascists, history became an important means of patriotic indoctrination, and one result was a tendency to play down the differences between Garibaldi and Cavour, or even to deny them altogether. It was not easy for any biographer to swim against the current and suggest that Cavour until nearly the end of his life showed little sign of wanting to unify Italy. It was not easy to suggest that he continued to oppose unification until he felt sure that it would not mean upsetting the monarchy or ending the dominant position of Piedmont: such ideas would have been thought eccentric or even politically dangerous.

Up to 1860 the idea of a united Italy had rather been the creed of Mazzini, a man who continued to be harried by Cavour's government as a major criminal and outlaw. Unification was therefore a perilous doctrine, for to everyone it meant revolution, while to most people it also spelt republicanism, and at the very least it would mean deposing all the dynasties in Italy save one. Equally suspect was any talk of a raid on Sicily, for this was another of Mazzini's favourite schemes, and the only people capable of carrying it out were dangerous revolutionaries on the Left. Though Garibaldi was not dogmatic in his republicanism, he was surrounded at Genoa in April 1860 by republican hotheads who stood to reap most of any benefit that was likely to be gained from such a revolutionary initiative. Their supposed intention was to conquer the Neapolitan forces and then use them to supplant Cavour in the leadership of the Italian revolution. As Farini said, 'a crisis at the moment would bring the radicals to power'.[2] For such reasons Cavour was justified in

[1] A. Omodeo, *Tradizioni Morali e Disciplina Storica* (Bari, 1929), p. 215.
[2] To Cavour, 25 Apr., MSS. Carte Farini (Biblioteca Classense, Ravenna).

opposing the expedition. Not a round of ammunition did he give to the Thousand; not a penny either, though pennies could have been easily and secretly given. Lack of money was to be a serious handicap to Garibaldi. Many volunteers had to be sent home because of it; ships and munitions had to be stolen.[1]

But almost at once a legend grew up about Cavour's help to the volunteers. This was founded on two indisputable facts: the first, that Cavour did not positively stop Garibaldi's departure; the second, that he did actively help the next expedition a month later and after half Sicily had been conquered. One can watch this legend appearing in the French Yellow Book on Garibaldi's expedition, which omitted a phrase in the original report of their ambassador calling it an unqualified Mazzinian plot; for, by the time the Yellow Book was published, the French attitude, like that of Cavour himself, had changed to recognition of Garibaldi's staggering and unforeseen success, and both of them now desired to make it more respectable and to profit from it.[2] Garibaldi himself added to the legend, because he found local authorities more co-operative if he wore a Piedmontese general's uniform to which he was no longer entitled,[3] and if he assured them that he was acting in connivance with the government. The conservative ministers of Europe contributed still more to the legend, for of course they tried their hardest to make out that Cavour was responsible for this atrocious act of revolution.

Cavour, however, was himself its most effective propagator. His elaborate smoke-screen was used to delude not only France and Naples but also Italian politicians of every colour into thinking he was really on their side, for he wished to keep open every avenue of escape until events had chosen for him a suitable policy. He explained to the French that 'if the Sicilian insurrection is crushed we shall say nothing; if it succeeds we shall intervene in the name of humanity and order'.[4] Whichever interpretation of his actions is adopted, Cavour must have been trying to deceive half the people he wrote to. Massimo d'Azeglio pointed this out and explained further that guilefulness had its disadvantages, for on the one hand other diplomats ceased to believe Cavour, while on the other hand he deceived even some of his own supporters. Azeglio's argument was thus one of expediency as well as morals:

---

[1] J. W. Mario, *Agostino Bertani e i suoi Tempi* (Florence, 1888), II. 48–9; C. Agrati, *I Mille nella Storia e nella Leggenda* (Verona, 1933), p. 16; G. Cadolini, *Memorie del Risorgimento dal 1848 al 1862* (Milan 1911), pp. 374–6.

[2] Matter, *Cavour*, III. 348.

[3] Cavour was at pains to show that Garibaldi's claim to be a Piedmontese officer was a mere usurpation (A. Zazo, *La Politica Estera del Regno delle Due Sicilie nel 1859–60* (Naples, 1940), pp. 316–17).

[4] 30 Mar., quoted in C. Maraldi, *Documenti Francesi sulla Caduta del Regno Meridionale*, ed. A. Omodeo (Naples, 1935), pp. 30–1; F. D. Guerrazzi, 'Discorso intorno alla Legge dell'Annessione', 18 Oct. 1860, compared Cavour's action with that of the government which had once allowed Theseus to go and face the Minotaur alone, and sent help only in the form of ropes to leash the monster when tamed (*Scritti Politici* (Turin, 1862), p. 747).

I should have preferred a more open conduct rather than resorting to so many artful tricks which have deceived no one. Garibaldi went straight ahead, risking his own life, and all credit to him. Whereas our conduct is better forgotten. All our cunning has been to no purpose. Deceit can gain something for the moment, but you lose far more in the long run when no one believes you any longer.[1]

Cavour's letters, like Bismarck's, must always be read with one eye on the possibility that their author had a reason for deceiving his correspondent, and sometimes with the further possibility in mind that he was using lies less to conceal policy than to disguise the absence of any policy.

Cavour's ascertainable motives at this time almost seem to cancel one another out. To be on safe ground we can say little more than that he did have perfectly sound reasons for not wanting the expedition to sail. Apart from its quasi-republican origin, there was the danger that it might involve him in war with Naples and Austria, and this at a time when he was mainly anxious to consolidate his newly-won provinces in northern and central Italy. It would also be likely to embroil him with France and invite Napoleon's intervention just when he was trying to inveigle the French garrison of Rome back to France.[2] Cavour's plans were for Rome and Venice rather than for Sicily. They certainly included another war in the near future, possibly quite soon, when the French might march on Antwerp and provide a further opportunity for Piedmontese aggrandizement; but he preferred to choose his own time for creating a revolutionary situation at home, and said that he did not want any change at Naples for some years.[3]

Another argument was that Garibaldi's success or failure in Sicily would be equally dangerous. If he became *Duce* of a revolutionary army and dictator of the two Sicilies, such success might challenge the hegemony of Piedmont, or even the crown itself, and certainly would weaken the conservatives. If, on the other hand, Garibaldi were to be captured or killed, the country would be likely to hold Cavour responsible. Success or failure therefore would compromise his government, and of course either event threatened him with the supreme danger that it might provoke further foreign intervention in the peninsula. It is thus easily understandable why, before the expedition set out, Cavour should have used every means in his power to stop it. As much as anything else there was the fact that he considered the idea to be a mad one, so mad indeed that perhaps he never seriously thought the Thousand would sail until they had actually weighed anchor. Only when the venture had succeeded did he send help and try to impose his own control over the revolutionaries, making a virtue out of necessity.

[1] Azeglio to Persano, 16 July, C. di Persano, *Diario Privato-Politico-Militare nella Campagna Navale 1860–1* (Florence, 1869), I. 81.
[2] Count Borromeo (Cavour's secretary) to Farini, 24 Apr., 'that the French have now decided to withdraw from Rome . . .' (MSS. Carte Farini).
[3] *Cavour-Nigra*, III. 270; Bianchi, *Storia Documentata*, VIII. 283.

But if the Sicilian expedition upset all his own plans, why then did he let it go at all? There are various possible answers. He had for one thing been assured by more persons than one that, in view of the collapse of the revolt in Sicily, it would not set out,[1] and without the government providing ships, money, and munitions he would have felt fairly safe in assuming that Garibaldi could not move.[2] A second possible and complementary answer is that, faced with such an awful decision, he could not make up his mind, but let events slide and buried his head in the sand for a fortnight while waiting for France's veto, or Garibaldi's defeat, or a miracle. Again, he knew that the king was half hoping for Garibaldi's success. Victor Emanuel on the one hand told the Garibaldians that 'his ministers meant to keep a tight hold on policy and not let the initiative be taken out of their hands by Garibaldi or anyone'; on the other hand he was looking for another prime minister, and would no doubt have been quite ready to use Garibaldi's success as a weapon against Cavour.[3] It was as much as the prime minister's position was worth to defy both monarch and public opinion simultaneously. At the same time Garibaldi's departure would have one incidental advantage in that it would clear most of the hotheads out of northern Italy, away from the political battle that was threatening over Cavour's cession of Nice and Savoy to France.

A parliamentary debate over Nice is another fact which helps to explain Cavour's inaction. Garibaldi first tried to raise the matter on 12 April and was ruled out of order, but a full-dress debate took place on 25–29 May. It is often forgotten that there was a sizeable ministerial crisis at the very moment of Garibaldi's expedition. General Fanti, the minister of war, Cavour's most important colleague, had threatened to resign over the cessions to France, and his resignation would certainly have brought down the cabinet. For a time Cavour was so discouraged that he wrote to ask if the Baron Ricasoli would think of forming a new ministry.[4] The few weeks before 5 May had confirmed that Garibaldi was extremely popular in the country, and the *corps diplomatique* at Turin agreed that Cavour might have fallen had he forcibly tried to stop the Thousand.[5] Cavour himself was afraid that he might fall whichever

¹ Talleyrand reported Cavour's words, 9 May, in Maraldi, *Documenti Francesi*, p. 47: 'Quant à Garibaldi, il m'a trompé grossièrement, brutalement, car il m'avait envoyé sa parole d'honneur de ne pas prendre part à cette expédition de Sicile. . . . Il était le centre des mécontents, et tant qu'il a été dans le pays, je me sentais comme un homme blessé: aujourd'hui je suis un homme guéri.'

² Guastalla to Cadolini, 16 May, MSS. Cadolini (Museo del Risorgimento, Rome), explained that money was exhausted and hence no reinforcements could be sent to support Garibaldi.

³ Farini to Cavour, 24 Apr., MSS. Carte Farini; *Cavour-Nigra*, III. 264, 269, 277; *Lettere Ricasoli*, V. 101.

⁴ *Cavour-Nigra*, III. 266–71, 292; *Notizie degli Archivi di Stato* (Rome), II (1942), 115.

⁵ Talleyrand, 9 May, quoted by Maraldi, *Documenti Francesi* p. 47: 'Mes collègues inclinent à penser que c'eût été une dangereuse expérience pour M. de Cavour d'entamer à Gênes une lutte sérieuse pour empêcher l'embarquement des volontaires. Quelle qu'en eût été l'issue il serait vraisemblablement tombé devant l'animadversion que cette acte aurait soulevé'; Hudson's dispatch of 6 Apr., P.R.O. 30/22/66; the Prussian minister at Turin thought that Cavour was just waiting until the debate on Nice was over before crushing Garibaldi and the revolutionaries (10 May, *Die Auswärtige Politik Preussens 1858–1871*, vol. II, pt. i, ed. C. Friese (Oldenburg, 1938), p. 379).

decision he took. In all the excitement of Garibaldi's departure it has gone without observation that the expedition sailed on the very day of the supplementary parliamentary elections into which Cavour's party was putting all the spare energy they had, otherwise Garibaldi might not perhaps have got away so lightly.

That these considerations were at the front of Cavour's mind appears from a letter he sent on 12 May, and its recipient, Costantino Nigra, was of all Cavour's correspondents the one whom he usually treated with entire frankness and honesty. As he wrote,

I regret Garibaldi's expedition as much as anyone. . . . I could not stop his going, for force would have been necessary. And the ministry is in no position to face the immense unpopularity which would have been drawn upon it had Garibaldi been prevented. With the elections taking place, and depending as I do upon the votes of every shade of moderate liberal to counter the opposition and get the French treaty through, I could not take strong measures to stop him. At the same time I omitted nothing to persuade Garibaldi to drop his mad scheme. I sent La Farina to see him, who assured me that Garibaldi had given up all thought of his expedition. Since the news from Palermo showed that the state of siege there had been lifted and the revolt was on the point of being extinguished, I thought Garibaldi would be obliged to stay at home whether he liked it or not.[1]

On another occasion Cavour gave a further clue in a private letter, when he wrote that 'if Garibaldi had been forcibly held back, he would have become very dangerous in internal politics'.[2] And public statements in official and semi-official newspapers were to much the same effect, namely that the government had tried every method of persuasion to stop Garibaldi, and indeed thought it had dissuaded him: according to some of these statements the use of force might have meant civil war, and even then might not have sufficed to stop him sailing.[3]

Yet Cavour cannot be judged only on his own testimony, for a month later he was hinting that he had been helping all the time, and if we regard all his earlier statements as meant to deceive someone or other, we might interpret them as a triumph of cunning and statesmanship. More convincing is confirmation from the British ambassador, a man who was closer to Cavour's real mind at the time than almost anyone else except Nigra and Farini—a man moreover who had no conceivable motive for untruthfulness. Hudson reported that 'if Garibaldi means to go, he is sufficiently strong and sufficiently supported by public opinion to be able to go whether the government likes it or not'.[4] And he later wrote:

At the outset nobody believed in the possibility of Garibaldi's success; and Cavour and *tutti quanti* thought the country well rid of him and of the unquiet spirits who

---

[1] *Cavour-Nigra*, III. 294.　　[2] *Lettere Ricasoli*, v. 64.
[3] *Gazzetta Ufficiale del Regno* (Palermo), 18 May; *L'Opinione* (Turin), 9, 11, and 14 May.
[4] To Russell, 4 May, P.R.O. 30/22/66.

went with him. The argument was, if he fails we are rid of a troublesome fellow, and if he succeeds Italy will derive some profit from his success.[1]

Another entirely reliable witness was Guido Borromeo, who was permanent secretary to the minister of the interior. In a note to Farini, the minister, he remarked that, a few hours before Garibaldi set out, Cavour did agree at last to risk the use of force against him, and let it be thought that he would get cabinet approval the following morning.[2] This is all the more likely to be true in that a telegram would have arrived a few hours earlier from naval units in Palermo harbour to confirm that the Sicilian insurrection, upon which Garibaldi relied, was at an end, so that Cavour must have thought himself at last on firmer ground. He made this remark about using force only hours after he himself arrived back in Turin after seeing the king at Bologna. But he was evidently too late in making up his mind. Or perhaps he was waiting until the election results showed that he could act without fear.[3]

One incident which is very important for an interpretation of Cavour's possible motives is the interview which he had at Genoa with one of the less politically radical of Garibaldi's generals, Giuseppe Sirtori, twelve days before the expedition set out. Of this interview we have two accounts, usually said to be contradictory. Sirtori himself three years later told parliament that Cavour had offered his help if the expedition went to Sicily, but opposition if they went to the Papal States,[4] and this statement has been taken as evidence that Cavour did actually help the Thousand. A second account of the interview was given by Dr. Agostino Bertani, also in the same parliamentary session of June 1863. Bertani told parliament how he remembered Sirtori coming back from that interview three years earlier with the story that Cavour had really said 'I don't know what to think or do', since he believed Garibaldi would be captured. Which of these was right? Was Cavour helpful, or discouraging? The answer given to this tiny point may affect our larger attitude to Cavour and to one of the most fundamental controversies in risorgimento history.

If it were a question of choosing between the two versions, Sirtori's account of Cavour's benevolence might well be thought the more reliable, since it is first-hand evidence even though it dates from three years after the event. Trevelyan went so far as to conclude that no modern historian had any right to repeat Bertani's tale, though to discredit it he used a legend that Bertani

---

[1] 28 June, ibid.

[2] Borromeo to Farini, 6 May, MSS. Carte Farini.

[3] The timing of these elections must have been a last-minute thought by Cavour, perhaps to win support against the revolutionaries; and when Depretis, the radical governor of Brescia, was told only on 29 April that he would have to prepare for elections on 6 May, he at once wrote to protest (MSS. Carte Depretis (Archivio di Stato, Rome)).

[4] *Atti Parlamentari*, 19 June 1863; C. Agrati, *Giuseppe Sirtori, Il Primo dei Mille*, ed. A. Omodeo (Bari, 1940), p. 189.

had said Cavour smiled as he spoke of Garibaldi's probable capture, and this gives a completely altered sense to the words in question. The legend appeared in 1869 during the bitter political controversy provoked by the publication of La Farina's letters and Persano's memoirs in defence of Cavour; to which Bertani replied in an acrid polemical work which distorted history in the opposite direction.[1] Going back to the parliamentary reports, it appears that the reference to smiling must have been introduced later, and that these parliamentary speeches were not at all the broil usually supposed, but a not unfriendly exchange, rather supplementing than contradicting each other. Bertani's statement at the time can hardly have been thought uncomplimentary to Cavour, for it was not greeted with cries of dissent like other parts of his speech. And in his very next sentence, not usually quoted, Bertani had added that if he himself had been in Cavour's shoes he might have thought and said much the same. Other sources confirm that it was generally believed in conservative circles that Garibaldi would be captured; and, indeed, this had been one good reason why Cavour had not wanted Garibaldi to go in the first place.[2] It is thus rather Sirtori's account which needs justification; for surely if Cavour had been really helpful as a result of this interview we should have heard about it earlier than 1863.

A completely different interpretation of the interview emerges if we look on the later recollections of Sirtori and Bertani as both true in so far as they went, and then supplement them with other indirect evidence. Much more reliable, for instance, than Sirtori's memory three years later is the diary of Crispi for this very day of the interview when he was in Genoa on the spot. Crispi there confirmed that Sirtori 'has great doubts' of the success of the expedition, while Cavour's friends 'are constantly coming and going, and trying to persuade Garibaldi to give up the attempt'.[3] This confirms Bertani's statement that Cavour thought the expedition to be madness. And exactly the same conclusion is reached in a letter Crispi wrote two days after the interview, which includes the remark that 'Piedmont can give us no help. . . . We are on the point of despair.'[4] Crispi at the time was Garibaldi's right-hand man at Genoa; and it is therefore important to know that he always strongly maintained in later years that Cavour had given no help to the *Mille* but had been glad to be rid of a bad lot.[5] Other minor details fit in with this view better

---

[1] A. Bertani, *Ire Politiche d'Oltre Tomba* (Milan, 1869), p. 61; and the legend was given more general currency in G. Guerzoni, *Garibaldi* (Florence, 1882), II. 30; *Discorsi Parlamentari di Agostino Bertani* (Rome, 1913), p. 46.

[2] Cavour to Brassier, 7 May: 'S'il est parti, ce que j'ignore encore, il m'a trompé et s'est conduit comme un mauvais drôle—d'ailleurs il ira avec les autres imbéciles se faire pendre, car après mes nouvelles tout est fini en Sicile' (*Auswärtige Politik Preussens*, II, pt. 1. 378–9).

[3] *The Memoirs of Francesco Crispi*, ed. T. Palamenghi-Crispi (London, 1912), I. 471.

[4] *Crispi: Lettere dall'Esilio (1850–1860)*, ed. T. Palamenghi-Crispi (Rome, 1918), p. 240.

[5] Letter of 1898, *Nuova Antologia* (Rome), Apr. 1941, p. 225; *Francesco Crispi: Ultimi Scritti e Discorsi Extra-parlamentari (1891–1901)*, ed. T. Palamenghi-Crispi (Rome, n.d.), pp. 235–6.

than with any other: a letter by Sirtori advising Garibaldi not to move;[1] another by Garibaldi himself explaining that the government could not help because of what he called 'false diplomatic considerations'.[2]

As for Cavour's own testimony, he never breathed a word about having offered help in this interview. But a cabinet minute shows that the very next day, 24 April, Cavour and his colleagues agreed to sequestrate the guns which Garibaldi had stored in Milan to be ready for his expedition. It was unanimously decided to refuse Garibaldi the guns he requires for the Sicilian insurrection, lest the European capitals should thereby be alarmed, in view of the imprudent publicity given by him and his friends in Genoa to the preparations he has in hand for Sicily. It was also resolved that any meeting of the émigrés in Genoa should be forbidden.[3]

There is little room for deceit or *arrière pensée* in a secret minute, and this fact makes it far better evidence of Cavour's intentions than remarks he made to third parties which they tried to recall three years after the event. The cabinet decision was also followed by immediate action, for Colonel Frapolli was at once dispatched by Cavour to dissuade Garibaldi from stirring; with such cogent arguments, moreover, that he was able to report back that the expedition had been called off.[4] These facts hardly indicate government offers of help. And finally there are the letters which Cavour wrote this same day, the 24th, to two of his closest colleagues—and he would have been more likely to tell the whole truth to them than to the revolutionary General Sirtori. These letters refer to his visit to Genoa the day before, and simply say he had there uncovered a dangerous Mazzinian agitation; he explained that he had given orders to prevent any insurrectionary movement, and added that in his opinion 'nothing serious is likely to develop'.[5]

Trevelyan points out how these two letters inexplicably contradict the interpretation he had favoured for the Sirtori interview. But the discrepancy is avoided if the affair is interpreted the other way. One can thus suppose that Cavour in Genoa recognized there was danger from Mazzini and tried to counter it, hoping that the old wedge which separated Mazzini from Garibaldi could be driven yet deeper. He was too prudent openly to reject this appeal from Garibaldi's chief of staff, Sirtori, especially when he knew from the

[1] 2 May, Agrati, *I Mille nella Storia*, p. 53.
[2] Garibaldi to Il Direttore dei Vapori Nazionali, 5 May, MSS. Carte Bertani (Museo del Risorgimento, Milan).
[3] MSS. 'Copia di Verbali delle Adunanze del Consiglio dei Ministri tenuta per Uso del Conte di Cavour' (Archivio di Stato, Rome); and it may be significant that no further entry in the minute book is recorded until after Garibaldi had set out on 8 May. The important fact that these minutes were not only private but almost personal to Cavour is suggested by the fact that he was the first to introduce the idea of cabinet minutes, and that they were discontinued during Lamarmora's intervening ministry.
[4] I. Raulich, *Rivista di Roma* (Rome), 1910, p. 306, quotes a note by Colonel Bruzzesi to say that Frapolli had even threatened to use force to prevent Garibaldi.
[5] *Cavour-Nigra*, III. 266, 269.

Genoese authorities and from Sirtori himself that the revolt in Sicily was collapsing and the expedition was unlikely to set out in any case. Help, therefore, might be offered gratuitously and with little risk. His principal fear was (Cavour's) lest Garibaldi should revert from his forlorn hope in Sicily and instead attack the Papal States through Tuscany, so destroying the credit of Piedmont with France. Accordingly he spoke fair words, hoping thereby to retain some influence over Garibaldi, hinting therefore at possible government help if the radicals behaved themselves and adhered to their Sicilian plan, but insisting chiefly on the chances of failure and the inadvisability of precipitate action.[1] Sirtori would have come back from this meeting and told people of Cavour's pessimism, which he himself fully shared, and it would have been this impression which remained uppermost in Bertani's mind. Whereas Sirtori, in happy retrospect after he had received military preferment at Cavour's hands, recalled rather the fair words, mistakenly associating with those words the concrete help which Cavour gave six weeks later in different circumstances.

So much for the *nihil obstat* which Cavour is supposed to have given on 23 April to the Sicilian exploit. A second controversial point which should be considered is the sequestration of the 12,000 firearms at Milan. These arms belonged to Garibaldi's party, but the government had previously agreed to store them at one of its own police arsenals in order that some official check might be imposed on the use to which they were put. Until now the authorities had allowed freedom of withdrawal unless Garibaldi should act against Cavour's wishes, and hence refusal at this moment of all moments confirms that Garibaldi's proposed expedition was disapproved of by the government. It was as early as 16 April that Garibaldi sent for the withdrawal of just 200 rifles from the store,[2] and to his surprise was refused by the governor of Milan, Massimo d'Azeglio. Azeglio took full responsibility himself for this refusal, but wrote at once to Farini, the minister of interior, asking the government to confirm his action. No reply came from the minister, and a week later Azeglio had to write again to Turin pressing for an answer. The minister's silence was assumed by Milan to be tantamount to the desired confirmation, and such, without any doubt, must have been intended. Farini was fully competent as minister of the interior to give orders to his subordinate governors, but he had passed the matter to Cavour, and Cavour had passed it back again saying that he left the decision entirely to Farini.[3] Neither wanted to commit himself, though each must have realized that silence would merely save his own reputation at the price of leaving Garibaldi disarmed and helpless.

---

[1] There is a possibly significant difference of wording in an account which Sirtori himself gave closer to the event in a letter to Conte Giulini of 3 May: 'What Cavour then said to me led us to hope for help from him' (Bianchi, *Storia Documentata*, VIII. 290).

[2] P. Fauché, *Giambattista Fauché e la Spedizione dei Mille* (Rome, 1905), pp. 80–9; A. Luzio, *Garibaldi, Cavour, Verdi* (Turin, 1924), pp. 105–9.

[3] Borromeo to Farini, 24 Apr., MSS. Carte Farini; Farini to Cavour, 27 Apr., ibid.

In fact the minutes of the cabinet already quoted show that the ministers, including Cavour whose actual signature confirms his position, were unanimous in approving Azeglio's action; though their approval was kept secret, and Cavour went on letting Azeglio take and keep responsibility for the matter, knowing he could either own or disown his subordinate's action and reap the credit however things turned out. Cavour's excuse was that at all costs it had to appear as if the government were not conniving; and this excuse, if correct, would at least prove that the motive of 'not being compromised' ranked higher with him than that of 'giving secret help'. But if he really wished to help short of being compromised, as is always maintained, he could have told Azeglio privately to disobey his official command; a discreet order to disobey orders was not unknown in the course of 1860. Cavour's excuse was obviously a mere pretext, for he must have known that in any case he was bound to be compromised if Garibaldi sailed; whereas the permission for arms to be withdrawn from government arsenals had been given before now without disaster and could easily have been given again.

The more immediate fear which possessed Cavour was that of throwing away good money on a desperate venture which was unlikely to succeed, and which if it did succeed would be likely to bestow far more benefit on his political opponents than on himself. There will always be scope for difference of opinion over what it might have been diplomatically possible for Cavour to do by way of help, because the answer to such a question depends on an interpretation of human nature as well as on inescapable inferences from documents; but financial help would surely have been easy, and he gave none. The Thousand were forced to set out with a few rusty, smooth-bore, converted flintlocks, the only advantage of which was that they did not fire and therefore imposed a tactic of bayonet charges which effectively struck terror into the Neapolitan soldiery. Of these weapons, given by the National Society, it was 'no exaggeration to say that nine out of ten would not fire at all', said Garibaldi.[1] Only a month later when Palermo had fallen did the government order Azeglio to release the new Enfield rifles from bond.

A third point which ought to be discussed is the alleged protection given to the Thousand by the Piedmontese fleet under Admiral Persano. One of the origins of this allegation is an almost certainly apocryphal document wherein Cavour is said to have told Persano to cruise between Garibaldi and the Neapolitan fleet, adding, 'I hope you understand me.' Only with much stretching can this be made to seem like an order to protect the expedition, but in any case we have only a suspect reference to the existence of such a document.[2] The known facts point rather the other way. On 3 May Persano was ordered to leave Tuscany and cruise near Sardinia, where Garibaldi's route

---

[1] *Garibaldi, Vittorio Emanuele, Cavour, nei Fasti della Patria: Documenti Inediti*, ed. G. E. Curàtulo (Bologna, 1911), p. 177; *Giuseppe Garibaldi: Scritti*, ed. C. Ciàmpoli (Rome, 1907), pp. 516–17.
[2] N. Bianchi, *Il Conte Camillo di Cavour: Documenti Editi ed Inediti* (Turin, 1863), p. 90.

would most likely lie.[1] Borromeo's evidence has already been given to suggest that on 5 May Cavour was at last resolved to use force; and this resolution would have been strongly confirmed when Garibaldi first landed not in Sicily but in Tuscany, which terrified Cavour with the prospect of an invasion of the Papal States, and also gave him the excuse he had so far lacked to win round public opinion against such folly. Then on 7 May the election returns showed that he would have a large parliamentary majority and so could act with less hesitation.

Cavour's actual order now was that Persano should arrest Garibaldi if he touched at any Sardinian port but not if he was encountered in the open sea.[2] The customary interpretation of this has been that it was not intended seriously but was another clever ruse to deceive European diplomacy into thinking that Piedmont was against the revolutionaries. It is, however, hardly likely that Cavour would have run the risk of deceiving his own admiral too. Persano at once wired for personal confirmation of such an important order, and the reply came back that 'the government' had decided for Garibaldi's arrest.[3]

Nine years later, when Persano published his memoirs, he cryptically interpreted this to mean that Cavour personally had been against the other ministers—in other words that Cavour had hoped that Persano would see through the wording of the telegram and disobey. But one must remember that nine years later everyone knew that Garibaldi had been successful; Persano was then a defeated and ostracized man who needed to justify himself, and the exigencies of national politics made it equally necessary to claim credit for the party of Cavour. If, instead of simply believing this later version, one looks at things as they appeared in 1860, it is surely unthinkable that Persano could have done anything else but arrest Garibaldi had the expedition put into port. Besides this there are still other difficulties in the story. It would, for instance, have been unique had Cavour let himself be overruled on such a matter by his own cabinet. Of course it is always probable that he was still unable to make up his mind, and was trying not to commit himself in writing. He may, for instance, have been hoping that Persano, like Azeglio and Garibaldi before him, would take action on his own responsibility one way or the other, ready to be disowned if necessary. Actually the confirmatory order reached Persano too late for him to be able to do much about it; though nine years later, when he had to explain how Garibaldi's two little paddle-steamers had eluded the vigilance of His Majesty's navy, he rationalized the matter as an example of his own astuteness and Cavour's patriotism.

Garibaldi for his part, in reviewing the admiral's memoirs, recollected that, when Persano arrived in Sicily later in May 1860,

---

[1] Persano, *Diario*, I. 14.
[2] Nazari-Micheli, *Cavour e Garibaldi*, pp. 97–8; *Cavour-Nigra*, III. 287.
[3] 11 May, Persano, *Diario*, I. 15; *Garibaldi, Vittorio Emanuele, Cavour*, ed. Curàtulo, pp. 145–8.

he assured me that he had had orders to follow and arrest me; and if he did not carry them out, it was because luckily our expedition, instead of coasting Sardinia as we had first planned, was switched via Tuscany by unforeseen circumstances, and so escaped the claws of the Piedmontese fleet.[1]

This version fits better with what we know of Cavour's other statements at the time, and can only be gainsaid if we assume that most of his public and private pronouncements were deceitful. Cavour repeated his orders for Garibaldi's arrest to Prince Carignano in Tuscany, and Ricasoli was told that 'Piedmontese warships have been ordered to stop Garibaldi if he is in Tuscan or Roman waters.'[2] He cannot possibly have thought that all these people would see through any deception that may have been intended. On 11 May he went so far as to order that Garibaldi should be arrested anywhere he could be found outside Sicilian waters; and all expeditions to reinforce him were to be prevented at all costs—the words 'at all costs' were underlined and repeated in more telegrams than one.[3]

The conclusion must be that Cavour played a less important and less helpful part than generally thought in the movement which conquered half Italy from the Bourbons. The facts only fit together if we assume, firstly, that there was a kind of hiatus in his policy; and secondly, that initially he did much more to hinder than to help the conquest of Sicily. In fact his chief contribution was in not absolutely vetoing the expedition, and it may be argued that even in this respect his attitude was forced upon him. Garibaldi himself wrote in 1861, 'if the government stopped short of an absolute veto on the Thousand, it did not neglect to raise up an infinity of obstacles to our departure', and this kind of remark was repeated by Garibaldi in later years.[4] Perhaps this confirms another report from various people who claimed to have witnessed a scene in which Cavour

tried to stop everything and halt Garibaldi. He became very excited as he spoke about his plans; and when someone objected that no one could be found who would dare to stop the expedition, Cavour exclaimed: 'If no one else will do it, I will go myself and seize Garibaldi by the scruff of his neck.'[5]

The question need not be raised whether Cavour is to be blamed for lack of courage or vision. It will be safe to consider that he could probably have

---

[1] Garibaldi to Barrili, 24 Aug. 1869, quoted by Curàtulo, ibid., pp. 143–4.

[2] Cavour to Carignano, telegram of 10 May, MSS. Ministero degli Affari Esteri (Rome), Régistre des Pièces Chiffrées; 11 May, *Il Risorgimento Italiano: Rivista Storica* (Turin), 1916, p. 249; Farini's telegram to Baron Ricasoli in cipher, MSS. Carte Bianchi-Ricasoli (Archivio di Stato, Florence), M/B.

[3] Farini to Ricasoli, 12 May, ibid.

[4] *Il Risorgimento Italiano: Rivista Storica*, 1908, p. 7; *Scritti di Garibaldi*, II. 414–15, 492.

[5] O. d'Haussonville, 'M. de Cavour et la Crise Italienne', *Revue des Deux Mondes* (Paris), Sept. 1862, p. 420; Chiala accepted this story, though himself one of Cavour's apologists (*Lettere di Cavour*, IV. clx), but there has been some criticism of it, notably in A. Dallolio, *La Spedizione dei Mille nelle Memorie Bolognesi* (Bologna, 1909), pp. 33–7.

done little else, and one must admire the great skill with which he quickly retrieved the situation and reasserted his influence over events. By 18 May he was already changing his policy to one of more active, if still half-hearted, co-operation with the revolutionaries. But in the decisive early half of this month his position had been almost impossibly difficult. He had been confronted with elections and a ministerial crisis together. He had all the worry of having to pilot through parliament the highly unpopular surrender of Nice and Savoy. On top of this the king was trying to undermine the parliamentary coalition on which he depended. Public opinion seemed to be leaving him for the more picturesque Garibaldi; while Garibaldi's success threatened to ruin his foreign policy and bring incalculable dangers to Italy. So, short of using force, he did his best to thwart the revolutionaries, though in the last resort he had not the courage or the strength to prevent them setting out, and in self-defence was compelled to allow something he inwardly regarded as a misfortune. He had weighed up the chances of success but had made a mistake in his calculations, and, had his advice been followed, southern Italy would not have fallen when it did.

Cavour did not usually lack daring, but on this occasion the suddenness of events threw him out of his equilibrium. It would be quite unfair to accept Brofferio's view that he was hoping for Garibaldi to be defeated by the Bourbons.[1] More acceptable is Rattazzi's interpretation that Cavour failed to stop the expedition, yet also failed to give it any even indirect help.[2] Far from helping Garibaldi while cleverly appearing not to (which is the traditional view), it seems that he gave no help while cleverly appearing as if he might do so at any moment. In reality he had no intention of squandering government resources on a buccaneering exploit that bid fair to ruin his own career and reputation. Even on a less severe interpretation of his motives, he was determined to avoid anything that might compromise him or be regarded as taking sides, at least until one or other of the combatants had actually won. This risked having the worst of both worlds, for Piedmont was inevitably compromised without having been able to exert herself adequately for the patriotic cause. What was more, the rift between Cavour and Garibaldi became unbridgeable, and the two chief architects of Italian unity were soon to be brought more than once within appreciable distance of civil war.

[1] A. Brofferio, *Il Conte di Cavour* (Turin, 1861), p. 61.
[2] Rattazzi to Lamarmora, 4 June 1860, MSS. Archivio Lamarmora (Biella), xcvii/155.

10

The Peasants' Revolt
in Sicily, 1860

A MONG the deeds of valour that made Garibaldi's conquest of Sicily so memorable, the importance of social revolt has generally been overlooked. G. M. Trevelyan, for instance, thought that there were no purely agrarian troubles in Sicily until after 1860. The few historians who suspected that there might have been elements of class struggle have had to admit that the economic structure of Sicily was far too backward for an orthodox class war to be clear cut. In any such society the literature of submerged rebellion has a poor chance of survival. Since there was almost total illiteracy in the country districts, the amount of documentation must always have been small.

Notwithstanding an increase in Sicilian trade during the ten years before 1860, agriculture over most of the island remained barely out of its nomad stage and depended on a hand-kissing population of serfs who had no contracts of labour and lived on the edge of starvation. The forests had almost disappeared; so had the artificial systems of irrigation on which a prosperous agriculture had long ago depended; and the roads were probably worse than they had been under the Romans. Sulphur mining, reported John Goodwin, the British consul, had more than doubled in output since 1850, mostly for the benefit of foreign owners and shareholders.[1] Apart from sulphur, agriculture was the primary and almost exclusive industry. Sicilian agriculture was still regulated by the system of *latifondi*, large estates which over the centuries had been produced by drought, malaria, and the lack of roads, rural houses, and public security. Goodwin thought that recent laws had resulted in considerable subdivision of land, which itself had 'brought immense tracts into regular cultivation',[2] but landowners were still few, and a landless peasantry was socially dangerous and economically unprotected in years of political revolution such as 1860.

Of the two main classes in agriculture, Commander Forbes wrote in July 1860 of an aristocracy that was 'ignorant and emasculated with dissipation, and workers degraded and demoralized to a degree without a parallel in

---

[1] Goodwin's journal for 18 June 1860, F.O. 165/134: Elliot, 23 July, F.O. 70/318.
[2] 20 July, F.O. 165/135.

Europe'.[1] The old Sicilian aristocratic families had been degenerating into a *noblesse titrée* worse instructed than their inferiors. They were reluctant to enter commerce, the church, or the professions, and the Bourbons would not readily admit them to the army; so they were usually poor, idle, without political knowledge or political courage. The new succession laws and the legal abolition of entails between 1812 and 1819 had permitted some fragmentation of property, and the post-war depression after the artificial stimulus of the British occupation of 1806–15 hit the big landed families. Their estates were smaller and mortgaged, their political influence except in local government was largely gone.

Goodwin remarked that 'two only of the nobles are men of fortune, none of them are men of energy, and none enjoy the public confidence'.[2] He estimated that, from 1812, the number of temporal peers had dwindled from 124 to 40, while the number of landowning families had grown from about 2,000 to 20,000; income levels likewise had fallen, from the Prince of Butera's £30,000 sterling a year in 1812, to a condition where no landowner not possessing sulphur mines had £5,000, and a scant hundred people in all Sicily had as much as £1,000.[3] Feudalism had by now been abolished in law, but had generally survived in fact, and was much more disadvantageous to the peasant than before. An interesting memorial was submitted to Garibaldi on 25 May:

Landowners are no longer poor aristocrats so much as grasping usurers. Property has not in fact been split up as the law demanded, but is still in just a few hands. Today we often look back on feudalism with regret, for in the latter days of the feudal system we had barons who were becoming more civilized, who would have been ashamed to enforce the full tithe of feudal obligation and were even kind to their tenants. In those days, agriculture, our sole occupation, prospered.[4]

However rose-coloured may have been this view of the past, there was more agreement about the present: as the governor of Girgenti remarked, 'agriculture in my province, as in the rest of Sicily, has been entirely abandoned'.[5] And, along with agriculture, the nobles too were in decay. That Bourbon officials in April 1860, when revolution began, had little appreciation of the fact that a Palermo revolt could be other than a feudal *fronde* after the style of 1812, and that their first reaction was even to arrest five leaders of the Palermo aristocracy, only shows that they had not realized what was happening. Goodwin tells that 'the five nobles all passed for royalists', and in fact there was to be little of imprisonment about their captivity; Castelcicala and other local officials were probably just trying to convince the young King Francis of Bourbon that they were in charge of the revolution. There was little chance

---

[1] C. S. Forbes, *The Campaign of Garibaldi in the Two Sicilies* (Edinburgh, 1861), p. 79.
[2] Goodwin to Elliot, 12 Apr., F.O. 70/318.   [3] 30 July, 5 Aug., F.O. 165/134.
[4] G. B. Marinagri to Crispi, 25 May, MSS. Archivio Crispi (Archivio di Stato, Palermo), fasc. 138. (These Crispi papers have recently been moved to the Archivio Centrale, Rome.)
[5] To Mordini, 3 Nov., MSS. Archivio Mordini (Barga), busta 30.

that the feudal constitution of 1812 would have satisfied the 20,000 families in 1860. Some of the noble class did make an almost invisible attempt to win a re-enactment of that constitution in the last days of Bourbon rule,[1] but history had passed them by. Crispi now wrote of these aristocrats as of some extinct species, 'who were not on the side of liberty, but were just anxious to live the grand life of courtiers and hence wanted freedom from Naples, so as to make Palermo the capital city of a separate kingdom'.[2] Few of the old grandees figured prominently in the revolution of 1860. There were indeed one or two expatriate returned exiles such as Marchese Torrearsa and the Duca della Verdura, who had learned new liberal ways as exiles in Turin and Florence. Others were mere figureheads to make the cause respectable, for instance, the Prince di San Giuseppe; or there was the future premier of Italy, Di Rudinì, who first fled post-haste to Naples and Genoa, and then returned when the revolt was over to become a leader of the ceremonial *Guardia Dittatoriale* and director of theatres. The liberal, Naselli, thus wrote that 'the most corrupt element of all in Sicily was the Palermo aristocracy who ask for nothing more than *panem et circenses*', and who were thinking not of revolution but just of building their new theatre.[3]

It is today a commonplace that the risorgimento was a middle-class movement of professional, mercantile, and landowning gentry, against which the reaction was to be largely composed of peasants led by the aristocracy. The middle-class landowners must have mostly come into Goodwin's 20,000 families, and in many or most cases probably opposed the revolution until Garibaldi became the best available defence of law and order. But the professional classes of the towns stood more solidly with those of the educated and travelled aristocrats who were shortly to champion the cause of united Italy. In Garibaldi's Thousand there were no peasants or aristocrats. Among the leading Sicilian revolutionaries there were the physician La Loggia, Monsignor Ugdulena the canon lawyer, Michele Amari the great medieval historian, Isidoro La Lumia the archivist and *letterato*, Vincenzo Errante the professor of literature, Orsini the professional soldier, Crispi the lawyer. There was also that most interesting family of arms manufacturers led by Luigi Orlando, who provided Rosolino Pilo with weapons in March for his expedition to Sicily, and who made the famous Ansaldo works at Sampierdarena into the arsenal of Garibaldi: Giuseppe Orlando was the chief engineer on Garibaldi's ship, the *Lombardo*, and Paolo was to become a minister in the revolutionary government.

In Sicily, men of the professions were less tied to conservatism than in many other countries; they were very rarely younger sons of the nobility, but were poor in money and esteem because their numbers were disproportionate to the society which they fed on. Educated above their station, oppressed by

---

[1] Lanza, 22 May, *Documenti Riguardanti la Sicilia* (Rome, 1861?), p. 197.
[2] *Il Precursore* (Palermo), 24 July.　　　[3] 8 Feb., MSS. Biblioteca Fardelliana (Trapani).

sovereigns who saw in them a chief source of discontent and instability, they were impelled to take desperate action when revolution exposed their special susceptibility to inflation and war conditions. They provided an important element in that small group of discontented intellectuals who organized and led the initial revolt, and they also bulked large in that dangerous body of educated unemployed who, after some weeks of interregnum, backed Garibaldi and then Cavour as the best hope of ending uncertainty and lack of governance.

In face of the systematic Bourbon persecution of *pennaiuoli* (scribblers), and remembering the fierce counter-revolution of 1849 when Ferdinand had marked his return to power by letting loose the mob against their liberal masters, many among the middle classes would have had some reason to wish Garibaldi success. Merchants could appreciate the freer trade and distant markets that unity would bring, and the political power which would secure legislation in their interests and break restrictive court monopolies. A few of them proved to have real liberal views, initiative, and capacity for self-sacrifice; yet most of them favoured revolution only when it could be seen as an economic proposition and if it could be achieved without undue damage or risk. In the revolutions of 1820 and 1848, for example, the middle classes had never had time to consummate their movement before the plebs profited from lack of government to rise against their betters; Poerio and his friends had therefore been driven in 1849 into hoping that Ferdinand would manage to repress the Calabrian risings, and had shown that they were ready to abjure liberal sentiments at the first sign of class war. In 1860, however, Garibaldi's march was very swift, and hence men such as Poerio were not compelled to fall back on established order when their employees and tenants again went land-grabbing.

An urban proletariat was not important in Sicily. In a pre-industrial age town-dwellers were capable of only rudimentary forms of organization and could be fairly easily contented in any emergency with doles and public works. Palermo lacked the *lazzaroni* class which at Naples battened on the royal court, the fish market, and the docks. There was little question in the island capital of any public right to common land, and hence class opposition was more diluted there than in the provinces. Outside Palermo, however, agrarian unrest was the same in 1860 as in every year of political upheaval. Not only was it more widespread than has been thought, it was an essential part of the political revolt, without which the latter might well not have succeeded.

The great mass of the peasants reaped no immediate gain from the risorgimento; the landowners won, and they marked their success by neglecting to enforce the laws which were designed for the sharing out of the communal lands; so far as we know, the number of small holdings actually decreased in the years after 1860. For this very reason among others, many in the lower strata of society, in so far as they had any political sympathies, sided with the Bourbons. It was natural for them to envy the landowners but to have no hatred of royal tyranny. Successive kings had been intelligent enough to cultivate popularity with the masses in order to set them against their masters. The successful royalist counter-revolutions of 1799 and 1849 had found a strong ally in popular ignorance and superstition. In general a paternalistic policy of *feste e farina* had thus sufficed in normal times to keep town-dwellers quiet. This explains how the spark was first kindled on the barricades not by the poor, not by a proletariat rising against starvation, but rather by lawyers, doctors, shopkeepers, and wealthier artisans.

Yet these facts leave out of account a parallel rising in the interior of the island, which was responsible for the dissolution of local government and the liquidation of the hated Bourbon police; and this process greatly helped Garibaldi's military success as much as it may have retarded political renewal afterwards. This unruliness, rick-burning, tax-avoiding, charter-destroying, land-occupation, often assassination, all helped the revolution in some ways just as they may have hindered it in others. Having next to no political views, the peasants were yet induced by one of Garibaldi's decrees on 2 June to think that he was in favour of land reform, and this was a deliberate calculation on his part. Support by the *contadini* had a military importance, for it led to Garibaldi being well informed of Bourbon troop movements, at the same time as it kept General Lanza quite in the dark about Garibaldi's series of surprise manœuvres on the way to Palermo. The peasantry therefore assisted Italy's most notable military success in the whole risorgimento. Psychologically it was invaluable for Garibaldi to find supporters everywhere, to be able in most places to avoid compulsory billeting. The squads of locally-recruited *picciotti* also had a distinct, if sometimes dubious, military importance. The speedy disillusionment of the peasants with patriotism must not conceal the fact that in the early days they contributed powerfully to the cause.

Sicily had been, along with the island of Sardinia, the only part of Italy to avoid the social impact of 1789 and the Napoleonic reforms. So the peasants had never won the land which would have integrated them into the social system as a conservative force. The *latifondista* with his armed *campieri* tyrannized over his serfs. He was in complete charge of local government, which is to say of the only effective part of government, and he regarded such a position as more a perquisite than a service. A Palermo newspaper referred to these local tyrants as acting like 'so many Machiavellis or Palmerstons'.[1] Baron Cusa wrote from Girgenti that 'the local authorities are completely unable to escape from the tyranny of the rich landowners'.[2] One minister remarked how 'the *monts-de-piété*, which had been set up originally to help poor farmers, had come into the hands of a few rich men who now used the

[1] *L'Unità Itallana* (Palermo), 26 Sept.
[2] 30 June, MSS. Carte Bianchi-Ricasoli (Archivio di Stato, Florence), N/P.

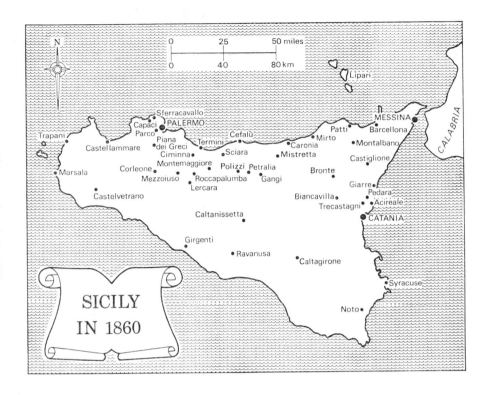

money of these same establishments to oppress the weak'.[1] The mayor of
Caltanisetta was none other than Barone Trabonella who owned most of the
local sulphur mines: there could be no alternative candidate.

With such a system of local government and land ownership there was bound
to be trouble in difficult times. The majority of Sicilians were landless
labourers, the class most of all depressed by the scarcity and high prices which
civil war brought in its train during 1860. The *comunisti* whom General Bixio
reviled and executed at Bronte as social revolutionaries could be seen in a
different light by Giuseppe Ferrari as 'the first victims of a social war'.[2] The
same Crispi who was ruthlessly to crush the Sicilian fasci in 1894 now wrote:
'In Bronte, Biancavilla, Polizzi, and many other villages, an inevitable insurrection broke out against the old regime, against the money-lenders, against
the fat *borghesia*. This was the war of the "berets" against the "hats", a war
that has always existed and will continue for ever.'[3] All over the south there

---

[1] 10 Oct., Arch. Palermo, b. 1589.
[2] In parliament, 11 Oct.
[3] To Ferrari, 22 Oct., Arch. Crispi, f. 152.

were smouldering fires of anger and vengeance against the userer, the land
agent or *gabelloto*, and the local notary.

In the Palermo newspapers of the time one can learn a fair amount about
'the enormous estates which are still referred to as "ex-fiefs" and which are
either not cultivated at all or at least are given over to a thoroughly unprofit-
able type of agriculture'.[1] *Il Rinnovamento Italiano* commented (6 February
1861): 'For the most part the land is abandoned and useless, just because
there is no market which will meet the costs of production, and expenses are
high because roads are lacking and transport slow.'[2] In the journal *Il Garibaldi*,
the economist Maggiore Perni spoke out in two articles of 11 and 16 June.

The forests have been destroyed and the mountain sides in Sicily are bare as the
Arabian desert; our rivers lack any embankments, and when torrents burst their
banks they may destroy in a single day what man has taken a year to build. The
latifondi belonging to the church or to villages are untilled and look like death
itself. Over immense areas, marshes and miasma make all life impossible. We have
no tools for agriculture, no agricultural education, and there is no meeting-point of
any kind between large and small proprietors. . . . Infamous, domineering userers
grant small-scale charity, but at the same time take all the crops for their own profit.
. . . The aristocracy is contemptible and ignorant. It never stands in defence of the
common people. . . . Traders and landowners have slavishly served the Bourbons so
as to be the more secure in their property, so as to obtain an official sanction for
their ill-gotten gains. . . . Meanwhile the poor hate governments which oppress them
and from which they have little to hope.

Another relevant comment comes from *L'Osservatore* (19 October):

In 1838 and 1841 Ferdinand introduced laws to break up these estates and so
encourage agriculture. He also once again forbade any remaining feudal exactions
by the baronage. . . . Yet his provisions for the distribution of land between villages
and then by lot between individuals have simply not been carried out. After so many
frustrated hopes it is understandable that the peasants of Biancavilla, Montemaggiore, and elsewhere have broken out into excesses against those responsible for
cheating them out of these legal benefits. Unfortunately the middle classes in small
villages have always been domineering towards labourers. Moreover these same
middle-class elements share out in succession among themselves the administrative
jobs in each village, and in this capacity have protected their own usurpation of the
communal lands. They have also bribed the intendants and other government
officials in order to slow up the process of land division.

These newspaper excerpts may make it easier to understand one aspect of
the revolution which broke out in April before Garibaldi decided to leave
Genoa—a revolution which was indeed to be the direct cause of his coming to

---

[1] *La Forbice* (Palermo), 30 Oct.
[2] Salvatore Maniscalco, a minister of the Bourbons, confessed on 9 February that 'we are spending
300,000 ducats a year on projects that are ill-conceived and badly executed. Very few rivers have
bridges, and at the present rate of construction very few will ever have them' (copy in F.O. 165/135).

Sicily. These journalistic comments may also help to disentangle the attitude of the common people from that of the intellectual, urban middle class who were to provide the brains of the political movement and be its chief beneficiaries. There is a sense in which both these groups had a common interest in *starting* a revolution, so as to obtain a turmoil from which to reach, the one a political objective, the other a social. But, once started, the triumph of either meant ruin to the other; for a successful political revolution would give the proprietors even more power over their tenants and labourers, while on the other hand social revolution spelt a *jacquerie*. From this fact grew quickly a wide diversity of aim which, as in 1849, split the revolutionary forces and might easily have opened the way to counter-revolution as on former occasions. But for the moment, in April 1860, both groups were ready for rebellion, and so Sicily for the second time in the risorgimento provided the example of that kind of dynamic popular initiative which was required to make Italy a nation.

On 4 April a rising in Palermo started off those sporadic outbursts of revolt which one month later induced Garibaldi to set out for Sicily and ended in the creation of a united Italy. Who were the men who rose and kept the guttering flame alight for that critical month? The names of Francesco Riso and Rosolino Pilo are well known; but in concentrating on the heroic but diminutive group of self-sacrificing liberals whose friends were to tell us of their deeds, we must not forget the perhaps more selfish and certainly less articulate common people without whose insurrection the rebellion could hardly have succeeded. The Bourbon governor, Prince Castelcicala, had reported back to Naples on 8 March that 'the spirit of sedition has reached even the plebeian classes of Palermo who now seem familiar with phrases such as "non-intervention", "popular sovereignty", "universal suffrage", and other strange ideas'.[1] One foreign observer of the initial outbreak said that it was the work almost entirely of 'lower orders and monks'.[2] The British consul noted that 'the combatants were workmen', and he went on to express his belief that

the movement was premature . . . and the best friends of the country tried to keep it down, not for the love of the government, but from the conviction that it would fail. The intended outbreak was not known to the liberals until 24 hours before it took place, when it was too late to prevent it. Not one of the liberals had anything to do with it.[3]

What makes this evidence more reliable is that Goodwin had not only spent thirty years living among the merchants and noble classes of Palermo, but was sufficiently in touch with the liberal would-be revolutionaries to be showing them privately the dispatches of the British foreign office.

---

[1] Arch. Crispi, f. 138.   [2] *The Westminster Review* (London), XIX (Apr. 1861), 140.
[3] Goodwin, 2 May, F.O. 165/134.

Outside Palermo, the first sign that the government might be incapable of maintaining order had been the cue for everyone with a grievance to rise and remedy it. A political motive existed strongly with some people, but equally or even more powerful were personal and family vendettas, inter- and intra-municipal rivalries, economic hardship and the lust for loot. Without these, rebellion would most likely have failed, for they served to harness the most powerful of all supports to the task of disrupting government services. Castelcicala reported on 6 April that 'bands are forming round Palermo and they are interrupting the flow of water to the grain mills'.[1] Others watched how the bands seized the government's money deposits in each village, and how officials were too terrified to remain in their jobs.[2] Numerous reports show that refusal to pay the official taxes, especially food taxes, was almost universal, and villages found the strongest of all motives to rise in the fact that revolt meant a tax-free holiday. The attitude of the various classes at Messina is suggested by this reference in a letter of the provincial intendant, dated 8 April:

Yesterday groups were forming here of the poorest citizens and of suspected criminals on the pretext of being unemployed, and this gave a good deal of worry to respectable people. We did everything possible to break them up, and I have arranged communal and provincial public works for tomorrow to keep them occupied, while traders and manufacturers will employ as much labour as they can on their own account.[3]

At Catania, after midday on the 8th there were reports of lower-class rebellion, and it was said that perverse elements of the population were creating general alarm and inciting to sack and theft.[4] One Catania newspaper later remarked how, if the moderates had not gone to extreme lengths to contain popular fury, the people would have risen that Easter Monday and massacred all Neapolitans in the town.[5] At Girgenti the British vice-consul spoke in similar terms on 9 April: 'On Saturday last the lower class of the people tried to make a demonstration with the intention of plundering the town, but were impeded doing so by a few influential persons.'[6]

Peasants and workmen were in the position of having everything to gain and little to lose; hence they rose with a fine abandon which did much to ensure the early success of the revolution. This was the fact which persuaded Garibaldi's government in almost its first measure to promise the peasants an equitable division of land, as well as the abolition of the food excise and the

[1] This elemental feature of a peasants' rebellion was later to accompany Garibaldi's invasion of the continent, where a major target was the mills, since private individuals had annexed the public waterways and tried by force to establish a monopoly on an essential service (*Il Nazionale* (Naples), 20 Sept.).
[2] I. La Lumia, *La Restaurazione Borbonica e la Rivoluzione del 1860 in Sicilia* (Palermo, 1860), p. 76; logbook of Bourbon staff officer, T. Battaglini, *Il Crollo Militare del Regno delle Due Sicilie* (Modena, 1938), II. 189.
[3] Arch. Palermo (Polizia), b. 1239.   [4] Castelcicala, 11 and 15 Apr., ibid. b. 1238.
[5] *Gazzetta di Catania*, 19 June. Easter Monday, 1282, was the date of the Sicilian Vespers.
[6] John Oates, 9 Apr., F.O. 70/315.

grist tax. This *macinato* had been payable by the peasant before his corn would be accepted in the communal mill. It had been the principal cause of the 1848 revolt, and now Marchese Torrearsa reported that 'the peasantry required the abolition of the duty as the condition of their joining his forces— a demand which was imperative.'[1] Property owners, on the other hand, had almost everything to lose and much less to gain. Some liberal landowners were in the forefront of the rebellion, but many others, so reported the viceroy in April, together with 'the more honest of the peasantry, had realized that revolution would be fatal to their interests and hence were helping to keep order in their respective villages'.[2] On the east coast towards the end of May, Mr. Jeans heard that 'at Giarre the moderate party, fearing to compromise the safety of the town, has made a species of counter-revolution'.[3] One of Ippolito Nievo's letters made the significant comment, 'We have been helped by auxiliary squads of volunteers made up for the most part of emeritus brigands who are ready to fight against the Bourbons just as an excuse to make war on the landowners. . . . So much so, that we are now forced to act as police against the very men who were our allies until yesterday.'[4] Such a statement carries considerable weight coming from a senior Garibaldian officer and one so perceptive. He was writing in July when various circumstances were turning the peasants' revolt into a reactionary movement, but we must be careful to keep the two phases distinct, and see that, in the critical months of April and May, the peasants had been the revolutionaries, whereas the reaction had rather come from their employers.

This first counter-revolutionary movement among property owners in April had been the despair of the liberals. Cordova lamented that 'the squads in the countryside cannot help but commit excesses, and selfish interest thus forces the landowners to side against them'.[5] D'Ideville spoke of 'le peu de sympathie qu'il [Garibaldi] rencontre dans la noblesse et la bourgeoisie sicilienne'.[6] This may have been one reason which made Cavour go slow on giving support to a Sicilian political revolution, for if not at once successful it would dangerously offend Sicilian property-owners, and also it might easily become social revolution, so inviting the horrified condemnation of Europe. In contrast with Cavour's careful calculation, it was the refusal of Garibaldi and Crispi to count the cost or think so logically which was to win Sicily and so unify the peninsula. It was, furthermore, the despised and feared *bassa gente*, on the point of starvation and despair, who were ready to risk all and continue the revolution through April, against all logic and against the opposi-

[1] Goodwin, 18 June, F.O. 165/134; La Masa found that he had to abolish it on his own initiative in the inland villages (G. La Masa, *Alcuni Fatti e Documenti della Rivoluzione dell'Italia meridionale del 1860* (Turin, 1861), p. xxxiii).

[2] 12 Apr., Arch. Palermo, b. 1238.   [3] 30 May, F.O. 165/134.

[4] 1 July, D. Mantovani, *Il Poeta Soldato Ippolito Nievo* (2nd ed., Milan, 1931), p. 357.

[5] 11 Apr., Bib. Fardelliana.

[6] H. d'Ideville, *Journal d'un Diplomate en Italie, 1859–1862* (Paris, 1872), I. 128 (diary for 20 July).

tion of almost everyone else; so doing, they kept a revolutionary situation open for Garibaldi one month later. On the other hand the interesting fact emerges that the revolution of 1860, which was to be rightly celebrated as the triumph of the middle classes, began with the bulk of them preponderantly in opposition.

The same fact that had caused dismay in Turin had been the main hope of the Neapolitan government in its efforts to put down the rebellion. A dispatch of 9 April from Naples reported that 'law and order is being defended at Palermo by the possessing classes who spontaneously offer us their help'.[1] Castelcicala's reports are full of these offers of help from proprietors. Arms were given out to them,[2] and he noted on 20 April that 'everywhere landowners rival the authorities in fighting against the insurgents who are only creating revolution as a weapon against property'. At Trapani and Termini, as early as the 8th, 'the leading citizens have official permission to form a civil guard and keep order'. From Noto on the 10th the intendant wrote that, 'thanks to the good sense of the majority who are opposed to disorder we have put down the few evil-doers who were creating public disorder as an excuse for robbery. . . . Employees, and the middle classes in general, but also the great mass of our villagers are together putting down the disorders committed by a few young good-for-nothings.'[3]

Almost everywhere a civic guard was formed, more to counter the revolutionary *squadre* than to fight the Neapolitans. It was well remembered how in the 1848 revolution the National Guard had done little against the Bourbons but much for internal public security—so much indeed that Filangieri had retained the new organization for some time after 1849. One is reminded of the cleavage in 1848 between radicals and liberals, for instance between the two ministers, Calvi and Stabile, which had been accurately reflected in the division between Calvi's *squadre* on the one hand, and the National Guard and the *compagnie d'armi* on the other. The intendant of Messina in 1860 now recorded that he had restored order by arming a

civic guard chosen from the wiser and more prudent property-owners of the town. . . . Respectable citizens are against any idea of disorder, which is wanted only by criminals and the very poor who have nothing to lose and much to gain from revolution. . . . Wherever seditious groups were found, they could not be put down except when some citizens took arms and joined the authorities.[4]

For example he described on the 12th how this had happened in the township of Barcellona and Milazzo. The same story almost exactly was told for Patti,

[1] Carafa telegram to Canofari, Carte Bianchi-Ricasoli, f. X.
[2] Messina intendant, 16 Apr., Arch. Palermo (Polizia), b. 1239.
[3] 10 Apr., ibid. *Il Nazionale*, 16 Aug., suggested that the government had been glad to leave unsolved the question of the common lands because it gave them a chance to divide the landless from the landowners.
[4] 16 Apr., Arch. Palermo (Polizia), b. 1239.

Corleone, Girgenti, and Caltagirone. At Catania the intendant described how he relied on the classes who remembered the excesses of 1848 and who feared lest 'the *bassa plebe*, those criminal vagabonds, might seize their chance to lay waste the town'. He had been able to dominate one demonstration on Easter day, but the real test came when a group of armed criminals arrived from the surrounding countryside 'on whom *i buoni* had no influence'.[1] A revealing letter to Torrearsa remarked on the motives of the people of Catania in being grateful to the soldiery for preventing a revolution: 'The citizens would like to have more liberty, but not if it means sacrifice or trouble on their part, and they are mostly afraid that liberty may mean more disorders and robberies.'[2] In the same way we find that at Catania, Messina, and Caltanissetta the mine-owners, contractors, and merchants in general, were very willing to take government subsidies to start up new enterprises and so absorb the unemployment which underlay much of the unrest.[3]

Towards the end of April the reports from the provinces clearly indicate a gradual return to order and more regular payment of taxes. Garibaldi was indeed to arrive none too soon, since the revolt was near the point of collapse. But the most important fact was that the government could never altogether extinguish the forces of disorder. Castelcicala's communiqués of 3 and 8 May reveal, for instance, that on 25 April houses were set alight at Caccamo; on the 29th bands fired on the *guardia urbana* at Ciminna; and the same day at Petralia Sottana a band descended from the mountains at dawn and slew the mayor. All these incidents were in the interior, where no government of Sicily had ever been really master, and where rebellion could lurk for years. At Petralia the citizens rose in self-defence and arrested the malefactors. The monitory news was officially published in the *Giornale Ufficiale* 'so that proprietors will see what kind of revolution this is and will support the government in suppressing it'.[4]

Apart from a few marauding *squadre* in the mountains, the country was mostly settling down. Castelcicala's policy had worked by giving doles and employment in the towns, by obtaining special shipments of flour from the Bourbon government in Naples, and in the provinces by setting proprietors against the landless labourers. But little was done for the two prime revolutionary classes, the town middle classes and the *contadini*. The former were known to be sometimes free-thinking liberals, but it was also believed of them, and the facts had shown with some justice, that they wanted liberty only if it did not mean risk, sacrifice, or trouble. Nevertheless, for many non-liberals in the commercial and professional classes, the time might come when the greater risk lay in the continuance of their allegiance to the Bourbons. It

[1] c. 20 Apr., ibid.
[2] 5 May, Bib. Fardelliana.
[3] Caltanissetta intendant, 14, 20 Apr., Arch Palermo, b. 1239; Castelcicala, 15 Apr., ibid. b. 1238.
[4] Castelcicala, 3 May, ibid.

might be, for instance, that the more probable danger of sack came less from the rebels than from the Neapolitan troops. It might be that the Bourbon regime offered no security at all except self-help, and that, caught between revolution and reaction, trade and confidence would languish, so that action meant risk but inaction ruin. Once the Bourbons had given currency to the first suspicion that they might not win, ordinary middle-of-the-road citizens might be inclined to look more favourably at a man such as Garibaldi who could possibly restore a different kind of law, order, and confidence. Palermo was a town of 250,000 inhabitants, and though it was officially stated that order had been restored, yet on 26 April H.M.S. *Assurance* arrived there to find the town 'much more disturbed than on the 17th . . . few shops are open', and firing was heard every night.[1] Vice-Consul Rickards wrote of Messina on the 30th: 'Almost all respectable young men are hid away or gone into the country. . . . Many of the shops are now open but business is entirely suspended.'[2] Goodwin remarked of Palermo on 2 May that the state of siege was causing much misery: 'Decent people beg in the streets. . . . The shops in the Toledo are still closed.'[3]

The landing of Garibaldi at Marsala on 11 May at once rekindled hope among the revolutionaries. His Sicilian friends had promised him immediate help from local auxiliaries, but at first no one dared to commit themselves. Only as he showed that his men could stand up to the royalist troops did the bands of *picciotti* join him,[4] and this was the signal for a general resumption of the revolt. Garibaldi had only a thousand soldiers of his own and an inadequate supply of arms, yet three weeks later a large army surrendered to him and almost all of the island had been won for the revolution. This astonishing result has always been hard to explain because it was not accompanied by a grass-roots movement of mass patriotic idealism.

A convincing explanation is that a leading part was taken by the peasants, again for other than political reasons. The murder of hated policemen and *macinato* collectors was everywhere the cause of a universal desertion from their posts by government officials, which in turn led to the dissolution of central as well as local government. An official publication of documents by the Bourbon authorities yields the following instances of the unleashed fury of an oppressed people. On 19 May, Intendant Vanasco of Girgenti notified Marshal de Rivera that 'armed bands have sprung up all over the province, and have attacked the smaller towns in order to seize stocks of cash in governmental or communal buildings, thereafter proceeding to occupy private property'. On the 20th, Brigadier Clary wrote from Catania that 'poverty has reached such a point that people are driven to excesses out of sheer desperation. Until now the presence of officials in government offices has kept

---

[1] Cmd. Aynesley, 28 Apr., F.O. 70/325.
[2] F.O. 70/315.   [3] F.O. 70/134.
[4] *Risposta del Generale Türr all'Opuscolo Bertani* (Milan, 1874), pp. 8–12.

the excesses in check . . . but now the authorities have simply disappeared.' On the 21st another document from Clary showed the fear that this could arouse: 'The sulphur miners here are indescribable. They are the worst brigands to be found anywhere in Calabria and Sicily. They dwell inside the mines just in order to escape from justice. In times of unrest they emerge, and are now marching en masse on Catania.'[1] This attack on Catania can therefore be seen as something more than the spontaneous rising by the oppressed and patriotic middle classes which some historians were to claim.

In May, much more than in April, there was something of a united front against the Bourbons, for many of the peasants thought Garibaldi a god come to deliver them, while the patriots thought him at least a hero, and ordinary citizens were much too frightened to oppose him. His arrival in Sicily provided middle-class liberals and non-liberals with another choice than merely that between ordered tyranny and free anarchy. Garibaldi's proclamations prudently called everyone to respect property, and if he did not yet offer a better regime of security than the Bourbons, his rule could hardly be worse than the lack of governance people had endured throughout April. Most of the liberals and patriots had understandably feared to commit themselves at first, mindful of many unsuccessful attempts to rebel in the past, and of the terrible Bourbonist counter-revolution in 1849. But, once the revolution had taken hold, it was too late to worry. If the Bourbons won again, they would certainly stir up the peasants to indulge in a counter-revolution of sack and slaughter, whereas Garibaldi alone could offer them present and effective aid against the outbreaks of social disorder. Every day that saw Garibaldi further entrench the fortunes of his revolt gave them further reason to back his cause. Hence the almost universal dislike of Sicilians for Neapolitans was at long last divorced from the social and economic compulsions which formerly had underpinned rule from distant Naples. The Bourbons in April stood for law and order; in May they were becoming increasingly associated with disorder, with sack and the destruction of property, with the threat of a useless continuance of civil war through the harvest months.

It may be added that, a few weeks later, a peasants' revolt for the second time played an important if negative part; because, once the peasants found that their local tyrants were surviving the collapse of the Bourbons, and that Garibaldi's decrees on land division were stillborn if not insincere, it followed that their own future lay no longer with the revolution but with counter-revolution. This fact was to be decisive in its effect on Sicilian public opinion, for it turned the largely non-political middle class in favour of Garibaldi and the dynasty of Savoy. In other words, the peasants had in the first place helped to bring the former government to a stop, so making Garibaldi's conquest feasible; and in the second place, the intensification of their own

[1] *Documenti Riguardanti la Sicilia*, pp. 695, 817, 819.

purely social war helped to turn former partisans of the Bourbons in favour of a united Italy.

During the month of May, however, this alteration of alignment was still in the future, and what needs explaining is the momentary formation of a united front against the Neapolitans. On 9 May a letter from Naselli in Palermo gives a clue. He declared that the Neapolitan soldiery had already managed to do 300,000 ducats worth of sack and damage since the insurrection began, and people were responding to this fact by coming from all over the island to enrol.[1] No better way could have been discovered of uniting all Sicilians behind the revolution. A manuscript by a Trentino among the *Mille* describes the havoc wrought by the Neapolitans in one village on the way to Palermo: 'Malcarnero (Valguarnera?) has been burnt to the ground and its inhabitants left without everything. But the loathsome Bourbon soldiers, when they started killing people here, paid the price of their infamy, and 30 Bourbon corpses, half burnt, half eaten by dogs, lie along their route of retreat. It is a terrible sight.' King Francis did in fact try to prevent too much wilful destruction.[2] But his generals on the spot had to cope with arrears of pay on a huge scale which Goodwin estimated at 100,000 lire,[3] and it was said on 24 April that the soldiers would not fight if they were forbidden to pillage as they went.[4] It does not need much imagination to see the great advantage, in comparison, of the fact that Garibaldi neither sacked nor was able to bombard. Termini was bombarded by the Bourbon forts on four occasions between the 16th and 26th; Palermo for three days after Garibaldi's entry, when a quarter of the city was, with some exaggeration, said to have been destroyed; Catania was horribly sacked between the 31st and 2 June; and Messina, the commercial capital of the island, was almost completely evacuated in fear on at least three occasions in six weeks.

Towards the end of May the situation was thus that many people, who would not otherwise have been likely to find themselves on the side of revolution, were hoping that the revolution would win and were even showing readiness to take arms against the Bourbon government. This change of heart was not sudden or complete, for timidity still came uppermost. At Messina, for instance, where even the Bourbon intendant thought that the majority sympathized with the rebels, citizens preferred not to start an insurrection until someone else had already won it for them. Instead of rising, the Messinese took to the hills or put their goods and families on board one of the ships in the harbour, so that, with 50,000 people fled, 'all business has ceased and the poorer classes are in serious distress'.[5] Fear of lower-class revolt thus created unemployment and so added fuel to lower-class agitation. It still remained

---

[1] Bib. Fardelliana.
[2] 27 May, *Documenti Riguardanti la Sicilia*, p. 222.   [3] 26 May, F.O. 70/316.
[4] *Garibaldi o la Conquista delle Due Sicilie: Raccontato da un Testimonio Oculare* (Leghorn, 1861), p. 127.
[5] Messina intendant, 27 May, Arch. Palermo (Polizia), b. 1239.

true that only those who had little to lose would rise unless the chances of material advantage were better than favourable: this meant the peasants, rather than the *borghesi*; it meant the professional middle class of Palermo rather than the rich merchants of Messina. At Termini the same fear of popular agitation led to the formation of a National Guard about 20 May, not to aid the revolution, but 'to stop an outburst of theft and assassination' which threatened to endanger the prospects of a good harvest.[1] This same National Guard would no doubt defend the revolution as soon as revolution became a going concern; but, until that moment, it was out to destroy the lawless bands which were doing more than anyone to bring the Bourbon government to a halt.

This combination of unemployment riots in the towns with anarchical *jacqueries* in the country thus had two results, which can be distinguished in point of time, but which both led in their separate way to Garibaldi's success. On the one hand was the dissolution of government; on the other there was a spreading lack of confidence in the capacity of the Bourbons to keep law and order. The generalization which would come nearest to fitting the facts about middle-class opinion is that the primary fear was of licence and disorder; the natural instincts were those of fear and self-interest; and an ambivalent attitude was then adopted, one which led to forming civic guards against the revolutionary *squadre*, at the same time that many of the same people may also have been beginning to hope for a quick Bourbon defeat. If the *squadre* were to be opposed because they endangered the harvest, so were the Bourbon troops who were specially commanded by King Francis to feed their horses on the ripening corn.[2] Opposition to the revolutionary *squadre* could be thought of as something else than opposition to an integral part of the revolution; indeed, once the initial and indispensable service of these bands was complete, it was the first object of Garibaldi to create a regular militia which would relieve his revolution of the embarrassment of their support.[3]

The change of mind appears in reports by the Bourbon commanders during the course of May. On the 13th, the Sicilian minister, Maniscalco, told Francis that 'the whole population now asks for a change in government, and the fear of revolutionary vendettas is turning even ordinary decent citizens into insurgents'.[4] On 15 May, Maniscalco added:

Public spirit is getting worse all the time. Palermo now fears either war reprisals on the one hand, or else the fury of the mob out for blood. . . . Everyone is terrified.

---

[1] 22 May, *Rapidi Cenni e Documenti della Rivoluzione del 1860 Riguardanti la Città di Termini* (Palermo, 1861), pp. 46–7.
[2] Francesco to Lanza, 20 May, *Documenti Riguardanti la Sicilia*, p. 184.
[3] 21 May, *The Memoirs of Francesco Crispi*, ed. T. Palamenghi-Crispi (London, 1912), I. 189; it was indeed the subject of the first decree which followed the assumption of dictatorship by Garibaldi, dated 14 May at Salemi (*Raccolta degli Atti del Governo Dittatoriale e Prodittatoriale in Sicilia* (Palermo, 1862), pp. 1–6).
[4] *Documenti Riguardanti la Sicilia*, p. 479.

Civil servants are leaving their jobs, and the voice of duty is no longer heard. What we are watching is a process of social disintegration. . . . Even men of good will are now turning in favour of the revolution, because they fear otherwise that they will be devoured.[1]

Salzano added to this the news that one of the most important features of the moment was a run on the banks by bondholders: 'Every day there are crowds in the bank selling their bond units, and to stop this would cause a riot.'[2] General Lanza was greatly worried by the strike of civil servants: 'Public offices are now closed and all functionaries have fled. To threaten them with dismissal would be fruitless, as fears aroused by the revolution are now much greater than those of unemployment.'[3] Obviously the fear of revolution was becoming over-shadowed by other and complementary sentiments: for instance, by the fear that the Bourbons could no longer perform the job of protection which alone justified their tyranny; or the fear of even larger-scale lower-class rebellion if the middle classes continued to stand aloof without actively intervening to capture the revolution for themselves.

By 2 June Garibaldi was in command of Palermo and most of the island, and the different social strata had to adjust their political alignment in response to this change in government. There was, first of all, a lull if only a temporary lull in class war: this was due to the excitement of the moment, to the sense of achievement in common, to the novelty of revolution and the fact that the criminal classes had gained from the profits of sack; also to the fact that there was much work to do in repairing the devastation and providing munitions of war. Rich and poor joined in the destruction of the edifice of tyranny. Priests, workmen, traders, and their clerks were all seen out at Castellammare pulling down the hated Bastille.[4] One observer was struck with the significant fact that 'despite the excitement and agitation in Palermo the town has never known so much order'.[5] At Catania an interregnum of seven days, without troops, without government, witnessed the revival of commerce and a new security for property.[6] Even outside the big cities, the minutes of the civic council of Partinico for 12 June contain the remark that 'our revolution destroyed as if by magic all the roots of our age-old dislikes and rivalries'.[7]

Yet this agreement evaporated once the work of destruction was accomplished and when civil war brought its usual aftermath of distress. The correspondent of the Turin newspaper *Opinione* said (20 June):

More than a quarter of Palermo is a heap of ruins. . . . Barricades are so numerous and so high that carriages and carts cannot move through the streets, while even pedestrians find some difficulty. Everywhere you find men armed with guns, scythes or

[1] Ibid., p. 481.   [2] 24 May, ibid., p. 325.
[3] 21 May, Arch. Palermo (Polizia), b. 1238.   [4] *La Forbice*, 27 June.
[5] 'Rivoluzione Siciliana del 1860', p. 96 (letter of 2 June), MSS. no. 220, Museo del Risorgimento (Rome).
[6] *Gazzetta di Catania*, 11 June.   [7] Arch. Palermo (Seg. di Stato), b. 1561.

spits. . . . Most of the shops are shut, and whole classes of the population are in serious want. There are beggars all over the place. Prices of food have rocketed, sometimes to four times their normal average. Even water must be purchased, because the aqueducts have largely been broken. . . . All the towns are refusing to re-employ those who had jobs under the Bourbons, which in places means dismissing the only people who can read and write. The government is isolated as though encamped in the middle of an unknown country.

There was an anti-Garibaldian political prejudice underlying this account; yet much of what it says must have been true. Despite some futile efforts to fix maximum prices,[1] the cost of living continued to increase,[2] and only a few workers were in any position to strike.[3] A most important class was affected by the inability to re-open several whole departments of government, and by the turning loose of the more compromised of the former Bourbon employees. The city merchants and industrialists memorialized Crispi, who was now Garibaldi's secretary of state, with the lamentation that the lack of trade with Naples had forced the closure of the best workshops of Palermo so that people were unemployed and demanding food.[4] Civil war still continued, with Bourbon soldiers remaining in the island for some months more, and a great number of deserters from both armies must have escaped to the *maquis*, preferring brigandage to military discipline. Arms and ammunition were circulating in quantity, at first distributed by the government for self-defence, later illegally sold and bartered by the troops. Convicts had been released both by the retreating Bourbons and by the victorious mob, and also by the new government which sometimes confused felons with political prisoners. Another dangerous class were 'young men who are idle and undisciplined because of interruption to their studies':[5] also 'the smugglers, a turbulent kind of men who may have helped to defeat Bourbon tyranny, but must be eliminated if a free regime is to endure'.[6] To confront these problems there existed only an improvised administrative system; the Bourbon police had been dissolved, and all available revolutionary troops were concentrated for the advance on Naples. Taxes could be left unpaid with impunity, for Garibaldi was compelled to rule, as Crispi described it, 'by love not by force',[7] and long years of Bourbon rule had inculcated 'sentiments of lawlessness, insubordination, and hence of hatred against the police'.[8]

These were circumstances conducive to all manner of excess, and it was hardly fair of Cavour and La Farina to blame Garibaldi for an inability to cope with them. On the whole one may be amazed that there was not more chaos. Many witnesses support Amari in recording the freedom of Palermo

---

[1] Decree at Catania, 8 June, in 12 June issue of *Giornale del Governo di Catania.*
[2] *L'Annessione* (Palermo), 28 Aug.   [3] *Il Precursore*, 2 Sept.
[4] 29 Aug., Arch. Palermo (Min. Int.), b. 1584.   [5] *La Forbice*, 18 Aug.
[6] *Il Precursore*, 19 Aug.   [7] Crispi in parliament, 6 Apr. 1861.
[8] Governor of Girgenti, 3 Nov., Arch. Mordini, b. 30.

from crime when compared with 1848, if we exclude pardonable offences like the smashing of the royal statues and the breaking of any windows which were not illuminated to celebrate Garibaldi's victories.[1] Amari added that even in the provinces, where the National Guard was usually weak because of municipal rivalries and the lack of an administration, there was exaggeration about this disorder by people who wanted the credit for suppressing it. Soldiers were sometimes called out to repress disorders, only to find nothing more amiss than that the local mayor was worried.[2] Depretis,[3] Forbes,[4] and Goodwin[5] were all severally impressed that there was surprisingly little disorder. It is not safe to generalize about the provinces, but Palermo did remain remarkably calm, and a comparison with post-1860 governments might show that, where Sicilians were concerned, there was a lot to be said for government 'by love and not by force'. The papal consul was once forced to ask for protection.[6] On another occasion a crowd outside the Questura compelled the police to yield up to summary execution some reputed police spies.[7] Of course there were also political demonstrations: for instance those organized by La Farina, who had been sent by Cavour to try and induce Garibaldi to cede Sicily to Piedmont, or those in an opposite sense, which were sponsored by Crispi.[8]

Outside the capital, matters were more serious, because the provinces had always been difficult to control. Throughout the revolution, communication between the main towns was preferably by sea, and even from quite near-by districts food used to come to Palermo by the sea route. In a country where the chief cities were still linked by mule paths and occasional fords over rivers, inland towns such as Caltanissetta were out of touch and always remained disorderly. Many villages in the interior had spontaneously formed committees to keep order and tide over the interregnum. That old Sicilian official, the captain at arms, with *compagnie d'armi*, reappeared, with the primary purpose of keeping order rather than of spreading rebellion. Self-help was the only help. The committees were hostile to the *squadre*, and everywhere personal rivalries and general lawlessness combined to give an opening to social unrest. Eber discovered at Roccapalumba that 'here as everywhere else you find traditional hostilities which turn everything into a question of personalities

---

[1] 3 Aug., *Carteggio di Michele Amari*, ed. A. d'Ancona (Turin, 1896), II. 109.

[2] Governor of Alcamo, 19 Sept., Arch. Mordini, b. 28.

[3] 24 July, MSS. Carte Bertani (Museo del Risorgimento, Milan).

[4] 'Not one of the least remarkable features amongst this unusually turbulent population was that life and property were unmolested' (Forbes, *The Campaign of Garibaldi*, p. 61).

[5] 'The conduct of the National Guard in preserving order during the past six months is deserving of high praise: the most perfect tranquility reigns in the capital and the provinces' (19 Nov., F.O. 165/135).

[6] 16 June, Arch. Palermo (Seg. di Stato), b. 1560.   [7] 27 June, ibid. b. 1561.

[8] Garibaldi was reported by Goodwin on 27 June to have threatened to remove his government out of Palermo and to where it would be out of reach of these attempts at popular dictation of policy (F.O. 165/134).

wherein patriotic feelings have no part'.[1] From Ravanusa the Capitano Giustiziere complained that, after being 'elected by the people' to an office he had held in 1848, he discovered that the governor of Girgenti had made another appointment to the same office.[2] All this was the inevitable accompaniment of revolution, and it weakened the conservative classes by adding one more division to that between liberals and reactionaries. La Farina wrote to Cavour that the wholesale change in personnel had created difficulties impossible to resolve without force.[3] One disappointed critic somewhat unfairly attributed to Crispi

the destruction of the former governmental structure and the appointment of new men without inquiry into their political principles. . . . In the interior of the island, where municipal rivalries are very much alive, the appointment to offices is very important, but outsiders might well not see what would happen if a distant government took over from local authorities the choice of magistrates and police officers. Hence the opposition to Crispi, who in this way has thrown an apple of discord into each village. Hence the absence of authority, the triumph of anarchy, and the distress of good honest citizens.[4]

Not many days went by in June without signs of reaction and agrarian unrest to show that the coming of Garibaldi had not been able to still such inherent rivalries any longer than the excitement of novelty might last. At Mistretta on 7 June there was a riot, and the governor was driven to create a permanent rota of 32 security guards to patrol night and day.[5] The 'proprietors of Castelvetrano' asked for a loan of mounted police.[6] From Alarinco on the 12th the National Guard reported that for a long time a group of criminals had been trying to turn the place upside down and had now brought it to the verge of civil revolution.[7] In the province of Catania, Mazzini's friend Nicola Fabrizi found by the 30th that every village showed signs of a full-scale political reaction.[8] From all over the island damage was reported to the telegraph poles and wires.[9] Special appeals had to be made for the horses and carriages of the postal service which had been stolen.[10] The inspectors of forests sent in much news of the destruction of woodland, and orders had to be dispatched to all governors to prevent the abusive cutting of wood for charcoal, especially as timber was so scarce in Sicily.[11] The peasants once again, just as in 1848, were invading and occupying the common lands.

[1] To Garibaldi, 28 June, Arch. Mordini, b. 28.
[2] To Garibaldi, 16 June, Arch. Palermo (Seg. di Stato), b. 1561.
[3] 5 July, MSS. Carte Farini (Biblioteca Classense, Ravenna).
[4] Tito Mannucci, *Un Consiglio imparziale al Prodittatore* (Palermo, 20 Aug. 1860).
[5] 18 June, Arch. Palermo (Seg. di Stato), b. 1561.   [6] Ibid., undated.
[7] Ibid. b. 1560.   [8] 30 June, Arch. Crispi, f. 152.
[9] 3 July, Min. Pub. Security to Min. Public Works, Arch Palermo (Polizia), b. 1512; 21 July, Min. Pub. Sec. to Min. Polizia, b. 1549.
[10] Garibaldi's proclamation, 11 June, Arch. Palermo (Seg. di Stato), b. 2095.
[11] 19 June, Min. Pub. Works to Min. Sec.; 22 June, Min. Sec. to all governors, Arch. Palermo (Polizia), b. 1547.

Popular discontent was first focused on Garibaldi's proclamation of conscription. Most citizens in the capital must have seen the need for this measure, the lack of which had spelt failure for the revolution of 1848, and most non-Sicilians were surprised at the extraordinary opposition it aroused. Apart from military needs, conscription could be a fine method of educating the masses and bringing them over to the side of order. *L'Annessione* thus wrote (26 June) that the masses in Sicily lacked education and civilization, but

when a peasant from some unknown village reaches Palermo, he enters a new environment which will educate him to ideas about national honour and the need for an ordered society. Discipline will there teach him, and work will cure him of laziness, while the proximity of more cultured people will act on him as a civilizing force.

But in the countryside the reluctance to be thus educated was enormous. Local authorities within a very few days had to advise modifications to the conscription law, permitting the sending of substitutes and the exemption of agricultural labourers during the harvest. Governor Scelsi of Cefalù on 13 June, only four days after taking office, told Crispi that, owing to the ineffective organization of the National Guard, there was not enough force available to carry the conscription decree into effect, and he would have to suspend it.[1] Scaglione reported from Patti on the 20th that the unwillingness to serve might trigger off a counter-revolution if they were not careful.[2]

The word 'counter-revolution' appears too often in these documents to be written off as accidental; and that the possibility was connected with disorder and growing social tension is suggested by a letter written to Crispi from Catania as early as 5 June. The letter shows that proprietors were now becoming bold enough to raise objections to some of the acts of the revolution, for example to the reduction of the food taxes and the replacement of local self-help committees by the government-organized militia; and it suggests that the allegiance of many to Garibaldi may have had an economic and social, rather than a political, significance.

Public security is our first priority as a government. Without it we shall be adversely criticized and Sicilians will begin to regret the sepulchral tranquillity of the Bourbon regime. It was a great mistake to have opened the prisons in Palermo and Catania, for this has released thieves and murderers amongst others. The public is furious at it, and landowners are already beginning to regret the past. Our victory has thereby been corrupted. . . . It is vital that you revive the *compagnie d'armi* and hand out some quick and exemplary punishments. . . . And why abolish the grist tax? It was not a heavy tax, but was universal and ancient, highly profitable to the state; its abolition has not reduced the price of bread, but has just helped a few middle-class speculators without aiding the really poor.[3]

---

[1] Arch. Crispi, f. 142.   [2] Arch. Palermo (Seg. di Stato), b. 1561.
[3] Vigo, Arch. Crispi, f. 135.

The districts of the sulphur mines were those suited by their remoteness and the character of the natives to the early re-emergence of social unrest. Caltanissetta was the largest town of this area, and there the governor wrote on 13 June that blood had been spilt, public archives had been rifled, and deposits of cash taken from government buildings; he feared that another civil war might be round the corner.[1] Nor was this the first mention of the possibility of civil war during the two initial weeks of liberation. Caltanissetta again on the 21st asked for more guards from Palermo to control the large and restless class of sulphur-miners.[2] On the 9th, the governor of Nicosia wrote that he could collect no taxes, and spoke of 'a civil war that threatens us everywhere and at any moment' because of unemployment in the mines. Every class of society, he added, had now observed that anarchy might be profitable to some individuals, but the 'terrifying sulphur-miners' were the most dangerous of all in this respect.[3] Such a statement may suggest the inference that the dominant economic class was driven almost against its will to support Garibaldi as soon as he became the established government and represented law and order.

Other villages in the sulphur districts had seen risings in June. At Comitini there had been several deaths.[4] Bivona reported riots against conscription on the 13th: the arrival of a civil governor was greeted here with joy as meaning an end to anarchy, but almost at once there were threats of kidnapping which were foiled only by the proprietors bribing members of the gangs to guard their homes. He had also been obliged to prevent people recruiting private armies.[5] A week later another report from the same district showed that the bands were being repressed by a body of militia organized by the governor and serving at their own expense.[6] This is a process by which the victors of the rebellion against Bourbon tyranny were splitting up into those who had nothing to lose and those who had everything to lose; and between these two the government of Garibaldi was compelled to stand with the owners of property.

Troops had also to be sent to Lercara, the site of the northernmost and richest sulphur mines of the island.[7] Here we know something of the trouble from a report made by the mine inspectors in 1861. All the mines round Lercara were unworkable because of underground and open-cast fires precisely during these months from March to October: a large area covering five villages was thus desolate, since the primitive mining system caused fumes that were lethal to vegetation, and so made alternative employment in agriculture impossible. Many casualties were also caused, since 'the workers were driven by such pressure to increase their earnings, that they took no account

---

[1] To Min. Sec., Arch. Palermo, b. 1561.   [2] ibid.
[3] Ibid. b. 1560.   [4] Goodwin, 23 June, F.O. 70/317.   [5] Arch. Palermo, b. 1560.
[6] 22 June, ibid.   [7] Undated draft report, Arch. Crispi, f. 138.

of the dangers involved . . . and so paid the penalty for their own ignorance and the immorality of managers who refuse to take necessary precautions'.[1]

The best-known example of lower-class revolt in 1860 was that at Bronte.[2] This was a village where there was always social unrest at any moment of political disturbance,[3] for Bronte was well known for the common rights once enjoyed by the villagers over the land, which had been mostly confiscated by the landowners without any offer of compensation.[4] Radice, who has written an account of this insurrection, says that the Brontesi had been struggling for their rights ever since the village had been given out in fief by Pope Innocent VIII in 1491. The Bourbons had much later used the revenues derived by the Palermo hospital from Bronte to endow the hated Nelson family with a duchy. The subsequent laws through which Ferdinand had intended to remove the relics of feudalism and divide up communal lands had been generally disobeyed, and the local authorities of Bronte had had every interest in cherishing the pretensions of the wealthy few to their encroachments on the rich volcanic land of the commune. In 1848 there had been the same conflict between the 'ducalist party' who supported the heirs of Nelson and those disinherited peasants who claimed rights on the estate. After 1848, some opposition leaders had been sent to prison, and others had lost costly legal suits against the duchess.

With the victory of Garibaldi, the villagers claimed that the fall of the Bourbon king should also mean the fall of his creature, the duchy of Bronte, and division of its lands among the inhabitants. Garibaldi was, in their eyes, a social as well as a political deliverer. He not only had abolished the grist tax, but his decree of 2 June promised a share in the communal lands to those Sicilians who rose in arms. Any village without enough land for this was empowered to draw on the crown *demanio*; alternatively, any land left over could be shared out by lots among non-combatants.[5] The difficulty was not immediately apparent to the peasantry that the ducalist party, their social enemy, might shift politically on to the same side as Garibaldi. In the subsequent murder trial, the defence lawyers tried to make out that the landowners in Bronte, unlike those elsewhere in the island, had been hostile to the revolution.[6] None the less it is clear that the division in the township ran along social and personal not along political lines. Nearly all the *classe civile* were for the absentee duchess in England, and her secretary was one of the

[1] 16 Mar. 1861, Arch. Palermo (Min. Int.), b. 4183.
[2] B. Radice, 'Nino Bixio a Bronte', *Archivio Storico per la Sicilia Orientale* (Catania), 1910, pp. 253–69.
[3] *L'Unità Italiana* (Genoa), 10 Aug., in issue for 15 Aug.
[4] *L'Osservatore* (Palermo), 19 Oct.   [5] *Raccolta degli Atti*, pp. 24–5.
[6] *Difesa Pronunciata d'innanzi la Corte d'Assise per la Causa degli Eccidii Avvenuti nell'Agosto 1860 in Bronte* (Catania, 1863); the *sindaco* was said to be reactionary by the Messina correspondent of *L'Unità Italiana* (Genoa), 25 Aug.

leading 'liberal' conspirators, while the revolutionary committee used to meet in her house. Once the political revolution had succeeded, the way was then open for personal vendettas and class war which used politics as a mere pretext. The ducalists denounced the opposition leader, Lombardo, to the governor of Catania as a Bourbonist: among the common people, however, spread the rumour that he was really a personal friend of Garibaldi, and his prestige and their pretensions rose accordingly and disastrously.

Violence began in Bronte after a decree on 17 June ordered the general exclusion from civic councils of all who had assisted the Bourbon reaction of 1849. Lombardo had hoped this would enable him to become president of the local council, but the nominations of 22 June vested power solidly in the hands of the ducalists. Governor Tedeschi, instead of placating Lombardo with some post like that of *giudice*, unwisely kept the minority out of all office, and the new office-holders rashly made no even token concessions to the popular demonstrations for land partition. Meanwhile, at the end of June, the British consul had persuaded Garibaldi's government to warn Tedeschi against possible disorders on the large estates of the duchess, for her factor Thovez had urgently enlisted British official intervention.[1] In the commune itself, four companies of National Guard were formed, of which three were ducalist, one of them being led by Thovez; the fourth was composed mainly of *contadini* under the lawyer Lombardo and his friends. On 8 July, Thovez and his company arrested four of the opposition leaders. Though Lombardo seems to have had no wish for his men to touch life or property, he found himself involved in an exploding class war. The malcontents of the province had smelt trouble, and possibly they helped to organize a mass demonstration when *contadini* came in from the surrounding countryside and carried out a macabre mock funeral before the houses of their prospective victims. On 30 July, Lombardo harangued them, promising that they would get their partition of land without illegal means. Meli, president of the council, refused to take strong action either way, for he feared to provoke tempers any further. The provincial governor did nothing but increase the forest guards from four to ten.[2]

On the night of 1 August, Lombardo's company had its turn to be on guard, and all night long there was a murmur like the sea as the peasants surrounded the village. The other companies of the National Guard deserted in fear, and Baron Meli, gout-ridden on a chair, announced that he would carry through the division of land that should by law have been made years earlier. But Lombardo was wrong if he thought he could then stop the peasants who, 'like wolves driven by hunger from the mountains', began to break into the houses. The night of the 2nd witnessed a Goya-like scene of a wild, frenzied dance

---

[1] British consul to Garibaldi, 30 June, and Min. Int. to governor of Catania, Arch. Palermo (M. Int.), b. 1584.
[2] 4 Aug., ibid.

lit up by the burning of municipal buildings with all their papers and property registers. On the 3rd the participants acclaimed Lombardo as their president, while he and his friends vainly tried to restrain them. In an orgy of terror the massacres began. One man was dragged through the streets by his feet after suffering the most filthy indignities, all the time pricked by knives, and then burned half alive in front of the house of his son. Vengeance against a much-hated class was perpetrated on the notary, Cannata, from whose burning body the heart and liver were snatched and then apparently eaten publicly in the market place as a ceremonial act of vendetta.[1] The well-to-do fled if they could, with the peasants' *berretti* on their heads for disguise. Jeans, the British vice-consul, reported that some 16 people were murdered. Yet, despite the previous half-century of strife, not a finger was laid on the ducal palace, per-haps (says Radice) because the British flag flew above it and people knew that Britain had helped the revolution, perhaps because popular fury was directed rather against other minor local gentry who were thought to be the chief offenders.

On 4 August arrived the chief of police from Catania with 80 of his National Guard, but was too terrified to do anything beyond arresting the enemies of the people on their behalf. He tried to save these intended victims by under-taking to escort them to Catania to be shot, but had to stand by while they were marched to the scaffold and cut in pieces. Then on the 5th arrived soldiers, after the British representative at Catania had seen the governor. For a while they faced the people, neither side wishing for a fight. Then the clergy came and besought the soldiers to enter the village in peace, which they did, and these wild citizens were suddenly tamed. On the 6th came General Bixio on Garibaldi's orders, and shot five of the ringleaders, including Lombardo, after summary trial. Garibaldi approved this action, even if he also continued to insist that local authorities should study the question of dividing up the *terreni demaniali* in order to stop any recurrence of such trouble elsewhere.[2] A stern example was required. British support for the revolution would thus be maintained,[3] and the 20,000 families of Sicilian landowners would be con-vinced that Garibaldi not only opposed these agrarian riots but knew how to suppress them.

An epilogue should tell that, three years later, out of hundreds imprisoned, the court of Catania sent 37 to life sentences in gaol for their share in this rising. It is ironic that when finally the land was in part shared out, these same peasants were at once ready to sell their lots to a new class of oppressors,

---

[1] M. Mandalari, in *Rivista di Roma* (Rome), 1901, p. 226; the author had received this from a senator who had been a local authority in Bronte.

[2] Bixio to governor of Catania, 12 Aug., *Epistolario di Nino Bixio*, ed. Emilia Morelli (Rome, 1939), I. 383.

[3] Governor of Messina, telegram 3 Aug., Museo del Risorgimento (Rome); Bixio to municipal council of Cesarò, 6 Aug., C. Pecorini-Manzoni, *Storia della 15ª Divisione Türr nella Campagna del 1860* (Rome, 1876), p. 402.

even to the extent of taking 40 lire and declaring it as 400 in order to circumvent a law which a benevolent government had made to try to save their interests.

What is so well documented at Bronte probably happened to some degree in many different parts of the island. At Corleone, labourers had been persuaded to stop work till the monasteries and landlords reduced the rents, and the dangerous situation existed of workmen earning nothing and next year's food supply going to waste, the fields lying unploughed.[1] This mutiny, as the governor of Corleone called it, was still continuing at the end of September. He reported that no one would work on the ex-fiefs, but that crops and manure heaps were being stolen, and people were threatening to annul existing contracts of tenure and *métayage* or change them arbitrarily in their own favour. A list of thefts notified in this area, which is preserved in the police files at Palermo, shows that livestock was chiefly involved. The local authorities appealed to Palermo for a few exemplary executions, since by reason of the presence in the nearby mountains of 'an anti-revolutionary band of sixty persons', good citizens could not be found in the neighbourhood who dared to pronounce sentence of death. Complaints of this kind continued to arrive from July to September. The local military commander reported on 17 September that he had been obliged to dissolve the National Guard as it was composed of both sides to this social dispute and hence was useless. Governor Paternostro found that 'the popular belief here identifies liberty with an end to taxation, an end to law-enforcement, and the ability for everyone to steal and act just in whatever manner they like'.[2]

At Montemaggiore there had been an outbreak of crimes against property as early as 19 June, a bare fortnight after liberation.[3] By 24 July the village was in a complete state of collapse. Crispi sent a special commission with full powers, which reported 'a complete state of anarchy . . . in which 18 lives have been claimed as a sacrifice by a bestial mob whose only wish is for a division of the ex-fiefs'. Order was then restored by means of a dozen summary executions.[4] Such outbreaks were said to be often confused with 'private vendettas and the rivalry between families'. Troops had to be sent to Altavilla, Parco, and Mezzoiuso. The archpriest of Montalbano had his house burned in July, and the malefactors proceeded in familiar fashion to set fire to all the papers they could find in the parish church.[5] At Sciara a mobile column had to restore filched land to the duke of Ferrandina after protests from the Spanish consul, for his family had opted for Spanish nationality.[6] Near Cefalù on 30

[1] Governor of Corleone, 6 Sept., Arch. Palermo (Polizia), b. 1547.
[2] Reports of 20 July, 9 and 25 Aug., and 6, 10, 12, 17, 22 Sept., ibid.
[3] Governor of Termini, 19 June, Arch. Palermo (Polizia), b. 1548.
[4] Crispi's draft order, Arch. Crispi, f. 152; governor of Termini, 22, 23, 25 Aug., Arch. Mordini, b. 28.
[5] 25 July, Arch. Palermo (Polizia), b. 1548.   [6] Governor of Termini, 28 Sept., ibid.

September a large number of people intruded on a council meeting: they presented a petition to the president calling for the restoration of 'rights which from time immemorial have been enjoyed here by individual villagers over the common lands of the village and which were taken from them arbitrarily. The president refused this petition on the pretext that it was not properly signed.' After which rebuff, some 400 took their animals forthwith to pasture the common lands.[1] At Gangi the civic council was compelled to appoint a commission to start breaking up the five ex-*feudi* of the village, and people threatened to revolt 'because they now recognize these infinite procrastinations as just designed to deceive them'.[2]

In Catania province, levellers' risings were reported in June at Pedara, at Trecastagní, S. Filippo d'Argirò, and at Castiglione. At Acireale, a riot developed after the Catania civic council had tried to reimpose the food taxes which had been slashed to win popular backing in the early days of revolution.[3] In Messina province, at Mirto, Alcara, and Caronia, various other manifestations of social unrest were found; and a witness declared that order had still not been restored when he returned to Sicily in May 1861.[4] Governor Ugdulena at Messina urgently sent off 40 ill-to-be-spared *carabinieri* to the island of Lipari, but they did not suffice, and he had to ask permission to send a further 30 together with 'a special commissioner responsible to myself who will hear the complaints of the people which often seem fully justifiable'.[5] Much the same story could be told for Patti and Mistretta.[6]

In the far west of Sicily, the governor of Trapani reported that hostages were being taken by the malefactors, and that a special commission already appointed would have to be replaced as none of its members dared to take firm action against crime.[7] At Capaci, 'twenty people have for a long time been formed into a band which treats law and authority as non-existent'.[8] Crispi was told that 'what has happened and is still happening at Piana dei Greci is quite horrible and in defiance of law'.[9] Depretis informed him that the fief of the Principessa di Niscemi 'was occupied by a hundred persons from Sferracavallo, who chased out her factor, divided up the land, marking it out with stones, and began to plough it': and he added 'we must take action quickly'.[10]

The anxiety of landowners was all the greater in that this was harvest time and the vintage would soon be due. Apart from olive oil, it seems to have been a good harvest this year, luckily for Sicily,[11] but that meant all the more need

---

[1] Governor of Cefalù, 2 Oct., ibid. b. 1547.   [2] Arch. Palermo (Min. Int.), b. 1585.   [3] Ibid. b. 1584.
[4] G. Buttà, *Un Viaggio da Boccadifalco a Gaeta 1860–1* (Naples, 1882), p. 156.
[5] 10 Oct., Arch. Mordini.
[6] Governor of Patti, 5 Aug., attributed the anarchic risings in several places in his district to the example of Bronte; governor of Mistretta, 18 Aug., referred to this continual anarchy (Arch. Mordini).
[7] 20, 29 Aug., Arch. Mordini.   [8] Laiacono, 26 Aug., Arch. Crispi, f. 155.
[9] Cenni, 28 Aug., ibid., f. 156.   [10] Depretis, 17 Aug., ibid., f. 138.
[11] Depretis to Garibaldi, 9 Aug., MSS. Archivio Curàtulo (Milan), doc. 928; Camera di Commercio, Palermo, to Min. Int., 17 Oct., Arch. Palermo, b. 1589.

to prevent crops being stolen or burnt. A three-year plague of locusts was fortunately just ending.[1] The revolution was, however, accompanied by widespread rick-burning and crop- and cattle-stealing. At Biancavilla, whence one committee had already gone to Naples to agitate for the division of land,[2] soldiers had to be withdrawn from the liberation war in order to supervise the threshing of rye.[3] At Marsala, Mr. Ingham, the doyen of the Marsala winegrowers, made complaints through the British consul that crops were being ravished, rents and debts repudiated, and a total lack of order was prevailing in the provinces of Palermo and Trapani, so that his large outlay on the year's vintage was in danger: he would have liked a few salutary executions, but Depretis promised only that he would try to protect the Ingham factories and estates.[4] A similar complaint was made later in September by another well-known name in the Marsala trade, Messrs. Woodhouse of Liverpool, who asked for a British gun-boat to be stationed off the port, and one was sent to protect their wine factories against 'the natives'.[5] Of all districts in Sicily, Marsala might have been expected to be the least susceptible to agrarian trouble: it was an area of intensive cultivation and even of long-established small holdings; prosperity was derived from foreign trade, and the population was said to be well-disposed to the merchant farmers on whom that prosperity depended. By September, moreover, the vintage was providing work and cheap food, and the forces of public security were increasing. On 9 October Garibaldi's secretary of the interior, Piraino, told the British that by now 'the authorities of the island are almost universally in the full and regular exercise of their functions and public order is nowhere seriously troubled'.[6]

It seems in general true that the main area of peasants' revolt was the inland, upland districts, and also that this revolt decreased after reaching a climax in August. One final example will suffice to show the forms it could take. At Vallelunga, near Caltanissetta, the mayor reported on 27 August: 'Between 4 April and 10 June all classes lived in complete harmony here. Everyone realized the difficulties of the times, and hence forgot the rancours which had been building up since 1849. But on 10 June all became chaos.' It was a perhaps not untypical story. A rumour started that the plebs had in mind to burn the communal registers, and so all 'good citizens' came round to the village piazza, where one family who thought itself particularly threatened tried to clear from the square a few peaceful labourers gathered on the steps of the church. No real violence happened, but the news spread and the peasants, 'thinking themselves threatened as a class', took arms. Thereat the irregular police, and also those 'private citizens who had armed themselves to enforce law and order, shut themselves up in their houses'. Some of the more

---

[1] *L'Annessione*, 3 July.   [2] *L'Osservatore*, 19 Oct.
[3] Governor of Catania to Min. Sec., 23 Aug., Arch. Palermo (Polizia), b. 1549.
[4] Ingham, 27 Aug., quoted on 6 Sept. by Goodwin, F.O. 165/134.
[5] 25 Sept., F.O. 70/327.   [6] Ibid.

peaceful inhabitants for a moment succeeded in dissuading the peasants from violence, but a shot was then heard, and the sound led to half an hour of general shooting. This was stopped by people crying 'Viva Italia! Viva Garibaldi!'; but it was clear that the rioters were the victors, and they disarmed their opponents, confiscating any keys so that they could search all houses for arms. The mayor added that, though they went on to burn the proceedings of the magistrate's court, they were to be praised for a scrupulous and almost religious respect paid to property. A few days later, some of the families which had fled were brave enough to return. On 1 July the provincial governor gave the writer of this report special powers, and he summoned the civic council to make emergency provisions. But as all members of the council were either priests or of the upper classes, the rest of the people objected, and the mayor, seeing that the objection was justified, submitted twelve names of *borghesi* to the governor. The latter, however, refused to approve them, and so the civic council was never able to meet because of the conflict it would have provoked. The trouble continued throughout the month, with some people always ready to flee into the countryside on the slightest suspicion of more violence, and the *contadini* always ready to assemble in the piazza at the warning blast of a horn.[1]

From these examples of the action of the peasants, taken deliberately from different parts of Sicily, little evidence can be found that there was anything concerted or organized; nor would one expect to find much theorizing or much doctrine of class struggle. The peasants' revolt never imperilled the success of the political, patriotic revolution, and indirectly did much to help it. Politically negligible, the peasants were in a way socially decisive. But it was not long before day-labourers realized that the new order had nowise changed the ownership of property, and they were still at the mercy of the *gabelloto*, the *notaio*, and the money-lender. Had they visualized this earlier, a yet more formidable *jacquerie* might have split the opposition to Bourbonism and cut across the political war of liberation, with negative results on the course of the risorgimento. Instead they clung with a pathetic confidence for these few weeks to the belief that a change of government must be a change for the better. An invocation to Garibaldi, contained in an anonymous seditious broadsheet posted at Corleone on 8 September, will help to correct the falsity of vision derived from the fact that all the known accounts of the political revolution inevitably come from the winning side, from the middle and literate classes. Ignoring the bad spelling and grammar, part of it reads:

People of Corleone, you have been turned into fleshless skeletons just because a few landowners have sucked out even the marrow from your bones. . . . Rise to your feet! Avenge the blood of your forebears who were allowed to die of hunger . . . kill all the

[1] Pres. Municipio to M. Sec., 27 Aug., Arch. Palermo, b. 1548.

cattle you can find! Burn hayricks wherever you can, and do any other damage you may. . . . If King Francesco was toppled from his throne in a single stroke, that was due to the common wish of all us Sicilians combined with the firmness and constancy of each individual. If you present a united front you can dethrone the proprietors, you can snatch from their mouths the bread they stole from yours and which they would like to go on stealing from you. Don't let yourselves be deceived by anyone. . . . Unity! Unity! Unity! . . . Long live God and Garibaldi!'[1]

One wonders who among the peasants would have been able to read this manifesto.

For all their trust in Garibaldi, this most numerous of all the classes in Sicily, most of them day-labourers in precarious employment, were to find that the political radicals who for the most part directed Garibaldi's government were in no sense levellers. Though Garibaldi later called himself a socialist, he never knew what the word meant in any technical sense. In his natural anxiety to win all the support he could get in Sicily, he sincerely intended some sort of division of the *terreni demaniali* and lowering the food taxes; and the wealthy, on the whole, acquiesced in these measures as not being very important or likely to survive.[2] He was liberal with doles or with the promise of doles.[3] He sometimes tried to fix maximum prices, in vain.[4] An empty decree established *asili infantili*, children's homes, in about thirty towns and large villages,[5] and another took over all debts of the local authorities in order to make possible the gradual abolition of the food excises which weighed so much more heavily on the poor than the rich.[6] In his policy of playing up to all classes, he tried to abolish the feudal practice of hand-kissing and the title of *eccellenza*, and at the same time created the socially chic Guardia Dittatoriale for idle aristocrats who liked unsoiled uniforms. But this did not amount to a policy. On one occasion Crispi's journal, the *Precursore*, did so far exceed itself as to proclaim (19 August) that Garibaldi's government was not just an emergency administration, but was bent on a policy of social reform. But this was an isolated opinion, and in practice Crispi's acts were to belie these words. By the beginning of October, one of his correspondents was exclaiming: 'When, oh when, will the government prove that our revolution is in the interest of the proletariat as well as of others?'[7]

The radical Crispi was ruthless in his suppression of agrarian outbreaks. His *Precursore* agreed at least in one respect with *L'Annessione* of his political enemy, La Farina, for it roundly abused 'the printers who, with unspeakable

[1] Enclosure from Governor of Corleone, 10 Sept., ibid. b. 1547.

[2] 15 June, M. Amari, *La Sicilia nel Risorgimento Italiano* (Palermo, 1931), p. 120.

[3] 5 June, *Giornale Officiale del Governo Provvisorio di Sicilia* (Palermo); decrees, 6, 9 June, *Raccolta degli Atti*, pp. 26–7, 36–7.

[4] *Giornale del Governo di Catania*, 8 June decree, in 12 June issue.

[5] 27 Sept. decree, specifying that they are for 'the poorer classes, hitherto hardly recognized by society, though they are the great mass of the people', *Raccolta degli Atti*, pp. 412–13.

[6] 17 Oct., ibid., p. 477.   [7] Carboni, 4 Oct., Arch. Crispi, f. 135.

wickedness, think they can get away with no evening work'.[1] As minister in charge of internal affairs, Crispi was stringent against begging and vaga-bondage,[2] and he circularized all provincial governors that 'police super-intendents must have no eye for anything except defending property, defend-ing individuals, and defending the inviolability of the home'.[3] Garibaldi's decrees indeed speak for themselves. Almost his primary concern had to be the restoration of order and the rigorous, even arbitrary, punishment of offences. One decree of 18 May set up a military court for the trial of ordinary civilian cases; one of 28 May made sack and theft punishable with death; one of 9 June prescribed that kidnappers could be shot; one of 30 June referred to martial law as having the purpose of preventing those scenes of popular fury which happened in the early, uncontrollable moments of the revolution.[4] A circular on 18 June to magistrates, by Guarneri who was in charge of the justice department, invoked a special rigour in punishing 'crimes against property and life which, in these times, must be deemed crimes against the state'.[5]

That this was the obvious and only policy to follow is proved by the con-currence of all radicals of whatever shade in supporting it, for in their eyes this was no time for social reform or for meeting the demands of the peasants. The radical *Forbice* remarked on the admirable consensus of view at Palermo, where 'there were no ultra-liberals, since we know from theory and practice that such people would have been fatal to the cause'.[6] Depretis, Garibaldi's pro-dictator, rejected out of hand the suggestion of a French speculator, Lafitte, that the government should take the chance to nationalize the sulphur mines.[7] Asproni was eager for the Palermo government to give full compensa-tion to the Rubattino company for the seizure of their ships, because 'tomorrow we may need to take other similarly illegal steps, and if Rubattino has no reason for complaint, then other proprietors will not take alarm'.[8] Ugdulena in parliament later looked back on this moment almost defensively: 'Gari-baldi's government was not a revolutionary government on the pattern of 1789 and did not confiscate the mortmain lands of the church, since we felt property in any hands was always sacred (*cries of dissent*).'[9]

Quite apart from personal inclination in this matter, it was by now abun-dantly clear to all that the revolution, by its own internal logic, had come to be based on the support of property-owners who found more security under the new order than under a continuance of the old. Garibaldi had been among the first to recognize that their support was much more important to him in

---

[1] *L'Annessione*, 30 June; *Il Precursore*, 2 Sept.
[2] His printed order recalling to magistrates article 302 of the penal code, 9 June, Arch. Palermo (Polizia), b. 1512.
[3] *Giornale Officiale*, 5 June.   [4] *Raccolta degli Atti*, pp. 12–13, 19, 40, 99.
[5] *Giornale Officiale*, 18 June.   [6] *La Forbice*, 22 June.
[7] Draft letter to Garibaldi, 30 July, MSS. Archivio Depretis (Archivio di Stato, Rome).
[8] 19 Aug., Arch. Crispi, f. 138.   [9] 5 Apr. 1861.

the long run than that of the peasants. They alone could make his laws effective. They had control of provincial government, of the local money deposits and the local taxes. Baron Trabonella, the mine-owner, not only sent a large contribution himself to the dictator in July, but 'persuaded' his miners, or some of them, to subscribe 60 *onze* of their meagre wages.[1] Such men were also Garibaldi's recruiting officers, and the dictator was obliged to go to them in each successive village, being prodigal with offers of rank and preferment so as to get them to allow or compel their own retainers and labourers to serve in his corps of irregulars.[2] His first need was for stable government, and hence he welcomed that the National Guard should develop out of the private security organizations employed by the landowners, even though this might eventually mean capitulation to one side in the social struggle which was now cutting across the political fight for freedom. The function of the National Guard was not to oppose the Bourbons but to defend property,[3] and by 15 June *L'Annessione* could write that 'the lower orders are beginning to feel the moral authority of the National Guard, which is carefully recruited only from honest folk'.[4]

Out of the Sicilian revolution of 1860, it is broadly true that the middle class emerged socially and politically victorious, yet enough has now been said to show that the bulk of the middle and upper classes had not at first backed Garibaldi. Their first instinct had been to adopt a timid abstention from compromising themselves, and as late as July several English observers noted that such people were unwilling to aid Garibaldi if it meant actual sacrifices.[5] Some few must have gained from a continuance of the state of anarchy, for example those traders in large-scale contraband from Malta and Africa who had evidently won over the customs officials and armed forces of Licata: even the National Guard was 'interested' in this illegal traffic, and the proprietors of Girgenti were lending money at usury to the smugglers.[6]

The leaders of the Garibaldian new order were perhaps the professional rather than the trading or agricultural classes. The *Mille* itself was composed almost exclusively of students and professional men, and it is not without interest that the advisory Consiglio di Stato formed by Garibaldi's government in October was of the same class. Goodwin thought this an absurdity:

The members consist of churchmen, lawyers, medical practitioners, journalists, professors and *employees*, all men of talent, learning and integrity, to whom but one objection can be taken, that they are men of theory rather than of practice. There is

---

[1] *L'Annessione*, 23 July.
[2] G. Cadolini, 'Garibaldi e l'arte della Guerra', *Nuova Antologia* (Rome), May 1902, p. 57.
[3] Goodwin, 6 Sept., F.O. 165/134.
[4] *L'Annessione*, 15 June.
[5] Goodwin, 19 July, F.O. 165/134; Admiral Mundy, *H.M.S. 'Hannibal' at Palermo and Naples during the Italian Revolution, 1859–1861* (London, 1863), p. 188.
[6] Director of Customs, 2, 5 Sept., Arch. Crispi, f. 138.

but one agriculturist in the number, and miners and merchants are left unrepresented.[1]

But these men of theory were none of them socialists; they were rather liberals who saw that the revolution would stand or fall in so far as it could attract the class of rich men who had bought up the land of the Lanza and Pignatelli families after this had been made possible by the new succession laws between 1812 and 1841—in other words the 20,000 families who made up the new rural landowning pseudo-aristocracy.

In the last resort it was the non-political, non-liberal middle class who probably controlled the ultimate fortunes of the revolution—not the peasants, nor the nationalists among the professional men of the capital, but the merchants of Messina and this new class of landowners. In April and May they had had every reason to fear the revolution because of its patent associations with social upheaval. But between June and August, the growing divorce between political revolution and the peasants' revolt changed their minds, and by a strange irony the revolutionary Garibaldi came to stand in their eyes for economic stability. Marc Monnier wrote of Messina on 19 June: 'Tous les rôles sont invertis, et les timorés, les alarmistes, les bons bourgeois, les ennemis des révolutions, attendent avec anxiété Garibaldi, qui seul peut sauver leurs caisses'.[2] Commerce at Messina in June was still at a standstill: on the 2nd, Russo wrote that sixty thousand people had run away from this town, leaving it almost empty.[3] Not even furniture had been left behind, said the Messina correspondent of the Florentine *L'Unità d'Italia* on 8 June; and he added that the police were hardly in evidence at all.

Still less would confidence in the continuance of Bourbon rule be inspired by the Neapolitan soldiers, of whom their own commander confessed that 'their state of discipline is horrible, and our soldiers are acting like wild animals'.[4] This explains how the Piedmontese consul could say on the 10th that Messina had finally decided against the Bourbons, even if it feared to rise against them so long as its houses and warehouses were dominated by the *cittadella*.[5] A month later there has been no change. 'Messina is in a terrible state. Her skilled workers are unemployed, even proprietors are in real want, and trade is languishing.'[6] One may easily imagine how every day that saw Garibaldi further establish his regime would have increased the general belief in the viability of the revolution and the welcome which it would receive. Michele Amari commented on the fear of continued disorder, and remarked that landowners as well as merchants recognized after the atrocities of Bronte that the Bourbons could no longer offer them security. 'Les excès des troupes napolitaines ont couronné l'œuvre de 12 ans de gouvernement détestable.'[7]

[1] 30 Oct., F.O. 165/134.
[2] Marc Monnier, *Garibaldi, Histoire de la Conquête des deux Siciles* (Paris, 1861), p. 165.
[3] *Documenti Riguardanti la Sicilia*, p. 661.   [4] 21 June, ibid., p. 889.
[5] 10 June, MSS. Archivio Storico, Ministero degli Affari Esteri (Rome).
[6] *La Costanza* (Palermo), 12 July.   [7] *Carteggio di Amari*, II. 119.

Unlike Tuscany, where the priests and nobles had still preserved some sort of ducalist party, there was no Bourbonist party left in Sicily, and former autonomists such as Marchese Torrearsa and Baron Pisani now led those who clamoured for annexation to Piedmont.[1]

The cause of Garibaldi gradually came to signify power and profit to these merchants and landowners. There had never yet been a government of Sicily acting entirely in their interests. Bourbon absolutism had been based on no logic except the interests of Naples and the royal house. It had always oppressed any powerful Sicilian interests, whether the feudal aristocracy in the eighteenth century, or their successors who for convenience have been labelled the 20,000 families. These people saw that Garibaldi at last enabled them to shake free from the shackles of protectionism and monopoly which had been crippling commerce.

Revolution also provided them with a chance to expropriate the huge church lands which the absence of French occupation in the time of Napoleon had left almost intact. Communal and state *demanii* too, all could be opened up and bought cheaply in a buyer's market. The great extent of these communal domains in Sicily was the capital asset which Filippo Cordova, La Farina's chief supporter, presented to Cavour as a primary reason for his annexation of the island. After 1860, their purchase by private individuals was to increase the extent of the *latifondi*, at the same time as it would divert capital away from the more socially useful activity of agricultural improvement, and a beginning in this direction was made under Garibaldi's *dittatura*. On 20 August, *L'Annessione* proposed the cession to all state creditors of *beni nazionali* so as to extinguish the public debt and restore idle land to life, while this same measure would create a capital asset for society at no cost to the economy. The village administration of Corleone, in other words the local landed gentry, asked permission to sell the communal lands in order to pay their many creditors, who in other words were the village authorities under another guise.[2] The land of the Jesuits and Redemptorist fathers on 17 June had been declared to constitute national property.[3] An edict of the pro-dictator, dated 2 September, declared that the sale of these public properties and those of the innumerable pious or charitable foundations would be of immense value in the improvement of agriculture and creating a market for land. The abolition of church tithes, announced on 4 October, was prefaced by the argument that Sicily was primarily agricultural and hence it was necessary to break up these mortmain properties.[4]

One provincial governor wrote to say what a fine effect all this was having on public morale, coupling to his remarks an approval of the abolition of the 10 per cent tax on civil service incomes, and a recommendation to abolish the

[1] Ibid. II. 115–16; III. 205.
[2] Governor of Palermo to Min. Int., 25 Sept., Arch. Palermo, b. 1585.
[3] 28 June, *Raccolta degli Atti*, p. 57.   [4] Ibid., pp. 423–8.

food subsidies 'in the interest of the poor themselves'.[1] Here was a revolutionary programme for the downtrodden middle classes. Among other relevant decrees of Garibaldi should be noted the early prescriptions of 16 and 27 June which pronounced for free trade and the free export of cereals, and that of 29 October which allowed the free export of vegetables: so ended a long-standing mercantile grievance. More significant still, on 15 June, his finance minister, Peranni, promised to make payment in full to government bondholders of the interest due for the current quarter.[2] This compared favourably with the action of the Bourbons in 1849, who not only had repudiated repayment of the forced loan contracted by the preceding liberal government, but even had exacted that part of it which had not yet been paid up at their restoration. Garibaldi's government at once took steps to pay interest on the 1848 loans, and also on subsequent Bourbon loans as well. The conservative *L'Annessione* joyfully exclaimed that 'this important act puts an end to many hesitations, because it calms a widespread apprehension at the same time as it establishes on a firm basis the credit, and hence ultimately the fate, of our revolution'.[3]

Thus the middle class of 1860, unlike that of 1848 and earlier rebellions, had managed to consolidate its position before it was forced back on counter-revolution in order to defend its property. On the other hand, the *popolani*, who had done so much directly and indirectly for victory, were to find themselves excluded from the fruits of their own success. After Garibaldi had gone, they were to discover in the title of *re galantuomo* just the representative of those gentry, the *galantuomini*, who had tyrannized over them for so long.[4] In all probability this result was inescapable. At the same time it should be admitted that a submerged and forgotten peasants' revolt played a necessary part in the revolution which consolidated the united kingdom of Italy.

[1] Governor of Girgenti, 3 Nov., Arch. Mordini, b. 30.
[2] *Giornale Officiale*, 14 June.   [3] *L'Annessione*, 22 June.
[4] A. C. de Meis, *Il Sovrano* (Bari, 1927), p. 15.

II

Victor Emanuel and Cavour, 1859–1861

DURING the six months after July 1859, while Cavour was in retirement, Victor Emanuel was said to be like a schoolboy on holiday.[1] Once again he felt himself to be the real ruler of the country. The new premier, Alfonso Lamarmora, was not one of his close friends, but was a loyal general who with considerable self-sacrifice had indulged the sovereign's military ambition during the recent war, and who was now prepared to accept the humiliation of being merely prime minister in name. Lamarmora took the job very reluctantly and knew that his master had little confidence in him,[2] but in his capacity as a general he had sworn always to obey the king, and received his appointment as an order. The real power in the cabinet was the royal favourite, Urbano Rattazzi.

Parliament never met during Lamarmora's six months' administration, and this fact permitted a noticeable return to a more royalist interpretation of the constitution than had prevailed under Cavour. The Villafranca negotiations had indicated that the king had little intention of behaving merely as a parliamentary sovereign whose decisions would be covered by ministerial responsibility. In July 1859, when he oddly reproached Cavour for leaving him in the lurch by resignation, what he meant was to reproach Cavour for not staying in office to carry out a policy laid down by the monarch and not the minister. That was the king's idea of constitutional government. From now onwards he took the direction of affairs more obviously into his own hands and was evidently delighted to do so. Foreign policy was to be formulated by himself, sometimes unknown to or even against the wishes of his ministers.[3] He cheerfully offered to buy the Romagna from the pope and Venice from Austria without apparently consulting the cabinet, and without any notion at

---

[1] Massari, *Diario*, p. 324.

[2] *Ricordi di Castelli*, p. 250; *La Liberazione del Mezzogiorno*, v. 454; on 17 Sept. 1859 Lamarmora asked Massimo d'Azeglio to take his place as premier because he could not get on with the king (MSS. Archivio Lamarmora (Biella), XCII/145).

[3] *Rassegna*, 1954, p. 417; C. Pischedda, *Problemi dell'Unificazione Italiana* (Modena, 1963), pp. 112–13; La Tour d'Auvergne, 6 and 10 Nov. 1859, M. Aff. Étrangères.

all of where the money could be found. In return for such purchases, he said he would be prepared to renounce Tuscany: it mattered little that the Tuscans voted to join his kingdom while the Venetians did not, for to take such a vote too seriously would have looked like an acceptance of popular sovereignty. If Franz Joseph and Pius IX did not agree to sell these territories, he intended to fight another war against Austria in the spring of 1860: he would try to persuade France once again to join him in this war, though if necessary was ready to fight on his own.[1]

Such a programme was entirely unrealistic. More seriously he thought of using Garibaldi to start a revolution in central Italy. Garibaldi had been twice exiled from Piedmont and once condemned to death by the Genoese courts, but his popularity was now an important political fact and his loyalty to the king could be relied upon. At a meeting in August 1859 the two of them reached broad agreement that Garibaldi should make ready to lead some kind of movement to threaten a revolution and an invasion of the Papal States; and the king would keep privately in touch with him, to encourage or restrain as events might decide.[2] This was at first sight an attractive scheme, since Garibaldi was quite ready to be repudiated if anything went wrong, while at the same time there was a chance of his becoming the revolutionary initiating force which Cavour had so far found it hard to create. Half a million lire from the privy purse was promised in order to provoke a revolution which would give an excuse for Piedmontese annexation of a further stretch of papal territory.[3]

A few weeks later, under strong French pressure, the king was compelled to back down. He had been playing with fire. In particular he had given Garibaldi the idea that the king's approval would be forthcoming for a much more revolutionary policy than would have been accepted by the cabinet. Garibaldi was ready to believe that the king should now make himself supreme *Duce* of the Italian patriotic movement and dispense with parliamentary restraints. Other people, Ricasoli among them, would soon be saying much the same. If Victor Emanuel had been either more actively ambitious or less sensible, he might have taken this advice, but for the moment he complied with French wishes and asked Garibaldi not to cross into papal territory.[4] It is clear that he was yielding to Napoleon and not to his ministers.

In the first few days of 1860, Victor Emanuel was again in touch with both Garibaldi and Rattazzi as part of a devious manœuvre aimed at undermining

---

[1] *Gran Bretagna e Sardegna*, VII. 218–20; Massari, *Diario*, p. 366.

[2] *Lettere di V. Emanuele*, I. 560; *Garibaldi, Vittorio Emanuele, Cavour nei Fasti della Patria*, ed. G. E. Curàtulo (Bologna, 1911), p. 341; G. Ardau, *Vittorio Emanuele e i Suoi Tempi* (Milan, 1939), II. 18–19, likened Victor Emanuel's attitude to Garibaldi in 1859 with his grandson's attitude in accepting the alliance of Mussolini in 1922.

[3] Pepoli in parliament, 24 Nov. 1862, *Atti Parlamentari: Camera*, p. 4517.

[4] *Scritti di Garibaldi* (ed. of 1872), II. 398–401; *Memorie di Giorgio Pallavicino* (Turin, 1895), III. 546, 560.

Cavour's reputation and the bases of his electoral support.[1] To one of his aides the king said he would rather see Garibaldi than Cavour as prime minister of his kingdom, and this extraordinary remark was probably not made entirely in jest.[2] He hoped to raise a fund for arming irregular troops under Garibaldi's command. He also intended to use Garibaldi's popularity to help in building up an alternative parliamentary coalition before the *camera* was recalled. The need for an alternative to Cavour's transformist majority in parliament induced the king to work secretly with members of the extreme parliamentary Left. This included Angelo Brofferio, about whom the king used to speak severely but who with little doubt received money from the court and whose vote in parliament the king tried to influence.[3] The political claims of Rattazzi were also supported by the king's mistress, Rosina Vercellana, as part of her campaign against Cavour.

Such dabbling with the Left, however, helped to bring a big swing of aristocratic and conservative opinion back to Cavour, and this swing was whole-heartedly backed by Cavour's former rival, Azeglio, who recognized that the king's active engagement in party politics, if allowed to continue any further, might dangerously expose the crown.[4] It was also backed by the French,[5] and even more decisively by the British. Sir James Hudson felt so certain that Cavour was the one safe man in politics that he used some unusually forthright language, and persuaded the king, or almost forced him, to give up the plan to arm Garibaldi's followers. A few days later Hudson succeeded in forcing the resignation of Lamarmora and virtually imposing Cavour as his successor.[6]

Victor Emanuel reappointed his former minister unwillingly, and only after receiving a promise that Cavour would never again challenge Rosina's position as *maîtresse en titre*. The king also insisted, as usual, on having a share in selecting the other ministers. Nevertheless this moment was an important stage in the development of constitutional practice, since it confirmed that his

---

[1] 'L'Italie Libérée: Lettres et Dépêches du Roi Victor-Emmanuel II', ed. F. Masson, *Revue des Deux Mondes* (Paris), Mar. 1923, p. 367; F. Bosio, *Ricordi Personali* (Milan, 1878), pp. 16–19; Massari, *Diario*, p. 458.

[2] Ibid., p. 463.

[3] *Cavour-Salmour*, p. 157; La Tour d'Auvergne, 1 June 1858, M. Aff. Étrangères; evidently it also had included Orsini who had been in communication with the king only a few days before his attempted assassination of Napoleon (*Die Auswärtige Politik Preussens*, vol. x, ed. H. Michaelis (Oldenburg, 1939), p. 6); A. Brofferio, *I Miei Tempi: Memorie* (Turin, 1860), XVI. 269.

[4] The Turin newspaper *Espero*, 9 Jan. 1860; *Azeglio-Galeotti*, p. 152; a letter of 10 Jan. in MSS. Archivio Depretis (Archivio di Stato, Rome), I/7, says that Azeglio resigned his position as honorary aide-de-camp to show his disapproval of the king.

[5] La Tour d'Auvergne, 23 Nov., 29 Dec. 1859, 4 Jan. 1860, M. Aff. Étrangères, where the king is said to be 'd'un caractère faible'; *Mémoires du Comte Horace de Viel Castel sur le Régne de Napoléon III* (Paris, 1885), VI. 36.

[6] *Gran Bretagna e Sardegna*, VII. 297, 299, 302, where Hudson reported that 'the King of Sardinia, who has no head for anything but a sword and a horse, looks forward with glee to drawing the one and riding the other, no matter where'; Massari, *Diario*, pp. 468, 471.

dabbling in high politics, like his generalship in the late war, had been too unsuccessful to win him much support for a presidential-type system of government. Cavour had to proceed with care. He knew that the king continued to pursue a private diplomacy apart from that of the cabinet, as he also knew that Rattazzi and Ricasoli were from time to time considered as alternative candidates for the premiership, and once or twice there were to be acrimonious disagreements which no doubt were intended to force his resignation. But he was determined to swallow almost any insult provided that he could curb the monarch's whims and keep him away from the reality of power. He had to put up with Victor Emanuel's jokes, for instance being served horsemeat for dinner and then asked to say how good the venison was;[1] he had to put up with bitter criticism in private: yet he was safe so long as he kept his temper and refused to be ruffled. The best answer to private court diplomacy was to have a private policy of his own, so he sometimes did not tell the king what he proposed to do, but just acted first and spoke later, realizing that the court party was too timid and too inexpert to join issue with him openly.[2]

Victor Emanuel was ill when Cavour returned to office, and this gave the new ministers time to set the pattern of their new relationship. For some weeks there is little sign that policy was seriously discussed between them and the monarch. For a brief moment Cavour seems to have flirted with the idea of changing his whole system of alliances, and he tentatively approached the Prussian government with the strange suggestion that they might make a military alliance together against France.[3] Napoleon, however, had much more to offer, at least for the moment, and Cavour realized that his safest policy was to revive the French alliance of January 1859. He was ready once again to agree to giving up Savoy and Nice, and in return could ask for compensation: as Venice could not be obtained without another war, he would settle for Tuscany and the Romagna.

Although the king eventually accepted Cavour's plan, he was far from enthusiastic about the sacrifices it would entail. Savoy was where his ancestors had come from, and the mountains above Nice contained hunting grounds which he was most unwilling to surrender.[4] As news of the proposed exchange of territory began to leak out and create a stir among public opinion, the king found himself in a stronger position and able to make difficulties. He was helped in this by the fact that Rattazzi and Ricasoli thought that a better bargain could have been made. Napoleon also caused gratuitous offence by insisting that French soldiers and officials should be present in Savoy and Nice when the population was called on to approve the cession in a plebiscite. Cavour managed to get some minor concessions from France on the royal

[1] *Cavour-Nigra*, III. 63.   [2] Massari, *Diario*, pp. 389, 494–5.
[3] *Die Auswärtige Politik Preussens*, vol. II, pt. i, ed. C. Friese (Oldenburg, 1938), p. 109.
[4] *Cavour-Nigra*, III. 284; ibid. IV. 158.

hunting grounds. Nevertheless he found general opinion in Piedmont to be most hostile to him over ceding Nice, for there was little noticeably French about the character of this small county. As the surrender of national territory weakened Cavour's position in parliament, the king was thus enabled to take a stronger and more independent attitude over other matters, and in addition a new and dangerous breach was opened up between Garibaldi and the government, for Nice was Garibaldi's birthplace. Hence Victor Emanuel was able to move once again towards a position where he was an arbiter between rival forces instead of a mere figurehead.

As early as February 1860, the king showed signs of wanting to launch another personal initiative by sending a private emissary to Rome, for annexation of the Romagna needed not only the permit of Napoleon III, but also that of its ruler, the pope, and Victor Emanuel had some reason to think that his own personal contacts with Pius IX would win a more favourable hearing than Cavour could ever obtain. Though it was clear by now that the pope would not sell the Romagna, possibly a compromise could be reached which would allow the Piedmontese to occupy this region while still continuing to recognize the suzerainty of Pius. Only when this too was shown to be unlikely did Victor Emanuel fall back on Cavour's policy of organizing a plebiscite in the area to indicate that the population wished to be annexed by Turin. He tried to excuse himself with the Roman authorities by explaining that, since Cavour's government had been in a sense imposed on him by the British, he was not able to act as freely and independently as he personally would have liked;[1] but his cheerful acceptance of annexation soon made this excuse look very slender.

Once again excommunication was pronounced. Just as on a previous occasion, the pope did not choose, or did not dare, to mention anyone by name in his anathema, though he left no doubt in practice that it applied to Victor Emanuel. The latter did not even seem to mind very much, nor was there much of a hostile reaction among the public in either Turin or Bologna.[2] Cavour in one respect positively welcomed this breach with Rome, for by depriving the monarch of a possible lever of independent power, it would inevitably strengthen the prime minister. To widen the breach still further, he arranged that Victor Emanuel should visit Bologna and so stress the personal involvement of the royal court in the policy of annexation.

Other state visits were also made to Milan and Florence to celebrate their union with Piedmont. When the Milanese crowds cheered louder for Cavour than for the king, the latter made no secret of his displeasure, and did not improve matters by asking Milan to raze to the ground the palazzo where his

---

[1] *Sclopis: Diario*, p. 215; a conversation by the king with Archbishop Charvaz is reproduced in *The Making of Italy 1796–1870*, ed. D. Mack Smith (New York, 1968), pp. 296–7.

[2] Cadogan's dispatch, ibid., p. 290; Massari, *Diario*, pp. 494–5; Talleyrand, 4 Apr. 1860, M. Aff. Étrangères; the pope had no use for the 'stupid *italianissimi*', and called Piedmont 'anti-Catholic, anti-pope, and almost anti-Christ' (*Pio e V. Emanuele*, II, pt. ii. 95–6).

father had been humiliated in August 1848.[1] In Florence, too, Cavour thought that the cheers were more for himself: he took a private satisfaction in the fact, and noted with some complacency that it was resented by the king.[2]

On 16 April, when the two of them were staying in the Palazzo Pitti in Florence, there was an angry scene between them. Both were unwell at the time and must have been tired after the journey, but it is also evident that the king had calculated that he now had a pretext to appoint a Tuscan as premier. Cavour had assumed that some gratitude was due to him for this new acquisition of territory and was shocked to hear himself bitterly criticized for the surrender of Savoy and Nice; moreover he attributed the criticism, no doubt correctly, to the influence and advice of Rattazzi. A few hours later the king partly apologized, but Cavour was not to be mollified by soft words. This was one of those moments, as in April and July 1859 and again later in April 1861, when the minister became quite beside himself with rage. The king, so Cavour now concluded, was a person whose unkindness and boorishness were intolerable: he therefore changed his plans and hurried back to Turin without visiting the other towns of Tuscany, telling a friend that as soon as he could settle the treaty with France he would resign. His experiences on these quick visits to Lombardy and Tuscany left him depressed about the future of the country, and for some days he was easily moved to tears. Back in Turin he made to Massari one of his more bitter and pessimistic remarks: 'How lucky I am to have known what Italy is like only after I had brought it into existence.'[3]

Hudson was one person who realized that the king was afraid of Cavour and anxious to get rid of him.[4] Popular indignation over Savoy and Nice had placed the government momentarily in difficulties, and so did Garibaldi's defiant accusation in parliament that the ministers had been acting unconstitutionally. The cabinet was divided, and the minister of war was threatening to resign on the grounds that Nice was Italian and that to surrender it would not only make Piedmont impossible to defend but would flout the principle of nationality on which the risorgimento depended. For a few days it seemed that the cabinet might fall. This must have emboldened Victor Emanuel, for he discussed the possibility of a new administration with senior local citizens in Florence and Bologna.

It was Cavour's fortune that the most likely alternative, a Ricasoli cabinet, might have endangered the continuance of the French alliance and so was hardly a serious possibility, while Rattazzi, whom the king without any doubt would have liked to appoint, did not carry broad enough support to form a viable coalition. Cavour was determined not to let Rattazzi back into power.

---

[1] *Sclopis: Diario*, pp. 220–1, 234–5; *Cavour-Nigra*, III. 114–15.
[2] Bollea, *Una Silloge*, p. 242; Maxime du Camp, 'Souvenirs Littéraires', *Revue des Deux Mondes*, June 1882, p. 802.
[3] *Carteggio Castelli*, II. 150; *L'Opera Politica del Senatore I. Artom nel Risorgimento Italiano*, ed. E. Artom (Bologna, 1906), p. 225; *Carteggi Ricasoli*, XIII. 313–14; *Liberazione del Mezzogiorno*, V. 470–1.
[4] *Gran Bretagna e Sardegna*, VIII. 92.

There were private grudges between them and they were now not even on speaking terms.[1] This was no doubt the main reason why in the end he decided not to resign but to swallow his pride and leave it to Victor Emanuel to dismiss him. A letter he wrote to the king to clarify his position has not been published, but it can be assumed that he did not mince his words about the hostile attitude at court towards his government.[2]

Victor Emanuel stayed for several weeks in central Italy after Cavour had returned home. He received the sword of Castruccio Castracane as a tribute to the hero of the battle of San Martino. He gave 100,000 lire for the refacing of Florence cathedral. At Siena early one morning he watched a special performance of the *palio*. And everywhere he was lavish in bestowing honours on those indicated to him as worthy or useful.

Whether during these two weeks he gave much encouragement to Garibaldi's volunteers in their plans for an invasion of Sicily is uncertain. One of the king's private envoys, unknown to Cavour, had visited Sicily in January, but his mission there had been not to encourage but to prevent revolution and to explain that no help could be expected from Turin.[3] King and minister seem to have agreed on this: they were not yet thinking of unifying Italy, but just of reinforcing the hegemony of Piedmont and stopping foreign intervention in the peninsula. Unification could be left to the future. France had by now agreed in principle to withdraw her soldiers from Rome provided that the Piedmontese did nothing to undermine the Bourbon dynasty in Naples and Sicily. This would explain why on 15 April, after a Sicilian revolution had in fact broken out with strong republican and Mazzinian overtones, Victor Emanuel wrote to King Francis at Naples with an offer to divide up Italy between their two monarchies. Part and parcel of this offer was that Francis would take over garrison duties in the Papal States, the assumption being that this would reassure the pope and allow French troops to leave Rome without fear of further Piedmontese aggrandizement.[4] If Victor Emanuel's offer had been accepted, Garibaldi's expedition would have become impossible or at least extremely difficult.

---

[1] Émile Ollivier, in *L'Empire Libéral* (Paris, 1899), IV. 595–6, quoted a letter from Rattazzi in 1870 criticizing the 'excessive adulation' given to Cavour. Rattazzi greatly admired Cavour's finesse and his quickness of perception but 'one could not say that Cavour had ever conceived, or was capable of conceiving, any grand project. . . . He had no scruples at all about the choice of means to use, or about his choice of men, and in general he had a poor opinion of people.' Rattazzi remembered Cavour as a convinced liberal, but as someone who had not believed in Italian unification until after Garibaldi's victories in Sicily.

[2] *Liberazione del Mezzogiorno*, I. 108; ibid. V. 475–6; *Cavour-Nigra*, III. 276–7.

[3] E. Brancaccio di Carpino, *Tre Mesi nella Vicaria di Palermo nel 1860* (2nd ed., Naples, 1901), p. 82; *Liberazione del Mezzogiorno*, I. 37; *Lettere di V. Emanuele*, I. 597; *I Fardella di Torre Arsa*, ed. F. de Stefano (Rome, 1935), p. 150; R. Salvo di Pietraganzili, *Il Piemonte e la Sicilia: Rivoluzioni e Guerre dal 1850 al 1860* (Palermo, 1902), p. 236.

[4] *Lettere di Cavour*, IV. cxx–cxxii; *Cavour e l'Inghilterra*, II, pt. ii. 57–8; G. Montanelli, *Schiarimenti Elettorali* (Florence, 1861), p. 10.

While travelling in central Italy the king had had a chance to see people with a different view of Italy than those he normally met, and to whom he could speak with a different and more 'Italian' voice than was customary in the provincial court circles of Turin. Ricasoli was one such person. Another was the radical *capopopolo*, Giuseppe Dolfi, to whom the monarch said that he was now prepared to adopt Mazzini's policy of national unification: Dolfi did not entirely believe him however.[1] Rumours were also current that Garibaldi was secretly in touch with the court in the hope of obtaining help for an expedition to Sicily. During most of April, Victor Emanuel was unhappy about the rising in Sicily, for its apparent republicanism was unacceptable, it had taken place against his advice, and it offered him no chance of intervention.[2] But in Florence and Bologna he had begun to recognize that Cavour's hostility towards the so-called republicans and radical patriots might be altogether too conservative and out of date. In some sections of the Piedmontese army, and even more among the students in Genoa and Pavia, there was soon talk about Victor Emanuel being more liberal and more Italian than his ministers.[3]

Cavour found it hard to counter these rumours, especially as he was not at all sure what the monarch's views were but was conditioned to assume that they would be at best confused and at worst mischievous. In any case it was hard to re-establish relations with the court after what had happened in the Palazzo Pitti. He used what means he could to indicate that any royal support for Garibaldi would be wrong. To the Prince di Carignano the king admitted that his ministers could not possibly be seen to give in to Garibaldi's pressure; but he also hoped that there was no need to stop private individuals going to Sicily and supporting the revolution if they wished to do so, and it might even be possible to give some covert help to the Sicilian rebels.[4] Without being actively implicated, and without giving way politically to the revolutionaries, there was good reason for making ready to accept the fruits of any success which they or Garibaldi might register.

Victor Emanuel, though he occasionally disparaged Garibaldi's military aptitude and was manifestly jealous of his huge success and popularity, had much more idea than Cavour of how to deal with this difficult but indispensable guerrilla general. Once the Thousand had set out for Sicily, the king swore on his word of honour that he had nothing to do with them, and even remarked that Garibaldi should be shown no pity if taken prisoner.[5] Yet on

[1] Dolfi to Linda White, 31 May 1860, MSS. Bodleian Library (Oxford); *Gran Bretagna e Sardegna*, VIII. 96.
[2] Türr to Bertani, 25 Apr. 1860, MSS. White Mario Papers (Museo del Risorgimento, Rome); *I Fardella di Torre Arsa*, p. 151.
[3] *Liberazione del Mezzogiorno*, V. 478; *Cavour-Nigra*, III. 266–7.
[4] *Liberazione del Mezzogiorno*, I. 62, 64, 66–7, 77.
[5] C. Maraldi, *Documenti Francesi sulla Caduta del Regno Meridionale*, ed. A. Omodeo (Naples, 1935), p. 53; A. Zazo, *La Politica Estera del Regno delle Due Sicilie nel 1859–60* (Naples, 1940), pp. 305–6.

the other hand he let it be known that he had given a large sum of money to help reinforcements reach Garibaldi in Sicily.[1] By his own admission he had disapproved of Garibaldi's initial expedition, and there exists abundant confirmation from Garibaldi that the king had tried to prevent him setting out.[2] It is safe to assume, however, that he was ready either to gain from Garibaldi's success or to disown his failure, at the same time as he hoped to use the fear of Garibaldian revolution as a means of extracting from France some tangible concession to monarchic, anti-revolutionary patriotism. Unlike Cavour he was at pains to keep friendly with the revolutionaries in case they should win. It was of particular help to them that he was at least anxious to hold the ring so that they should have a fair chance to try their luck.

Garibaldi's quite unexpected success quickly made the radicals very well worth while supporting actively, especially when, again contrary to Cavour's expectation, Garibaldi turned out to be far from a republican but a loyal monarchist whose chief aim was to make Victor Emanuel king of a united Italy. The king was thus reinforced in his resistance to Cavour.[3] He was probably being advised by Rattazzi to adopt a much more radical policy than that of his official government. He soon established direct means of communication with Garibaldi, the go-betweens including Count Amari, Captain Trecchi, and Count Litta. Their employment as message-carriers could not be kept entirely secret, and the French minister noted that their missions to and from Sicily were entirely outside Cavour's control.[4] Written messages were sometimes specially marked for eventual return to the king and for no copies to be taken by anyone.[5] Garibaldi was told to trust the king and no one else, and was requested if possible to send word before making any new move. Subsequently some people tried to make out that the king had personally guided the main stages of Garibaldi's revolution by a kind of remote control; others were to say the very reverse, that he continued to hinder the revolution developing. On occasion he had to speak in two different senses, with the result that it is hard to be sure what his real views were at any one moment; but probably his main wish was just to keep on good terms with the revolutionaries whatever happened, so that he could contrive to be the gainer, win or lose.[6] Whether he gave much practical help, as distinct from mere words and promises, is harder to say.

[1] F. Guardione, *Il Dominio dei Borboni in Sicilia dal 1831 al 1861* (Turin, 1907), II. 458, where the king is quoted as saying he had just given the astronomic sum of 3 millions to Bertani; Giuseppe Finzi, who represented the more 'Cavourian' of Garibaldi's supporters, testified to having received 10,000 lire from the king (*Una Lettera del Deputato Finzi* (Naples, 1870), p. 8).

[2] *Garibaldi, Vittorio Emanuele, Cavour*, ed. Curàtulo, p. 154; *Giuseppe Garibaldi: Scritti Politici e Militari*, ed. D. Ciàmpoli (Rome, 1907), p. 137; *Cavour-Nigra*, IV. 98.

[3] *Carteggi Ricasoli*, XIII. 304–5.   [4] Talleyrand, 9 and 23 July 1860, M. Aff. Étrangères.

[5] *Lettere di V. Emanuele*, I. 612–13.

[6] D. Mack Smith, *Cavour and Garibaldi, 1860* (Cambridge, 1954), pp. 125–7.

Cavour's attitude was equally ambiguous, because he too both needed the revolution yet was afraid of it. He could see the usefulness of the king's special relation with Garibaldi, yet was frightened where it might lead. 'Victor Emanuel', so he wrote to a friend in France, 'is going too fast for me; I do not like to play double or quits when my country is one of the stakes.'[1] To the Prussian minister he confessed that, if he decided to fight against Garibaldi, he would lose, and the king would then have to abdicate; better to wait before committing himself until he was sure if Garibaldi's army was going to be destroyed by the Bourbons or not.[2] The king, on the other hand, could adopt a bolder policy with many fewer inhibitions. But to act the revolutionary was not Cavour's natural *métier*, and he could never be sure that Victor Emanuel and Rattazzi were not using Garibaldi for purposes which might include over-turning the existing cabinet. It could even be feared that their policy of double or quits might include sending positive encouragement for another attempt by Garibaldi to invade the Papal States. This would be a move which would threaten the French alliance and so be clean contrary to governmental policy, but it was a move which Victor Emanuel was evidently prepared to accept.[3]

Throughout July and August, Ricasoli, who had a good deal of influence at court after the annexation of Tuscany, insistently demanded a more revolu-tionary attitude, not so much in support of Garibaldi as in rivalry with him. Ricasoli's argument was that, if such an attitude were not adopted, success would make Garibaldi stronger and more popular than the sovereign, and this would be a terrible humiliation for the monarchy. Worse still, it might open the way to social revolution. The king summoned Ricasoli to put his case at Turin. Fortunately for Cavour, however, the Tuscan leader succeeded in antagonizing Victor Emanuel by his tactless complaint that the king was not doing anything, as well as by references to Garibaldi's successes and the way that the radicals were dimming the military glory which the king had acquired the previous year at San Martino.[4]

Cavour nevertheless took Ricasoli's advice seriously, and to regain the initiative he decided to carry out at Naples a conservative and 'Piedmontese' revolution before Garibaldi could cross the Straits of Messina and start moving up the peninsula. This policy proved in the end a mistake, or at least a failure, but its acceptance by the king gave Cavour his chance to destroy any possibility of an alliance between the court and the radicals of the Left. Cavour's argument was this: Garibaldi must not be allowed to reach Naples first, or else he would have all the credit for making Victor Emanuel into the

[1] Nassau William Senior, *Conversations with Distinguished Persons during the Second Empire from 1860 to 1863*, ed. M. C. M. Simpson (London, 1880), I. 50, quoting a letter to Mme de Circourt.
[2] *Auswärtige Politik Preussens*, II, pt. i. 588.
[3] G. Manacorda, 'Vittorio Emanuele II e Garibaldi nel 1860, secondo le Carte Trecchi', *Nuova Antologia* (Rome), June 1910, pp. 413, 426; *Carteggi Ricasoli*, XIV. 182–3.
[4] Ibid. XIV. 47: 51–4, 307, 311.

monarch of a united Italy; that would result in the king losing face disastrously; better to go down fighting; better that the patriotic cause should lose than that Garibaldi should win and threaten conservatism and the hegemony of Piedmont.[1]

Confused though this policy may have been in logic, and politically dangerous in its potential effect of threatening to split the patriotic movement, the king accepted it because he could not help but recognize that Cavour and Ricasoli were safer allies than Garibaldi; and they in their turn continued to play on his resentment against the 'republicans' who had won Sicily in his name, but who had in the process diminished his own credit and renown.[2] Orders were therefore sent to the Piedmontese navy to hinder Garibaldi's crossing to the mainland. Secret consignments of arms were landed by the navy in Calabria; others were distributed to the Abruzzi and to carefully selected citizens in the town of Naples. Money was also sent in abundance with which to corrupt the local notables, and Victor Emanuel's Neapolitan cousin, the count of Syracuse, agreed to defect in return for a bribe.[3] Support was likewise promised by Liborio Romano, the chief minister of the Bourbons, and also by General Nunziante, the most reputable Neapolitan general, who received in return a hint that he would be given high rank in the Piedmontese army. Naturally the king's messengers to Garibaldi said nothing of these plans to forestall the radical revolution. Indeed, once the radicals knew the full scale of this counter-revolution against them, the whole success of the patriotic movement was endangered.

But the scheme never for a moment looked like succeeding, so the result was only to antagonize Garibaldi without anything gained to show for it. The conservatives could hardly compare with the radicals in revolutionary zeal. Nunziante cravenly fled when his reactionary politics were attacked by some Neapolitan liberals who were not in the secret. Liborio Romano was serving not two masters but three, and soon informed Garibaldi about the way the Piedmontese were plotting against him. Fortunately Victor Emanuel's private envoys managed to parry this by convincing Garibaldi that any apparent hostility came from Cavour's government and not from the monarch personally. The king's private diplomacy thus had successes as well as failures: the principal failure was that it made Garibaldi confident that he would be allowed to continue up to Naples and even as far as Rome provided he could beat the Bourbon army; its chief success was to convince Garibaldi that the king would ultimately be on his side rather than on Cavour's. This kept the radical revolutionaries loyal to the throne. They sent to tell the king when they intended to cross the Straits of Messina; and, after they had captured the Neapolitan fleet, it was at once placed at Victor Emanuel's disposal.

---

[1] *Cavour-Nigra*, IV. 122–3.
[2] *Lettere di V. Emanuele*, I. 613.
[3] Bollea, *Una Silloge*, p. 355; *Liberazione del Mezzogiorno*, II. 2, 8, 66.

Certainly the king must in part have been deceiving Garibaldi. Probably he was also in part deceiving Cavour. In other words he may have been encouraging both these men in policies which were inconsistent with each other and now threatened to collide: his own determination being to accept whichever succeeded and to disown whichever lost. He was faced with a situation where Garibaldi, though everyone said he would fail, had continuously won and in fact had conquered almost half of Italy against all the odds; whereas Cavour had failed to stop Garibaldi leaving for Sicily and then failed to stop him advancing on Naples. On this reasoning, there was some point in letting Garibaldi believe in a possible invasion of the Papal States, because just conceivably such an invasion might succeed, while, if it failed, the attempt could be repudiated and nothing, except Garibaldi himself, would be lost.

Such a subtle and ambiguous policy needed more delicate handling than the king was capable of. While it kept the revolutionaries loyal, it also made them over-confident in opposing Cavour's government. Trecchi and other emissaries from Turin gave Garibaldi the clear impression that Victor Emanuel wanted him to come out openly against Cavour and make a public request for the latter's resignation. Possibly this was a misunderstanding, but much more likely the king dropped some miscalculated hints and Rattazzi saw a chance to edge his rival out of power. People who had reason to know felt sure that Victor Emanuel was deliberately trying to widen the breach between Cavour and Garibaldi. This would help to explain why Garibaldi on his arrival at Naples, where he found positive evidence that Cavour had been trying to prevent his victory, wrote to ask the king that a new prime minister should be found who would unite and not divide the patriotic movement.[1]

Such a startling demand placed the king in a position where he could no longer continue with his dual policy. But already, even before the message had time to reach Turin, he had been compelled to change his policy. For Cavour at the end of August succeeded in persuading the French to come once more to his rescue and help to deliver Italy from the revolutionaries: the suggestion was that Napoleon should permit the Piedmontese to march through the Papal States in order to arrest the revolutionary armies before they could cross the frontier which divided Naples from Rome.[2] This was a brilliantly calculated idea which, at the same time as it held out the possibility of annexing further territory, also recaptured the initiative for the conservatives and for Cavour personally. It gave him a sufficiently strong position from which to confront the king with an offer of resignation which was in effect a threat. The king had to recognize that his prime minister alone possessed the skills and the imagination necessary for success on this scale. Cavour

[1] *Cavour-Nigra*, IV. 212–13; *Liberazione del Mezzogiorno*, II. 316–17; Mack Smith, *Cavour and Garibaldi, 1860*, pp. 243–6.
[2] *Carteggi Ricasoli*, XIV. 269.

alone would have the nerve to invade papal Umbria, cross into Naples, and force Garibaldi to surrender the south. In other words, Cavour now had much more to offer than Rattazzi. Nor was there any more to be gained from backing Garibaldi, since Napoleon put an absolute veto on any advance of the volunteers which would bring them closer to the Papal States.

The king had some regrets at the exposure of his private diplomacy and at being forced to capitulate to his ministers, but he no longer had much choice; under pressure he adopted Cavour's new policy, and undertook to accept the consequences even if they meant civil war and opposing Garibaldi by force.[1] Yet he wisely continued to keep open his lines of communication with the radicals. When on 14 September he replied to Garibaldi with a refusal to change the government, he added the somewhat ominous phrase 'for the moment'; a copy of this letter was then sent to Cavour which omitted these compromising words, and a jocular but perhaps more than half-serious postscript added that he would be glad if ministers would stop conspiring behind the monarch's back.[2] At the same time Vimercati was sent to reassure Garibaldi of Victor Emanuel's good will and to say that there was more to be gained for Italy if they now all worked together: Vimercati's message also contained an argument carefully calculated to appeal to the Left, for it said that the volunteers would be needed for another war against Austria very shortly.[3]

The intention to invade the Papal States was leaked by Cavour to the Rothschilds, and so was known within hours by the British foreign office. So familiar to the British was the king's pursuit of a personal policy that their reaction was to wonder if he had his ministers' approval.[4] Victor Emanuel himself was overjoyed that fighting was about to begin. Unlike in 1859, however, and no doubt because he was fighting against the head of the church, he agreed to allow his generals to keep the practical responsibilities of command. The campaign presented only moderate difficulty. The papal army was too small to give any trouble, and summary execution of civilian opponents, whether priest or peasant, terrified into submission most of those who were minded to defend their property against the invading forces.[5] The Neapolitan frontier

[1] *Liberazione del Mezzogiorno*, II. 258–9; *Garibaldi, Vittorio Emanuele, Cavour*, ed. Curàtulo, p. 175; *Memorie di Pallavicino*, III. 605–6; Solaroli to Massari, 12 Oct. 1860, MSS. Archivio Massari (Museo del Risorgimento, Rome); *Cavour-Nigra*, IV. 235–6—the phrases indicating the possibility of civil war were carefully omitted by Chiala in *Lettere di Cavour*, IV. 16.

[2] *Liberazione del Mezzogiorno*, V. 488–9; *Garibaldi, Vittorio Emanuele, Cavour*, ed. Curàtulo, p. 353.

[3] Ibid., p. 352.

[4] *Liberazione del Mezzogiorno*, V. 248; the British knew on 31 August of Cavour's plans to invade Naples against 'the Mazzinists' (letter of Hammond, Broadlands Archives, and of Cowley on 1 Sept., F.O. 519/10).

[5] Luigi Zini, *Storia d'Italia dal 1850 al 1866: Documenti* (Milan, 1869), II, pt. ii. 706; E. Della Rocca, *Autobiografia di un Veterano* (Bologna, 1897), II. 46, 52–3; *Italia e il suo Dramma Politico nel 1861* (Leghorn, 1861), pp. 34–5, 46; G. di Revel, *Da Ancona a Napoli: Miei Ricordi* (Milan, 1892), p. 40; T. Sandonnini, *In Memoria di Enrico Cialdini* (Modena, 1911), p. 12.

was reached in ten days' time, and this brought the conservative and radical wings of the patriotic party into direct confrontation.

Ricasoli was eager for parliament to give the king dictatorial powers for the last stages of national unification.[1] Some other members of parliament, on the contrary, distrusted Victor Emanuel and thought that if he were formally accorded full powers he might use them improperly, and Cavour on the whole agreed with this view. Yet it was no moment for too close an observance of constitutional restraints. Cavour privately expressed the conviction that the invading army need not bother too much with the niceties of the law, and eventually he was advocating that the king should after all act as a dictator.[2]

What surprised some people was that the prime minister did not accompany the sovereign to Naples as he had done to the other regional capitals, Florence, Milan, and Bologna. If he had been able to study the facts at first hand, Cavour might have been able to devise a more realistic policy towards the south, and his presence alongside the king would have made it possible to avoid a dangerous duality of government between Turin and the royal headquarters. But their two quarrels at Monzambano in July 1859 and at Florence the following April had not been forgotten by the minister. He wrote to a friend that, as far as his personal relations were concerned, 'I ask of Victor Emanuel only one favour, to be allowed to remain as far away from him as possible.'[3] It was a relief to stay at Turin where he could escape backstairs intrigue at court and royal interference in his decisions. He also was honest enough to admit that the king would be better at dealing with the Garibaldians on his own.

In general the two of them were agreed on being generous to Garibaldi provided he made no trouble, but they were determined to be inexorable should there be any opposition, even to the point of being prepared to 'exterminate' his followers.[4] In practice, as soon as he saw no chance of reaching Rome, Garibaldi realistically gave up any idea of making difficulties, and did all he could to effect an easy transference of power. Yet the king had assured Cavour that he knew Garibaldi intimately and was certain there would be trouble; hence the monarch was ready to make an example of him and his rabble. This attitude did not help to ease the process of transition, and it contrasted sharply with Garibaldi's generosity and realism. Somewhat ungratefully, Victor Emanuel blamed the Garibaldians for misgoverning Naples. He lacked the imagination to recognize that government under conditions of civil war was very hard, and he could not foresee that his own government at Naples with far greater force at its disposal would not show up too well by

---

[1] *Carteggi Ricasoli*, xv. 103, 119; dictatorship would 'show our gratitude to the king and be a splendid proof of Italian good sense. . . . Dictatorship would make a stupendous inauguration for a new monarchy.'

[2] Ibid. 137; *Liberazione del Mezzogiorno*, iii. 21, 287, 319.

[3] Ibid. 302; Cavour to Lamarmora, 15 Oct., Archivio Lamarmora, xciii/147.

[4] *Liberazione del Mezzogiorno*, iii. 64; Chiala omits the word 'exterminate' (*Lettere di Cavour*, iv. 35).

comparison. He went further and even questioned Garibaldi's honesty, sincerity, and military competence.[1] He assumed that the military feats of the Piedmontese army would soon put Garibaldi's reputation in the shade, and sulked when things turned out differently.[2]

Cavour in remote Turin was so thoroughly misinformed that he thought the Neapolitans had decisively turned against Garibaldi, just as he went on calling Garibaldi himself a secret republican and a disgrace to the name of Italy; for some reason he also thought Garibaldi would be grateful to the king for saving the volunteers from a crushing defeat by the Bourbons.[3] This ignorance and attempt to govern from a distance was at the root of much of the trouble which now ensued. Farini and Fanti, the two ministers accompanying the king to Naples, were known to be enemies of Garibaldi and were quite certainly chosen for this very reason. A proclamation which they wrote for the sovereign to make to his new subjects carefully avoided even a word of thanks to the man who had just conquered half of Italy. Farini refused to speak to Garibaldi when they met, or to shake hands, or indeed even to look at him.[4] The king too, although for the most part he behaved well in a difficult situation, on one occasion, when he had agreed to show the national gratitude to Garibaldi's army by formally reviewing the volunteers, failed to turn up, and this must have been a deliberate slight.

On 7 November, Garibaldi and the king were due to drive together into Naples. The guerrilla leader was so upset by the gratuitous offensiveness of the royal entourage that he had at first been reluctant to appear at all, but the king sensibly realized that the royal prestige might suffer if Garibaldi did not join him, and he made a special request of a kind that the radical leader rarely refused. They rode in an open carriage through a torrential downpour of rain. The only thing, apart from the rain, that marred their meeting was that Garibaldi refused all the gifts and honours pressed on him. The one honour he had coveted was to be allowed to continue to govern as the king's lieutenant at Naples. Even among the conservatives some recognized that there would have been certain advantages in such an arrangement, for Garibaldi in only two months' rule had created a great impression on southerners, an impression which perhaps no subsequent administration was ever to achieve; but politically his continuance in power was impossible, because an important motive in the Piedmontese take-over of Naples was to destroy Garibaldi as a

---

[1] *Lettere di V. Emanuele*, I. 630, 652; *Il Principe Napoleone nel Risorgimento Italiano*, ed. A. Comandini (Milan, 1922), p. 200; H. d'Ideville, *Journal d'un Diplomate en Italie* (Paris, 1872), I. 54; *Archivio Storico Italiano* (Florence), 1955, p. 365.

[2] *Ricordi di Castelli*, p. 339; A. Oriani, *La Lotta Politica in Italia* (Bologna, 1941), III. 99.

[3] *Cavour-Nigra*, IV. 238; *Liberazione del Mezzogiorno*, III. 9; Chiala prints both these letters, but with the harsher passages deleted.

[4] *Liberazione del Mezzogiorno*, III. 326; Cavour had been advised that to send Farini would be a disaster, by C. Di Persano (*Diario Privato-Politico-Militare* (Turin, 1870), III. 98); also by Di Revel (*Da Ancona a Napoli*, p. 83); and by Mancini (*Garibaldi, Cavour, Verdi*, ed. A. Luzio (Turin, 1924), pp. 294, 296).

potential source of power. A day later he secretly left for Caprera, avoiding any emotional crowd scenes which might have embarrassed his royal successor. Some of the foreign vessels in the bay realized what was happening and saluted his ship as he left, but not the Piedmontese navy. The king was glad to see him go and leave the monarchy without competition.

The new ruler of Naples at once made some effort to ingratiate himself with his subjects. Against his will, on Farini's advice he went to venerate the blood of the miracle-working saint, San Gennaro (Januarius); it was embarrassing that the ampoule of blood had liquefied in Garibaldi's honour, and the comparison would look odious if the same did not happen for Victor Emanuel. He was seen to kiss the relic five times, and the miracle duly took place. Yet this was not enough. A bare week showed that this somewhat uncouth and ungracious monarch would not look well in any comparison with the radical, charismatic dictator. In the streets there were demonstrative shouts of 'Down with Victor Emanuel'. This was an affront which he had not expected and which he did not easily accept, but he had too little warmth or geniality, too little of courtesy or even of majesty for the great majority of Neapolitans.[1] Their evident dissatisfaction, and the fact that they thought him a poor substitute for Garibaldi, brought out some of the petty elements in his nature.

After a few days he was rarely to be seen in public, and when he appeared he was surrounded by guards and officials who carefully protected him from the public. This was utterly unlike the tradition set by the Bourbons and followed by Garibaldi. Victor Emanuel chose to live outside Naples so long as the weather was warm enough, and only appeared in town for an occasional quick half-hour. He told Cavour that he was 'absolument assassiné d'affaires', but in fact almost every day he went hunting instead of meeting people. It caused offence that he departed early from a state ball, and that he left the opera house before the singing of a hymn composed in his honour. When 100,000 people lined the main street of Naples for a long-announced procession, he capriciously altered the route to escape the crowds, and there was much disappointment especially among those who had hired balconies and bought flowers to strew in his path. Privately, and regrettably even in public, he spoke of Neapolitans as contemptible *canaille*—this was one of his favourite words for people he despised and disliked. Their reply was 'take us or leave us; Naples is like this, and if you do not like it, then go away and leave us in peace'.[2] Evidently the attempt to build up the king as someone more impressive than Garibaldi was not succeeding, and the result was a collapse of confidence and liking on both sides. The price of government bonds, which

[1] Maxime du Camp, 'Naples et la Société Napolitaine sous le Roi Victor-Emmanuel', *Revue des Deux Mondes*, Sept. 1862, p. 5; Charles Grün, *L'Italie en 1861* (Bruxelles, 1862), II. 279; *Liberazione del Mezzogiorno*, III. 332; ibid. V. 537.

[2] Ibid. IV. 2; ibid. V. 540; *Epistolario La Farina*, II. 445, 450–1; Louise Colet, *L'Italie des Italiens* (Paris, 1863), III. 149; D. Lioy, *Due Anni di Vita Politica* (Naples, 1863), pp. 81, 85.

remained stable after the arrival in Naples of Garibaldi's 'reds', was soon down by over 30 per cent.[1] Cavour begged the king to come home before things got even worse.

For Cavour suddenly realized that, away from the restraints of Turin, Victor Emanuel was enjoying a sense of independence and was again diverging from his government on important points of policy. One interesting divergence was over the king's proposal to adopt a less hostile attitude to Mazzini. The republican leader, who was still under sentence of death in Piedmont, was living at Naples when the Piedmontese arrived there, and the king decided to use his new sense of power to grant this greatest of Italian patriots an amnesty. Cavour, on the other hand, had been looking forward to hanging Mazzini in public, and he particularly feared the effect it would have on Napoleon if Mazzini were pardoned. Though he had been telling the king to act as a dictator and to rule by martial law, he now sent a sharp reminder that parliament had not granted the full powers which an amnesty would require.[2]

This is one of the points on which the king showed not only more generosity but more common sense than his minister, and in fact there was little need to fear any hostile reaction coming from Napoleon.[3] The king's attitude was that Mazzini should be left alone.

'If Piedmont can succeed in making Italy, Mazzini will not want to stop us; if we fail, better he should do it than no one. I may not be able to make a career as a schoolmaster, but I would know how to be a farm bailiff; I would become Monsieur Savoia and clap my hands at his success.'[4]

Cavour's attitude, on the other hand, was quite unusually intolerant at this moment. Chiala's edition of his letters is heavily bowdlerized wherever Cavour seems to behave badly, but we know that he was urging the king to use the army to put down party differences in Naples by main force, and was referring to this area as the most corrupt part of Italy and one which would have to be ruled by martial law.[5]

When Cavour threatened to resign rather than permit an amnesty, the king decided not to make an issue of it. Other points of conflict, however, were more difficult. Victor Emanuel had been allowed to leave Turin before he and Cavour had had time to secure clear agreement over policy, and inevitably so, because the way things would develop was impossible to guess. Another hasty decision by Cavour, which in the end he himself admitted to have been a mistake, was to choose Luigi Carlo Farini to accompany the monarch as minister *ad latus*. Farini had neither the strength of character nor the political imagination and resilience for such a delicate situation, and his known animus

---

[1] *Liberazione del Mezzogiorno*, IV. 86.   [2] Ibid. III. 319.   [3] Ibid. 404.
[4] Nisco heard him say this on 1 September (N. Nisco, *Storia Civile del Regno d'Italia*, IV. 339); N. Nisco, *Francesco II, Re* (Naples, 1887), p. 129; other versions in Massari, *Diario*, p. 223; *Rivista Storica del Risorgimento Italiano* (Turin), 1899, p. 830; compare his remark to Queen Victoria, quoted in her Journal for 1 Dec. 1855, 'si je l'attrape je l'embaumerais'.
[5] *Lettere di Cavour*, IV. 120; *Cavour-Nigra*, IV. 292–3.

against Garibaldi was far more hindrance to him than help. The choice of
Farini and Fanti suggests that Cavour feared above everything else the king's
unreliability where concessions to Garibaldi might be concerned. Fanti also
held the additional post of army commander and military aide-de-camp to the
king, and this enabled him to act without feeling entirely bound by cabinet
decisions. Others among the king's immediate entourage were even less open
to control from remote Turin: such people included Della Rocca of the household staff; there was also Captain Trecchi who constituted a direct means of
contact between the king and the Garibaldians, and Trecchi was perhaps to
play quite an important part behind the scenes in the conflicts of policy which
now arose.

   These conflicts were such that Farini was soon asking to resign. Fanti, too,
threatened resignation; so did General Cialdini; so did the minister of justice,
Cassinis, after he had been sent to Naples to reinforce the government team
and had realized in what an impossible situation he had been placed. Cavour
himself threatened resignation repeatedly. The main disagreements were
over what to do with Garibaldi's army of volunteers. Farini had no very clear
orders here, for the simple reason that Cavour had had no time to consider
the various possibilities open to him. Perhaps neither of them had quite
realized how strong was the resentment and jealousy on the part of their own
senior generals towards these volunteers who had just won such a brilliant
and unorthodox campaign.

   The king once again showed that he could be more generous and sensible
than his advisers. He reminded them that he was now monarch of more than
just Piedmont and he was not prepared to be merely the mouthpiece of a
military clique.[1] His own idea, and he was proud of it, was that the Garibaldians should be kept in permanent existence as a separate corps.[2] He
angrily told Cavour how Fanti had publicly humiliated some of Garibaldi's
men who were now unemployed and sometimes starving; how Fanti had ridiculed them for cowardice, when these were men who had voluntarily left
jobs and homes in order to shed their blood for Italy.[3] Cavour was horrified,
and his first reaction was to threaten resignation if Fanti's severe view prevailed; but a few days later he was also threatening to resign when the king
seemed to go too far the other way. The morale of the army leaders had to be
carefully fostered, but if possible without incurring the odium of ingratitude
towards the volunteers. This was a delicate balance which could not be manipulated far away in Turin. Prodded by Cavour, Farini tried to make the king
move over to the army view that there should be no more concessions to the
Garibaldians.[4]

   Another issue over which Cavour threatened to resign was his belief that

[1] *Liberazione del Mezzogiorno*, III. 316.   [2] *Cavour: Questione Romana*, I. 86.
[3] *Lettere di V. Emanuele*, I. 652–3; Di Revel, *Da Ancona a Napoli*, p. 89.
[4] *Liberazione del Mezzogiorno*, IV. 11.

Filippo Cordova and Giuseppe La Farina, two other noted opponents of Garibaldi, should be sent to take over Sicily from Garibaldi's regime. Nothing could have been more calculated to cause division. The king, who could see things from closer at hand, remonstrated on the grounds that provocation and party strife must be minimized: some of the cabinet agreed with him on this, and so on reflection did Farini, but Cavour was adamant. The premier, as many people recognized, was not a good judge of men or a wise chooser of subordinates. He also was determined to crush *garibaldinismo*. No irremediable damage was done in fact, for Cordova and La Farina met such fierce opposition in Sicily that their stay there lasted only a few days; but the episode cannot have helped to reconcile the radicals and Sicilian autonomists to the sudden changes of a new regime. Victor Emanuel's protest is testimony to his lack of dogmatism and political prejudice when the occasion demanded.

By early December, Cavour was trying to insist that the king should not be allowed to take any further decisions but should return to Turin at once. The monarch had hoped to wait until his troops had captured Gaeta and eclipsed the military successes of Garibaldi, but, as this achievement eluded him, he too was anxious to leave what he called the nauseating scenes of degradation in Naples. He first made a quick visit to Sicily. At Palermo, when the populace in traditional fashion unhorsed his carriage so as to draw it themselves, he was so offended that he got out and walked: as he angrily and somewhat pompously remarked, 'I am not a singer or ballerina; I prefer men to act like men and not animals.'[1] On the whole, however, he much preferred Sicily to Naples, and perhaps for this reason he made a better impression there than on the mainland. His ministers had to hurry him away from the island as soon as he showed signs of wanting to assert himself and actually govern. Cassinis at one point read him a lesson in constitutional law, pointing out that a constitutional sovereign reigned but did not govern, since responsible ministers ought to be the ones to take decisions on policy and be held to account for them. No doubt this was said in a somewhat playful tone, but a mild threat was contained in it, for Cassinis had reason to think that the king once again had in mind to find alternative ministers from the Left: the minister apprehensively explained to Victor Emanuel that the Left might opt for a republic, and hence it would be wise to give firm support to Cavour and the conservatives.[2]

At the end of December, ministers and king returned from Naples. Gaeta had still not fallen, and indeed held out until the following February when it was bombarded into submission, so the king had none of the hoped-for military triumph to accompany his return to Turin. His failure to impress the

---

[1] *Ricordi di Castelli* (Diary of Solaroli), p. 349; M. Puccioni, *Storielle, Ricordi, Memorie* (Florence, 1940), p. 113.
[2] *Liberazione del Mezzogiorno*, III. 393; ibid. IV. 35–6.

Neapolitans, and his inability to take any serious political or military initiative while he had been away from Turin, left him henceforward more than ever submissive to Cavour's direction. It was noted that he now took greater care to speak well of his prime minister, especially when he thought that his words might be repeated, and perhaps the difficulties encountered at Naples had taught him to set a higher value on his minister's advice.

Cavour for his part knew better than to push his victory over Victor Emanuel too far. As Vimercati said, the king could be fairly easily manipulated provided that you first suggested a policy to him and then flattered him into thinking that it was his own idea.[1] If Mme Rattazzi is correct, Cavour secretly despised the king, but to his face he was now ready to praise the monarch's energy, his military skill, his gift at dealing with people.[2] Cavour was not normally a flatterer and there may have been some element of irony here, but it is also true that the king was more susceptible to such flattery, provided it were not too gross, than he himself liked to imagine.

Both of them were quickly at work thinking of what should be the next step in the unification of Italy. According to the Prussian minister, the king admitted that his only thoughts once again were of fighting,[3] for Cavour had told him that another European war was in the offing, and he assumed, on not very much evidence, that his army would shortly be ready for the next fight against Austria.[4] He talked with Kossuth, the Hungarian leader, about joint preparations for this war, and also spoke of the Hungarians as his 'allies'.[5] To the suspicious British, on the other hand, he gave his word that he had no agreement with the Hungarian rebels, and he promised that if Cavour gave any private undertaking to Kossuth it would be overruled: wars and treaties were constitutionally part of his royal prerogative, and hence ministers would here have to defer to him.[6] Unfortunately this was the moment when Cavour's gun-running activities in the Balkans were exposed. The Piedmontese minister to Turkey and his embassy secretaries had worked hard to paint out the offending marks which showed that the guns came from Piedmont, but it was too late for concealment.[7] Such signs of wanting to keep Europe in turmoil helped to neutralize some of the enthusiasm in other countries for the proclamation of Victor Emanuel as king of a united Italy.

Yet Victor Emanuel felt under some compulsion to follow an aggressive

---

[1] *Cavour: Questione Romana*, I. 86.

[2] Ibid. 136; *Cavour-Nigra*, IV. 279; *Carteggio Castelli*, I. 327; Mme Rattazzi, *Rattazzi et son Temps* (Paris, 1881), I. 579.

[3] *Die Auswärtige Politik Preussens*, vol. II, pt. ii, ed. C. Friese (Oldenburg, 1945), p. 162.

[4] *Sclopis: Diario*, p. 307.

[5] L. Chiala, *Politica Segreta di Napoleone III e di Cavour in Italia e in Ungheria (1858–1861)* (Turin, 1895), p. 125.

[6] De Vecchi di Val Cismon, 'Paolo Solaroli a Londra nel Dicembre 1860', *Rassegna*, Nov. 1934, p. 1203.

[7] *Episodi Diplomatici del Risorgimento Italiano dal 1856 al 1863 Estratti dalle Carte del Generale Giacomo Durando*, ed. C. Durando (Turin, 1901), pp. 102–3; *Cavour e l'Inghilterra*, III. 172.

policy, for Garibaldi's conquest of southern Italy had brought into being a new feeling of patriotism. The king had assured Garibaldi at Naples that the volunteers would be again required in the spring of 1861, so Garibaldi provocatively anounced to his followers that half a million soldiers should be ready by March to fight for their king.[1] Strong objections against this kind of talk came from Britain and France, who advised the king to use his influence on behalf of a more realistic and pacific policy. Several emissaries then shuttled unostentatiously between the palace and the island of Caprera in order to make Garibaldi keep quiet.[2] The latter's indignant reaction was to call the court corrupt and Cavour a puppet of France; the king had sometimes been helpful in the past, so Garibaldi admitted, 'but unfortunately he has done less than he might: he could have done more, and by God he must do more'. He should dismiss the corrupt government of Cavour and himself take over personal direction of the national movement.[3]

No one inside the country had ever before spoken like this in public of Victor Emanuel. When Garibaldi unexpectedly arrived in Turin to protest against the shabby treatment of his volunteers, some people began talking of a possible *coup d'état*. The radical leader asked for an audience at the palace and was apparently refused, but rumour confirmed a report by the secret French police that the king went to visit him privately.[4] Such condescension, if the rumour was true, would have been most unusual, but Victor Emanuel had a considerable and sometimes justified confidence in his ability to deal with people face to face. This time, however, Garibaldi did not prove to be so amenable as before. Rattazzi was also sent twice to counsel moderation and returned empty-handed, for Garibaldi was fiercely loyal to his former officers in the volunteer army and thought that the government was going back on the king's pledge to help them. An angry confrontation then occurred in parliament between Cavour and Garibaldi.[5] A few days later it was the king who, at Garibaldi's request, tactfully presided over a formal reconciliation between these two men at the palace, but the bitterness of the occasion was not forgotten.

In March 1861, parliament created the new title 'Victor Emanuel II, by grace of God and by will of the nation'. Outside Piedmont there was strong feeling against the numeration of Victor Emanuel *the second*, since its implication was that there existed no new nation but only an extension of Piedmont; it seemed to follow from such a title that the plebiscites, in other words the expressed will of the people, had been of no practical account. Some of the

---

[1] *Garibaldi, Vittorio Emanuele, Cavour*, ed. Curàtulo, p. 341.
[2] *Auswärtige Politik Preussens*, II, pt. ii. 162; *Gran Bretagna e Sardegna*, VIII. 309, 319–20.
[3] Garibaldi to Türr, 15 Feb. 1861, MSS. Museo del Risorgimento (Rome), 221/30/9; *Scritti di Garibaldi*, IV. 351–2; *Cavour: Questione Romana*, II. 120.
[4] Rayneval, 11 Apr. 1861, M. Aff. Étrangères, Correspondance Italie; Bollea, *Una Silloge*, p. 442; *Sclopis: Diario*, pp. 320–1.
[5] Garibaldi's speech is translated in *The Making of Italy*, ed. Mack Smith, pp. 347–52.

After the parliamentary clash of 18 April 1861, with Rattazzi, left, in the Speaker's chair—
CAVOUR: The debate is over. Are we friends now?
GARIBALDI: Friends yes, but not for life.

Piedmontese patriots, and not only those on the Right, used this as convenient evidence for their insistence that the kingdom still perpetuated some aspects of the divine-right monarchy of earlier days.[1] When Ricasoli resented the new title as an insult to the Italian people, Cavour and the king on the contrary maintained that ideas of popular sovereignty were dangerous sophistry, and the title of Victor Emanuel *the first* would be dishonourable to a dynasty which had so many centuries of splendid history.[2]

Cavour at this point resigned so as to allow the formation of a new and more Italian cabinet with representatives of south and central Italy. He advised the king to consult Ricasoli, Rattazzi, and Farini about the new appointments, for this would have been the practice in Britain; but must have been dismayed when Victor Emanuel asked Ricasoli to become premier in order to prove 'that there are other politicians than Cavour in Italy'. This decision was taken after the monarch had been seen taking a carriage ride with Rattazzi.[3] Since it had no relation at all to the balance of parliamentary groups, it indicated once again that not even during Cavour's lifetime did the

[1] La Farina in parliament, 1 Dec. 1862, *Atti parlamentari*, p. 4678.
[2] *Cavour: Questione Romana*, II. 56; *Carteggi Ricasoli*, XVI. 115; A. Monti, *Il Conte Luigi Torelli* (Milan, 1931), p. 487; F. Campanella, *Monarchia e Repubblica* (Florence, 1882), p. 21.
[3] Minghetti's diary for 20 Mar., ed. A. Bertelli, *Archivio Storico Italiano*, 1955, p. 361.

monarch fully accept the doctrine that ministers were responsible to parliament.[1] He hardly saw the new Italian nation as a liberal state in Cavour's sense of the word. Indeed he had not liked it when Cavour wanted to call parliament in January; though, as he told a friend, the calling of parliament would not signify much, since 'I have all the parties in my own hand and I despise the lot of them'.[2]

Ricasoli upset the king's plan by refusing. He would not come to power as the result of a private grudge at court against a man who had served the crown so well.[3] Cavour therefore returned to office. He was the necessary man, and it is almost astonishing in retrospect that the king had thought he could be dispensed with. Two months later, however, came Cavour's tragic and unexpected death at the age of fifty-one. His last cabinet meeting, which was presided over by the king at the royal palace, saw another fierce quarrel between them.[4] Victor Emanuel henceforward had another chance to reassert himself and check the drift towards parliamentary government and prime-ministerial predominance.

[1] The public legend, on the contrary, insisted that 'Victor Emanuel never tried to supplant Cavour by any of his rivals' (D. Zanichelli, *Studi di Storia Costituzionale e Politica del Risorgimento* (Bologna, 1900), p. 224).

[2] *Lettere di V. Emanuele*, I. 676; Della Rocca, *Autobiografia*, II. 117.

[3] *Carteggi Ricasoli*, XVI. 155; Mme Rattazzi, *Rattazzi et son Temps*, I. 562, says that the king asked Rattazzi as well to form a ministry, who also refused for he recognized that Cavour alone would have a majority in parliament.

[4] F. Crispolti, *Politici, Guerrieri, Poeti: Ricordi Personali* (Milan, 1938), p. 18.

12

Cavour and the Problem
of Regionalism

THE unification of Italy into a single state did not mean the obliteration of regional differences. Patriotic and regional loyalties continued to coexist alongside each other as a fundamental fact of Italian life, and their coexistence was eventually to receive constitutional recognition in 1947 when the regions were given varying degrees of autonomy. The possibility of making partial and temporary provision for local autonomy had been at the back of Cavour's mind during the last year of his life, but he was unable in 1860–1 to decide quite how far to go. Unification came about so fast and so unexpectedly that he had not had time to be sure of what kind of administrative organization the country needed. The result was that a centralized system of administration, inherited largely from Piedmontese practice, was adopted almost by default and remained a fundamental fact of Italian life.

What administrative structure would suit Italy was not a subject easy to discuss until the basic political issues had been settled, for until 1860 it could not even be assumed that political unification was practicable, nor whether the union would include Rome, Naples, and Sicily. It must be kept in mind that only some 2·5 per cent of the population of the peninsula were Italian-speaking —in other words not many more than still used Latin as a practical language.[1] Not until after 1860, moreover, could Italians easily travel to see other neighbouring regions of their own country, for the great bulk of the population, even in relatively advanced Piedmont, could not move without a permit from the police.[2] The result of these two facts was that even those who were most politically aware knew surprisingly little of other areas than their own.

Mazzini, the great prophet of Italian patriotism, had no first-hand information of the south except what he was able to gather during a few weeks at Naples in 1860 and a short spell in prison ten years later at Gaeta. Strong believer though he was in unification, Mazzini knew that the differences between one region and the next were so strong that a centralized system of administration on the Piedmontese pattern might be unrealistic or even might

[1] T. De Mauro, *Storia Linguistica dell'Italia Unita* (Bari, 1963), p. 41.
[2] *Raccolta delle Leggi, Regolamenti e Decreti* (Milan, 1860), I. 639.

positively distort the national genius.[1] Alessandro Manzoni, the most revered name of the century in Italian culture, never travelled as far south as Rome, let alone to Naples. Cavour paid three visits to Milan, but can hardly have spent much more than ten days there all told. He made one quick visit to Florence, though he did not move a great deal outside the palazzo where he was staying, and he never travelled further south than Leghorn. The 'Etruscan race', said Cavour, was utterly unlike that of Emilia;[2] but this was a judgement made on very little evidence. Cavour's ignorance about the rest of Italy was even claimed by him as a positive advantage, for without it he might not have had the courage to confront the difficulties of making a nation out of such diverse material.[3] Another leading Piedmontese politician, General Lamarmora, who as prime minister in 1859–60 ruled over Lombardy as well as Piedmont, does not seem to have known that there was a German-speaking population south of the Alps which would constitute a serious problem for Italian nationalism.[4]

In view of the restrictions on travel, it is not surprising that a reciprocal ignorance and misunderstanding separated the north from the south, region from adjacent region, and even town from neighbouring towns. Visconti Venosta was one of the few northerners to travel through the south before 1860, and at Naples what he saw convinced him that Mazzini's central doctrine about an idealized '*popolo italiano*' must be unrealistic; in southern Sicily the peasants insisted that he must be an Englishman, because the word 'Italian' meant little to them, and only Englishmen were thought eccentric enough to move so far off the beaten track.[5]

Massimo d'Azeglio was quite exceptional in having visited Sicily where his brother was a priest. In fact he went there three times. He had also lived for fairly long periods in Milan, Rome, and Florence, and hence knew much more than Cavour about the rest of Italy. This makes it the more interesting that Azeglio was not happy about annexing Naples; he blamed Cavour here for acting rashly out of sheer ignorance, and thought that the south might well split off again one day.[6] Nor was he in favour of administrative centralization for Italy.[7] Nor indeed was he in favour of Cavour's scheme to make Rome the Italian capital. Azeglio's reluctance over Rome was shared by other eminent Italian politicians such as Gino Capponi, Luigi Menabrea, Lamarmora, Casati, Giuseppe Pasolini, Jacini, Giorgini, and Ferrari; and it is not without interest that Lamarmora and Menabrea, both of them future prime ministers,

---

[1] *Scritti di Mazzini*, III. 333–5 (article dated 1861), where he advocated creating about twelve regional units in Italy.

[2] *Cavour-Nigra*, I. 214.   [3] *Carteggio Castelli*, II. 150.   [4] *Lettere di Cavour*, VI. 686.

[5] G. Visconti Venosta, *Memoirs of Youth, 1847–1860* (London, 1914), pp. 205–8.

[6] *Carteggi E. d'Azeglio*, II. 308; *Lettere Inedite di Massimo d'Azeglio al Marchese Emanuele d'Azeglio*, ed. N. Bianchi (Turin, 1883), p. 319; *Massimo d'Azeglio e Diomede Pantaleoni: Carteggio Inedito*, ed. G. Faldella (Turin, 1888), p. 489; *Cinquantasette Lettere di Massimo d'Azeglio dal Carteggio di G. B. Giorgini*, ed. M. Puccioni (Florence, 1935), pp. 136, 139.

[7] *Azeglio, Rendu*, p. 150.

thought that Cavour's annexation of Naples had been either an outright mistake or at least very premature.[1] Yet neither their views nor Azeglio's were listened to seriously by Cavour, and, after Azeglio left office at the age of fifty-four, it seems that only twice in the last fourteen years of his life was this elder statesman consulted by the king. Furthermore not even he knew the various regions well enough to be able to compare and choose between their methods of administration and codes of law. Few Italians had any well-founded views on the questions of whether the disparity of social and economic conditions would be aggravated or relieved if a uniform system of laws was applied to the whole country, let alone on the further question of which system of laws might be best.

Even Sardinia was little known by the Piedmontese, though they had ruled this island since 1720 and though it provided the kings of the house of Savoy with their regal title. This ignorance was mainly due to the fact that the big estates in Sardinia were in the hands of absentee landlords. Communications were difficult, and the journey from Genoa could take twelve to fifteen days as late as 1835, while the island was also thought of as a kind of remote penal settlement where convicts would provide cheap agricultural labour.[2] On the rare occasions when Sardinian affairs were seriously discussed in the Turin parliament, the feudal customs of the island were found quite baffling, and the authorities had to admit ignorance on some fairly basic facts where detailed knowledge would have been required for efficient administration. Cavour once reassured parliament that talk about poverty in this island was gravely exaggerated, and if Sardinians were unemployed it must be because they were work-shy; he added that there would soon be 'gigantic' improvements in Sardinia's prosperity.[3] Yet, when local residents begged him to come and study the facts on the spot, he had to decline; he never visited Sardinia, and his gigantic improvements were an illusion that never began to materialize.

Politicians of course knew well enough that certain regional differences in Italy were important and potentially dangerous. The Piedmontese had plenty of experience of fierce opposition from Genoa,[4] and they had been shocked to discover in 1848 that Lombardy and the Veneto had distinct interests of their own which might not square at all with those of Turin.[5] Neapolitans knew all about the regional feeling of Sicilians, and vice versa, since centuries of

[1] R. Bonfadini, *Vita di Francesco Arese con Documenti Inediti* (Turin, 1894), p. 300; *Azeglio*, Rendu, pp. 221, 313; Verax, *Alfonso Lamarmora: Commemorazione* (Florence, 1879), p. 130; *Sclopis: Diario*, p. 368; S. Jacini, *Un Conservatore Rurale della Nuova Italia* (Bari, 1926), II. 44–5; Jacini's and Casati's speeches in the senate, and the negative votes registered on 27 January 1871.
[2] E. Della Rocca, *Autobiografia di un Veterano* (Bologna, 1897), I. 96–7.
[3] *Cavour: Discorsi*, VII. 44–6, 57–8, 70.
[4] *Correspondance Diplomatique de Joseph de Maistre, 1811–1817*, ed. A. Blanc (Paris, 1864), I. 281–2; A. Vieusseux, *Italy and the Italians in the 19th Century* (London, 1824), I. vii; Vincenzo Ricci accused Piedmont of ruling in Genoa by the same right that Austria ruled in Lombardy *(Le Biografie dei Deputati Italiani ovvero i Deputati Italiani innanzi al Tribunale del Popolo* (Genoa, 1865),'p. 11).
[5] *Carteggio Casati-Castagnetto, 19 Marzo–14 Ottobre 1848*, ed. V. Ferrari (Milan, 1909), pp. 56–7.

mutual hostility coloured popular attitudes.[1] These examples of regional animosities were a basic fact which had to be taken into account by anyone planning a single constitution for a united Italy. Nevertheless, local loyalties could be looked upon in two quite different ways, either as something which tended to pull Italy apart, or else as providing diversities of experience which could be a positive enrichment for the life of the country. Most politicians tended to think that regionalism would have to be crushed before Italy could claim nationhood; yet some rather saw it as one of the great glories of Italy, which should be not only accepted but positively encouraged; still others, and these may have been the most realistic, saw it as at least something unavoidable, which had therefore to be recognized and made the best of.

A federal constitution was one possible answer, and this idea attracted some of the foremost intellectuals in Italy. Gioberti and Balbo in Piedmont had in the 1840s agreed that the regional differences inside Italy were fundamental, something to be accepted and up to a point welcomed when thinking about a constitution. Niccolò Tommaseo, a Venetian from Dalmatia, and Giuseppe Montanelli, a Tuscan, also recognized the importance of avoiding too much imposed uniformity, for they feared the suppression of local cultures and local individuality. Giuseppe Ferrari, a refugee from Lombardy, likened the Piedmontese conquest of Italy to that of Alaric the Goth: he insisted that the municipal loyalties and traditions of Italian history could not be argued out of existence, and that only some kind of federal union would prove sufficiently resilient to contain the diversity of his fellow-countrymen.[2]

Another Lombard, Carlo Cattaneo, one of the most intelligent and knowledgeable Italians of his generation, wanted to create not a single unified state but a 'United States of Italy'. Cattaneo felt that the spirit of patriotism among Italians was so frail that a unitary state might well be unrealistic; he also feared that a closely united Italy would become authoritarian in the process of forcing the regions into a common mould. Hence he thought the acquisition of Venice and Rome less important than the establishment of firm liberal foundations for resurgent Italy, and indeed the striving to annex more territory might well create conditions which were inconsistent with liberalism.[3] Few others went as far as this in their federal views, though a number of pamphlets appeared in the years 1860–2 carrying variant or dilute versions of the same message.[4]

[1] Giustino Fortunato, *Pagine e Ricordi Parlamentari* (Rome, 1947), II. 308.

[2] G. Ferrari, *Histoire des Révolutions d'Italie* (Paris, 1858), IV. 503; Ferrari's speech to parliament in October 1860 is translated in *The Making of Italy 1796–1870*, ed. D. Mack Smith (New York, 1968), pp. 341–5.

[3] *Epistolario di Carlo Cattaneo*, ed. R. Caddeo (Florence, 1954–6), III. 231, 518; ibid. IV. 30.

[4] C. Busi, *In Feodere Unitas* (Florence, 1860); H. Cernuschi, *Réponse à une Accusation Portée par M. de Cavour* (Paris, 1861); F. Malvica, *Intorno l'Unità d'Italia* (Palermo, n.d.); *Quale possa quale debba essere il Migliore Destino Politico dell'Italia* (Vicenza, 1861); C. L. di B., *L'Unità e la Confederazione, Riguardate sotto l'Aspetto del Mantenimento della Libertà* (Florence, 1862); *L'Italia Disfatta dalla Rivoluzione Piemontese* (Malta, 1862).

The popular support for federalism is impossible to gauge, since the general public was allowed to have little view in the matter, and the plebiscites of 1860, 1866, and 1870 were phrased (and then carefully supervised) so as to exclude any possibility other than a unitary state.

At the other extreme from Cattaneo was Giuseppe La Farina and the National Society. La Farina argued that the main point of the patriotic movement was to establish Italy as a great power, and for this she would need to be made into a state with a strong centralized direction. Regionalism was, for this loyal servant of Cavour, something divisive and debilitating. In La Farina's view, Italy had to be 'a unitary state, come what may, even if it means paying the price of losing our liberty',[1] and Piedmont had to be coerced into the role of an Italian Prussia which would dominate and unify the peninsula. La Farina teased the Americans for their out-of-date belief in a federal constitution, and justified his attitude by stating that any European army would easily beat an American army just because federalism inevitably spelt military weakness.[2] He even claimed to deny the very existence of regional sentiment in Italy, insisting that there was no other nation in existence which had so few internal differences.[3]

Such statements do not bear close scrutiny, but they were far from being entirely pointless. La Farina, like Mazzini in this at least, consciously over-estimated the strength of Italian patriotism because he recognized patriotism as a supreme good, and he hoped that this over-estimate might serve as a weapon of war against the regionalism which he inwardly feared might ruin his dream. Such an explanation, at all events, will reconcile what would otherwise seem a paradox, because as a Sicilian he had spent his youth fighting in the middle of regional differences and hatreds. The very fierceness of La Farina's reiteration of Italy's need for strong central government suggests that he was afraid of what might happen without it. In other words, although his opinion and Cattaneo's were at opposite extremes, at root both these men had a first-hand conviction that regionalism was one of the main problems to confront the new kingdom of Italy.

One could go further today and assert that patriotism was, for all except a select few, much weaker than regionalism during the risorgimento. If this seems another paradox, it is so only superficially and only because we have been conditioned by a hundred years of patriotic historiography to think the contrary. Many events are hard to explain unless it is accepted that patriotism was more a result than a cause of the national movement, in other words that patriotism was less the reason why successive revolutions broke out than the end product which those revolutions brought about. After Garibaldi had

[1] G. La Farina, *Sulle Presenti Condizioni d'Italia* (Turin, 1862), p. 15.
[2] *Il Piccolo Corriere d'Italia* (Turin), 4 Oct. 1861.
[3] La Farina, *Credo Politico* (7th ed., Turin, 1860), p. 7.

moved to Naples in 1860, Maxime du Camp noted in his diary that the people in the streets were crying 'Viva l'Italia', but he heard one ask his neighbour what this word Italy meant.[1] Even politically-conscious Neapolitans, among them many liberals, had shown earlier that they were prepared to fight to impose their rule on Sicilian liberals, whereas Sicilians of all classes in 1860 had been fighting not so much *for* Italy as *against* Naples. In Sicily, too, the word 'L'Italia', or rather 'La Talia', was thought by some people to be the name of the king's wife.[2]

The closer the risorgimento is studied the more it comes to look like a complex mixture of individual movements, of which one, but only one among many, was a patriotic revolt against the Austrians. Other revolts were against being taxed, against compulsory military service, against censorship; others were various manifestations of class war; there were movements against the church, and also against anticlericalism; there was the rivalry between neighbouring towns, as there was the perpetual tension between towns and countryside, and in the rural areas between peasants and shepherds; there was the struggle for economic freedom; there was above all the struggle for food and jobs. This kind of motive could be said by a level-headed and honest observer to be more effective than patriotism.[3] Every one of these individual revolts can be found as an accompaniment to Garibaldi's war against the Bourbons of Naples, a war which he himself considered a patriotic war to create an Italian nation.

Garibaldi's quite astonishing victories are impossible to understand without recognizing the further contribution of purely regional movements or manifestations of local and not national patriotism. Some of the great moments of the risorgimento were local revolts, for instance the five days of Milan in 1848, the defence of Venice in 1849, the Sicilian revolts which in 1848 and 1860 triggered the two most important nation-wide revolutions of all. Feelings of Italian nationalism were certainly present on these occasions, but less prominently than subsequent rhetorical interpretations of national history allowed people to think.

To take one example, there was no patriotic insurrection at Milan in 1859, even when a few miles away at Magenta the French were winning perhaps the most decisive victory of the whole risorgimento. The attempt by the National Society that same year to instigate a nationalist revolution at Parma was gravely disappointing; so was their similar attempt the following spring in Florence; so it was again in Umbria in the autumn, and the same in the Marches where the society thought it had a strongly entrenched position; and

---

[1] Maxime du Camp, 'Naples et la Société Napolitaine sous le Roi Victor-Emmanuel', *Revue des Deux Mondes* (Paris), Sept. 1862, p. 8.

[2] Corrado Tommasi-Crudeli, *La Sicilia nel 1871* (Florence, 1871), p. 50; G. Rothan, 'Un voyage à travers l'Italie', *Souvenirs Diplomatiques: L'Allemagne et l'Italie 1870–1871* (Paris, 1885), II. 412, says that in Naples the cry 'Viva la costituzione' was thought to mean 'Long live the queen'.

[3] Giuseppe Saredo, *La Vita Locale in Italia* (Siena, 1867), pp. 11–12.

in each case their failure came as a cruel shock to Cavour who had relied on La Farina and his friends to inform him about the strength of Italian patriotism outside Piedmont.[1] At Naples, too, Cavour ordered a revolution to begin in August 1860, and, to his extreme disgust, nothing happened: this can be compared with the more spontaneous and successful revolution at Palermo in April, a revolution which the National Society had not encouraged and in which regional feelings were much stronger than nationalism.[2] There was no serious popular revolt at Venice in 1866, not even when the Italian army was in the Veneto and the bulk of the Austrian army had withdrawn north of the Alps;[3] nor was there one in Rome at the time of either Aspromonte or Mentana, nor in 1870, though in each case the Italian patriots tried their best.[4]

Such facts are rarely mentioned in historical studies of the period, or are at best glossed over, and this partly because of a mistaken notion that they are somehow discreditable. What is mentioned is the heroism; whereas historians rarely recall the great difficulty Manin experienced finding a single newspaper in Piedmont or indeed anywhere in the whole of Italy which would support his National Society. Of course Manin and his followers, while not wanting to advertise their own failures, continued on the contrary to exaggerate their estimates of patriotic zeal as an entirely legitimate device for generating enthusiasm and self-sacrifice. Nevertheless their failures, as well as the concealment of these failures by later historians, contain important clues for an understanding of what happened in the risorgimento.[5]

To stress this other side of the story would thus help to explain how the final victories of the risorgimento caught everyone by surprise. Until the last moment most contemporary politicians would have thought it almost inconceivable that patriotism could triumph over regionalism with such apparent decisiveness, and the sheer unexpectedness of the victory forced Cavour to improvise hurriedly on the crucial issue of whether centralization or decentralization would best suit Italy. Wherever he lacked strong convictions he usually preferred to deal with each individual case as it arose. On this occasion a succession of improvised steps thus established what in the end could be seen as a highly centralized pattern of government. Such centralization, moreover, came about despite the fact that Cavour himself and most subse-

---

[1] F. de Dominicis, 'L'Ordinamento Provvisorio della Lombardia nel 1859', *Il Risorgimento Italiano: Rivista Storica* (Turin), 1911, pp. 576, 579; *Carteggi Ricasoli*, XIV. 363–4; R. Grew, *A Sterner Plan for Italian Unity* (Princeton, 1963), pp. 380, 472.
[2] *Scritti Politici di Giuseppe La Farina*, ed. A. Franchi (Milan, 1870), II. 295; *Liberazione del Mezzogiorno*, II. 164, 169, 251.
[3] *Scritti di Garibaldi*, v. 335–6; S. Jacini, *Due anni di Politica Italiana: Ricordi ed Impressioni* (Milan, 1868), p. 106, where he also adds that there was little enthusiasm in the rest of Italy for the acquisition of Venice.
[4] *The Roman Journals of Ferdinand Gregorovius 1852–1874*, ed. G. W. Hamilton (London, 1911), pp. 295, 391.
[5] *Daniele Manin e Giorgio Pallavicino: Epistolario Politico (1855–1857)*, ed. B. E. Maineri (Milan, 1878), pp. 207, 309–10; A. Oriani, *La Rivolta Ideale* (Bologna, 1912), pp. 65–6.

quent politicians deplored a centralized administration as at once illiberal and inefficient. That this happened was in part due to the inner fear of regionalism, the fear that Italy was so precariously constituted that she might fall apart again if a unified system were not quickly imposed on her.

As each region in turn was annexed, much the same reaction can be found. Lombardy towards the end of 1859 was given a modified version of the centralized Piedmontese administrative system, and this had to be done without recourse to the legislature. It was said at the time to be just an emergency measure until Lombard representatives were elected to a joint parliament and could discuss the matter there, but, before parliament could meet, the fact had already been accomplished. Substantially the same legislation was then extended to Emilia by royal decree, subsequently validated by parliament without discussion.[1] It was also extended subsequently to Umbria and the Marches; then to Naples, Sicily, and Tuscany; and finally, after Cavour's death, to Venice and Rome. La Farina had won, Cattaneo had lost, and in each case procedure was by executive decree so as to avoid delay and to dispense with the need for some potentially embarrassing debates.

Cavour's attitude to what happened is not entirely clear, and in particular the question of why he let it happen needs some explanation. In practice, when he was himself in power, Cavour seems to have been temperamentally a centralizer who did not relish delegating powers; Alessandro Luzio, who among historians was perhaps in the best position to know, even called him 'a formidable centralizer'.[2] Yet in his early years he had been no lover in theory of administrative centralization. He had even on one occasion condemned it outright as the root cause of the ills of modern society, because he believed that true liberalism would never be attained in Italy until there was a radical devolution of power, and until ordinary citizens could be actively involved at local level in the processes of self-government.[3]

Even in office, when the demands of practical politics inevitably confused such issues of principle, Cavour was still sufficiently an admirer of British practice to talk of wanting to change the existing law so that greater powers could be given to the localities.[4] His secretary, Isacco Artom, thought that, at least until after the war of 1859, he was ready to accept a federal solution to the Italian problem.[5] This remarkable testimony has been almost forgotten, partly

[1] 9 Apr. 1860, *Atti del Parlamento: Discussioni della Camera*, p. 108; C. Ghisalberti, *Contributi alla Storia delle Amministrazioni Preunitarie* (Milan, 1963), p. 225.
[2] *Nuova Antologia* (Rome), July 1920, p. 22.
[3] *Cavour: Discorsi*, I. 256; ibid. II. 185–8; *Gli Scritti del Conte di Cavour*, ed. D. Zanichelli (Bologna, 1892), I. 326; E. De Marchi, 'Il Decentramento negli Scritti del Cavour', *Occidente* (Milan), III (May 1947), 32.
[4] Ministerial circular of 18 Apr. 1858, quoted by A. Cuniberti, *Riflessioni e Proposte sulle Questioni del Discentramento delle Regioni* (Bologna, 1871), pp. 28–35; *Lettere di Cavour*, II. 426.
[5] I. Artom and A. Blanc, in their introduction to *Œuvre Parlementaire du Comte de Cavour* (Paris, 1862), p. 7.

because Cavour's disciples after 1861 would have condemned as utterly inexpedient the association of his name with the discredited and dangerous doctrines of federalism. But Artom knew him intimately, and Baron Talleyrand, the French minister in Turin, heard Cavour more than once say that until 1859 he favoured a federal system for Italy;[1] other testimony can also be found to support their personal memories.[2] Cavour was much too little of a doctrinaire to hold any absolute principles about centralization or decentralization until he could foresee the circumstances in which these principles would have to be applied. He was ready to confess, at all events in private, that he knew much more about England than about southern Italy,[3] and he certainly knew far less about Rome than about Switzerland or Paris; in other words there was good reason for him to keep an open mind and be ready to take advice.

In May 1859, when Lombardy was being invaded, Cavour suddenly realized he would have to be ready to choose what kind of administration to impose on this first of the other regions to be incorporated into the *regno subalpino*. The Lombards had voted by plebiscite in 1848 to join Piedmont; hence it could be claimed that the main formalities for annexation had already been completed; the one snag was that in 1848 the Lombards had made their vote conditional on the subsequent summoning of a constituent assembly to decide what kind of government would suit the two provinces when they were united. The Piedmontese had at the time accepted this condition, but perhaps not in good faith, and to many of them in 1859, including Cavour, a constituent assembly was unthinkable, as it might call in question the monarchy, the *statuto*, and the whole structure of their own existing state. To a pragmatic politician such as Cavour, the most important aim was to annex Lombardy quickly and with as little fuss as possible. A leisurely comparative study of the two administrative systems might ideally be desirable, especially as his concentration on foreign policy had kept the Piedmontese system unreformed and defective;[4] but hostilities in May 1859 made any adequate study impossible.

An advisory committee was therefore hurriedly chosen, co-opted by Count Giulini from among the Lombard refugees living in Piedmont, and their allotted task was to make a quick report on the problem. The committee recommended leaving many existing Lombard institutions intact, and even that a customs barrier should continue to separate Lombardy and Piedmont; their idea was that the two regions should both gradually adapt by each taking what was best from the administrative practice of the other. Possibly Cavour intended, if only he had been given time, to accept some such arrangement and to make substantial concessions in the direction of local administrative

---

[1] Dispatch of 24 Aug. 1860, translated in *The Making of Italy*, ed. Mack Smith, p. 319.
[2] G. Montanelli, *Schiarimenti Elettorali* (Florence, 1861), pp. 10–11, where, writing in Cavour's lifetime, he stated that Cavour had been a federalist until 1859, and had finally been converted to unitarism by Garibaldi's victories in Sicily; Prince von Bülow, *Memoirs* (London, 1932), i. 654.
[3] C. Lacaita, *An Italian Englishman, Sir James Lacaita* (London, 1933), p. 157.
[4] *L'Opinione* (Turin), 28 July 1859; H. von Treitschke, *Cavour* (Leipzig, 1942), pp. 212, 214.

autonomy for Milan, but in practice, when the war ended and Cavour resigned, not much notice was taken of Giulini's recommendations.[1]

The law enacted for Lombardy on 24 October 1859 was to remain the basis of the local government system in Italy down to contemporary times. Rattazzi, its main author, thought of it as the most liberal piece of legislation ever issued by Victor Emanuel.[2] But he deliberately hurried it into effect during the parliamentary vacation, together with a great many other highly contentious laws, and authorized it somewhat dubiously under the full powers which parliament had granted six months earlier for the purpose of fighting the war. Such haste looked very suspicious to some people. Letitia Rattazzi in her biography of her husband admitted that he might have gone too far and too fast out of an excess of zeal, but she also insisted that, even though Milan might have been in some respects ahead of Turin in its system of administration, he was right to demand that the hegemony of Piedmont should prevail,[3] and hence that in substance the law properly reflected the realities of politics.

Rattazzi's law brought into Lombardy the Piedmontese practice by which local government was centrally controlled, more so indeed than under Austrian rule hitherto: provincial administration was to come under the prefects, while village and town administration would come under the mayors or *sindaci* who like the prefects were to be government appointees. As well as extending to Lombardy the prefectoral system, Rattazzi also introduced other fundamental laws under these war-time emergency powers, along with an extra 40 million lire for the armed forces, and all this despite the fact that the peace treaty of Zürich had been signed.[4] A comprehensive education act empowered the government to prescribe the methods of teaching, the time-table, and the texts to be used in an essentially state-controlled system of education.[5] On the same day another fundamental law vested the minister of justice with quite considerable authority over the judges and the judicial system. Also on the same day was issued a public security law which created a preventive censorship hitherto unknown in Piedmont; it also compelled hotels, cafés, and bookshops to obtain a police licence, and wage-earners to obtain police permission before changing their jobs.[6] The fact that such important laws were issued on

[1] *Atti della Commissione Giulini per l'Ordinamento temporaneo della Lombardia (1859)*, ed. N. Raponi (Milan, 1962), pp. xxxvii, 10–11, 25, 115, 352; B. Malinverni, 'Alcune Lettere del Conte Cesare Giulini', *Il Risorgimento* (Milan), XI (June 1959), 128–9; *Il Risorgimento Italiano: Rivista Storica*, 1911, pp. 576–81.
[2] G. Saredo, *La Nuova Legge sulla Amministrazione Comunale e Provinciale* (Turin, 1889), I. 82; P. C. Boggio and A. Caucino, *Legge Provinciale e Comunale commentata* (Turin, 1860), p. 53.
[3] Mme Rattazzi, *Rattazzi et son Temps* (Paris, 1881), I. 442.
[4] The peace treaty was signed by the king on 10 November, and ratified on 1 December, between which dates a great mass of legislation was hastily introduced, including 23 decrees on the one day 20 November.
[5] *Raccolta delle Leggi, Regolamenti e Decreti*, I. 263–5; that this was illiberal compared with the laws of Bourbon Naples was maintained by E. Cenni, *Delle Presenti Condizioni d'Italia e del suo Riordinamento Civile* (Naples, 1862), p. 229.
[6] *Raccolta delle Leggi*, I. 639–43, 652–3.

the same day and in this excessively arbitrary manner suggests a deliberate hurry in order to take advantage of the emergency powers before parliament could meet.

This legislation, despite Rattazzi's claims for it, did not strike other people as particularly liberal, and understandably there was a great deal of opposition in Lombardy to what was the first important sample of administrative centralization. More than half the Lombard members of the National Society resigned when they saw where La Farina's principles, without their knowledge, had been leading them.[1] Casati and Cattaneo, though bitter enemies of each other, agreed in their sense of outrage over such a scant regard for Lombard opinion, since apparently not even the highest officials in Lombardy, and not even the Lombards in Rattazzi's cabinet, had been consulted.[2] When parliament met, some of the deputies complained that the new legislation was in many respects less enlightened than the Austrian legislation which it replaced, and claimed that the nation had a right to be consulted through its representatives before so many and such important laws were imposed on them.[3] Pamphlets tried to argue that the Piedmontese were taking Lombardy back into the Middle Ages and treating a proud province as conquered territory.[4]

This was an extreme view, but there was general agreement over seeing, behind Rattazzi's attitude, a dangerous authoritarianism, especially when the same pattern was repeated in education, in the courts, in local government: this pattern was broadly typical of Piedmontese legislation, and revealed 'a wish to regulate everything, to organize things *a priori* and on a uniform scale'. These so-called liberal laws were, to some critics, a manifest denial of individual liberty. The Piedmontese, it was said, could be without qualification praised for their military virtues and their parliamentary system; but their laws were far from being the best or the most enlightened available in Italy, and in administration their habit of expecting every little decision to be taken for them by the government in Turin was an example to be shunned and not copied.[5]

The irritation in Lombardy, coming on top of his own earlier experience of opposition from Genoa, no doubt helped to persuade Cavour, when he

[1] *Scritti di La Farina*, II. 388–90.

[2] *Il Politecnico: Repertorio mensile di Studi* (Milan), IX (1860), 15–17; *Carlo Cattaneo: Scritti Politici ed Epistolario*, ed. G. Rosa and Jessie White Mario (Florence, 1894), II. 276; ed. M. degli Alberti, *Rassegna Contemporanea* (Rome), Dec. 1908, pp. 569–70; F. Catalano, 'Motivi Politici e Sociali nella Lotta per l'Autonomia Lombarda', *Belfagor* (Florence), XVII (1962), 157–60.

[3] *Atti Parlamentari: Camera*, pp. 179, 187.

[4] A. Lonati, *Difesa della Lombardia Avvilita e quasi Ripudiata come Troppo Povera* (Milan, 1859), pp. 12, 24, 27; M. Formentini, *Sulla Organizzazione Politica e Amministrativa del Regno d'Italia* (Milan, 1863), pp. 28–9.

[5] Ibid., p. 26; *Due Mesi di Sessione Parlamentare e il Programma della Maggioranza* (Bologna, 1860), pp. 18–19; G. Saredo, *Marco Minghetti* (Turin, 1861), pp. 49–51; C. Norsa, *Sul Compartimento Territoriale e sull'Amministrazione del Nuovo Regno d'Italia* (Milan, 1863), pp. 4–5.

returned to office in January 1860, that it might be wise to try a different tack with the annexed provinces of central Italy. His subsequent decision to study a plan for regional constitutional units may well have something to do with the fact that he resumed power as an opponent of Rattazzi and had to search for alternative policies. He agreed in parliament that Rattazzi might have been right in theory when he tried to get a unified administrative system, but had been wrong to proceed in such a hurry and under out-of-date emergency regulations. Cavour himself would be ready to go a little more slowly. And yet he refused to submit the question to a full parliamentary discussion, because that would mean not waiting one or two years but twenty or more.[1] The problem of unifying the various regions, he was eventually to admit, was quite as difficult as that of acquiring Venice or Rome.[2] As an indication of the way his mind was moving, he issued an official statement of policy referring to the 'administrative autonomy' which Tuscans would continue to enjoy in a united Italy.[3] Ricasoli took exception to this phrase on the grounds that regional autonomy would seem to perpetuate the old state differences in a new and unwelcome guise; but Cavour, who could hardly understand such an apparent change of attitude in Florence, angrily insisted on the word 'autonomy', and his quite unusual touchiness almost suggests an irritability at having been caught out in a piece of deceit.[4] At all events his published views at this moment do not square with the centralized system which he and his successors eventually were to enforce.

Autonomy, of course, had a number of possible meanings. Cavour in parliament later tried to explain away his use of this particular expression, but whatever his reason for using it, whether it was designed to appeal to the French who wanted Italy divided and weak, or to the electors who thereby might be induced to vote for his coalition in the imminent parliamentary election, it helped to perpetuate a dangerous ambiguity which in turn seems to have been based on some degree of intellectual muddle. Ricasoli and Cavour, though they continued to fight each other over this theme, seem in fact to have been almost in agreement, only neither could find the correct formula to express their similarity of view. Both believed in forming a strong Italy, at the same time as both feared governmental over-centralization and claimed to want some kind of administrative regional devolution. Cavour, who at one moment was insistent about accepting some degree of regional autonomy, before long was fiercely denouncing both the fact and the term. At different moments he claimed to want a 'perfect unification of the state' but

---

[1] *Discorsi Parlamentari del Conte Camillo Di Cavour*, ed. G. Massari (Rome, 1872), pp. 65, 77, 104–5; R. Bonghi, *La Vita e i Tempi di Valentino Pasini* (Florence, 1867), pp. 826–7, developed the point that Cavour returned to power on the swing against Rattazzi's policy of centralization.

[2] *Lettere di Cavour*, IV. 201.

[3] *Carteggi Ricasoli*, XII. 375–6.

[4] *XXXV Lettere Politiche di Bettino Ricasoli a Leopoldo Galeotti*, ed. G. Mazzone (Bologna, 1895), p. 46.

also local 'self-government'. Ricasoli brought even more confusion into the argument, for he could not bear the idea of regional autonomy, yet he wanted Tuscany to remain some kind of entity with a real life of its own and with its old institutions preserved as much as possible.[1]

One reason why such ambiguities were allowed to persist was that Cavour had too many other problems to attend to. He chose to leave these administrative questions in the hands of two successive ministers of the interior, Luigi Carlo Farini who held office from January to October 1860, and Marco Minghetti who followed for the next twelve months. Farini and Minghetti both started from an assumption, which must first have been agreed with the prime minister, that considerable delegation of powers was desirable. They both agreed that local authorities should have more control than Rattazzi had permitted over education, public works, and taxation. Farini and Minghetti both came from central Italy, and hence were more open to non-Piedmontese influences than Rattazzi had been, as they were anxious to study existing practice in other states of Italy before simply extending Rattazzi's law of October 1859 to the rest of the country.

In the summer of 1860, Farini appointed another committee to discuss the various possibilities. This committee included in its deliberations the subject of regional 'administrative autonomy', which they interpreted to mean the possibility of creating a system of large regions interposed between the central government and the existing provinces and communes which were the basis of local government. These regions might be made to coincide with the old state frontiers, for instance Lombardy, Piedmont, Naples, and so forth, but not necessarily. As to their range of competence, one possibility was to make these regional administrations just a delegation or extension of state authority in the localities; an alternative was that there should also exist elected regional assemblies which carried with them some degree of political autonomy and self-government.[2] Cavour probably had a fairly open mind on the issue at this stage, but his remarks on Tuscan and Sicilian autonomy suggest that he must have favoured some degree of regional self-government, and it is unthinkable that Farini would have continued to think along these lines without active encouragement from the prime minister.

After Minghetti succeeded Farini, a good deal of further discussion took place, while special studies were also made of local government in other countries of Europe and even as remote as Brazil.[3] Minghetti's final proposals were presented early in 1861. While disavowing any idea of wanting to permit

[1] Ibid., pp. 41–4, 48; *I Toscani del '59*, ed. R. Ciampini (Rome, 1959), p. 202; *Carteggi Ricasoli*, XI. 316.

[2] A. Petracchi, *Le Origini dell'Ordinamento Comunale e Provinciale Italiano* (Venice, 1962), I. 298–303; C. Pavone, *Amministrazione Centrale e Amministrazione Periferica da Rattazzi a Ricasoli (1859–1866)* (Milan, 1964), pp. 62–6; B. Chapman, 'The Problem of Regionalism in Italy' (D.Phil. diss., Oxford, 1951), pp. 88, 90, 94.

[3] MSS. notes in Archivio Minghetti (Biblioteca dell'Archiginnasio, Bologna), 106/A/70.

political autonomy in the old regional capitals, he proposed that a system of regions should be set up with fairly wide powers. In strong contrast to Rattazzi's law of October 1859, Minghetti would also have liked the mayor in each town or village to be elected rather than nominated by the government; and also he wanted the nominated prefect to be deprived of some of his coercive power over provincial affairs. A good deal was left vague in Minghetti's scheme; his presentation of it also suggested a certain lack of conviction, or an excessive haste in preparation, or the need to reconcile some sharp conflicts of interest which existed behind the scenes.

A powerful influence in favour of a unified and central system of administration came from the Piedmontese bureaucracy with its traditions of centralism. There was quite a strong feeling among many politicians at Turin that the Piedmontese had been the architects of unification, and that the laws and institutions tried and proven at Turin should have a preference over those from elsewhere.[1] Rattazzi himself did not go quite so far as this: in public he now said that he did not want to impose Piedmontese laws on the other states of Italy; nevertheless he could not accept Minghetti's idea of regionalism, and he privately claimed for Piedmont, 'qui a été l'individualité la plus marquée dans la race italique', certain rights of primacy which allowed her to predominate to some extent over other parts of Italy.[2] At a time when some reputable politicians were seriously suggesting that Naples or Florence might be a better capital city for Italy than either Turin or Rome,[3] there was at Turin a particular sensitivity to see that the primacy of Piedmont was recognized and maintained.

Every other kind of argument was also brought up in an attempt to block the introduction of the regions, and some of the arguments raised serious doubts. It was said that the regions would be inefficient, that they would be yet one more wheel in the mechanism of government. It was said that they would be an illiberal innovation in that they would inevitably curtail the existing liberty of towns and provinces.[4] Other arguments spoke of the danger of federalism, and the possibility that regions were wanted by some people just as a means of preserving the old sub-nationalities which had been such a curse in Italian history; they would thus be a source of weakness at a

---

[1] C. Boncompagni, *L'Unità d'Italia e le Elezioni* (Turin, 1861), pp. 35–6; C. Gonella, *Del Potere Regionale, ossia dell'Andamento Amministrativo del Nuovo Regno d'Italia* (Turin, 1861), pp. 53–4.

[2] Rattazzi to Minghetti, 3 Dec., Libreria del Senato (Rome), MS. A/4/X/10; 8 June speech in parliament, *Atti del Parlamento*, p. 499; Mme Rattazzi, *Rattazzi et son Temps*, I. 538.

[3] C. Casati, *Roma o Firenze: qual esser debba la Capitale dell'Italia* (Turin, 1861), pp. 10–11; E. Cenni, *Napoli e l'Italia* (Naples, 1861), p. 92; C. Crisci, *La Situazione Politica in Italia: Quistione di Governo e di Organizzazione* (Naples, 1861), p. 22; *Scritti d'Azeglio*, III. 383.

[4] Pompeo Quarto, *Poche Parole sul Progetto del Ministro Minghetti di Dividere il Regno d'Italia in Regioni* (Naples, 1861), pp. 7–8; *La Centralizzazione: Studio dell'Avvocato Domenico Mantovani-Orsetti* (Turin, 1862), p. 29.

time in world history when larger and larger aggregates of power were being created everywhere else.[1]

If Cavour had any strong views either way, they would almost certainly have resulted in a clearer decision than was in fact made. His own theoretical statements might have been expected to range him on the side of decentralization. In particular he had always assumed that the delegation of powers to local authorities would be a much cheaper form of administration,[2] and he knew better than anyone else that Italy had a desperate need at this moment for economies in public expenditure. He read and commented on Minghetti's proposals before they were published, yet did not propose any substantial alterations in them;[3] on the contrary, he said he agreed with Minghetti in wanting 'self-government' for towns and provinces, and allowed others to think that he would have liked the same also for groups of provinces formed into larger regional units.[4]

Cavour, for these reasons, is sometimes said to have been in full agreement with Minghetti over the latter's proposal to create the regions, and Minghetti certainly tried to give this impression;[5] but a good deal of contemporary evidence suggests that the premier was at least unenthusiastic.[6] His own gifts and his own interests were far less apparent in the field of administration than in politics, and this could be a sufficient reason why he did not show much active support of his colleagues on this occasion. Quite likely it was an issue over which he was uncertain, or which he had had insufficient time to consider, so that he was deliberately waiting to see the reaction of public opinion before committing himself; and Artom, for one, thought Cavour not sorry to discover that there would be support in other parts of Italy for a greater degree of administrative unification than at first he had been prepared to accept.[7]

Gaspare Finali, who often heard Cavour discussing the question with Minghetti, noted that the prime minister always seemed doubtful and unenthusiastic when talking about it; and Finali added the perhaps relevant point that Cavour, in his early study on the Irish problem, had become convinced that home rule would be a mistake.[8] Possibly, therefore, when he held out

[1] L. Carbonieri, *Della Regione in Italia* (Modena, 1861), pp. 48, 346–7; G. B. Giorgini, *La Centralizzazione: i Decreti d'Ottobre e le Leggi Amministrative* (Florence, 1861), pp. 12–13, 51.

[2] *Cavour: Discorsi*, VI. 422; *Lettere di Cavour*, IV. 112.

[3] Ibid. 237–44; E. Artom, 'L'Antico Disegno delle Regioni', *Nuova Antologia*, Jan. 1922, pp. 37–8; Archivio Minghetti, MS. 105/7.

[4] *Carteggi Ricasoli*, XIII. 315.

[5] L. Lipparini, *Minghetti* (Bologna, 1942), I. 252; *Discorsi Parlamentari di Marco Minghetti*, ed. L. Pullé (Rome, 1888), I. 104.

[6] Philo Junius, *L'Amministrazione in Rapporto all'Unità Politica d'Italia* (Milan, 1863), p. 9; Bonghi, *Vita di Pasini*, p. 828; *Lettere Ricasoli*, V. 334–5; *L'Opinione*, 8 Dec. 1860; D. Zanichelli, *Studi di Storia Costituzionale e Politica nel Risorgimento Italiano* (Bologna, 1900), p. 218.

[7] Artom et Blanc, *Œuvre Parlementaire de Cavour*, p. 19; Bersezio, *Il Regno*, VII. 582; ibid. VIII. 16.

[8] G. Finali, *Il Conte di Cavour: Commemorazione fatta a Cesena nella Festa Nazionale del 1894* (Cesena, 1894), p. 22; Count Cavour, *Thoughts on Ireland, its Present and its Future*, trans. W. B. Hodgson (London, 1868), p. 103.

hopes of establishing home rule in Tuscany or Sicily, this may have been a deliberate or half-conscious stratagem to win support in other Italian regions for his policy of annexation. It would also appeal to the French who were anxious not to have a too strongly centralized Italy. Cavour had to take careful note of Napoleon's opinions, and it is likely that this was an important reason why he allowed Minghetti to prepare a scheme along these lines.[1]

Domestic politics were almost certainly another strong influence in making it hard for him to take a firm line one way or the other. A meeting of ministers took place on 25 November 1860, and a short cabinet minute stated, somewhat unusually, that when a parliamentary discussion took place on Minghetti's scheme the government would not make it a '*questione di gabinetto*'.[2] Clearly the cabinet was divided, and almost certainly one can infer from this minute that Cavour had not openly taken sides. His preferred technique of government was to work with coalitions that contained people of various views: apart from Farini and Minghetti, his majority also included Cassinis and La Farina who lacked any enthusiasm for regional devolution, and understandably Cavour would not have wanted to risk dividing this composite majority at such a critical moment by pushing too hard on a controversial issue.

Here were the beginnings of 'transformism' at work. Believing in the '*juste milieu*', Cavour did not like raising principles of disagreement round which a polarized party system could arise; he preferred to steal part of his opponents' policy and discover a compromise which would keep his transformist coalition in being at the same time as it inhibited the coalescence of any rival grouping. This fear of dividing his majority over *regionismo*, which was the first important controversy to be raised in the new kingdom, was specially noted by De Sanctis of the Left and Bonghi of the Right as an important reason why parties failed to develop in Italy; it must have been one reason why parliament was not called upon to discuss this and other major issues.[3] Depretis, too, who was in time to become one of the leading parliamentarians in modern Italian history, recognized Cavour's difficulty in being supported by a coalition which was insufficiently cohesive and insufficiently liberal; Depretis hinted that Cavour burked this particular controversy so as to avoid party divisions and stay in office.[4] Later under Depretis, transformism became a set method of government, an almost standard means of avoiding awkward decisions, a means of preventing the growth of an organized opposition. It would be surprising if he had not learnt part of his technique from the frustrating experience of being in opposition to Cavour.

[1] *Cavour-Nigra*, IV. 186, 245.
[2] *L'Opera Politica del Senatore I. Artom nel Risorgimento Italiano*, ed. E. Artom (Bologna, 1906), p. 282.
[3] F. de Sanctis, *Scritti e Discorsi Politici* (Naples, 1939), I. 269–70; Bonghi, *Vita di Pasini*, p. 831.
[4] *Discorsi Parlamentari di Agostino Depretis*, ed. G. Zucconi and G. Fortunato (Rome, 1891), IV. 526; *Giacomo Dina*, II. 12–13; Lipparini, *Minghetti*, II. 10.

It is more than possible that Cavour had at first encouraged Farini and Minghetti to devise a system of regional government, and then changed his mind as he learnt more about Italy and what regionalism might mean in practice. Such experience came first from Tuscany. When Tuscany was annexed in March 1860, Cavour had at first been anxious that this province should retain some autonomy, and Ricasoli therefore remained as governor of Tuscany for another year: in practice, however, the events of this year revealed to Cavour some of the disadvantages of *regionismo*. Ricasoli was not an efficient governor, nor had he a head for finance, and he was highly disrespectful towards Cavour personally, as he was also contemptuous of the 'stupid, pedantic, useless bureaucracy of Turin'. Ricasoli attacked the Piedmontese for being too little Italian, too provincial, too domineering, and above all for being unable to see that Tuscans wanted to be Italians rather than just efficient automatons in the Piedmontese style.[1] When Ricasoli asked for serious changes before northern legislation was applied to Tuscany, here was obvious danger; and so Cavour, who in March had claimed to want Tuscan autonomy more than Ricasoli did, was declaring by the end of the year that a unified administration was essential at once. The separate governorship of Ricasoli, he said, was impossible; the 'iron baron' had been administering his region 'like a Turkish pasha', and could not be allowed to continue.[2]

Sicilians in 1860 provided Cavour with a lesson which told in exactly the same sense. In Sicily, as in Tuscany, he began by favouring local autonomy, even advocating that the island should be allowed a separate regional parliament.[3] But as Garibaldi's conquest progressed, it became clear that local insular patriotism was a possible threat to national sentiment. La Farina, when he was expelled from Sicily by Garibaldi in June, returned to Turin full of anger against the autonomist sentiments of Palermo, and tried to push Cavour towards treating both the autonomists and the Garibaldians as a dangerous enemy. Scores, even perhaps hundreds, of pamphlets were produced at Palermo to argue that Sicily had a special personality of her own requiring individual treatment, or which claimed that her laws were better than those of other regions; and some even advocated that Sicily should have not only her own parliament, but her own armed forces and recognition of her own specific nationality.[4]

This kind of reasoning was unwittingly encouraged in August 1860 by the publication at Palermo of Farini's remarks in favour of administrative auto-

---

[1] *Carteggi Ricasoli*, VIII. 137; ibid. XV. 197.

[2] *Liberazione del Mezzogiorno*, III. 178; Bollea, *Una Silloge*, pp. 364, 376–7.

[3] R. Romeo, 'Michele Amari', *Dizionario Biografico degli Italiani* (Rome, 1960), II. 649; *Carteggio di Michele Amari*, ed. A. d'Ancona (Turin, 1896–1907), II. 389; ibid. III. 230–1; C. Avarna di Gualtieri, *Ruggero Settimo nel Risorgimento Siciliano* (Bari, 1928), pp. 198–9.

[4] *Appendice all'Opuscolo 'Sull'Annessione ed Autonomia'* (Palermo, 1860), p. 20; S. M. Ganci, 'L'autonomismo Siciliano nello Stato Unitario', *La Sicilia e l'Unità d'Italia: Atti del Congresso sul Risorgimento a Palermo* (Milan, 1962), I. 227, 234, 238.

nomy. Farini's endorsement of what so many Sicilians wanted was hailed there with enormous enthusiasm,[1] and Cavour's friends at Palermo industriously spread the news as propaganda to win adherents to the cause of annexation to Piedmont. Cavour additionally made certain calculated remarks which must have been designed to appeal to the autonomist vote in the forthcoming plebiscite. If only Sicilians would vote annexation to Piedmont, he promised them 'a real regional self-government' and 'a very large decentralization of administration'.[2] Until the plebiscite took place on 21 October, it was important to create as little offence to *sicilianità* as possible.

Before giving up his post as dictator of Sicily, Garibaldi appointed a committee of distinguished Sicilians to discuss the implications of annexation and what this promised self-government might mean in practice. Their report, influenced without doubt by Cavour's remarks, was presented in November and made certain precise demands for autonomy, including an elected regional assembly and special laws which would not apply elsewhere in Italy. But Cavour had by this time changed his policy and had no intention now of allowing Sicily her own assembly.[3] What had happened in the interval was that he had been given his huge majority in the plebiscite and had discovered a unitary state to be within his grasp. Moreover he had been surprised and frightened to be informed that an autonomous Sicily might give encouragement and political power to Garibaldi and the political enemies of Piedmont. Whatever the real reason for his change of attitude, some people soon began to think and say in the newspapers that Cavour's earlier promises must have been a deliberately false prospectus in order to win a resounding vote, since with no doubt many votes must have been given for annexation under the impression that regional self-government was part of his policy.

At Naples, too, there were similar misunderstandings on both sides. Cavour had had no very clear idea of what he would find in these southern provinces, for until the summer of 1860 the prospect of reaching Naples had seemed remote. The advice he received from the Neapolitans exiled in Turin was unreliable. For example, when he eventually annexed the south, he did so only after being persuaded that the arrival of efficient, moral government by northerners could in twenty years' time turn this largely barren wilderness into the richest part of Italy.[4] This was the same kind of optimistic ignorance which had sustained him in his treatment of Sardinia. But by the autumn he was greatly disconcerted to discover how strong was the desire for some kind of

[1] *Giornale Officiale di Sicilia* (Palermo), 30 Aug. 1860; and correspondence from Palermo in *La Perseveranza* (Milan) of 5 Sept.; R. Salvo di Pietraganzili, *Garibaldi e la Sicilia: Patri Ricordi del 1860* (Palermo, 1905), p. 347.

[2] *Liberazione del Mezzogiorno*, III. 144–5; ibid. IV. 220; *I Fardella di Torre Arsa*, ed. F. de Stefano (Rome, 1935), pp. 150–1.

[3] *Carteggio di Amari*, II. 137, 141.

[4] De la Rive, *Cavour*, p. 439; Artom's note in *Nuova Antologia*, Nov. 1901, p. 148; *Rivista Contemporanea* (Turin), May 1961, p. 283; the king told Cavour that the Abruzzi was 'le pays le plus fertile du monde' (*Bollettino Storico-Bibliografico Subalpino* (Turin), LX (1963), 526).

local autonomy:[1] considerable publicity was therefore given in the Neapolitan press to Farini's and Minghetti's supposed views in favour of creating partially autonomous regions, and here too, just as in Sicily, the news had caused great satisfaction.[2]

At a later stage, however, what was happening in Tuscany, and experience of Garibaldi's dangerously independent politics in Sicily, made Turin suspicious of any talk along these lines. Cavour chose Farini to be the first governor of Naples, but gave him secret orders to see if it would be possible to impose Piedmontese laws with a minimum of delay. Farini was told that, if need be, he should assume dictatorial powers without hesitation in order to overcome local opposition, and Cassinis was also sent to Naples with a clear mandate to introduce immediately and as something 'absolutely vital' the legislation which was already accepted in northern and part of central Italy.[3] Once in Naples, however, it was not so easy to accept the wisdom of such a policy. Farini at the end of November followed Garibaldi's Sicilian example and set up an advisory committee of Neapolitan *notabili* to advise him on the special interests of Naples. Cavour, when he heard of it, insisted that this body should be given nothing serious to do, since Farini's task was not to consult Neapolitan opinion but to impose unity on 'the most corrupt part of Italy', and any local advice could only weaken this determination.

Farini's appointment of an advisory *consulta* had resulted from the fact that his government had run into grave difficulties not foreseen at Turin. Cavour had assured Farini that he would find himself welcomed as a deliverer from the tyranny of Garibaldi, and neither of them had any idea that Garibaldi's name might still be popular nor that the deliverers would be regarded as another and less welcome despotism. Farini on his arrival soon reached the startling conviction that the 99 per cent majority in the plebiscite could not have been a vote for Italy but had been a protest against Bourbon misrule, as the 99 per cent majority in Sicily had been a vote against Neapolitan rule of any kind; indeed the believers in a united Italy turned out, to his great astonishment, to be very few.[4] The opposition he encountered was occasionally very fierce indeed. Farini was sometimes obliged to imprison and exile people without trial, or even to carry out summary executions. Conditions were very different here from those in 'Italian Italy', so he wrote to Minghetti,[5] and this persuaded him to go slowly in enforcing the policy which had been decided in remote Turin: hence he appointed his advisory

---

[1] Bonghi, in *Il Nazionale* (Naples) of 12 Sept. 1860; Liborio Romano, in a letter of 7 Aug. 1860 to Dragonetti, MSS. Carte Bianchi-Ricasoli (Archivio di Stato, Florence), N/P; Pavone, *Amministrazione Centrale e Periferica*, p. 84.

[2] Lipparini, *Minghetti*, I. 246; *Giornale Officiale* (Naples), 10, 27, 30 Nov., 8 Dec.

[3] Cassinis to Mancini, 30 Oct. 1860, MSS. Museo del Risorgimento (Rome); Cassinis to Farini, 1 Nov., MSS. Carte Farini (Biblioteca Classense, Ravenna); *Liberazione del Mezzogiorno*, III. 21, 122, 282, 287, 377.

[4] Ibid. 328; *Epistolario La Farina*, II. 451.   [5] 12 Dec. 1860, MSS. Carte Farini.

consulta in order to conciliate local feelings and make the change-over less abrupt and thorough than Cavour had wished.

Once Cavour realized that the south was so different from what he had imagined, he reacted in quite another way, for here too he began to fear that any grant of local autonomy would be tantamount to handing over to either Garibaldi or the partisans of the *ancien régime*. Cavour's closest Neapolitan friend, Massari, reported that Farini was imperilling the process of unification by appointing so many southerners to government posts, and the only hope was at once to put the country into the hands of northern Italians who had a finer sense of morality and efficiency. A kind of panic seized Turin, for a parliament would probably be meeting in Piedmont within three months, and it was thought important to create a unified and effective administrative structure before southern deputies could arrive there with their different political traditions and ideas of political behaviour. Cavour had to admit that Naples was not ready for his ideas on self-government. Accordingly he sent renewed instructions that Farini should use force if necessary and disregard local criticism. On La Farina's advice, he recognized that this was an occasion where rigid martial law was necessary, and there was little to be gained by further talk of compromising with the autonomists.[1]

Evidently the Neapolitan refugees in Turin had seriously misled Cavour about public opinion in the south. At one moment his pessimism seems to have reached a point where he lamented that Garibaldi had compelled him to annex Naples.[2] But it was too late to repine at the facts. To meet the emergency his cabinet decided unanimously that it was essential to hurry through the process of legal unification and above all to do this before parliament could question what was being done. Even Minghetti must presumably have agreed to this decision. In such conditions of emergency there would be no time to study local conditions or consult local opinion, so Rattazzi's law of 23 October 1859 was hastily published in Naples with a few minor changes. Parliament eventually met on 18 February, but in the previous two days 53 different decree-laws were rushed into print in Naples, and these completely altered the legal structure of government in the south.[3]

They covered an enormous range. Against one of them which introduced the jury system into the south, there was a protest by some liberal southerners on the grounds that the jury system might mean a major perversion of justice in a region where juries were more easily intimidated than magistrates. Here was a question of fact on which local opinion might profitably have been consulted, but Cassinis, though we know he had himself been doubtful on this very point, could not let himself seem to weaken, and he made the inaccurate

---

[1] *Liberazione del Mezzogiorno*, III. 163; ibid. IV. 68, 127–8; *Cavour-Nigra*, IV. 292.

[2] Mme Rattazzi, *Rattazzi et son Temps*, II. 427–8.

[3] Cassinis to Mancini, 30 Jan. 1861, MSS. Museo del Risorgimento (Rome); *Collezione delle Leggi e dei Decreti emanati durante il Periodo della Luogotenenza nelle Provincie Napoletane, Anno 1860* (Naples, 1861), I, pt. i. 256, 555–768.

and unhelpful reply that juries worked perfectly well in Sardinia.[1] This was one small example of what could happen when people used the argument of haste and urgency to conceal their ignorance.

Another law unilaterally abolished the concordat of 1818 with the Holy See. There was no time to investigate the possibility that the position of the church might have special features in the south which rendered some modifications advisable in the anticlerical legislation of Piedmont. So the religious houses were mostly abolished, their property confiscated, and this brought about considerable hardship quite apart from creating a large new element of opposition at a moment when conciliation was vital. To those who expressed doubt whether Cavour had powers to introduce this mass of legislation, especially as it was done in a way quite obviously designed to circumvent parliamentary discussion, the official answer came that 'government actions should not be judged on any strict interpretation of the law, but in the light of circumstances'.[2] To those who wondered if it would not have been expedient to make some concessions to religion and the pope, Cavour replied with a clear negative, for he mistakenly thought that he held most of the trump cards. As a result, he gratuitously convinced Pius that it was not worth compromising with someone so insensitive and disingenuous.[3] This was a major catastrophe.

Naples, Sicily, and Tuscany each posed problems for Cavour which were novel, complicated, and urgent, and about which he had insufficient factual information or reliable advice. By the beginning of 1861 he had still not turned finally against any idea of setting up regional governmental institutions. That Minghetti's regional units might be allowed some kind of self-government had been Cavour's belief as late as 15 January, and he had particularly asked that this policy should be given publicity at Naples where the parliamentary elections were about to take place.[4] On 1 February he still wrote of wanting 'to introduce decentralization to the very limits of what is reasonable', and the king's speech to parliament on 18 February spoke once again of wanting 'the most extensive administrative liberties'.[5]

But by this time Cavour was receiving urgent advice from his friends in Naples that Minghetti's policy of regionalism would be a disaster. If he was sincere in what he said, it was in the second half of February that he finally changed his opinion, and the main influence upon him must have been what was happening in Naples. Costantino Nigra, who was his closest and most trusted collaborator, had been sent to Naples in January to discover the true

---

[1] Speech by Amari, 5 Apr. 1861, in *Atti Parlamentari: Camera*, p. 200; Cassinis to Mancini, 30 Oct. 1860, MSS. Museo del Risorgimento (Rome).

[2] Speech by Cassinis on 5 Apr. 1861, *Atti Parlamentari*, p. 201.

[3] *Lettere di Cavour*, IV. 137, 187.

[4] *Liberazione del Mezzogiorno*, IV. 220 (the elections were on 27 January).

[5] *La Politica Italiana dal 1848 al 1897: Programmi di Governo* (Rome, 1899), I. 153; *Lettere Ricasoli*, V. 361.

facts on the spot, and was soon begging Cavour to put Minghetti's proposals right out of his mind: if Neapolitan autonomy were allowed to survive, it would not only prejudice the unity of the kingdom but might make effective government of any kind impossible.[1] By the beginning of March, Cavour had entirely renounced his earlier support for local self-government: it would be fatal and ruinous; and, what was more, he had been surprised to receive strong advice from some southerners against allowing regional autonomy.[2] Another discovery was that there simply did not exist sufficient talent in Italy with the necessary experience and skills to staff so many regional governments: Cavour was in despair that he might not be able to find a single southerner capable of filling a post in his cabinet at Turin.[3]

Another awkward fact was that *regionismo* was being taken up and exploited by the opposition, by Mazzini and Cattaneo on the far Left and by the clericals and reactionaries on the Right. Regionalism appealed to a number of quite different interests: for example to those who thought that a unitary state would be wrong and federalism right; to those who thought that decentralization would make political unification more acceptable, as well as to others who wanted it as a means of preserving some of the class structure and politics of the *ancien régime*.[4] It also appealed to those who saw regional autonomy as a means of conserving local patronage systems, or of keeping the hegemony of regional capitals such as Florence in their ancient battle against the merely provincial capitals such as Pisa, Lucca, and Siena.[5] To still others, regionalism was a useful stick with which to beat the government or with which to constitute a possible alternative coalition against that of Cavour.

To combat these miscellaneous forces, the prime minister found that the idea of a powerful, centralized Italy commanded widespread support among many of his own friends, all the more strongly in that the contrary view was being adopted by their opponents. Above all this was so in Piedmont, where, even among Cavour's followers, there was a palpable movement away from purely libertarian ideas and in favour of a greater degree of force and authority.[6] In central Italy, Ricasoli had by now given up his earlier toying with regionalism, for he too had seen what it might mean in Sicily and Naples. Some of his friends were insisting that centralization and even authoritarianism were necessary laws of modern society; while others thought that the region would

---

[1] *Cavour-Nigra*, IV. 334.

[2] Ibid. 352; *Cavour e l'Inghilterra*, II, pt. ii. 194.

[3] *Gran Bretagna e Sardegna*, VIII. 324; *Archivio Storico Italiano* (Florence), 1955, p. 361.

[4] F. de Blasiis, *Progetto di Legge Organica Comunale e Provinciale* (Turin, 1861), p. 3; G. Ghezzi, *Saggio Storico sull'Attività Politica di Liborio Romano* (Florence, 1936), pp. 178-83, 202-10, 216-17; E. Albèri, *L'Italia Uscente l'Anno 1860* (Florence, 1861), p. 4.

[5] *Carteggio di Amari*, III. 224; *Carteggi Ricasoli*, XVI. 103; *Liberazione del Mezzogiorno*, III. 131; G. B. Giorgini, *Dell'Unità d'Italia in Ordine al Diritto e alla Storia* (Milan, 1861), p. 60 (Giorgini was born at Lucca, and represented Siena in parliament); Pavone, *Amministrazione Centrale e Periferica*, p. 134.

[6] *Carteggio Castelli*, I. 382; Boncompagni, *L'Unità d'Italia*, pp. 10, 30; *Giacomo Dina*, II. 12.

at least be 'a danger to national unity and a diminishment to the liberties of the individual provinces inside each region'.[1] In southern Italy, too, a similar view was increasingly favoured by Spaventa, Mancini, and Massari, who all came from outlying provinces of the *Napoletano* and therefore preferred government from Turin to government from the regional capital, Naples; also in Sicily by La Farina and Cordova who, having their homes in eastern Sicily, welcomed centralized rule from Turin as a means of escape from the dominance of Palermo. It was thus common to find the opponents of regionalism among the representatives of the small towns: Toscanelli representing Pontedera, Giorgini from Massa-Carrara, Caracciolo from Cerignola, Leopardi from Sulmona.

A still further factor in swaying Cavour's mind may have been the news of civil war in the United States of America. Lincoln was elected president in November 1860 and South Carolina seceded in December: to some Italian observers this seemed proof that the American union was moribund. Coming not long after a civil war in Switzerland, it suggested that federal states were doomed and that Italy needed a very different type of constitution if she were to survive.[2] The surrender of Fort Sumter, the first engagement of the American civil war, took place on 13 April 1861 when Minghetti's scheme for creating the regions was being discussed in committee at Turin. Already by this time another civil war was beginning in the southern provinces of Italy, thinly concealed under the term 'suppression of brigandage'. This Italian civil war was going to need the full force of an organized state to defeat it. Moreover a quick victory would have been an inestimable asset in persuading the rest of Europe that the new Italy was a viable state deserving diplomatic recognition. All this made Minghetti's theoretical talk about regional autonomy look academic or even dangerous.

During the last months of Cavour's life, faced with this and an infinity of other questions, the prime minister seemed to lack the energy to impose solutions on his colleagues or to dominate parliament as he had been accustomed to do; he rather gave the impression of wanting to put off decisions and to avoid public debate. His closest friends, for example Costantino Nigra, found him more remote. Parliament seemed almost to be turning against him.[3] As Giuseppe Ferrari told parliament, Italy had completed in a few

---

[1] L. Carbonieri to Minghetti, 2 Dec. 1860, MSS. Archivio Minghetti; G. B. Giorgini, *La Centralizzazione*, pp. 6, 46, 51; G. B. Giorgini, *Dell' Unità d'Italia*, p. 15; C. Busi, *L'Unità Politica e le Autonomie Amministrative* (Florence, 1861), p. 7; Leone Carpi, *Del Riordinamento Amministrativo* (Bologna, 1860), p. 39.

[2] Carbonieri, *Della Regione in Italia*, pp. 62, 237; Gonella, *Del Potere Regionale*, p. 30; Ernesto d'Amico, *Sopra l'Ordinamento Amministrativo del Regno d'Italia* (Palermo, 1861), p. 23; Boncompagni, *L'Unità d'Italia*, p. 10; *Piccolo Corriere d'Italia*, 4 Oct. 1861.

[3] Hudson, 12 Apr. 1861, P.R.O. 30/22/68: 'It will be, I think, a misfortune were he to fall before he has settled the Roman Question. But I imagine this to be the general impression in parliament, for altho' Cavour is admired and feared and followed, he is not loved. People fear a return of the French, and they do not trust Cavour implicitly. They dread a second edition of Nice and Savoy, and say if

months a process that had taken France more than a thousand years, from the time of Clovis to that of Napoleon I, and to deal with so many complex problems was beyond the capacity of Cavour's administrative staff or even of his own fertile brain. This must be one of the reasons why he had not given any firm lead on the subject of regions but left the question in Minghetti's hands. At a cabinet meeting on 9 May, it was agreed to drop any idea of making the regions into autonomous bodies, but still to retain as official policy their establishment as administrative entities with delegated powers from Turin. This decision was confirmed ten days later, just before Cavour's fatal illness, though it was already clear that a majority in parliament might be hard to find for even such a watered-down project. The parliamentary committee discussing it was clearly intending to make a thoroughly negative report. Cavour on 21 May still talked of a possible compromise, but does not seem to have been greatly perturbed by the possibility of rejection: he had more serious things to think of.[1]

Cavour's death on 6 June altered the picture quite conclusively, for his successor, Ricasoli, knew his own mind by now much more clearly on this issue and ensured that Minghetti's project never reached the point of a parliamentary discussion. Along with the regions, Ricasoli also discarded Minghetti's other ancillary idea for increased local self-government in provinces and villages. A few months later, the prefectoral system, in almost precisely the version practised in Piedmont, had been extended to most of the other regions of Italy. Finali recalls how Ricasoli returned after midnight from a cabinet meeting where his colleagues had been unanimous in thinking this step wrong or over-hasty; but the premier simply announced that he had decided to exert his powers and disregard cabinet opinion.[2] Most parliamentarians were evidently quite ready to accept such a decision, and only Minghetti resigned from the cabinet on the issue. The same parliament which a year earlier had been doubtful about Rattazzi's law of October 1859, now saw it extended with a few slight modifications to the rest of Italy, and no one forced a debate on this process in either house.

One of the weak points of the centralized system of Italian politics was to be that parliamentary business was often jammed by purely local *affari di campanile*, as they were already being termed;[3] so much so, that important

---

he brings the French in we shall never get them out again. . . . For the present doubtless he is a necessity, but there is a tiny cloud of opposition rising on the political horizon no bigger than Ricasoli's wig which I believe will overshadow the Goschen of Cavour and force him to flee to his tents at Leri'; *Carteggi Ricasoli*, XVI. 157; *Cavour-Nigra*, IV. 358; *Piccolo Corriere d'Italia*, 6 June 1861.

[1] Cabinet minutes, in *Opera Politica del Artom*, pp. 309, 313; *Lettere di Cavour*, IV. 232; Minghetti's diary, in Petracchi, *Origini dell'Ordinamento Comunale e Provinciale*, I. 355-7.

[2] G. Finali, *Memorie*, ed. G. Maioli (Faenza, 1955), p. 232; but see E. Ragionieri's comments in *Studi Storici* (Milan), Apr. 1960, p. 500.

[3] F. Petruccelli della Gattina, *I Moribondi del Palazzo Carignano* (Milan, 1862), p. 31.

state business had to be inadequately discussed or not discussed at all. Sidney Sonnino, a conservative reformer who was himself to become prime minister, fastened on this fact as the chief reason why parties failed to form in Italy and hence for the failure of parliamentary institutions to work.[1] The practice of transformism contributed to keeping the problem of regionalism like all other major policy issues away from too direct a parliamentary scrutiny. Giuseppe Ferrari once tried to raise in parliament the question of the different requirements of each region, implying that they therefore needed different treatment and different laws: he was ruled out of order by Rattazzi, at that time speaker of the house, on the grounds that 'any discussion of the integrity of the kingdom is *ultra vires*'. D'Ondes Reggio tried on another occasion to do the same, and insisted that centralization was obviously proving a hindrance to effective government: he too was forced into silence by the then speaker, Cassinis, who ruled that any question of provincial or regional autonomy was now, and henceforth, beyond the competence of parliament.[2] The personal views of both Rattazzi and Cassinis on this issue were well known.

D'Ondes Reggio therefore had to remain content with pointing out that every one of the main laws on local government, those of 1848, 1859, and 1861, had been enacted not by parliament but by successive governments employing royal decrees and acting under emergency regulations. Not even the unifying law of 1865 was brought before parliament for approval, even though parliament was in session on the day of its publication; it may be noted that the law of 1865 differed only in small details from that of 23 October 1859, and both of them were a good deal more centralizing and less liberal than Minghetti's abortive proposals of 1861. But the issues concerned were too delicate and too controversial to be decided by parliamentary means, and the deputies passively accepted this as being the most convenient mode of operation.

Later prime ministers of Italy, almost without exception, continued to pay lip-service to the urgent need for changing the resultant practice and moving in the direction of administrative devolution. Some of them, indeed, called this the most urgent of all problems facing the nation. But all of them failed to take sufficient action, and for much the same reasons as had prevailed with Cavour. There was the fear that even a minor degree of regional self-government might aid the political opposition, or, worse still, weaken the union. There was the conviction that every parliamentary coalition was too carefully poised for any minister to risk a fundamental debate on such a contentious topic as regional devolution. Moreover elections had to be won; therefore ministers could not afford to diminish the authority of the prefects in each locality or encourage too much local self-government. The prefect and the *sindaco* were important government servants, and were particularly useful when it came to 'making' the elections. It was therefore desirable to have

[1] S. Sonnino, *Del Governo Rappresentativo in Italia* (Rome, 1872), pp. 14–15, 22.
[2] 4 Apr. 1861, *Atti Parlamentari: Camera*, p. 351; 23 June 1864, ibid., pp. 3080, 3083.

them nominated by the minister of the interior. Minghetti's proposal had contained the excessively liberal suggestion that the *sindaco* should be elected from below, and that the prefect's powers over the elected element in the provincial administrations should be weakened; but neither of these suggestions had much appeal to successive conservative governments after 1861.

Such a degree of centralization had perhaps not been intended by Cavour, but at the time of his death he had been moving some way in that direction, driven to it by an emergency situation and also by certain facets of his own temperament. Other politicians went much further than he did. To most people the victories of the risorgimento were astonishing and unexpected; nor was there any absolute certainty that the nation would survive intact and overcome its internal differences. From Sicily there now came rumours of another 'Sicilian Vespers' to chase out the Italian invaders.[1] At Naples the position was such that Azeglio anxiously suggested that unification might have been premature and the southern provinces might split off again. One of the real problems for Italians, said Azeglio with his usual pungency, was to find how they could dislike each other less: not even the best cook, he said, could make a good dish with stinking meat; and several times he spoke of the union with Naples as like going to bed with a victim of smallpox.[2] This was a degree of pessimism which, while it showed that some responsible observers were not altogether happy about the union, pushed others to the opposite extreme where they were ready to accept a greater degree of centralization than any of the principal political thinkers of the risorgimento would ideally have liked.

The suppression of the proposal to set up regions was, in other words, due in part to the very strength of regional feelings and to the realization that patriotic sentiment needed time to develop. Setting myth and rhetoric aside, the mass of the people had been indifferent to the risorgimento, if not actively hostile, and it was possible for contemporaries to say that no other modern nation had made fewer efforts and fewer sacrifices in the cause of patriotism.[3] Hence arose the assumption that a strong and centralized government was required if the nation were to survive. Subsequently, by another piece of

---

[1] Minghetti's diary, ed. A. Bertelli, *Archivio Storico Italiano*, 1955, p. 360.

[2] *Azeglio e Pantaleoni: Carteggio*, p. 430; *Lettere d'Azeglio a sua Moglie Luisa Blondel*, ed. G. Carcano (Milan, 1870), p. 523; C. di Persano, *Diario Privato-Politico-Militare* (Turin, 1871), IV. 80; *Carteggi E. d'Azeglio*, II. 469; Azeglio's famous letter to Matteucci is translated in *The Making of Italy*, ed. Mack Smith, p. 367.

[3] Giorgini, *Dell'Unità d'Italia*, pp. 33–4; L. Galeotti, *La Prima Legislatura del Regno d'Italia: Studi e Ricordi* (2nd ed., Florence, 1866), p. 87; *La Stampa* (Turin), 26 Aug. 1862; M. Formentini, *Sulla Organizzazione del Regno d'Italia*, p. 63; Mameli, speech in parliament, 20 June 1881, *Atti Parlamentari*, p. 6326; G. Fortunato, *Il Mezzogiorno e lo Stato Italiano* (Florence, 1926), I. 7–9, 273–4, 298; L. C. Fregoso, *Del Primato Italiano sul Mediterraneo* (Turin, 1872), p. 211; A.Z., *Verità ingrate sull'Ordinamento Militare Italiano* (Rome, 1895), p. 41; C. Tivaroni, *Storia Critica del Risorgimento Italiano* (Turin, 1894), VI. 469. The contrary myth, however, became historical orthodoxy, namely that few peoples had made greater patriotic exertions (G. Volpe, *Italia Moderna 1815–1915* (Florence, 1943), I. 43).

irony, the very imposition of an over-centralized administration was self-defeating in so far as its effect in the long run was to accentuate regionalism and a regional opposition against central government.[1] Cavour's greatest German admirer, Heinrich von Treitschke, drew the lesson for Germany that national unity would be helped and not hindered by strong regional autonomy.[2] The centralized system imposed on Italy in 1861 was not a coherent and deliberate programme so much as an emergency attempt to meet an immediate and largely unexpected problem. As such it failed to satisfy the real needs of the country and provided just one more source of division and discontent. But this was hardly something for which responsibility can attach to Cavour.

[1] Petruccelli della Gattina, *I Moribondi del Palazzo Carignano*, p. 45; Cenni, *Delle Presenti Condizioni d'Italia*, p. 265, maintained that 99·9 per cent of Neapolitans and Sicilians were autonomists by 1862; A. Salandra, *La Politica Nazionale e il Partito Liberale* (Milan, 1912), pp. 76–8; B. Chapman, 'Regionalism in Italy', p. 136; G. Maranini, *Storia del Potere in Italia 1848–1967* (Florence, 1967), pp. 131–2.

[2] Treitschke, *Cavour*, p. 215; for his admiration of Cavour, see also *Heinrich von Treitschke's Briefe*, ed. M. Cornelius (Leipzig, 1918), II. 458.

13
Constitutional Monarchy, 1861–1865

UNDER a simple and direct exterior, King Victor Emanuel was not so straightforward as the conventional stereotype admitted. He liked to strike an attitude, to act a role, and knew that this was expected of him. Hence it is sometimes hard to know which was the act and which the reality. At the time of Cavour's death, Sir James Hudson wrote of him:

Ten years have improved his character. Experience has softened him. Responsibility has moderated him. From a mere soldier and hunter he is rising into the politician. He spoke of war as a sad necessity. He (today) had lost altogether that tone of a sabreur which 5 years ago was one of his characteristics.[1]

Hudson was soon to change this opinion. A more precise and more subtle view came from one of the king's former mistresses whom he subsequently bestowed in marriage on his favourite Italian politician:

Victor Emanuel was a soldier and a gentleman, which is not to say he was a ladies' man. Simple though he may have been, he was susceptible to flattery provided it was not too crude. He was adroit, intelligent, and quite sharp under an appearance of straightforward good nature. Beneath his brusque, soldierly behaviour, there was more shrewdness than you might think. He was avid for popularity, though he used to pretend the contrary. He had little education, but intuition taught him much that he never learnt at school. His manners were rather gauche and embarrassed; only when he was with women could this rough soldier throw off his shyness.[2]

As to his political importance, there were many different views. At one extreme Count Vitzthum, the Saxon diplomat, reached the point of stating that Victor Emanuel was the real maker of Italy, much more for instance than Cavour. Vitzthum thought that from 1861 onwards, despite what might appear, he was effective dictator of the country: if he observed constitutional forms, it was only so that he might bend them to his will, and in fact Cavour, Rattazzi, Ricasoli, and Lamarmora were puppets in his hand.[3] The fact that

---

[1] 30 June 1861, P.R.O. 30/22/68.
[2] Mme Rattazzi, *Rattazzi et son Temps* (Paris, 1881), I. 469–70.
[3] K. F. Vitzthum von Eckstädt, *St. Petersburg und London in den Jahren 1852–1864* (Stuttgart, 1886), I. 271.

this could be said by a not unobservant politician has a certain interest, even though those closer to events knew that, as far as Cavour at least was concerned, the reverse was nearer to the truth.[1]

There was undeniably a good deal of sound common sense in Victor Emanuel's make-up, and this helped to earn the loyalty of many different kinds of people. On the other hand it had been demonstrated at Naples in 1860 that his slight eccentricities, if not kept well under control, could sometimes make him unpopular. No one, except once or twice Cavour and Ricasoli, dared to interfere in his private behaviour. Since his wife's death he had developed the singular habit, whenever inveigled into a public banquet or into entertaining guests, of eating absolutely nothing, not even opening his napkin, but keeping his hands on the pommel of his sword and looking sulky and bored, to the confusion of his guests and hosts. When forced, not very willingly, to visit his new subjects in central and southern Italy, he would make very few concessions. If he was in a good mood and wanted to impress people, he could charm almost anyone, but equally he could put on a calculated pose of indifference which caused offence and dismay.

His ministers were anxious for him to undertake a number of leisurely tours to see the rest of Italy and show himself to the populace. Yet he hated being away from Turin and often acted badly in consequence. Sometimes on these visits he would put the local dignitaries out of countenance by refusing to let them read him a loyal address; sometimes he deigned to turn up at a public function for just a bare ten minutes. He disliked having his hand kissed, and his reaction when southerners prostrated themselves before him was 'j'aurai envie de leur flanquer un coup de pied au cul'. On a quick visit to Rimini in 1861, after only five minutes he suddenly abandoned a public dinner, leaving his entourage to seize and carry off what food and drink they could, and the subsequent passage of the royal train to Ancona turned into a memorably drunken orgy. At Ancona he was again unwilling to carry out the arranged schedule, and local delegations were put off and told to return the next morning, which they did only to find that he was already *en route* for Bologna. At Foggia in 1863, where once again, as in Palermo, the populace unhorsed his carriage for the privilege of drawing it themselves, he could not endure the thought that this might make him look ridiculous, so he testily insisted on entering the town on foot in the dark and the rain.[2]

This kind of presumption and capriciousness was not serious in its results except when allowed to intrude into politics, but unfortunately it was in

---

[1] Rayneval, 25 Mar. 1861, M. Aff. Étrangères, that the king 'subit l'ascendant de M. de Cavour malgré son aversion pour lui'; Mme Rattazzi, *Rattazzi et son Temps*, I. 443.

[2] H. d'Ideville, *Journal d'un Diplomate en Italie: 1859–1862* (Paris, 1872), I. 294–7; G. Rothan, *Souvenirs Diplomatiques: L'Allemagne et l'Italie 1870–1871* (Paris, 1885), II. 406–18; *Souvenirs du Général Cte Fleury* (3rd ed., Paris, 1897), I. 236–7; *Lettere di V. Emanuele*, I. 653; G. Di Revel, *Da Ancona a Napoli* (Milan, 1892), p. 58; General P. H. Sheridan, *Personal Memoirs* (London, 1888), II. 442; R. Mundy, *H.M.S. 'Hannibal' at Palermo and Naples 1859–61* (London, 1863), pp. 316–17.

politics, and especially in the field of military and foreign policy, that Victor Emanuel felt specially gifted and specially competent to act. This brought out a weak point in the national constitution. On the one hand it was quite clear that this particular sovereign had only a limited enthusiasm for the doctrine of ministerial responsibility to parliament; yet on the other hand he was not prepared to devise and consistently maintain any effective alternative to it. Politicians often tried to cover up what might have been interpreted as unconstitutional behaviour on his part: Cavour, Rattazzi, Ricasoli, Minghetti, Massari, Castelli, all were well aware of the need to conceal certain facts. So were those historians who subsequently altered any compromising documents which happened to survive. Luigi Chiala was a grave offender in this respect. Chiala showed a more critical sense than some other historians, but he once noted that he could not accept the French minister's evidence about the king's attempt to work behind Cavour's back, since the monarch's observance of constitutional niceties had to be beyond question.[1]

In fact, however, there was less of a parliamentary monarchy under Victor Emanuel than there had been under Charles Albert during the latter's few months of constitutional government in 1848–9. Not for Victor Emanuel the doctrine that a king reigns but does not govern. He gladly accepted the other much more convenient doctrine that the king could do no wrong, but without admitting all the constitutional implications that normally followed from it. Nor would he accept that his governments should necessarily reflect the wishes of a majority in parliament. Successive governments after Cavour's death fell just by a decision at court and without any indication from a parliamentary vote.[2] By the *statuto* of 1848, the ministers were his ministers, and parliamentary laws could be vetoed if he disliked them enough.

When speaking to Englishmen, Victor Emanuel sometimes affected a great admiration for Queen Victoria and for the way she never over-stepped her prerogative, though he never spoke like this to others and he did not even bother to condole with her on the death of the prince consort. To his friends he rather confessed to admire the Emperor Napoleon III who had a much more enlarged view of the royal prerogative. Like Napoleon, and almost certainly copying him, Victor Emanuel developed the practice of having a private policy of his own from which his ministers were often entirely excluded, and sometimes he seems to have done this more because he thought it proper to his regal dignity than because he disagreed with his cabinet. He liked to have private ambassadors alongside those of his government, for this flattered his vanity and increased his sense of personal power. He had also observed how

[1] L. Chiala, *Ancora un po' più di Luce sugli Eventi Politici e Militari dell'Anno 1866* (Florence, 1902), p. 627; F. Cognasso, *Vittorio Emanuele II* (Turin, 1942), pp. 374–5.
[2] I. Artom, 'Ricordi di Vittorio Emanuele II', *Rivista Storica del Risorgimento Italiano* (Turin), 1899, p. 747; S. Spaventa, *Lettere Politiche (1861–1893)*, ed. G. Castellano (Bari, 1926), p. 43; F. Crispolti, *Corone e Porpore: Ricordi Personali* (3rd ed., Milan, 1937), p. 12.

Cavour had employed private envoys to check and sometimes to thwart the official representatives of the diplomatic service.

That Victor Emanuel had these personal ambassadors was common knowledge in the world of European diplomacy, though the fact was less often put to his credit than he imagined. Sometimes they were junior officials in an embassy who might even possess private ciphers for correspondence with the king on official matters without his ministers knowing. Sometimes they were allowed to help successive cabinets by providing an extra source of information. Alternatively they might be told to spy on official ambassadors or even to act in direct defiance of cabinet policy, and the result of this was to lower the reputation and effectiveness of Italian diplomacy abroad.

H.M. [wrote Hudson] has a strong predilection for blackguards of the spy genus, male and female, who merely get money from him and tell him just as much as whets his curiosity and suits their purpose. Their information is drawn to suit the king's tastes which are warlike; and this again throws him still further into the arms of the Rattazzi and Garibaldi party.[1]

According to Mme Rattazzi, they were not all of them rogues, though some were just exploiting the king's vanity in order to fatten their purses and their self-importance. Her husband, as prime minister, had been glad if he merely had to pay their bills and not remedy their mistakes. If ever any minister was bold enough to hint to the king that their existence was an embarrassment or a danger, the monarch could cheerfully deny all knowledge of them even when written evidence of their activities was in the minister's hands.[2]

Probably not a great deal of positive harm was done by these men, for they were not notoriously able, and their doings were often known and discounted by both foreign governments and the Italian foreign service. The illusion of power satisfied Victor Emanuel almost as much as the reality. Foreign ambassadors quickly learnt to interpret his hyperbolic language. He would regularly talk to them as though he bore the whole weight of government on his own back, and as though his ministers were incompetents whom he had to humour with the mere appearance of authority. According to General Petitti, who was a close acquaintance, almost no conversation with the king could take place without hearing this kind of vain talk about his political prowess: just occasionally some credit might be given to Cavour or Rattazzi, but the king used to add that even these two men needed firm direction from himself, while the rest of his ministers were totally incapable and had to be watched night and day.[3] No doubt such remarks would have been intended to impress, but not many people can have been deceived. As he lacked friends who could criticize him to his face, the result was more likely to have been self-deception. In other words Victor Emanuel deluded himself into an excessive

---

[1] 26 Jan. 1862, P.R.O. 30/22/69; K. F. Vitzthum von Eckstädt, *London, Gastein und Sadowa 1864–1866: Denkwürdigkeiten* (Stuttgart, 1889), pp. 160–1.

[2] Mme Rattazzi, *Rattazzi et son Temps*, II. 326.   [3] Chiala, *Ancora un po' più di Luce*, p. 627.

belief in his own power and cleverness; hence he was encouraged to pursue some highly suspect ventures by means of secret diplomatic initiatives which hindered rather than helped his country.

If it had not been for these secret ventures, such boastful talk would not have been taken very seriously by anyone who knew him well. His chaplain once explained that he was content to play the king for one month a year, while for the rest he was too idle and too much concerned with minor pleasures to have enough time for politics; and this reputation for idleness did him no good.[1] Even if he had wanted to put the clock back to the days of absolutism, he would have been prevented by his lack of application and single-minded determination. The absence of these qualities became, if anything, more noticeable with advancing years. In 1861, Victor Emanuel was only forty-one, but was ageing and putting on weight; he was beginning to tint his hair and his enormous upturned moustache, as was noticed by careful observers who saw the colours running when exposed to the rain. Less often now did he preside over cabinet meetings.[2] Letters had a habit of getting lost in the enormous pockets of his baggy trousers, to be forgotten until his valet went through his suits and found them.[3]

Victor Emanuel could never have played the tyrant, and not only because he was too fond of a quiet life; he also possessed too much sense. After 1861 there existed less of a basis than there had been ten years earlier for a restoration of full monarchical power. The aristocrats did not form a solid faction, and many of them had been alienated by the king's anticlericalism as well as by his manifest distaste for etiquette, honours, and the fine points of rank; so he tended to disregard them.[4] Senators were all appointed by him personally, and among them there was in general a strong monarchical loyalty, even a nostalgia for absolutism, but the rank of senator was sought more as an honour than a public service, and was accorded rather to emeritus functionaries and politicians than to build up an active party of king's friends. Senators did not like the expense and trouble of moving into Turin from their country estates, and it was often very hard to find a quorum for debates in the upper House.[5]

Cavour was eight years in all as premier. In 1861–2, Ricasoli his successor held office for eight months, and was followed by Rattazzi for another eight months, by Farini for only three, then Minghetti for over a year. The king's attitude to these successive prime ministers was briefly stated by Hudson.

---

[1] Crispolti, *Corone e Porpore*, p. 13; *Carteggi E. d'Azeglio*, II. 306.
[2] E. Re, *I Verbali del Consiglio dei Ministri (1859–1903)* (Rome, 1942), p. 6 of offprint.
[3] *Cavour: Questione Romana*, I. 182–3.
[4] L. Chiala, *Politica Segreta di Napoleone III e di Cavour in Italia e in Ungheria (1858–1861)* (Turin, 1895), p. 113.
[5] Sclopis to Cavour, 29 Apr. 1861, MSS. Archivio Ministero degli Affari Esteri (Rome), Gabinetto, b. 178; Elliot, 18 Mar. 1864, F.O. 45/57; Mme Rattazzi, *Rattazzi et son Temps*, II. 54.

His scale of affection for the leading public men is about as follows. He was afraid of Cavour. He respects Ricasoli. He loves Rattazzi. He despises Farini. He hates Minghetti.[1]

Cavour had once expressed a wish that Minghetti should succeed him, but Cavour's cabinet colleagues, when suddenly confronted with the emergency of his death, agreed on the name of Ricasoli, and they took it on themselves to advise the king so. The monarch himself would almost certainly have preferred Rattazzi to the formidable 'iron baron', but the death of Cavour was such a catastrophe that it was important to find a consensus candidate. There were also advantages in choosing someone who did not come from Piedmont.

Ricasoli was known to be a loyal monarchist and patriot, but he nevertheless made some conditions for acceptance: one was that he should not have to wear court uniform or receive any salary; another, mindful of the king's liking for private intrigues abroad, was that the prime minister should also be in charge of the foreign office.[2] Ricasoli was too proud to be a courtier. He even treated the king with some condescension, having none of Cavour's elasticity of temper and formal deference. Victor Emanuel had always thought him a little strange, even a bit mad, and familiarity did not improve their view of each other. Ricasoli was a Tuscan, and experience had taught him to dislike and distrust the ambience of Turin: in his eyes people from Piedmont were too conscious of their own superiority, as well as being pedantic, aesthetically uneducated, even a little inhuman. This did not make for ease of relations. The king, who 'hates speaking Italian',[3] took time to adjust to men of other regions who had other traditions and habits than those to which he was accustomed.

Cavour towards the end of his life had been approaching a solution of the Roman question which would have brought him close to effective possession of Rome as the Italian capital. Napoleon had been extremely anxious to withdraw the French garrison from the Papal States where, ever since 1849, they had been guarding the pope. He therefore proposed in April 1861 that, in return for repatriating these troops, Cavour should promise not to attack the Papal States and to stop Garibaldi doing so. Secretly the emperor explained that, after a six months' delay, he might turn a blind eye to any patriotic revolution inside the Papal States that might prepare the way for the annexation of Rome. Cavour hoped that the six months could be reduced to three.[4] One serious difficulty however was Cavour's public announcement that Rome

---

[1] 8 Sept. 1861, P.R.O. 30/22/68.
[2] *Cavour: Questione Romana*, II. 245; *Lettere di V. Emanuele*, I. 697.
[3] Elliot, 17 Sept. 1864, P.R.O. 30/22/70.
[4] Hudson, 24 May 1861, P.R.O. 30/22/68; *Das Ende des Kirchenstaates*, ed. N. Miko (Vienna, 1964), I. 33–4; *Archivio Storico Italiano* (Florence), 1955, p. 367; *Cavour: Questione Romana*, I. 177; ibid. II. 233–6; L. Lipparini, *Minghetti* (Bologna, 1947), II. 361; Türr's evidence, quoted by G. Giacometti, *L'Unité Italienne 1861–1862: Aperçus d'Histoire Politique et Diplomatique* (Paris, 1898), p. 176.

would one day be the national capital; this announcement made it much harder for Napoleon to withdraw his troops, simply because he could no longer pretend to be ignorant about Italy's intention to overthrow the pope's temporal power. The French wanted to go home, but Cavour, by this '*sottise*', had made it difficult for them to leave.[1]

Apart from this public statement, Cavour had been cautious about telling other people the full extent of his plans for Rome. In particular he had evidently not kept the king fully informed, partly because he feared the latter's indiscretion; partly also because he knew that Victor Emanuel was especially anxious to solve this particular problem 'off his own bat', as Hudson said, and so might make difficulties; partly, too, because he thought that the king was not clever enough to understand the complexities of the Roman question.[2] Ricasoli did not find it easy to take up where Cavour had left off, especially as Cavour had wanted to do everything personally and work through instruments rather than collaborators, as Azeglio put it.[3] Even Cavour's closest disciples had encountered an aristocratic disdain and untrustfulness, even an unfriendliness sometimes, in his attitude towards them.[4] Very few people knew his policy and almost no one understood at first hand the more important problems of Italian politics. The lack of trained personnel in responsible jobs made Ricasoli's task difficult, and it was made worse still by the fact that he himself was less yielding and diplomatic than Cavour, as he was also notably less eager than his predecessor for a continuance of the French alliance on which the country was still morally dependent.

Worst of all was that the pope, far from being ready to compromise as Cavour had supposed, resolutely maintained his excommunication of the Italian leaders. Pius reacted with sharp hostility when he found out that a disobedient priest had charitably given Cavour absolution on his death-bed. The pope refused to recognize the kingdom of Italy, and continued to recognize as legitimate the supplanted dynasties of Tuscany and Naples; he still opposed not only Italian patriotism but the idea of a free press and what he called 'the perilous system of parliamentary government'.[5] The continued papal opposition to Italy came as an unwelcome shock to the French. Napoleon depended on Catholic support in France, and this dependence, together with his lack of confidence in Ricasoli, made him decide to change his plans and leave French troops to defend the pope against attack or subversion.

---

[1] *Carteggi e Bibliografia di Costantino Nigra*, ed. A. Colombo et al. (Turin, 1930), p. 275; *Azeglio*, Rendu, pp. 208, 219; *Die Auswärtige Politik Preussens*, vol. v, ed. R. Ibbeken (Oldenburg, 1935), p. 411.

[2] *Cavour: Questione Romana*, I. 173.

[3] *Azeglio*, Rendu, p. 197; *Azeglio-Torelli*, p. 130; Rayneval, 10 June 1861, M. Aff. Étrangères; L. Zini, *Storia d'Italia dal 1850 al 1866* (Milan, 1869), I, pt. iii. 921.

[4] *Lettere di Cavour*, I. 581; *Cavour-Nigra*, IV. 359; Massari, *Diario*, p. 291; *Giacomo Dina*, III. 622; d'Ideville, *Journal*, I. 240, reporting Cavour's words to him, 'Mais, mon cher prince, me dit-il, y pensez vous? On n'invite pas Nigra.'

[5] *Pio IX e V. Emanuele*, II, pt. ii. 246–7, 270–1, 298, 300.

Victor Emanuel realized that Rome was therefore out of reach for the time being. He did not mind too much about being excommunicated. Apparently he continued to hear mass regularly, and he had a proud confidence that the five saints who had once belonged to the house of Savoy would override the pope and protect his spiritual welfare. Sometimes he reached the point of boasting that God was manifestly on his side against Pius, as proof of which he mentioned that the facts were there to show that the risorgimento was succeeding.[1] But the idea of open battle against the pope offered much less chance of military glory than another war against Austria for Venice, and this gave rise to a difference of policy with his government. Ricasoli made it clear that the government was ready to forget about Venice, but wanted to concentrate on persuading Europe to permit the annexation of Rome. Victor Emanuel, however, decided to adopt the opposite policy and postpone the Roman question until a later date when opinion in France might have altered.

Because of this difference of view, and within six weeks of Cavour's death, the king was writing to Napoleon to arrange a private means of communication between them which Ricasoli would not know about. The main intermediary would be Count Ottaviano Vimercati. For ten years this man was to hold the post of military attaché at Paris and was specially charged during this period with execution of the king's private affairs.[2] With the British and the Prussians, on the other hand, the king had less success in using such irregular channels. General Solaroli went on several secret missions to London, but with nothing to show for them. Victor Emanuel confided to the British that he would discontinue Cavour's warlike and revolutionary policies, and yet the truth was that he had every intention of showing himself a more successful revolutionary than either Garibaldi or Cavour. Vague schemes were adumbrated for a revolt in Herzegovina and to land Garibaldi in Dalmatia. There were plans to stir up a revolt by the Hungarians against Austria and by the Serbs against Turkey.

Some kind of action in the Balkans had been at the back of Cavour's mind. He had dreamt of the 'latin races' one day recovering their predominance in the Mediterranean, and he had at one point hoped for another war against Austria in the spring of 1861, preferably one which would involve the whole of Europe from Turkey to Scandinavia.[3] Victor Emanuel intended to translate some such scheme into practical politics, and he preferred to do so as part of a personal initiative for which he would get the credit and about which his government would know little. Ricasoli was not sufficiently revolutionary or heroic for him, and at the same time was too ready to depict Italy's dependence on France as something humiliating. So the king, through Vimercati's

---

[1] Costa de Beauregard, *Prologue d'un Règne: la Jeunesse du Roi Charles-Albert* (Paris, 1892), p. 349; *Lettere di V. Emanuele*, II. 857.
[2] Ibid. I. 710–11; *Carteggio Castelli*, I. 504.
[3] *Liberazione del Mezzogiorno*, V. 519; *Cavour: Questione Romana*, I. 170; ibid. II. 119.

good offices, sent Rattazzi on a private visit to France to arrange a much more bellicose policy.

In the previous two years the king had developed a genuine affection for Rattazzi, often asking his advice, and Rattazzi was said to be the sole politician who had access to the private royal residence where lived the king's new illegitimate family.[1] Cavour had won effective power for himself by using parliament to control the king; Rattazzi was rather prepared to win power by supporting the king, if necessary against or irrespective of parliament. This admirably suited Victor Emanuel, who had learnt from his experience with Cavour how powerless the monarch might become if he did not always have a possible alternative government as a covert threat to the coalition in office; hence Rattazzi was held *in pectore* as a check on Cavour and then on Ricasoli.

As well as an alternative government, the king was also thinking of an alternative policy to that of Ricasoli, namely to bring about a war against Austria to obtain Venice: success here would show him equal to Cavour in diplomacy and to Garibaldi in war. In October 1861 Rattazzi was therefore sent to win the support of Napoleon for this idea. Before going, Rattazzi called on Ricasoli, though without telling the prime minister that he had orders from Victor Emanuel to propose to the French that they should sign nothing less than an offensive and defensive alliance against Austria.[2] Rattazzi at this moment held the office of president or speaker of the lower House of parliament, and it was constitutionally unheard of for such an official to act in this way without the prime minister's knowledge. His was also a foolish mission, since there was no conceivable reason for France to want to fight Austria, and Rattazzi merely alerted the French to the dangerously conspiratorial attitudes of the Italian court.

Napoleon had no intention at all of helping Italy against the Austrians, but he used this indiscreet approach as a means of inducing the king to permit Rattazzi to supplant Ricasoli, since in this way he could bring Italy back under French influence. Rattazzi returned from Paris to Turin with a fairly explicit message that Victor Emanuel should assert his royal authority and dismiss the existing prime minister.[3] The king set to work at once. He first asked Ricasoli to accept Rattazzi in the cabinet, and met a stubborn refusal, for the premier had now heard about their intrigues to provoke war in the Balkans and realized

---

[1] D'Ideville, *Journal*, I. 61; *Cavour-Salmour*, p. 158; Mme Rattazzi, *Rattazzi et son Temps*, II. 601; Bersezio, *Il Regno*, IV. 358; Apponyi to Rechberg, 26 Feb. 1862, MSS. Haus-, Hof- und Staatsarchiv (Vienna), reported that Rattazzi was backed by the king's three current mistresses, Rosina, the Countess Della Rocca, and Signora Bensa.

[2] A. Luzio, *Aspromonte e Mentana: Documenti Inediti* (Florence, 1935), p. 121; G. Durando, *Episodi Diplomatici del Risorgimento Italiano dal 1856 al 1863*, ed. C. Durando (Turin, 1901), pp. 135–6; *Lettere di V. Emanuele*, I. 722.

[3] Mme Rattazzi, *Rattazzi et son Temps*, I. 604–9.

the great damage this was doing to Italy's good name.[1] So, early in 1862, the king sent word to Paris that he would get rid of Ricasoli; and added that he, Victor Emanuel, without Ricasoli's knowledge, had decided upon war: he was preparing day and night for revolutions in Greece, Serbia, and Hungary. To his great astonishment, however, his envoy met a very cold reception from Napoleon who was horrified to find French advice so misunderstood. The emperor wrote urgently to say that no idea of war against Austria could possibly be entertained. Yet the king refused to accept this demurrer, for he was convinced that he, just like Cavour, could compromise the French and force them into supporting him. He did not know that Napoleon was passing his plans to the Austrians and assuring them that he thoroughly disapproved of Italian aggressiveness.[2]

Meanwhile a number of other people at Turin had been told about the plan to get rid of Ricasoli. Rattazzi advised caution and not to dismiss the government out of hand, but to work more insidiously so as not to reveal that it was a palace intrigue; as Rattazzi explained, the monarchy could rely on support in Piedmont against a Tuscan prime minister, but not so much in other regions, and hence there might be danger unless a plausible crisis was manufactured in order to provoke Ricasoli's resignation.[3] Early in February, through the medium of Rattazzi and despite the latter's supposedly neutral office as speaker, the king approached one of Ricasoli's ministers, Cordova, who agreed to weaken the cabinet from inside and report to the court on its private deliberations. Specific overtures were also made by Rattazzi to Farini and also to the 75 deputies of the Left to induce them to desert the government. The king even secretly subsidized an avowedly anti-government newspaper which now launched a provocative political programme on behalf of enlarging the scope of monarchical authority.[4]

The prime minister knew more or less what was going on. He recognized that this royal intrigue with one member of the cabinet against the premier would undermine both monarchy and government if it became known. Already there were reports that even in Piedmont, and far more elsewhere, public opinion was turning sharply against the king.[5] Loyally Ricasoli did what he could to cover the crown's responsibility and conceal from parliament what Hudson called the determined and systematic opposition of the king to his prime minister.[6] Victor Emanuel's behaviour, said Ricasoli in private, was shameless and dishonourable; as well as being unconstitutional, it risked a war which might destroy the country; and yet it was a premier's duty to persuade

[1] *Carteggi di Alfonso Lamarmora*, ed. A. Colombo et al. (Turin, 1928), pp. 148–9, 195–6.
[2] L. Thouvenel, *Pages de l'Histoire du Second Empire* (Paris, 1903), pp. 343–4; L. Thouvenel, *Le Secret de L'Empereur* (Paris, 1889), II. 232; *Lettere di V. Emanuele*, I. 728–31.
[3] Luzio, *Aspromonte*, pp. 130–7.
[4] Nicotera, 27 Nov. 1862, *Atti Parlamentari: Camera, Discussioni*, p. 4579; *Carteggi di Lamarmora*, pp. 107, 139–40, 145.
[5] *Carteggi E. d'Azeglio*, II. 306.   [6] 1 Mar. 1862, F.O. 45/21.

the king to take politics more seriously, to save him from the results of his own folly while not making a public issue of what was happening.[1] According to Ricasoli, it was wishful thinking to state, as the king positively assured Prince Napoleon,[2] that the Italian army was ready for war: Victor Emanuel had absolutely no means of estimating this kind of fact, and was merely being exploited by courtiers and ruffians who had their own reasons for deluding him and stirring up trouble. The king himself, not Garibaldi and the reds, was the real danger for Italy, while Rattazzi was a weak man who as prime minister would allow the king to misbehave as he liked.[3]

After receiving a unanimous vote of confidence from parliament, Ricasoli decided to force the issue, for Victor Emanuel could hardly continue his intrigue much further without exposing the existence of a royalist plot, and this the ministers wanted to conceal. They went to call on the king with a request for Cordova's resignation; but Cordova had been ahead of them and warned him of their intentions. So the monarch at first refused to see them; he just let it be known that he could not agree with what he stated (quite erroneously) to be their alliance with the 'extreme Left', while their policy of peace was not that which he and Cavour had followed since 1849. Neither side could now back down. The king, advised by Rattazzi, would have been content to keep Ricasoli and so conceal the true facts from the public, but only if he could continue with the secret war policy on which he had set his heart and which he now insisted was the only policy in Italy's interests. What the monarch wanted was 'mighty events': and as he said these words his voice took on a note of great vivacity.[4]

Ricasoli, very properly, insisted on resigning. On the other hand Rattazzi's view of the constitution was quite different, since he blamed Ricasoli for thus forcing the king into the open where this disregard of parliament would become obvious: in Rattazzi's opinion the monarchy had presumably to be supported by ministers even despite such a major difference of policy. Yet Rattazzi's own newspaper publicly mentioned that the king had been speaking ill of his government; the same paper criticized parliament for supporting Ricasoli and for thus compelling the king to bring this disagreement into the open.[5] Here was a fundamental issue of the balance of power between the crown and parliament, and the king recognized as much in an interview reported by Hudson. His Majesty

said at once without the slightest hesitation, 'Cordova was the spy. He told me everything. He told me of the midnight meeting of the Ricasoli cabinet. He told me of the 4 propositions on which alone Ricasoli would consent to serve me. Had I not

[1] *Carteggi E. d'Azeglio*, II. 494–5.

[2] *Il Principe Napoleone nel Risorgimento Italiano*, ed. A. Comandini (Milan, 1922), p. 228.

[3] *Carteggi di Lamarmora*, p. 143; *I Documenti Diplomatici Italiani*, Ser. I, vol. II, ed. W. Maturi (Rome, 1959), pp. 58–9, 87.

[4] *Lettere Ricasoli*, VI. 416–21; ibid. VII. 28.

[5] R. Mori, *La Questione Romana 1861–1865* (Florence, 1963), p. 80.

turned out Ricasoli he would have upset me, and perhaps my family. Those 4 propositions would have deprived me even of the shadow of royalty. They were artfully planned. I determined to forestall them. I did so and Ricasoli fell, and the Tuscans hate me.'[1]

Victor Emanuel was evidently determined to claim a dominant role for himself in the making of policy. When Ricasoli, basing himself on Cavour's practice, contested that view, he had to go, and this without any hostile parliamentary vote; on the contrary, parliament had given a unanimous vote for the government a few days earlier. A note was sent from the king to inform Ricasoli of his replacement by Rattazzi, and this note was to be carefully remembered in court circles as a precedent on how a monarch should act in similar circumstances.[2] When parliament was finally summoned to hear about the change of government, Giovanni Lanza claimed that, though the sovereign technically had a constitutional right to dismiss a minister, this was a right which by now had effectively disappeared in ten years of constitutional practice, and it was quite improper to allow such an extra-parliamentary ministerial crisis while parliament was actually in session.[3] Ricasoli, on the other hand, gave no public hint of the king's involvement, but invented a plausible excuse. In his own way he was a true royalist and realized that the dynasty might lose some of its authority if everyone knew that the king had behaved badly. With some satisfaction he was at last able to leave Turin and the 'corrupt' world of court intrigue.[4]

Victor Emanuel received ample parliamentary condonation when Ricasoli's majority refused to challenge Rattazzi.[5] The king had been ready for some time with the name of his new prime minister. Rattazzi, not without reason, was known as 'the favourite of Rosina', and it was in the house of the king's mistress that he took his oath of office.[6] He at once showed himself pliant to the royal wishes, and accepted, though not without certain regret, the king's nominees to some of the other cabinet posts in a government which deliberately included both Left and Right.[7] The new cabinet contained two generals who were royal aides-de-camp, Giacomo Durando and Agostino Petitti, also the incompetent Admiral Persano who was a particular favourite of the king's, as

---

[1] 30 Nov. 1862, P.R.O. 30/22/69; 27 Mar. 1862, F.O. 45/22.
[2] Domenico Farini, *Diario di Fine Secolo*, ed. E. Morelli (Rome, 1962), II. 1006.
[3] M. Mancini and U. Galeotti, *Norme ed Usi del Parlamento Italiano* (Rome, 1887), p. 736; O. d'Haussonville, 'M. de Cavour et la Crise Italienne', *Revue des Deux Mondes* (Paris), Sept. 1862, p. 429.
[4] *Carteggi di Lamarmora*, p. 157.
[5] A. Gallenga, *Episodes of my Second Life* (London, 1884), II. 327–8.
[6] Lipparini, *Minghetti*, II. 283; Hudson, 8 Mar. 1862, P.R.O. 30/22/69.
[7] Mme Rattazzi, *Rattazzi et son Temps*, I. 615; *Carte di Lanza*, II. 277; on 29 Mar. 1862, Hudson reported that the king sent Solaroli six times to enlist his help in forming a cabinet, but the Englishman declined: 'I told him the king has created the difficulty and has burnt his fingers' (P.R.O. 30/22/69).

well as Cordova whose loyalty and guile had been so usefully proved, and Depretis of the Left Centre. The presence of the latter, a friend of Garibaldi and a man whom the aristocratic Cavour had scorned, may be explained by the fact that the king was already negotiating with the Garibaldians to precipitate his war against Austria. To counter Hudson's suspicions about the new government, Rattazzi strenuously denied that there had been any court conspiracy to get rid of Ricasoli; any such rumour was absolutely untrue and just designed to make trouble.[1]

Another thing Rattazzi had also been obliged to accept, though again he denied it vigorously,[2] was the king's scheme to employ Garibaldi. It was settled that the guerrilla leader should recruit another private army which would be paid and armed by the government; this army would then be encouraged to attack the Austrian empire somewhere on its Dalmatian frontier in the hope that another international crisis could be manufactured from which Italy might gain Venice.[3] The king simultaneously had a private ambition to make his second son monarch of Greece, and Garibaldi's army might here be of some help. The plan had yet another incidental advantage that it would get Garibaldi out of the way along with other dangerous hotheads on the Left. With a certain lack of logic, the king explained to Kossuth, the Hungarian revolutionary, that, even if the Garibaldians were defeated, their venture would gain time for Italy. By the autumn his army would be ready to fight Austria. War in 1862, in his view, was quite inevitable.[4]

Rattazzi saw Garibaldi within a few hours of obtaining the premiership, and probably a second time soon afterwards;[5] the king also saw Garibaldi twice early in March, and minister and monarch both thought that the radical leader agreed to the plans which they outlined to him. Other members of the cabinet were not apparently informed, and this was soon to prove a disaster: the other ministers merely knew, as did many other people, that the king was personally involved in some project, yet as Rattazzi would say nothing to them about it, they feared to cross the monarch by voicing their doubts.[6] 'The most positive assurances' were given by the king that no enterprise in the Balkans was under consideration, yet there was soon abundant proof to the contrary. Rattazzi, when tackled on the subject, admitted privately that the government was helping to arm Garibaldi's volunteers, but tried to make out that this was part of a campaign against brigandage in the southern provinces of Italy. Such an improbable story was not easily believed. When Hudson later spoke to the king and accused him of having made 'over-

---

[1] *Carteggi E. d'Azeglio*, ii. 505.   [2] Ibid. 507.

[3] Report by Rattazzi's confidant, Cirilio Monzani, *Nuova Antologia* (Rome), Jan. 1900, p. 11.

[4] Ludwig Kossuth, *Meine Schriften aus der Emigration* (Leipzig, 1882), iii. 683–4; Hudson, 20 Apr. 1862, P.R.O. 30/22/69, who heard via the king's son that 'the king and his advisers hoped to get rid of Garibaldi'.

[5] 12 Apr., ibid.; Luzio, *Aspromonte*, p. 138.   [6] Durando, *Episodi Diplomatici*, p. 274.

tures to a gentleman in a Red Shirt to promote a little family interest south of the Danube', his interlocutor good-humouredly admitted the fact.[1]

Garibaldi and his men were once again to be cast in the role of victims in a court intrigue. Some of them were arrested in May near the Austrian frontier at Sarnico, and at Brescia the police fired on a demonstration which was taking place in Garibaldi's support and killed a number of people. Possibly this reflected another misunderstanding between the government and the radicals. According to the king, it suddenly became clear that Garibaldi was deceiving him and that, under cover of an expedition across the Adriatic, the party of action was planning an invasion of the Austrian Tyrol. This explanation cannot be ruled out as untrue, especially as the Garibaldians had now learnt not to place too much confidence in the king's good will and seriousness of purpose. But it is unlikely that they would ever have attacked Austria without some degree of governmental, or at least of royal, connivance. One of the king's envoys had certainly sounded out the French about the feasibility of an attack on the Tyrol. Some element of guilty conscience may also be betokened by the fact that Garibaldi was not arrested after this so-called *putsch* at Sarnico, and that the government arranged with the judiciary that the arrested men should quickly be released. It became public knowledge that a large sum of money had recently been placed at Garibaldi's disposal by the government. Though the king claimed to some people that he had been deceived, to others he went on speaking in June as though Garibaldi were still acting under his orders.[2]

The episode of Sarnico, like that other far more serious clash later in the year at Aspromonte, has been generally blamed on Garibaldi, and royalist biographers continue to assert that the king was not behind him;[3] but some degree of connivance is beyond question and was indeed admitted. Garibaldi since 1859 had been told repeatedly by the king that the volunteer movement would have to accustom itself to secret support and public condemnation by officialdom. When Garibaldi went off to Sicily in June 1862, once again Rattazzi pretended to be entirely in the dark, though he and the king in fact knew all about it; a naval ship was put at Garibaldi's disposal and a cache of arms was built up for him at Messina.[4] People who saw these arms pass without question through the customs offices accepted that there must have been official complicity, and when Garibaldi's close friend, the Marquis Pallavicino, was unexpectedly appointed as prefect of Palermo, this strange

[1] 30 Nov. 1862, P.R.O. 30/22/69; 22 Feb., ibid.; 18 Apr., F.O. 45/23.
[2] *Il Principe Napoleone*, ed. Comandini, pp. 229–30; M. Rosi, *I Cairoli* (Bologna, 1944), p. 106; *New York Evening Post*, 9 June 1900; Thouvenel, *Pages de l'Histoire*, p. 344; *L'Opera di Stefano Türr nel Risorgimento Italiano Descritta dalla Figlia* (Florence, 1928), I. 213; *Discorsi Parlamentari di Francesco Crispi*, ed. C. Finocchiaro-Aprile (Rome, 1915), I. 142.
[3] G. Ardau, *Vittorio Emanuele II e i suoi Tempi* (Milan, 1939), II. 91; Cognasso, *Vittorio Emanuele*, p. 260.
[4] Mori, *Questione Romana*, pp. 127–9; *Carteggio Castelli*, II. 269–70; Hudson, 9 Aug. 1862, P.R.O. 30/22/69; *Lettere di V. Emanuele*, I. 767.

choice told in the same sense. After Garibaldi made public statements that his programme was to march on Rome, eventually a public condemnation came from the king, but only four weeks later. Even then, without let or hindrance, some 4,000 volunteers were allowed to form and drill in the Ficuzza forest outside Palermo, and moved slowly across Sicily, while for a whole month government troops either did not dare or did not want to stop them. At Catania, though 16 battalions of royal troops were stationed there and many more were in Messina, Garibaldi took over the town and did not even seem in a hurry. He told people that the king was behind him, showing them a mysterious document, and he was believed. He also added that it was all arranged for government troops to use the excuse of his own expedition in order to march on Rome and arrive there before he did.[1]

The exact truth is hard to disentangle. It is not impossible that Garibaldi was deceiving the king, though any deception is more likely to have been the other way round. There is no doubt that the king was behind Garibaldi up to a point, though his intention may only have been for Sicily to be a stepping-stone for an expedition to place his son on the throne of Greece. It is unlikely that the king can have wanted a Garibaldian march on Rome to succeed, and he wrote privately to advise against any such attempt;[2] but on previous occasions he had written this kind of letter just for the record. Victor Emanuel no doubt aimed to find an excuse to intervene himself in the Papal States. He wished to show Napoleon that revolutionary fever in Italy was ungovernable, in the hope that the royal troops would be allowed to take Rome in return for halting a revolution which he had secretly encouraged.

If this seems too absurd to be true, it should be remembered that Cavour had successfully used similar tactics in 1860, as it should also be noted that some such idea had been recently suggested to the king by Prince Napoleon himself, while Gioacchino Pepoli in August was officially negotiating along these lines in Paris on the king's behalf.[3] Garibaldi had good reason to think that he could rely on any successful *putsch* being supported by the court. He knew that, even though his own policy to march on Rome was public knowledge, the authorities had still provided him with weapons in Sicily: why, then, should the king be treating him any differently than in 1860 when the volunteers had been allowed to chance their arm?[4] Why otherwise also should the foreign minister be so indiscreet as to choose this moment to promise parliament that Rome would soon be in Italian hands?[5]

[1] Mordini, 27 Nov. 1862, *Atti Parlamentari: Camera, Discussioni*, pp. 4588–9; *Risposta di Giorgio Pallavicino al Deputato Pier Carlo Boggio* (Turin 1862), pp. 20–1.
[2] Elpis Melena (Baroness Schwartz), *Garibaldi: Mitteilungen aus seinem Leben* (Hanover, 1884), I. 198; *Lettere di V. Emanuele*, I. 748.
[3] *Nuova Antologia*, Jan. 1900, pp. 22, 27; *Carteggi di Nigra*, ed. Colombo, p. 289.
[4] G. E. Curàtulo, *Scritti e Figure del Risorgimento Italiano* (Turin, 1926), pp. 14, 16.
[5] 20 July 1862, *Atti Parlamentari: Camera, Discussioni*, p. 3462; worse still, he referred to the Italian-speaking areas of Switzerland as 'not yet united to the mother country' (ibid., p. 3457).

The episode came to a tragic end when towards the end of August Garibaldi sailed from Sicily to land on the mainland in Calabria. Until this moment the army and navy must have understood that they were expected to let him proceed; otherwise their inactivity is inexplicable. General Cugia and Admiral Albini found it very hard subsequently to explain their conduct in letting this private army cross the Straits of Messina, and merely mentioned the undeniable fact that the orders they received had been dubious and ambiguous.[1] Garibaldi was thus able to embark his men openly at Catania while naval ships stood by, and only after his departure did troops occupy the town. Just possibly the military commanders thought that, despite Garibaldi's unambiguous pronouncements, the volunteers were sailing to Greece, and in that case had orders to let them go; more likely the king was still naïvely hoping that Napoleon would now be spurred to make some concession over Rome; almost certainly Admiral Persano and General Petitti, ministers of the navy and of war, like the prime minister himself,[2] had good reason to fear that the king had compromised himself by private support of Garibaldi, and hence they were loath to take any unequivocal decision either way which might expose the crown. Once the volunteers were on the mainland of Italy, the pressure on the government from conservatives, and especially from Generals Lamarmora and Cialdini, became overwhelming, and a French naval squadron was ominously ordered to Naples.[3] French intervention would have been intolerably humiliating. General Cialdini was therefore ordered into action, and on 29 August Garibaldi was permanently crippled when the royal troops opened fire on him at Aspromonte.

Some light is thrown on these events by a report from Sir James Hudson who saw the king just before Garibaldi set sail from Catania:

I have known the king so long and so intimately that a conversation between us is certain to end in a confidential manner. . . . I said Garibaldi is a very honest man who doubtless believes he is serving the interests of the crown in taking up arms against the king's government. . . . 'Garibaldi, sir, says he acts under your inspirations'.

'Inspirations, forsooth,' said the king. 'He does more than I ever told him to do. Yes, he had my orders to a certain extent, but he adds something of his own to them and makes a mess of everything.'

'Garibaldi, sir, is a sea captain and probably knows as much of politics as Your Majesty does of navigation.'

'I will destroy him,' growled the king.

'Well sir, and what will be the result of that measure?'

'Why I shall be the most unpopular man in Italy. But the emperor [Napoleon] who is the cause of all this mischief, his turn will come too, later it is true, but it will come.'

---

[1] 27 Nov., ibid., pp. 4541–3.
[2] *Carteggi di Lamarmora*, pp. 204–5; Durando, *Episodi Diplomatici*, pp. 272–4.
[3] *Carteggi di Nigra*, ed. Colombo, p. 238.

'Pray sir, has Garibaldi any ships with him?'

'Yes, five Americans, one of them armed.'

'Do you intend to allow him to embark on board those ships?'

'I cannot prevent him if he goes in American vessels.'

'But sir, those ships are in your ports and cannot violate your Municipal Law.'

To this the king replied, 'I am not strong in Municipal Law. The deputy Musolino has been to see me and he has proposed as a remedy that I shall permit Garibaldi to lay down his arms and pass into Calabria or to Naples, whence he is to make a peaceable promenade to Rome accompanied by an enormous mass of Italians.'

'But Your Majesty has not given any countenance to that scheme.'

'No,' said the king, 'none whatever'.

The proposal by Colonel Musolino, a parliamentary deputy from Calabria and himself a former Garibaldian volunteer, had in fact been already put to the king by Prince Napoleon, and then was referred to the emperor by Pepoli on behalf of Victor Emanuel. The proposal may indeed help to explain why the authorities waited before acting until they saw that there was no insurrection in the Papal States and that no 'enormous mass of Italians' was forthcoming. Hudson was not an entirely detached observer, for he was sure that Rattazzi had come to power unconstitutionally as a royal puppet, and he was frightened over where Italian politics might be heading; he also knew that Musolino, after talking to the king, had been telling everyone that Victor Emanuel admitted to being behind Garibaldi. He thus concluded:

Rattazzi, ever the pliant tool of the king, has consented to all the expeditions to the east, first at Sarnico and now in Sicily. . . . The king is the first to feel the effects of his own intrigues and imprudence and is now drifting helpless on the tide of those events which he created and cannot control save by the loss of his own agent, and at the risk of his own popularity.[1]

From the diary of Giacomo Durando, the foreign minister, much the same story emerges, and it is clear that cabinet ministers suddenly and unexpectedly found themselves in a dangerous crisis about which they had been told not very much. Public opinion was deeply shocked by the news of Garibaldi's wound, and people at once suspected, what Durando by now knew all too well to be a fact, that the king and Rattazzi were implicated. Ricasoli spoke of Garibaldi being the victim of governmental perfidy.[2] Victor Emanuel came to a cabinet meeting to confess he was involved up to a point, his explanation being that, at Sarnico and again in Sicily, Garibaldi had deceived him.

At another meeting the ministers discussed in private how far an enquiry into these events could be permitted to go before the king's complicity would be exposed. Their instinctive initial feeling had been that they could not avoid bringing Garibaldi to justice, but in the light of what was said on this occasion they decided to release him and probe no further.[3] Durando's diary merely

[1] 10 Aug. 1862, P.R.O. 30/22/69.   [2] *Lettere Ricasoli*, VII. 101.
[3] Durando, *Episodi Diplomatici*, pp. 272–3.

hints at their reason for this change of mind, though chiefly they were worried
that the mysterious document in Garibaldi's possession might reveal the king's
private policy and double-dealing.[1] Meanwhile strong pressure came from
France and Prussia for condign punishment not only of Garibaldi but of the
naval, military, and civilian officials who had allowed Garibaldi to cross the
Straits, and clear warning was given that the dynasty might fall if it could not
dominate the revolutionaries.[2] After several months the serving officers were
quietly acquitted, but, in order to keep a balance, some attempt was also made
to build Aspromonte up into a famous victory against the forces of anarchy
and disorder, and 76 medals were issued for courage in face of the enemy. A
few of Garibaldi's volunteers, after being taken prisoner, had unfortunately
been summarily executed by the army, and for them the royal amnesty arrived
too late, while those who had deserted from the army to join him had still to
endure years of imprisonment, even though precisely similar behaviour had
been positively encouraged in 1860.[3] The king himself, after two weeks of
panic, quickly recovered his good spirits.[4]

No permanent damage had been done, yet there had been a fairly severe
setback to his plans. Not only did his reputation lose by the fact of civil war,
but Napoleon now moved sharply away from his customary italophilia.
Hitherto the making of Italy had depended essentially on French support.
But the amnesty for Garibaldi was a virtual confession that the king had been
in league with the revolutionaries in their attempt to dispossess the pope, or at
least that he did not dare repudiate them. At first Victor Emanuel did not
entirely realize the importance of this change in French policy. Moreover he
obstinately kept his overconfidence in the strength of the Italian army, and
gladly concurred with Rattazzi's desperate hope that the British would
compensate for one setback by helping him to purchase Venice from Austria.

In this mood of over-confidence, sharpened now by the need to succeed in
some glorious enterprise, Victor Emanuel turned again to his wider Mediterranean ambitions. He had recently married his daughter to the king of Portugal, and he now further examined the possibility of making his second son,
Amedeo of Aosta, king of Greece. Within a few weeks of Aspromonte he told
Rattazzi to send several Italian warships to Greece to be ready for a possible
coup, while Terenzio Mamiani, the Italian ambassador in Athens, secretly
got in touch with a faction of Greek revolutionaries who were planning to

[1] Massimo d'Azeglio, in *Lettere ad Antonio Panizzi di Uomini Illustri*, ed. L. Fagan (Florence, 1880),
p. 480.
[2] *Die Auswärtige Politik Preussens*, vol. II, pt. ii., ed. C. Friese (Oldenburg, 1945), pp. 739–40, 749;
Luzio, *Aspromonte*, p. 182.
[3] Elliot, 22 May 1864, P.R.O. 30/22/70: 'Minghetti . . . did not dispute the truth of what I asserted
as to the majority of those men having deserted with a bona fide conviction that they were acting
as the king wished'; *Archivio Storico Italiano*, 1955, p. 382.
[4] Durando, *Episodi Diplomatici*, p. 279.

overthrow the existing Greek government.[1] Apart from the possibility of a throne for his son, the king thought that Greece would be a convenient point of entry for Italy into Balkan affairs.

General Durando, the foreign minister, was not completely informed about this adventurous idea. He knew the king was sending money to Greece, and on one occasion, after making some difficulties, he was obliged to give one of the royal secret agents, Enrico Bensa, the cover of a position in the consular service. Bensa was the husband of one of the monarch's current mistresses. Durando's embassy officials in Athens reported back in great alarm when Bensa told them that he intended to use the embassy ciphers, and even more when they found that an Italian naval sloop, though technically under their orders, had disappeared at his command on some unknown errand. When they protested, the foreign minister was in the humiliating position of having to reply that he knew nothing about what was going on, and such facts would have to be accepted without protest. Another royal agent in the Balkans, Marco Antonio Canini, created further trouble by similarly acting against official policy, at the same time as he compromised the government by saying that he was acting in their name.[2] In October the king and Rattazzi, again by-passing their own foreign office, informed Paris that Italian troops were being sent to Greece. When Durando heard of this he protested, for not only would it be a defiance of treaty obligations, but the Italian army was not nearly so strong as the king thought, and the French would be extremely angry; the king had also omitted to note that the constitution in Greece stated that the monarch should be Greek Orthodox in religion.

In reply the king reproached the minister for being insufficiently revolutionary to understand such a far-seeing project. The court had evidently not considered the possibility that Britain and France would refuse to tolerate Italian revolutionary action in the Balkans. The British had already been once turned against Italy by Cavour's reckless attempts at gun-running along the Danube. They too, like the French and unbeknown to the king, were now sufficiently alarmed to be thinking of fighting in defence of Austria against Italian aggression.[3] Durando pointed out that the king's plan would certainly fail, and would weaken rather than strengthen Italy's status in eastern Europe.[3]

At this point, in December 1862, Rattazzi's government collapsed in face of growing parliamentary suspicion after the shame of Aspromonte. The prime minister had just assured parliament that he continued to enjoy the king's

[1] *I Documenti Diplomatici Italiani*, Ser. i, vol. iii, ed. Maturi-Sestan (Rome, 1965), pp. 133, 135, 178; Costas Kerofilas, *La Grecia e l'Italia nel Risorgimento Italiano* (Florence, 1919), pp. 101–5, 159.

[2] W. Maturi, 'Le Avventure Balcaniche di Marco Antonio Canini nel 1862', *Studi in Onore di Gioacchino Volpe* (Florence, 1958), ii. 585–6, 631–4.

[3] Mori, *Questione Romana*, p. 76; Lipparini, *Minghetti*, ii. 343.

[4] Durando, *Episodi Diplomatici*, pp. 279, 285, 288, 293–5, 300.

confidence,[1] but he had not realized that Victor Emanuel might come to see him as a convenient scapegoat for Aspromonte and for its unfortunate results in alienating the French. When this possibility at last occurred to him he asked for a dissolution of parliament so that he could 'make the elections', perhaps recognizing, as Cavour had done earlier, that reliance on parliamentary support would now provide his only chance of resisting the royal will to power; but the king saw what he was up to and refused his request.

Rattazzi now forgot his own use of court pressure to oust Ricasoli, and made an angry protest against this palpable intervention by the crown in politics. The cabinet went as a body to present their resignation; Victor Emanuel accepted it and dismissed them in profound and embarrassed silence. Rattazzi followed Ricasoli's example and loyally retired without asking for a parliamentary vote which might have curtailed the royal freedom of action in appointing a successor. Behind the scenes, however, some angry words were exchanged.[2] Among Rattazzi's followers as well as Ricasoli's there was reason to fear that the king's private entourage of army officers and household officials were becoming a dangerous force in politics and must somehow be brought under parliamentary control.[3]

When a parliamentary deputation called on the king, as was customary at the end of each year, its members were surprised to be given a sharp lecture and told that he was not at all satisfied with their conduct. They were informed that it was their duty as parliamentary deputies to have greater confidence in him, for he was trying to pursue the national interest in ways they did not and could not know. In private he explained his anger to one senator, tracing it to the fact that he had been on the point of carrying out a very important secret enterprise when the parliamentary leaders, instead of helping him, had precipitated this political crisis.[4] To Prince Napoleon he complained that it was very hard for a sovereign to contend with a system where governments were continually changing. If the various factions did not give up some of their sterile criticism and bickering, he might have to take 'une résolution énergique'; it might even be necessary to risk another and perhaps premature war against Austria in order to re-establish national unity. And he added the threat that France would suffer from this as much as Italy.[5] Prince Napoleon must have known his father-in-law well enough by now not to take such posturing too seriously.

The king's first thought for a new premier was another Piedmontese, Ponza di San Martino, whom he thought could be relied on to take strict measures with the extreme Left. Too embarrassed to discuss this directly, he sent one

[1] 1 Dec., *Atti Parlamentari: Camera, Discussioni*, p. 4684.
[2] Durando, *Episodi Diplomatici*, p. 369; *Bismarck: Die Gesammelten Werke*, vol. IX, ed. W. Andreas (Berlin, 1926), p. 286.
[3] *Documenti Diplomatici Italiani*, II. 205–6; *Carteggio Castelli*, I. 458, 492–3; *Lettere di V. Emanuele*, I. 729.
[4] *Sclopis: Diario*, pp. 351–2.   [5] *Il Principe Napoleone*, ed. Comandini, pp. 232–3.

of his friends to invite San Martino and explain to him that he was determined to have not another short-term administration but one which had enough time to 'prepare for the future'. So out of touch was the king with parliamentary leaders that he was greatly surprised when San Martino made a condition that there should be rigid economies in the state and at court. Ten successive years of budgetary deficits had almost entirely ruined the country's credit, hence San Martino insisted that the army would have to be reduced and there should be no further talk of Venice or Rome.[1] If the king had been in closer touch he might also have realized how strong would have been the opposition in other regions to yet another Piedmontese prime minister. But in any case these conditions were unacceptable to him. The annexation of Venice was the field he had chosen in which to demonstrate his political skill, and the army was his chosen instrument. So the money would simply have to be found.

He therefore turned to Giuseppe Pasolini, a man who stood somewhat outside the various parliamentary groupings, and who had the great advantage of believing, or at least telling the king he believed, that it was the sovereign who should make policy while ministers merely obeyed orders.[2] Pasolini was told that 'the king wished to have no party-leader as premier but someone outside party strife who might therefore remain longer in office'.[3] Devoted monarchist that he was, Pasolini agreed to help, but he thought it prudent to give a warning, because this kind of non-political administration was hardly in line with political developments over the past fifteen years.

After a visit to the palace, Sir James Hudson noted that the king was having great difficulty in finding a government, for he wanted no one as a minister who had been against Rattazzi and this left only a small choice. 'His Majesty nothing daunted continues his crusade against the parliamentary majority.' Hudson allowed that the king might conceivably be a good soldier, but 'no power living, no circumstances ever will make him a politician'; indeed 'the man was, I really think, half mad'. The Englishman had been told outright that the Italian army would surprise Europe when the day came for it to fight, but he was no longer impressed by these exaggerated heroics.[4]

With Pasolini's help, the king's choice finally fell on Luigi Carlo Farini, Cavour's former colleague. It was an astonishing decision, for Farini had recently been showing obvious signs of mental derangement and experienced some difficulty in speaking; nor was the king unaware of his condition.[5] Even

[1] Mme Rattazzi, *Rattazzi et son Temps*, I. 648; *Sclopis: Diario*, p. 339; *Lettere di V. Emanuele*, I. 751.

[2] *Giuseppe Pasolini 1815–1876: Memorie Raccolte da suo Figlio* (3rd ed., Turin, 1887), p. 359.

[3] Ibid., pp. 320–1.

[4] 2 Dec., F.O. 45/27; 2 Dec., P.R.O. 30/22/69; that the king refused to have any minister who had opposed Rattazzi is confirmed by S. Jacini, *Un Conservatore Rurale della Nuova Italia* (Bari, 1926), I. 147.

[5] *Il Principe Napoleone*, ed. Comandini, p. 233; Luzio, *Aspromonte*, p. 154; D. Mack Smith 'Vittorio Emanuele e i suoi Primi Ministri', *Rassegna*, Apr. 1954, p. 414.

Rattazzi was amazed by this choice of Farini, but, as Mme Rattazzi later explained, the king deliberately chose *'une nullité'* as prime minister, a man whom he himself referred to as a 'pompous ass', under cover of whose purely nominal position he could pursue his own day-dream of leading the country triumphantly into war.

One of Victor Emanuel's constant delusions, which he had inherited from Cavour, was that Hungary was on the verge of revolt and could be induced to rise against Austria whenever it might suit Italian policy. An unknown but very considerable amount of money, both from the government and also apparently from the king's private income, had been poured into this fruitless cause since 1859, much of it through the agency of Hambro's bank in London. In January 1863, General Türr, one of the king's aides-de-camp and a favourite messenger to Paris and Vienna, was sent to see Napoleon with a private message on this subject, but was refused an audience. The Italian ambassador in Paris, annoyed at these intrigues behind his back, took some pleasure in reporting that the repeated sending of private emissaries had thoroughly annoyed the French.[1] Pasolini, now foreign minister, was evidently in the dark about Türr's mission, and soon he, like his predecessor, was reduced to asking private individuals in foreign capitals to find out what the king was up to.[2] He was utterly opposed to the king's continual activity in the Balkans, but could do little more than try to neutralize it behind the scenes.[3] Neither he, however, any more than Durando before him, thought that such behaviour warranted their resignation. They had to admit that this private royal diplomacy was ruining Italy's finances and her influence in the outside world, but were ready to accept it and so far as possible conceal the facts from the rest of the world, since to uncover the crown was the worst sin in the book. The result was that Italy continued to have a dual foreign policy, part of which was irresponsible, uncontrollable, and took no account of some of the essential facts of Italy's weakness and of the European situation.

The British and, probably through them, the French police had by now come across the odd fact that Victor Emanuel was in touch with Mazzini for a joint action of some kind in support of a revolutionary war against Austria. When Napoleon complained to Francesco Arese, the king's friend, the latter denied the story as untrue, though in private he guessed otherwise; nor was he certain whether he ought to tell the king that this intrigue had been found out. Victor Emanuel had in fact given the excuse to Mazzini's friends, when they doubted his good faith, that he had to keep negotiations secret or else his ministers might force him to desist; and Arese therefore had some justification for concluding that he had better feign ignorance.[4]

Farini was kept in office as long as his mental illness could be concealed,

[1] *Documenti Diplomatici Italiani*, II. 60; ibid. III. 280–1.
[2] R. Bonfadini, *Vita di Francesco Arese con Documenti Inediti* (Turin, 1894), p. 321.
[3] *Carteggi E. d'Azeglio*, II. 585–6.   [4] Bonfadini, *Vita di Arese*, pp. 317, 435–6.

but rumours began to circulate, and the time came when the prime minister rushed into the king's private rooms, laid violent hands on him, and demanded that war should immediately be declared against Russia. Pasolini, who found himself the senior man in the cabinet, refused to continue the pretence any longer, and the ministry fell.[1] Minghetti agreed to assume office in this difficult emergency, after being warned that otherwise the king might take some regrettable step in the direction of arbitrary power.[2] He kept much the same cabinet, and so continuity was not destroyed.

Minghetti was informed about what plans were afoot in the Balkans. He was told by the king that General Türr and Colonel De Sonnaz were to visit eastern Europe in connection with revolutionary projects devised by the sovereign, and that the government was expected to provide both these men with funds. No secret was made to Minghetti of the fact that Napoleon had insisted that the king should stop any Hungarian revolt, but Victor Emanuel explained that to accept the emperor's advice would be quite impossible: during the previous two years he had worked hard to prevent any rising in Hungary, but now revolution was unstoppable. Napoleon's protest rather gave the king an exciting sensation that Italy was now feared abroad, and from this it was a short step to thinking that he was strong enough to contemplate war.[3] Unfortunately his two secret envoys could find nothing serious to do in eastern Europe, but merely created quite unnecessary alarm and displeasure among would-be friendly governments. When protests arrived from Turkey and France about Türr's activity, the foreign minister had to reply lamely that the king's aide-de-camp was on a private visit, and this was not easy to credit.[4]

When the threat of war did not succeed in making Austria cede Venice in peace, the king moved one step closer to actual hostilities. He intended to make a martial speech from the throne at the opening of parliament. His ministers counselled against this, but he could not be prevented from other private initiatives. Karl Usedom now spoke of the court camarilla as determined on some adventurous escapade; they were, he said, the secret government of the country, and were ready to sacrifice Minghetti at any moment.[5] Other foreigners in Turin, Hudson, Elliot, Eugene Sartiges, Joseph Malaret, and the Duke of Brabant, all reported back that in private the king 'indulged in language of the most warlike character'; 'he had full confidence in his destiny'; 'he is in fact panting for the moment when he may be allowed to make war'. He again insisted that he was ready to fight Austria single-handed,

[1] Hudson, 28 Mar. 1863, P.R.O. 30/22/70; *Documenti Diplomatici Italiani*, III. 395.
[2] *Lettere di V. Emanuele*, I. 769.   [3] Ibid. 759.
[4] *Documenti Diplomatici Italiani*, III. 535, 547, 565–6; Hudson (on 1 June 1863, P.R.O. 30/22/70) alleged that the king wanted Türr away because he was having an affair with Türr's wife; she, incidentally, and Mme Rattazzi, were both putat've daughters of Sir Thomas Wyse.
[5] *Die Auswärtige Politik Preussens*, vol. III, ed. R. Ibbeken (Oldenburg, 1932), p. 433.

or even Austria and France simultaneously; and Italy and France together could easily beat the whole of the rest of Europe.[1] This was ridiculous bravado. On another occasion he raised once again with the British, as an alternative, that they might help him persuade Austria to sell Venice for a thousand million francs, in other words £40 millions, and he did not stop to wonder where the money could be found.[2]

Another strange adventure was Victor Emanuel's employment of a down-at-heel actress to go secretly and put this last proposition to Marshal Benedek, the Austrian commandant in Verona. Laura Bon had one, possibly two, children by the king, but had long since been pensioned off, and Cavour had tried to prevent her ever coming to Turin. In the king's eyes she had the advantage of possessing, or boasting that she possessed, an intimate relationship with Napoleon as well as himself, and it seems another with Marshal Benedek. When she arrived in Verona on a personal mission in his name to ask for nothing less than an Austrian alliance, Benedek was astonished at the monarch's lack of *savoir-faire*: he treated the lady courteously, but asked her what the king would say if a similar message came to him in reverse through a Piedmontese general; whatever might be true in Piedmont, these questions in Austria were conducted by politicians and not by generals or by women of the *demi-monde*.[3]

Almost as strange was Victor Emanuel's obscure dealings with Mazzini and members of the extreme Left. These people always had a fascination for him. He resented their independence, and could treat them brutally whenever he feared them as rivals; but his own instincts for war and revolution brought him often much closer to them than to the conservatives, and he took a cynical amusement in their susceptibility to the gifts of money, power, and social success which he was able to offer as political bribes.[4] His own talent for affability, his dislike of court etiquette, as well as his rough, barrack-room language, gave him a greater success among the humble than among the old aristocracy. His success with the radical Left was sometimes of considerable advantage to Italy, and Rattazzi, Garibaldi, Depretis, Nicotera were among members of the Left who at different moments fell for his charm. One former republican, Francesco Crispi, in 1864 coined the talismanic phrase that 'the monarchy unites us, while republicanism would divide us'. Crispi must have been angling for power when he added in justification of this manifesto that the king had been entirely unintrusive and neutral in domestic

[1] Elliot, 11 Oct. 1863, F.O. 45/43; 1 Jan. 1864, F.O. 45/56; 2 Apr. 1864, P.R.O. 30/22/70; *Sclopis: Diario*, pp. 353–4; *Documenti Diplomatici Italiani*, III. 545; *Il Problema Veneto e L'Europa*, vol. III, ed. G. Dethan (Venice, 1967), pp. 407, 426–7.
[2] Elliot, 17 Nov. 1864, F.O. 45/60.
[3] *Benedeks Nachgelassene Papiere*, ed. H. Friedjung (3rd ed., Dresden, 1904), pp. 329–32; G. Piccini, *Memorie di una Prima Attrice (Laura Bon)* (Florence, 1909), p. 199.
[4] His continued relations with Brofferio are mentioned in *Sclopis: Diario*, pp. 384–5, and in *Carte di Lanza*, III. 326.

politics since 1860; Victor Emanuel was completely above party differences, said Crispi, and so could be trusted. In private, however, this ambitious radical said almost the opposite.[1]

Nothing much came of the king's negotiations with Mazzini in 1863–4, which were carried out through the medium of Emilio Diamilla Müller and Giuseppe Pastore, one of the court lawyers; the two national leaders exchanged photographs and at one moment it was almost settled that a secret meeting between them should be arranged.[2] Probably the king's motives were a mixture of curiosity, vanity, and a desire to compromise the revolutionaries, to keep them quiet and learn of their projects so that he could stop them interfering with his own. He flattered himself that his threats and bribes were the only things that kept the Left away from revolution and civil war. The republicans, he said, were much stronger in Italy than people said, but he intended to keep them in reserve as conceivable allies for when war should come.[3] He informed Minghetti of his relations with Mazzini; and Minghetti did not try to stop him, because he knew the king would continue anyway, and the ministers wanted to keep on friendly terms with the court.[4]

For some weeks in 1864, Victor Emanuel was in fairly close touch with Garibaldi about another wild project for an armed expedition to Transylvania and the Polish areas of the Austrian empire. He denied this when taxed with it, and indeed claimed to the Prussian ambassador that he was now on Austria's side and working against Garibaldi.[5] For a short while he was probably in secret touch with the Austrians, because the presence in Vienna of the disreputable Bensa was noted early in 1864, but the king was also serious about fomenting revolt in Galicia and Hungary, and judging from Bollea's catalogue of the royal archives there exist dozens of receipts for money sent to aid this cause.[6] Only when Austria proved unyielding did he fall back on the probability of war. There were then a number of personal exchanges with Garibaldi through Baron Alessandro Porcelli and General Klapka. Minghetti knew of these negotiations, but he can hardly have been enthusiastic over them. Attempts were made to keep them secret from Mazzini, for the same

---

[1] Crispi, 17 Nov. 1864, *Atti Parlamentari: Camera, Discussioni*, p. 6759; F. Crispi, *Repubblica e Monarchia: A Giuseppe Mazzini, Lettera* (Turin, 1865), pp. 5, 68; his anti-monarchic views are in *Francesco Crispi: Pensieri e Profezie*, ed. T. Palamenghi-Crispi (Rome, 1920), pp. 102, 113.

[2] *Politica Segreta Italiana (1863–1870)* (2nd ed., Turin, 1891), pp. 26, 48–9; *Roma e Venezia: Ricordi Storici d'un Romano: Appendice al volume 'Politica Segreta Italiana'* (Rome, 1895), pp. 220–1; A. Boullier, *Victor-Emmanuel et Mazzini: Leurs Négociations Secrètes et leur Politique* (Paris, 1885), pp. 37–49.

[3] A. Monti, *Vittorio Emanuele II* (Milan, 1941), p. 336; *Scritti di Mazzini*, LXXIX. 255, 303; ibid. LXXXI. 13; ibid. LXXXIII. 119–24; *Politica Segreta Italiana*, p. 92.

[4] M. Minghetti, *La Convenzione di Settembre: Un Capitolo dei miei Ricordi* (Bologna, 1899), pp. 28–9.

[5] *Auswärtige Politik Preussens*, v. 189; Lipparini, *Minghetti*, II. 371.

[6] Ibid. 364; *Il Risorgimento Italiano: Rivista Storica* (Turin), 1917, p. 480; Lamarmora commented in January 1870, 'After all the many millions that Italy has been called upon to spend in order to get a revolution in Hungary, I wonder if a single Hungarian shot has been fired in our cause' (*Complemento alla Storia della Campagna del 1866*, ed. Corpo Stato Maggiore (Rome, 1909), II. 102),

reason that they would not have been approved. Strong opposition came from those of Garibaldi's friends who resented that the king had deceived him before; by leaking rumours of court intrigues to the press, these men were eventually able to prevent Garibaldi going off on what would have been a wild goose chase and might well have led to his death.[1] Sir Henry Elliot, the new British minister, unkindly assumed that the king's real motive was just to get Garibaldi away from Italy to where the radicals might lose their reputation, and 'nothing would give the king greater pleasure than to know that Garibaldi was knocked on the head'.[2]

Minghetti's government survived for over a year, during which it succeeded in restoring the French alliance but only at the cost of another head-on clash with the throne. The king was paid in his own coin when Minghetti arranged with France the convention of September 1864. Under this convention it was agreed to carry out Cavour's scheme of 1861: the French would withdraw their troops from Rome, while Italy undertook to defend the pope against any attack from outside, and the Italians would move their capital from Turin to some other town in order to make it seem that they had truly given up their ambitions to capture Rome. This last provision to abandon Turin was concealed from Victor Emanuel while negotiations proceeded, since the politicians were frightened that he would not agree to it unless confronted with a *fait accompli*. As Minghetti explained, he was no ordinary king, and ministers could not impose on him the ordinary restrictions of constitutional government; hence he would have to be deceived on this crucial issue.[3] If the prime minister was correct in such a judgement, obviously there was some radical defect in the working of the constitution.

Not since Cavour's day had any ministry treated Victor Emanuel so disrespectfully. His first reaction when he heard was that he ought to refuse to sign their convention, but he asked Minghetti not to tell this to the other ministers while he consulted his private advisers on the subject.[4] Rattazzi indeed advised him to defy his own government and refuse to sign, and many of the Piedmontese conservatives seem to have thought the same; they realized that removal of the capital would signify the end of Piedmontese predominance, and they feared that the monarchy would be less strong if the seat of government were elsewhere. At the same time they recognized that the cabinet had placed the king in a position where if he refused his assent he would be publicly involved on one side of a political controversy, and there

---

[1] G. Guerzoni, *Garibaldi* (Florence, 1882), II. 393–404; A. Elia, *Note Autobiografiche e Storiche di un Garibaldino* (Bologna, 1898), pp. 154–5; *Garibaldi, Vittorio Emanuele, Cavour, nei Fasti della Patria*, ed. G. E. Curàtulo (Bologna, 1911), pp. 364–5.
[2] 22 July 1864, P.R.O. 30/22/70.
[3] Minghetti, *Convenzione di Settembre*, pp. 29, 72; *Carteggio Castelli*, I. 509–10.
[4] *Giacomo Dina*, II. 749.

was even talk of an enforced abdication.[1] Victor Emanuel realized the danger and decided not to push his opposition too far, especially as he could not wish it to be generally known that he had been thus deceived. He sent Menabrea to see Napoleon in the hope that there was some chance of changing the clause about the capital, but on this point the ministers were ready to make a very firm stand. Finally he gave his agreement. All he could do was to use his influence to ensure that the capital was not moved to Naples, as a majority of ministers wanted, but rather to Florence.[2]

The convention of September, and the decision to move to Florence, came as a blow to the king's pride. As he self-admiringly told several people, long experience had by now given him a position above parties where he could see to the heart of things, and his ministers ought to take him into their confidence and defer more readily to his judgement: rumour might say that he spent his time hunting and womanizing, but people should know by now that he was a serious statesman and could be expected to feel the true interests of Italy better than any merely party politician.[3] He was particularly upset when there were demonstrations in Turin against the removal of the capital. Turin was his favourite city and the most loyal to the monarchy, but it now came close to rebellion. At one point the police began shooting against an unarmed mob; by mistake they killed some of Della Rocca's troops who incredibly had been drawn up on the opposite side of the central square; the soldiers, thinking themselves attacked, fired back, and the result was what the British minister called the 'September massacres'.[4]

General Della Rocca, who Minghetti had placed in charge of keeping order in the town, was a royal aide-de-camp who for fifteen years had been closer to the king than anyone else in public life. Della Rocca was not a man of any political judgement at all. He now excused his own incompetence by taking it on himself to advise the king to dismiss the government for causing such havoc, and his advice was accepted. Just as with the fall of Ricasoli and Rattazzi, the attitude of parliament, where Minghetti still had a majority, was not considered important. Della Rocca was sent in person to instruct Minghetti to resign. Minghetti asked to have such an order in writing, and when this request was met he did as he was told.[5] As Azeglio remarked, a small demon-

---

[1] Mme Rattazzi, *Rattazzi et son Temps*, I. 669, 676; *Sclopis: Diario*, pp. 365, 367, 369–72.

[2] Cabinet minute, translated in *The Making of Italy 1796–1870*, ed. D. Mack Smith (New York, 1968), p. 405.

[3] *Lettere di V. Emanuele*, I. 789–90; ibid. II. 805.

[4] H. G. Elliot, *Some Revolutions and other Diplomatic Experiences* (London, 1922), pp. 176–7; 20 Jan. 1865, and 9 Feb., P.R.O. 30/22/70; *Risposta del Senatore Generale Della Rocca alle Osservazioni degli Onorevoli Deputati (ex-Ministri) Minghetti, Peruzzi, Pisanelli e Visconti-Venosta* (Turin, 1865), p. 1.

[5] *La Stampa* (Turin), 25 Sept. 1864, p. 2, where the fact that they had not resigned but had been dismissed was published by the government, so leaving the crown 'uncovered' by the doctrine of ministerial responsibility.

stration in the streets of Turin had succeeded in turning a government out of office.[1]

Victor Emanuel asked Rattazzi to form another government, only to find that Rattazzi wanted to repudiate the convention and keep the capital at Turin.[2] Against this there was plenty of other advice even in court circles which supported the move to Florence as now inevitable if the dynasty were not to fall.[3] To reverse such a public act would cause grave difficulties elsewhere in Italy where it would reanimate all the resentment against 'Piedmontization'. It would inhibit France from withdrawing her troops, with the result that Rome would be placed outside Italy's grasp. There were also powerful strategic reasons for the move. He therefore appointed as premier General Lamarmora, another Piedmontese and someone he personally disliked, but a man whose great sense of duty would accept this logic and obey the king's express command. Once again, as at previous moments of crisis in March 1849 and July 1859, Victor Emanuel turned to an army leader to form a government. His next planned phase for the risorgimento was to be another war against Austria, and it would suit well to have a general in office. Lamarmora's government, which was largely composed of Piedmontese, was chosen without any reference to the balance of parties in parliament,[4] but with support at court he was going to last longer than any prime minister since Cavour.

[1] *Azeglio*, Rendu, pp. 285–6; E. Della Rocca, *Autobiografia di un Veterano* (Bologna, 1897), II. 163–4; Minghetti, *Convenzione di Settembre*, pp. 198–201, 269–72. The formula used by the *Gazzetta Ufficiale* on 24 Sept. was 'since His Majesty thinks that the ministers should resign, they have [agreed . . .'; some people thought that the king's dismissal of Minghetti saved the country from revolution (*Le Opere di Giorgio Arcoleo: Diritto Costituzionale*, ed. G. Paulucci di Calboli Barone and A. Casulli (Milan, 1935), III. 257).

[2] Mme Rattazzi, *Rattazzi et son Temps*, II.1–5.   [3] *Carteggio Castelli*, I. 521; ibid. II. 4–5.

[4] M. A. Canini, 'Rassegna Politica', *Rivista Contemporanea* (Turin), XLIV (1866), p. 392; M. Vinciguerra, *I Partiti Italiani dal 1848 al 1955* (Rome, 1956), p. 64.

14

The King and the War of 1866

THE war against Austria in 1866, though it won Venice for Italy, was a military catastrophe, and the defeats of Custoza and Lissa inflicted a psychological wound that for decades generated much dangerous nationalist hysteria.[1] The two senior officers in the armed forces were singled out as scapegoats. Admiral Persano was condemned after trial before the senate. General Lamarmora was treated less savagely, but his career was ruined. Other contributory factors in these defeats were, after this convenient transference of guilt, left uninvestigated.

Lamarmora as prime minister in 1864–6 had had the task of preparing for war. Victor Emanuel told the Prussian ambassador in 1865 that Lamarmora's government owed its strength to the fact that it depended on the monarch rather than on parliament;[2] and yet Lamarmora was not someone he believed in. Rattazzi, the favourite, was still consulted privately on political matters and was clearly being groomed to resume office.[3] Contemporaries used the word 'antipathy' for the king's attitude towards his prime minister, and the fact that such hostility was fairly widely known was unfortunate. 'The king's dislike of an honest minister is, I am afraid, past cure', wrote Sir Henry Elliot.[4] Their differences went back to 1859, to Lamarmora's criticism of the king's military competence. More recently they had been increased by the unwillingness of Lamarmora and the generals to support the king's plans to foment war in the Balkans or to agree with him that Italy was strong enough to fight Austria on her own.[5]

On the other hand Lamarmora had some compensatory advantages. Much more than Rattazzi he was widely respected for being honest and straightforward. Unlike Cavour he was neither clever nor disobedient. As a military

---

[1] Bonghi, 15 May 1883, *Atti Parlamentari: Camera*, p. 3101: 'I want a war for Italy, because I know how much the defeats of Custoza and Lissa still weigh on us'; E. T. Moneta, *Custoza e Lissa* (Milan, 1910), p. iii.

[2] *Die Auswärtige Politik Preussens*, vol. v, ed. R. Ibbeken (Oldenburg, 1935), p. 600; the fact was widely recognized (A. Monti, *Il Conte Luigi Torelli* (Milan, 1931), p. 192).

[3] A. Luzio, *Profili Biografici e Bozzetti Storici* (Milan, 1927), II. 297–8; *Carteggio Castelli*, II. 55, 96; *Sclopis: Diario*, p. 391.

[4] 18 Feb. 1865, P.R.O. 30/22/70; M. Minghetti, *La Convenzione di Settembre* (Bologna, 1899), p. 73; G. Di Revel, *Sette Mesi al Ministero: Ricordi Ministeriali* (Milan, 1895), pp. 2–3.

[5] *Aus dem Leben Theodor von Bernhardis* (Leipzig, 1897), VII. 84–5.

officer he had a deep loyalty to the crown and was ready to conceal Victor Emanuel's occasional intervention in controversial issues. Hence the king kept him in office, despite a contrary vote in parliament, and even though some people saw such treatment of parliament as constitutionally improper.[1]

Victor Emanuel never forgot that foreign policy was a field where the monarch had a special competence. Between the various possible alliances in Europe he kept a fairly open mind. The most obvious possibility was France. It could be assumed that, whenever the French should decide to occupy Belgium and the Rhineland, Italy ought to fight alongside France against Prussia and Austria; and yet Napoleon was becoming uncomfortably peaceable, and his countrymen had lost some of their friendliness for united Italy.[2] Alternatively there was Austria. The king started from the assumption that Austria in a level fight could beat the Prussians; hence he chose to speak to Count Vitzthum of his deep feelings of friendship for Austria. He even made private enquiries in Vienna about a possible *entente*, and was supported in this initiative by some of the ultra-conservatives at court who backed Habsburg Austria for its authoritarian politics.[3] The main obstacle was whether Austria, to buy his support, was ready to sacrifice Venice and the Trentino.

When the Prussians put up another alternative, that of a joint war against Austria, this seemed a better bet, and Lamarmora eventually signed an offensive alliance with Bismarck in April 1866. The important thing was to have a war, and as soon as possible. Victor Emanuel was constantly tempted by the thought of leading his forces to victory, and the army officers of the *casa reale* carefully pandered to this temptation. Though Prussia was reputedly less strong than Italy and would probably be defeated by Austria, Italy and Prussia could surely win together against a divided Austrian army.[4] Outsiders were less confident of this: some of them privately said that war would mean bankruptcy and possible defeat; others had in mind the almost unmentionable possibility that most Italians had hardly heard of Venice and would not want war.[5] But anyone who hinted to the king that he might be entering on a perilous gamble was silenced by being called an ignorant fool. Victor Emanuel had for some time been sure that the army was in splendid condition and that he himself as its commander-in-chief was an instrument of divine providence

[1] M. Mancini and U. Galeotti, *Norme ed Usi del Parlamento Italiano* (Rome, 1887), p. 737.

[2] H. Oncken, *Die Rheinpolitik Kaiser Napoleons III, von 1863 bis 1870, und der Ursprung des Krieges von 1870–71* (Stuttgart, 1926), I. 218; *Auswärtige Politik Preussens*, V. 189; *Carte di Lanza*, III. 304; *Carteggio Castelli*, II. 115.

[3] K. F. Vitzthum von Eckstädt, *London, Gastein und Sadowa 1864–1866* (Stuttgart, 1889), p. 109; A. Lamarmora, *Un po' più di Luce sugli Eventi Politici e Militari dell'Anno 1866* (Florence, 1873), p. 51; A. Luzio, 'La Missione Malaguzzi a Vienna', *Il Risorgimento Italiano* (Turin), XV (1922), 131–2, 193; Cowley to Clarendon, 12 May 1866, F.O. 27/1616.

[4] *Rassegna*, 1963, p. 94; G. Guerzoni, *La Vita di Nino Bixio* (Florence, 1889), p. 311.

[5] Clarendon, 4 June 1866, Clarendon MSS. (Bodleian Library, Oxford), dep c 143; *Carteggi Ricasoli*, XXII. 25; *Lettere Ricasoli*, VII. 273; *Carteggio Castelli*, II. 127; Mme Rattazzi, *Rattazzi et son Temps* (Paris, 1887), II. 54–5.

to humble the might of Austria. He seemed 'quite drunk with over-confidence'.[1]

Ordinary Italians had no means of knowing the truth when the experts thought victory inevitable. General Bixio, who as a member of parliament had made a detailed study of the subject, agreed that the army was splendid, the navy was 'incontestably superior', and the Italian commanders were 'the envy of Europe'.[2] Francesco Crispi urgently demanded in parliament that Italy be given 'a baptism of blood'.[3] Even though Austria was now ready to give up Venice without war, the view of Italian officialdom was 'that Venice got without fighting would not be worth having', and Bixio said he would prefer 100,000 Italians to die in battle rather than accept a peaceful cession. Italians would soon become dominant in the Mediterranean and chase the British from their illegal possession of Malta.[4] This belief shows that the course of the risorgimento had run too easily. How far Italy had depended on French support was almost forgotten. Italians had come to rely on a virtual guarantee by which France and Britain secured them against loss;[5] few of them paused to think how much this might have masked the realities of their military capability, especially when the king assured them that all was well.

All later reports on the war of 1866 glossed over the fundamental lack of military preparations, because it was feared that a serious enquiry might have exposed parliament, army, and the king himself. Lack of planning had in part been due to the instability of Italian political practice and to the fact that ministers had a divided responsibility to the king and parliament. In six years, seven different ministers had been in charge of the war office, and nine that of the navy; all of these ministers were generals or admirals hand-picked for the job by the king. Yet finance was the responsibility of civilian ministers who were restricted by their greater degree of accountability to parliament. Victor Emanuel did not like intrusion by civilians into the arcana of war preparation. Parliamentary discussion of military matters was in fact kept to a minimum, and very little informed criticism of the executive was ever heard

---

[1] *Carteggio Castelli*, II. 138; *Lettere di V. Emanuele*, II. 857; *Il Principe Napoleone nel Risorgimento Italiano*, ed. A. Comandini (Milan, 1922), p. 228.

[2] *Epistolario di Nino Bixio*, ed. E. Morelli (Rome, 1949), III. 9; Guerzoni, *Bixio*, pp. 271, 318; P. Villari, *Saggi di Storia, di Critica e di Politica* (Florence, 1868), p. 387; the army was said to be the one really efficient organization in Italy (*Epistolario di Giuseppe La Farina*, ed. A. Franchi (Milan, 1869), II. 528.

[3] *Discorsi Parlamentari di Francesco Crispi*, ed. C. Finocchiaro-Aprile (Rome, 1915), I. 717, and his statement was greeted with cries of 'Bravo! Benissimo!'

[4] Elliot, 26 May 1866, Clarendon MSS., dep c 98; Bixio's speech of 17 Dec. 1864, quoted by A. Savelli, *L'Anno Fatale per l'Italia (1866)* (Milan, 1916), p. 94; C. Cantù, *Della Indipendenza Italiana: Cronistoria* (Turin, 1877), III. 187: L. C. Fregoso, *Del Primato Italiano sul Mediterraneo* (Turin, 1872), pp. 53, 187.

[5] Russell to Elliot, 27 Dec. 1863, P.R.O. 30/22/110: 'If Italy was defeated we should save her from any other penalty for her rashness than that of paying an indemnity to Austria for the expenses of the war.' Some Italians, oddly, claimed that Italy had won the Crimean War for the Allies (A. Oriani, *La Rivolta Ideale* (Bologna, 1912), p. 129).

in parliament or the press, while of course the king could sign the treaty of alliance without any reference to parliament.[1]

As a result there was almost no serious debate on the fundamental question of whether the available resources of the country made a policy based on war realistic. Pure assumptions served in place of argument. Successive prime ministers knew that the king was wrong when he said that Italy could fight against Austria on her own, but if possible they preferred not to contradict him too forcibly. Lamarmora, who for a long time had been minister of war under Cavour, remembered that governments had been obliged to allocate funds to the army in secret, or at least without parliamentary sanction,[2] but it did not occur to him that this might have contributed to foster a dangerous illusion. Hence parliament was allowed to believe that great deeds might be possible without having to pay for them.[3]

How much was being spent on the armed forces is not all that easy to discover, but the strange fact emerges that the amount decreased in each of the four years before 1866.[4] Even as late as February 1866 a decision was taken to take positive disarmament one stage further,[5] and this despite a plethora of belligerent speeches. An active diminution of military strength continued until March 1866 when suddenly the decision was taken to go into reverse and prepare for war in three months' time. Whatever the king deluded himself into thinking, the army at the outbreak of war was hopelessly under strength, under-trained, and under-equipped—a fact which appears strikingly from a comparison with the army of Prussia, a smaller country than Italy, but much stronger than he chose to think.[6] Without adequate parliamentary criticism, however, advance warning could have come only from serving officers who were either party to the deception or who would have ruined their careers by telling. The minister of the navy had usually been an army general who had no technical competence: hence no plans at all for a naval campaign had been prepared; there was in 1866 no adequate base in the Adriatic on which war against Austria could have been based; nor even had the fleet been allowed to take part in manœuvres. When an anonymous pamphlet protested, nothing could be done because the truth was too inconvenient to be officially noticed.[7]

[1] Gen. G. Ulloa, *L'Esercito Italiano e la Battaglia di Custoza: Studi Politico-Militari* (Florence, 1866), p. 10; *Le Opere di Giorgio Arcoleo*, ed. G. Paulucci di Calboli Barone (Milan, 1935), III. 250; *Il Parlamento dell'Unità d'Italia (1859–61)* (Rome, 1961), II. 680, 747–9.

[2] A. Lamarmora, *Agli Elettori del Collegio di Biella* (Turin, 1860), pp. 61–2; royal decree of 13 Nov. 1859, *Raccolta delle Leggi, Regolamenti e Decreti* (Milan, 1860), p. 703.

[3] F. Uccelli, *Della Presente Mediocrità Politica* (Florence, 1866), p. 68.

[4] C. de Cesare, *La Politica, l'Economia, e la Morale dei Moderni Italiani* (Florence, 1869), p. 257; P. Pieri, *Le Forze Armate nella Età della Destra* (Milan, 1962), p. 342.

[5] Ibid., p. 71; D. Farini, *Diario di Fine Secolo*, ed. E. Morelli (Rome, 1961), I. 5.

[6] Luzio, *Profili Biografici*, II. 304; P. Silva, *Il Sessantesei: Studi Storici* (Milan, 1917), pp. 308–9.

[7] *Quistione Vitale o Cenni sulla Marina Italiana Dedicati al Parlamento Nazionale* (Naples, ?1863), pp. 20, 29, 53, 63–4; Pieri, *Le Forze Armate*, pp. 432–3.

Quite as dangerous was the fact of arriving at a long-sought-after moment with a higher command which was inexperienced, badly trained, and torn by jealousies and factions. The system was one in which promotion was achieved through seniority or favouritism, and not only had incompetents been brought into positions of power, but the real extent of their incompetence was unknown to politicians and the public at large.

Thus Admiral Persano, who commanded the fleet, enjoyed special backing at court, and this obscured his lack of every essential quality of a commander. Earlier in his career, when given command of the largest ship in the navy, he almost immediately ran it aground just outside Genoa harbour. Soon afterwards his refusal to accept a pilot in the Thames estuary had been brought to the notice of a disciplinary court, and it was typical of him that he boasted of this breach of regulations. On another occasion he had wrecked his ship on a reef off Sardinia when the king and the royal family were aboard, and again he took credit for saving their lives. Such incidents would have ruined the career of any other man. Persano was unpopular in the service: his insubordination and lack of attention to duty were legendary; nevertheless his superior officers found he was under the protection of an '*altissimo personaggio*', not mentioned by name,[1] but who must have been a member of the royal family. Persano's juniors, notably Rear-Admiral Galli della Mantica, who was probably the best officer in the fleet, resigned rather than continue to serve with him. Persano was the man whom Rattazzi, with the king's encouragement, appointed minister of marine in 1862. Later the same year he had to leave office with Rattazzi, but, with just a few hours to spare before his resignation was accepted, he appointed himself the only full admiral in the fleet, and thus this incompetent man held command by seniority when war broke out.[2]

In April 1866 there was a belated rush to prepare for hostilities. The king still had romantic thoughts of a revolutionary war in the Balkans. He disregarded the fact that his generals and the prime minister were against this idea, but got privately in touch with Garibaldi to make secret plans.[3] He discussed with the Hungarian, Lajos Kossuth, their old scheme for an insurrection in Hungary, and spoke about it with his other Hungarian aide-de-camp, General Türr, who was sent secretly to discuss it further with Bismarck. The secretary-general of the foreign office, Marcello Cerruti, assisted in this project, but was under orders from the king not to inform the prime minister. Karl Usedom, the ambassador of Prussia, came to see Victor Emanuel more than once without Lamarmora's knowledge: he too was told not to inform the

---

[1] Vice-Admiral Serra, 7 and 10 Dec. 1857, MSS. Archivio Lamarmora (Biella), xcvii/156.
[2] D. Guerrini, *Come ci Avviammo a Lissa* (Turin, 1907), i. 272–5; C. Randaccio, *Storia delle Marine Militari Italiane* (Rome, 1886), ii. 25; *La Guerra in Italia nel 1866: Studio Militare* (Milan, 1867), pp. 358–61; N. Romualdi, *Il Processo Persano* (Milan, 1938), pp. 77, 90–1; *Carteggi Ricasoli*, xxii. 266–7; A. Iachino, *La Campagna Navale di Lissa 1866* (Milan, 1966), p. 87; B. Orero, *Da Pesaro a Messina: Ricordi del 1860–61* (Turin, 1905), pp. 96–7.
[3] *Scritti di Garibaldi*, ii. 502–3.

cabinet of their talks, but to wait until the outbreak of war permitted the king to act with fewer constitutional restrictions.[1]

Nothing materialized from this persistent illusion about a Hungarian revolt. In any case, so Usedom noted, Victor Emanuel liked to talk about taking practical initiatives but knew too little about politics to carry them very far.[2] An essentially timid person under the surface, he preferred not to override his ministers so long as he could act behind their backs; and his preferred action was just talk, even though talk could be damaging enough when it fed Prussian suspicions of Italian policy. There is not much doubt that when the Prussians sent an official note to Lamarmora asking for revolutionary action in the Balkans, this was because the king had told Usedom that he wanted to push his own government in that direction; and Lamarmora's refusal to accept this note had damaging effects for Italy when it was known in Berlin.

In April, as soon as war was decided, Lamarmora asked to be allowed to return to his military duties. Victor Emanuel toyed with the idea of himself assuming dictatorial powers,[1] but found little support, so he dutifully though very unwillingly accepted that Ricasoli was the only man who could become prime minister without dividing the country. General Cialdini sensibly recommended that the change should be made at once so that Lamarmora, as the senior general in the army, could prepare for the campaign. Ricasoli was therefore sounded out, but was unwilling to accept until there was no doubt that war would come. After his last experience of government he was reluctant to expose himself again to the intrigues of Rattazzi and the court. It is at first sight strange that the king did not intervene more firmly at this point, for Ricasoli was not the man to refuse if Victor Emanuel had insisted; or else, if Lamarmora had to remain in office, another general should have been selected to prepare the army for war. No one except the king could have decided this cardinal point one way or the other. But, after dismissing him so curtly in February 1862, it was not easy for Victor Emanuel to say openly to Ricasoli's face that the national interest demanded his immediate return to power. Nor did the king show any signs of realizing how much depended on this decision. Nor was Lamarmora the man to persist in offering advice when that advice had been once rejected.

Lamarmora was therefore obliged to continue in office, and Ricasoli did not succeed him until three days before war began on 23 June. The result was that political and military preparations were both entirely defective: because Lamarmora had no time to co-ordinate strategy, whereas Ricasoli, coming to

[1] S. Türr, 'Fürst Bismarck und die Ungarn: Reminiscenzen aus dem Jahre 1866', *Deutsche Revue* (Stuttgart), Mar. 1900, p. 318; L. Chiala, *Cenni Storici sui Preliminari della Guerra del 1866 e sulla Battaglia di Custoza* (Florence, 1870), II. 21; *Aus dem Leben Bernhardis*, VII. 37; *Carteggio Castelli*, II. 572.

[2] *Die Auswärtige Politik Preussens*, vol. VI, ed. R. Ibbeken (Oldenburg, 1939), p. 564; *Carteggio Castelli*, II. 110.

[3] *Carteggi Ricasoli*, XXII. 9.

power after most decisions had been taken, had no time to recognize that there were some major flaws in the structure of command. Ricasoli talked with Lamarmora on 30 May and again on 11 June, but otherwise they evidently did not meet at all to concert policy.[1] It is surprising that this satisfied either of them or the king.

The main reason why Italy came badly out of the war was that the king never made clear who was in command and indeed seems to have gone out of his way to cloud the issue. The constitution recognized him as commander-in-chief; and though Charles Albert had taken only nominal command in the war of 1849, Victor Emanuel in 1859 had refused to follow his father's example. Cavour and Lamarmora had strongly objected to this, without avail. They knew that he lacked the ability and experience. For another thing, a constitutional monarch who took up an active command could not take credit for victory without also taking responsibility for defeat: and, if answerable for defeat, he might have to abdicate just as a minister would resign. This was a delicate point of constitutional law which it would have been impolitic to let parliament discuss, and nothing had therefore been done after 1859 to clarify it.[2] The commander-in-chief had hardly even bothered to turn up at military manœuvres.[3] Despite courage, a cool head, and plenty of attacking spirit, he entirely lacked the ability to command a large army of 300,000 men, and yet was unwilling for anyone else to have the laurels which the war was expected to bring. In 1866 he did not possess quite the self-confidence to impose his authority as he had done in 1859, nor yet the realism of Charles Albert to look for a more expert alternative. Only on rare occasions can any doubts about his military capacity have been allowed to reach his own ears.

The king therefore announced that he himself would take over supreme command. He was prepared to have a chief of staff who would in fact assume most of the practical responsibility, though his preference would be for a mere executive who carried out orders and remained unobtrusive: he did not want in this post either of the two senior generals, Alfonso Lamarmora or Enrico Cialdini, for they would try to interfere, and 'after two days we would be at each others' throats'. His first preference, as in 1859, was for his old friend General Enrico Della Rocca: this man enjoyed no military reputation whatever, but owed his promotion to influence at court, and represented all that was most amateurish and ineffective in the Italian military machine.[4] Victor Emanuel was told that Della Rocca's appointment would be widely disliked, so as an alternative he suggested General Petitti, a younger and more accommodating man who would be less meddlesome and critical than either of the

[1] Ibid. 6–8.   [2] Mancini and Galeotti, *Norme ed Usi del Parlamento*, pp. 662–3.
[3] C. Massei, *L'Italia e la Politica di Napoleone III Durante e Dopo la Guerra dell'Indipendenza* (Leghorn, 1867), II. 267.
[4] A. Guarnieri, *Otto Anni di Storia Militare in Italia (1859–1866)* (Florence, 1868), pp. 320–1, 494.

two prima donnas of the army. Cialdini and Lamarmora were at a pinch prepared to accept Petitti, though neither was enthusiastic and both were unhappy about the king's decision to command in person.[1]

Later reticence, both by the generals themselves and by the historians who edited their writings, managed to conceal their real opinions, but Lamarmora, Cialdini, and Petitti were all secretly disturbed by the king's delusions about being a great general,[2] nor were they anxious to accept the ambiguous position of chief of staff under him. Cialdini was bold enough to raise the matter directly with the sovereign, but found him unmoveable as well as being irritated that his military competence was being called in question. Cialdini now became alarmed; though anxious not to wound the king's *amour propre*, in private he said that success or failure would depend on Lamarmora taking effective command. Lamarmora, on the other hand, would gladly have deferred to Cialdini, partly because he recognized Cialdini as the better strategist, and also because he himself as prime minister would have insufficient time to supervise the strategic planning of the campaign. The minister of war, General Pettinengo, agreed with both the others in a lack of enthusiasm for Petitti. Everyone except Victor Emanuel himself was quite sure that Della Rocca would have been a disaster.

It was for the king to decide, but weeks went by in casual discussion, and it seems that he never thought of summoning the military and political leaders to settle the matter in a council of war. This would not have been his way of conducting business. Military historians later contrived to put the whole blame on Lamarmora and Cialdini by inaccurately stating that each of them obstinately refused to serve under the other.[3] It was to be said that the king had more military talent than his generals allowed, and that, if only he had openly accepted full responsibility himself, the army would at least have had a commander.[4] The generals would almost certainly have accepted any firm decision on his part, but his own timidity made him uncertain about asserting himself except in claiming the title of commander-in-chief. Finally he conceded that the chief of staff should have more authority and initiative than in 1859, though not so much as Chrzanowski had been allowed in 1849; appearances would have to be carefully preserved, and he refused to contemplate an arrangement where he could not give effective orders. This was an ambiguous decision which meant in effect that no one was in unfettered command.

---

[1] L. Chiala, *Ancora un po' più di Luce sugli Eventi Politici e Militari dell'Anno 1866* (Florence, 1902), pp. 560–70; Chiala, *Cenni Storici sui Preliminari*, pp. 263–6; T. Sandonnini, *In Memoria di Enrico Cialdini* (Modena, 1911), p. 82; *Schiarimenti e Rettifiche del Generale Alfonso Lamarmora* (Florence, 1868), pp. 10–11.

[2] A sentence of Cialdini's was omitted by Chiala, though later printed by Luzio, *Profili Biografici*, II. 303, which warned Lamarmora against a possible '*colpo di testa* from the king who somehow has persuaded himself that he is a great general'.

[3] V. Giglio, *Il Risorgimento nelle sue Fasi di Guerra* (Milan, 1948), II. 303.

[4] P. Calza, *Nuova Luce sugli Eventi Militari del 1866* (Bologna, 1924), pp. 144–5; A. Pollio, *Custoza (1866)* (4th ed., Rome, 1935), p. 24.

Lamarmora in the end accepted the post of chief of staff, but reluctantly, and only because war would otherwise have begun without anyone appointed to this essential job.[1] It was a most unfortunate choice because until the outbreak of war he was simultaneously premier and foreign minister. Nor was he an experienced field commander. As the war of 1859 had shown, he furthermore lacked the malleability of temperament and the confidence in the king's judgement needed for tactful treatment of the commander-in-chief. The king did not precisely specify Lamarmora's powers, presumably because he wished to retain for himself an undefined element of responsibility. At the last moment General Pettinengo asked him to change his mind and give Lamarmora the full executive authority that Chrzanowski had possessed, but the request was refused.[2]

Lamarmora subsequently claimed that his own lack of effective authority had seriously contributed to Italy's defeat.[3] From the very first day of the campaign the king set up a separate headquarters of his own where Lamarmora and Petitti were rarely to be seen. This royal headquarters, only a few miles away from Lamarmora's, contained a brilliant and 'fabulously numerous' retinue, but not a single map of the Veneto, and its general staff was not notable for military skill and experience. How these officers spent their time and what precisely their authority and their duties were, are questions that have still not been clarified, though one official later recalled hearing the campaign discussed with indifference.[4] What is indisputable is that Lamarmora and the king kept their staffs in different places, without arrangement for co-ordination, and both of them retaining the capacity to issue commands.

The root difficulty here was an unresolved constitutional problem, since the king carried over into war the techniques of government which he had practised in peace. Only after defeat had made things clearer was Ruggero Bonghi able to bring this point under public scrutiny. He claimed that a constitutional or an absolutist monarch would work better on his own than any mixture between the two. A constitutional monarchy which neither governed effectively nor allowed others to do so was bound to prove inadequate; in effect it permitted the Italian army in 1866 to have three commanders in the field, each of whom possessed an undefined element of independence, quite apart from their equally undefined relationship to the prime minister and the minister of war in Florence.[5]

[1] Chiala, *Ancora un po' di Luce*, p. 570.
[2] E. Della Rocca, *Autobiografia di un Veterano* (Bologna, 1898), II. 244; *Lettere di V. Emanuele*, II. 1034, shows that the king continued to insist on being treated as commander-in-chief.
[3] Lamarmora's report of 20 Dec. 1868, *Complemento alla Storia della Campagna del 1866*, ed. Corpo Stato Maggiore (Rome, 1909), II. 39–40; Lamarmora, *Un po' più di Luce*, p. x.
[4] *Aus dem Leben Bernhardis*, VII. 110–11; L. Dal Verme, 'Il Generale Govone a Custoza', *Nuova Antologia* (Rome), Jan. 1902, pp. 277–8; Di Revel, *Sette Mesi al Ministero*, p. 3.
[5] R. Bonghi, 'L'Alleanza Prussiana e l'Acquisto della Venezia', *Nuova Antologia*, Apr. 1869, pp. 671, 674, 712; R. Bonghi, *Come Cadde la Destra*, ed. F. Piccolo (Milan, 1929), p. 250.

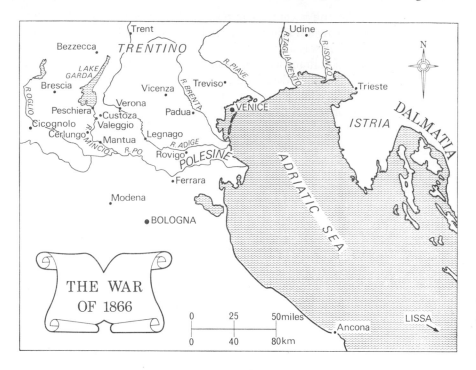

Another issue needing the commander-in-chief's consideration was the military strategy to be adopted. Here too there was a noticeable absence of drive, and this was almost certainly due to the knowledge that the Austrians would be fighting on two fronts, so that Italian troops would outnumber theirs by more than two to one. Yet the general assumption throughout the risorgimento had left the army unprepared for such a position of numerical superiority; training had been based on a defensive war, or at best on just a limited attack against the fortresses of the Quadrilateral.[1] The plan finally adopted was chosen almost by accident and not long before the declaration of war. The Italian forces were split into two armies, one under Cialdini to attack from the south across the river Po, the other under Lamarmora to attack from the west over the river Mincio. The king said once to one of his generals that he had always been against dividing his forces, but he said this after it had proved wrong.[2] In fact he seems to have proposed some such division himself,[3] and before the fatal 24 June there is no other evidence that he was unhappy about the choice.

---

[1] *La Campagna del 1866 in Italia*, ed. Corpo Stato Maggiore (Rome, 1875), I. 116; Col. P. Valle, *Sulla Difesa d'Italia* (Pavia, Jan. 1866), p. 104, barely considers the possibility of an offensive strategy.
[2] U. Govone, *Il Generale Giuseppe Govone* (Turin, 1902), p. 265.
[3] Chiala, *Ancora un po' di Luce*, p. 564; *Complemento*, II. 44.

The decision to have two almost separate armies reflected a conflict of personalities, because Cialdini was a difficult man who liked to work on his own and had no very high opinion of either Lamarmora or of the king.[1] In part it also reflected a division inside the higher command over two possible areas and types of attack. The Commission for Defence had reported in the previous year that the chief area of battle should be over the Mincio, especially as the Po was between 300 and 400 metres wide; moreover, even after a successful crossing of the Po an attacking force would run into difficulty in the Polesine where rivers would slow any advance and marshland could easily be flooded.[2] Cialdini disagreed; he wanted to attack over the Po, avoiding the Quadrilateral, co-ordinating his advance with the navy in the Adriatic and with a landing by Garibaldi's volunteers somewhere on the Dalmatian coast.

The Piedmontese generals, however, who dominated the military establishment, had been brought up on the fear of an attack by the Austrians against Turin, and had concentrated their training on the region between the Mincio and Adige rivers. This was the area bounded by the Austrian fortresses of Verona, Mantua, Peschiera, and Legnago which in Lamarmora's eyes were the main target. He and his colleagues, recognizing Cialdini's ability and impatience of superior orders, were ready to let him create a diversion on the Po; but they knew almost nothing about the navy, and had never bothered to prepare any scheme for combined operations in the Adriatic. They also were determined to curtail any action by Garibaldi, and preparations for arming volunteer units were therefore left to the last possible moment.[3] Garibaldi had become in popular esteem a rival to the king, as Garibaldi's volunteers were a rival to the regular army; this rivalry could not be allowed to continue, and hence the best available general on the Italian side was muzzled from the start.

The army general staff was never consulted and asked to reconcile these plans. Perhaps there was some jealousy here, for the general staff was under the special protection of Della Rocca; but it is still strange that General Ricci and Colonel Federici, heads of the *stato maggiore*, were allowed no part at all in the whole war. Nor did the royal commander-in-chief suspect that there might be an inherent conflict between the two different plans, otherwise he would have allowed Lamarmora to resign earlier as prime minister so as to study them in more detail. When General Petitti reported that Cialdini had a good chance of crossing the Po and taking Rovigo, it was agreed to strengthen the proposed diversion by allocating eight divisions to it, as compared with only twelve divisions kept for the more important Mincio front where the king and Lamarmora were in command. Yet the precise aims of these two virtually independent armies were at no stage exactly prescribed, and their

[1] *Aus dem Leben Bernhardis*, VII. 29, which quotes Cialdini calling Lamarmora mediocre; Elliot, 18 Aug. 1866, F.O. 45/89, ascribed to Cialdini 'an excessive ambition, an impatience of a superior, an ungovernable temper, and an overbearing disposition towards inferiors'.
[2] *Campagna del 1866*, I. 32–3.
[3] Ibid. 23–4; G. Guerzoni, *Garibaldi* (Florence, 1882), II. 413–15.

co-ordination in practice was left to chance. The fact that Cialdini's attack had originally been designed to coincide with wider operations in the Adriatic was soon forgotten.

Everyone continued to believe that there was no great urgency. There might well be no war at all, because Bismarck would have to start hostilities by 8 July or else the Italo-Prussian treaty would lapse. Moreover the Austrians tried to keep Italy out of the war by saying they would cede Venice in peace:[1] the king refused to accept this offer, but he must have realized from it that after 8 July Italy might well get what she wanted, with or without war, and this knowledge must have taken away the sense of precipitancy which military preparations required. Early in June the Austrians went further still and promised that even if they won a war against Italy they would not alter the territorial alignment of the peninsula. Napoleon added to this his personal guarantee that the Italian *status quo* would not be changed to Italy's disadvantage, and this must have contributed to create a sense of false security. Napoleon also suggested that, in return, if the Italians insisted on fighting, they should at least be prepared not to fight too strenuously, for he did not want either Prussia or Austria to win the war decisively.[2] These facts all subtracted something from the single-mindedness of Italian preparations. By mid-June, furthermore, Lamarmora knew that Austria was concentrating on her northern front against Germany, whereas on her southern Italian front she was determined not to accept a serious battle.[3] Hence the division of the Italian forces between the Mincio and the Po seemed quite acceptable.

The lack of urgency was such that General Pollio, who later wrote the best military study of the Custoza campaign, could find nothing worthy of being called a plan of campaign when hostilities began on 23 June,[4] and this despite the fact that here was a war which everyone had for years called necessary and inevitable. Clearly the king was not going to be bothered with strategy, and Lamarmora as prime minister had been more concerned with diplomatic preparation. Some kind of rough co-ordination between the two armies was agreed on 17 June when Lamarmora had a private meeting with Cialdini at Bologna, but that was only after the war in Germany had already begun. Pollio assumes that, at this meeting, both generals were deceiving each other, though more likely it was rather a question of misunderstanding. No written note was taken of anything they may have decided. Several days later the king approved Lamarmora's account of their deliberations and confirmed the idea of a two-pronged attack.

By his own account, Cialdini came away from Bologna with an impression that he was to carry out not a diversion but the main attack. He was to cross

---

[1] Lamarmora, *Un po' più di Luce*, p. 208.   [2] Ibid., p. 310.
[3] Ibid., pp. 333–4; A. Lamarmora, *I Segreti di Stato nel Governo Costituzionale* (Florence, 1877), pp. 11, 112.
[4] Pollio, *Custoza*, p. 28.

the Po on the night of 25–26 June, aiming to capture Rovigo and then Padua, while Lamarmora was to draw off the bulk of the enemy forces by a diversionary movement over the Mincio on the 24th. On the other hand Lamarmora's later recollection was that, since either of the two Italian forces individually outnumbered the whole Austrian *Süd-Armee*, one and perhaps both could be expected to succeed, and the arrangement was thus that they could each improvise in the light of events. They must have reckoned on meeting little resistance, for there was mention of linking up at Anguillara, which was a hundred kilometres beyond the Quadrilateral and only some 35 kilometres from the Adriatic.[1] Almost certainly it was agreed, as both later confirmed, that each army should develop its plan as occasion allowed and with a certain degree of autonomy.[2] Almost certainly Lamarmora, whatever he subsequently said, was not absolutely clear on what might seem a fundamental point, whether he would first have to attack at least one or two of the fortresses of the Quadrilateral. So greatly did he outnumber the Austrians that he could afford to wait and see whether they decided to concentrate against him or against Cialdini.

This lack of co-ordination was their first mistake. A second mistake was that, especially in view of the need to improvise, they omitted to set up a telegraph system outside the ordinary telegraph service and which would have kept each army in touch with the way events developed. The third and fundamental error was to leave the hierarchy of command confused. Cialdini concluded that he had been given 'full powers' to act on his own, though the only written orders said 'ample powers to act as he thought fit under the circumstances'; he imagined he had a separate command, whereas Lamarmora called it just a '*corpo staccato*'.[3] It is clear that neither Victor Emanuel nor Lamarmora felt strong enough to be firm with Cialdini, or indeed with each other. All three men acted as though they could not order one another to do things; they just 'requested' or 'urgently begged' for action.

Victor Emanuel waited for a week after Bismarck's declaration of war before Lamarmora was allowed to follow suit, and this was read at Berlin, not doubt correctly, to mean that the Italians were going to leave the labouring oar to their ally. So confident was the king, that he did not leave Florence until 20 June. All told he claimed to have some 350,000 soldiers. Of these, he and Lamarmora on the Mincio had over 100,000 front-line troops against the

---

[1] Chiala omits this fact, perhaps because it makes the tactics of his hero, Lamarmora, even harder to understand, but the letter is quoted by Luzio, *Profili Biografici*, II. 306; *Risposta alla 2ᵃ Parte dell'Opuscolo 'Il Generale Lamarmora e la Campagna del 1866'* (Bologna, 1868), p. 44, gives Cialdini's recollection that Lamarmora arrived at Bologna with no plan of attack, and simply accepted Cialdini's.

[2] *Schiarimenti e Rettifiche*, pp. 17–18; *Risposta del Generale Cialdini all'Opuscolo 'Schiarimenti e Rettifiche del Generale Lamarmora'* (Bologna, 1868), pp. 17–18.

[3] *Risposta del Generale Cialdini*, p. 31.

Archduke Albrecht's 75,000.[1] He was content to know that his other army under Cialdini, with a further 75,000 men, had a well-studied scheme of attack, even though apparently he did not know the quite vital fact of when that attack was timed to begin. There was no chance on this occasion of being outclassed by Garibaldi, who at the last minute was assigned a third area of attack in the Trentino. Most of the volunteers had been kept waiting in the extreme south of Italy so that they could not be brought quickly into action; and, despite official denials, the equipment given to Garibaldi was poor and unsuited to his allotted task.[2]

Despite the king's confidence, almost everything went wrong that could possibly go wrong. He and Lamarmora thought that they could cross the Mincio and meet no opposition before reaching the Adige. They also assumed that Cialdini's moves could not fail to synchronize with their own. These assumptions were left to pure chance. The Archduke Albrecht, however, left little to chance. He had carefully taken up his command not three days earlier, as the king and Lamarmora had done, but six weeks before war began.[3] He had had time to know his generals well, and they all knew the terrain thoroughly from their annual manœuvres. By the simple expedient of attacking first, he destroyed any chance of synchronization between the two armies on which the Italians were depending, and astonishingly this was completely unexpected. Lamarmora had advanced blindly, without scouts, indeed with most of the cavalry in the rear, and his staff officers far away on the wrong side of the river Mincio.

The main failures at Custoza were Lamarmora's responsibility, for in the early stages of the morning of 24 June the king made no attempt to interfere with his strategy or lack of it. At no time in the day did Lamarmora succeed in imposing any direction on the fighting. Most of his twelve divisions were never brought into any action at all. Evidently he quite lost his head, and instead of trying to improvise a headquarters where the other generals could find him, he spent the day galloping about the field in search of individual divisional commanders. At one point in the afternoon he was found twenty kilometres away from the centre of the battle, where he had gone to consult with Petitti and his staff about preparing for a retreat, having left his other generals to fight on their own as best they could.

The king and Lamarmora did not stay together. Victor Emanuel continued to keep a completely separate, though equally disorganized, headquarters, and soon he was giving orders on his own initiative which sometimes contradicted Lamarmora's. It may be, though the evidence is only a single state-

---

[1] *Lettere di V. Emanuele*, ii. 907; *Campagna del 1866*, i. 339.

[2] *Scritti di Garibaldi*, ii. 500; General P. Schiarini, 'La Campagna del 1866', *Garibaldi Condottiero*, ed. Corpo Stato Maggiore (Rome, 1932), p. 310; L. Zini, *Storia d'Italia dal 1850 al 1866* (Milan, 1869), iii. 1331–2.

[3] *Österreichs Kämpfe im Jahre 1866*, ed. Generalstabs-Bureau für Kriegsgeschichte (Vienna, 1868), ii. 8.

ment made subsequently by the king himself, that he had foreseen the Austrian attack. Patriotic historians continued to assert that he remained in the front line for the whole day, but in fact he left the field of battle in the late morning and spent the rest of the day nearly 25 kilometres away on the far side of the Mincio. He undoubtedly kept a cooler head than either his chief of staff or Della Rocca, but it is also understandable that Lamarmora should have found his presence an embarrassment.[1]

Only 725 Italian soldiers were killed at the battle of Custoza. In other words, despite all its later notoriety, it was in itself not even remotely a major defeat, and the Archduke Albrecht was quite expecting that the Italians would return to fight the next day and bring their superior numbers into play. But a chain of unfortunate events turned a minor reverse into a real catastrophe. Failure of the commanders to restore morale resulted in a panic and a complete dispersal of some units. This created an unwarranted impression on both Lamarmora and the king. By late afternoon the army was falling back over the Mincio, leaving hundreds of wounded behind on the field, and the bridge at Valeggio was then destroyed under a completely unjustified fear that the Austrians might be in pursuit.[2] Exaggerated reports of this retreat then reached Cialdini, who waited a further day for more explicit information, and then took the decision that his troops should not cross the Po but would fall back towards Modena. News of Cialdini's movement persuaded the king and Lamarmora to turn their own army's withdrawal into a full-scale retreat, because they feared that the whole of the Austrian forces would now be concentrated on an attack over the Mincio. A large army was thus routed by one less than half its size before most Italian divisions had been engaged. This happened despite the fact that the enemy were not even in pursuit and despite the fact that the Austrians had suffered far more casualties.[3]

How such a disaster can have been allowed to occur has been a considerable puzzle. The main characters in the drama were inevitably confused at the time, and later tried too hard to justify their own conduct for the true facts to emerge with clarity. Some of the relevant details are still uncertain. The official war-office history, written largely by Colonel Corsi in 1868–9, had its publication delayed, partly it seems because Cialdini made difficulties about what it said, but in part, almost certainly, so that the king's share of responsibility should not be exposed. The first volume came out only in 1875, long after the Austrian and Prussian histories of the campaign, the second volume not until 1895; two further volumes by Colonel Cavaciocchi were

---

[1] *Complemento*, I. 48, 51–3; ibid. II. 30; Giglio, *Il Risorgimento nelle sue Fasi di Guerra*, II. 362.
[2] *La Campagna del 1866 nei Documenti Militari Austriaci*, ed. A. Filipuzzi (Padua, 1966), pp. 156, 161, 175; *Lettere del Generale Pianell e Ricordi Familiari* (Naples, 1901), p. 334.
[3] *Nuova Antologia*, Jan. 1902, p. 307; ibid., June 1966, pp. 180–1; the falsification of history soon turned Custoza into 'one of the most bloody battles in all modern history' (P. Porro, *Note sulla Storia d'Italia*(Milan, 1885), VI. 543).

later put out in 1909, though they too were far from being entirely satisfactory or free of political motivation.[1]

Lamarmora had protested against this delay in publication which he regarded as designed to off-load the main responsibility on to himself. At one point he began to publish his own self-defence, and did so with considerable discretion, yet a second volume with his account of events after 17 June was forbidden publication by the king.[2] Later independent histories by Generals Pollio, Del Bono, and Calza were to agree with different degrees of emphasis in chiefly blaming Lamarmora's carelessness on the 24th, and also in blaming Cialdini for his repeated disobedience and especially his refusal to hold the line of the Po. But none of these historians, and indeed only Chiala in his spirited but still heavily expurgated defence of Lamarmora, so much as hinted that the crown might also be implicated. Any private comments on the subject by the main participants in the campaign were all guarded and inexplicit, while the pamphlet war which broke out between the generals after 1866 took care not to mention the king's involvement. The documents quoted in the important memoirs of General Di Revel cannot be relied upon for accuracy where they concern Victor Emanuel.[3]

Yet to some outside observers it was fairly obvious that the fundamental mistake was the king's refusal, after he had turned down the initial advice of Lamarmora, Cialdini, and Petitti, to make clear who was in command.[4] One important result of the confusion of authority was that Cialdini heard about the reverse on the Mincio in two telegrams which came from the king and which Lamarmora did not see. It was these telegrams which turned a withdrawal into a retreat. The first of them, sent at 16.30 on the 24th from Cerlungo, said that the battle was still uncertain but the Archduke's entire force was fighting on the Mincio, and Cialdini was told to cross the Po 'at once' so as to relieve the pressure. Cialdini replied that at such a late stage he could not risk altering a quite complicated manœuvre which was now synchronized to take place at three different locations on the Po. The king's second telegram was sent at 22.20 and was more alarming, for it reported that his army had given way and was retreating 'horribly tired' and with 'immense losses', though the king was hoping to resume the offensive when his men had been rested.

Whether or not Cialdini could, without inviting disaster, have suddenly changed his plans and bridged the Po at once is open to argument, but the general state of training and of communications suggests that the result would have been chaotic. Cialdini thought he had been given ample authority

---

[1] Luigi Cadorna, *Il Generale Raffaele Cadorna nel Risorgimento Italiano* (Cernusco, 1945), pp. 217–18; Sandonnini, *In Memoria di Cialdini*, p. 96.

[2] S. Jacini, *Un Conservatore Rurale nella Nuova Italia* (Bari, 1926), II. 78.

[3] Compare the same document quoted in Di Revel's *Sette Mesi al Ministero*, p. 8, and in his *La Cessione del Veneto: Ricordi di un Commissario Regio Militare* (Milan, 1890), p. 13.

[4] *Le Général Lamarmora et l'Alliance Prussienne* (Paris, 1868) p. 191.

to act as he saw fit. He also had to assume that the whole of the Austrian forces might soon be waiting for him on the north bank, and this would make the crossing of such a wide river impossible, since his whole plan had pre-supposed that the enemy would be drawn away to the Mincio. As he saw events on the 25th, the 'disaster' on the Mincio altered everything, and there would be positive danger in any further advance. The news of a major battle, instead of the mere demonstration on the Mincio which he had expected, led him to think that Lamarmora and the king had been acting against the spirit of their agreement and, out of jealousy, had been trying to gain for themselves the honours of war: this astonishing supposition cannot have helped mutual confidence.[1]

A third telegram to Cialdini was quoted by German sources. They alleged that it told him of 'an irreparable disaster', as a result of which his army should fall back to 'cover the capital'.[2] This not very plausible telegram was attributed to Lamarmora and was used to pin the main responsibility for the retreat on him, but he denied writing it, and Cialdini later confirmed that he had not heard from Lamarmora on the 24th.[3] The text of no such telegram was found in the archives when search was made in 1909. One officer who claimed to have seen the text said that it was not from Lamarmora but from the royal headquarters, and that it had been destroyed after the war by one of the king's friends.[4] Possibly the king may have been referring to such a telegram when, ten days after the battle, he told the Prussian military attaché that a 'traitorous rumour' had caused Cialdini's withdrawal: but von Bernhardi noted privately that there was no need to hypothesize any rumour, since the king's own published report about the battle would have been quite enough by itself to cause Cialdini to change his plans and retreat.[5]

Assuming that no such third telegram was sent, it is important to note that this view of von Bernhardi's was confirmed by others. General Petitti, for example, agreed that it was the king's momentary alarm, when he witnessed the disorderly flight of groups of soldiers over the Mincio, which led to the telegrams being sent from his private headquarters; these in turn caused Cialdini to pause, and set in train the events by which a minor reverse became a major defeat.[6] Although the king's alarm was fully understandable, Lamarmora was wiser than his sovereign when he waited until he could tell Cialdini something more than a panic account of what was happening. What is particularly strange is that, before sending these telegrams, the king's headquarters at Cerlungo had not first checked them with the chief of staff. Lamarmora was in fact only two kilometres away at 15.00, and this fact was

[1] *Carteggi Ricasoli*, XXII. 105.
[2] W. Rüstow, *Der Krieg von 1866 in Deutschland und Italien* (Zürich, 1866), p. 149; *L'Opinione* (Turin), 17 Dec. 1866, p. 3.
[3] Chiala, *Ancora un po' di Luce*, p. 595.   [4] *Complemento*, I. 71.
[5] *Aus dem Leben Bernhardis*, VII. 132-3.
[6] Chiala, *Ancora un po' di Luce*, pp. 415-16, 597.

known at Cerlungo; moreover messengers passed with ease from one head-quarters to another in the next two hours.[1]

Indisputably it was the king's report of the battle, unknown to Lamarmora, that made Cialdini change his plans. Not only would Cialdini not cross the Po, but early in the morning of the 25th he began to withdraw from the river towards Ferrara. In the afternoon of the 25th, still having heard no more from the main army, he called his generals together and put before them his own view that a full withdrawal from the Po would be necessary unless Lamarmora sent more hopeful information before nightfall. He then waited several hours before confirmatory news of the battle came from Lamarmora in a telegram which arrived about 19.00. Cialdini later stated that he assumed that this telegram had been dispatched that same afternoon,[2] though in fact it had been sent during the previous night and almost certainly while Lamarmora was asleep.[3] When the message reported 'condition of the army deplorable', this represented the situation as some people had seen it the previous evening; but it now confirmed Cialdini in his decision to fall back.

If only Cialdini had known, by the afternoon of the 25th the main army had been able to recover some of its poise and recognize that, since the Austrians were not in pursuit, the defeat of Custoza had not been serious. The king was one of the first to realize this. Even in the afternoon of the 24th, after his unnecessarily alarmist telegram, a report by one of his aides has been quoted as evidence that the king hoped to give the Austrians a trouncing the next day. This one phrase was interpreted by the official historians of the campaign into proof that the king alone saw the situation correctly and he alone was determined not to retreat. From the context, however, it is likely he was not referring to the Austrians at all, but to the flood of Italian fugitive soldiers who were blocking the roads; and, if he was speaking of the enemy, it cannot have been a considered remark about a serious practical possibility, but could only have been intended to raise morale at a moment when some units were disintegrating.[4] The king's own later statements on the point are contradictory, a fact which no doubt reflects the general confusion. At one moment he said he had been opposed to any withdrawal;[5] at another he accepted a retreat as essential,[6] and subsequently he recalled the perfectly good logistic reasons which had compelled him to fall back.[7] Victor Emanuel's lack of defeatism must surely have helped the army to recover some of its combativeness, but

[1] *Complemento*, I. 55–7.
[2] *Risposta all'Opuscolo 'Il Generale Lamarmora e la Campagna del 1866'* (Bologna, 1868), pp. 16–17; *La Campagna del 1866*, ed. Corpo Stato Maggiore (Rome, 1895), II. 7.
[3] *Complemento*, II. 70–1; ibid. I. 67.
[4] Dal Verme, *Nuova Antologia*, Jan. 1902, pp. 289–91, 307–8, where it seems, at least to judge from the reference to Chiala, that the important testimony of Captain Sforza Cesarini must have been not from a contemporary diary but from later recollection; A. Cavaciocchi, 'Dopo Custoza', *Nuova Antologia*, Jan. 1910, p. 152; *Complemento*, I. 81.
[5] Ibid. 80.   [6] Ibid. 74.
[7] *Campagna del 1866 nei Documenti Austriaci*, ed. Filipuzzi, pp. 408–9.

this was far outweighed by his characteristic indecision. There is no convincing evidence that he had any practical alternative strategy to suggest, nor that he disagreed when Lamarmora and Della Rocca wanted to retreat.

At some time after 16.00 on the 25th, when General Govone had pointed out that the Austrians were not following but were actually destroying the remaining bridges over the Mincio, Lamarmora momentarily changed his mind and decided to forget any idea of further retreat. So long as Cialdini remained on the Po, the two armies could still threaten the archduke with a pincers movement.[1] At much the same time, however, Cialdini had made his own independent decision to fall back, basing himself on what he did not know to be out-of-date information. At 19.00, Cialdini received yet another telegram from the king, this one arriving after only a seven-hour delay. It warned him that Albrecht would be moving the main Austrian forces from the Mincio to the Po, and added that Cialdini's army would now be advised to wait a day before crossing the Po.

By the time this arrived, however, the king had decided definitely to fall back and give up all idea of retrieving the setback of Custoza. At 18.30 on the 25th a fourth telegram was dispatched to Cialdini from royal headquarters which makes nonsense of the supposition that the king opposed the idea of retreat. It confirmed that the Mincio line would be untenable, and the king was going to fall back for over 40 kilometres so that he could form a new base on the far side of the river Oglio. This would enable him eventually to transfer his troops to the Po where he would join Cialdini, but he explained that the operation would take at least a week, and he was hoping that Cialdini would be able to hold a bridgehead north of the Po until reinforcements could arrive in a week or more's time.[2] In Cialdini's view, such a plan for a bridgehead was utterly unrealistic. There could be no chance of crossing the Po if the king gave up the idea of a simultaneous diversion on the Mincio; had it been otherwise, the whole plan of campaign would have been easier from the start. In any case the message arrived too late to alter his decision.

The official history of the campaign agrees with the king and Lamarmora in thinking that Cialdini should have disregarded the news from the Mincio and continued with his attack. This conclusion is based in part on an improbable and much later story that Cialdini once told someone he wished that he had done so; though his close friends never heard him say anything of the kind, and, if the story has any truth, he can only have expressed the general wish that it had been possible to synchronize a pincers movement by the two Italian armies. General Pollio, who also criticizes Cialdini's unwillingness to cross the river, used the king's order and Cialdini's refusal as proof that Victor Emanuel's strategic instinct was much better than that of his generals. Pollio

---

[1] *Campagna del 1866*, II. 11–12; *Complemento*, II. 70–1.

[2] *Complemento*, I. 74; though, despite the evidence of this document, on p. 81 the editors continue to assert that the king was firmly against any retreat.

adds that it was a pity the king did not insist on his own view and give up playing the constitutional sovereign: but Pollio elsewhere directly controverted his own argument by stating that the whole plan for attacking over the marshlands of the Po delta was misconceived and would have led to certain disaster.[1]

More easily criticizable was Cialdini's decision that he would withdraw altogether from the Po and fall back on Ferrara and Modena. News of Lamarmora's retreat might have justified him in not crossing the river, but hardly in falling back; and it was his withdrawal which removed a threat to the Austrians and so contributed to turning a reverse into a rout. His own force was as strong as the whole Austrian army, and his continued presence on the Po would have constituted a menace which would have given Lamarmora time to regroup and launch another attack. Only the false news of a 'disaster' on the Mincio could begin to justify his unfortunate decision to fall back.

However it is judged, Custoza indicates that, as well as a failure in communications, as well as a sheer lack of ability among the commanders, there was also a dangerous misunderstanding over the location of command, and this because the residual powers of the crown could not be either discussed or precisely defined. When the king told Cialdini on the 24th to cross the Po at once, this apparently did not need validation by his chief of staff, yet Lamarmora later referred to it as being a formal order.[2] Cialdini, on the other hand, claimed that the king was merely a nominal commander and any formal orders would come from Lamarmora.[3] Della Rocca, who dutifully took his views from Victor Emanuel, did not think of the sovereign as just a nominal commander,[4] and this would support Lamarmora's interpretation. Lamarmora never once issued Cialdini with any precise instruction, though the king from his neighbouring headquarters did so. As Cialdini pointed out, relying on merely verbal agreements without written orders could easily lead to this kind of difficulty.

Forty years later the official history failed to unravel the confusion in its attempt to defend Victor Emanuel's reputation. While it was at pains to exculpate the king on the grounds that Lamarmora had an unfettered command, it simultaneously and inconsistently blamed Lamarmora for not staying at the king's headquarters in order to transmit the royal orders. It used the strange phrase that the king during this campaign 'almost always' kept within the bounds of his constitutional authority.[5] The confusion was compounded when it maintained that news of Cialdini's retreat on the 25th *caused* Victor Emanuel to fall back from the Mincio; though its own documents show that

---

[1] Pollio, *Custoza*, pp. 27, 275, 280, 288; Moneta, *Custoza e Lissa*, p. 158, agrees that the order to cross the Po was an absurdity.
[2] Luzio, *Profili Biografici*, II. 307.
[3] *Risposta del Generale Cialdini all'Opuscolo*, pp. 8, 35-7.
[4] *Complemento*, II. 214.   [5] Ibid. I. 81-2.

this retreat from the Mincio had been ordered before Cialdini had taken any decision. News of Cialdini's withdrawal reached Lamarmora's headquarters only on the morning of the 26th, and it came to him as a shock to discover that the king's two alarmist telegrams on the 24th, neither of which he had seen, had set off this sad sequence of events.[1] He urgently 'begged' Cialdini to stay on the Po so as to give the main army time to get a better position, but his telegram arrived only when Cialdini had already moved back.[2]

Mutual recrimination began at once. According to Di Revel, the king complained bitterly of all his generals, especially of Lamarmora, and also, for some reason, of the prime minister. But Di Revel, guarded though he was, had to admit that 'the king makes operations very difficult by his inopportune interference'.[3] General Govone heard Victor Emanuel deplore that political considerations prevented him from commanding his own army, and Govone, who was a man of good judgement, thought that the king showed more sense and a better grasp of the situation than Lamarmora did.[4] On the other hand, Lamarmora wanted the monarch to leave the army in order to permit a properly unified command. Victor Emanuel refused to do this and complained to Petitti that it would damage his prestige; but Petitti, who as adjutant general was in a position to know, agreed here with Lamarmora and Di Revel, and was brave enough to tell the king that his presence was responsible for the prevalent 'anarchy' in the higher command. According to Petitti the king had never intended to let anyone else possess effective power and so diminish royal prestige. Lamarmora later recalled that his own advice had been more readily listened to in 1848 as a colonel than it was in 1866 as the senior general. As chief of staff in 1866, he had been 'in a more or less subordinate position'. When he realized that Victor Emanuel and Cialdini intended to continue acting on their own initiative without allowing the chief of staff an over-all co-ordinating authority, he decided to resign so that the king could find an alternative way of creating a unity of command.[5]

All his life long, Lamarmora was angry at being made the sole scapegoat for Custoza, but his only effective self-defence would have meant publicly criticizing the king. Being the man he was, he went out of his way not to involve the crown. Petitti and Di Revel, neither of whom had the slightest *parti pris* against the monarchy, both thought that Lamarmora had a genuine grievance. So did another good monarchist, General Bixio, who poured scorn on Lamarmora's generalship, but also saw the grave danger that, in self-defence, he might be tempted to expose the king's part in the whole sorry affair. Bixio and Cialdini agreed with Lamarmora that Victor Emanuel should

[1] *Carteggi Ricasoli*, XXII. 97.

[2] *Schiarimenti e Rettifiche*, p. 22; *Risposta del Generale Cialdini all'Opuscolo*, p. 29.

[3] Di Revel, *Sette Mesi al Ministero*, p. 13; Di Revel, *Cessione del Veneto*, p. 13.

[4] Govone, *Generale Govone*, pp. 265, 269.

[5] É. Ollivier, *L'Empire Libéral* (Paris, 1903), VIII. 509; Chiala, *Ancora un po' di Luce*, pp. x, 570, 598, 628.

leave the front and return to Florence.[1] Cialdini wrote privately to Lamarmora on the 26th that the king's separate headquarters was the main obstacle they had to contend with. What was worse, Victor Emanuel

understands absolutely nothing at all of what is going on, and this may yet be our ruin. . . . After what has happened you must surely agree now with what I told you repeatedly, that without unity of command we shall get nowhere. The king is wholly ignorant and incompetent. He should have stayed at home like Franz Joseph instead of taking up a command whose duties he cannot seriously discharge. You alone are in a position to tell him so, and I cannot think how he will react. It would have been a thousand times less humiliating if he had recognized this himself without having to be told.[2]

Unfortunately it was too late, for to go back to Florence would now have been an open acknowledgement of his own partial responsibility for the defeat. Moreover, Victor Emanuel knew that the king of Prussia held the title of supreme commander and Moltke was only chief of staff; he could not bear to think that people might be making unfavourable comparisons between him and Wilhelm. Yet, as Émile Ollivier was to explain, Wilhelm was an altogether more serious soldier, much less of a boaster, who above all did not fear to accept good advice; whereas Victor Emanuel was

an incorrigible braggart . . . who thought that there was nothing more to the art of war than courage, of which he had more than anyone. . . . He conceived himself to be a great captain and would allow no one to doubt the fact. What really worried him was that people would attribute to his chief of staff the glory which he wanted all for himself.[3]

This opinion was more or less shared by Napoleon III, who in 1859 had been well placed to judge, and who laughingly commented in June 1866 that Victor Emanuel would never understand the first thing about war.[4]

The supreme test was whether he could lead the Italian forces and inspire them to recover from their reverse at Custoza. That depended in the first instance on achieving an exact understanding of what had happened and of how any deficiencies could be remedied, but this he was simply unable to do. As soon as he realized that his telegrams to Cialdini had had such a bad effect, he tried to correct them by going too far to the other extreme and announcing that Custoza had after all not been a defeat: his somewhat boastful communiqué in this sense received unfortunate publicity, and it compared badly with the Archduke Albrecht's more sober report.[5] Austrian troops were

---

[1] *Epistolario di Bixio*, III. 67, 73, 109.   [2] Luzio, *Profili Biografici*, II. 307.
[3] Ollivier, *Empire Libéral*, VIII. 252, 254; the king was certainly copying Wilhelm, though he was very sensitive lest people should think so (A. Luzio, *Aspromonte e Mentana* (Florence, 1935), p. 430).
[4] Oncken, *Rheinpolitik Napoleons*, I. 285.   [5] *Carteggi Ricasoli*, XXII. 76, 100.

occupying part of Lombardy. Three Italian army corps had retreated well into Lombardy across the river Oglio, and the king's headquarters between 26 June and 11 July was at Cicognolo which was 50 kilometres west of the Mincio; yet despite this he reached the point of announcing that he had placed the Austrians in a very difficult position; in 'a few days' he would take Trieste and move on Vienna.[1] Such confidence helped to prevent the commander-in-chief seeing that there was any serious problem still to be solved, and the result over the next few weeks was to be a disaster far worse than Custoza.

Victor Emanuel at first made some attempt to assert himself. After categorically refusing to withdraw from military affairs as his senior generals advised, at some point on the 25th or 26th he further decided to by-pass Lamarmora and claim a more effective authority as supreme commander. This intention, in view of the recent battle, might have been more than justifiable if done openly, wholeheartedly, and after discussion; but that would have been against his nature. He even proposed to by-pass the prime minister, and sent a private message to Rattazzi asking this opposition leader to come to advise him. Possibly he had in mind to appoint Rattazzi to Ricasoli's office. Rattazzi, however, did not want to be placed in a false position in defiance of parliament, and found an excuse not to come.[2]

Against Rattazzi's opinion, and apparently without consulting the prime minister, the king decided to accept Lamarmora's resignation and appoint a new chief of staff. His first choice was Della Rocca,[3] the corps commander whose inaction and inability had contributed as much as anything to making Custoza a defeat. Only when Della Rocca refused did he ask Cialdini instead. This second invitation, which was a request and not an order, he gave at a secret meeting with Cialdini which was intended to be without Lamarmora's knowledge, but the latter heard of it from Cialdini, and commented that the king was typically trying to play them off against each other.

Petitti agreed with Lamarmora that the royal proposal, even though both of them thought Cialdini the right choice, would retain precisely the same weakness as before, just because Victor Emanuel still intended to stay at headquarters as at least nominal overlord; and Lamarmora insisted that 'it is impossible to command an army with a monarch at one's side who will neither take decisions himself nor let others take decisions either'.[4] Cialdini, when he realized the king's intention, replied that Lamarmora was the only general under whom everyone was ready to serve. He complained that Victor Emanuel was in a psychological condition where he would not give the kind of firm orders which would compel obedience. Cialdini ended by saying that he would take the job, but only if Victor Emanuel left the front altogether.[5] The king

[1] *Lettere di V. Emanuele*, II. 915; *Il Problema Veneto e l'Europa, 1859–1866*, vol. I, ed. R. Blaas (Venice, 1966), p. 871; *Revue des Deux Mondes* (Paris), May 1925, p. 96.
[2] Mme Rattazzi, *Rattazzi et son Temps*, II. 119–21. [3] *Complemento*, II. 206.
[4] Ibid. I. 79; *Carteggi Ricasoli*, XXII. 85, 97; Chiala, *Ancora un po' di Luce*, p. 344.
[5] Ibid., p. 351; Di Revel, *Sette Mesi al Ministero*, p. 13.

absolutely refused to leave and changed back to thinking that Lamarmora, a more obedient man, should remain in office. Here was an absurd situation. Cialdini was recommending Lamarmora whom he well knew to be a bad general and whose demoralization was now obvious to all; Lamarmora persisted in recommending Cialdini whom he knew to be insubordinate; the king was evidently ready to accept either, even though blaming both for leading the army to defeat. His final choice of Lamarmora suggests that the prestige of the throne was more important to him than winning the war.

Ricasoli at this point arrived at royal headquarters. He had been prime minister for barely a week, and was only beginning to see that Italy's high hopes had been frustrated because of fundamental weaknesses in the higher command. At first he was sure that Lamarmora should be superseded, but three desultory days of talks convinced him that the answer was not so simple. He agreed that, of all the generals in the army, only Cialdini and Lamarmora had the authority to act as chief of staff, but both of them now wanted Victor Emanuel out of the way. While discussions proceeded, the army did nothing, because it lacked a commander, and this was something which the Prussians found hard to forgive. Rumours now began to circulate that the king had prearranged with France that Italy would not fight too hard.[1] Only on 3 July was the situation somewhat clarified. Since Cialdini had refused to take over except on evidently impossible terms, and since he refused to take orders from anyone else except Lamarmora, things would have to remain as they were. Ricasoli told his brother that Lamarmora would continue as before, with one slight change:

The king has promised to abstain from any interference in military operations and to leave his generals full liberty of action, provided only that they keep up appearances as far as he is concerned and allow the army and the nation to go on thinking that the monarch is still in charge, because when a king of Prussia is in command of his army, a king of Italy can be no less.[2]

This was ten days after Custoza, during which period vital time had been lost. Tempers had also been roused. The king was deeply upset at being criticized. He knew that people were expecting him to impose a solution, yet he lacked the imagination and self-confidence to know the answer and enforce it. He did not approve of interference from civilians in military affairs, especially from the prime minister. There was further annoyance in some quarters when Ricasoli brought up once again the provocative suggestion that Garibaldi was being insufficiently used. Lamarmora, while he welcomed that a decision had at last been taken, would have preferred the choice to fall on someone else than himself: everyone had made it clear that they had little confidence in him, and yet, because of miscellaneous private jealousies and

[1] A. Verona, *La Guerra d'Italia del 1866* (Como, 1867), p. 45.
[2] *Carteggi Ricasoli*, XXII. 130; *Campagna del 1866*, II. 52–3; *Complemento*, II. 82–3.

the king's determination to remain generalissimo, he had to stay in a position for which he had lost the required self-assurance.

On 3 July, and still before the Italian forces had given any serious sign of life, the whole shape of the war suddenly changed when the Prussians soundly defeated the Austrians at Königgrätz and the way was opened to Vienna. The Austrians reacted by withdrawing most of their forces from Italy, a move which looked to Victor Emanuel as almost deliberately contemptuous of the Italian army. Bismarck positively demanded that the king should impede the Austrian retreat and launch an immediate attack: if the Italians let the Austrians leave Italy, so he unambiguously added, Prussia might be forced to make a peace which would give Italy less than she wanted. Italy was a country with a larger population than Prussia, yet had let her ally take on the great bulk of the Austrian army; Victor Emanuel had entered the war late and not without arousing some suspicion that he had arranged in advance not to fight seriously; his chosen strategy against the Quadrilateral seemed designed to let Prussia do all the work; and then, with immensely superior forces, he had remained completely inactive after the unimportant and indecisive battle of Custoza. This inactivity, said Bismarck, could only be explained by the fact that Austria had secretly promised before the war to cede Venice. The king had obviously been playing a thoroughly dishonourable game.[1]

The Prussian demands for an attack were awkward enough, but on 4 July Napoleon intervened and put a very different but equally unwelcome pressure on Italy to bring the war to an end. French interests demanded that Napoleon should try to save Austria from a thorough defeat which might upset the balance of power. This came as an immense blow to Victor Emanuel, who was suddenly faced with the prospect of an unsatisfactory peace after an unsatisfactory war: the French proposed that he should get Venice, but only as a humiliating concession, as a gift from Austria to France and then from France to Italy, just as Lombardy had been given to Piedmont in 1859; he would be prevented from winning Trent and Trieste on which he had set his heart; and his army would have suffered a defeat for which the monarchy itself could hardly escape all responsibility. Both his allies, France and Prussia, were threatening to humiliate him further if he did not obey their presumptuous and mutually contradictory behests, and yet to submit to either demand would be in itself one more public humiliation.[2]

Nearly six weeks were still left between 4 July and the end of the war, during which a military success might have altered this depressing picture. But, despite Ricasoli's compromise, even now there was no one person in

---

[1] *Bismarck: Die Gesammelten Werke,* vol. V, ed. F. Thimme (Berlin, 1928), p. 549; ibid. VI. 34, 50; *Aus dem Leben Bernhardis,* VII. 164; *Lamarmora et l'Alliance Prussienne,* p. 188.

[2] Oncken, *Rheinpolitik Napoleons,* I. 317, 327; G. Del Bono, *Come Arrivammo a Custoza e come ne Ritornammo* (Milan, 1935), p. 170.

complete control, nor was this essential question of the higher command further clarified during the weeks that followed. As early as 1 July, Lamarmora, supported by Govone, had hoped to attack on the Mincio, but Cialdini had been allowed to veto this move. Evidently Cialdini had agreed to Lamarmora's reappointment only on the private understanding that he himself, though junior as a general, should once again have a virtually independent command of his own, and he wanted no competition from the other Italian army on the Mincio.[1] Nor did the king or Lamarmora feel confident enough to resist him. Cialdini at last began his own attack on 5 July by assaulting Borgoforte on the river Po: he had calculated that this small fortress would fall in a few hours, but he had omitted to check on the map some elementary facts about its position, and the fort held out for two weeks.[2] At Cialdini's special request, Lamarmora meanwhile kept his own forces waiting on the west side of the river Oglio where they had fallen back after Custoza. Not even the news of Napoleon's ultimatum stirred them from their lethargy. General Cucchiari sent a shocked note over the heads of his superiors to Ricasoli, in which he complained of the contemptible incompetence and pusillanimity which allowed this to happen even though four-fifths of the Italian forces had still not come under fire. The Austrians found it quite incomprehensible.[3]

The division of authority in the army was made worse by a political difference between the king and his civilian ministers. This, too, was directly due to the fact that the king insisted on staying with the army rather than in Florence. While cabinet ministers at Florence could clearly see the political reasons for pushing the attack as hard as possible and occupying the Veneto and the Trentino, Victor Emanuel feared this might offend the French. Once again his private communications with Paris resulted in a dual foreign policy with all its weaknesses and uncertainty. His lack of combativeness and his submission to Napoleon's patronizing commands antagonized Bismarck and were a threat to the prestige of the monarchy itself.[4]

The cabinet's contrary view was eventually accepted on 14 July. Not until the night of 11–12 July had Victor Emanuel moved his headquarters from Cicognolo to Ferrara, and at Ferrara on the 14th he presided over a meeting of all the leading generals and politicians. It was agreed as a matter of urgency that Italy could not afford the war to end before obtaining one military success. Cialdini was therefore given an even stronger independent command, this time of fourteen divisions or 150,000 men, with the aim of occupying the Veneto and reaching the river Isonzo before peace was made. The king

---

[1] *Schiarimenti e Rettifiche*, p. 43; Chiala, *Ancora un po' di Luce*, pp. 350, 355, 401; Govone, *Generale Govone*, p. 282.

[2] *Risposta alla 2ᵃ Parte dell'Opuscolo 'Il Generale Lamarmora e la Campagna del 1866'*, p. 35; *Ricordi di Castelli*, pp. 359, 361; Cialdini's responsibility for the delay is argued in *Risposta all'Opuscolo di Bologna e alla Lettera del Generale Sirtori* (2nd ed., Florence, 1868), pp. 110–12, 120–3.

[3] A. Hold, *Geschichte des Feldzuges 1866 in Italien mit Benützung autentischer Quellen* (Vienna, 1867), p. 189; *Carteggi Ricasoli*, XXII. 267–8.   [4] Ibid. 207–8– *Carteggio Castelli*, II. 141.

would remain in the rear as commander of the remaining six regular divisions, with Lamarmora in the still ambiguous position of his chief of staff, while Garibaldi's volunteers, it was hoped, would proceed to occupy the Trentino. Lamarmora continued to hold his post for another month, but complained that he was now allowed to know little of what was going on.[1] Victor Emanuel continued to speak in uncomplimentary terms about Cialdini, Ricasoli, and Lamarmora. Though his authority had been shaken, he had certainly not altered his intention of achieving some military glory for himself, and was determined to follow closely on Cialdini's heels so that he could appear dramatically on the scene whenever battle was joined.[2]

One other decision taken at Ferrara was to order Admiral Persano into action to defeat the Austrian fleet and support Cialdini's advance. Until this moment the navy had not been mentioned in any of the king's dispatches; it had simply been forgotten. No naval officer was on the planning staff at head-quarters. Indeed never in his life does Victor Emanuel appear to have had a naval officer among his personal aides. The superiority of the Italian fleet had simply been taken for granted, since it possessed a great superiority in size and fire power. There had even been an assumption in some quarters, at all events by Cavour, that since the Austrian navy was mostly manned by Italians they would refuse to fight against their compatriots.[3]

Persano's competence to command the navy had been questioned by many people: somewhat late in the day the government thought of appointing Galli della Mantica instead, but they had lost his address.[4] So Persano was the man on whom the country depended to obliterate the memory of Custoza. A month earlier he had been ordered to attack and destroy the Austrian fleet wherever it was to be found; he had reported in reply that the fleet was ready to move and that the order to attack would be carried out 'to the letter', but then had done nothing.[5] Even several weeks later when the Austrian admiral sailed up to the roadstead of Ancona, where the much larger Italian fleet was established, Persano failed to engage. Again on 5 July he had been ordered to attack at once and not stop short of victory, yet he continued to avoid the enemy in a way which completely justified Bismarck's worst suspicions. At Ferrara on 14 July, Persano's relegation was finally discussed, but the remarka-able decision was taken just to threaten him with dismissal if he did not at once take some offensive action.

The battle of Lissa bore an uncomfortable resemblance to Custoza. In both the Italians with greatly superior forces were beaten. The naval commanders, like the generals, were notoriously jealous of each other, and there was a complete lack of confidence in Persano. He had prepared no strategic plan,

---

[1] *Complemento*, I. 86; ibid. II. 82, 84–5.
[2] Pettinengo's diary, ed. A. Colombo, *Atti del X Congresso della Società Nazionale per la Storia del Risorgimento Italiano: Trieste, 1922* (Aquila, 1923), p. 55.
[3] *Preussens Auswärtige Politik 1850 bis 1858*, ed. H. von Poschinger (Berlin, 1902), III. 389.
[4] *Complemento*, II. 78.   [5] Guerrini, *Come Arrivammo a Lissa*, vol. II (1908), pp. 87, 89.

despite the fact that the navy had been waiting years for this war to begin. Only after 14 July did he decide to attack Lissa. This was an island only some 130 kilometres from the Italian coast, and he well knew it to be the key to the Austrian defences in the Adriatic, yet he had not attempted until now to find out essential topographical details, nor even now did he consult sailors in his fleet who knew the island well. Only after the threat of dismissal did he on 15 July at last ask the admiralty for a map. Cavour had once procured maps and details of the fortifications at Lissa, but nothing could now be found in the archives, and Persano accordingly embarked on this expedition with minimal preparations.[1] Worse still, he then allowed himself to be caught by the enemy before his plan of battle was ready, much as Lamarmora had done. At the last moment he unexpectedly changed his flagship, and his orders therefore went largely unobserved, with the result that he never at any moment succeeded in imposing any direction on the conflict. After a short engagement on 20 July, he broke off the fight when he still had a heavy superiority in numbers and while many units of his navy had not yet come under fire.

The news of Lissa shocked everyone. To some extent it involved the crown, because Victor Emanuel was thought to be Persano's protector.[2] Without a naval victory, any advance of the army towards Venice and Trieste was hampered. Three times in ten days did Cialdini again send his resignation. He still refused to obey orders but complained that the king and Lamarmora were interfering with his 'independent' command, for example when they asked him to send some of his troops to assist Garibaldi's campaign in the Trentino. If only Garibaldi had earlier been given enough men and equipment, Trent would have been captured by now; or alternatively Cialdini, if his advance had been adequately supported, might have reached Trieste and the Isonzo; but the king wanted both objectives simultaneously, and also brought up a third projective for himself to assault Verona. At one point after Lissa he ordered Lamarmora to send half of Garibaldi's volunteers from the Trentino to land on the Dalmatian coast.[3] These were wild and contradictory last-minute improvisations. All of them came to nothing. Not only did he fail to impose any unity of direction on army movements, but he lacked the self-confidence to react against Cialdini's threats to resign. While refusing to exert full powers himself, he still refused to appoint anyone else as generalissimo, and hence he made victory less likely at the same time as he exposed the crown to bear yet more of the responsibility for defeat.

Meanwhile the Prussians sent a further demand that the Italians should 'make war seriously and not perfidiously', or at least should give some explana-

[1] *L'Ammiraglio C. Di Persano nella Campagna Navale dell'Anno 1866* (Turin, 1872), pp. 133, 135; G. Quarantotti, 'Prima di Lissa e Dopo', *Rassegna*, 1951, p. 600; Iachino, *Campagna di Lissa*, p. 316.
[2] *Carteggi Ricasoli*, XXII. 354–5.
[3] *Atti del X Congresso: Trieste*, 1922, p. 55.

tion why they had spent so long doing nothing.[1] The defeat of Lissa must have helped to decide Bismarck on 26 July to carry out his threat and accept an independent armistice, and soon heavy Austrian forces were returning from the German front back into Italy. The Italians affected outrage at Bismarck's 'treachery', but he had warned them what would happen if they did not fight more aggressively. They, too, were negotiating privately with the common enemy, though they managed to keep the fact secret: this was no time for the niceties of diplomatic usage, and Bismarck had good reason not to trust his ally too far.[2] Victor Emanuel spoke bravely but unrealistically of Italy continuing the war alone: better be beaten, he said, than be dishonoured by failing to reach Trent or Trieste and having to accept Venice as a present from France.[3] By 3 August, Cialdini's column had almost come to a stop; it had run out of provisions, the soldiers were in rags, and a hundred thousand pairs of boots were urgently required. Obviously the planning staff had never envisaged an offensive war. Moreover, without German support, even defence might now be impossible. Nevertheless, despite this great emergency, on 6 August Lamarmora had to complain to Ricasoli that unity of command was still lacking; Cialdini would have to be given supreme command as a matter of urgency.[4]

The fine hopes of many years were crumbling. Countless rhetorical speeches were being deflated as the reality of military weakness could no longer be hidden, and the fact that Italians had been allowed to think themselves invincible made this reality very bitter.[5] Politicians and generals were already blaming each other. In a private letter Ricasoli wrote that he had struggled to save the prestige of the crown but had failed, and he hinted that the king's responsibility for Custoza could not be concealed for ever.[6] There were ugly scenes when the king arrived on 5 August at Padua, as people suddenly realized that the Italians might possibly lose the war after all. Enthusiasm vanished, the flags disappeared, and at Udine the liberators were welcomed in glacial silence. This was not at all what the king had expected, but, as Lamarmora pointed out, his insistence on acting as commander had unnecessarily involved him in personal responsibility for a national humiliation.[7]

Victor Emanuel blamed everyone except himself. He blamed Ricasoli for meddling in strategy, for lack of respect, and for not treating the king as commander-in-chief.[8] To the Prussian representative he complained that Lamarmora had no brains, while Persano was a known incompetent and the king had accepted him as naval commander only because a constitutional

[1] *Aus dem Leben Bernhardis*, VII. 172–4.
[2] Ibid. 233; R. Lill, 'Beobachtungen zur Preussisch-Italienischen Allianz (1866)', *Quellen und Forschungen aus Italienischen Archiven* ((Tübingen), XLIV (1964), 506–7.
[3] *Ricordi di Castelli*, p. 371.   [4] Chiala, *Ancora un po' di Luce*, pp. 641–2.
[5] *Lamarmora et l'Alliance Prussienne*, p. 261; Guarnieri, *Otto Anni di Storia Militare*, p. 395.
[6] *Carteggi Ricasoli*, XXIII (1968), 99; Cadorna, *Generale Cadorna*, p. 253.
[7] Silva, *Il Sessantasei*, p. 311; *Lettere Ricasoli*, VIII. 274; *Complemento*, II. 105; *Rassegna*, 1919, p. 384.
[8] *Lettere di V. Emanuele*, II. 1034.

king's hands were tied. He also blamed Cialdini for ruining everything by disobeying orders and not crossing the Po after Custoza; yet this must have been merely to find a scapegoat, for it did not stop the king agreeing to make Cialdini effective commander of the army in August. The Germans too were blamed, for Bismarck was abandoning the war just when the king's troops were apparently poised for a great and decisive victory. Even if Prussia made peace, he nevertheless was sure that Italy would manage to win Trent and the Isonzo. He repudiated with bristling indignation Bismarck's brutal hint that he, the king, did not know how to fight. He had been a soldier for twenty years. The Germans had had more luck than the Italians. They had encountered an easy terrain. If Moltke had had to overcome the endless strategic difficulties that faced Victor Emanuel, it would have been a different story.[1]

Ricasoli and Cialdini wanted to go on fighting long after the war had lost all point and there was no possibility of victory. The king too, as late as 8 August, was saying that to make peace was quite out of the question, even though he was already evacuating his own family from Padua as the Austrians advanced. He and Ricasoli were slow to realize that, if they went on fighting, they would not only fail to get the Trentino and Istria, but the Austrians would certainly hold Venice, and that would be a blow from which Italy and the monarchy might not recover.[2] Their attitude, in other words, was the very height of irresponsibility. Lamarmora was the one person with the common sense and courage to admit that the war was over, a fact for which he was subsequently blamed by the nationalists. On his own responsibility he accepted a virtual Austrian ultimatum and ordered Garibaldi to withdraw from the Trentino. As he explained, it was better that he as a responsible minister should accept the odium attached to such a task: the king wept at Lamarmora's generosity, but, while he could not resist this logic, he evidently could not make up his own mind one way or the other, and perhaps he was at last glad to admit the usefulness of ministerial responsibility.[3]

By the terms of the peace settlement, Austria agreed to give Venice to France, who then handed it to Italy, and this unkind arrangement was palliated by a plebiscite which, in the presence of Italian troops, gave the customary 99·99 per cent affirmative majority. There was a great deal of rejoicing at these figures, but though only 69 negative votes were registered, under the surface there were politicians and journalists who found little of the enthusiasm that they had expected to find among politically-conscious Italians.[4] Victor Emanuel too was far from happy. The glory of battle and victory had eluded

---

[1] *Aus dem Leben Bernhardis*, VII. 178–9, 222–4.

[2] *Ricordi di Castelli*, pp. 373, 375; *Carteggi Castelli*, II. 129–30; Chiala, *Ancora un po' di Luce*, p. 639.

[3] G. Massari, *Il Generale Alfonso Lamarmora* (Florence, 1880), p. 365; Del Bono, *Come Arrivammo a Custoza*, pp. x, 233–4.

[4] S. Jacini, *Due Anni di Politica Italiana: Ricordi ed Impressioni* (Milan, 1868), p. 106; *Scritti di Garibaldi*, V. 335–6; *La Stella d'Italia: Nove Secoli di Casa Savoia* (Milan, 1879), VI. 761; G. Gorini, *Cronaca Mensile* (Milan), III (30 Nov. 1866), 287.

him. Only with reluctance did he participate in the celebrations to the extent that his ministers wanted. Ricasoli acidly noted that he liked to avoid giving out medals or reviewing his troops, but preferred to go off hunting; and on 7 November, when 100,000 people waited for him in the city of Venice, they saw less of him than was announced in the official reports.[1] The king grumbled that he alone had been always right, yet no one listened to him. He was amazed that Venice had been won despite the incompetence of his generals, despite Italians being so crazy.[2] He told an Austrian that Cialdini, if he had not been an old friend, would have been shot for refusing to cross the Po on 25 June. He was now convinced that not himself but Lamarmora must have sent those telegrams and ordered Cialdini's fatal retreat, and this legend was soon accepted.[3]

The myths were thus already being constructed which were to conceal the real reasons for successive failures in this war, and some historians were thus to find Italy's defeat quite inexplicable.[4] The initial conviction of infallibility, which had been the chief ingredient in those failures (as well as the chief reason for their catastrophic psychological effect), had if possible to be restored as a means of reviving self-confidence. Having found two convenient victims in Persano and Lamarmora, there were good reasons not to probe too much further and above all not to dim 'the epic grandeur of the king'.[5] Responsible politicians could already state that the battle of Custoza had greatly increased the prestige of the monarchy.[6] There was nothing wrong with the army, said the king, indeed it was 'the one good thing left in Italy'.[7] One monarchist historian, Gioacchino Volpe, persuaded himself that Lissa and Custoza had not been military defeats, while Antonio Monti succeeded in erecting Lissa into 'a great moral victory'. Already the legend was growing of an Italy which had made possible Moltke's success, which had then been cheated by Napoleon out of an easy victory and so deprived unjustly of her right to expand.[8]

Another and less dangerous myth grew up about Garibaldi. His volunteers

---

[1] *Carteggi di Ricasoli*, XXIII. 291, 365; ibid. XXIV (1970), 252, 283.

[2] Malaret to Drouyn de Lhuys, 17 Aug. 1866, M. Aff. Étrangères; *Nuova Antologia*, May 1961, p. 23.

[3] *La Campagna del 1866 nei Documenti Austriaci*, ed. Filipuzzi, pp. 408, 416; C. Belviglieri, *Storia d'Italia dal 1814 al 1866* (Milan, 1869), VI. 205; *Stella d'Italia*, VI. 721; Porro, *Note Sulla Storia*, VI. 575.

[4] F. Donaver, *Il Re Galantuomo* (Genoa, 1886), p. 114; F. Petruccelli della Gattina, *I Fattori e i Malfattori della Politica Europea Contemporanea* (Milan, 1881), I. 290.

[5] L. Pollini, *Il Padre della Patria* (Milan, 1942), p. 213; A. Lumbroso, *La Battaglia di Lissa nella Storia e nella Leggenda* (Rome, 1910), p. 29; Major C. Corsi, *Conferenze d'Arte Militare Tenute in Milano* (Milan, 1866-8), in 1159 pages of lectures to the staff college never once mentioned the king's part in this war as commander-in-chief.

[6] *Carteggi Ricasoli*, XXII. 182.

[7] F. Chabod, *Storia della Politica Estera Italiana: Le Premesse* (Bari, 1951), p. 683.

[8] Monti, *Vittorio Emanuele II* (Milan, 1941), p. 352; Pollini, *Padre della Patria*, p. 192; G. Volpe, *Il Risorgimento dell' Italia* (Rome, 1934), pp. 170, 172; G. Volpe, *Pagine Risorgimentali* (Rome, 1967), II. 217-18, where he imprudently asserts that 'almost all Italians' at the time thought that

were described by the king contemptuously as *canaille révolutionnaire*, and blamed for lack of fighting spirit. Garibaldi's victory at Bezzecca, and his famous telegram, 'Obbedisco', are among the few memorable achievements of the campaign, and his obedience under difficulties should have been a lesson to Cialdini and the regular army; but the king's hostile judgement of the volunteers was accepted by the very people who had deliberately given Garibaldi no time to prepare his campaign, who had left him unsupported and poorly armed, and who had then ordered him unwillingly to retreat when almost within sight of Trent.[1] It was important for the conservatives that the official version of events should remain the accepted story, and for the same reason a request by the Left to have a parliamentary inquiry into the campaign was decently buried in the same way as that on the war of 1848 had been.[2]

A few months later Victor Emanuel had recovered his good humour. He had accepted Cialdini's demand that never again would Lamarmora be given an active command in the army.[3] Already he was planning another war. This time he thought it should probably be in alliance with his late enemy. When he met the Austrian plenipotentiary to discuss the cession of the Veneto, he explained how he disliked both France and Prussia. Perhaps Austria would join him in fighting against Bismarck, in other words against the ally whose victory at Königgrätz had just won Venice for Italy. What the object of such a war would be was not said, and perhaps that did not matter much to the author of this scheme. How unsuccessful it might have been can be guessed. One paragraph of General Möring's report of this conversation may be quoted for what it reveals of the king's character. Victor Emanuel asked Möring to speak to Franz Joseph:

'Promise me you will personally tell him all I have said. Tell him that I will join him with 400,000 or 450,000 men against Prussia. To go against France would be more difficult, and for my part I would prefer the French to be on our side. Tell the emperor that he can count on my word of honour when I give it to him as a king and a soldier. The one thing which truly gives me pleasure is fighting wars. I do not like governing, and would rather leave that to my ministers. They are always coming to ask my advice and to make me take decisions. Whenever possible I run away from them and go hunting, for I love exercise in the open air. I ride a great deal. I always have a horse ready and saddled so that I can go off hunting. . . .'[4]

Dalmatia and Istria should have been ceded to Italy; *Il Generale Osio* (Milan, 1909), p. 128; S. Bortolotti, *La Guerra del 1866* (Milan, 1941), pp. 29, 31; F. Predari, *Storia Politica, Civile, Militare della Dinastia di Savoia* (Turin, 1869), II. 422; *Francesco Crispi: Ultimi Scritti e Discorsi Extra-Parlamentari (1891–1901)*, ed. T. Palamenghi-Crispi (Rome, n.d.), p. 281.
[1] A. Tamborra, 'La Guerra del 1866 in un Colloquio tra Vittorio Emanuele II e il Gen. Möhring', *Rassegna*, 1963, p. 94; *Complemento*, II. 41; C. Tivaroni, *L'Italia degli Italiani 1866–1870* (Turin, 1897), III. 33.
[2] The *Relazioni e Rapporti Finali sulla Campagna del 1848 nell'Alta Italia* was released for publication only in 1910.
[3] *Complemento*, II. 209.   [4] *Rassegna*, 1963, pp. 94–5.

To Napoleon the king sent word that he would like an alliance with France; he asked the French to put pressure on Franz Joseph to cede Italy the Trentino and to join in a war to stop Prussia dominating Europe. He threatened Prince Napoleon that if they did not help him he would join Bismarck and make things hard for France.[1]

It looked from this kind of talk as though Italy would soon be condemned to fighting another major European war. What could not yet be known was whether Victor Emanuel would pause long enough to learn anything at all from the painful lessons of 1866. His own failures had been just one among many causes of the defeats of this year, but there were powerful forces dedicated to denying that he carried any responsibility at all whenever things turned out badly. In the Italy of 1866 the king had a huge responsibility. By law, and by his own wish, he had to supervise foreign policy; he had to decide on peace and war; he had to choose the ministers and the leaders of the armed forces; he had, in time of war, to see that the whole machine worked effectively and, if possible, to inspire Italians as Garibaldi knew how to inspire them. In addition he insisted on acting as commander-in-chief and on not being bound to accept his ministers' advice. But so long as he was not prepared to accept the doctrine of ministerial responsibility, he could not both accept the glory of success and dissociate himself from the humiliation of failure. Victor Emanuel's best service to his country would have been to hold a thorough investigation into what had happened so that the machinery of government could be made to work better in future.

---

[1] E. d'Hauterive, 'La Mission du Prince Napoléon en Italie (1866): Lettres Inédites', *Revue des Deux Mondes*, May 1925, pp. 118–19.

15

Victor Emanuel and the Occupation of Rome

TOWARDS the end of 1866 Victor Emanuel suffered a slight stroke, though the fact was successfully concealed. Acquaintances had been noticing a tendency to corpulence, though they also noted that his intelligence remained quick and his conversation agreeable. No one had ever thought him a clever person, nor at any stage in his life did he read any books, but he could usually charm and impress when he took the trouble. Legend made him out to be a strong character with a capacity for firm decision, but the legend was wrong. Among his other failings, those who knew him well would admit that he was lazy and wilful; they knew that he concealed an inner timidity under an incorrigible braggadocio; they were aware that he was not always loyal to his friends and servants.[1] Nevertheless he possessed 'un excellent coeur'. When he went to the trouble to apply himself, whenever he listened to enough advice and took time for second or third thoughts, his judgement was sound.[2]

To preserve the prerogatives of the crown remained one of Victor Emanuel's persistent aims. Indeed the frustrating campaign of 1866 convinced him that the monarchy needed to cut not less but more of a figure in national and international politics. By September 1866 the prime minister had discovered that the king was contemplating the appointment of a more personal ministry under General Menabrea and Rattazzi. Foreign ambassadors were reminded that they had better keep in direct touch with the palace as well as, or instead of, with Ricasoli and his ministerial colleagues. This was nothing very new. Every one of the premiers of the reign had sooner or later been forced to resign because of the king's liking for a personal policy of his own: this had been true of De Launay, Azeglio, Cavour, Lamarmora, Ricasoli, Minghetti,

---

[1] H. d'Ideville, *Journal d'un Diplomate en Italie* (Paris, 1872), I. 63; G. A. H. de Reiset, *Torino 1848: Ricordi sul Risorgimento*, ed. R. Segàla (Milan, 1945), pp. 290–1; A. Lumbroso, *Il Carteggio di un Vinto* (Rome, 1917), p. 373; É. Ollivier, *L'Empire Libéral* (Paris, 1905), X. 80, 132; *Aus dem Leben Theodor von Bernhardis* (Leipzig, 1897), VII. 225.

[2] *La Campagna del 1866 nei Documenti Militari Austriaci*, ed. A. Filipuzzi (Padua, 1866), pp. 413–14; *Carte di Lanza*, IV. 124; *Aus dem Leben Bernhardis*, VII. 54–5; G. Di Revel, *Sette Mesi al Ministero* (Milan, 1895), p. 177; *Thiers au Pouvoir (1871–1873): Texte de ses Lettres*, ed. G. Bonniols (Paris, 1921), p. 178; G. Bapst, *Le Maréchal Canrobert: Souvenirs d'un Siècle* (Paris, 1904), III. 232, 248: 'le maréchal le jugeait très supérieur à M. de Cavour'.

and even the favourite Rattazzi. Ricasoli was now to go through the experience a second time as the advice of his political enemies was frequently and privately sought at court.[1]

The annexation of Rome was the one remaining political ambition for Victor Emanuel. He used to say that he and he alone knew how to solve the problem of Rome; he hinted as much to the pope himself. Notwithstanding his excommunication, he told Pius IX that his conscience was clear, that the papal anathema on him was unjust, and that the pope was struggling against God's will. The king liked to refer to himself as God's chosen instrument, since it was evident that only someone under divine guidance could have suc- ceeded in such a difficult task as unifying Italy. In his view the pope, by holding to the temporal power, was guilty of indulging unworthy material ambitions. Pius disagreed and claimed that not God but Napoleon III had made possible the creation of this impious state of Italy.[2]

In private the pope used to refer sorrowfully to 'povero Vittorio'; the latter in return spoke of 'ce pauvre diable de Saint Père'. Respect and affection were not lacking in their regard for each other. Several times the king, usually with his ministers' approval, sent emissaries to Rome to discuss a possible arrange- ment about the future of Rome. He once claimed that the pope had informed him that Italy might have Rome as her capital,[3] but such a boast is implausible; and equally implausible was his reason for the failure of this possibility to materialize, since he tried to put all the blame on his ministers for interfering and not leaving him a free hand. The knowledge that he could transfer blame to his ministers gave him an enhanced sense of personal irresponsibility, and it enabled him to excuse himself to the pope on the grounds that as a parliamen- tary monarch his hands were tied. Pius replied by condemning parliamentary government as 'vicious in itself, and certainly unsuitable for Italy'; the king should at least help the church by ensuring that parliament was kept in its place; at any rate he ought to place his veto on dangerous proposals such as the introduction of compulsory education.[4]

At the end of 1866 or early in 1867, probably without Ricasoli's knowledge, the king got directly in touch with the Austrians and once again proposed to them an alliance, but without much success.[5] In December 1866 the French evacuated their garrison from Rome according to the terms of the convention of September 1864. Italy in return promised not to occupy papal territory, nor to let others invade it, and to do what could be done to prevent any

[1] *Carteggi Ricasoli*, XXIII. 441; Mme Rattazzi, *Rattazzi et son Temps* (Paris, 1887), II. 122–3, 160, 162; *Carteggio Castelli*, II. 157; *Souvenirs du Général Cte Fleury* (Paris, 1898), II. 323–5.

[2] *Pio e V. Emanuele*, III, pt. ii. 52, 185–6, 194, 197; *Lettere di V. Emanuele*, II. 857.

[3] *Les Origines Diplomatiques de la Guerre de 1870–1871*, ed. Ministère des Affaires Étrangères, vol. XIX (Paris, 1926), pp. 380–1.

[4] K. F. Vitzthum von Eckstädt, *London, Gastein und Sadowa 1864–1866* (Stuttgart, 1889), pp. 119–20, 125; *Pio e V. Emanuele*, III, pt. ii. 97–8, 225–6.

[5] Kübeck, 8 Feb. 1867, MSS. Haus-, Hof- und Staatsarchiv (Vienna); A. Sandonà, *L'Irredentismo nelle Lotte Politiche e nelle Contese Diplomatiche Italo-Austriache* (Bologna, 1932), I. 42.

rebellion in Rome. Few Italian politicians, however, had the slightest intention of keeping such a promise; nor had the king.[1] The very day that the French troops withdrew he authorized a secret plan to subvert the Papal States from within. An organizing committee was appointed which was in touch with Garibaldi and received subsidies from the secret service funds. The king's intention was that, after a decent interval, a rising would be organized in Rome which would provide an excuse for him to intervene and 'restore law and order'. Patriotic propaganda did not allow him to suspect that the Romans would not rise in rebellion to join the rest of Italy.[2]

Ricasoli broadly agreed with the king over Rome, but less over other political questions, especially as there were people in court circles who thought with the pope that Italians needed more authoritarianism than was provided by the existing parliamentary system.[3] Victor Emanuel, according to Sir Henry Elliot, the British representative, was indifferent to everywhere else in Italy save Piedmont: the court was peopled 'by Piedmontese favourites, for the most part characters inspiring the very reverse of respect'.[4] As a Tuscan and a man of principle, Ricasoli could not like this, nor as premier could he approve when he caught the king engaging in domestic politics behind the minister's back.[5] In November 1866, Napoleon advised the king to show more energy and assume personal direction of government. A few weeks later, at a reception for members of parliament, Victor Emanuel startled his audience by asserting that their policy of economizing on the army was entirely wrong; his remarks on this occasion had to be toned down before they were published in the official Gazette.[6]

Ricasoli hastily consulted British precedents about how to limit royal interference in parliamentary government. He realized that parliament was not working as well as at Westminster. Parties were incoherent, unstable, and irresponsible, and some people wanted the king to exercise his authority and repair the defect. Ricasoli in part agreed, though he also was quite sure that to increase royal authority beyond a certain point would make things worse. The Italian political system worked best on the doctrine that 'the king can do no wrong'; in other words a sovereign should act only through his ministers, or else there might be a dangerous dualism in policy and the crown would be deprived of the useful cushion provided by ministerial responsibility. Yet Ricasoli was ready to experiment with minor changes in the system. Some liberal politicians proposed increasing the powers of the senate and reducing

---

[1] *Carteggi e Bibliografia di Costantino Nigra*, ed. A. Colombo et al. (Turin, 1930), p. 125; *Carteggio Castelli*, II. 172, 371; *Politica Segreta Italiana (1863–1870)* (2nd ed. Turin, 1891), p. 193.
[2] *Carteggio Castelli*, II. 183–5, 192, 194; E. Montecchi, *Mattia Montecchi nel Risorgimento Italiano* (Rome, 1932), p. 189; L. Lipparini, *Minghetti* (Bologna, 1947), II. 369.
[3] *Carte di Lanza*, III. 373, 547–9; *Carteggio Castelli*, II. 204.
[4] Elliot, 17 Nov. 1866, F.O. 45/90.   [5] *Carteggi Ricasoli*, XXIV. 491, 495.
[6] *Gazzetta Ufficiale del Regno d'Italia* (Florence), 1 Jan. 1867; Elliot, 1 Jan., F.O. 45/104; *Souvenirs du Général Fleury*, II. 308.

the number of deputies in the lower House. Some wanted to shorten parliamentary sessions, others to introduce a more rigid censorship of the press. Ricasoli agreed that these points were worthy of discussion; he also admitted that the monarchy as the embodiment of the nation should up to a point be magnified and reinforced so that it could set a new tone for public life.[1]

Finance was one of the more delicate points at issue between court and cabinet, especially the crucial fact that the monarch wanted more spent on the army. A number of present and former ministers were bold enough to disagree strongly with him on this point, for experience had taught them that current expenditure on the armed forces might be twice as much as Italy could afford and was kept so high only out of a false view of what befitted a Great Power. Such a dangerous imbalance of expenditure was supported by the king and by the vested interest of a narrow circle of Piedmontese generals who monopolized power in the ministry of war. Yet this imbalance might well be the major flaw in the whole system, the main cause of popular disaffection, of parliamentary corruption, and economic backwardness.

Among the heirs of Cavour, Sella, Lanza, and Jacini were realists who understood that the reiterated superlatives of patriotic rhetoric, explicable though they may have been as a means of consolidating national sentiment, had obscured the inescapable fact of Italy's poverty, with the result that governments were being forced to continue wasting money on a sterile and perhaps unattainable search for military prestige. Many people must have said this in private who would not say it in public. Concealment of the true facts had resulted in leading Italy into Lissa and Custoza, which in other words meant that military expenditure, far from increasing Italy's reputation as had been promised, had diminished it.[2] The main justification for this colossal expenditure on arms was thus false in logic. The most urgent problems of Italian society, which in the main were problems of national finance, education, and living standards, remained unsolved, and to a large extent this was the result of sheer intellectual confusion.

The king's civil list was an especially sensitive point for the government. Victor Emanuel himself lived simply, but he had no sense of economy, and in order to keep the full panoply of royalty he had cheerfully taken over the upkeep of the palaces and hunting grounds which had belonged to half a dozen deposed dynasties. He even bought or rented new estates to satisfy his inexhaustible mania for hunting. He adored being able to make lavish gifts to his mistresses.[3] He boasted of how he used to bribe politicians and

---

[1] *Lettere Ricasoli*, IX. 235–6, 240–3, 257; *Carteggi Ricasoli*, XXIV. 81, 88–9; *Sclopis: Diario*, pp. 404–5, 412; R. Mori, *Il Tramonto del Potere Temporale 1866–1870* (Rome, 1967), p. 111.

[2] S. Jacini, *Due Anni di Politica Italiana* (Milan, 1868), p. 94; S. Jacini, *Pensieri sulla Politica Italiana* (Florence, 1889), pp. 59–60; *Carteggi Ricasoli*, XXIV. 500; *Carteggio Castelli*, II. 146; P. Calza, *Nuova Luce sugli Eventi Militari del 1866* (Bologna, 1924), p. 180.

[3] Di Revel, *Sette Mesi al Ministero*, pp. 85, 204.

how he employed a private police force of his own.[1] He was surrounded by all kinds of sharks who exploited his gullibility and generosity,[2] and the management of his household expenditure was subject to no greater system of accountability than his father's had been.[3] The frequency with which Letitia Rattazzi in her memoirs refers to the malpractices in the *casa reale* suggests that her husband may have owed some of his influence at court to an ability to extricate the monarch from his financial difficulties; in particular she mentions that the king was brought into disrepute over some most unattractive financial dealings in ecclesiastical land and in the grant of railway concessions to foreign companies.[4] In 1864 much play had been made with the king's generous gesture of agreeing to give up 3 million lire a year from his civil list, but this reduction came after his official income had been raised from 4 millions to 10 and then to 17. The reduction was simply a gesture, and expenditure was not reduced; the household treasurer merely resorted to the accumulation of debts which he then called on the government to settle.[5]

Ricasoli was by nature neither courtier nor parliamentarian, and no premier could succeed for long who was neither one nor the other. In face of what Lanza and Giacomo Dina called 'parliamentary anarchy',[6] he was ready to introduce a greater element of authority, and to this extent he had the court behind him. When he tried to tighten up press censorship and curtail the right of public assembly, Ricasoli was defeated in parliament by 136 votes to 104, but Victor Emanuel refused to let him resign. The king's view was that 'parliament is quite insane and is not carrying out the nation's mandate',[7] so he permitted his prime minister to appeal to the electorate. Ricasoli was thereby induced to presume on what he mistakenly thought to be a position of strength, and proceeded to read the king a lesson, pointing out that the style of life at court was turning public opinion against the monarchy as an institution. The king should not pile up debts, nor keep disreputable company, nor grant titles for unworthy motives, but should fill his allotted role by setting a better public example and by spending more on art and less on women. Victor Emanuel denied most of Ricasoli's accusations in a dignified reply which showed keen resentment at such prying into his private affairs. Though

---

[1] H. Oncken, *Die Rheinpolitik Kaiser Napoleons III, von 1863 bis 1870 und der Ursprung des Krieges von 1870–1871* (Leipzig, 1926), III. 388; *Lettere di V. Emanuele*, I. 791; Bollea, *Una Silloge*, p. 31.
[2] Mme Rattazzi, *Rattazzi et son Temps*, I. 589.
[3] *Carteggi di Alfonso Lamarmora*, ed. A. Colombo et. al. (Turin, 1928), pp. 120, 125; Elliot, 18 Apr. 1867, F.O. 45/105: 'members of the king's household . . . are not called upon to furnish any accounts'.
[4] Mme Rattazzi, *Rattazzi et son Temps*, I. 587, 642–3; ibid. II. 10–11.
[5] It was a larger civil list than in any western country, G. Pallavicino, *Su le Questioni del Giorno* (Milan, 1874), p. 105; A. Gallenga, *Italy Revisited* (London, 1876), I. 394; *Discorsi Parlamentari di Agostino Bertani*, ed. L. Fera (Rome, 1913), pp. 358–61.
[6] *Carte di Lanza*, IV. 101; *Giacomo Dina*, III. 88; *Carteggio Castelli*, II. 211.
[7] Mori, *Tramonto del Potere Temporale*, p. 109; G. Sardo, *Storia del Parlamento Italiano* (Palermo, 1969), VI. 145–6.

he confessed to having been blackmailed for several years by journalists who threatened to write about him, and to being surrounded by 'a *camorra* dedicated to sucking him dry', nevertheless suggestions about introducing economies into the royal household were clearly unwelcome.[1]

A general election was held in March 1867, in which Ricasoli campaigned on a promise to tackle 'profitless parliamentary discussions, weakness of government, and the perpetual mutability of ministers and programmes'.[2] His followers did quite well, but not well enough to alter the familiar pattern of government; he still was obliged to depend on a largely amorphous coalition which, if a prime minister ever introduced any issue of major principle, was liable to dissolve. He was also vulnerable to court intrigues, and this vulnerability encouraged the king to get rid of him and try a different style of government altogether.

The alleged pretext was Ricasoli's decision that a heavy tax on flour was needed to balance the budget and meet current military expenditure. This was no more than a pretext, since one of the king's friends introduced the same tax a year later. The real reason was that Ricasoli wanted Quintino Sella as finance minister, and Sella laid it down as an absolute and urgently necessary condition that the king should reduce his civil list to only 10 millions a year, besides accepting some degree of public financial accountability for the *casa reale*.[3] The king refused to accept such a recommendation and suggested instead that Ricasoli appoint to this key ministry one of the private financiers who were employed by the court.

When the cabinet resigned on this issue, it caused some alarm inasmuch as no parliamentary vote had gone against them since the elections. Indeed Ruggero Bonghi, who was an expert on constitutional law and practice, stated that seven successive governments in Italy had been obliged to resign quite irrespective of parliament.[4] Ricasoli announced curtly that he had resigned 'for reasons which parliament does not need to know', and deputies were discreet enough to pursue the matter no further; they must have felt that an open debate might touch the throne or break up the loose alliance of the conservative *onesti* and give power to the radicals.[5] Victor Emanuel privately spoke with fear and contempt of Sella; he criticized the retiring premier as an imbecile and blamed him for letting parliament get out of control.[6]

---

[1] *Lettere di V. Emanuele*, II. 1165; *Carteggi Ricasoli*, XXIV. 134; *Lettere Ricasoli*, IX. 302, 315-16,323-4.

[2] I. Ghiron, *Annali D'Italia (1867–1870)* (Milan, 1890), III. 17.

[3] *Epistolario Inedito di Quintino Sella*, ed. A. Segre (Turin, 1930), pp. 55, 294; *Carte di Lanza*, IV. 123; N. Nisco, *Storia Civile del Regno d'Italia, Scritto per Mandato di Sua Maestà* (Naples, 1892), VI. 60-1; *Lettere Ricasoli*, IX. 367-8.

[4] R. Bonghi, *Come Cadde la Destra*, ed. F. Piccolo (Milan, 1929), p. 171; *Rivista Contemporanea* (Turin), XLIX (Apr. 1867), 160.

[5] M. Mancini and U. Galeotti, *Norme ed Usi del Parlamento Italiano* (Rome, 1887), pp. 693, 738; *Giacomo Dina*, III. 85-7.

[6] Kübeck to Beust, 15 Apr., MSS. Haus- und Hof-Archiv.

The king had been caught off guard, and the crisis therefore came upon him before he had prepared an alternative ministry. He now turned once again to the older generation of loyal servants of the crown, hoping to find a combination which would permit the return of Rattazzi into the cabinet. On the king's behalf, Rattazzi first went to ask Count Sclopis to accept the premiership, explaining that the royal desire was to have an essentially Piedmontese administration. Piedmont was where the king felt most at home, just as the Piedmontese dialect remained the language he used in his family and at court. When Sclopis pleaded age, they turned to General Di Revel and General Menabrea. None of these three men had any personal following in parliament, but they were convenient figureheads; all were close to the court and could be relied upon to allow the king his own way in policy. Di Revel made the mild objection that he had always voted against Rattazzi in parliament and hence their association would look strange, but he was notified in reply that Rattazzi would do whatever the king told him to.[1]

In the end Victor Emanuel decided to make Rattazzi premier again. Even among strong royalists this caused a sense of shock, for it was surprising to find the monarchy siding so openly with a minority faction; the king's authority, at least in the country at large, derived from being thought above party conflicts, but here he was 'stuck in them up to his neck'.[2] The new premier's wife was socially unaccepted: the illegitimate daughter of Lady Wyse, she had notoriously been a mistress of the king's, and in most years she also received a large annual pension from Napoleon III which some people thought should have excluded her husband from office.[3] Rattazzi was furthermore associated with the disasters of Aspromonte and Novara. But at court they were delighted to have him back, for his presence gave Victor Emanuel a new sense of command. '*Quei signori*' in parliament had been making government difficult, but now they would be kept in their place; and if any politician tried to make trouble, added the king, the royal archives contained enough compromising letters which he could use to blackmail them into silence.[4] He did not think finance would be an obstacle. How to restore financial stability, he explained, was a problem which had personally exercised him for five months, and he had worked out a complete plan which, incidentally, would enable him to increase the army budget still further.[5]

The new ministers at once aroused the never entirely dormant feelings of hostility towards Piedmont, and these were now coupled with the fear of a

[1] Di Revel, *Sette Mesi al Ministero*, pp. 74–6; *Sclopis: Diario* pp. 410–3.
[2] *Carteggio Castelli*, II. 226, 235, 244.
[3] Elliot, 23 Dec. 1865, Clarendon MSS. (Bodleian Library, Oxford), dep c 98; N. Bazzetta de Vemenia, *I Savoia e le Donne* (Milan, 1923), p. 112.
[4] Kübeck, 15 Apr. 1867, MSS. Haus- and Hof-Archiv, reported the king as saying 'Je les tiens tous en main, et en gardant toute une archive de lettres qu'ils m'ont écrites à différentes époques, je les fais taire et marcher, car je suis à même de les compromettre devant le public et ils le savent'.
[5] Kübeck, 3 May, ibid.; *Lettere di V. Emanuele*, II. 1195.

possible palace revolution. References were made in parliament to 'certain forces working against the constitutional system which we are not allowed to name', and some people admitted privately that the reputation of the crown as an impartial influence above party politics had been destroyed.[1] Within three weeks of becoming premier, Rattazzi had to fight a duel with a leading Bolognese politician, after the king in person had been obliged to appoint a *jury d'honneur* to investigate a provocative indiscretion by Mme Rattazzi. His cabinet was the least impressive government Italy had yet known, a fact which was probably not unconnected with the part taken by the crown in its selection. According to a British diplomat, it was made up of nonentities, and the foreign minister, Senator Pompeo Campello, was 'so entirely ignorant of all matters belonging to his own department as to make it a mere waste of time to attempt to hold any conversation with him concerning them'.[2] Such a choice must have been deliberate. The king intended to be his own foreign minister in order to annex Rome and complete the risorgimento. That parliamentary government might in the process be weakened did not matter very much.

His self-confidence was impressive but not well founded, for his notions on foreign policy were only a little less inconsequential than his views on finance. He told the Prussians emphatically that he wanted another alliance with them against all comers but especially against France. To the Austrians, however, he said he wanted an alliance with them against Prussia: he explained to Vienna that he disliked the idea of being allied to either Napoleon or Bismarck, since both were always playing a double policy, something which was entirely contrary to his own nature and practice; they were both untrustworthy, whereas he himself never deceived anyone.[3] And yet his main trust had to be in France, because he hoped for at least a tacit connivance by Napoleon III in the annexation of Rome. He had received plenty of advice that this would be difficult to obtain, but he preferred to follow his own instincts in the matter.

Foreign ambassadors very soon learnt not to take too seriously his statements of friendship or enmity. They knew perfectly well that it was his habit to have a secret policy distinct from that of his official cabinet, but the best thing was to pay not too much attention to it. Victor Emanuel was never more upset than when people did not believe his word of honour, and he used to insist almost to the point of obsession on his own trustworthiness. But Baron Kübeck did not believe him, nor did Count von Beust. Elliot had been warned by no less a body than the Italian foreign office that the king's words were often meant only to astound, impress, or mystify, and London was therefore

[1] *Carteggi E. d'Azeglio*, II. 416; Sardo, *Storia del Parlamento*, VI. 172.
[2] Edward Herries, 8 Aug. 1867, F.O. 45/106.
[3] *Die Auswärtige Politik Preussens*, vol. VIII, ed. H. Michaelis (Oldenburg, 1934), pp. 252, 365, 373; ibid., vol. IX, ed. H. Michaelis (Oldenburg, 1936), pp. 94–5; Kübeck, 15 Apr. and 3 May, MSS. Haus- und Hof-Archiv; *Rassegna*, 1963, p. 94.

warned that not much attention should be paid to them. Other British ministers said much the same. Count Usedom referred to 'die inkonsequente Versatilität' of Victor Emanuel's character which made him essentially not to be trusted. Bismarck, who did not often agree with Usedom, was entirely at one on 'der wohlbekannten Unzuverlässigkeit des Königs', and used to say that Victor Emanuel could be made to do anything by playing on his weak points, which were women and money.[1]

French politicians took him a little more seriously. Yet the Baron de Malaret spoke of

ce langage coloré, toujours excentrique, souvent excessif, qui lui est particulier et qui a l'inconvénient ou l'avantage d'enlever aux paroles de Sa Majesté une grande partie de l'importance et de la portée politique qu'elles auraient certainement sous une autre forme.

Malaret added that the king would have more importance if he could be more serious. General Fleury commented on 'son caractère mobile', and the 'cachoterie du Roi qui manque toujours de franchise'; Fleury's practice had been to pretend to treat with the king, but in fact to rely only on the ministers.[2]

Vanity, lack of seriousness, unreliability, all these had their part to play in the tragedy which was to lead to disaster at Mentana. In 1867, as in 1862, Garibaldi was chosen to be instrument and victim of the policy which the king now hatched with Rattazzi. They had been unequivocally warned by Napoleon that French troops would have to reoccupy Rome if the pope's security were threatened; nevertheless they thought they could force Napoleon's hand by engineering a rebellion in the Papal States which would look like a spontaneous outburst of patriotic fervour.[3] When foreign governments complained that Garibaldi was again being allowed to recruit volunteers, Rattazzi tried to convince them that these men were intending to emigrate to the Argentine. When pressed he also informed them that a general insurrection 'en masse' would soon break out in Rome, of course without any connivance from the government.[4] What he took care not to say, and indeed what he formally and mendaciously denied,[5] was that he was providing the revolution-

---

[1] Elliot, 6 June 1865, F.O. 45/70; Elliot, 16 Nov. 1866, F.O. 45/90; Paget, 13 March and 5 June 1869, Clarendon MSS., dep c 488; *Memoirs of Prince Chlodwig of Hohenlohe Schillingsfürst* (London, 1906), I. 351; *Auswärtige Politik Preussens*, IX. 94; *Bismarck: Die Gesammelten Werke*, vol. VI[b], ed. F. Thimme (Berlin, 1931), p. 107; Kübeck, 3 May 1867, MSS. Haus- und Hof-Archiv; F. von Beust, *Aus Drei Viertel-Jahrhunderten: Erinnerungen und Aufzeichnungen* (Stuttgart, 1887), II. 320.

[2] *Les Origines Diplomatiques de la Guerre*, vol. XIII (1922), pp. 190, 285, 399–401; *Souvenirs du Général Fleury*, II. 323, 325.

[3] Ibid., 306; Ollivier, *Empire Libérale*, X. 94; *Giacomo Dina*, III. 105.

[4] Paget, 14 Oct. 1869, F.O. 45/107; Mori, *Tramonto del Potere Temporale*, p. 225; *Les Origines Diplomatiques de la Guerre*, vol. XVIII (1925), pp. 8–9.

[5] *Discorsi Parlamentari di Urbano Rattazzi*, ed. G. Scovazzi (Rome, 1880), VII. 177.

aries with funds and arms to make up for the fact that so few volunteers and contributions were forthcoming for this great enterprise against the pope.[1] In public he repeated 'a thousand times' that he stood absolutely by his promise to protect the Papal States.[2]

Some people in Italy realized that this looked like a replica of Aspromonte, and were appalled. Among Garibaldi's friends there were some who suspected, and rightly, that they were being exploited by the king and Rattazzi. Many conservatives were strongly averse to another deal with the Garibaldians, for if Garibaldi once reached Rome he might proclaim a constituent assembly or a republic, and in that case the established order would be destroyed. Some of them were praying that this anticlerical revolutionary would be beaten by the papal zouaves; win or lose, a Garibaldian expedition looked like being a disaster for the monarchy and for the country.[3]

But the king privately had no intention of letting Garibaldi win. On the contrary, Garibaldi's invasion of the Papal States would be merely an excuse for the Italian army to cross the frontier in pursuit, so that the temporal power and the forces of radicalism could be destroyed in one single blow. This was the same excuse as Cavour had made to Napoleon in August 1860 and Rattazzi again in July 1862, though it might have been guessed that the French were hardly likely to be caught the same way again.

Victor Emanuel later explained to Malaret that his plan had been to let Garibaldi arrive in Rome with some 30,000 volunteers, and then himself attack and 'massacre them so that not one would be left'. This story was not believed by the Frenchman, who had learnt that 'everyone in Italy knows that the king very rarely speaks the truth'.[4] Possibly Malaret was right to be sceptical. Nevertheless the king on different occasions gave exactly the same explanation of his motives to Karl Vitzthum, to Hugues Fournier the French foreign minister, and to the Crown Prince Friedrich Wilhelm. The repeated words 'massacre', 'exterminate', and 'bloodbath' may possibly have been his usual tall talk, but with no doubt the king intended to enter Rome as the conqueror of both Garibaldi and the pope at once.[5] Of the two, he probably preferred the pope. Often he expressed his dislike of the Garibaldians; the worst thing of all, he said to the British representative, would be to have a

[1] G. Finali, *Memorie*, ed. G. Maioli (Faenza, 1955), pp. 294–5; *Carteggi Politici Inediti di Francesco Crispi (1860–1900)*, ed. T. Palamenghi-Crispi (Rome, 1912), pp. 262–3; G. Cadolini, 'Roma e Mentana', *Nuova Antologia* (Rome), Nov. 1913, pp. 47, 50, 62; F. Cavallotti, *Storia della Insurrezione di Roma nel 1867* (Milan, 1869), p. 73; P. Balan, *La Politica Italiana dal 1863 al 1870 Secondo gli Ultimi Documenti* (Rome, 1880), pp. 142–3; *Carteggio Castelli*, II. 235, 276.

[2] *Discorsi di Rattazzi*, VII. 109.

[3] *Carteggio Castelli*, II. 249–50, 261, 273.

[4] *Les Origines Diplomatiques*, XIX. 379–81; Ollivier, *Empire Libérale*, X. 173.

[5] *Les Origines Diplomatiques de la Guerre*, vol. XXIX (1932), p. 469; ibid. XVIII. 303–4; *Die Auswärtige Politik Preussens*, vol. X, ed. H. Michaelis (Oldenburg, 1939), pp. 6–7; Oncken, *Rheinpolitik Napoleons*, III. 496; F. Chabod, *Storia della Politica Estera Italiana* (Bari, 1951), p. 678; Cavour had also used the word 'exterminate' for Garibaldi, though it was deleted in *Lettere di Cavour*, IV. 35.

revolutionary government in Rome, and to prevent it 'he would run the risk of any consequences'.[1]

In October, since another expedition of volunteers was more and more obviously being prepared, the French again threatened to return their garrison troops to Rome if it was not stopped, but Victor Emanuel and his ministers were quite sure of themselves and were already printing proclamations to the Roman people and discussing how much of papal territory they would occupy. Towards the middle of the month, in execution of what was now said to be a prearranged plan, they informed Napoleon that Italian soldiers would soon cross the papal frontier in order to check the volunteers. The king explained that he had tried to stop Garibaldi's irregulars, but national feeling was running too high for him to use force against them on Italian soil. Once they were on papal territory he could suppress them, and he would do so because only in that way would he save his own dynasty and ensure papal independence.[2]

Napoleon, on the contrary, could not possibly afford to let the world think that France was cynically conniving at an Italian conquest of Rome. Rattazzi shamelessly protested that any French intervention at Rome would violate the convention of September 1864, and he was being strongly advised to disregard what he persisted in thinking was French bluff.[3] Possibly it was at this point that he asked for help from Bismarck. The latter of course promised nothing, though this did not stop Rattazzi hinting to the French that the Germans had advised him to proceed and take Rome. Bismarck duly put the record straight and informed the French of this request by the Italians, fully realizing how the news would turn Napoleon against them. Not even the falsification of the official Italian documents could conceal what Rattazzi had been trying to do.[4]

On 17 October, Garibaldi 'escaped' from Caprera, where a naval cordon was guarding him. Rattazzi with Victor Emanuel's consent[5] was planning to invade the Papal States on the 18th, but quite unexpectedly he resigned. Evidently the king and the army leaders lost their nerve at the last moment, and so the prime minister, finding his advice rejected, withdrew 'in order to leave the king free to choose what policy to adopt'.[6] Victor Emanuel confidently said that he now knew what to do, and instructed General Di Revel to

[1] Paget, 14 Oct. 1869, F.O. 45/107; *La Campagna del 1866 nei Documenti Austriaci*, ed. Filipuzzi, pp. 395, 414.

[2] *Lettere di V. Emanuele*, II. 1224; *Les Origines Diplomatiques*, XIX. 10, 17; G. Gadda, *Ricordi e Impressioni della Nostra Storia Politica nel 1866–1867* (Turin, 1899), pp. 268, 273, 275.

[3] *Les Origines Diplomatiques*, XIX. 22; *Carteggio Castelli*, II. 282, 287; Mori, *Tramonto del Potere Temporale*, pp. 228–9.

[4] *Les Origines Diplomatiques*, XIX. 42–3, 211–12; *Auswärtige Politik Preussens*, IX. 303; *Il Risorgimento Italiano: Rivista Storica* (Turin), 1914, pp. 447–8.

[5] The king's connivance was reported by the minister of education, Michele Coppino (*Bollettino Storico-Bibliografico Subalpino* (Turin), XXXV (1933), 215–16.

[6] *Das Ende des Kirchenstaates*, ed. N. Miko (Vienna, 1964), I. 272; *Discorsi di Rattazzi*, VII. 213–17.

take full powers; conscription notices were posted, and Rattazzi's orders to occupy the Papal States were rescinded. Di Revel, however, could not see where
this would lead; he advised the king not to by-pass parliament or act under martial law, but to appoint a new and regular government under General Cialdini.[1]

Let down by his first choice, the king took this advice and turned to
Cialdini, another former royal aide-de-camp. As prime minister elect,
Cialdini spent five days trying to form a cabinet, and he also had a private
talk with Garibaldi. Various interpretations can be placed on the fact that
Garibaldi did not thereafter stop his preparations, but on the contrary hastened the movement of his volunteers towards the papal frontier, and no
obstacles were placed in his way. Subsequently it was said that Cialdini failed
to persuade enough people to take the responsibility of becoming ministers
at such a dangerous moment for the state, and his failure gave an excuse for
the king to withdraw his appointment. Other evidence suggests that this was
only a cover for the fact that Cialdini, like Rattazzi, wanted to invade the
Papal States and defy the French. The king at the last moment refused to let
him do this, but also refused to adopt the only other obvious policy, which
would have been to use his influence to make Garibaldi give up his plans.
There can be small doubt that the protraction of the crisis through these five
days was by collusion with the court. Either the king could not make up his
mind, or he was playing for time.[2]

Victor Emanuel then sent Di Revel to ask General Lamarmora to form a
government. Lamarmora was too dutiful a monarchist ever to publish the
fact, but he made the unacceptable condition that the king should abdicate:[3]
only in this way could the monarchy compound for a series of dangerous
errors of judgement and a repeated refusal to accept constitutional advice.
Victor Emanuel in some desperation turned back to Rattazzi and General
Durando, who said they would accept office if allowed to continue with the
plan to invade. They must have hoped that Napoleon was still bluffing when
he threatened to stop them. But the king could not lightly contemplate the
possibility of fighting against Napoleon. His judgement on this occasion may
well have been wiser than that of his advisers; the objection to it was that his
decision came too half-heartedly and much too late. In talking to the British
ambassador, Rattazzi blamed the king for simply not being able to make up
his mind, and the charge is plausible; equally interesting was the king's
excuse, namely that he would have agreed to fight against Napoleon if only
he had not suddenly discovered that he had no more than 80,000 soldiers
under arms in the whole of Italy.[4]

[1] Di Revel, *Sette Mesi al Ministero*, pp. 185–7; *Lettere di V. Emanuele*, II. 1231.
[2] *Discorsi Parlamentari di Francesco Crispi*, ed. C. Finocchiaro-Aprile (Rome, 1915), I. 808; A. Luzio,
Aspromonte e Mentana (Florence, 1935), pp. 387–8.
[3] *Ende des Kirchenstaates*, ed. Miko, I. 360; *Carteggio Castelli*, II. 295.
[4] Paget, 27 and 28 Oct. 1867, F.O. 45/108; Kübeck, 8 Nov., MSS. Haus und Hof-Archiv, agreed
that 'il ne sut à quel parti s'arrêter et flottait entre la peur de la France et du parti révolutionnaire'.

While waiting for his successor to be named, Rattazzi had remained all this time in interim charge of the government and continued to assist the volunteers in the hope that Garibaldi would have time to complete his revolution.[1] Victor Emanuel claimed that he ordered Rattazzi to arrest Garibaldi and Rattazzi had agreed to do so, but that the order was then disobeyed: in this way the blame for the catastrophe of Mentana was to be placed on disobedience by Garibaldi and the outgoing prime minister. Just conceivably, however, this disobedience was all a pre-arranged plan to which the king had secretly assented, for Victor Emanuel continued to be in personal touch with his ex-premier, Rattazzi, and his sharp criticism of this man in the presence of some people contrasts strangely with his continued praise of him to others.[2] On the other hand, if the king was speaking the truth, he was in a dangerous situation where he had refused the advice not only of a constitutional premier, but of several premiers elect, and of the most prominent soldier in the army. Not many options now remained open to him, so he turned to General Menabrea with not a request but an order to form a government of ultra royalists.

The French relief expedition of 2,000 men left Toulon on 26 October, the same day that Garibaldi's volunteers overran a small papal unit at Monterotondo. Menabrea's cabinet was formed on the 27th. At a special meeting with the king and other party leaders it was then decided to disown Garibaldi in a last-minute bid to keep the French from landing. Presumably it was also hoped that, by averting French intervention, the rebels might thereby win time to enter Rome to the applause of the populace. But such hopes were based on a misunderstanding of the feelings in both Rome and Paris.

One miscalculation followed another. Once the French had landed, the Italian army was ordered to cross the papal frontier. While the Garibaldians were at first told that the king wanted to support the volunteers, the French were told that he meant to help in 'restoring order',[3] but if it was believed that Napoleon would permit such a face-saving gesture to protect the monarchy from incrimination, the assumption was wrong. Nor did the much-heralded spontaneous rising occur which had been intended to prove to the French that the pope's subjects were burning to be free. On 3 November, Garibaldi was easily beaten at Mentana, and there was no sign of any widespread support for him among the local population.[4] Menabrea tried to throw all the

---

[1] Mori, *Tramonto del Potere Temporale*, pp. 247–50.

[2] *Carteggio Castelli*, p. 310; *Les Origines Diplomatiques*, XIX. 61; Kübeck, 8 Nov. 1867, MSS. Haus-und Hof-Archiv, chronicles warm praise of Rattazzi given by the king to a deputation on 24 Oct., 'un vrai patriote et mon ami'.

[3] Ibid.

[4] *Lettere Ricasoli*, X. 14; Cadolini, in *Nuova Antologia*, Nov. 1913, pp. 48–9: Ollivier, *Empire Libérale*, X. 159; *The Roman Journals of Ferdinand Gregorovius 1852–1874*, ed. F. Althaus (London, 1911), p. 295, 'The tumult which was expected to break out yesterday evening, and which had been announced the day before, was, it is said, put off on account of the rain' (diary for 23 Oct.).

blame on Rattazzi, explaining to the French that Rattazzi's government had deceived them and had been helping Garibaldi,[1] but Napoleon was unimpressed. An ultimatum from Paris forced the Italian army to retreat, and an unfortunate episode thus reached its humiliating conclusion.

When the king's responsibility for these events was hinted at in parliament, ministers dutifully suppressed such an obnoxious suggestion and with perfect propriety refused to allow the throne to be brought into debate.[2] Royalist propaganda claimed that the king had 'saved the country'.[3] But some people blamed him for both instigating revolution and then causing that revolution to fail. If such a weakness in the constitution persisted, it might well lead to other disasters in future.[4] Undoubtedly the monarchy suffered in repute as a result of Mentana. So did the morale of the nation suffer. For over a year the government had been subsidizing a Roman liberation committee without any visible result save to bring back a French occupation of Rome and to provide further proof of the fragility of Italian patriotism. The Prussians learnt from what had happened that Italy would be worth nothing as an ally; the Austrians called Victor Emanuel's conduct deplorable beyond words.[5]

Napoleon was furious with him, especially after hearing of his 'fornication' with Germany. The king's disregard of the emperor's need to consider Catholic opinion in France was unforgiveable; the Italians by their clumsiness had cost Paris a lot of money and had exposed to the French public a serious weakness in their government's foreign policy. Napoleon's fury was such that he began to speak of undoing the unification of Italy and dividing it into three states: there was talk of an Austrian archduke in Naples, and even of restoring the Bourbons.[6]

Another unfortunate result of Mentana was to break Garibaldi's confidence in Victor Emanuel. Four or five times since 1860 the radicals had been pushed by the king towards various martial enterprises, but had invariably been let down, and it was especially humiliating when Mazzini could say 'I told you so'. After Mentana the government did what it could for Garibaldi's wounded, and after a respectable interval gave an amnesty to Garibaldi himself; but when the king asked him to go off on another 'distant venture which is certain to succeed', the unwontedly sharp reply came from Caprera that the sovereign, having led Italy to dishonour, could not be trusted again.[7]

Royalist historians sometimes claim that Garibaldi never lost his faith in the monarchy,[8] but in fact, to judge by alterations made in later versions of

[1] *Les Origines Diplomatiques*, XIX. 153.
[2] *Discorsi di Rattazzi*, VII. 225; Sardo, *Storia del Parlamento Italiano*, VI. 227.
[3] D. Zanichelli, *Studi di Storia Costituzionale e Politica* (Bologna, 1900), pp. 225–6.
[4] *Carte di Lanza*, IV. 145–6; *Carteggio Castelli*, II. 296, 300; A. Monti, *Il Conte Luigi Torelli* (Milan, 1931), p. 281; G. Gorini, *Cronaca Mensile* (Milan), IV (30 Oct. 1867), 314–23.
[5] Kübeck, 8 Nov. 1867, MSS. Haus- und Hof-Archiv; *Ende des Kirchenstaates*, ed. Miko, I. 391.
[6] Ibid. 353, 360, 391; Oncken, *Rheinpolitik Napoleons*, II. 489; *Carteggio Castelli*, II. 330.
[7] *Garibaldi, Vittorio Emanuele, Cavour*, ed. G. E. Curàtulo (Bologna, 1911), p. 369.
[8] A. Monti, in *Nuova Antologia*, Apr. 1941, p. 219.

his memoirs, Garibaldi reverted a good deal of the way towards republicanism. He concluded that Victor Emanuel must have been motivated less by patriotism than by selfish, dynastic objectives, to attain which the monarchy had been even prepared to leave Italy weak and servile. According to Garibaldi the king was living on a huge civil list which the nation just could not afford, and was no longer respected by honest folk. 'Acting under the cover of his ministers' responsibility, he has been the root cause of the various ills which afflict our country, despised as we are abroad, poor and desperate at home.' If the monarch could not break free from his closed circle of adulation, if he could not stop truckling to imperial France, the dynasty might be near its end.[1]

General Luigi Menabrea, after being ordered into office at the end of October 1867, remained prime minister for over two years, longer than anyone since Cavour. He was much admired as an upright, honest man, though was hardly at home in the world of parliamentary debate. It was unusual for a senator to hold the premiership. Like De Launay before him and Pelloux later, Menabrea was one of those loyal Savoyard generals and senators who became prime minister in times of trouble when the king needed a reliable soldier in charge. Himself the senior royal aide-de-camp, he selected his ministers from the court party, notably Senator Cambray-Digny who was Grand Master of Ceremonies to the king, Senator Gualterio, soon to be head of the royal household, and General Bertolè Viale who had been in parliament only since March. Together they formed what was recognized as a personal, almost extra-parliamentary administration. It was a withdrawal away from parliamentary government in the direction of 'constitutional government' as the term had been understood before Cavour exalted the status of the *camera*. Menabrea had been one of Cavour's leading opponents. He had questioned both the annexation of Naples and Cavour's anticlerical laws, nor was he particularly happy with the idea of Rome as the capital of Italy.[2] Inevitably such a man became the target of parliamentary attack.

Menabrea was in fact twice defeated in the *camera* at the end of 1867. The king was not unready this time, but had secretly been at work since the beginning of November preparing an alternative cabinet under General Durando in case he needed to fall back on someone with more parliamentary experience.[3] According to the French ambassador at Florence, Victor Emanuel was not a man to give Menabrea his entire support, for the king knew that the royal prerogative would best be served if he 'persevered in his habit of more or

[1] *Scritti di Garibaldi* II. 392–3, 398; ibid. VI. 107, 423; *Epistolario di Giuseppe Garibaldi*, ed. E. E. Ximenes (Milan, 1885), I. 341; ibid. II. 257; G. Sacerdote, *La Vita di Giuseppe Garibaldi* (Milan, 1933), p. 935; *Garibaldi: Poema Autobiografico*, ed. G. E. Curàtulo (Bologna, 1911), pp. 183, 219; G. E. Curàtulo, *Il Dissidio tra Mazzini e Garibaldi: Documenti Inediti* (Milan, 1928), p. 326.
[2] *Sclopis: Diario*, p. 368.
[3] *Carteggio Castelli*, II. 308.

less conspiring against his official govenment'.[1] Yet neither would he automatically give way to a vote in parliament, especially when Menabrea's ministers formally recommended that he should disregard parliamentary wishes and confirm them in office.[2] Sella and others, on the contrary, maintained that, after two parliamentary votes, his reappointment of Menabrea was a constitutional impropriety.[3] To a group of senators, the king gave the partially but not entirely convincing excuse for this move that there were many groups in parliament and hence no single 'opposition' to which he could turn as an alternative.[4] To the Austrian minister he referred to the deputies in more forceful terms and spoke 'of parliamentary difficulties which make government so difficult in Italy'; perhaps there would be no other solution than to put away forty of the worst deputies. 'But I will succeed in the end', he said; 'I know *ces mauvais drôles* and how to make them behave'.[5] The Prussians were warned that a *coup d'état* by the army was not far off.[6]

One detached observer who spoke with the king at the end of December 1867 was Lord Clarendon, the British politician, who reported on his Florentine visit in a private letter to Lord John Russell.

I saw many other persons, the burthen of whose song was the same, viz. that the king was the great obstacle, that he was ignorant and false, and an intriguer whom no honest man could serve without damage to his own reputation. I made no démarche to see H.M., but hearing that I was at Florence he sent for me and kept me for 2 hours. He began by attacking the Emperor savagely for his intervention, and upon my asking why the Convention [of September 1864] had not been observed he threw the whole blame upon Rattazzi, who he said had furnished arms, men and money to Garibaldi, and had applied for the assistance of Prussia without his knowledge.[7]

Clarendon added that he believed not a word of this excuse. In other notes made at the time about this same interview, Clarendon quoted the king as saying that Rattazzi had 'infamously betrayed him', and at one moment the king had given orders for Rattazzi to be put under arrest. Victor Emanuel pledged the Englishman his 'solemn assurance' that the convention of September 1864 would in future be respected by Italy, in other words that he would guarantee the Papal States against any invasion.[8]

In answer to my enquiries as to how the Emperor could feel more certain than heretofore that the Convention would be observed and the Pope's safety secured, His Majesty said that with his present ministry he could guarantee both, as no movement could take place unless it was encouraged by the government, and that the

---

[1] *Les Origines Diplomatiques de la Guerre*, vol. xx (1927), p. 125.
[2] Mancini and Galeotti, *Norme ed Usi del Parlamento*, p. 688.
[3] Paget, 3 Jan. 1868, F.O. 45/124; *Giacomo Dina*, III. 197; *Les Origines Diplomatiques*, xx. 70.
[4] *Carteggio Castelli*, II.327.
[5] Kübeck, 2 Jan. 1868, MSS. Haus- und Hof-Archiv.
[6] *Aus dem Leben Bernhardis*, VII. 146, 171.   [7] 1 Jan. 1868, Russell Papers, P.R.O. 30/22/16E.
[8] 23 Dec. 1867, Clarendon MSS., dep c 555.

rabble which composed the volunteers could easily be stopped and had had a lesson which they would not forget.[1]

An interesting, though second-hand, account of Clarendon's visit to Florence was given by the Austrian minister, to whom the British politician talked more unguardedly. Evidently the king had told Clarendon outright, among other things, that he now had decided to join France in fighting one day against Prussia. Clarendon spoke of having seen Lamarmora, Rattazzi, Ricasoli, Minghetti, and all the parliamentary leaders. In talk with these men,

the thing which most struck him was the complete discredit into which the king has fallen with everyone. There is universal agreement that Victor Emanuel is an imbecile. He is a dishonest man who tells lies to everyone. At this rate he will end by losing his crown and ruining both Italy and his dynasty. Lamarmora informed Clarendon that, when invited to take office, he had to say that he could never return to power until the king abdicated. Everyone agrees that the present parliament makes government almost impossible, but they also agree that anything would be better than to see absolute power in the hands of such a person as Victor Emanuel.

I asked Lord Clarendon if he thought a *coup d'état* possible, but he does not think the king has enough drive for it, nor that he would find enough people to help him, since he has alienated the devotion and confidence of everyone.[2]

Clarendon was about to visit Pius IX, and Victor Emanuel authorized him to convey an assurance that Italy would always respect the pope's present territorial possessions. Clarendon later commented:

I gave this message to His Holiness who smiled and said, 'Le pauvre roi, he is almost in as much danger as myself. He perhaps meant what he said, but his habit of lying is so inveterate that he cannot be trusted'.[3]

Whether 'lying' is too strong a word may be judged from the fact that a week later the king tried to convince Sir Augustus Paget that 'the pope was organizing a force for the purpose of attacking Italy and getting back his lost provinces'.[4]

The divisions inside parliament made it possible to keep Menabrea in office for two years, and there was little further sign of rebellion from the deputies. On the contrary, the same people who had voted for Ricasoli, and then for Ricasoli's opponent, Rattazzi, eventually voted with equal composure for Menabrea.[5] In a sense the king was thus the victim of transformism, who found himself with a defective system and was forced to find ways to make it work. At the same time it was also one of the consequences of this degree of royal intervention in politics that a strong opposition coalition could never be

---

[1] 24 Dec. 1867, Archives of the Duke of Norfolk (Arundel).
[2] Kübeck, 31 Dec. 1867, quoted by Mori, *Tramonto del Potere Temporale*, pp. 567–8.
[3] 1 Jan. 1868, P.R.O. 30/22/16E.   [4] Paget, 31 Dec. 1867, F.O. 45/109.
[5] S. Sonnino, *Del Governo Rappresentativo in Italia* (Rome, 1872), pp. 11–12.

formed, because most moderate politicians would not risk exposing the monarchy to criticism. At one point the king 'was supposed to be up to his old tricks, and to have in view the overthrow of the present cabinet', but when the rumour reached his ears he let it be known that he would back Menabrea 'through thick and thin'; above all he hoped that the prime minister would manage, by avoiding any parliamentary vote of confidence, to retain the political centre of gravity inside the royal household and to leave the head of state with full freedom of manoeuvre.[1]

To one leading senator Victor Emanuel railed at 'the very defective qualities' (*cattive disposizioni*) of his fellow-countrymen, and threatened that he might abdicate and leave them to get on with things as best they could without him. He asked the same man, somewhat cryptically, to tell the Piedmontese that they should seize their chance and take over government of the country.[2] To Paget,

the king spoke with the utmost scorn of Italian politicians . . . 'There were only two ways', His Majesty said, 'of governing Italians, by bayonets and bribery; they did not understand and were quite unfit for the constitutional regime'.[3]

This sweeping condemnation of parliamentarians and the parliamentary system did not even exclude Rattazzi, who after 1867 was no longer welcome at the palace even though his advice was sometimes sent for privately.[4] The king's closest political friend was now Filippo Gualterio who ran the royal household and the civil list, and whose authoritarian views were greatly suspect among the deputies. A motion was presented in parliament, based on experience of Westminster, that the monarch should not make political appointments to his household where there might be a clash with majority wishes in parliament, but the motion had to be withdrawn as improper and unconstitutional.[5]

Court finance was still a delicate matter. Victor Emanuel had in 1867 made another gesture of surrendering 4 millions from his civil list. Less publicized was the fact that he had made this conditional on receiving another and much larger sum in return, with which to pay off his debts, and he again threatened to make a scandal and accumulate new debts if this were not done.[6] Sella was convinced that here was a major cause of Italy's grave financial problems, and in parliament, without actually mentioning the king by name, called upon him to set the nation a better example of economy and morality.[7] Yet Victor

[1] Paget, 19 Dec. 1868, Clarendon MSS., dep c 488; *Lettere di V. Emanuele*, II. 1440.
[2] *Sclopis: Diario*, pp. 414, 426.   [3] 27 May 1869, Clarendon MSS., dep c 488.
[4] Mme Rattazzi, *Rattazzi et son Temps*, II. 219, 297.
[5] T. Villa, *Discorsi Parlamentari*, ed. C. Rinaudo (Turin, 1910), I. 53–6; *Lettere di V. Emanuele*, II. 1273, 1282, where the documents suggest that Gualterio must have been acting privately for the king before he ceased to be minister of the interior; W. Maturi, *Interpretazioni del Risorgimento* (Turin, 1962), p. 189, says that Gualterio had more power than the prime minister.
[6] *Lettere di V. Emanuele*, II. 1196; *Epistolario di Nino Bixio*, ed. E. Morelli (Rome, 1949), III. 123.
[7] *Discorsi Parlamentari di Quintino Sella*, ed. F. Mariotti (Rome, 1890), V. 234; A. Guiccioli, *Quintino Sella* (2nd ed., Rovigo, 1887), I. 211.

Emanuel was still determined to support the army in their request for increased expenditure on the armed forces, ignoring the fact that for eight years the national budget had, largely for this reason, been in heavy deficit.[1] After the Venetian fiasco he urgently needed a success in foreign policy, and hence the army must be increased.

To provide some of the money, Menabrea decided to introduce the much-hated *macinato* tax on flour and to lease off to a private company the government monopoly of tobacco. A scandal over peculation arising from this tobacco concession involved a number of deputies, and there is some evidence from Rattazzi that the king himself profited very handsomely from the contract. Mme Rattazzi maliciously added, of course without offering proof, that the king regularly purloined several millions a year from the army appropriations, and that in 1868 he took for himself as much as 20 millions, a piece of sharp practice which was with difficulty concealed in the budget.[2] This may well be untrue or at least exaggerated, but the king certainly was involved with financiers of highly dubious reputation and eventually died with his personal finances in grave disorder.[3]

In foreign policy it was widely known that he was fretting for another war, and many of the conservatives were fully behind him even though they knew that the coffers were bare. A war, as one politician remarked, 'would cover everything'. Paget reported the king's thoughts to be 'full of battles gone by, and of imaginary battles to come, with himself at the head of his army'.[4] There were proposals for setting up Italian colonies in Borneo, Sumatra, and along the Red Sea. He agreed with Mazzini that Britain might be compelled to give up Malta.[5] Quixotically he tried to push his second son, the duke of Aosta, on to the throne of Spain. When the duke had more sense than to accept, the king thought of his nephew, the fifteen-year-old duke of Genoa who was then at school in England, but the boy's mother adamantly refused.

An indispensable condition for a successful foreign policy was to ally with one of the major European powers. Victor Emanuel continued to be in some doubt over which would be best. He felt sure that a war was inevitable between France and Prussia, but for a while was not entirely sure whether it would be best to join one side or stay neutral. Several times in 1868 and 1869

---

[1] *Les Origines Diplomatiques*, XIX. 337; *Carteggio Castelli*, II. 336–7, 377.

[2] Mme Rattazzi, *Rattazzi et son Temps*, II. 281–4, 287–8, 293; F. Petruccelli della Gattina, *Storia d'Italia dal 1866 al 1880: Demolizioni, Rabberci, Disinganni* (Naples, 1882), p. 46; L. Anelli, *I Sedici Anni del Governo dei Moderati (1860–1876)* (Como, 1929), pp. 168–9.

[3] N. Colajanni, *Banche e Parlamento* (3rd ed., Milan, 1893), pp. 236–7; N. Quilici, *Banca Romana* (Milan, 1935), pp. 143–5, 601; D. Farini, *Diario di Fine Secolo* ed. E. Morelli (Rome 1961), I. 378; G. Tozzoni, *Il Re e la Sinistra al Potere* (Rome, 1876), pp. 66–7; Finali, *Memorie*, p. 448; *Lettere di V. Emanuele*, II. 1526; it is interesting that Cognasso has printed no correspondence between the king and the disreputable Bernardo Tanlongo, the main offender in the Banca Romana scandal, though some is known to exist.

[4] 13 Mar. 1869, Clarendon MSS., dep c 488; *Carteggio Castelli*, II. 353–5, 360, 381.

[5] A. Boullier, *Victor-Emmanuel et Mazzini: Leurs Négociations Secrètes et leur Politique* (Paris, 1885), p. 37.

he asked the Prussians about an alliance against France, but they had learnt never to take him or his suggestions very seriously.[1] Simultaneously he was telling the Austrians that they could count on Italian soldiers to fight against Prussia: the number of these notional soldiers was increased from time to time, until he was speaking of as many as half a million, though Count von Beust had good reason to doubt if so many existed.[2] After Austria had for so long been the traditional enemy of Italy, Victor Emanuel on one occasion produced the imaginative idea of proposing a dynastic alliance, and with some courage suggested that his eldest son, Umberto, should marry the daughter of the Habsburg archduke who commanded the Austrian army in 1866. Unfortunately the lady was tragically burnt to death when, surprised by her governess as she was secretly smoking, her clothes caught fire. A gesture had nevertheless been made, and the king was sensible enough to see that new possibilities would open up for Italian foreign policy as soon as unhappy memories of the past could be forgotten. Now that Venice had been won, he was strongly opposed to those Italians who nourished further irredentist ambitions, and there is little doubt that at this point he inclined more to Vienna than to Berlin or even to Paris.

As early as December 1867, Napoleon proposed to Victor Emanuel that they should consider secretly allying with each other.[3] Mentana was less than two months in the past and a French alliance would thus have been hard for the general public to swallow, but there was no need for the general public to know. In private Victor Emanuel used to speak of Napoleon as '*ce cochon*', and in this same month tried to convince Garibaldi that he was burning to revenge himself on France;[4] nevertheless his favourite child was the wife of Prince Napoleon, and the fact that one of the great powers wanted him as an ally was too flattering to be ignored. Napoleon asked for negotiations to be kept out of the official foreign office correspondence.[5] Such conspiratorialism appealed to the king's penchant for personal diplomacy. Menabrea was informed, but not the other ministers, and messages were secretly taken to Paris by Vimercati and Türr. Both messengers, like Menabrea himself, were soldiers, for it was a tradition of *casa Savoia* to use military men as confidants. It was an additional advantage in this case that they were jealous of each other.

---

[1] *Auswärtige Politik Preussens*, IX. 594, 859; ibid. X (1939), 6, 185–6; *Bismarck the Man and the Statesman: Being the Reflections and Reminiscences of Otto Prince von Bismarck* (London, 1898), II. 112.

[2] Beust, *Aus Drei Viertel-Jahrhunderten*, II. 320; Kübeck, quoted in A. Stern, *Geschichte Europas von 1848 bis 1871* (Stuttgart, 1924), IV. 189.

[3] De Vecchi di Val Cismon, 'Dai *Ricordi Diplomatici* di Costantino Nigra', *Nuova Antologia*, Jan. 1934, pp. 181–2; *Il Risorgimento Italiano: Rivista Storica*, VII (1914), 239–40.

[4] *Aus dem Leben Bernhardis*, VII. 128; *Garibaldi, Vittorio Emanuele, Cavour*, ed. Curàtulo, p. 369; Bapst, *Canrobert: Souvenirs*, p. 233, quoted the king as saying 'Qu'est-ce que ce bougre-là. Le dernier venu des souverains. Un intrus parmi nous'; *Auswärtige Politik Preussens*, X. 79–80.

[5] Ibid. 118.

Negotiations continued throughout 1868 and 1869 for what Victor Emanuel considered to be the most thoroughgoing piece of monarchic diplomacy in his whole reign, and eventually it was agreed in principle that France, Austria, and Italy should make a secret triple alliance against Prussia and perhaps Russia. More realistically than before, Victor Emanuel now mentioned putting only 200,000 Italian soldiers into the pool. He now admitted that the finances could not stand a war, so it was arranged that his expenses in fighting would be reimbursed by France, and this absence of any financial burden had the additional advantage that, by article 5 of the *statuto*, it would give him more authority to act without parliamentary consent. France would be fighting for the Rhine frontier; Austria would be seeking new territories in the Balkans and along the Danube; while Italy would be compensated by the Trentino and concessions on her north-eastern frontier up to the river Isonzo. Napoleon refused to cede Nice, though he was ready to allow some frontier rectifications there.[1] A further request for Italian troops to be allowed to occupy most of what was left of the Papal States was refused outright, but hints were made that some agreement might eventually be reached over solving the Roman question in Italy's favour.[2] Victor Emanuel would also be allowed special commercial privileges at Bizerta, and since Switzerland might hopefully take the other side, there was a conditional arrangement that the canton of Ticino might also fall to him.[3]

In May 1869, to strengthen the cabinet, Menabrea was allowed to bring in Minghetti and Luigi Ferraris; Minghetti first asked for, and was given, an assurance that rumours about a secret alliance were false.[4] It almost looks as though the king up to this point had imagined he might avoid having to present any treaty to his ministers for their approval, but that he could simply sign it personally so long as it placed no financial burden on the state. As soon as he realized that a counter-signature might be necessary, he gave his word of honour to the French to play out this '*comédie*' and ensure that his ministers would make no difficulties: he would wait until some political incident justified the closure of parliament; then he would inform the cabinet of the alliance, and any minister who did not agree would be dismissed.[5]

Until there arose this need for ministerial approval, it seems that he had intended to sign without securing any concessions over Rome. This exem-

---

[1] *Nuova Antologia*, Jan. 1934, pp. 186–8; *Les Origines Diplomatiques de la Guerre*, vol. XXII (1928), p. 422; ibid., vol. XXIII (1928), pp. 33–4; Oncken, *Rheinpolitik Napoleons*, III. 87–90, 167–8; *L'Opera di Stefano Türr nel Risorgimento Italiano, Descritta dalla Figlia* (Florence, 1928), I. 165, 171–2.

[2] *Les Origines Diplomatiques*, XXIII.393; *Nuova Antologia*, Jan. 1934, p. 182; Paget, 27 May 1869, Clarendon MSS., dep c 488, reported the king as confirming that the French troops would be leaving Rome before the end of 1869.

[3] *Les Origines Diplomatiques*, XXIII. 399.

[4] *Ende des Kirchenstaates*, ed. Miko, I. 483; Minghetti's involvement in the process of transformism is discussed by L. Burckhardt, *Partei und Staat im Risorgimento* (Basel, 1958), pp. 20, 33–6.

[5] Oncken, *Rheinpolitik Napoleons*, III. 194–5, 198.

plifies one drawback to his technique of personal diplomacy, namely that decisions might be taken with insufficient knowledge of what the Italian public would tolerate. Cut off from full use of Italian ambassadors abroad, he also might have to act without adequate knowledge about the aims and interests of the other states with which he was negotiating. The need to rely on Vimercati, essentially an amateur diplomat of limited talent and prejudiced views, a man indeed who may even have been in Napoleon's employment,[1] was most unfortunate, and sometimes it is clear that the king was for this reason acting in the dark. Vimercati's private intention, incidentally, was that an alliance with imperial Paris and Vienna would increase the power of Victor Emanuel and diminish that of parliament.[2]

This suggests that these negotiations for a triple alliance with the two emperors can be thought of in terms of the king's wish to reduce the importance of '*quei signori*' and '*ces mauvais drôles*' in parliament. And yet, short of a *coup*, parliament could not be entirely ignored. Despite his constitutional prerogatives, if the various opposition factions ever came together, they could wield considerable pressure through the fact of parliamentary control of taxation. Unless the king was prepared to assert himself and shift the balance of the constitution still further, ministers would have to be told of commitments he had made or intended to make in Italy's name, and, if war did not follow quickly, they might have to defend his actions in public debate.

Towards the middle of 1869 they were in fact informed individually. No member of the cabinet seems to have complained that negotiations had been conducted secretly, and the royal prerogative to negotiate was not questioned, a fact which shows how far constitutional conventions had changed since the death of Cavour. All the ministers apparently agreed to accept the alliance as offensive as well as defensive, though, repudiating Vimercati's advice, they insisted on one indispensable condition, namely that Italian patriotic feeling be first satisfied by France promising to withdraw her troops at a given date from the Papal States. They made other minor conditions, but the king privately told the French that no notice need be taken of them.[3] Over the withdrawal of French troops he was ready to accept their view. Napoleon explained that he would have to wait until the French elections were over before he offended Catholic opinion by withdrawing his troops, though he hoped that it might be possible early in 1871. As a result, Victor Emanuel agreed not to press for a formal treaty, but simply sent a personal letter to the

---

[1] E. Di Nolfo, 'Monarchia e Governo Durante la Crisi Diplomatica dell' Estate del 1870', *Un Secolo da Porta Pia* (Naples, 1970), p. 18 of offprint; Oncken, *Rheinpolitik Napoleons*, I. 182, where Bismarck called Vimercati 'ein ganz unglaubwürdiger Intrigant ... Was er sagt ist, wenn nicht anderweit unterstützt, des Berichtens nicht wert.'

[2] Mori, *Tramonto del Potere Temporale*, pp. 378–9; *Les Origines Diplomatiques de la Guerre*, vol. XXV (1929), p. 387.

[3] Mori, *Tramonto del Potere Temporale*, p. 384; *I Documenti Diplomatici Italiani*, Ser. I, vol. XIII, ed. W. Maturi (Rome, 1963), pp. 165–6.

emperor promising to enter into an alliance as soon as arrangements could be made on this one point.

Napoleon was not entirely pleased, for he could envisage the possibility of an eventual clash of national interest. Though at one moment he had evidently intended to withdraw his troops, on reconsideration he preferred to leave this question unresolved, and in the process of negotiating his attitude hardened. He criticized Victor Emanuel for slowness in the negotiations, as well as for frequent changes of mind, and above all for dangerous indiscretions: it was these indiscretions in Florence which alerted Prussia and others to what was happening, hence making it more difficult for Napoleon to desert the pope.[1] No formal treaty was therefore signed. Negotiations ended when he and Victor Emanuel declared in private letters that they were bound 'morally' if not formally to join each other in a European war.[2]

Parliament turned against Menabrea's government in November 1869, but broad agreement with France had by this time been reached and there was less need to continue the experiment in personal government. In domestic politics the experiment had not been a great success. Giovanni Lanza said that Italy had never before been worse governed. Even Sclopis, a loyal conservative monarchist and Menabrea's friend, knew that the king's extravagant expenditure on the army was threatening the country with ruin, and Massari found in his travels that Italy's reputation abroad was lessened by 'the want of confidence inspired by the king'.[3] Menabrea and his colleagues still hoped that, despite another hostile vote in parliament, they would be able to remain in office. The king suggested that they should test public feeling in an election, but the conservatives realized that this would be to invite a major political defeat.[4] The court was quite out of touch with public opinion.

Only a Lanza-Sella coalition looked like commanding a majority in the existing parliament, and the trouble was that both these men had ranged themselves strongly against the court party over the issue of the tobacco concession and the king's financial extravagance. At the end of November, Victor Emanuel sent General De Sonnaz to find out, first, whether Lanza would join the cabinet under Menabrea; failing that, whether he would consider taking over himself with a mostly unchanged administration and without touching the

---

[1] *Bismarck: Die Gesammelten Werke* (1930), VI[a]. 206; Oncken, *Rheinpolitik Napoleons*, III. 224–5, 233–4; Mori, *Il Tramonto del Potere Temporale*, p. 386.

[2] A. Stern, *Geschichte Europas*, IV. 365; *Lettere di V. Emanuele*, II. 1446–7; *Les Origines Diplomatiques*, XXV. 432; ibid., vol. XXVI (1929), p. 420; Oncken, *Rheinpolitik Napoleons*, III. 251; Général Lebrun, *Souvenirs Militaires 1866–1870* (Paris, 1895), p. 59.

[3] Paget, 17 Dec. 1868, Clarendon MSS., dep c 488; *Sclopis: Diario*, pp. 442–3: *Carte di Lanza*, IV. 272; scores of examples of Menabrea's interference with freedom of the press and with the judiciary are in A. Comandini, *L'Italia nei Cento Anni del Secolo XIX* (Milan, 1929), IV. 1106–43.

[4] Guiccioli, *Sella*, I. 207; *Carteggio Castelli*, II. 406–7, 413–14; Paget, 25 Nov. 1869, F.O. 45/145, reported that the king's anxiety to keep Menabrea was due 'to the accommodating spirit evinced by His Excellency in regard to certain family affairs of His Majesty of a very delicate nature'.

army and navy. These conditions obviously reflect the king's determination to have his war against Prussia. But Lanza refused both suggestions and asked for an audience to discuss the matter. The king would not see him and charged Menabrea to form another cabinet. Lanza at this point was bold enough to warn the king that he was taking a dangerous step and the future of parliamentary government might be in the balance; in particular, attention was drawn to the need for drastic economies. Victor Emanuel replied, with somewhat artificial surprise, that he had no idea the economic situation was so serious; he was ready to abdicate rather than lead the country into bankruptcy, but would be grateful if Lanza could form a government and save the country.[1]

Lanza knew by now that he held a strong hand. He repeated that the army and the court would have to reduce their expenditure; also the king would have to follow British precedent and change the ministers of his household so that contradictory advice would not be given to him in private. According to Lanza, these private advisers had undermined the parliamentary system by using the crown as an instrument of party politics. Unwilling to accept such stark advice, the king tried one more alternative and asked General Cialdini to form an administration. Cialdini, as a former aide-de-camp of the king, was looked upon as representing the armed forces and their insistence on rearmament. By early December, he had his ministers ready, but at the last moment some of them backed down when they realized where he was leading them. Menabrea was once again ordered to stay in office. A person close to the king at this moment was Cavour's old friend, Michelangelo Castelli: and great believer though Castelli was in a strong and warlike monarchy, he feared that the king was leaning dangerously towards Gualterio's opinion that the army alone could save the country from collapse.[2]

In the last resort, after three weeks of political crisis in which he had been unable to make up his mind, Victor Emanuel accepted Lanza's conditions. This was one of the major decisions of his reign. Menabrea, Gualterio, and Cambray-Digny lost their offices in the royal household. Severe reductions were accepted in the army. The new cabinet also persuaded the king, at least temporarily, to renounce his ambition to place a relative on the throne of Spain—an ambition, said Paget, 'which oddly enough he appears to consider complimentary to his family'. It was a fact that 'he don't like Lanza, and can't bear Sella who, when he was last minister, showed a certain determination to curtail the royal expenditure and a disposition to reform the royal morals'; all the same, Paget was impressed by the common sense and constitutional propriety which the king showed in the end.[3] Victor Emanuel, almost without

---

[1] Bersezio, *Il Regno*, VIII. 340; *Carteggio Castelli*, II. 434–5; *Carte di Lanza*, IV. 319; ibid. VI. 365–6; ibid. III. 289, 309, 456–7, mentions previous talk of possible abdication.

[2] *Rassegna*, 1921, p. 489; *Carteggio Castelli*, II. 440; *Carte di Lanza*, IV. 322.

[3] 23 Dec. 1869, Clarendon MSS., dep c 488.

noticing it, had decided to accept a new style of government much closer to
that of Cavour. Lanza had gently taught him a lesson in constitutionalism.
From now on he came much less often to cabinet meetings. Gradually he
accepted that he had lost some of his prerogative of appointing senators and
choosing the time for elections.[1] Possibly he was glad to be relieved of the
responsibility.

On one important point Victor Emanuel scored a private victory, and this
no doubt explains why he was prepared to accept Lanza and the wishes of
parliament: for he did not tell the new ministers the most important fact of
all, namely that he had made a conditional pledge to fight alongside France
and Austria against Prussia. He forbade the Austrian ambassador to mention
this pledge to his new ministers, giving the reason that they were not experienced enough for such high policy. He was convinced that, when the
time came, they would have no option but to accept the fact that he had committed the country to war, or that otherwise he would be able to count on a
wave of patriotic hysteria to support the appointment of a more belligerent
cabinet. War would change everything and solve everything. He went so far
as to discuss with the Austrians the possibility of having to extend the war
and march on Paris to help Napoleon against a republican revolution.[2] What
he entirely failed to appreciate, however, was that Lanza's reduction in the
armed forces made his private foreign policy a complete day-dream. These
military economies, which had immediate results that he did not even bother
to check, saved Italy in August 1870 from being involved by the king on the
losing side of a major European war.

Napoleon's rash provocation of Prussia is in part explicable by his reliance
on the moral commitment by Austria and Italy to a triple alliance.[3] When the
Franco-Prussian War began in July 1870, Victor Emanuel was indeed eager
to fight; he could not be expected to regard his commitment as one of those
symptoms of clumsy amateur diplomacy from which a responsible foreign
minister might have saved him. The Archduke Albrecht, as well as General
Lebrun and the French general staff, were basing their plans on the occupation of Munich by the Italian army in fulfilment of what Napoleon called
their '*anciennes promesses*', though the king's glib talk of half a million soldiers
was gradually scaled down to 200,000, then to 100,000, and finally to 60,000

---

[1] 8 Dec. 1869, F.O. 45/145; *Carte di Lanza*, VI. 13, 386, 398; G. Tupini, *Il Senato* (Bologna, 1946),
p. 105; the list of senators in the *Manuale Parlamentare* shows that Minghetti had 26 new conservative senators named in the last months of his premiership during February–March 1876, while
Depretis consolidated the victory of the Left with 53 nominations in May 1876, so bringing the
total to about 400—these were ministerial, rather than royal, nominations.
[2] S. William Halperin, *Diplomat under Stress: Visconti-Venosta and the Crisis of July 1870* (Chicago,
1963), pp. 69–71; Oncken, *Rheinpolitik Napoleons*, III. 273–4.
[3] The Empress Eugénie, quoted by M. Paléologue, *Les Entretiens de l'Impératrice Eugénie* (Paris,
1928), p. 60.

as the limit of what Italy could provide.[1] Whether the king had remembered to warn his own general staff to prepare for a campaign in Bavaria is not known, but probably the thought never occurred to him. Nevertheless, in June 1870 he reassured the Austrians that the triple alliance between them was as good as signed.[2]

On 3 July came the news of the Hohenzollern candidature to the throne of Spain, news which was unexpectedly to trigger off war. Victor Emanuel now repeated his assurance of military support to the French, though not even at such a late hour did he permit anything to be said to his ministers about the commitment he had made in Italy's name. Visconti Venosta, who was one of the most level-headed foreign ministers in all modern Italian history, was gratuitously described by the king as 'too much of a lightweight to be trusted with such matters'. In a final indiscretion, the monarch told the Austrian envoy, of all people, that as soon as the war was arranged he would dismiss his government and reappoint a more personal administration; this was the reason why his existing ministers could be allowed to remain in ignorance.[3] Rattazzi was once again in close touch with the court, and Lanza knew it. The prime minister must have become aware that some kind of secret commitment to war had been made under the previous administration; his own government, on the contrary, was based on the firm assumption that Italy had 'an un-qualified need for peace', and he commented acidly that Victor Emanuel, who liked to assume that he had been responsible for unifying Italy, was going to be the man who destroyed it again through military defeat.[4]

The Franco-Prussian War appeared to Victor Emanuel as a heaven-sent reward for years of private diplomacy, but its outbreak caught him unawares before he had had time to appoint a more warlike administration. The first news of the crisis arrived when he was at his hunting lodge in the remote mountains of the Val d'Aosta. He stayed there ten days more, which suggests that he did not know quite how to proceed. Meanwhile the 'promises' to France, for which he now took personal responsibility, were revealed in his absence to the ministers. He ominously remarked that 'in this grave situation I do not want to find myself embarrassed by objections from the cabinet'.[5] No doubt he feared to be present when ministers were apprised of the situation. He also must have wanted to be near Turin and Rattazzi, with whom he was now said to be having frequent talks. Possibly he wanted to be far away from Florence while a parliamentary attack was organized by Gualterio

[1] Oncken, *Rheinpolitik Napoleons*, III. 361; *Documenti Diplomatici Italiani*, XIII. 35, 96; *Les Origines Diplomatiques de la Guerre*, vol. XXVIII (1931), p. 531.
[2] *Ende des Kirchenstaates*, ed. Miko, I. 566–7.
[3] Oncken, *Rheinpolitik Napoleons*, III. 387.
[4] *Carteggio Castelli*, II. 465; *Documenti Diplomatici Italiani*, XIII. 88.
[5] E. Mayor des Planches, 'Re Vittorio Emanuele II alla Vigilia della Guerra del Settanta', *Nuova Antologia*, Apr. 1920, pp. 351–2.

and Menabrea aimed at replacing Lanza by one of the king's friends.[1] When this attack failed, he complained to Napoleon that more warning should have been given so that he could have put into operation his plans for a *coup*. Paget conjectured what must be happening and commented that 'Victor Emanuel is no joke under these circumstances'.[2]

Lanza's cabinet was in difficulty. Either they would have to join the war, or else the crown's personal complicity would be publicly exposed, which could lead only to dictatorship or abdication. Fortunately the more extreme conservatives made it clear that they would prefer Lanza to remain rather than see the ill-fated Rattazzi return to office.[3] Fortunately, too, Lanza's economy measures had rendered the armed forces 'barely sufficient for internal security', and Italy's credit touched almost its lowest point when government funds fell to much less than half their par value; so the French realized that there might not be a great deal to be expected from Italian assistance.[4]

But the king never doubted, nor did Generals Cialdini and Menabrea, that France was easily going to defeat Prussia; hence, despite Italy's weakness, they thought that they could join the war and seize their chance to obtain Rome, the Trentino, a foothold in North Africa, and perhaps Nice. Lamarmora and Sella were among the few who had learnt from the events of 1866 that the Germans might win. Visconti Venosta was not so sure, yet he still disagreed fundamentally with the king and looked on a war between France and Prussia as the most frightening possibility; he thought that Italy should stay neutral if at all possible, though he was not a strong enough character to stand up to the court party as soon as he knew that the king was bound by secret promises.[5]

Until Victor Emanuel decided to return to Florence on 17 July, the cabinet had only a vague idea what he had committed them to; they could find nothing in the archives and Menabrea would tell them nothing, but they promised to do what they could 'to get Your Majesty out of any difficult situation in which you may find yourself'.[6] Victor Emanuel's correspondence with Napoleon had been private, and he suddenly discovered that he had kept no copies, so he could not even tell Lanza what precise promises had been made. This was one disadvantage of not using normal diplomatic channels. Hurriedly he, Menabrea, and Vimercati tried to recall the sequence of negotiations, and they decided that Italy was committed to fight provided that French troops withdrew from the Papal States and provided that the Austrians also agreed to

[1] *Ende des Kirchenstaates*, ed. Miko, I. 616; Sardo, *Storia del Parlamento Italiano*, VI. 369–70; Mori, *Tramonto del Potere Temporale*, p. 482.

[2] *Les Origines Diplomatiques*, XXIX. 112; Paget, 16 July 1870, F.O. 391/23.

[3] *Ende des Kirchenstaates*, ed. Miko, I. 616.

[4] Ibid. 641; *Les Origines Diplomatiques*, XXIX. 21.

[5] S. Castagnola, *Da Firenze a Roma: Diario Storico-Politico del 1870–71* (Turin, 1896), p. 5; Bersezio, *Il Regno*, VIII. 361; *Documenti Diplomatici Italiani*, XIII. 88–91; Di Nolfo, *Un Secolo da Porta Pia*, p. 28 of offprint; Halperin, *Diplomat under Stress*, p. 190.

[6] *Carte di Lanza*, VI. 418; Ollivier, *Empire Libérale*, XV. 452; *Nuova Antologia*, Apr. 1920, p. 351; *Documenti Diplomatici Italiani*, XIII. 71, 124.

join the war. While the cabinet investigated these two essential points, some of the army reservists were recalled.

Victor Emanuel was meanwhile engaged in a parallel series of negotiations with Paris, about which his government knew little. Agreement was reached through Vimercati that he would protect the pope, and in return the French promised to withdraw their troops again from the Papal States. The ministers were then informed and accepted a triple alliance on these terms, since they felt Italy was committed by the king's '*obligation d'honneur*'.[1]

Thus near was Italy to fighting a war for which she entirely lacked the resources and which would almost certainly have brought defeat, abdication, perhaps revolution, and certainly a reinforcement of the papal claim to be temporal ruler of Rome. How she was saved from this disaster is a larger story that concerns much more than the history of the king. If the alliance was not activated, one reason was that both Paris and Vienna were suspicious of Florence, especially when they realized that the king was saying one thing to France and the opposite to Austria; suspicion was created by the fact that he and his ministers were known not to agree with one another over policy, and his private agents were known to be working in Paris and Vienna without reference to Italy's official ambassadors.

Above all, Napoleon still disbelieved the king's word and feared that behind his promise to respect the papal frontier lay a determination to annex Rome. Victor Emanuel explained that it was his ministers who were dragging their feet and who wanted annexation of Rome to be a condition of entering the war, whereas he himself would in any case fight alongside France '*jusqu'au bout*'. This at least was the message he tried to convey, though in private he could not conceal his secret intention to use France's difficulties in order to occupy the rest of central Italy. 'La perfidie des Italiens' was known at Paris, and, luckily for the king, it helped to delay the formal signing of an alliance.[2]

Victor Emanuel did not know about this when at the end of July he confirmed to the Austrians that he had made up his mind to dismiss Lanza and declare war. Count Vitzthum, the Saxon diplomat who was in the service of Austria, had been invited to see him secretly without Visconti Venosta knowing. The king informed Vitzthum that Lanza was an idiot, that Visconti Venosta would always do as he was told, and the other ministers except Sella were complete nonentities who did not count. He expressed some concern that the news of his intention to annex part of Switzerland had leaked out. According to his own account he had personally intervened behind the scenes to make the Italian press support the war. He claimed that he was closer than

---

[1] E. Bourgeois and E. Clermont, *Rome et Napoléon III (1849–1870)* (Paris, 1907), p. 277; *Les Origines Diplomatiques*, XXIX. 11, 111–12, 129, 163–4, 181, 183; Oncken, *Rheinpolitik Napoleons*, III. 463, 466.

[2] Ibid. 482, 487, 500; *Les Origines Diplomatiques*, XXIX. 220.

his ministers to Italian public opinion, and knew that there was no more time to lose if Italy were to make use of the war and enlarge her frontiers. He had ensured that his army would be ready to fight by 15 August, and Napoleon had by now received his promise to that effect, nor would he embarrass the emperor by waiting for the formal consent of France to his occupation of Rome. He would look ridiculous if, having called up his soldiers, he did not fight.[1]

Vitzthum did not take these remarks too seriously. For one thing it was obvious that the king was completely deluding himself if he thought that the Italian army could so easily be put on a war footing. Hints had also been dropped that the king himself might prefer to see how the war went before taking any irrevocable step, and possibly he might in time have discovered that Italy had less to gain from France than from a grateful Germany.[2] The first positive news from the front was a false report that the French had won a battle at Saarbrück; and this report so impressed the cabinet that they voted to intervene in the war on France's side, either directly or by way of armed mediation.[3] This remarkable decision, which only Sella and perhaps Govone were against, shows how civilian ministers could be browbeaten by the king into believing his confident assertion that France was bound to win. Fortunately Sella managed to gain time by threatening that he would resign and bring the whole issue of peace or war into the open; so the cabinet agreed to put off a final decision and not to register their vote in a formal cabinet minute.

Meanwhile, without Visconti Venosta or the cabinet knowing, the king once again sent Vimercati to see Napoleon with a message that all was virtually settled and the king was ready now to dismiss Lanza if necessary.[4] Victor Emanuel was determined to have his war. After Sella's brave act of opposition the king sneeringly remarked to him that a politician who came from a family of cloth merchants could not be expected to have the courage and sense of honour needed for such a moment of destiny.[5] On 3 August, in the senate, General Cialdini and a group of conservatives launched another bitter attack on the government; they demanded in explicitly racialist terms that Italy and France should unite against the Germans. Their attack, with little doubt, had been instigated by the court, and as late as 5 August the king was personally expressing his delight that the partisans of the French alliance

---

[1] Bourgeois and Clermont, *Rome et Napoléon*, p. 330; Oncken, *Rheinpolitik Napoleons*, III. 494, 496–8.

[2] H. von Sybel, *The Founding of the German Empire by William I* (New York, 1898), VII. 482–3, where some interesting unpublished memoirs are summarized; F. Engel Janosi, 'La Questione Romana nelle Trattative Diplomatiche del 1869–1870', *Nuova Rivista Storica* (Città di Castello), XXV (1941), 40.

[3] Guiccioli, *Sella*, I. 277; Castagnola, *Da Firenze a Roma*, pp. 6–7; *Documenti Diplomatici Italiani*, XIII. 389; Chabod, *Politica Estera Italiana*, p. 654.

[4] Ollivier, *Empire Libérale*, XV. 514.

[5] Guiccioli, *Sella*, I. 268; Luigi Luzzatti, *Memorie Autobiografiche e Carteggi* (Bologna, 1930), I. 307.

had finally triumphed in Italy. Vimercati was at this moment giving the king's latest message to Napoleon and doing his utmost to commit Italy to war without the cabinet knowing what he was up to.[1]

But by this time the French had already suffered the first of the succession of reverses that led a month later to the capitulation of Napoleon at Sedan. Visconti Venosta, who until 6 August believed that France would win and had been intimidated by his sovereign into preparing to join the war, was thus emboldened to move away from this colossal miscalculation.[2] Vimercati and Türr continued until the end of August to urge that the king take full powers and disown the cabinet so that Italy could join what seemed to them, or so they pretended, an obviously winning cause; but these confidential agents of the king were deceiving him and, whatever may or may not have been true earlier, must now have been working rather in the interests of Napoleon.[3] Victor Emanuel was a little more hesitant than they were, though still eager to fight if only Napoleon could show that France was going to win. He excused himself from immediate intervention on the grounds that the danger of revolution in Italy compelled him to wait before declaring his support,[4] but even as late as October, long after intervention had become quite impossible, he and the generals were trying to persuade Lanza to fight.[5]

Sella and the other ministers, despite the fact that they had saved the crown and Italy by providing time for second thoughts, received no thanks at court but were criticized privately and to their faces in front of other people. Not only had they refused to fight, but they were continuing to press for economies in the civil list and trying to reduce the independent activity of household officials. Early in September the king told Lanza that the monarch, as head of the armed forces, should have the deciding voice in choosing a new minister of war, and Lanza replied by simply offering his resignation.[6]

This at last brought the king up against the unwelcome fact that other party leaders had lost confidence in the monarchy and there was no alternative premier. His chief animosity was directed at Sella whom he attacked for, of all things, not having warned him that the Prussians were going to win.[7]

---

[1] L. Chiala, *Pagine di Storia Contemporanea dal 1858 al 1892* (Turin, 1892), I. 51–2; *Documenti Diplomatici Italiani*, XIII. 255, 261; Isacco and Ernesto Artom, *Iniziative Neutralistiche della Diplomazia Italiana nel 1870 e nel 1915*, ed. A. Artom (Turin, 1954), pp. 26, 77.

[2] *Documenti Diplomatici Italiani*, XIII. 394, 428–9.

[3] *L'Opera di Türr nel Risorgimento*, I. 179; Türr's wife enjoyed a large pension from Napoleon (E. A. Vizetelly, *The Court of the Tuileries 1852–1870* (London, 1907), p. 213); Eugénie hinted the same of Vimercati (C. Lacaita, *An Italian Englishman, Sir James Lacaita* (London, 1933), p. 245).

[4] *Documenti Diplomatici Italiani*, XIII. 286–7; Oncken, *Rheinpolitik Napoleons*, III. 519; E. Tavallini, *La Vita e i Tempi di Giovanni Lanza: Memorie Ricavate da suoi Scritti* (Turin, 1887), II. 34; *Carte di Lanza*, VI. 420–1; Ollivier, *Empire Libérale*, XVI. 526, 532.

[5] *Déposition de Monsieur Thiers sur le Dix-Huit Mars* (Paris, 1872), p. 12, where Thiers reported on his 'discussions extrêmement vives' at Florence.

[6] *Carte di Lanza*, VI. 73; Tavallini, *Vita di Lanza*, II. 40; Castagnola, *Da Firenze a Roma*, pp. 32–3.

[7] Guiccioli, *Sella*, I. 316; this helps to explain the back-handed compliment by Sella in Bollea, *Una Silloge*, p. 455, where the king is called 'il più furbo degli Italiani'

If only the monarch had been shrewd enough to choose the other side, a Prussian victory might well have won him Savoy, Nice, and Rome.[1] Instead, by reneging on promises to join France, he was likely to lose his reputation as a man of courage and honour. He felt guilty about deserting Napoleon just when the French were beginning to suffer defeat, but he secretly knew how lucky he had been in escaping a major disaster. Later he tried to locate the incriminating letter in which he had first promised to support the French, and he also tried to ensure that no one had a copy of it which might be used to bring his conduct into question.[2]

On 20 September, taking advantage of the fall of Napoleon, the king's soldiers bombarded the Porta Pia and entered Rome, so bringing the risorgimento to a fitting if not very heroic conclusion. Even after the French soldiers had left the Papal States, there had been no serious popular revolution against the pope's regime. Some initial lack of enthusiasm was, however, amply compensated when a plebiscite gave the customary 99 per cent majority against Pius.[3] Visconti Venosta had until the last moment been strongly against the occupation of Rome, but finally changed his mind along with his other colleagues. He then showed his talents as a foreign minister by justifying the attack on the Holy City as necessary to preserve the pope's spiritual authority and to safeguard the prestige of the Italian monarchy.[4] Fortunately for Italy, the other Catholic powers of Europe, piqued by the pope's proclamation of his own infallibility, rather encouraged than discouraged this brutal termination of the temporal power. Somewhat reluctantly the king agreed to move the capital of Italy from Florence to Rome. Alfredo Oriani, who happened to overhear his slightly irritable remark as the royal entourage reached the Rome railway station, related how a disgruntled aside was deftly altered for publicity purposes in order to sound like the arrival of a conquering hero.[5]

Victor Emanuel showed a good deal of moral courage in defying the pope and involving himself once more in excommunication from the church. The previous year, stricken with what was thought might be a fatal illness, he had been momentarily reconciled with the faith: in the presence of witnesses he had confessed that he had been against the spoliation of the papacy by his government, and he promised in future to do all he could to heal the breach between church and state.[6] But by September 1870 he had convinced himself

[1] *Bismarck: Gesammelten Werke*, VI[b]. 452.
[2] Ollivier, *Empire Libérale*, XVI. 523, 540; *Carteggio Castelli*, II. 491.
[3] C. Vallauri, 'Roma nel 1870', *Il Venti Settembre nella Storia d'Italia*, ed. G. Spadolini (Rome, 1970), p. 169; the interesting comments of a very hostile witness of the plebiscite are translated in *The Making of Italy 1796–1870*, ed. D. Mack Smith (New York, 1968), pp. 413–15.
[4] *Ende des Kirchenstaates* (1969), ed. Miko, Santifaller, and Schmidinger, III. 6.
[5] A. Oriani, *La Lotta Politica in Italia* (5th ed., Bologna, 1941), III. 333–4; 'finalment i suma', thus became 'finalmente ci siamo e ci resteremo'.
[6] *Pio e V. Emanuele*, III, pt. ii. 213–15; G. Massari, *La Vita ed il Regno di Vittorio Emanuele II di Savoia* (Milan, 1878), II. 349, a volume which is one of the more satisfactory of the king's biographies, even though it could be called a 'nauséabond panégirique' by Émile Ollivier (*Empire Libérale*, X. 73).

again that, whatever the pope might say, the annexation of Rome by Italy was willed by God.[1]

In the last few years of his life, Victor Emanuel again made some attempts to assert himself as a maker of policy. Lanza remained prime minister until 1873, but was determined from now on to have as little as possible to do with the court.[2] When the Left came to power in 1876, they allowed the king a freer rein. He continued to tell foreign ambassadors to come and visit him privately, and even Italian ambassadors in foreign capitals were informed that they should keep in touch with him, if necessary by-passing the foreign minister altogether. Ministers would come and go, he told Andrassy and Baron Haymerle, but the king was always there and was a reliable man who kept his promises. To others he repeated that it was the monarch who in fact ran the country and who alone could be trusted.[3] He tried once more to make an alliance with Austria; but, as an insurance, he also made another offer to Bismarck for an offensive and defensive alliance with Germany against Austria (keeping this offer secret from the Italian ambassador in Berlin); and yet he still was angry when the Austrians would not trust his word.[4] He would not have liked to know that Franz Joseph thought him insufficiently a gentleman.[5]

What worried him was that he had not crowned his life work with a victory that would give himself and his army the power and prestige which they lacked and which he thought they deserved. It was a pity that, after taking Rome, there was no territory left which he thought he could conquer.[6] He was strongly against the irredentist movement which wanted further cessions of territory by Vienna, because he now thought of Austria as a friendly, conservative, ultra-monarchical power with whom he and the house of Savoy needed good relations. On the other hand he told the British that he might possibly play a more active role in the Eastern Question, and he hoped they would not mind: 'for himself, he could not remain passive, it was contrary to his nature'.[7]

[1] *Lettere di V. Emanuele*, II. 1495.   [2] *Carte di Lanza*, VI. 236.

[3] R. Lill, 'Die Deutsch-Italienischen Beziehungen 1869–1876', *Quellen und Forschungen aus Italienischen Archiven* (Tübingen), XLVI (1966), 435; A. Guiccioli, 'Diario', *Nuova Antologia*, July 1935, p. 214; Chabod, *Politica Estera Italiana*, pp. 665, 673, 677–8; *Dizionario Biografico degli Italiani* (Rome, 1960), I. 388–9; Senator Gadda's remark, quoted in G. Rensi, *Gli 'Anciens Régimes' e la Democrazia Diretta* (Bellinzona, 1902), pp. 87–8.

[4] Chabod, *Politica Estera Italiana*, pp. 682–3; on the subject of these offers it is interesting to compare Crispi's denial in Chiala, *Pagine di Storia Contemporanea*, II. iii, of the very thing which in other circumstances he boasted of doing (*Francesco Crispi: Politica Estera*, ed. T. Palamenghi-Crispi (Milan, 1929), p. 31); Crispi, who was the king's last ministerial appointment, believed strongly in rearmament and a forceful foreign policy (ibid., pp. 35, 69).

[5] 'Victor-Emmanuel a souvent oublié de se conduire en gentilhomme. Ce n'était pas, chez lui, manque de noblesse naturelle; mais il était débraillé dans ses sentiments comme il l'était dans ses habits et dans ses manières' (quoted by Paléologue, *Les Entretiens de l'Impératrice Eugénie*, p. 168).

[6] F. Martini, *Confessioni e Ricordi 1859–1892* (Milan, 1929), p. 153; *Crispi: Politica Estera*, pp. 9–10.

[7] Paget, 5 May 1876, F.O. 45/286.

Lord Salisbury, when on a visit to Rome, found Victor Emanuel and his son Umberto eagerly hoping that war would soon spread through the Balkans, though the Italian foreign minister privately explained to this visitor that war would be the reverse of government policy.[1] To Paget, the king explained the kind of thing he had in mind:

'I know the answer to the Eastern Question, and I do wish people would let me tackle it. I have already asked the Austrian and German emperors to let me intervene. My idea would be to take the Sultan of Turkey and put him down in some remote part of central Asia. Then I would say to Austria and Russia, "Gentlemen, help yourselves to anything you want." I would keep just a little for Italy. And England too, she could take anything that suited her.'

Paget paid no attention, and replied tactfully that this project 'had certainly the merit of being energetic'.[2]

Victor Emanuel remained true to himself until the last. A week before he died he told a group of politicians that Italy needed more than just respect, she needed to be *feared* and must therefore increase her military strength. In reporting his *boutade*, the London *Times* took the unusual course of adding that the real words he had used 'were too strong to be allowed a free transmission through the wires'.[3] This tradition of forceful foreign policy was a legacy which he transmitted to his successor. He himself had fought personally in four wars, while his son Umberto was to fight in none. Yet father handed on to son much the same harsh military upbringing which he himself had received, with little affection, and absolutely no practical education in the responsibilities of constitutional government.[4] Of Victor Emanuel's two sons, King Umberto was to be the founder of the Italian empire in Africa; Amedeo was eventually placed on the perilous and somewhat tarnished throne of Spain, but prudently abdicated after three years, asking the pope to absolve him from his wicked oath to the Spanish constitution and protesting that he had been coerced into it by his father.[5]

At the time of Victor Emanuel's death in January 1878, the Italian constitution had still not found an entirely stable balance between legislature and executive. Yet the *statuto* had become a much more sophisticated instrument of government than at the time of its enactment thirty years earlier, and the

[1] Salisbury from Rome to Lord Derby, 30 Nov. 1876, Salisbury Papers (Christ Church College, Oxford).
[2] Paget, 2 Jan. 1876, F.O. 45/284; he also told others that with 200,000 soldiers he 'could solve the Eastern Question' on his own (*La Patria negli Scritti e nei Discorsi di Paolo Boselli*, ed. P. Barbèra (Florence, 1917), p. 292).
[3] *The Times*, 5 Jan. 1878, p. 5; *Atti Parlamentari: Senato, Discussioni*, p. 2298; P. Turiello (*Governo e Governati in Italia* (2nd ed., Bologna, 1889), II. 234-5) welcomed the king's remarks, and was glad to think that Italy would be hated as well as feared.
[4] *Sclopis: Diario*, p. 495; d'Ideville, *Journal d'un Diplomate*, I. 63-4; Oncken, *Rheinpolitik Napoleons*, II. 586.
[5] *Pio e V. Emanuele*, III, pt. ii. 333.

lower House of parliament had by 1878 achieved a paramount place in the political system. This was due chiefly to Cavour, but also to Azeglio, Lanza, Sella, and other younger collaborators of Cavour's; nor should one forget that Victor Emanuel, however much he resented and tried to halt the process, possessed enough sense and enough indolence not to push his prerogative beyond a certain point.

The unification of Italy had come about, not by spontaneous revolution as Mazzini would have liked, but by a succession of wars. These wars, some of the most bitter of which were civil wars, had not created an optimum milieu for the development of representative institutions. Victor Emanuel therefore found that circumstances, as well as his own temperament, encouraged him to disregard parliament whenever he dared. Even after unification, his scale of values put first the acquisition of prestige for himself and Italy. Prestige was in his eyes more urgent than helping his country to achieve a sense of community or of political consciousness, let alone the development of an indigenous parliamentary tradition which would work efficiently in an Italian context. Possibly, when in his later years he said that high policy was too important to be openly debated in parliament,[1] he thought he was making a realistic assessment of the facts. Probably, however, it was not realism but velleity, not fact but a nostalgic monarchist romanticism. Certainly by this attitude he was impeding rather than assisting the solution of Italy's major problems.

One of the king's friends admitted privately in 1878 that, when a truly impartial history could be written, it would show him as a good king, but would detract a great deal from the artificial glorification which was already metamorphosing him into a legendary hero.[2] This was to ask too much, since strong political and sentimental forces were at work building up the legend, to such a point indeed that the risorgimento could eventually be described as 'the most important fact of the nineteenth century' and Victor Emanuel as its supreme and infallible guide, 'the Agamemnon of our Iliad', 'the grandest and most glorious sovereign in the history of Christian Europe'.[3] In retrospect this hardly looks a serious claim, but it was a very dangerous one, since nationalist fantasies often came to obscure the practical facts on which policy had to be founded.

Such exaggeration must be balanced by remembering that the warlike propensities and absolutist traditions of *casa Savoia* survived through Victor Emanuel's reign, and neither one nor other can be considered beneficial to the state. He was able to hand over to his son and grandson a residual power which allowed them to intervene decisively at crucial moments in domestic politics,

---

[1] *Carte di Lanza*, VII. 121.

[2] Persano, letter edited in Lumbroso, *Carteggio di un Vinto*, p. 571.

[3] D. Zanichelli, *Politica e Storia: Discorsi e Studi* (Bologna, 1903), pp. 85, 96; A. Monti, *Figure e Caratteri del Risorgimento* (Turin, 1939), pp. 243–5; A. Oriani, *Quartetto*, ed. Benito Mussolini (Bologna, 1923), p. 35.

and this was a power which, not always wisely, they were to exercise in support of Crispi, Salandra, Mussolini, and Marshal Badoglio. Failure to curtail the extent of monarchical authority was to be one element in a process which brought with it military defeat, financial collapse, defective political education, economic and social backwardness. Victor Emanuel had said that Italians could be governed only by bayonets or bribery, and hence hardly lived up to his public reputation of being a good constitutional king. He showed more courage and occasionally more good judgement than his successors were to do, and he had a more attractive and forthright personality, yet equally he showed less sense of responsibility and less intelligent awareness of what he was doing. His passion for war, his incompetence as a military commander, his secret and thoroughly irresponsible opposition to his prime ministers, not to mention what Sir James Hudson called his 'predilection for blackguards' and 'his crusade against the parliamentary majority', these were unfortunate aspects of his reign, particularly so in that he ruled at a time when, because traditions of Italian political life were being formed, his contribution was the more obvious and consequential. Deliberately or by default, for good or ill, he probably did as much as Cavour to shape the political institutions and practice of united Italy.

Index

DUE